More Than Just

Internet Resources

Step 1 Connect to NY Math Online **macmillanmh.com**

Step 2 Connect to online resources by using *QuickPass* codes. You can connect directly to the chapter you want.

NY4921c1

Enter this code with the appropriate chapter number.

For Students

Connect to the student edition *eBook* that contains all of the following online assets. You don't need to take your textbook home every night.

- Personal Tutor
- Extra Examples
- Self-Check Quizzes
- Multilingual eGlossary
- Concepts in Motion
- Chapter Test Practice
- Test Practice
- Study to Go
- Math Adventures with Dot and Ray
- Math Tool Chest
- Math Songs

For Teachers

Connect to professional development content at macmillanmh.com and the *eBook Advance Tracker* at AdvanceTracker.com

For Parents

Connect to macmillanmh.com for access to the *eBook* and all the resources for students and teachers that are listed above.

Macmillan McGraw-Hill

New York Math Connects

5

Authors
Altieri • Balka • Day • Gonsalves • Grace • Krulik
Malloy • Molix-Bailey • Moseley • Mowry • Myren
Price • Reynosa • Santa Cruz • Silbey • Vielhaber

Macmillan/McGraw-Hill

About the Cover

Developing fluency with fractions, decimals, and polyhedral solids are featured topics in Fifth grade. The mathematical symbols shown on the mountain goat's snowboard will help students gain momentum as they carve their way through higher levels of math. Have students locate parallel and intersecting lines on the ski lift, and use at least one of the symbols on the snowboard to describe the ski lift chairs.

The McGraw·Hill Companies

 Macmillan/McGraw-Hill

Send all inquiries to:
Macmillan/McGraw-Hill
8787 Orion Place
Columbus, OH 43240-4027

ISBN: 978-0-02-107492-1
MHID: 0-02-107492-5

New York Math Connects, Grade 5

Printed in the United States of America.

1 2 3 4 5 6 7 8 9 10 027/055 16 15 14 13 12 11 10 09 08 07

Contents in Brief

Focal Points and Connections
See page iv for key.

Focal Points

The Curriculum Focal Points identify key mathematical ideas for this grade. They are not discrete topics or a checklist to be mastered; rather, they provide a framework for the majority of instruction at a particular grade level and the foundation for future mathematics study. The complete document may be viewed at www.nctm.org/focalpoints.

KEY
G5-FP1 Grade 5 Focal Point 1
G5-FP2 Grade 5 Focal Point 2
G5-FP3 Grade 5 Focal Point 3
G5-FP4 Grade 5 Focal Point 4 Connection
G5-FP5C Grade 5 Focal Point 5 Connection
G5-FP6C Grade 5 Focal Point 6 Connection
G5-FP7C Grade 5 Focal Point 7 Connection

G5-FP1 *Number and Operations* and *Algebra:* **Developing an understanding of and fluency with division of whole numbers**

Students apply their understanding of models for division, place value, properties, and the relationship of division to multiplication as they develop, discuss, and use efficient, accurate, and generalizable procedures to find quotients involving multidigit dividends. They select appropriate methods and apply them accurately to estimate quotients or calculate them mentally, depending on the context and numbers involved. They develop fluency with efficient procedures, including the standard algorithm, for dividing whole numbers, understand why the procedures work (on the basis of place value and properties of operations), and use them to solve problems. They consider the context in which a problem is situated to select the most useful form of the quotient for the solution, and they interpret it appropriately.

G5-FP2 *Number and Operations:* **Developing an understanding of and fluency with addition and subtraction of fractions and decimals**

Students apply their understanding of fractions and fraction models to represent the addition and subtraction of fractions with unlike denominators as equivalent calculations with like denominators. They apply their understandings of decimal models, place value, and properties to add and subtract decimals. They develop fluency with standard procedures for adding and subtracting fractions and decimals. They make reasonable estimates of fraction and decimal sums and differences. Students add and subtract fractions and decimals to solve problems, including problems involving measurement.

G5-FP3 *Geometry* and *Measurement* and *Algebra:* **Describing three-dimensional shapes and analyzing their properties, including volume and surface area**

Students relate two-dimensional shapes to three-dimensional shapes and analyze properties of polyhedral solids, describing them by the number of edges, faces, or vertices as well as the types of faces. Students recognize volume as an attribute of three-dimensional space. They understand that they can quantify volume by finding the total number of same-sized units of volume that they need to fill the space without gaps or overlaps. They understand that a cube that is 1 unit on an edge is the standard unit for measuring volume. They select appropriate units, strategies, and tools for solving problems that involve estimating or measuring volume. They decompose three-dimensional shapes and find surface areas and volumes of prisms. As they work with surface area, they find and justify relationships among the formulas for the areas of different polygons. They measure necessary attributes of shapes to use area formulas to solve problems.

Connections to the Focal Points

G5-FP4C *Algebra:* Students use patterns, models, and relationships as contexts for writing and solving simple equations and inequalities. They create graphs of simple equations. They explore prime and composite numbers and discover concepts related to the addition and subtraction of fractions as they use factors and multiples, including applications of common factors and common multiples. They develop an understanding of the order of operations and use it for all operations.

G5-FP5C *Measurement:* Students' experiences connect their work with solids and volume to their earlier work with capacity and weight or mass. They solve problems that require attention to both approximation and precision of measurement.

G5-FP6C *Data Analysis:* Students apply their understanding of whole numbers, fractions, and decimals as they construct and analyze double-bar and line graphs and use ordered pairs on coordinate grids.

G5-FP7C *Number and Operations:* Building on their work in grade 4, students extend their understanding of place value to numbers through millions and millionths in various contexts. They apply what they know about multiplication of whole numbers to larger numbers. Students also explore contexts that they can describe with negative numbers (e.g., situations of owing money or measuring elevations above and below sea level).

Authors

Mary Behr Altieri
Putnam/Northern
    Westchester BOCES
Yorktown Heights,
    New York

Don S. Balka
Professor Emeritus
Saint Mary's College
Notre Dame, Indiana

Roger Day, Ph.D.
Mathematics Department Chair
Pontiac Township High School
Pontiac, Illinois

Philip D. Gonsalves
Mathematics Coordinator
Alameda County Office
    of Education and
    California State
    University East Bay
Hayward, California

Ellen C. Grace
Consultant
Albuquerque,
    New Mexico

Stephen Krulik
Professor Emeritus
Mathematics Education
Temple University
Cherry Hill, New Jersey

Carol E. Malloy, Ph.D.
Associate Professor of
    Mathematics Education
University of North
    Carolina at Chapel Hill
Chapel Hill, North
    Carolina

Rhonda J. Molix-Bailey
Mathematics Consultant
Mathematics by Design
Desoto, Texas

Lois Gordon Moseley
Staff Developer
NUMBERS: Mathematics
    Professional
    Development
Houston, Texas

Brian Mowry
Independent Math Educational
    Consultant/Part-Time Pre-K
    Instructional Specialist
Austin Independent School District
Austin, Texas

NY Math Online Meet the Authors at macmillanmh.com

Authors

Christina L. Myren
Consultant Teacher
Conejo Valley Unified
    School District
Thousand Oaks, California

Jack Price
Professor Emeritus
California State
    Polytechnic University
Pomona, California

Mary Esther Reynosa
Instructional Specialist for
    Elementary Mathematics
Northside Independent
    School District
San Antonio, Texas

Rafaela M. Santa Cruz
SDSU/CGU Doctoral
    Program in Education
San Diego State University
San Diego, California

Robyn Silbey
Math Content Coach
Montgomery County
    Public Schools
Gaithersburg, Maryland

Kathleen Vielhaber
Mathematics Consultant
St. Louis, Missouri

Contributing Authors

Donna J. Long
Mathematics Consultant
Indianapolis, Indiana

FOLDABLES **Dinah Zike**
Educational Consultant
Dinah-Might Activities, Inc.
San Antonio, Texas

Master the New York State Standards in 3 Easy Steps

1 Practice the Standards Daily

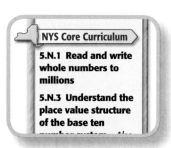

NYS Core Curriculum

5.N.1 Read and write whole numbers to millions

5.N.3 Understand the place value structure of the base ten

- Each lesson addresses New York State Standards covered in that lesson.

NYSMT PRACTICE

- Questions aligned to the standards in a format like those on the New York State Mathematics Test provide you with ongoing opportunities to sharpen your test-taking skills.

② Practice the Standards throughout the Chapter

- Every chapter contains two full pages of NYSMT Practice.

 **NYSMT Practice**

③ Practice the Standards Before the Test

- If you've followed steps 1 and 2, you should be more than ready for the test. But just in case you want to make sure, use pages NY1–NY21 to practice questions that are organized by standard. Lesson references are included for you should you need a little refresher.

GET READY FOR THE New York State Test

New York Reviewers

Each New York Reviewer gave feedback and suggestions for improving the effectiveness of the PreK–8 Math Connects program.

 Paula Barnes
Mathematics Teacher
Minisink Valley CSD
Slate Hill, NY

 Joanne DeMizio
Asst. Supt., Math and Science Curriculum
Archdiocese of New York
New York, NY

 Roberta Grindle
Math and Language Arts
Academic Intervention Service Provider
Cumberland Head Elementary School
Plattsburgh, NY

Consultants

Glencoe/McGraw-Hill wishes to thank the following professionals for their feedback. They were instrumental in providing valuable input toward the development of this program in these specific areas.

Mathematical Content

Viken Hovsepian
Professor of Mathematics
Rio Hondo College
Whittier, California

Grant A. Fraser, Ph.D.
Professor of Mathematics
California State University, Los Angeles
Los Angeles, California

Arthur K. Wayman, Ph.D.
Professor of Mathematics Emeritus
California State University, Long Beach
Long Beach, California

Assessment

Jane D. Gawronski, Ph.D.
Director of Assessment and Outreach
San Diego State University
San Diego, California

Cognitive Guided Instruction

Susan B. Empson, Ph.D.
Associate Professor of Mathematics
and Science Education
University of Texas at Austin
Austin, Texas

English Learners

Cheryl Avalos
Mathematics Consultant
Los Angeles County Office of Education, Retired
Hacienda Heights, California

Kathryn Heinze
Graduate School of Education
Hamline University
St. Paul, Minnesota

Family Involvement

Paul Giganti, Jr.
Mathematics Education Consultant
Albany, California

Literature

David M. Schwartz
Children's Author, Speaker, Storyteller
Oakland, California

Vertical Alignment

Berchie Holliday
National Educational Consultant
Silver Spring, Maryland

Deborah A. Hutchens, Ed.D.
Principal
Norfolk Highlands Elementary
Chesapeake, Virginia

Consultants and Reviewers

Reviewers

Each Reviewer reviewed at least two chapters of the Student Edition, giving feedback
and suggestions for improving the effectiveness of the mathematics instruction.

Ernestine D. Austin
Facilitating Teacher/Basic
　Skills Teacher
LORE School
Ewing, NJ

Susie Bellah
Kindergarten Teacher
Lakeland Elementary
Humble, TX

Megan Bennett
Elementary Math Coordinator
Hartford Public Schools
Hartford, CT

Susan T. Blan3kenship
5th Grade Teacher – Math
Stanford Elementary School
Stanford, KY

Wendy Buchanan
3rd Grade Teacher
The Classical Center at Vial
Garland, TX

Sandra Signorelli Coelho
Associate Director for
　Mathematics
PIMMS at Wesleyan University
Middletown, CT

Joanne DeMizio
Asst. Supt., Math and
　Science Curriculum
Archdiocese of New York
New York, NY

Anthony Dentino
Supervisor of Mathematics
Brick Township Schools
Brick, NJ

Lorrie L. Drennon
Math Teacher
Collins Middle School
Corsicana, TX

Ethel A. Edwards
Director of Curriculum and
　Instruction
Topeka Public Schools
Topeka, KS

Carolyn Elender
District Elementary Math
　Instructional Specialist
Pasadena ISD
Pasadena, TX

Monica Engel
Educator Second Grade
Pioneer Elementary School
Bolingbrook, IL

Anna Dahinden Flynn
Math Teacher
Coulson Tough K-6 Elementary
The Woodlands, TX

Brenda M. Foxx
Principal
University Park Elementary
University Park, MD

Katherine A. Frontier
Elementary Teacher
Laidlaw
Western Springs, IL

Susan J. Furphy
5th Grade Teacher
Nisley Elementary
Grand Jct., CO

Peter Gatz
Student Services Coordinator
Brooks Elementary
Aurora, IL

Amber Gregersen
Teacher – 2nd Grade
Nisley Elementary
Grand Junction, CO

Roberta Grindle
Math and Language Arts
　Academic Intervention
　Service Provider
Cumberland Head
　Elementary School
Plattsburgh, NY

Sr. Helen Lucille Habig, RSM
Assistant Superintendent/
　Mathematics
Archdiocese of Cincinnati
Cincinnati, OH

Holly L. Hepp
Math Facilitator
Barringer Academic Center
Charlotte, NC

Martha J. Hickman
2nd Grade Teacher
Dr. James Craik Elementary
　School
Pomfret, MD

Margie Hill
District Coordinating Teacher
　for Mathematics, K-12
Blue Valley USD 229
Overland Park, KS

Carol H. Joyce
5th Grade Teacher
Nathanael Greene Elementary
Liberty, NC

Stella K. Kostante
Curriculum Coach
Roosevelt Elementary
Pittsburgh, PA

Pamela Fleming Lowe
Fourth Grade eMINTS Teacher
O'Neal Elementary
Poplar Bluff, MO

Lauren May, NBCT
4th Grade Teacher
May Watts Elementary School
Naperville, IL

Lorraine Moore
Grade 3 Math Teacher
Cowpens Elementary School
Cowpens, SC

Shannon L. Moorhead
4th Grade Teacher
Centerville Elementary
Anderson, SC

Gina M. Musselman, M.Ed
Kindergarten Teacher
Padeo Verde Elementary
Peoria, AZ

Jen Neufeld
3rd Grade Teacher
Kendal
Naperville, IL

Cathie Osiecki
K-5 Mathematics Coordinator
Middletown Public Schools
Middletown, CT

Phyllis L. Pacilli
Elementary Education Teacher
Fullerton Elementary
Addison, IL

Cindy Pearson
4th/5th Grade Teacher
John D. Spicer Elementary
Haltom City, TX

Herminio M. Planas
Mathematics Curriculum
　Specialist
Administrative Offices-
Bridgeport Public Schools
Bridgeport, CT

Jo J. Puree
Educator
Lackamas Elementary
Yelm, WA

Teresa M. Reynolds
Third Grade Teacher
Forrest View Elementary
Everett, WA

Dr. John A. Rhodes
Director of Mathematics
Indian Prairie SD #204
Aurora, IL

Delores M. Rushing
Numeracy Coach
Dept. of Academic Services-
　Mathematics Department
Washington, DC

Daniel L. Scudder
Mathematics/Technology
　Specialist
Boone Elementary
Houston, TX

Laura Seymour
Resource Teacher Leader –
Elementary Math & Science, Retired
Dearborn Public Schools
Dearborn, MI

Petra Siprian
Teacher
Army Trail Elementary School
Addison, IL

Sandra Stein
K-5 Mathematics Consultant
St. Clair County Regional
　Educational Service Agency
Marysville, MI

Barb Stoflet
Curriculum Specialist
Roseville Area Schools
Roseville, MN

Kim Summers
Principal
Dynard Elementary
Chaptico, MD

Ann C. Teater
4th Grade Teacher
Lancaster Elementary
Lancaster, KY

Anne E. Tunney
Teacher
City of Erie School District
Erie, PA

Joylien Weathers
1st Grade Teacher
Mesa View Elementary
Grand Junction, CO

Christine F. Weiss
Third Grade Teacher
Robert C. Hill Elementary School
Romeoville, IL

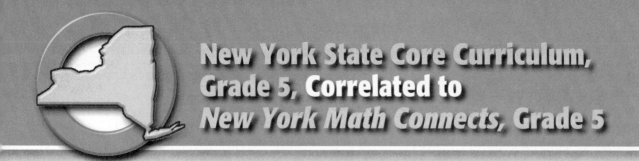

Lessons in which the standard is the primary focus are indicated in **bold**.

Process Strands and Performance Indicators		Lesson	Page
Problem Solving Strand			
Students will build new mathematical knowledge through problem solving.			
5.PS.1	Know the difference between relevant and irrelevant information when solving problems.	23, **3–9**	68–69, **136–137**
5.PS.2	Understand that some ways of representing a problem are more efficient than others	1–8, 4–5, 4–8, 6–7, 8–7, 9–8, 10–9, 11–6, 12–7	48–49, 166–167, 180–181, 266–267, 360–361, 400–401, 456–457, 496–497, 544–545
5.PS.3	Interpret information correctly, identify the problem, and generate possible strategies and solutions	**1–3**, 2–3, 2–5, 4–3, 4–8, 5–5, 6–7, 7–2, 8–7, 9–8, 10–9, 12–7, 13–5, 14–9, 15–5	**24–25**, 68–69, 74–75, 158–161, 180–181, 206–207, 266–267, 282–283, 360–361, 400–401, 456–457, 544–545, 576–577, 648–649, 682–683
Students will solve problems that arise in mathematics and in other contexts.			
5.PS.4	Act out or model with manipulatives activities involving mathematical content from literature.	**4–5**	**166–167**
5.PS.5	Formulate problems and solutions from everyday situations	1–5, 1–8, 4–8, 6–7, 7–2	32–35, 48–49, 180–181, 266–267, 282–283
5.PS.6	Translate from a picture/diagram to a numeric expression	5–1, 5–3	193–195, 198–201
5.PS.7	Represent problem situations verbally, numerically, algebraically, and/or graphically	5–3, 5–4	198–201, 202–204
5.PS.8	Select an appropriate representation of a problem	4–8, 5–5, 7–2	180–181, 206–207, 282–283
5.PS.9	Understand the basic language of logic in mathematical situations	**8–3, 13–2**	**344–345, 562–563**
Students will apply and adapt a variety of appropriate strategies to solve problems.			
5.PS.10	Work in collaboration with others to solve problems	P	P2–P3, P8–P9
5.PS.11	Translate from a picture/diagram to a number or symbolic expression	Explore 1–4, 1–4	26–30
5.PS.12	Use trial and error and the process of elimination to solve problems	1–8	48–49
5.PS.13	Model problems with pictures/diagrams or physical objects	Explore 1–4, 1–4, Explore 2–6, 3–5, Explore 4–3, Explore 4–6, 5–1, Explore 5–6, Explore 6–1, Extend 6–1, Explore 6–2, 11–2, 14–5	26–30, 78–79, 120–121, 156–157, 168–169, 193–195, 208–209, 235–236, 240–241, 242–243, 482–483, 628–629

LA = Looking Ahead to Next Year   CC = Cross Curricular   P = Projects   CSB = Concepts and Skills Bank

Process Strands and Performance Indicators		Lesson	Page
5.PS.14	Analyze problems by observing patterns	**9–6**	**394–395**
5.PS.15	Make organized lists or charts to solve numerical problems	**15–3**, 15–4	**674–675**, 677–680
Students will monitor and reflect on the process of mathematical problem solving.			
5.PS.16	Discuss with peers to understand a problem situation	P	P6–P9
5.PS.17	Determine what information is needed to solve problem	5–2	196–197
5.PS.18	Determine the efficiency of different representations of a problem	5–2	196–197
5.PS.19	Solve addition, subtraction, multiplication, and division problems, including those arising in concrete situations, that use positive and negative integers and combinations of these operations.	1–3, 10–5	24–25, 442–443
5.PS.20	Understand valid counterexamples	LA	LA6–LA9
5.PS.21	Explain the methods and reasoning behind the problem solving strategies used	10–9, 13–5	456–457, 576–577
5.PS.22	Discuss whether a solution is reasonable in the context of the original problem	2–2, 2–3, 3–3, 4–2, **12–2**	64–69, 112–115, 152–155, **522–523**
5.PS.23	Verify results of a problem	1–3, 8–7	24–25, 360–361
Reasoning and Proof Strand			
Students will recognize reasoning and proof as fundamental aspects of mathematics.			
5.RP.1	Recognize that mathematical ideas can be supported using a variety of strategies	2–7, 2–8, 3–2, 5–2, 5–6	84–91, 108–111, 196–197, 210–213
5.RP.2	Understand that mathematical statements can be supported, using models, facts, and relationships to explain their thinking	Explore 2–6, 2–7, Explore 3–2, Explore 4–3, Explore 4–6	78–79, 84–87, 106–107, 156–157, 168–169
Students will make and investigate mathematical conjectures.			
5.RP.3	Investigate conjectures, using arguments and appropriate mathematical terms	2–5	74–75
5.RP.4	Make and evaluate conjectures, using a variety of strategies	2–8	88–91
Students will develop and evaluate mathematical arguments and proofs.			
5.RP.5	Justify general claims or conjectures, using manipulatives, models, expressions, and mathematical relationships	3–5, 5–6, 11–2	120–121, 210–213, 482–483
5.RP.6	Develop and explain an argument verbally, numerically, and/or graphically	7–9	320–321
5.RP.7	Verify claims other students make, using examples and counterexamples when appropriate	P	P4–P5
Students will select and use various types of reasoning and methods of proof.			
5.RP.8	Support an argument through examples/counterexamples and special cases	10–5, 13–2	442–443, 562–563
Communication Strand			
Students will organize and consolidate their mathematical thinking through communication.			
5.CM.1	Provide an organized thought process that is correct, complete, coherent, and clear	2–4, 3–6	70–72, 122–124

LA = Looking Ahead to Next Year   CC = Cross Curricular   P = Projects   CSB = Concepts and Skills Bank

Process Strands and Performance Indicators		Lesson	Page
5.CM.2	Explain a rationale for strategy selection	2–5, CC, 9–8, 11–6	74–77, 400–401, 496–497
5.CM.3	Organize and accurately label work	2–4	70–72
Students will communicate their mathematical thinking coherently and clearly to peers, teachers, and others.			
5.CM.4	Share organized mathematical ideas through the manipulation of objects, numerical tables, drawings, pictures, charts, graphs, tables, diagrams, models, and symbols in written and verbal form	6–3, 6–6, 7–3, 7–4, 7–5, 7–6	248–249, 260–262, 284–292, 294–303
5.CM.5	Answer clarifying questions from others	P	P4–P5
Students will analyze and evaluate the mathematical thinking and strategies of others.			
5.CM.6	Understand mathematical solutions shared by other students	P	P4–P5
5.CM.7	Raise questions that elicit, extend, or challenge others' thinking	P	P6–P7
5.CM.8	Consider strategies used and solutions found by others in relation to their own work	P	P6–P7
Students will use the language of mathematics to express mathematical ideas precisely.			
5.CM.9	Increase their use of mathematical vocabulary and language when communicating with others	13–1, 13–4	557–560, 570–574
5.CM.10	Use appropriate vocabulary when describing objects, relationships, mathematical solutions, and rationale	13–1	557–560
5.CM.11	Decode and comprehend mathematical visuals and symbols to construct meaning	13–1, 13–7, 13–8	557–560, 582–590
Connections Strand			
Students will recognize and use connections among mathematical ideas.			
5.CN.1	Understand and make connections and conjectures in their everyday experiences to mathematical ideas	13–2	562–563
5.CN.2	Explore and explain the relationship between mathematical ideas	3–1, 4–6	103–105, 170–173
5.CN.3	Connect and apply mathematical information to solve problems	4–6, 5–5	170–173, 206–207
Students will understand how mathematical ideas interconnect and build on one another to produce a coherent whole.			
5.CN.4	Understand multiple representations and how they are related	7–8	312–317
5.CN.5	Model situations with objects and representations and be able to draw conclusions	Explore 6–1	235–236
Students will recognize and apply mathematics in contexts outside of mathematics.			
5.CN.6	Recognize and provide examples of the presence of mathematics in their daily lives	1–1, 3–4, 3–6, 3–9, Explore 4–3	17–19, 116–118, 122–124, 136–137, 156–157
5.CN.7	Apply mathematics to problem situations that develop outside of mathematics	1–1, 2–6, 3–7	17–19, 80–82, 126–129
5.CN.8	Investigate the presence of mathematics in careers and areas of interest	CC	40–41, 76–77, 130–131, 178–179, 216–217, 258–259, 304–305, 355–356, 408–409, 462–463, 498–499, 542–543, 594–595, 636–637, 664–665

LA = Looking Ahead to Next Year   CC = Cross Curricular   P = Projects   CSB = Concepts and Skills Bank

Process Strands and Performance Indicators		Lesson	Page
5.CN.9	Recognize and apply mathematics to other disciplines and areas of interest	CC	462–463, 498–499, 542–543, 594–595, 636–637, 664–665
Representation Strand			
Students will create and use representations to organize, record, and communicate mathematical ideas.			
5.R.1	Use physical objects, drawings, charts, tables, graphs, symbols, equations, or objects created using technology as representations	Extend 5–6, Extend 6–6, Extend 7–8, Explore 9–2, Explore 9–9, Explore 12–6	214–215, 264–265, 318–319, 376–377, 402–403, 536
5.R.2	Explain, describe, and defend mathematical ideas using representations	P	P2–P3
5.R.3	Read, interpret, and extend external models	Explore 6–2	242–243
5.R.4	Use standard and nonstandard representations with accuracy and detail	12–1	517–521
Students will select, apply, and translate among mathematical representations to solve problems.			
5.R.5	Use representations to explore problem situations	3–5	120–121
5.R.6	Investigate relationships between different representations and their impact on a given problem	11–2	482–483
Students will use representations to model and interpret physical, social, and mathematical phenomena.			
5.R.7	Use mathematics to show and understand physical phenomena (e.g., determine the perimeter of a bulletin board)	Explore 14–1, 14–1	607–611
5.R.8	Use mathematics to show and understand social phenomena (e.g., construct tables to organize data showing book sales)	CC	76–77, 130–131, 178–179, 408–409, 542–543
5.R.9	Use mathematics to show and understand mathematical phenomena (e.g., find the missing value that makes the equation true: $(3 + 4) + 5 = 3 + (4 + \underline{})$)*	2–7, 3–7	84–87, 126–129

LA = Looking Ahead to Next Year   CC = Cross Curricular   P = Projects   CSB = Concepts and Skills Bank

New York State Core Curriculum, Grade 5

Content Strands and Performance Indicators		Lesson	Page
Number Sense and Operations Strand			
Students will understand numbers, multiple ways of representing numbers, relationships among numbers, and number systems.			
Number Systems			
5.N.1	Read and write whole numbers to millions	**1–1**, 1–2	**17–19**, 20–23
5.N.2	Compare and order numbers to millions	**1–2**, 9–9	**20–23**, 404–407
5.N.3	Understand the place value structure of the base ten number system 10 ones = 1 ten 10 tens = 1 hundred 10 hundreds = 1 thousand 10 thousands = 1 ten thousand 10 ten thousands = 1 hundred thousand 10 hundred thousands = 1 million	**1–1**, 1–2, Explore 1–4, 1–4, 1–5, 3–1, 4–1, 9–5	**17–19**, 20–23, 26–30, 32–35, 103–105, 149–151, 391–393
5.N.4	Create equivalent fractions, given a fraction	**9–3**, P	**382–384**, P8–P9
5.N.5	Compare and order fractions including unlike denominators (with and without the use of a number line) *Note: Commonly used fractions such as those that might be indicated on ruler, measuring cup, etc.*	**8–5, Explore 9–9**, 9–9	**350–353**, 402–407
5.N.6	Understand the concept of ratio	**LA**	**LA10–LA13**
5.N.7	Express ratios in different forms	**LA**	**LA10–LA13**
5.N.8	Read, write, and order decimals to thousandths	**1–5, 1–6, 1–7**	**32–39, 42–46**
5.N.9	Compare fractions using <, >, or =	**8–5**	**350–354**
5.N.10	Compare decimals using <, >, or =	**1–6**	**36–39**
5.N.11	Understand that percent means part of 100, and write percents as fractions and decimals	**CSB**	**R56**
Number Theory			
5.N.12	Recognize that some numbers are only divisible by one and themselves (prime) and others have multiple divisors (composite)	**9–1, Explore 9–2, 9–2**, 9–3, 9–4	**373–384**, 386–389
5.N.13	Calculate multiples of a whole number and the least common multiple of two numbers	**9–7**	**396–399**
5.N.14	Identify the factors of a given number	**9–1**	**373–375**
5.N.15	Find the common factors and the greatest common factor of two numbers	**9–1**, 9–4	**373–375**, 386–389
Students will understand meanings of operations and procedures, and how they relate to one another.			
Operations			
5.N.16	Use a variety of strategies to divide three-digit numbers by one and two-digit numbers Note: Division by anything greater than a two-digit divisor should be done using technology.	**3–4, 3–6**	**116–118, 122–124**
5.N.17	Use a variety of strategies to divide three-digit numbers by one and two-digit numbers Note: Division by anything greater than a two-digit divisor should be done using technology.	**4–1, Explore 4–3, 4–3, 4–4, Explore 4–6, 4–6, 4–7**	**149–151, 156–164, 168–176**

LA = Looking Ahead to Next Year   CC = Cross Curricular   P = Projects   CSB = Concepts and Skills Bank

New York State Core Curriculum, Grade 5

Content Strands and Performance Indicators		Lesson	Page
5.N.18	Evaluate an arithmetic expression using order of operations including multiplication, division, addition, subtraction and parentheses	Explore 3–2, 3–2, 3–7, 5–7, **LA**	106–111, 126–129, 218–222, **LA18–LA21**
5.N.19	Simplify fractions to lowest terms	**9–4**	**386–389**
5.N.20	Convert improper fractions to mixed numbers, and mixed numbers to improper fractions	**8–1, Explore 8–2, 8–2, 8–4**	**333–342, 346–348**
5.N.21	Use a variety of strategies to add and subtract fractions with like denominators	**Explore 10–1, 10–1, Explore 10–2, 10–2, P**	**421–431, P2–P3**
5.N.22	Add and subtract mixed numbers with like denominators	**10–7, 10–8, 10–10**	**448–454, 458–461**
5.N.23	Use a variety of strategies to add, subtract, multiply, and divide decimals to thousandths	**Explore 2–6, 2–6, 3–8, 4–7, LA**	**78–82, 132–135, 1 74–176, LA2–LA5**

Students will compute accurately and make reasonable estimates.

Estimation

5.N.24	Round numbers to the nearest hundredth and up to 10,000	**2–1**	**61–63**
5.N.25	Estimate sums and differences of fractions with like denominators	8–6, 10–6	356–359, 444–446
5.N.26	Estimate sums, differences, products, and quotients of decimals	**2–2**, 3–8, **4–2**	**64–67**, 132–135, **152–155**
5.N.27	Justify the reasonableness of answers using estimation	**2–2, 3–3, 4–2**	**64–67, 112–115, 152–155**

Algebra Strand

Students will represent and analyze algebraically a wide variety of problem solving situations.

Variables and Expressions

5.A.1	Define and use appropriate terminology when referring to constants, variables, and algebraic expressions	**5–1, 5–7**	**193–195, 218–222**
5.A.2	Translate simple verbal expressions into algebraic expressions	5–1, 5–3, 5–4, 5–6, 5–7	193–195, 198–204, 210–213, 218–222

Students will perform algebraic procedures accurately.

Variables and Expressions

5.A.3	Substitute assigned values into variable expressions and evaluate using order of operations	**5–1, 5–3, 5–4**, 5–6, 5–7, **LA**	**193–195, 198–204**, 210–213, 218–222, **LA22–LA25**

Equations and Inequalities

5.A.4	Solve simple one–step equations using basic whole-number facts	**Explore 6–1, 6–1, Extend 6–1, Explore 6–2, 6–2**, 6–6	**235–247**, 260–262
5.A.5	Solve and explain simple one-step equations using inverse operations involving whole numbers	**6–2**	**244–247**
5.A.6	Evaluate the perimeter formula for given input values	**Explore 14–1, 14–1**	**607–611**

Students will recognize, use, and represent algebraically patterns, relations, and functions.

Patterns, Relations, and Functions

5.A.7	Create and explain patterns and algebraic relationships (e.g.,2,4,6,8...) algebraically: 2n (doubling)	**3–1, 4–1,** 5–3, 5–4, Explore 5–6	**103–105, 149–151,** 198–204, 208–209

LA = Looking Ahead to Next Year   CC = Cross Curricular   P = Projects   CSB = Concepts and Skills Bank

xvii

Content Strands and Performance Indicators		Lesson	Page
5.A.8	Create algebraic or geometric patterns using concrete objects or visual drawings (e.g., rotate and shade geometric shapes)	**3–1, 4–1**, 6–7, CC	**103–105, 149–151,** 260–267, 594–595
Geometry Strand			
Students will use visualization and spatial reasoning to analyze characteristics and properties of geometric shapes.			
Shapes			
5.G.1	Calculate the perimeter of regular and irregular polygons	**14–1**, P	**608–611**, P4–P5
Students will identify and justify geometric relationships, formally and informally.			
Geometric Relationships			
5.G.2	Identify pairs of similar triangles	**CSB**	**R58–R59**
5.G.3	Identify the ratio of corresponding sides of similar triangles	**CSB**	**R58–R59**
5.G.4	Classify quadrilaterals by properties of their angles and sides	**13–4**	**570–574**
5.G.5	Know that the sum of the interior angles of a quadrilateral is 360 degrees.	**CSB**	**R61**
5.G.6	Classify triangles by properties of their angles and sides	**13–3**	**566–569**
5.G.7	Know that the sum of the interior angles of a triangle is 180 degrees	**CSB**	**R60**
5.G.8	Find a missing angle when given two angles of a triangle	**CSB**	**R60**
5.G.9	Identify pairs of congruent triangles	**CSB**	**R58–R59**
5.G.10	Identify corresponding parts of congruent triangles	**CSB**	**R58–R59**
Students will apply transformations and symmetry to analyze problem solving situations.			
Transformational Geometry			
5.G.11	Identify and draw lines of symmetry of basic geometric shapes	13–1	557–560
Students will apply coordinate geometry to analyze problem solving situations.			
Coordinate Geometry			
5.G.12	Identify and plot points in the first quadrant	**6–4, 6–5**, Extend 6–6, P	**250–252**, 254–257, 264–265, P6–P7
5.G.13	Plot points to form basic geometric shapes (identify and classify)	6–4, 6–5, 13–6, 13–7, 13–8, 13–9	250–252, 254–257, 578–593
5.G.14	Calculate perimeter of basic geometric shapes drawn on a coordinate plane (rectangles and shapes composed of rectangles having sides with integer lengths and parallel to the axes)	**Explore 14–1**	**607**
Measurement Strand			
Students will determine what can be measured and how, using appropriate methods and formulas.			
Units of Measurement			
5.M.1	Use a ruler to measure to the nearest inch, $\frac{1}{2}$, $\frac{1}{4}$, and $\frac{1}{8}$ inch	**Explore 11–1,** **11–1**	**475–480**
5.M.2	Identify customary equivalent units of length	**11–1**	**477–480**
5.M.3	Measure to the nearest centimeter	**Explore 12–1**	**515–516**

LA = Looking Ahead to Next Year   CC = Cross Curricular   P = Projects   CSB = Concepts and Skills Bank

Content Strands and Performance Indicators		Lesson	Page
5.M.4	Identify equivalent metric units of length	**12–1**	**517–521**
5.M.5	Convert measurement within a given system	**11–1, 11–3, 11–4, 11–5, 12–1, 12–2, 12–3, 12–4, 12–6** P	**477–480, 484–490, 492–495, 517–530, 537–541**, P2–P3
Tools and Methods			
5.M.6	Determine the tool and technique to measure with an appropriate level of precision: lengths and angles	Explore 13–3, 14–8	564–565, 644–647
Students will use units to give meaning to measurements.			
Units			
5.M.7	Calculate elapsed time in hours and minutes	**11–7**	500–503
5.M.8	Measure and draw angles using a protractor	Explore 13–3	564–565
Students will develop strategies for estimating measurements.			
Estimation			
5.M.9	Determine personal references for customary units of length (e.g., your pace is approximately 3 feet, your height is approximately 5 feet, etc.)	11–1	477–480
5.M.10	Determine personal references for metric units of length	Explore 12–1, 12–1	515–521
5.M.11	Justify the reasonableness of estimates	2–2, 3–3	64–67, 112–115
Statistics and Probability Strand			
Students will collect, organize, display, and analyze data.			
Collection of Data			
5.S.1	Collect and record data from a variety of sources (e.g., newspapers, magazines, polls, charts, and surveys)	7–1, 7–3, 7–4, 7–5, 7–6, 7–8, Extend 7–8, 12–6, P, CSB	279–281, 284–292, 294–307, 312–319, 537–541, P2–P3, P8–P9, R64
Organization and Display of Data			
5.S.2	Display data in a line graph to show an increase or decrease over time	**7–7**, Extend 7–8, Explore 12–6	**306–310,** 318–319, 536
Analysis of Data			
5.S.3	Calculate the mean for a given set of data and use to describe a set of data	**CSB**	**R63**
Students will understand and apply concepts of probability.			
Probability			
5.S.4	Formulate conclusions and make predictions from graphs	7–3, 7–6, 7–7, 7–8, Extend 7–8, 7–9	284–288, 299–303, 306–310, 312–321
Students will compute accurately and make reasonable estimates.			
Estimation			
5.S.5	List the possible outcomes for a single-event experiment	15–1, Explore 15–2, **15–3**	661–663, 666–667, **674–675**
5.S.6	Record experiment results using fractions/ratios	**15–2, Extend 15–2,** 15–4	**668–673,** 677–680
5.S.7	Create a sample space and determine the probability of a single event, given a simple experiment (e.g., rolling a number cube	**15–2**	**668–672**

LA = Looking Ahead to Next Year   CC = Cross Curricular   P = Projects   CSB = Concepts and Skills Bank

Contents

Start Smart

H.O.T. Problems

WRITING IN MATH 3, 5, 7, 9, 11, 13

CHAPTER 1 Use Place Value

Focal Points and Connections
See page iv for key.

G5-FP7C *Number and Operations*

NYSMT PRACTICE 23, 31, 35, 39, 46, 55, 56, 57

H.O.T. Problems
Higher Order Thinking 19, 23, 30, 35, 38, 45

WRITING IN MATH 19, 23, 25, 27, 30, 31, 35, 38, 45, 49

Contents

CHAPTER 2

Solve Addition and Subtraction Problems

NYSCC

Focal Points and Connections
See page iv for key.

G5-FP2 *Number and Operations*

NYSMT PRACTICE 67, 73, 87, 91, 97, 98, 99

H.O.T. Problems
Higher Order Thinking 63, 66, 72, 82, 87, 90

WRITING IN ►MATH 63, 66, 69, 72, 73, 75, 79, 82, 87, 90, 97

CHAPTER 3

Multiply Whole Numbers

NYSCC

Focal Points and Connections
See page iv for key.

G5-FP1 *Number and Operations and Algebra*
G5-FP7C *Number and Operations*

NYSMT PRACTICE 111, 118, 119, 124, 129, 135, 143, 144, 145

H.O.T. Problems
Higher Order Thinking 105, 110, 115, 118, 124, 128, 135

WRITING IN ►MATH 105, 107, 110, 115, 118, 119, 121, 124, 128, 135, 137, 143

Contents

CHAPTER 4 Divide Whole Numbers

NYSCC

Focal Points and Connections
See page iv for key.

G5-FP1 *Number and Operations and Algebra*
G5-FP7C *Number and Operations*

CHAPTER 5 — Use Algebraic Expressions

Focal Points and Connections See page iv for key.

G5-FP4C *Algebra*

NYSMT PRACTICE 201, 205, 213, 222, 229, 230, 231

H.O.T. Problems
Higher Order Thinking 195, 200, 204, 212, 221

WRITING IN ▶MATH 195, 197, 200, 204, 205, 207, 209, 212, 215, 217, 221, 229

Contents

CHAPTER 6 Use Equations and Function Tables

NYSCC

Focal Points and Connections
See page iv for key.

G5-FP4C *Algebra*

CHAPTER 7

Display and Interpret Data

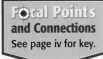

F⊙cal Points and Connections
See page iv for key.

G5-FP6C *Data Analysis*
G5-FP4C *Algebra*

NYSMT PRACTICE 288, 293, 298, 310, 327, 328, 329

H.O.T. Problems
Higher Order Thinking 281, 287, 292, 297, 303, 309, 317

WRITING IN ►MATH 281, 283, 287, 292, 293, 297, 303, 309, 317, 319, 321, 327

Contents

CHAPTER 8
Develop Fraction Concepts

NYSCC

Focal Points and Connections
See page iv for key.

G5-FP2 *Number and Operations*
G5-FP4C *Algebra*

NYSMT PRACTICE   342, 349, 353, 367, 368, 369

H.O.T. Problems
Higher Order Thinking 335, 341, 348, 353, 357

WRITING IN ▸MATH 335, 337, 341, 345, 348, 349, 353, 358, 361, 367

CHAPTER 9
Use Factors and Multiples

NYSCC

Focal Points and Connections
See page iv for key.

G5-FP2 *Number and Operations*
G5-FP4C *Algebra*

NYSMT PRACTICE 381, 389, 390, 399, 405, 415, 416, 417

H.O.T. Problems
Higher Order Thinking 375, 381, 384, 393, 399, 405

WRITING IN ▸MATH 381, 389, 390, 399, 405, 415, 416, 417

Contents

CHAPTER 10 — Add and Subtract Fractions

Focal Points and Connections
See page iv for key.

G5-FP2 *Number and Operations*
G5-FP4C *Algebra*

NYSMT PRACTICE 431, 447, 451, 461, 469, 470, 471

H.O.T. Problems
Higher Order Thinking 425, 431, 446, 450, 454, 461

WRITING IN ►MATH 422, 425, 427, 431, 443, 446, 447, 450, 454, 457, 461, 469

CHAPTER 11
Use Measures in the Customary System

Focal Points and Connections
See page iv for key.

G5-FP5C *Measurement*

NYSMT PRACTICE 480, 487, 491, 495, 503, 509, 510, 511

H.O.T. Problems
Higher Order Thinking 480, 486, 490, 495, 502

WRITING IN MATH 476, 480, 483, 486, 490, 491, 495, 497, 502, 509

Contents

CHAPTER 12 — Use Measures in the Metric System

Focal Points and Connections
See page iv for key.

G5-FP5C *Measurement*

CHAPTER 13

Identify, Compare, and Classify Geometric Figures

NYSCC

Focal Points and Connections
See page iv for key.

G5-FP3 *Geometry and Measurement and Algebra*

NYSMT PRACTICE 574, 575, 581, 590, 591, 592, 593, 601, 602, 603

H.O.T. Problems
Higher Order Thinking 560, 569, 573, 580, 586, 589, 593

WRITING IN ▶MATH 560, 563, 565, 569, 573, 575, 577, 580, 585, 589, 593

Contents

CHAPTER 14 — Measure Perimeter, Area, and Volume

Focal Points and Connections
See page iv for key.

G5-FP3 *Geometry and Measurement and Algebra*
G5-FP5C *Measurement*

H.O.T. Problems

Contents

CHAPTER 15 Use Probability to Make Predictions

NYSCC

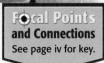

Focal Points and Connections
See page iv for key.

G5-FP6C *Data Analysis*

NYSMT PRACTICE 670, 676, 680, 687, 688, 689

H.O.T. Problems
Higher Order Thinking 663, 671, 680

Writing In ▶MATH 663, 667, 671, 675, 676, 680, 683, 687

Contents

Looking Ahead

Problem-Solving Projects

H.O.T. Problems
Higher Order Thinking LA5, LA9, LA13, LA17, LA21, LA25

WRITING IN ►MATH LA5, LA9, LA13, LA17, LA21, LA25

Student Handbook

Built-In Workbook

Reference

In March, you will take your Grade 5 New York State Mathematics Test. This test is divided into two books, Book 1 and Book 2. You will apply the concepts and skills that you have learned throughout the year in order to answer multiple-choice, short-response, and extended-response questions.

Book 1

This book contains multiple-choice questions only in which you will select the correct response from four answer choices. Your teacher will provide you with an answer sheet to fill in your answer choices.

Book 2

This book contains short-reponse and extended-response questions in which you will write an answer to open-ended questions. You are required to show your work to receive full credit. In some cases, you will be required to explain, in words, how you arrived at your response. You can write your responses directly in this test book.

How Can I Get Ready?

The New York State Test you will take in March covers the New York Core Curriculum for Grade 5 Mathematics. The following pages give you practice questions similar to those found on the test. You can use these practice pages in the weeks before the test to determine if you are ready. If you are struggling with any of the items, lesson references are provided so you can go back and review from the pages in your textbook.

Post March

1 Which point represents the coordinate $3\frac{2}{3}$ on the number line? **(Lesson 8-5)** **(4.N.7, 5.PS.7)**

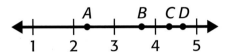

A Point A

B Point B

C Point C

D Point D

2 What number goes in the box to make this equation true? **(Lesson 9-3)** **(4.N.8, 5.CM.11)**

$$\frac{2}{3} = \frac{\blacksquare}{36}$$

A 6

B 10

C 12

D 24

3 What decimal is shown by the shaded portion in the model below? **(Lesson 1-4)** **(4.N.10, 5.PS.8)**

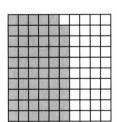

A 0.41

B 0.59

C 0.6

D 0.64

4 Maria completed 4 out of her 8 homework assignments. Which fraction represents her completed homework? **(Lesson 8-5)** **(4.N.8, 5.CN.7)**

A $\frac{4}{5}$

B $\frac{3}{4}$

C $\frac{5}{8}$

D $\frac{1}{2}$

5 Which dollar amount represents forty-two dollars and twenty-seven cents? **(Lesson 1-5)** **(4.N.11, 5.CN.9)**

A $27.42

B 27.42¢

C $42.27

D 42.27¢

6 What is the product of 27 and 19? **(Lesson 3-6)** **(4.N.19, 5.PS.9)**

A 46

B 60

C 456

D 513

7 Find the sum of the shaded regions in the fraction circles below. **(Lesson 10-1)** **(4.N.23, 5.PS.13)**

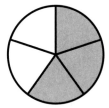 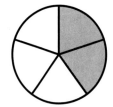

A $\frac{3}{5}$

B $\frac{2}{5}$

C 1

D 2

8 Which fraction represents the following decimal? **(Lesson 8-1)** **(4.N.24, 5.PS.18)**

0.17

A $\frac{17}{10}$

B $\frac{17}{100}$

C $\frac{1}{7}$

D $\frac{7}{1}$

SHORT RESPONSE

9 Jenna wants to buy dinner at the concession stand at the football game. If she wants to purchase a hot dog, a soft pretzel, a candy bar, and a soda, how much will she spend according to the prices given?
(Lesson 2-6) **(4.N.25, 5.PS.1)**

Hot dog	$1.75
Soft pretzel	$1.15
Candy bar	$0.85
Soda	$1.50

EXTENDED RESPONSE

10 Five friends want to put their change together to buy a card for their basketball coach. If Jake has $0.25, Kiry has $0.78, Ben has $0.92, Nikita has $0.45, and Cameron has $0.37, how much do they have to spend on the card? **(Lesson 2-6)**
(4.N.12, 4.N.25, 5.PS.14)

Order the amounts from least to greatest.

11 Choose the correct order of the fractions given from least to greatest.
(Lesson 8-5) **(4.A.2, 5.CN.2)**

$$\frac{1}{9}, \frac{1}{2}, \frac{1}{3}, \frac{1}{5}, \frac{1}{8}$$

A $\frac{1}{9}, \frac{1}{8}, \frac{1}{5}, \frac{1}{3}, \frac{1}{2}$

B $\frac{1}{2}, \frac{1}{3}, \frac{1}{5}, \frac{1}{8}, \frac{1}{9}$

C $\frac{1}{9}, \frac{1}{2}, \frac{1}{3}, \frac{1}{5}, \frac{1}{8}$

D $\frac{1}{8}, \frac{1}{5}, \frac{1}{3}, \frac{1}{2}, \frac{1}{9}$

12 Choose the symbol that makes a true sentence. (Lesson 1-7) **(4.A.2, 5.PS.17)**

$$0.77 \underline{\hspace{2cm}} 0.71$$

A $<$

B $>$

C $=$

D $\neq$

13 Choose the most accurate words for the following lines. (Lesson 13-1)
(4.G.6, 5.RP.3)

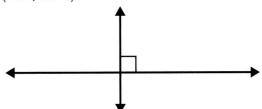

A parallel

B parallel and intersecting

C parallel and perpendicular

D perpendicular and intersecting

14 Classify the following angle.
(Lesson 13-3) **(4.G.8, 5.RP.4)**

A acute

B right

C obtuse

D straight

15 Classify the following angle.
(Lesson 13-3) **(4.G.8, 5.RP.4)**

A acute

B right

C obtuse

D straight

16 Classify the following angle.
(Lesson 13-3) **(4.G.8, 5.RP.4)**

A acute

B acute

C acute

D straight

17 Identify the vertex of $\angle ABC$.
(Lesson 13-3) (4.G.7, 5.RP.4)

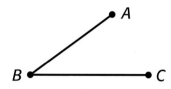

A point B

B $\overline{AB}$

C $\overline{CB}$

D point A

18 Choose the word that matches the following definition. (Lesson 13-1) (4.G.8, 5.RP.4)

2 lines that never meet

A perpendicular lines

B intersecting lines

C straight lines

D parallel lines

19 The graph shows the cost of using a computer at a coffee shop. If Regina's total cost was $45, for how many hours did she work on the computer?
(Lesson 7-3) (4.S.4, 5.R.5)

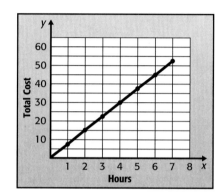

A 3   **C** 5

B 4   **D** 6

20 Which type of graph would be best for displaying the height of a plant over the past several weeks? (Lesson 7-8) (4.S.1, 4.S., 5.R.5)

A bar graph   **C** histogram

B circle graph   **D** line graph

EXTENDED RESPONSE

21 The list shows the birth month of the students in Mrs. Barr's geometry class. (Lesson 7-4) (4.S.2, 5.RP.1)

September	October	July
June	February	October
October	July	July
October	October	February
February	March	December
March	June	March
September	August	September

How many of the students were born in September?

Which months are not represented?

Month	Tally	Frequency
Jan		0
Feb	|||	3
Mar	|||	3
Apr		0
May		0
Jun	||	2
Jul	|||	3
Aug			1
Sep	|||	3
Oct	|||||	5
Nov		0
Dec			1

Number Sense

1 *Three-hundred five million, two hundred twenty-eight thousand, four hundred fifteen should be written as:* (Lesson 1-1) **(5.N.3, 5.CN.4)**

  A 305,228,415

  B 375,228,415

  C 350,228,415

  D 35,228,415

2 The number 2.25 could be expressed as: (Lesson 9-5) **(5.N.11, 5.R.6)**

  A $2\frac{2}{5}$

  B $\frac{2}{25}$

  C $2\frac{1}{4}$

  D $2\frac{1}{2}$

3 Brian recorded how many pencils his teacher gave out for an entire week. On Monday she gave out 2 pencils, Tuesday she gave out 3, Wednesday she gave out 1, Thursday she gave out 2, and Friday she gave out 5. Which expression represents the total amount of pencils she gave out throughout the week? (Lesson 5-1) **(5.N.18, 5.PS.19)**

  A $2 + 3 + 1 - 2 - 5$

  B $2 + 3 + 1 + 2 + 5$

  C 14

  D $2 - 3 - 1 - 2 - 5$

4 What fraction is represented by the model below? (Lesson 8-1) **(5.N.19, 5.PS.6)**

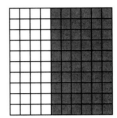

  A $\frac{1}{5}$

  B $\frac{1}{4}$

  C $\frac{1}{2}$

  D $\frac{3}{5}$

5 What fraction is represented by the model below? (Lesson 8-2) **(5.N.20, 5.PS.11)**

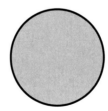

  A $\frac{1}{2}$

  B $\frac{3}{2}$

  C $\frac{3}{4}$

  D $\frac{7}{4}$

6 Which symbol will make a true number sentence when it is placed in the blank? (Lesson 9-9) (**5.N.2, 5.RP.8**)

$$\frac{5}{8} \underline{\hspace{2cm}} \frac{5}{6}$$

A <

B >

C =

D ÷

8 What decimal is shown in the model below? (Lesson 1-4) (**5.N.8, 5.R.2**)

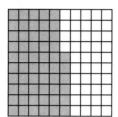

A 0.54

B 0.56

C 0.6

D 0.64

7 Which expression is equal to the product 3 × 5? (Lesson 5-3) (**5.N.18, 5.R.9**)

A 3 + 5 + 3 + 5 + 3

B 3 × 3 × 3 × 3 × 3

C 5 × 5 × 5

D 3 + 3 + 3 + 3 + 3

SHORT RESPONSE

9 Randy runs the race in 45.273 seconds. Mica runs the race in 42.948 seconds. Round to the nearest second to find about how many more seconds it takes Randy to run the race than Mica. (Lesson 2-6) (**5.N.26, 5.CN.1**)

10 Find the sum of $4\frac{3}{8} + 2\frac{1}{8}$. Write the answer in simplest form. (Lesson 10-5) (**5.N.22**)

EXTENDED RESPONSE

11 Order the following numbers from greatest to least and explain how you determined the order. (Lesson 1-6) (**5.N.10, 5.CM.2**)

0.01, 0.25, 0.04, 0.15, 0.2

12 A school cafeteria has 272 chairs and 34 tables. If the same number of chairs are placed at each table, how many chairs will be at each table? **(Lesson 4-4)**
(5.N.17, 5.PS.2)

  A 6

  B 8

  C 10

  D 12

13 Jarvis completed 3 out of his 5 homework assignments. Which fraction is less than $\frac{3}{5}$? **(Lesson 8-5) (5.N.5, 5.PS.5)**

  A $\frac{4}{5}$

  B $\frac{3}{4}$

  C $\frac{5}{8}$

  D $\frac{1}{2}$

14 A concession stand sold 188, 205, 299, 211, and 314 hot dogs during the first five home football games. What is the best estimate for the total number of hot dogs that were sold during the first five games? **(Lesson 2-2) (5.N.24, 5.N.27)**

  A 1,300

  B 1,200

  C 1,100

  D 1,000

15 The lengths of two radio commercials that air together are 2.2 minutes and 2.45 minutes. Which time is equal to the total time it will take to air both commercials? **(Lesson 2-6)**
(5.N.23, 5.CN.6)

  A 2.67 minutes

  B 4.47 minutes

  C 4.65 minutes

  D 4.67 minutes

16 Which point represents the coordinate $4\frac{1}{3}$ number line?
(Lesson 8-5) (5.N.9, 5.RP.2)

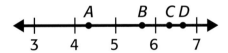

  A Point *A*

  B Point *B*

  C Point *C*

  D Point *D*

17 What number sentence is shown by the model below? **(Lesson 10-1)**
(5.N.13, 5.N.21)

  A $\frac{3}{6} + \frac{1}{6} = \frac{2}{3}$

  B $\frac{1}{6} + \frac{1}{3} = \frac{1}{2}$

  C $\frac{1}{3} + \frac{1}{4} = \frac{7}{12}$

  D $\frac{1}{2} + \frac{1}{3} = \frac{5}{6}$

18 In a recent year, between 142,000 and 143,000 pounds of material were recycled in one school district. Which of the following could be a number of pounds of material that were recycled? (Lesson 1-2) **(5.N.2, 5.PS.3)**

   A 143,930 pounds

   B 141,616 pounds

   C 143,094 pounds

   D 142,860 pounds

19 An electronics store sells an average of 145 video games in one day. How many games could they sell in 365 days? (Lesson 3-6) **(5.N.16, 5.R.4)**

   A 1,825

   B 5,292

   C 16,425

   D 52,925

20 What number goes in the box to make this equation true? (Lesson 9-3) **(5.N.4, 5.CN.3)**

$$\frac{5}{9} = \frac{\blacksquare}{36}$$

   A A

   B 5

   C 10

   D 20

21 Find the greatest common factor of 24, 30, and 42. (Lesson 9-1) **(5.N.14, 5.N.15)**

   A 2

   B 6

   C 8

   D 12

SHORT RESPONSE

22 Identify the prime numbers from the list below. (Lesson 9-2) **(5.N.12, 5.PS.20)**

6, 7, 8, 9, 10, 11, 12, 13, 14, 15, 16, 17

23 Ben has played piano for $4\frac{11}{12}$ years and Alana has played for $2\frac{1}{12}$ years. Estimate how many more years Ben has played the piano than Alana. (Lesson 10-4) **(5.N.25, 5.PS.3)**

EXTENDED RESPONSE

24 The Art Club is selling 12-ounce boxes of chocolate candy for a fundraiser. There are 36 boxes of candy in a case. Write a proportion that represents the problem. Calculate how many ounces of chocolate are in one case. (Looking Ahead 4) **(5.N.6, 5.N.7)**

25 Magdalena hiked along a 5-mile trail. She completed 4 of the miles before noon. Which fraction is greater than $\frac{4}{5}$?
(Lesson 8-5) **(5.N.5, 5.PS.5)**

A $\frac{1}{2}$

B $\frac{5}{8}$

C $\frac{3}{4}$

D $\frac{7}{8}$

26 In one minute, the average adult's heart beats 72 times. How many times will the average adult's heart beat in one hour? (Lesson 3-6) **(5.N.16, 5.R.4)**

A 8,640

B 4,320

C 864

D 432

27 Which expression is equal to the product 4×6? (Lesson 5-3)
(5.N.18, 5.R.9)

A $2 \times 2 \times 2 \times 3$

B $2 + 2 + 2 + 3$

C $4 \times 3 \times 2 \times 2$

D $2 + 2 + 2 + 2 + 2$

28 *Eight-hundred six million, three hundred forty-one thousand, nine hundred seventeen* should be written as: (Lesson 1-1)
(5.N.3, 5.CN.4)

A 860,341,917

B 806,341,917

C 806,314,917

D 800,341,917

29 At 8 A.M., the outside temperature was 44°F. By 10 A.M., the temperature rose 9°. The temperature rose an additional 15° by 2 P.M., and by 8 P.M., the temperature had dropped 12°. Which expression represents the temperature in degrees Fahrenheit at 8 P.M.?
(Lesson 5-1) **(5.N.18, 5.PS.19)**

A $44 + 9 - 15 - 12$

B $44 + 9 + 15 + 12$

C $44 + 9 + 15 - 12$

D $44 - 9 + 15 - 12$

30 What number sentence is shown by the model below? (Lesson 10-1)
(5.N.13, 5.N.21)

A $\frac{3}{8} + \frac{1}{8} = \frac{1}{2}$

B $\frac{3}{8} + \frac{1}{4} = \frac{5}{8}$

C $\frac{3}{8} + \frac{1}{4} = \frac{1}{2}$

D $\frac{5}{8} + \frac{1}{4} = \frac{7}{8}$

31 The number 5.75 could be expressed as: (Lesson 9-5) (5.N.11, 5.R.6)

A $5\frac{4}{5}$

B $5\frac{3}{4}$

C $5\frac{1}{2}$

D $5\frac{1}{5}$

32 Find the greatest common factor of 18, 27, and 36. (Lesson 9-1) (5.N.14, 5.N.15)

A 2
B 3
C 6
D 9

33 What number goes in the box to make this equation true? (Lesson 9-3) (5.N.4, 5.CN.3)

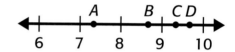

$$\frac{3}{8} = \frac{\blacksquare}{24}$$

A 6
B 9
C 12
D 18

34 Which point represents the coordinate $9\frac{1}{3}$ on the number line? (Lesson 8-5) (5.N.9, 5.RP.2)

A Point A
B Point B
C Point C
D Point D

SHORT RESPONSE

35 Philip paid $14.78 at a restaurant and Monique paid $11.17 at the same restaurant. Round to the nearest dollar to find about how much more Philip paid than Monique. (Lesson 2-6) (5.N.26, 5.CN.1)

36 Find the sum of $7\frac{1}{5} + 2\frac{3}{5}$. Write the answer in simplest form. (Lesson 10-5) (5.N.22)

EXTENDED RESPONSE

37 Order the following numbers from least to greatest and explain how you determined the order. (Lesson 1-6) (5.N.10, 5.CM.2)

0.56, 0.65, 0.05, 0.06, 0.6

38 The number of attendees at a baseball game was between 3,400 and 3,600. Which of the following could be a number of attendees at the game? (Lesson 1-2) (5.N.2, 5.PS.3)

A 3,476

B 3,704

C 3,760

D 3,806

39 A pet store carries 8 puppies. Of these, 3 are golden retrievers. Which fraction is less than $\frac{3}{8}$? (Lesson 8-5) (5.N.5, 5.PS.5)

A $\frac{2}{3}$

B $\frac{3}{5}$

C $\frac{1}{2}$

D $\frac{1}{4}$

SHORT RESPONSE

40 Eli has 324 more pages to read in his book. If he reads 9 pages a day, how many days will it take him to finish his book? (Lesson 4-3) (5.N.17)

41 A rectangular city park is 780 feet long by 625 feet wide. How much more area does this park cover than another rectangular park that is 500 feet long by 430 feet wide? (Lesson 14-2) (5.N.16, 5.M.5)

EXTENDED RESPONSE

42 Karen brought in $1\frac{3}{4}$ packages of cookies to share with the class. Grady brought in $2\frac{1}{4}$ packages. Explain how to estimate the total amount of packages. (Lesson 10-6) (5.N.24)

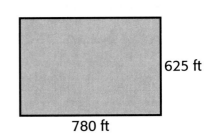

625 ft

780 ft

43 Regina completed $\frac{1}{8}$ of her math homework during study hall. She completed another $\frac{5}{8}$ before dinner. What fraction of her homework does she have left to complete? Explain how you solved the problem. (Lesson 10-2) (5.N.21)

Measurement

1 Suppose Beth started jogging at 3:52 P.M. and jogged for 45 minutes. At what time did she finish jogging? (Lesson 11-7) **(5.M.7, 5.CN.1)**

   A 4:32 P.M.

   B 4:37 P.M.

   C 4:42 P.M.

   D 4:47 P.M.

2 Jacob left his house at 11:25 A.M. He returned home two hours and 30 minutes later. At what time did he arrive home? (Lesson 12-1) **(5.M.7, 5.CN.1)**

   A 1:55 A.M.

   B 1:50 P.M.

   C 1:55 P.M.

   D 12:55 P.M.

3 Dario walked 4 kilometers. How many meters did he walk? (Lesson 12-1) **(5.M.4, 5.CN.7)**

   A 4,000 meters

   B 400 meters

   C 40 meters

   D 4 meters

4 Which of the following is equal to 4 quarts? (Lesson 11-4) **(5.M.5, 5.PS.2)**

   A 7 pints

   B 12 cups

   C 14 cups

   D 16 pints

5 Which of the following units would be most appropriate for finding the perimeter of the rectangle shown below? (Lesson 12-1) **(5.M.6, 5.M.4, 5.PS.8)**

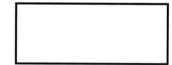

   A liters

   B millimeters

   C grams

   D kilograms

6 The 5th grade basketball team practices from 3:45 P.M. until 5:05 P.M. this afternoon. How long will the team practice? (Lesson 11-5) **(5.M.7, 5.CN.1)**

   A 55 min

   B 1 h 5 min

   C 1 h 15 min

   D 1 h 20 min

7 Estimate to the nearest $\frac{1}{4}$ of a centimeter, the length of the pencil.
(Lesson 11-1) (5.M.1, 5.PS.6)

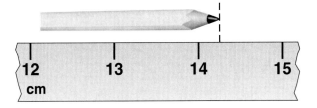

A 14 centimeters

B $14\frac{1}{2}$ centimeters

C $14\frac{1}{4}$ centimeters

D 15 centimeters

8 Which is *closest* to the measure of the angle shown below?
(Lesson 13-3) (5.M.8, 5.PS.11)

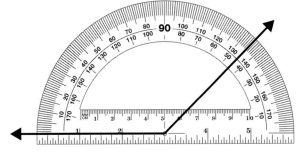

A 45°

B 55°

C 135°

D 145°

SHORT RESPONSE

9 The temperature at 9:15 A.M. was 20°C. By 2:00 P.M., the temperature was 32°C. How many degrees Celsius did the temperature rise? How much time had elapsed?
(Lesson 11-5) (5.M.7, 5.PS.19)

10 Brittany needs 16 ounces of milk for a recipe. How many cups of milk does she need? (Lesson 11-4) (5.M.5, 5.PS.17)

EXTENDED RESPONSE

11 Jamel and his father were to pick up three of his teammates and then drop them off at school for football practice. Below is a diagram of the path that Jamel and his father took. (5.PS.18)

Estimate to total distance Jamel and his father traveled. (Lesson 2-2) (5.M.11)

What was the actual distance? Was your estimate reasonable? (Lesson 2-6) (5.M.2, 5.M.11)

If it takes approximately 2 minutes to travel 1 mile and they spent 3 minutes at each stop, how long did the trip take them? (Looking Ahead 1) (5.M.7)

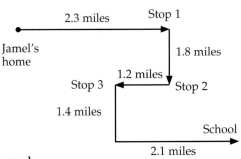

12 Use a ruler to measure the length of the paper clip. (Lesson 11-1) (5.M.1, 5.R.1)

  A 1.5 inches
  B 0.5 inch
  C 2.0 inches
  D 150 inches

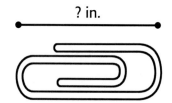

? in.

13 Which is the best estimate for the length of a baseball bat? (Lesson 11-1) (5.M.9, 5.PS.8)

  A 30 centimeters
  B 3 feet
  C 30 feet
  D 3 yards

14 Which is the best estimate for the height of a fifth grader? (Lesson 11-1) (5.M.10, 5.PS.8)

  A 1.5 meters
  B 5 meters
  C 15 meters

15 The outside walls of the Pentagon in Washington, D.C., each have a length of 921 feet. What is the perimeter in yards? (Lesson 14-1) (5.M.2, 5.CN.8)

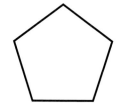

  A 926 yards
  B 307 yards
  C 1,535 yards
  D 4,605 yards

SHORT RESPONSE

16 Shana is making art smocks. Each smock requires 0.75 yard of fabric. Shana has 6 yards of fabric. How many smocks can she make? Show your work or draw a picture to explain your answer. (Lesson 11-1) (5.M.9, 5.PS.9)

EXTENDED RESPONSE

17 Use your ruler to help you solve this problem. Measure the sides of the shape below to the nearest centimeter. (Lesson 12-1) (5.M.4, 5.CM.3)

What is the perimeter of the shape?

What is the perimeter in millimeters?

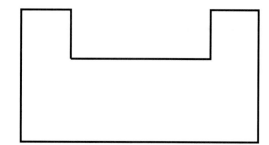

Algebra

1 The table shows the price of trail mix per pound.

Number of Pounds	Cost ($)
1	2.50
2	3.25
3	4.00
4	4.75
5	5.50
6	▨

What is the cost of 6 pounds of trail mix? (Lesson 9-6) **(5.A.7, 5.PS.14)**

A $5.75

B $6.00

C $6.25

D $6.50

2 Carrie earns $6 each week doing chores. Which expression can you use to find how much Carrie will earn in w weeks? (Lesson 5-3) **(5.A.7, 5.RP.5)**

A $6w$

B $6 + w$

C $6 - w$

D $w \div 6$

3 If the pattern continues, what will be the next number? (Lesson 6-3) **(5.A.7, 5.PS.14)**

$$3, 9, 15, ?$$

A 18

B 21

C 27

D 45

4 Which rule could have been used to create the table shown below? (Lesson 5-6) **(5.A.8, 5.R.3)**

x	1	2	3	4
y	4	8	12	16

A $y = x + 4$

B $x = y + 4$

C $y = 4x$

D $x = 4y$

5 What single transformation is shown below? (Lesson 13-8) **(5.A.8, 5.CM.10)**

A translation

B reflection

C rotation

D not here

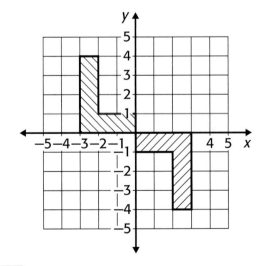

6 What is the perimeter of a hexagon with a side length of 12 centimeters? Use $P = ns$ where n is the number of sides. (Lesson 14-1) **(5.A.6, 5.CN.5)**

A 18 centimeters

B 48 centimeters

C 56 centimeters

D 72 centimeters

7 Identify the variable in the following expression. (Lesson 5-1) (5.A.1, 5.CM.10)

$$5a + 12 - a + 7a + 25A$$

A 5
B 12
C 7
D a

8 Identify the variable in the following expression. (Lesson 5-1) (5.A.1, 5.CM.10)

$$2x + 5$$

A 5
B 2
C x
D +

9 Find the perimeter of the rectangle. Use $P = 2\ell + 2w$. (Lesson 14-1) (5.A.6, 5.CN.5)

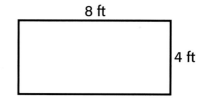
8 ft
4 ft

A 12 feet
B 18 feet
C 24 feet
D 36 feet

10 Find the perimeter of a square with a side length of 9 yards. Use $P = 4s$. (Lesson 14-1) (5.A.6, 5.CN.5)

A 12 feet
B 18 feet
C 24 feet
D 36 feet

SHORT RESPONSE

11 What number is missing in the table shown? (Lesson 5-6) (5.A.8, 5.PS.14)

input	output
12	7
15	10
17	▩
20	15
22	17

12 What rule can generate the next number of the sequence shown below? (Lesson 5-6) (5.A.7, 5.PS.14)

Multiply the previous term by 2.
$$24, 48, 72, 96, ?$$

EXTENDED RESPONSE

13 The set of number is a sequence. (Lesson 6-6) (5.A.7, 5.PS.14)

$$..., 48, 24, 12, ...$$

Describe the pattern.
What are the next two numbers in the sequence?
What are the previous two numbers in the sequence?

Geometry

1 What is the perimeter of the cube formed by the pattern below? (Lesson 14-1) **(5.G.1, 5.CM.4)**

  A 25 feet

  B 70 feet

  C 125 feet

  D 150 feet

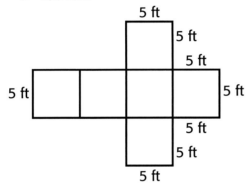

2 In the figure below, *ABCD* is a parallelogram. The diagonal cuts the parallelogram into two congruent triangles. What is the corresponding part of segment *AB* in △*BDC*? (Concepts and Skills 3) **(5.G.10, 5.RP.6)**

  A $\overline{AB}$

  B $\overline{CD}$

  C $\overline{BD}$

  D $\overline{BC}$

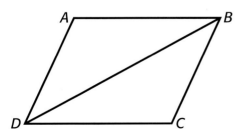

3 Which term most accurately describes the relationship between the two objects? (Concepts and Skills Bank 3) **(5.G.2, 5.CM.10)**

  A equal

  B congruent

  C similar

  D alike

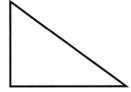

4 Find the missing angle measure in the quadrilateral. (Concepts and Skills Bank 5) **(5.G.5, 5.PS.6)**

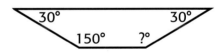

  A 30°

  B 60°

  C 120°

  D 150°

5 Choose the statement that is true for the following diagram. (Concepts and Skills 3) (5.G.9, 5.CM.1)

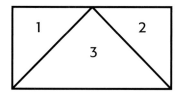

A △1≃△2

B △1≃△3

C △2≃△3

D not here

6 Classify the following triangle in terms of sides and angles. (Lesson 13-3) (5.G.65.CM.10)

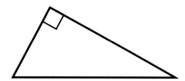

A isosceles right

B equilateral

C equiangular

D scalene right

SHORT RESPONSE

7 Sketch all lines of symmetry in the figure. How many lines of symmetry exist? (Start Smart 4) (5.G.11, 5.R.1)

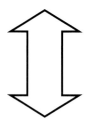

8 Kurt made a triangular garden in the corner of his yard. One angle is 40°. What is the measure of the third angle of Kurt's triangle? (Concepts and Skills Bank 4) (5.G.7, 5.G.8, 5.PS.6)

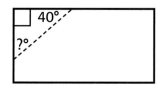

9 Which statement below best describes the figures shown? (Concepts and Skills Bank 3) (6.G.9, 5.CM.10)

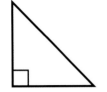

A The figures are congruent.

B The figures are similar.

C The figures are congruent and similar.

D The figures are neither similar nor congruent.

10 What is the perimeter of the diagram? (Lesson 14-1) (5.G.3, 5.CM.3)

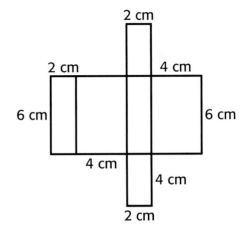

A 20 centimeters

B 26 centimeters

C 52 centimeters

D 76 centimeters

SHORT RESPONSE

11 Label the following figures below by properties shown. (Lesson 13-4) (5.6.4, 5.CM.10)

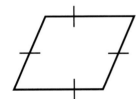 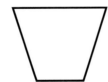 

12 Edmundo plotted the polygon *JKLM* on the coordinate plane (Lesson 13-4) (5.G.4, 5.CM.11)

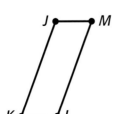

- Classify ∠*J* and ∠*M*.

- Classify the polygon *JKLM* using the name that most accurately describes it.

Statistics and Probability

1 The graph shows the cost of renting a jet ski for x hours. If Reggie's total cost was $30, for how many hours did he rent the jet ski? **(Lesson 7-3)** **(5.S.4, 5.R.5)**

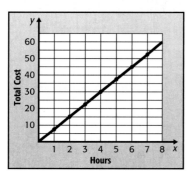

A 3   **C** 5

B 4   **D** 6

2 What is the mean of the following set of quiz scores? **(Concepts and Skills Bank 7)** **(5.S.3, 5.PS.5)**

$$8, 9, 7, 6, 10, 9, 7$$

A 7   **C** 8

B 7.5   **D** 8.5

3 The Venn diagram shows the factors of 51 and 34. What is the greatest common factor of 51 and 34? **(Lesson 8-3)** **(5.S.4, 5.PS.13)**

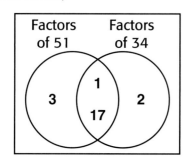

A 1   **C** 3

B 2   **D** 17

4 The line graph shows the height of a plant after several weeks. What was the height of the plant during week 4? **(Lesson 7-3)** **(5.S.4, 5.R.7)**

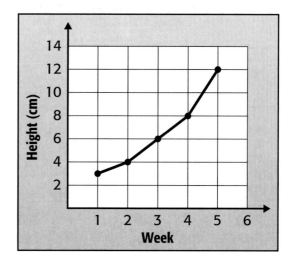

A 12 cm

B 8 cm

C 6 cm

D 4 cm

5 Sam kept track of the number of Calories that he burned per minute while running on the treadmill. How long did it take him to burn 60 Calories? **(Lesson 7-3)** **(5.S.4, 5.R.7)**

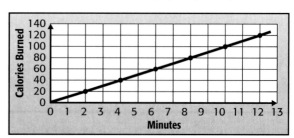

A 4 minutes

B 6 minutes

C 8 minutes

D 10 minutes

6 The line graph below shows the number of cars passing a particular intersection for the first ten days of a month.

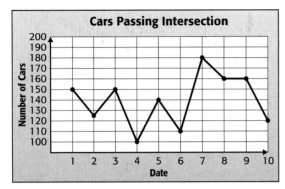

How many cars pass the intersection on the 5th of the month? (Lesson 7-3)
(5.S.4, 5.CN.6)

A 120   **C** 140

B 130   **D** 150

7 Lee used the newspaper to make the following table of high and low temperatures for 5 days.

Day	Mon	Tues	Wed	Thurs	Fri
High	72°F	78°F	81°F	83°F	85°F
Low	62°F	58°F	65°F	65°F	61°F

Which double line graph best presents the data? (Lesson 7-3) (5.S.1, 5.R.5)

A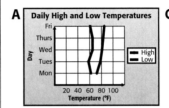

C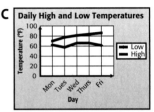

B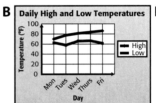

D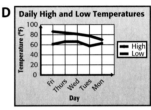

SHORT RESPONSE

8 Find the mean for the data in the table at the right.
(Concepts and Skills Bank 7) (5.S.3, 5.PS.9)

9 Sean made this frequency table to show the time it took his classmates to run 100 meters. (Lesson 7-4) (5.S.1, 5.S.4, 5.PS.15)

How many students ran 100 meters in less than 16 seconds?

How many students took 17 seconds or longer to run 100 meters?

How many students did Sean survey?

In what interval did the greatest number of times occur?

How many students ran 100 meters in 15.0 – 16.9 seconds?

Campers Buying Lunch	
Monday	114
Tuesday	98
Wednesday	65
Thursday	158
Friday	234
Saturday	234
Sunday	287

Time	Tally	Frequency
13.0-13.9	|||	3
14.0-14.9	卌		6
15.0-15.9	卌 卌		11
16.0-16.9	卌 卌 |||	13
17.0-17.9	||||	4
18.0-18.9	||	2

To the Student

As you gear up to study mathematics, you are probably wondering, "What will I learn this year?"

- **Number and Operations:** Estimate and find quotients of whole numbers, including quotients of multidigit numbers.

- **Number and Operations:** Add and subtract fractions with unlike denominators.

- **Geometry and Measurement:** Find volume and surface area of three dimensional figures.

Along the way, you'll learn more about problem solving, how to use the tools and language of mathematics, and how to THINK mathematically.

How to Use Your Math Book

Have you ever been in class and not understood all of what was being presented? Or, you understood everything in class, but got stuck on how to solve some of the homework problems? Don't worry. You can find answers in your math book!

- **Read** the **MAIN IDEA** at the beginning of the lesson.

- **Find** the **New Vocabulary** words, **highlighted in yellow**, and read their definitions.

- **Review** the **EXAMPLE** problems, solved step-by-step, to remind you of the day's material.

- **Refer** to the **EXTRA PRACTICE** boxes that show you where you can find extra exercises to practice a concept.

- **Go** to **NY Math Online** where you can find extra examples to coach you through difficult problems.

- **Review** the notes you've taken on your **FOLDABLES**.

- **Refer** to the **Remember** boxes for information that may help you with your examples and homework practice.

TREASURE HUNT

Let's Get Started

Use the Treasure Hunt below to learn where things are located in each chapter.

❶ What is the title of Chapter 1?

❷ How can you tell what you'll learn in Lesson 1-1?

❸ What is the title of the feature in Lesson 1-1 that tells you how to read a numer on a place-value chart?

❹ Suppose you're doing your homework on page 22 and you get stuck on Exercise 13. Where could you find help?

❺ List the new vocabulary words that are presented in Lesson 1-1.

❻ What is the key concept presented in Lesson 1-4?

❼ How many examples are presented in Lesson 1-6?

❽ In the margin of Lesson 1-6, there is a Vocabulary Link. What can you learn from that feature?

❾ What is the Web address where you could find extra examples?

❿ What problem-solving strategy is presented in the Problem-Solving Strategy in Lesson 1-8?

⓫ What is the Web address that would allow you to take a self-check quiz to be sure you understand the lesson?

⓬ On what pages will you find the Study Guide and Review for Chapter 1?

⓭ Suppose you can't figure out how to do Exercise 17 in the Study Guide on page 51. Where could you find help?

MATH?
SYMBOLS

New York

Start Smart

Let's Review!

Ladybug, the state insect

Problem Solving

Lake Champlain

Two popular tourist spots in New York are Lake Champlain and Seneca Lake. Lake Champlain, also known as the sixth Great Lake, covers 435 square miles. Seneca Lake has an area of 68 square miles.

How much larger is Lake Champlain than Seneca Lake?

You can use the four-step problem-solving plan to solve many kinds of problems. The four steps are Understand, Plan, Solve, and Check.

Understand

- **Read the problem carefully.**
- **What facts do you know?**
- **What do you need to find?**

You know the sizes of Lake Champlain and Seneca Lake. You need to find how much larger Lake Champlain is than Seneca Lake.

Did you Know?

The Finger Lakes are said to resemble the fingers on a hand. The three longest finger lakes are Cayuga Lake (40 mi), Seneca Lake (38 mi), and Keuka Lake (20 mi).

Plan

- **Think about how the facts relate to each other.**
- **Plan a strategy to solve the problem.**

Lake Champlain has an area of 435 square miles, and Seneca Lake has an area of 68 square miles. To find how much larger Lake Champlain is than Seneca Lake, you can use subtraction.

Solve

- **Use your plan to solve the problem.**

$$
\begin{array}{r}
435 \text{ square miles} \\
- 68 \text{ square miles} \\
\hline
367 \text{ square miles}
\end{array}
$$

Lake Champlain
Seneca Lake

So, Lake Champlain is 367 square miles larger than Seneca Lake.

Check

- **Look back.**
- **Does your answer make sense?**
- **If not, solve the problem another way.**

You can check the subtraction by using addition.

Seneca Lake		difference		Lake Champlain
68	+	367	=	435

This is the size of Lake Champlain. So, the answer is correct.

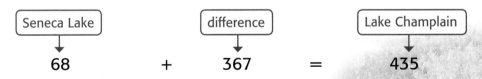 CHECK What You Know

1. List and describe the steps of the four-step problem-solving plan in order.

2. **WRITING IN ►MATH** Use the lake facts on the previous page to write a real-world problem. Ask a classmate to solve the problem using the four-step plan.

Number and Operations

New York's Coney Island

The historic Wonder Wheel on Coney Island in New York was constructed in 1920. It stands 150 feet tall and can hold 144 people.

After riding for five minutes, passengers will have completed about $1\frac{1}{2}$ revolutions along the outer wheel. The models show the fraction $1\frac{1}{2}$.

Did you Know?

The Wonder Wheel Stands out from other Ferris wheels because it has both an inner and an outer wheel.

CHECK What You Know · Fractions · · · · · · · · · · · ·

Draw a model to represent each fraction.

1. $2\frac{3}{4}$ **2.** $3\frac{2}{3}$ **3.** $\frac{5}{8}$

4. $1\frac{5}{6}$ **5.** $\frac{4}{5}$ **6.** $4\frac{1}{3}$

CHECK What You Know — Estimation

The New York Aquarium on Coney Island has 8,000 animals representing 350 species, including northern fur seals. A full-grown northern fur seal can weigh over 600 pounds.

For Exercises 7-9, use the table that shows the possible weight of four different northern fur seals.

Weight of Northern Fur Seals				
northern fur seal	A	B	C	D
weight (lb)	95	480	582	409

7. About how much more does northern fur seal C weigh than northern fur seal A?

8. About how much more does northern fur seal B weigh than northern fur seal D?

9. Estimate the combined weight of all of the northern fur seals.

CHECK What You Know — Multiplication and Division

The table shows the admission prices to the New York Aquarium on Coney Island.

Admission Prices	
Ticket	Price ($)
Adult	12
Senior	8
Child	8

10. On Monday, Karen bought 4 adult tickets to the Aquarium. What was the total cost of the tickets?

11. Mrs. Coughlin spent $112 on children's tickets. How many tickets did Mrs. Coughlin purchase?

12. Ryan bought children's tickets for himself and 3 friends. How much did Ryan spend on tickets?

13. **WRITING IN ►MATH** Use the information about admission prices to write a real-world multiplication or division problem.

Algebra

New York's Natural World

The beaver is the state mammal of New York. A hard worker, the beaver cuts down trees to build lodges and dams. A beaver can cut down 120 trees in a year. The sentence $120 \div 12 = \blacksquare$ represents the number of trees a beaver can fell in a month. So, a beaver can chop down 10 trees in a month's time.

 **CHECK What You Know** Multiplication and Division ··········

Replace each ■ with a number to make a true number sentence.

1. $48 \div \blacksquare = 12$

2. $8 \times 7 = \blacksquare$

3. $9 \times 7 = \blacksquare$

4. $8 \times 11 = \blacksquare$

5. $40 \div \blacksquare = 5$

6. $5 \times 7 = \blacksquare$

7. $36 \div 3 = \blacksquare$

8. $45 \div \blacksquare = 9$

9. $4 \times 9 = \blacksquare$

10. $49 \div \blacksquare = 7$

Did you Know?

Bald eagles use the same nest year after year, building upon it as time goes on. Some nests weigh as much as 2 tons and span 9 feet!

The bald eagle is also a resident of New York. In the early spring, a female bald eagle usually lays about 2 eggs per clutch.

Number of clutches	Number of baby bald eagles
1	2
2	▦
3	6
4	8
5	▦

11. How many baby bald eagles would be in two clutches?

12. How many baby eagles would be in five clutches?

Bald eagles weigh about 10 pounds. Kemp's ridley sea turtles, found in coastal waters, weigh 10 times that amount. So, the sea turtle weighs 10 × 10, or 100 pounds.

Replace each ▦ with a number to make a true sentence.

13. 10 × ▦ = 100

14. ▦ × 7 = 700

15. 15 × 100 = ▦

16. 10 × ▦ = 30

17. 12 × 10 = ▦

18. ▦ × 100 = 900

19. WRITING IN ►MATH
Choose a number between 1 and 10. Multiply the number by 10 and 100. Explain how you found your answers.

Measurement

Baseball Measures Up!

Did you Know?

The final score of this game was San Francisco 8 New York 6. The game lasted 23 innings.

In 1964, the San Francisco Giants defeated the New York Mets in one of the longest games in Major League Baseball history. The game lasted 7 hours and 23 minutes.

CHECK What You Know   Time

1. An inning of a baseball game begins at 6:45 P.M. and ends at 7:25 P.M. How long was the inning?

2. Tomas and his family drive to the ballpark. They leave their house at 10:10 A.M. and arrive at the stadium 1 hour and 25 minutes later. What time do Tomas and his family arrive at the stadium?

3. Lily and her brother went to the concession stand at 2:37 P.M. If they arrived back at their seats at 2:56 P.M., how long were they gone?

CHECK What You Know · Temperature · · · · · · · · · · · · · · · · · · ·

For Exercises 4-7, use the table at the right that shows the temperatures in New York City on a recent day.

New York City's Temperature	
Time	Temperature (°F)
7:20 A.M.	61
2:45 P.M.	75
8:15 P.M.	84

4. Find the temperature difference between 2:45 P.M. and 7:20 A.M.

5. Between 7:20 A.M. and 12:50 P.M., the temperature rose 11 degrees. What was the temperature at 12:50 P.M.?

6. If the temperature was 74°F at 10:00 P.M., how many degrees did the temperature fall from 8:15 P.M.?

7. **WRITING IN ►MATH** Find yesterday's high and low temperatures in your city or town and then write a real-world problem based on those temperatures. Ask a classmate to solve the problem.

CHECK What You Know · Mass ·

A baseball has a mass of about 143 grams. There are 108 stitches on each baseball, and the life span of a baseball in the Major Leagues is 6 pitches!

Match the object with the appropriate unit of mass.

8. car   **a.** 1 gram

9. gorilla   **b.** 1,800 kilograms

10. paper clip   **c.** 160 kilograms

11. **WRITING IN ►MATH** Explain whether you would measure the weight of a beach ball in grams or kilograms.

Lesson 4

Geometry

Spectacular Shapes!

The state capitol building of New York has two prominent isosceles triangles in the front. An isosceles triangle has at least two sides that are the same length and at least one line of symmetry.

 **CHECK What You Know** Angles

Different angles can be found in buildings. Remember that 90°, 180°, 270°, and 360° are associated, respectively, with $\frac{1}{4}$ turn, $\frac{1}{2}$ turn, $\frac{3}{4}$ turn, and 1 full turn on a circle.

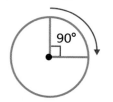 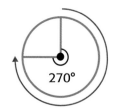 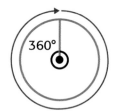

Use the photo of the capitol to solve each problem.

1. Describe any angles that appear to be less than 90°.

2. Describe any angles that appear to be exactly 90°.

3. Describe any angles that appear to be greater than 90°.

CHECK What You Know — Symmetry

Write the number of lines of symmetry for each figure.

4.

5.

6.

7.

8.

9.

CHECK What You Know — Classification

Examples of parallel lines can be found in the state capitol building. Parallel lines are lines that are the same distance apart and never intersect.

Identify each figure and the number of pairs of parallel sides.

10.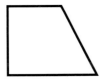

11.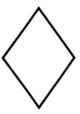

12.

13.

14. **WRITING IN ►MATH** Use the photo below of The Dairy in Central Park in New York City to describe any shapes, angles, and types of lines that appear to be in the building.

Data Analysis

Lesson 6

Island Life

Did you Know?

Fire Island has 30 miles of beach shoreline.

Fire Island, which is located off the southern side of Long Island, is a favorite vacation spot for many New Yorkers. More than 800,000 visitors journey to Fire Island each summer.

CHECK What You Know — Outcomes

1. Diego and his family will participate in two fun activities at Fire Island during their weekend stay. Make a list to show all of the different combinations of things they can do.

Fire Island Activities	
kayaking	fishing
surfing	bird watching
hiking	clamming

2. During their stay at the island, Antonia's family will go fishing, kayaking, and hiking. Make a list to show the different orders they can do these activities.

CHECK **What You Know** **Bar Graphs**

Classes may take field trips to Fire Island and explore its animal life, plantlife, sand samples, variety of seashells, etc.

For Exercises 3–8, use the graph at the right that shows the number of students who went on the fifth grade field trip to Fire Island.

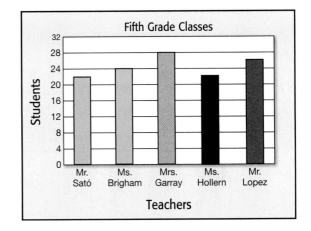

3. Which two fifth grade classes had the same number of students go on the field trip?

4. Identify the mode for this graph.

5. What is the total number of students who went on the field trip?

6. What is the total number of students in Mrs. Garray's and Mr. Lopez's class?

7. How many more students in Mr. Lopez's class went on the field trip than in Ms. Hollern's class?

8. WRITING IN ►MATH Explain how to find the median for this graph.

CHAPTER 1

Use Place Value

BIG Idea What is place value?

Place value is the value given to a digit by its position in a number.

Example The total land area of Arizona is 113,635 square miles. The **place-value chart** shows the value of each digit.

Place-Value Chart

hundred thousands	ten thousands	thousands	hundreds	tens	ones
1	1	3	6	3	5

What will I learn in this chapter?

- Use place value to read, write, compare, and order whole numbers.
- Use place value to read, write, compare, and order decimals.
- Solve problems using the *guess and check* strategy.

Key Vocabulary

place value

standard form

expanded form

decimal

NY Math Online Student Study Tools at macmillanmh.com

FOLDABLES®
Study Organizer

Make this Foldable to help you organize information about place value. Begin with a sheet of 11″ × 17″ paper.

① **Fold** the paper in half to make a two column chart.

② **Fold** one side of the paper upwards to create a 3″ tab.

③ **Glue** the outer edges of the 3″ tab to create a pocket.

④ **Fold** the top edge down to create a 2″ crease. Unfold to create a heading space for the two column chart.

⑤ **Label** the columns as shown. Use the pockets to store your notes.

Whole Numbers	Decimals

ARE YOU READY for Chapter 1?

You have two ways to check prerequisite skills for this chapter.

Option 2

NY Math Online > Take the Chapter Readiness Quiz at macmillanmh.com.

Option 1

Complete the Quick Check below.

QUICK Check

Write each number in word form. (Prior Grade)

1. 8

2. 15

3. 23

4. 44

5. 160

6. 371

Write the number that represents each point on the number line. (Prior Grade)

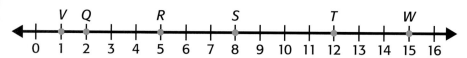

7. Q

8. S

9. R

10. T

11. V

12. W

Write each sentence using the symbols <, >, or =. (Prior Grade)

13. 8 is less than 12.

14. 25 is greater than 10.

15. 136 is equal to 136.

16. 471 is greater than 470.

17. The high temperature yesterday was 64°F. The high temperature today is 70°F. Write *64 is less than 70* using symbols.

Place Value Through Billions

▶ GET READY to Learn

Parker Ranch in Hawaii spreads across 150,000 acres, making it one of the largest ranches in the United States. There are different ways to represent this number.

You can read it as:
• one hundred fifty thousand

You can write it as:
• 150 thousand
• 100,000 + 50,000

A **place-value chart**, like the one below, shows the value of the digits in a number. In greater numbers, each group of three digits is separated by commas and is called a **period**.

Thousands Period			Ones Period		
hundreds	tens	ones	hundreds	tens	ones
1	5	0 ,	0	0	0

A digit and its **place**, or **place value**, name a number. For example, in 150,000, the digit 5 is in the ten thousands place. Its **value** is 5 × 10,000, or 50,000.

EXAMPLE   Place Value

① **Name the place of the underlined digit in 3̲65,200. Then write the value of the digit.**

The digit 3 is in the hundred thousands place. The digit represents 3 × 100,000, or 300,000.

The **standard form** of a number is the usual or common way to write a number using digits. The **expanded form** of a number is a way of writing a number as the sum of the *values* of its digits.

Lesson 1-1 Place Value Through Billions   **17**

 **Real-World EXAMPLE**   **Expanded Form**

② SPORTS The Bristol Motor Speedway in Tennessee has about 147 thousand seats. Write this number in standard form and in expanded form.

Standard Form: 147,000

Expanded Form:

value of 1 → 100,000   1 is in the hundred thousands place.
value of 4 → 40,000   4 is in the ten thousands place.
value of 7 → 7,000   7 is in the thousands place.

So, in expanded form, 147,000 = 100,000 + 40,000 + 7,000.

EXAMPLE   **Word Form**

③ Read and write 1,650,072,900 in word form.

Remember

To read a number, say the number in the period and then the period name.

Billions			Millions			Thousands			Ones		
hundreds	tens	ones	hundreds	tens	ones	hundreds	tens	ones	hundreds	tens	ones
		1	6	5	0	0	7	2	9	0	0

Word Form: one billion, six hundred fifty million, seventy-two thousand, nine hundred

---

CHECK What You Know

Extra Practice, p. R2

Name the place of the underlined digit. Then write the value of the digit. See Example 1 (p. 17)

1. 6̲57,230

2. 15̲,389,000

3. 49̲1,306,200,513

Use place value to write each number in standard form. See Example 2 (p. 18)

4. 12 million, 324 thousand, 500

5. 500,000 + 30,000 + 1,000 + 40 + 6

Write each number in expanded form. Then read and write in word form. See Examples 2, 3 (p. 18)

6. 34,617

7. 205,801,300

8. Weld County, Colorado, has four thousand four square miles. Write this number in standard form.

9. **Talk About It** Explain the steps you take to write 514,903,365 in word form.

Name the place of the underlined digit. Then write the value of the digit. See Example 1 (p. 17)

10. 3̲1,567

11. 2̲06,943

12. 5̲7,926,458

13. 814̲,210,307,000

14. 179,7̲03,341,650

15. 4̲1,653,000,241

Use place value to write each number in standard form. See Example 2 (p. 18)

16. 14 million, 286 thousand, 700

17. fifty billion, one hundred million, ninety-five

18. 800,000,000 + 30,000,000 + 2,000,000 + 50,000 + 4,000 + 600 + 70

Write each number in expanded form. Then read and write in word form. See Examples 2, 3 (p. 18)

19. 5,962

20. 2,040,391

Read and write each number in word form. See Example 3 (p. 18)

21. 9,200,340

22. 107,000,523,094

23. The top animated film of all time earned $436,471,036 in the United States. Write this amount in word form.

24. The U.S. Mint produces about 13 billion coins each year. What is this number in standard form?

Real-World PROBLEM SOLVING

Science The space probe *Cassini* took seven years to travel to Saturn and its largest moon, Titan.

25. How far did the probe travel to Saturn? Write the distance in standard form.

26. How do you read the cost of the mission?

27. Write the speed of the probe as it approached Titan in expanded form.

Facts About the Space Mission	
Distance to Saturn	934 million miles
Distance to Titan	2,200,000,000 miles
Cost of mission	$3,300,000,000
Speed of probe approaching Titan	13,700 miles per hour

Source: CNN

H.O.T. Problems

28. **OPEN ENDED** Write a number in both standard and expanded form that has 7 in the ten billions place and 5 in the hundred millions place. Then read your number.

29. **WRITING IN ►MATH** Explain how place value and periods are useful in reading whole numbers through 999 billion.

1-2

Compare Whole Numbers

GET READY to Learn

You can ride the roller coaster if you are 42 inches or taller. So, you will compare your height to 42 inches.

Must be 42 inches tall to ride.

When you compare numbers, they are either equal or *not* equal. If two quantities are equal, they form an **equation**. If two quantities are *not* equal, they form an **inequality**.

Words	Symbol
less than	<
greater than	>
equal to	=

One way to compare numbers is to use a number line.

• Numbers to the right are greater than numbers to the left.
• Numbers to the left are less than numbers to the right.

EXAMPLE   Use a Number Line

1 **Replace ● with <, >, or = to make 214 ● 209 a true sentence.**

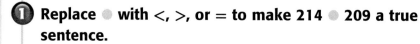

209 is to the left of 214.   214 is to the right of 209.

209 is *less than* 214. ⟵ **Say** ⟶ 214 is *greater than* 209.

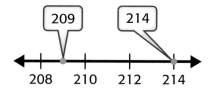

So, 214 > 209.

You can also use place value to compare whole numbers.

Step 1 Line up the digits at the ones place.

Step 2 Starting at the left, find the first position where the digits are different. The number with the greater digit is the greater whole number.

Real-World EXAMPLE   **Use Place Value**

2 ROLLER COASTERS The Daidarasaurus roller coaster is 7,677 feet long. The Ultimate roller coaster is 7,442 feet long. Which roller coaster is longer?

Step 1 Write the numbers, lining up the digits in the ones place.

    7,677
    7,442

Step 2 Compare the digits in each place value, starting from the left.

    7,677
    7,442

In the thousands place, 7 = 7.   In the hundreds place, 6 > 4.

Since 6 > 4 in the hundreds place, 7,677 > 7,442. You can check the reasonableness by using a number line.

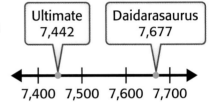

So, the Daidarasaurus roller coaster is longer.

> **Remember**
>
> If the first digit of one number has a greater place value than the first digit of another number, then you can compare without lining up the digits.
>
> For example,
> 584 > 68.
> hundreds↙   ↘tens

CHECK What You Know

Use the number line. Replace each ● with <, >, or = to make a true sentence. See Example 1 (p. 20)

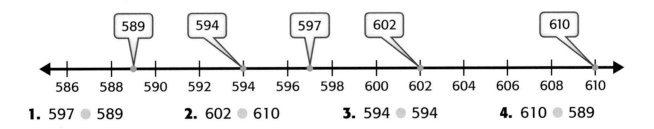

1. 597 ● 589   **2.** 602 ● 610   **3.** 594 ● 594   **4.** 610 ● 589

Replace each ● with <, >, or = to make a true sentence. See Example 2 (p. 21)

5. 14 ● 9   **6.** 86 ● 79   **7.** 134 ● 1,340

8. 4,260 ● 4,209   **9.** 23,681 ● 24,681   **10.** 5,655,710 ● 5,654,911

11. The Colorado River is 1,450 miles long. The Arkansas River is 1,460 miles long. Which river is longer?

12. **Talk About It** Discuss the steps you would take to compare 81,520 and 81,516.

Lesson 1-2 Compare Whole Numbers   **21**

Use the number line. Replace each ● with <, >, or = to make a true sentence.
See Example 1 (p. 20)

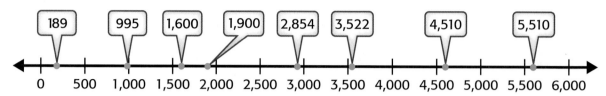

13. 1,600 ● 1,900   **14.** 995 ● 189   **15.** 2,854 ● 4,510   **16.** 3,522 ● 995

17. 189 ● 189   **18.** 5,510 ● 4,510   **19.** 4,618 ● 982   **20.** 189 ● 1,900

Replace each ● with <, >, or = to make a true sentence. See Example 2 (p. 21)

21. 284 ● 290

22. 860 ● 780

23. 1,076 ● 1,224

24. 3,743 ● 3,842

25. 10 ● 1,040

26. 2,072 ● 1,955

27. 62,300 ● 62,980

28. 4,678 ● 4,678

29. 14,092 ● 14,060

30. 364,250 ● 356,350

31. 114,208,600 ● 112,300,792

32. 7,655,240,000 ● 7,655,420,000

33. 10,856,432,021 ● 10,856,432,020

34. About 213 million songs were downloaded in 2004, and about 320 million were downloaded in 2005. In which year were more songs downloaded?

35. A giant ball of twine in Kansas has a mass of 7,893 kilograms. A giant ball of twine in Minnesota has a mass of 7,802 kilograms. Which ball has the larger mass?

Real-World PROBLEM SOLVING

Social Studies Time lines are used to show the order of events.

1541
Coronado's expedition to the Great Plains.

1640
Horses begin to spread throughout North America.

1500 1550 1600 1650 1700 1750 1800

1609
Spanish founded Santa Fe, New Mexico.

1706
Spanish founded Albuquerque.

Replace each ● with < or > to make a true sentence.

36. 1541 ● 1609

37. 1609 ● 1640

38. 1706 ● 1640

39. In 1750, horses reached the northern part of the Great Plains. Did this happen before or after the Spanish founded Albuquerque? Explain.

H.O.T. Problems

40. CHALLENGE Use the digits 4, 7, 1, 9, 3, and 8 one time each to write the greatest and least possible whole numbers in standard form.

41. OPEN ENDED Find a missing digit that makes 26,3■4 > 26,351 a true sentence.

42. NUMBER SENSE Is the statement *x* billion > *y* million *sometimes*, *always*, or *never* true for values of *x* and *y* that are greater than zero? Explain.

43.  Write a word problem about a real-world situation which you solve by comparing whole numbers.

NYSMT Practice > 5.N.1, 5.N.2

44. The Pacific Ocean covers about 64,000,000 square miles. How is this number written in words? **(Lesson 1-1)**

   A Sixty-four thousand

   B Sixty-four million

   C Sixty-four billion

   D Sixty-four trillion

45. Which is a true statement about the dimensions of the box? **(Lesson 1-2)**

height = 135 cm
width = 74 cm
length = 282 cm

   F The height is greater than the length.

   G The height is greater than the width.

   H The length is less than the height.

   J The width is equal to the height.

Spiral Review

Name the place value of the underlined digit. Then write the number it represents. (Lesson 1-1)

46. 1,2̲68   **47.** 15̲,809   **48.** 4̲94,268   **49.** 12̲3,475,689

50. The deepest place in the ocean is 35,838 feet below sea level. Read and write this number in word form. **(Lesson 1-1)**

Use place value to write each number in standard form. (Lesson 1-1)

51. 39 billion, 402 million, 1 thousand, 755

52. six hundred nineteen thousand, twenty-eight

Problem-Solving Investigation

<u>MAIN IDEA</u> I will use the four-step plan to solve a problem.

 5PS.3 Interpret information correctly, identify the problem and generate possible strategies and solutions *Also addresses 5.PS.19, 5.PS.23.*

P.S.I. TEAM +

TERESA: The table shows the prices, including tax, of the toys sold at Toy Central.

Item	Price
Yo-Yo	$4
Jump rope	$6
Bubbles	$2

I can spend exactly $10 on toys. Which of the following combination of toys can I *not* buy?

• 2 yo-yos and 1 bubbles

• 3 bubbles and 1 yo-yo

• 1 jump rope and 3 bubbles

YOUR MISSION: Determine which combination of toys Teresa cannot buy.

Understand	You know she can spend $10 on toys and the prices of the toys. You need to determine which combination of toys she *cannot* buy.
Plan	You can solve the problem by finding the total cost of each combination of toys.
Solve	2 yo-yos and 1 bubbles: $(2 \times \$4) + (1 \times \$2)$ or $10 ✓$ 3 bubbles and 1 yo-yo: $(3 \times \$2) + (1 \times \$4)$ or $10 ✓$ 1 jump rope and 3 bubbles: $(1 \times \$6) + (3 \times \$2)$ or 12 So, Teresa *cannot* buy 1 jump rope and 3 bubbles.
Check	Look back at the problem. The combination of 1 jump rope and 3 bubbles costs $12. Since $12 > $10, the answer makes sense.

Use the four-step plan to solve each problem.

PROBLEM-SOLVING SKILLS
• Use the four-step plan.

1. Latvia has 101 movie screens for every one million people. Sweden has 137 movie screens, and the United States has 105 movie screens for every one million people. Which country has the greatest number of movie screens for every one million people?

2. **Measurement** A swimmer set three world records. His times were 53.6 seconds, 24.99 seconds, and 1 minute 55.87 seconds. He swam in the 200-meter, the 50-meter, and the 100-meter backstroke competitions. What were his times for each race? Explain.

3. The cost of one jump rope is shown. If Ofelia has $15, does she have enough money to buy six jump ropes?

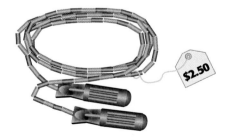

4. Parker cut his pizza into 6 equal slices and ate 3 of them. Tanisha cut her pizza into 8 equal slices and ate 3 of them. If the pizzas were the same size, who ate more? Explain how you know.

5. Shane spent 20 minutes on reading homework. He spent half as many minutes completing his social studies homework. He spent 10 minutes longer on his math homework than his reading homework. How many minutes did he spend on homework?

6. **Measurement** Use the map below. Ty went from his house to school and then to Art's house. Polly went from her house to school and then to Juanita's house. Who traveled farther?

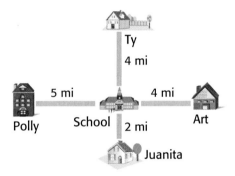

7. Todd has $85 to spend on athletic shoes. The shoes cost $50. If he buys one pair, he gets a second pair for half price. How much money will he have left if he purchases two pairs of the shoes?

8. A relative gives you twice as many dollars as your age on each birthday. You are 11 years old. How much money have you been given over the years by this relative?

9. Twelve students are going on a field trip. Each student pays $6 for a ticket and $3 for lunch. Find the total cost for tickets and lunches.

10. **WRITING IN ►MATH** Write a problem that you can solve using the four-step plan.

Math Activity for 1-4
Fractions and Decimals

Fractions and decimals are related. In a place-value chart, the place to the right of the ones place has a value of $\frac{1}{10}$ or one tenth. The next place value has a value of $\frac{1}{100}$ or one hundredth. Numbers that have digits in the tenths place, hundredths place, and beyond are called **decimals**. A **decimal point** is used to separate the ones place from the tenths place.

MAIN IDEA

I will use models to relate decimals to fractions.

NYS Core Curriculum

5.N.3 Understand the place value structure of the base ten number system *Also addresses 5.PS.11, 5.PS.13.*

New Vocabulary

decimal

decimal point

Fraction	Words	Decimal	Model
$\frac{1}{10}$	one tenth	0.1 decimal point tenths place	

ACTIVITY

1. **Use a model to show $\frac{3}{10}$. Then write it in words and as a decimal.**

   Step 1 Shade 3 rows in a 10 × 10 grid.

   Step 2 The model shows three tenths or 0.3.

You can use a similar model for $\frac{1}{100}$.

Fraction	Words	Decimal	Model
$\frac{1}{100}$	one hundredth	0.01 decimal point hundredths place	

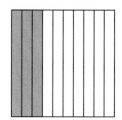

ACTIVITIES

② Use a model to show $\frac{9}{100}$. Then write it in words and as a decimal.

Step 1 Shade 9 of the 100 small squares.

Step 2 The model shows nine hundredths or 0.09.

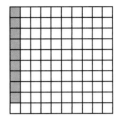

③ Use a model to show $\frac{34}{100}$. Then write it in words and as a decimal.

Step 1 Shade 34 of the 100 small squares.

Step 2 The model shows thirty-four hundredths. Notice that there are 3 tenths and 4 hundredths shaded. As a decimal, this is written 0.34.

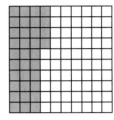

Think About It

1. The model at the right shows a thousandths cube. What fraction of the model is shaded? Then write as a decimal.

2. Model $\frac{80}{100}$. Then name the fraction as a decimal in two different ways.

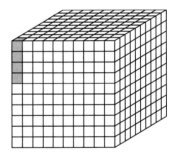

CHECK What You Know

NYSCC • NYSMT
Extra Practice, p. R2

Use a model to write each fraction in words and as a decimal.

3. $\frac{7}{10}$ **4.** $\frac{9}{10}$ **5.** $\frac{5}{100}$ **6.** $\frac{63}{100}$

Write the decimal for each model. Write the related fraction.

7. 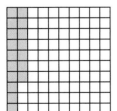   **8.** 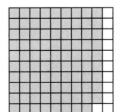   **9.**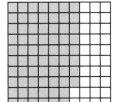

10. **WRITING IN ►MATH** Explain why $\frac{45}{100}$ is written as a decimal with a 4 in the tenths place and a 5 in the hundredths place.

Represent Decimals

MAIN IDEA

I will represent fractions that name tenths, hundredths, and thousandths as decimals.

NYS Core Curriculum

5.N.3 Understand the place value structure of the base ten number system *Also addresses 5.PS.11, 5.PS.13.*

NY Math Online

macmillanmh.com
• Extra Examples
• Personal Tutor
• Self-Check Quiz
• Concepts in Motion

GET READY to Learn

Each year, about $\frac{9}{10}$ of the days are sunny in Yuma, Arizona. In Redding, California, about $\frac{88}{100}$ of the days are sunny.

Fractions with denominators of 10, 100, 1,000, and so on can easily be written as decimals.

Fractions to Decimals — Key Concept

Model	Fraction	Decimal
Nine tenths are shaded.	$\frac{9}{10}$	0.9
Eighty-eight hundredths are shaded.	$\frac{88}{100}$	0.88
Sixteen thousandths are shaded.	$\frac{16}{1,000}$	0.016

Fractions that name tenths, hundredths, and thousandths have 1 digit, 2 digits, and 3 digits to the right of the decimal point.

EXAMPLE Fractions as Decimals

 Write $\frac{35}{100}$ as a decimal.

$\frac{35}{100}$ is 35 hundredths. Since the fraction names hundredths, there should be two digits to the right of the decimal point.

So, $\frac{35}{100} = 0.35$.

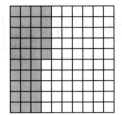

Real-World EXAMPLE Fractions as Decimals

Remember

The decimals 0.056 and 0.560 are not the same. The decimal 0.560 is read *five hundred sixty thousandths*.

② **INSECTS** A bee hummingbird weighs only about $\frac{56}{1,000}$ of an ounce. Represent this fraction as a decimal.

The fraction names thousandths, so there should be 3 digits to the right of the decimal point.

So, $\frac{56}{1,000} = 0.056$.

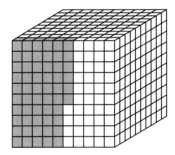

✓CHECK What You Know

Use a model to write each fraction as a decimal. See Examples 1, 2 (p. 29)

1. $\frac{4}{10}$ 2. $\frac{2}{10}$ 3. $\frac{58}{100}$ 4. $\frac{74}{100}$

5. $\frac{6}{100}$ 6. $\frac{5}{100}$ 7. $\frac{795}{1,000}$ 8. $\frac{9}{1,000}$

9. In a class survey, $\frac{60}{100}$ students said that they have a pet. Write this result as a decimal.

10. Describe a rule for writing fractions like $\frac{8}{100}$ and $\frac{32}{1,000}$ as decimals.

Use a model to write each fraction as a decimal. See Examples 1, 2 (p. 29)

11. $\frac{3}{10}$

12. $\frac{9}{10}$

13. $\frac{86}{100}$

14. $\frac{99}{100}$

15. $\frac{107}{1,000}$

16. $\frac{387}{1,000}$

17. $\frac{51}{1,000}$

18. $\frac{80}{1,000}$

19. $\frac{60}{100}$

20. $\frac{22}{1,000}$

21. $\frac{4}{100}$

22. $\frac{1}{1,000}$

23. Mrs. Carroll bought $\frac{8}{10}$ pound of turkey. Write this fraction as a decimal.

24. A runner decreased his time by $\frac{5}{100}$ of a second. Express this decrease as a decimal.

25. About $\frac{7}{10}$ of a person's body weight is water. Write this fraction as a decimal.

26. It rains only 9 hundredths of an inch each year in Ica, Peru. Write this number as a decimal.

Measurement Write the customary measure for each metric measure as a decimal.

27. 1 kilometer

28. 1 millimeter

29. 1 gram

30. 1 liter

Metric Measure	Customary Measure
1 kilometer	$\frac{62}{100}$ mile
1 millimeter	$\frac{4}{100}$ inch
1 gram	$\frac{35}{1,000}$ ounce
1 liter	$\frac{908}{1,000}$ quart

H.O.T. Problems

31. **OPEN ENDED** Write a fraction that has a denominator of 100. Then write the fraction as a decimal and draw a model to represent the decimal.

32. **FIND THE ERROR** Ryan and Janelle are writing $\frac{95}{1,000}$ as a decimal. Who is correct? Explain.

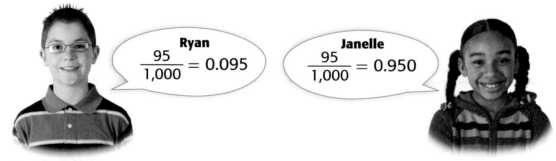

Ryan
$\frac{95}{1,000} = 0.095$

Janelle
$\frac{95}{1,000} = 0.950$

33. **WRITING IN ►MATH** Explain how the word form of a fraction can help you write the fraction as a decimal.

Name the place of the underlined digit. Then write the value of the digit. (Lesson 1-1)

1. 42,924,603

2. 953,187

3. **MULTIPLE CHOICE** In which number does 6 have a value of 60,000,000? (Lesson 1-1)

A 1,862,940   C 564,103,278

B 16,743,295   D 693,751,842

For Exercises 4 and 5, use the graph that shows the size of three Alaskan parks. (Lesson 1-1)

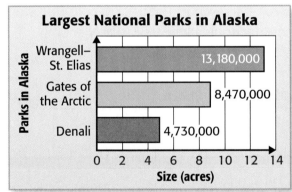

Largest National Parks in Alaska

Parks in Alaska

Wrangell– St. Elias — 13,180,000
Gates of the Arctic — 8,470,000
Denali — 4,730,000

0   2   4   6   8   10 12 14
Size (acres)

Source: *Scholastic Book of World Records*

4. Write the number of acres of Wrangell–St. Elias in expanded and word form.

5. Write in words how you would read the number of acres in Denali park.

Replace each ● with <, >, or = to make a true sentence. (Lesson 1-2)

6. 84 ● 90   7. 542 ● 524

8. 925 ● 1,024   9. 6,132 ● 6,231

10. The attendance at Friday's baseball game was 45,673. Sunday's game attendance was 45,761. Which game had a greater attendance? (Lesson 1-2)

11. A fifth grade teacher has 24 students in class. She wants to give each student 3 pencils. If she has 56 pencils, how many more pencils does she need? (Lesson 1-3)

Use a model to write each fraction as a decimal. (Lesson 1-4)

12. $\frac{1}{10}$ 13. $\frac{85}{100}$

14. $\frac{492}{1,000}$ 15. $\frac{39}{1,000}$

16. **MULTIPLE CHOICE** Which decimal represents the shaded part of the figure? (Lesson 1-4)

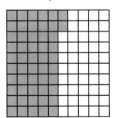

F 0.0052   H 0.52

G 0.052   J 5.2

17. Write *four hundredths* as a decimal. (Lesson 1-4)

18. **WRITING IN ►MATH** Describe the difference between 142 thousands and 142 thousandths. Explain how you know. (Lessons 1-2 and 1-4)

Place Value Through Thousandths

MAIN IDEA

I will read and write decimals in standard form, expanded form, word form, and short word form.

NYS Core Curriculum

5.N.3 Understand the place value structure of the base ten number system

5.N.8 Read, write, and order decimals to thousandths

NY Math Online

macmillanmh.com
• Extra Examples
• Personal Tutor
• Self-Check Quiz

GET READY to Learn

In 2004, Natalie Coughlin of the United States set an Olympic record. She swam the 100-meter backstroke in 59.68 seconds.

You can read the time as:
• fifty-nine and sixty-eight hundredths seconds

You can write the time as:
• 59 and 68 hundredths seconds

You have seen that the place-value chart used for whole numbers can be extended to include decimals like 59.68. The decimal point separates the ones place and the tenths place.

Place-Value Chart

tens	ones	tenths	hundredths	thousandths
5	9	6	8	0

The digit 6 is in the tenths place. Its value is 0.6.

The digit 8 is in the hundredths place. Its value is 0.08.

EXAMPLE Place of Digits in Decimals

1 Name the place of the underlined digit in 0.247. Then write the value of the digit.

The digit 7 is in the thousandths place. The digit represents 0.007.

Just as with whole numbers, you can also write decimals in standard form and expanded form.

EXAMPLE   Standard and Expanded Form

(2) Write *five and six hundred fourteen thousandths* in standard form and in expanded form.

Standard Form: 5.614

Expanded Form:

value of 5 → 5	5 is in the ones place.
value of 6 → 0.6	6 is in the tenths place.
value of 1 → 0.01	1 is in the hundredths place.
value of 4 → 0.004	4 is in the thousandths place.

So, in expanded form $5.614 = 5 + 0.6 + 0.01 + 0.004$.

To write decimals in word form, use the word *and* for the decimal point and use the place value of the last digit in the number.

Real-World EXAMPLE   Decimals in Word Form

(3) Measurement Five tree taps produce enough maple sap to make 1 gallon, or about 3.79 liters of syrup. Read and write the number of liters in word form.

tens	ones	tenths	hundredths	thousandths
	3	7	9	

The place value of the last digit, 9, is hundredths.

Word form: three and seventy-nine hundredths

Remember

As with whole numbers, understanding place value can help you read decimals and write them in word form.

Representing Decimals		Concept Summary
Form	**Definition**	**Example**
Standard Form	The usual way or commom way of writing a number using digits.	10.49
Expanded Form	A way of writing a number as the sum of the values of its digits to show place value.	$10 + 0.4 + 0.09$
Word Form	A way of writing a number using words.	Ten and forty-nine hundredths

Name the place of the underlined digit. Then write the value of the digit. See Example 1 (p. 32)

1. 6.<u>1</u>4

2. 32.09<u>5</u>

Write each number in standard form. See Example 2 (p. 33)

3. 5 and 87 hundredths

4. 20 + 6 + 0.9 + 0.01 + 0.004

Write each number in expanded form. Then read and write in word form. See Examples 2, 3 (p. 33)

5. 19.4   **6.** 35.19   **7.** 1.608   **8.** 2.085

9. A spider can travel one and two tenths miles per hour. Write this as a decimal.

10. **Talk About It** Discuss how place value is used to read decimals.

NYSCC • NYSMT
Extra Practice, p. R3

Name the place of the underlined digit. Then write the value of the digit. See Example 1 (p. 32)

11. 63.4<u>7</u>   **12.** 9.<u>5</u>6   **13.** 4.07<u>2</u>   **14.** 81.<u>4</u>53

Write each number in standard form. See Example 2 (p. 33)

15. 13 and 9 tenths

16. fifty and six hundredths

17. 10 + 1 + 0.9 + 0.02 + 0.003

18. 7 + 0.1 + 0.005

Write each number in expanded form. Then read and write in word form. See Examples 2, 3 (p. 33)

19. 4.28   **20.** 0.917   **21.** 69.409   **22.** 20.05

23. 13.09   **24.** 0.25   **25.** 92.301   **26.** 2.047

27. An athlete completes a race in 57.505 seconds. Name all the places the digit 5 appears in the number.

28. There was three and five hundredths inches of rain yesterday. Write this number in standard form.

29. A baseball player had a batting average of 0.334 for the season. Write this number in expanded form.

30. The table shows the amount of salt that remains when a cubic foot of water evaporates. Read each number that describes the amount of salt. Then write each number in words.

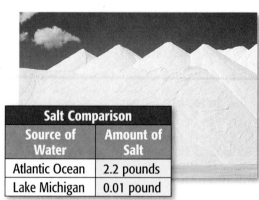

Salt Comparison	
Source of Water	**Amount of Salt**
Atlantic Ocean	2.2 pounds
Lake Michigan	0.01 pound

H.O.T. Problems

31. OPEN ENDED Write a number that has 6 in the thousandths place. Then write the number in expanded form and word form.

32. WHICH ONE DOESN'T BELONG? Identify the decimal that does not belong with the other three. Explain your reasoning.

five and thirty-nine hundredths	5.39	5 + 0.3 + 0.09	5 and 39 tenths

33. ◖ **WRITING IN** ►**MATH** Name an advantage of using 0.8 instead of $\frac{8}{10}$.

NYSMT Practice 5.N.3, 5.N.8

34. Which decimal is represented in the model below? (Lesson 1-5)

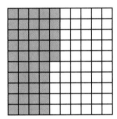

A 45

B 4.5

C 0.45

D 0.045

35. Which decimal represents the total value of 5 nickels, 1 quarter, and 3 dimes when compared to 1 dollar?

F 0.08

G 8.0

H 0.80

J 0.008

Spiral Review

Use a model to write each fraction as a decimal. (Lesson 1-4)

36. $\frac{6}{10}$ **37.** $\frac{29}{100}$ **38.** $\frac{541}{1,000}$ **39.** $\frac{7}{100}$

40. The ticket prices for a children's play are shown in the table. Mrs. Rodriguez bought 4 children's tickets, 2 adult tickets, and 1 senior ticket. If she gives the cashier $40, how much change should she receive? (Lesson 1-3)

Children	$4.00
Adults	$6.00
Seniors	$3.00

Replace each ● with <, >, or = to make a true sentence. (Lesson 1-2)

41. 830 ● 813   **42.** 5,670 ● 590   **43.** 23,904,156 ● 23,904,156

44. About 234 million bushels of apples were produced in the United States in a recent year. Write this number in expanded form. (Lesson 1-1)

1-6 Compare Decimals

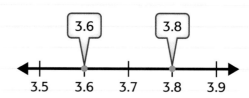 **GET READY to Learn**

Luis downloaded two songs onto his MP3 player. Which song is longer?

Song	Length (min)
1	3.6
2	3.8

MAIN IDEA

I will compare decimals.

NYS Core Curriculum

5.N.8 Read, write, and order decimals to thousandths

5.N.10 Compare decimals using <, >, or = *Also addresses 5.N.3.*

New Vocabulary

equivalent decimals

NY Math Online

macmillanmh.com
• Extra Examples
• Personal Tutor
• Self-Check Quiz

Comparing decimals is similar to comparing whole numbers.

Real-World EXAMPLE Compare Decimals

1 MUSIC Refer to the table above. Which song is longer?

One Way: Use a number line

```
        ┌─────┐              ┌─────┐
        │ 3.6 │              │ 3.8 │
        └──┬──┘              └──┬──┘
           ▼                    ▼
◄──────┬───●───┬───┬───●───┬──────►
      3.5 3.6 3.7 3.8 3.9
```

Numbers to the right are greater than numbers to the left. Since 3.8 is to the right of 3.6, 3.8 > 3.6.

Another Way: Use place value

Step 1	Step 2	Step 3
Line up the decimal points. 3.6 3.8	Compare the digits in the greatest place. 3.6 3.8 The ones digits are the same.	Continue comparing until the digits are different. 3.6 3.8 In the tenths place, 6 < 8. So, 3.6 < 3.8.

So, song 2 is longer.

Vocabulary Link

equi-

Everyday use equal

Decimals that have the same value are **equivalent decimals**.

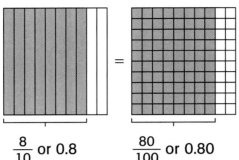

The shaded part of each model is the same. So, 0.8 = 0.80.

$\frac{8}{10}$ or 0.8 $\frac{80}{100}$ or 0.80

The model shows you can *annex*, or place zeros, to the right of a decimal without changing its value.

EXAMPLES   **Compare Decimals**

2 **Replace ● with <, >, or = to make 0.450 ● 0.45 a true sentence.**

0.450 = 0.45**0**   Annex a zero. The value does not change.

So, 0.450 = 0.45.

3 **Replace ● with <, >, or = to make 8.69 ● 8.6 a true sentence.**

8.69 → 8.69
8.6   → 8.6**0**   Annex a zero to the right of 8.6 so that it has the same number of decimal places as 8.69.

Since 9 > 0 in the hundredths place, 8.69 > 8.6.

CHECK What You Know

Replace each ● with <, >, or = to make a true sentence.

See Examples 1–3 (pp. 36–37)

1. 0.5 ● 0.7

2. 0.62 ● 0.26

3. 3.7 ● 3.70

4. 4.40 ● 4.44

5. 0.003 ● 0.102

6. 9.624 ● 9.618

7. 8.001 ● 8.001

8. 0.375 ● 0.42

9. 6.500 ● 6.5

10. Each year, Wadis Halfa, Sudan, gets about 2.5 millimeters of rain, and Luxar, Egypt, gets about 0.76 millimeter of rain. Which place gets more rain each year?

11. Talk About It   Describe how you know if two decimals are equivalent.

Replace each ● with <, >, or = to make a true sentence.

See Examples 1–3 (pp. 36–37)

12. 4.4 ● 4.1   **13.** 0.39 ● 0.37   **14.** 0.57 ● 0.65

15. 2.15 ● 2.150   **16.** 0.1 ● 0.006   **17.** 0.652 ● 0.647

18. 0.09 ● 0.001   **19.** 7.304 ● 7.30   **20.** 2.800 ● 2.8

21. 6.57 ● 6.6   **22.** 0.91 ● 0.90   **23.** 11.341 ● 11.34

24. 4.972 ● 4.972   **25.** 124 ● 124.1   **26.** 3.06 ● 3.814

27. 0.7 ● 0.007   **28.** 36.504 ● 36.6   **29.** 5.09 ● 5.10

30. A cat's normal body temperature is 101.5 degrees Fahrenheit. A rabbit's normal body temperature is 103.1 degrees Fahrenheit. Which animal has a lower normal body temperature?

31. Measurement Monisha lives 2.16 miles from school and 2.08 miles from the mall. Is Monisha's home closer to school or the mall?

For Exercises 32–34, use the table at the right that shows the cost of posters of famous works of art.

Poster Prices	
Poster	**Cost ($)**
From the Lake, No. 1, Georgia O'Keeffe	16.99
Relativity, M.C. Escher	11.49
Women and Bird in the Night, Joan Miro	18.98
Waterlillies, Claude Monet	15.99

32. Does the poster *Relativity* or the poster *Women and Bird in the Night* cost more?

33. Which poster costs less: *From the Lake, No. 1* or *Waterlillies*?

34. Which poster costs less than *Waterlillies*?

H.O.T. Problems

35. OPEN ENDED Write two decimals that are equivalent to 18.7. Tell why.

36. CHALLENGE How many times greater is 46 than 0.46? Explain.

37. **WRITING IN ►MATH** Discuss the similarities and differences between comparing whole numbers and comparing decimals.

38. Which of the following numbers is greater than 7.02? (Lesson 1-6)

A 7.021

B 7.020

C 7.002

D 7.0

39. Which of the following lists three decimalls between 8.6 and 9.2? (Lesson 1-6)

F eight and seven tenths, 8.61, 8.5

G eight and seven hundredths, 9.1, 9.0

H eight and eight tenths, 9.21, 9.01

J eight and seventy-five hundredths, 8.80, 9.19

Spiral Review

Use place value to write each number in expanded form. (Lesson 1-5)

40. 0.85   **41.** 2.09   **42.** 5.074   **43.** 16.731

44. The model at the right has $\frac{6}{10}$ of its squares shaded. Write the decimal that is represented by the shaded portion. (Lesson 1-4)

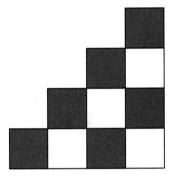

45. Della wants to score 32 goals this soccer season. So far, she has scored 26 goals and there are 3 games left this season. If she scores the same number of goals in each of the remaining games, how many goals must she score per game to score 32 goals? (Lesson 1-3)

Replace each ● with <, >, or = to make a true sentence. (Lesson 1-2)

46. 743 ● 842   **47.** 10,361 ● 1,542   **48.** 25,972 ● 52,955

49. The graphic shows the fastest speeds recorded for different activities. Which activity had the fastest speed? (Lesson 1-2)

Name the place of the underlined digit. Then write the value of the digit. (Lesson 1-1)

50. 4,<u>6</u>92,013

51. 1<u>8</u>,925

52. <u>2</u>7,904,611,000

ACTIVITY	SPEED (MILES PER HOUR)
luge	85.38
water skiing	143.08
horse running	43.26

Problem Solving in Science

Fun in the Sun

The Sun is amazing. It is a star that is 4.5 billion years old. At its center, the temperature is 27 million degrees Fahrenheit. That's about 67,000 times hotter than an oven! The Sun is not only incredibly hot, but also very large. If it were hollow, 100 Earths could fit inside of it. Because the Sun is so big, it has a lot of gravity. This gravity pulls on the 8 planets and keeps them in orbit.

Each planet's orbit is a different shape. Orbital eccentricity describes the shape of a planet's orbit. Scientists use decimals to measure orbital eccentricity. If a planet's orbit is perfectly circular, its orbital eccentricity is 0.0. The more oval-shaped the planet's orbit, the closer the decimal is to 1.0. Because each orbit is different, the planets are not always the same distance from the sun. Scientists describe these distances from the sun as averages.

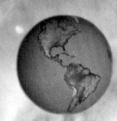

Planet	Average Distance from Sun (miles)	Orbital Eccentricity
Mercury	35,983,093	0.205
Venus	67,237,910	0.007
Earth	92,955,820	0.017
Mars	141,633,330	0.055
Jupiter	483,682,810	0.094
Saturn	886,526,100	0.057
Uranus	1,783,935,996	0.046
Neptune	2,795,084,800	0.011

 ## Real-World Math

Use the information on page 40 to solve each problem.

1. What planets are more than one billion miles from the Sun?

2. Is Neptune's orbit more circular than Earth's orbit? Explain your reasoning.

3. Which planet's orbit is closest to a circle? Write its orbital eccentricity in word form.

4. Which planet's orbit is closest to an oval? Write its orbital eccentricity in expanded form.

5. Which planet is more than one hundred million miles from the Sun, but less than two hundred million miles from the Sun?

6. The temperature of the Sun at its center is 27 million degrees Fahrenheit. Write this number in standard form.

7. Which 4 planets have orbits that are the most circular? Order these four planets from most circular to least circular.

Did You Know?

If you drove 60 miles per hour, it would take you 176 years to get to the Sun.

Order Whole Numbers and Decimals

GET READY to Learn

The table at the right shows the capacities of National League Football stadiums. You can use place value to order the capacities from greatest to least.

Stadium	Capacity
INVESCO Field Englewood, CO	76,100
Ford Field Detroit, MI	65,000
Qwest Stadium Seattle, WA	67,100

Real-World EXAMPLE   Order Whole Numbers

1 **STADIUMS** Refer to the table above. Order the capacities of the stadiums from greatest to least.

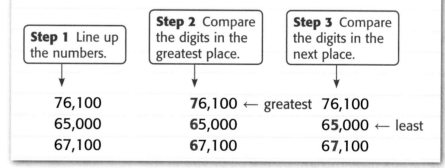

One Way: Use place value

Step 1 Line up the numbers.

Step 2 Compare the digits in the greatest place.

Step 3 Compare the digits in the next place.

76,100   **7**6,100 ← greatest 76,100
65,000   **6**5,000   **6**5,000 ← least
67,100   **6**7,100   **6**7,100

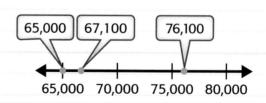

Another Way: Use a number line

65,000   67,100   76,100

65,000 70,000 75,000 80,000

So, the capacities from greatest to least are 76,100, 67,100, and 65,000.

Real-World EXAMPLES

Order Whole Numbers and Decimals

2 **SPORTS** Ava's scores for three gymnastics events are shown in the table. Order her scores from least to greatest.

Event	Score
Beam	9.375
Bars	8.950
Floor	9.275

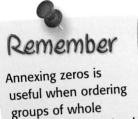

Remember

Annexing zeros is useful when ordering groups of whole numbers and decimals.

Step 1 Line up the decimal points.	**Step 2** Compare the digits in the greatest place.	**Step 3** Compare the digits in the next place.
9.275	**9**.275	9.**2**75
8.950	**8**.950 ← least	8.950
9.375	**9**.375	9.**3**75 ← greatest

The scores from least to greatest are 8.950, 9.275, and 9.375.

3 **MAIL** Four packages weighing 22.7, 23.84, 22, and 23.9 pounds were mailed. Order the weights from greatest to least.

Step 1 Line up the decimal points.	**Step 2** Annex zeros so all numbers have the same final place value.	**Step 3** Compare and order using place value.
22.7	22.7**0**	23.90
23.84	23.84	23.84
22	22.**00**	22.70
23.9	23.9**0**	22.00

The weights from greatest to least are 23.9, 23.84, 22.7, and 22.

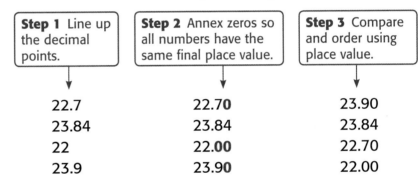

CHECK What You Know

Order each set of numbers from least to greatest. See Examples 1–3 (pp. 42–43)

1. Miles traveled: 567, 643, 590, 645

2. Rainfall in inches: 0.76, 0.09, 0.63, 0.24

3. Height of flowers in inches: 8.9, 8.59, 8.705, 8.05

4. Lengths of boxes in centimeters: 52.8, 51, 51.01, 52.47, 51.008

5. The length of insects in centimeters are: 1.35, 0.9, 1.48, and 1.8.
   Order the sizes of the insects from greatest to least.

6. **Talk About It** Discuss different steps that make ordering numbers easier.

Order each set of numbers from least to greatest. See Examples 1–3 (pp. 42–43)

7. Ages of teachers: 45, 32, 29, 30

8. Temperatures in °F: 106, 99, 101, 110

9. Baseball game attendances: 7,342, 7,249, 7,300, 7,248

10. Yearly salaries: $32,547, $33,200, $32,830, $32,829

11. Kilometers ran: 4.9, 3.7, 3.4, 4.2

12. Cost of snacks: $2.43, $2.34, $2.05, $2.18, $1.99

13. Masses of bottles in grams: 9.14, 7.99, 9.02, 8.95, 8.91

14. Race times in seconds: 43.789, 67.543, 86.347, 78.432, 34.678

15. Heights of trees in meters: 9.8, 10, 10.2, 9.6, 11

16. Weights of dogs in pounds: 25.4, 26.2, 26, 25.8, 27

17. The table shows the total number of students enrolled in some universities in a recent year. Which university had the greatest number of students enrolled? Which university had the least number of students enrolled?

University Enrollment	
University	**Number of Students**
Michigan State University	44,836
New York University	39,408
Purdue University	40,108
The Ohio State University	50,995
University of South Florida	42,238
University of Washington	39,199

Source: Institute of Education Sciences

18. The following measures are the long jump distances of the top six finishers in the 2004 Summer Olympics. Which distance was greater than 8.32 meters, but less than 8.59 meters?

8.25 m, 8.47 m, 8.59 m,
8.24 m, 8.32 m, 8.31 m

19. The table shows the heights of the tallest indoor waterfalls. Order the heights from greatest to least.

Location	Height (meters)
Hotel Windsor, Michigan	18.3
International Center, Michigan	34.7
Mohegan Sun, Connecticut	26.1
Orchid Hotel, India	21.3
Trump Tower, New York	27.4

Source: Scholastic Book of World Records

The table shows facts about snakes common to different regions of New York.

Snake	Average Adult Body Length (cm)	Average Hatchling Body Length (cm)
Northern Copperhead	76	21.5
Queen Snake	61	15.2
Timber Rattlesnake	121.6	29.5
Black Rat Snake	144.9	30.5

Source: *Smithsonian National Zoological Park*

20. List the average hatchling, or baby, body lengths from least to greatest.

21. Write the names of the snakes in order from greatest to least adult body length.

22. The average length of an adult eastern milk snake is 76.2 centimeters. Write a sentence comparing its length to the length of the snakes listed in the table.

H.O.T. Problems

23. **OPEN ENDED** Write an ordered list of five numbers whose values are between 50.98 and 51.6. Tell whether your list is from least to greatest or greatest to least.

24. **FIND THE ERROR** Diego and Abigail are ordering the numbers 0.088, 0.007, 0.4, and 0.19 from least to greatest. Who is correct? Explain.

Diego
$0.4 < 0.007 < 0.19 < 0.088$

Abigail
$0.007 < 0.088 < 0.19 < 0.4$

25. **WRITING IN** ►**MATH** Write a real-world problem that can be solved by finding the least number from: 12.33, 12.2, 11.79, 11.9, and 12.05.

26. Matt completed his first race in 15.163 seconds. The time of his second race was 15.24 seconds. Which of the following choices correctly shows the relationship between 15.163 and 15.24? (Lesson 1-6)

A 15.163 < 15.24

B 15.163 > 15.24

C 15.24 < 15.163

D 15.24 = 15.163

27. The table shows the seating capacity of the three largest stadiums in the world. Which is a true statement? (Lesson 1-7)

Stadium	Maximum Seating
Maracaña Municipa (Brazil)	205,000
Rungrado (North Korea)	150,000
Strahov (Czech Republic)	240,000

F The Maracaña Municipa is larger than the Rungrado.

G The Strahov is smaller than the Maracaña Municipa.

H The Maracaña Municipa is the largest stadium.

J The Strahov is the smallest stadium.

Spiral Review

Replace each ● with <, >, or = to make a true sentence. (Lesson 1-6)

28. 46.49 ● 46.5

29. 2.79 ● 2.37

30. 10.56 ● 10.65

Write each number in word form. (Lesson 1-5)

31. 7.3

32. 0.81

33. 2.99

34. 5.046

35. Mihir has $29 in his piggy bank. He receives $35 for his birthday. Does he have enough money to buy a computer game that costs $68 including tax? (Lesson 1-3)

For Exercises 36–38, use the table. It shows the world's largest freshwater aquariums. (Lesson 1-1)

Largest Freshwater Aquariums	
Aquarium	Size (sq ft)
Tennessee Aquarium, Tennessee	130,000
The Freshwater Center, Denmark	91,494
Great Lakes Aquarium, Minnesota	62,382

36. Describe the size of the Tennessee Aquarium in expanded form.

37. How many square feet is The Freshwater Center? Write in expanded form.

38. Describe the size of the Great Lakes Aquarium in word form.

Decimal War

Comparing Decimals

Get Ready!

Players: 2 players

Get Set!

- Each player creates ten game sheets like the one shown at the right, one for each of ten rounds.

- Make a spinner as shown.

Go!

- One player spins the spinner.

- Each player writes the number in one of the blanks on his or her game sheet.

- The other player spins the spinner, and each player writes the number in a blank.

- Play continues until all blanks are filled.

- The person with the greatest decimal scores 1 point. If players have the same decimal, each player scores 1 point.

- Repeat for ten rounds.

- The person with the greatest number of points after ten rounds is the winner.

You will need: spinner with digits 0 through 9 paper

Problem-Solving Strategy

MAIN IDEA I will solve problems by using the *guess and check* strategy.

 NYSCC **5.PS.12 Use trial and error and the process of elimination to solve problems** *Also addresses 5.PS.2, 5PS.5.*

The Bactrian camel has two humps, while the Dromedary camel has just one. Zach counted 19 animals with a total of 27 humps. How many camels of each type are there?

Understand	**What facts do you know?** • Bactrian camels have two humps. • Dromedary camels have one hump. • There are 19 camels with 27 humps. **What do you need to find?** • How many camels of each type are there?
Plan	You can use the *guess and check* strategy to solve the problem. Use combinations of 19 total camels to guess.

Solve	**Guess:** 10 Bactrian camels and 9 Dromedary camels
	Check: $10 \times 2 = 20$ humps 20 humps + 9 humps = 29 humps
	         $9 \times 1 = 9$ humps Too high. Try fewer Bactrian camels and more Dromedary camels.
	
	Guess: 7 Bactrian camels and 12 Dromedary camels
	Check: $7 \times 2 = 14$ humps 14 humps + 12 humps = 26 humps
	       $12 \times 1 = 12$ humps Too low. Try more Bactrian camels and less Dromedary camels.
	
	Guess: 8 Bactrian camels and 11 Dromedary camels
	Check: $8 \times 2 = 16$ humps 16 humps + 11 humps = 27 humps
	       $11 \times 1 = 11$ humps ✓ This guess is correct.
	
	So, there are 8 Bactrian camels and 11 Dromedary camels.

Check	Look back at the problem. $8 + 11 = 19$ camels and $16 + 11 = 27$ humps. So, the answer is correct.

Refer to the problem on the previous page.

1. Are there any other combinations of each type of camel that Zach could have seen? Explain your reasoning.

2. Suppose you saw 18 camels with a total of 22 humps. How many of each type did you see?

3. Explain how the guess and check method helped you solve this problem.

4. Explain why you should record your guesses and their results in the *solve* step of the problem-solving plan.

PRACTICE the Strategy

NYSCC • NYSMT
Extra Practice, p. R4

Solve. Use the *guess and check* strategy.

5. Vanessa sees 14 wheels on a total of 6 bicycles and tricycles. How many bicycles and tricycles are there?

6. Cole spent $66 on rookie cards and Hall of Famer cards. How many of each type of card did he buy?

Baseball Card	Cost
Rookie	4 for $6
Hall of Famer	2 for $9

7. A teacher is having three students take care of 28 goldfish during the summer. He gave some of them to Mary. Then he gave twice as many to Brandon. He gave twice as many to Kaylee as he gave to Brandon. How many fish did each student get?

8. Measurement Bike path A is 4 miles long. Bike path B is 7 miles long. If April biked a total of 37 miles, how many times did she bike each path?

9. Stacie counts 26 legs in a barnyard with horses and chickens. If there are 8 animals, how many are horses?

10. Len bought 2 postcards and received $1.35 in change in quarters and dimes. If he got 6 coins back, how many of each coin did he get?

11. The sum of two numbers is 30. Their product is 176. What are the two numbers?

12. A tour director collected $258 for tour packages. Tour package A costs $18 and tour package B costs $22. How many of each tour package were sold?

13. Ticket prices for a science museum are shown in the table. If $162 is collected from a group of 12 people, how many adults and students are in the group?

Customer	Cost
Adult	$18
Student	$12

14. WRITING IN MATH Refer to Exercise 11. How did you use the *guess and check* strategy to find the numbers?

Study Guide and Review

NY Math Online | macmillanmh.com
• STUDY *TO GO*
• Vocabulary Review

FOLDABLES Study Organizer GET READY to Study

Be sure the following Big Ideas are noted in your Foldable.

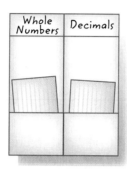

Key Concepts

Place Value (pp. 17, 32)

• **Place Value** is useful for reading and writing whole numbers and decimals.

9,000,000,000 → nine billion

5.38 → five and thirty-eight hundredths

• Whole numbers and decimals can be written in different forms.

Standard Form: 2,006,000

Expanded Form: 2,000,000 + 6,000

Word Form: two million, six thousand

Compare and Order Whole Numbers and Decimals (pp. 20, 36)

• Use a number line or place value to compare and order numbers.

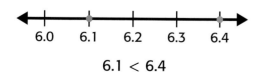

6.0   6.1   6.2   6.3   6.4

6.1 < 6.4

Key Vocabulary

decimal (p. 26)

equation (p. 20)

equivalent decimals (p. 37)

expanded form (p. 17)

inequality (p. 20)

place value (p. 17)

standard form (p. 17)

Vocabulary Check

State whether each sentence is *true* or *false*. If *false*, replace the underlined word or number to make a true sentence.

1. The symbol > means <u>greater than</u>.

2. The number 50.02 written in <u>standard form</u> is 50 + 0.02.

3. The number 7,105 is <u>equal to</u> 7,501.

4. The digit 4 in 24,510,000,000 is in the <u>millions</u> place.

5. A <u>decimal</u> is a number that has at least one digit to the right of the decimal point.

6. Eight and two hundredths written as a decimal is <u>0.802</u>.

Lesson-by-Lesson Review

1-1 Place Value Through Billions (pp. 17–19)

5.N.1,
5.N.3

Example 1
Name the place of the underlined digit in 2̲4,900. Then write the value of the digit.

place: ten thousands
value: 20,000

Example 2
Use place value to write the following number in standard form and expanded form.

ten million, twenty thousand, four hundred sixteen

Standard: 10,020,416
Expanded: 10,000,000 + 20,000 + 400 + 10 + 6

Name the place value of the underlined digit. Then write the number it represents.

7. 195̲,489   **8.** 6̲,720,341

Use place value to write each number in standard form.

9. 94 billion, 237 million, 108

10. 8,000,000 + 50,000 + 2,000 + 600

Write each number in expanded form. Then read and write in word form.

11. 4,302   **12.** 1,279,018

13. Measurement Montana has an area of 147,165 square miles. Write this number in word form.

1-2 Compare Whole Numbers (pp. 20–23)

5.N.2

Example 3
Replace ● with <, >, or = to make 3,249,800 ● 3,210,756 a true sentence.

Step 1 Line up the digits.   3,249,800
                             3,210,756

Step 2 Compare each place value, starting at the left.

In the ten thousands place, 4 > 1.

Since 4 > 1 in the ten thousands place, 3,249,800 > 3,210,756.

Replace each ● with <, >, or = to make a true sentence.

14. 98 ● 70

15. 234 ● 1,510

16. 8,960 ● 8,960

17. 814,789,002 ● 814,789,020

18. Is the population of Jacksonville or San Francisco greater?

City	Population
Jacksonville, Florida	777,704
San Francisco, California	744,230

Study Guide and Review

1-3 **Problem-Solving Investigation: The Four-Step Plan** (pp. 24–25)

5.PS.3

Example 4

On Sunday, Li ate 2,072 Calories. On the same day, her brother ate 2,141 Calories. Who ate more Calories on Sunday?

Understand   Li ate 2,072 Calories. Her brother ate 2,141 Calories. Find who ate more.

Plan   Use place value to determine who ate more Calories on Sunday.

Solve   Line up the digits.   2,072
Compare place   2,141
value starting
at the left. Li's   In the
brother ate   hundreds
more Calories.   place,
   $1 > 0$.

Check $2,072 < 2,141$ ✓

Solve. Use the four-step plan.

19. Measurement There are three long tunnels that go under Boston Harbor. The Summer Tunnel is 5,653 feet long. The Callahan Tunnel is 5,070 feet long. The Ted Williams Tunnel is 8,448 feet long. Order the lengths of the tunnels from least to greatest. Which tunnels are shorter than 5,670 feet in length?

20. How much more money is spent on strawberry and grape jelly than the other types of jelly each year?

Yearly Jelly Sales (thousands)	
Strawberry and grape	$371
All others	$285

1-4 **Represent Decimals** (pp. 28–30)

5.N.3

Example 5

Use a model to write $\frac{41}{1,000}$ as a decimal.

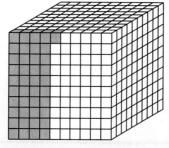

The fraction names thousandths, so there should be 3 digits to the right of the decimal point.

$$\frac{41}{1,000} = 0.041$$

Use a model to write each fraction as a decimal.

21. $\frac{19}{100}$ **22.** $\frac{8}{10}$

23. $\frac{644}{1,000}$ **24.** $\frac{2}{100}$

25. four tenths

26. thirteen thousandths

27. Tommy made six tenths of the free throws he attempted this season. Write the fraction of free throws that he made as a decimal.

1-5 Place Value Through Thousandths (pp. 32–35)

5.N.3,
5.N.8

Example 6
Write *eleven and eighty-five hundredths* in standard form.

tens	ones	tenths	hundredths
1	1 .	8	5

Standard Form: 11.85

Example 7
Write 7.394 in expanded form and word form.

Expanded: 7 + 0.3 + 0.09 + 0.004

Word: seven and three hundred ninety-four thousandths

Use place value to write each number in standard form.

28. five and nine tenths

29. 0.7 + 0.01 + 0.002

Write each number in expanded form. Then read and write in word form.

30. 0.53 **31.** 0.068

32. 1.22 **33.** 9.745

34. Measurement The winner of an inline skating race finished in 40.375 minutes. Write this time in word form.

1-6 Compare Decimals (pp. 36–39)

5.N.8,
5.N.10

Example 8
Replace ● with <, >, or = to make 5.613 ● 5.619 a true sentence.

Step 1 Line up the decimal points.
5.613
5.619

Step 2 Starting at the left, find the first place the digits are different.
5.61**3**
5.61**9**

> In the thousandths place, 3 < 9.

Since 3 < 9 in the thousandths place, 5.613 < 5.619.

Replace each ● with <, >, or = to make a true sentence.

35. 0.1 ● 0.11 **36.** 0.49 ● 0.71

37. 3.6 ● 3.16 **38.** 9.02 ● 9.020

39. 0.843 ● 0.846 **40.** 4.25 ● 4.025

41. Measurement The table shows the speeds of two fish.

Fish	Speed (mi per h)
Bluefin tuna	43.4
Wahoo	48.5

Is the bluefin tuna or the wahoo faster? Tell why.

Study Guide and Review

1-7 Order Whole Numbers and Decimals (pp. 42–46)

5.N.8

Example 9
Order 60.11, 60, and 61.038 from least to greatest.

Step 1 60.11
60
61.038
Line up the decimal points.

Step 2 60.11**0**
60.**000**
61.038
Annex zeros so all numbers have the same final place value.

Step 3 60.000
60.110
61.038
Compare and order using place value.

The numbers in order from least to greatest are 60, 60.11, and 61.038.

Order each set of numbers from least to greatest.

42. 56, 46, 58, 76

43. 13.84, 13.097, 13, 12.655, 13.6

44. Refer to the table. List these countries from the greatest to least number of bikes per person.

Country	Bikes per Person
China	0.37
Germany	0.88
Japan	0.63
Netherlands	1.10
United States	0.49

Source: *Scholastic Book of World Records*

1-8 Problem-Solving Strategy: Guess and Check (pp. 48–49)

5.PS.12

Example 10
Logan buys 10 T-shirts and spends a total of $96. Long-sleeved shirts cost $12. Short-sleeved shirts cost $8. How many of each did he buy?

Use the *guess and check* strategy.

Guess: 5 $12 shirts, 5 $8 shirts
Check: 5 × 12 = 60, 5 × 8 = 40
$60 + $40 = $100   too high

Guess: 4 $12 shirts, 6 $8 shirts
Check: 4 × 12 = 48, 6 × 8 = 48
$48 + $48 = $96 ✓

So, he bought 4 shirts for $12 each and 6 shirts for $8 each.

Solve. Use the *guess and check* strategy.

45. The table shows admission costs to an art exhibit.

Customer	Cost
Adult	$5
Child	$3

It costs a total of $37 for 9 people. How many adults and children are in the group?

46. Will ran 120 minutes in the past two days. He ran 20 more minutes the second day than the first day. How many minutes did he run each day?

Chapter Test

Name the place value of the underlined digit. Then write the number it represents.

1. 2<u>3</u>7,961
2. <u>8</u>04,510,327
3. 6.4<u>5</u>7
4. 0.89<u>2</u>

5. **MULTIPLE CHOICE** Write 4 million, 76 thousand, 850 in standard form.

   A 4,076,085
   B 4,076,850
   C 4,760,850
   D 4,076,850,000

6. A car wash costs $7 for cars and $12 for trucks. If $370 is collected from 40 vehicles, how many cars and trucks were washed? Use the *guess and check* strategy.

Write each number in word form.

7. 18,709
8. 3,524,064
9. 23.16
10. 5.921

11. **MULTIPLE CHOICE** What part of the model is shaded?

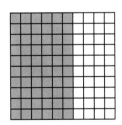

   F 0.006   H 0.6
   G 0.06   J 6.0

Write each fraction as a decimal.

12. $\frac{31}{100}$
13. $\frac{4}{10}$
14. $\frac{985}{1,000}$
15. $\frac{16}{1,000}$

For Exercises 16 and 17, use the table. It shows the length of the largest of each type of whale.

Type of Whale	Length (feet)
Fin whale	90
Sei whale	72
Right whale	60
Blue whale	80

16. Is the sei whale or fin whale longer?

17. Which is smaller: the right whale or the blue whale?

18. China has 4,639 movie theaters. France has 4,365. Which country has more?

Replace each ● with <, >, or = to make a true sentence.

19. 8.9 ● 8.2
20. 0.15 ● 0.4
21. 1.251 ● 1.201
22. 0.7 ● 0.700

Order each set of numbers from least to greatest.

23. 170, 181, 178, 171
24. 2.587, 2.43, 2.09, 2.23, 2.568

25. **WRITING IN ►MATH** The table shows tips that a server earned for four days.

Day	Tips ($)
Monday	$40.98
Tuesday	$55.30
Wednesday	$46.20
Thursday	$36.50

On which day(s) did the server earn more than $46? Explain.

NYSMT PRACTICE

The table shows the number of laps Michael swam each day over the past 4 weeks. If the pattern continues, how many laps will he swim each day during the fifth week?

Week	1	2	3	4	5
Laps	10	12	14	16	?

A 16 laps   **C** 18 laps

B 17 laps   **D** 20 laps

Read the Test Item

Look for a pattern to find the number of laps during week 5.

Solve the Test Item

Find the increase in laps between each of the first 4 weeks.

Week	1	2	3	4	5
Laps	10	12	14	16	?

+2 +2 +2 +2

The number of laps per day increases by 2 each week. During the fifth week, Michael will swim 16 + 2, or 18 laps per day. The answer is C.

PART 1   Multiple Choice

Read each question. Then fill in the correct answer on the answer sheet provided by your teacher or on a sheet of paper.

1. At a school function, there are 12 parents for every 1 teacher. If there are 72 parents at the function, how many teachers are there?

   A 5   **C** 7

   B 6   **D** 8

2. Start with 168,905.252. Increase the digit in the ten thousands place by 3, and decrease the thousandths digit by 2. What number results?

   F 148,905.234

   G 171,905.250

   H 198,905.232

   J 198,905.250

3. What fraction is equivalent to the decimal 0.058?

A $\frac{58}{10}$

B $\frac{58}{100}$

C $\frac{58}{1,000}$

D $\frac{58}{10,000}$

4. The population of the city where Lydia lives is eight million, six hundred twenty thousand, four hundred one. Which is the standard form of this number?

F 8,602,401

G 8,620,401

H 8,620,410

J 80,620,401

5. What portion of the squares is shaded? Express your answer as a decimal and a fraction.

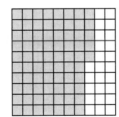

A 0.25, $\frac{25}{100}$

B 0.4, $\frac{40}{100}$

C 0.6, $\frac{60}{100}$

D 0.75, $\frac{75}{100}$

PART 2 Short Response

Record your answers on the sheet provided by your teacher or on a sheet of paper.

6. Write the number of students in the fifth grade in word form.

Grade Sizes	
Grade	Number of Students
5th Grade	237
6th Grade	215

7. Eduardo wants to save $770 to buy a new refrigerator. He saves $110 per month. Write a number sentence to show how many months it will take him to save enough money.

PART 3 Extended Response

Record your answers on the answer sheet provided by your teacher or on a sheet of paper. Show your work.

8. Draw a model to represent $\frac{5}{10}$. Then determine if $\frac{5}{10}$ is greater than, less than, or equal to $\frac{1}{2}$. Explain.

9. A machinist needs to cut a hole with a diameter of twenty-nine thousandths inch. By mistake, he cuts the hole 0.03 inch. Did he cut the hole too large or too small? Explain.

NEED EXTRA HELP?									
If You Missed Question...	1	2	3	4	5	6	7	8	9
Go to Lesson...	1–3	1–1	1–4	1–1	1–5	1–1	1–8	1–4	1–5
NYS Core Curriculum	5.PS.3	5.N.1	5.N.3	5.N.1	5.N.3	5.N.1	5.PS.12	5.N.3	5.N.3

CHAPTER 2 Add and Subtract Whole Numbers and Decimals

BIG Idea How are adding whole numbers and adding decimals the same?

The steps for adding and subtracting whole numbers and decimals are similar. In both cases, you add or subtract digits with the same place value.

Example Chicagoland Speedway's track length is 1.5 miles. Indianapolis Motor Speedway's track length is 2.5 miles. How much longer is the Indianapolis track than the Chicagoland track?

$$
\begin{array}{r}
2.5 \\
- 1.5 \\
\hline
1.0
\end{array}
$$

What will I learn in this chapter?

- Round whole numbers and decimals.
- Estimate sums and differences by rounding.
- Add and subtract whole numbers and decimals.
- Use properties of addition to add whole numbers and decimals mentally.
- Solve problems by using the *work backward* strategy.

Key Vocabulary

round

estimate

compatible numbers

compensation

NY Math Online > **Student Study Tools** at macmillanmh.com

CHICAGOLAND SPEEDWAY

FOLDABLES®
Study Organizer

Make this Foldable to help you organize information about whole numbers and decimals. Start with a sheet of 11″ × 17″ paper.

1 **Fold** the short sides toward the middle.

2 **Fold** the top to the bottom. Then open the paper.

3 **Cut** along the second fold to make four tabs.

4 **Label** each of the tabs as shown.

+ Whole Numbers   + Decimals
− Whole Numbers   − Decimals

You have two ways to check prerequisite skills for this chapter.

Option 2

NY Math Online > Take the Chapter Readiness Quiz at **macmillanmh.com**.

Option 1

Complete the Quick Check below.

QUICK Check

Name the place-value position of each underlined digit. (Lessons 1-1 and 1-5)

1. 5_2

2. 13_8_

3. 4._3_

4. _9_01

5. 1.2_1_6

6. _2_,785

Add. (Prior Grade)

7. 7 + 3

8. 2 + 9

9. 60 + 11

10. 52 + 30

11. 7 + 4 + 1

12. 8 + 5 + 1

13. The Pham family has 3 dogs, 1 cat, and 6 fish. The Weber family has 2 dogs, 3 gerbils, and a turtle. How many more pets does the Pham family have than the Weber family?

Complete to correctly rename each number. (Prior Grade)

14. 8 tens = 7 tens + __?__ ones

15. 2 hundreds = 1 hundred + __?__ tens

16. 5 hundreds = __?__ hundreds + 10 tens

17. 13 ones = 1 ten + __?__ ones

18. 16 tens = 1 hundred + __?__ tens

2-1 Round Whole Numbers and Decimals

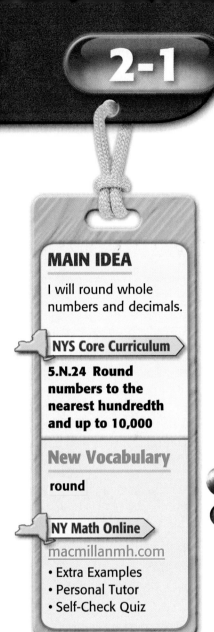

> ## GET READY to Learn

A new species of lobster that measures 5.9 inches long was discovered 7,540 feet deep in the South Pacific Ocean.

Anna described the lobster: "It's about 6 inches long. It was found about 7,500 feet deep in the ocean."

When you **round** a number, you find its approximate value. You can round whole numbers and decimals.

Real-World EXAMPLE   Round Whole Numbers

1 **TRAVEL** Steve Fossett was the first person to travel 20,626 miles around the world alone in a hot air balloon. **Round 20,626 to the nearest thousand. Is it closer to 20,000 or 21,000?**

Step 1 Underline the digit in the place to be rounded. In this case, the 0 in the thousands place is to be rounded.	2<u>0</u>,626
Step 2 Look at 6, the digit to the right of the underlined digit.	2<u>0</u>,**6**26
Step 3 If this digit is 5 or greater, add 1 to the underlined digit. Since 6 > 5, add 1 to the 0.	2<u>1</u>,626
Step 4 Replace all digits after the underlined digit with zeros.	21,000

To the nearest thousand, 20,626 rounds to 21,000. The number line shows that 20,626 is closer to 21,000 than to 20,000.

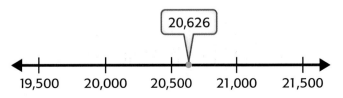

20,626

← 19,500   20,000   20,500   21,000   21,500 →

When you round decimals, identify the place being rounded. Determine whether the original number is closer to that place or the next higher place.

 **EXAMPLE** Round Decimals

2 **Round 46.73 to the nearest tenth. Is it closer to 46.7 or 46.8?**

Step 1 Underline the digit in the tenths place, 7.   46.<u>7</u>3

Step 2 Look at 3, the digit to the right of 7.   46.<u>7</u>3

Step 3 If the digit is 4 or less, do not change the underlined digit. Since 3 < 5, keep the digit 7 the same.   46.<u>7</u>3

Step 4 Drop the digit after the underlined digit.   46.7

So, 46.73 rounds to 46.7. On the number line, 46.73 is closer to 46.7 than to 46.8. So, the answer is reasonable.

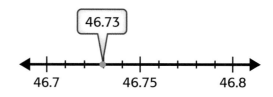

Remember

You can use a number line to check if the answer is reasonable.

 **CHECK What You Know**

Round each number to the underlined place. See Example 1 (p. 61)

1. <u>4</u>2

2. 8,<u>3</u>17

3. <u>5</u>,729

4. 1,0<u>9</u>6

Round each decimal to the place indicated. See Example 2 (p. 62)

5. 28.6; ones

6. 4.35; tenths

7. 110.079; hundredths

8. 67.142; ones

9. An ice sheet that covers most of Antarctica is about 1.34 miles thick. To the nearest tenth mile, how thick is the ice?

10. **Talk About It** Explain how to round 74.685 to the nearest hundredth.

Round each number to the underlined place. See Example 1 (p. 61)

11. <u>1</u>9

12. 6<u>8</u>1

13. <u>7</u>35

14. <u>3</u>,705

15. 106,<u>9</u>50

16. 5,<u>7</u>50

17. 24,<u>9</u>21

18. 6<u>9</u>2,300

Round each decimal to the place indicated. See Example 2 (p. 62)

19. 6.2; ones

20. 8.17; tenths

21. 0.053; hundredths

22. 19.25; ones

23. 36.81; ones

24. 9.045; tenths

25. 2.526; hundredths

26. 57.009; hundredths

27. A recent Tour de France bike race was 2,274 miles long. How long was the race rounded to the nearest hundred miles?

28. The African bush elephant weighs between 4.4 tons and 7.7 tons. What are its least weight and greatest weight, rounded to the nearest ton?

Real-World PROBLEM SOLVING

Science The table shows what a 95-pound student would weigh on the Sun and on different planets.

Round the weight on the Sun or each planet to the place indicated.

Place	Weight (lb)
Jupiter	224.58
Mars	35.815
Sun	2,571.84

29. Mars; tenths

30. the Sun; thousands

31. Jupiter; tens

32. Jupiter; tenths

H.O.T. Problems

33. **OPEN ENDED** Write two different numbers that when rounded to the nearest tenth will give you 18.3.

34. **NUMBER SENSE** Explain what happens when you round 9,999.999 to any place.

35. **WRITING IN ▶MATH** Describe two real-world situations in which it makes sense to round numbers.

2-2 Estimate Sums and Differences

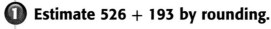

MAIN IDEA

I will estimate sums and differences by rounding and using compatible numbers.

NYS Core Curriculum

Preparation for 5.N.26 Estimate sums, differences, products, and quotients of decimals

5.N.27 Justify the reasonableness of answers using estimation *Also addresses 5.M.11, 5.PS.22.*

New Vocabulary

estimate

compatible numbers

NY Math Online

macmillanmh.com
• Extra Examples
• Personal Tutor
• Self-Check Quiz

GET READY to Learn

The table shows the final results of the Skateboard Vert competition in a recent X Games.

Dias scored *about* 10 more points than Hendrix.

Place	Athlete	Points
1	Sandro Dias (Brazil)	88.67
2	Renton Milar (Australia)	80.33
3	Neal Hendrix (U.S.)	79.67

When you do not need an exact answer or when you want to check whether an answer is reasonable, you can **estimate**. One way to estimate is to use rounding.

EXAMPLE Use Rounding with Whole Numbers

① **Estimate 526 + 193 by rounding.**

Round each number to the nearest hundred. Then add.

526	→	500	526 is closer to 500 than 600.
+ 193	→	+ 200	193 is closer to 200 than 100.
		700	

So, 526 + 193 is about 700.

You can also use compatible numbers to estimate sums and differences. **Compatible numbers** are numbers that are easy to add or subtract mentally.

EXAMPLE Use Compatible Numbers

② **Estimate 458 − 340 by using compatible numbers.**

Find two numbers that you can easily subtract.

458	→	450	458 is close to 450.
− 340	→	− 350	340 is close to 350.
		100	

So, 458 − 340 is about 100.

You can round numbers to any place value that makes estimation easier. If you round numbers to a lesser place value, you are likely to get a more accurate estimate.

Real-World EXAMPLE Use Rounding with Decimals

③ **TEMPERATURE** The average January temperature for Knoxville, Tennessee, is 37.6°F. In Newark, New Jersey, the average is 31.3°F. Estimate the difference in average temperatures.

One Way	Another Way
Round to the nearest ten.	Round to the nearest whole number.
$\begin{array}{r} 37.6 \rightarrow 40 \\ -31.3 \rightarrow -30 \\ \hline 10 \end{array}$	$\begin{array}{r} 37.6 \rightarrow 38 \\ -31.3 \rightarrow -31 \\ \hline 7 \end{array}$

Depending on how the numbers are rounded, the difference in temperatures is about 10°F or about 7°F. The actual difference is 6.3°. So, rounding to the nearest whole number gave the more accurate estimate.

CHECK What You Know

Estimate each sum or difference. Use rounding or compatible numbers. See Examples 1–3 (pp. 64–65)

1. $\begin{array}{r} 28 \\ +13 \\ \hline \end{array}$

2. $\begin{array}{r} 598 \\ -103 \\ \hline \end{array}$

3. $\begin{array}{r} 10.08 \\ +5.6 \\ \hline \end{array}$

4. $104 + 328$

5. $2.65 - 0.766$

6. $37.58 - 21.25$

7. $3,256 + 670$

8. $2,521 - 1,247$

9. $475.6 - 58.5$

10. $751.2 + 82.3$

11. The world's largest cherry pie weighed 37,740 pounds. The world's largest apple pie weighed 30,115 pounds. About how much more did the cherry pie weigh?

12. **Talk About It** Tell when it might be appropriate to estimate rather than get the exact answer. Give a real-world example.

Estimate each sum or difference. Use rounding or compatible numbers. See Examples 1–3 (pp. 64–65)

13. 59
   − 31

14. 1,324
   + 2,064

15. 7.6
   + 1.9

16. 824
   − 637

17. 6,820
   + 195

18. 52.85
   − 9.09

19. 150.9 + 310.6

20. 19.8 + 9.93

21. 24.86 − 12.49

22. 4.087 − 1.692

23. 3.872 + 12.49

24. 986 − 99

25. 4,201 − 592

26. 791.3 + 38.6

27. 321.75 − 16.65

28. The graphic shows the average speeds of two airplanes in miles per hour. About how much faster is the Foxbat than the Hawkeye? Show your work.

Plane	Speed (mph)
Hawkeye	375
Foxbat	1,864

29. Sophia has $20. She buys a hair band for $3.99, gum for $1.29, and a brush for $6.75. Not including tax, estimate how much change she should receive. Show your work.

H.O.T. Problems

30. **OPEN ENDED** Write a word problem that you can solve by subtracting. Estimate the difference two different ways. Identify which method, if any, gives a more accurate estimate.

31. **FIND THE ERROR** Samuel and Marlina are estimating 529.16 + 110.48 by rounding. Whose estimate is correct? Explain.

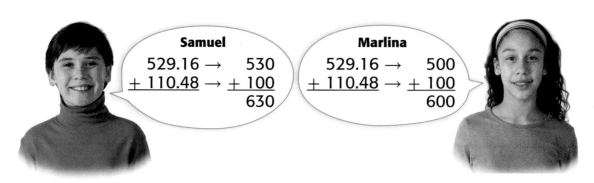

Samuel
529.16 →   530
+ 110.48 → + 100
              630

Marlina
529.16 →   500
+ 110.48 → + 100
              600

32. **WRITING IN ►MATH** Suppose you round all addends down. Will the estimate be greater than or less than the actual sum? Explain.

33. The table shows the lengths of four trails at a horseback riding camp. Which is the best estimate for the total length of all the trails? (Lesson 2-2)

Trail	A	B	C	D
Length (mi)	2.6	1.8	4.2	3.3

A 8 mi

B 12 mi

C 14 mi

D 15 mi

34. Mr. Jackson bought a plasma television that was on sale for $1,989. The regular price was $2,499. Which is the best estimate of the amount of money Mr. Jackson saved by buying the television on sale? (Lesson 2-1)

F $500

G $1,000

H $3,000

J $4,000

Spiral Review

35. The price of a jacket is $50.49. What is the price of the jacket to the nearest dollar? (Lesson 2-1)

36. The Soda Shop sold 12 more milkshakes on Friday than it sold on Thursday. A total of 100 milkshakes were sold. How many were sold on Thursday? Solve. Use the *guess and check* strategy. (Lesson 1-8)

37. An ice cube floats in water because it is less dense than water. Density is the measure of mass per unit of volume. List the names of the substances in the table from least to greatest density. (Lesson 1-7)

Substance	Density (g/cm³)
Aluminum	2.7
Cork	0.4
Ice cube	0.9
Water	1.0

Replace each ● with <, >, or = to make a true sentence. (Lesson 1-6)

38. 0.0561 ● 0.15

39. 40.900 ● 40.9

40. 17.22 ● 17.223

Use place value to write each number in standard form. (Lesson 1-5)

41. 13 and 9 tenths

42. $10 + 1 + 0.9 + 0.02 + 0.003$

43. Shanti has 85 baseball cards. She buys 12 more cards and sells 19 cards. How many baseball cards does Shanti have now? (Lesson 1-3)

Problem-Solving Strategy

MAIN IDEA I will solve problems by using the *work backward* strategy.

 **5.PS.3 Interpret information correctly, identify the problem, and generate possible strategies and solutions** *Also addresses 5.PS.1, 5.PS.22.*

The Nature Club raised $125 to buy and install nesting boxes for birds at a wildlife site. Each box costs $5. It costs $75 to rent a bus so the members can travel to the site. How many boxes can the club buy?

Understand	**What facts do you know?** • $125 is available to buy and install the nesting boxes. • Each box costs $5. • The bus costs $75. **What do you need to find?** • How many boxes can the club buy?
Plan	You can work backward to find the number of boxes that can be bought. Start with $125, the amount the Nature Club has raised. Then subtract the costs. Recall that subtraction "undoes" addition and that division "undoes" multiplication.
Solve	First, undo the addition of the cost of the bus by subtracting the cost of the bus. $125 − $75 = $50 Then undo the multiplication of the cost of the boxes by dividing by the cost for each box. $50 ÷ $5 = 10 So, ten boxes can be bought.
Check	Look back. Since, 10 × $5 = $50 and $50 + $75 = $125, the answer is correct.

68 Chapter 2 Add and Subtract Whole Numbers and Decimals

Refer to the problem on the previous page.

1. Explain how using the *work backward* strategy helped you find the number of nesting boxes the club could buy.

2. Suppose the club had $150 to spend. How many boxes could the club buy?

3. What is the best way to check your solution when using the *work backward* strategy?

4. Explain when you would use the *work backward* strategy to solve a problem.

> **PRACTICE** the Strategy

NYSCC • NYSMT
Extra Practice, p. R5

Solve. Use the *work backward* strategy.

5. Students sold raffle tickets to raise money for a field trip. The first 20 tickets sold cost $4 each. To sell more tickets, they lowered the price to $2 each. If they raise $216, how many tickets did they sell in all?

6. Amy collected 15 more cans of food than Peyton. Ling collected 8 more than Amy. Ling collected 72 cans of food. How many cans of food did Peyton collect?

7. Jeanette's sister charges $5 per hour before midnight for babysitting and $8 per hour after midnight. She finished babysitting at 2:00 A.M. and earned $36. At what time did she begin babysitting?

8. Seth bought a movie ticket, popcorn, and a drink. After the movie, he played 4 video games that each cost the same. He spent a total of $19. How much did it cost to play each video game?

Movie Costs
Popcorn $4
Drink $3
Ticket $8

9. **Measurement** Mandy needs to arrive at softball practice by 5:00 P.M. It takes her 15 minutes to pick up her teammates and then 30 minutes to get to the field. What time must Mandy leave home to be on time for practice?

10. Chet has $4 in change after buying a bike and a helmet. How much money did Chet have originally?

$90

$30

11. Rosa is 3 years older than Omar. Omar is 2 years older than Francesca. Francesca is 8 years younger than Roberto. If Roberto is 21 years old, how old is Rosa?

12. **WRITING IN ▸MATH** Suppose Molly scored 7 more goals than Papina and Stew scored 2 more than Molly. If Stew scored 15 goals, what operation(s) can you use to find the number of goals Papina scored? Solve then explain your selection(s).

2-4 Add and Subtract Whole Numbers

MAIN IDEA

I will add and subtract multi-digit numbers.

NYS Core Curriculum

Reinforcement of 4.N.14 Use a variety of strategies to add and subtract numbers up to 10,000 *Also addresses 5.CM.1, 5.CM.3*

NY Math Online

macmillanmh.com

• Extra Examples
• Personal Tutor
• Self-Check Quiz

GET READY to Learn

In a recent year, the two longest-running Broadway plays were *Cats* with 7,485 performances and *The Phantom of the Opera* with 7,829 performances.

The total number of performances is found by adding.

Always estimate first. Then add or subtract the digits in each place-value position. Start at the ones place.

EXAMPLES   Add or Subtract Whole Numbers

1 **Find 415 + 280.**   Estimate $400 + 300 = 700$

Step 1	Step 2	Step 3
Add the ones.	Add the tens.	Add the hundreds.
415	415	415
+ 280	+ 280	+ 280
5	95	695

Since 695 is close to the estimate, the answer is reasonable.

2 **Find 3,972 − 741.**   Estimate $4,000 - 1,000 = 3,000$

Step 1	Step 2	Step 3
Subtract the ones.	Subtract the tens.	Subtract the hundreds and thousands.
3,972	3,972	3,972
− 741	− 741	− 741
31	31	3,231

Since 3,231 is close to 3,000, the answer makes sense.

Real-World EXAMPLE   Add with Regrouping

3 **BROADWAY** **Refer to the beginning of the lesson. How many performances of *Cats* with 7,485 and *Phantom of the Opera* with 7,829 were there?**

Estimate 7,000 + 8,000 = 15,000

Remember

To add or subtract whole numbers, write the numbers in a column and line up the digits by place value.

Step 1 Add the ones.	**Step 2** Add the tens.	**Step 3** Add the hundreds. Add the thousands.
$\begin{array}{r}\overset{1}{7,}485\\ +\ 7,829\\ \hline 4\end{array}$ Rename 14 ones as 1 ten, 4 ones.	$\begin{array}{r}\overset{1\,1}{7,485}\\ +\ 7,829\\ \hline 14\end{array}$ Rename 11 tens as 1 hundred, 1 ten.	$\begin{array}{r}\overset{1\,1\,1}{7,485}\\ +\ 7,829\\ \hline 15,314\end{array}$

The total number of performances was 15,314. This answer is close to the estimate. So, the answer is reasonable.

EXAMPLE   Subtract with Regrouping

4 **Find 834 − 561.**   **Estimate** 800 − 600 = 200

Step 1 Subtract the ones.	**Step 2** Subtract the tens.	**Step 3** Subtract the hundreds.
$\begin{array}{r}834\\ -\ 561\\ \hline 3\end{array}$	$\begin{array}{r}\overset{7\,13}{8\not{3}4}\\ -\ 561\\ \hline 73\end{array}$ 3 < 6, so rename 8 hundreds as 7 hundreds, 10 tens. Then, 10 tens + 3 tens = 13 tens.	$\begin{array}{r}\overset{7\,13}{8\not{3}4}\\ -\ 561\\ \hline 273\end{array}$

Since 273 is close to the estimate, the answer makes sense.

CHECK What You Know

Add or subtract. **See Examples 1–4 (pp. 70–71)**

1. 20,612 + 1,186

2. 611 − 32

3. 2,679 + 8,170

4. 4,200 − 1,652

5. 7,015 + 4,938

6. 67,315 − 28,502

7. The Everest Marathon starts at 17,100 feet above sea level and ends at 11,300 feet above sea level. What is the difference?

8. **Talk About It** Discuss how place value and regrouping are used when adding and subtracting whole numbers.

Add or subtract. See Examples 1–4 (pp. 70–71)

9. 407 + 162

10. 2,655 − 41

11. 10,375 + 1,503

12. 2,900 + 1,062

13. 851 − 705

14. 7,319 − 410

15. 739 + 3,824

16. 6,284 − 1,839

17. 4,762 + 594

18. 29,238 + 51,698

19. 215,075 + 6,025

20. 382,500 − 17,986

21. The main section of the Great Wall of China is 2,150 miles long. It also has 2,195 miles of branching walls. What is the total length of the wall? Show your estimate and exact answer.

New York Data File

New York is the 27th largest state in the United States. A few states that are similar to New York in size are shown. **Show your estimate and your exact answer.**

22. How much larger is Georgia than Arkansas?

23. What is the total area of North Carolina and New York?

24. Which is larger, the areas of North Carolina and Georgia combined, or the areas of Arkansas and New York combined?

New York

Place	Area (sq mi)
North Carolina	53,821
Georgia	59,411
Arkansas	53,182
New York	54,475

Source: Enchanted Learning

H.O.T. Problems

25. OPEN ENDED Write an addition problem where the estimated sum when rounded to the thousands place is the same as the exact sum.

26. WHICH ONE DOESN'T BELONG? Identify the expression that does not belong with the other three. Explain your reasoning.

| 1,296 − 516 | 608 + 172 | 420 + 360 | 1,049 − 179 |

27. CHALLENGE Arrange the digits 1, 2, 3, 4, 5, and 6 into two whole numbers so that their difference is as close to 1 as possible. Use each digit once.

28. WRITING IN ►MATH Write a real-world problem in which the answer is found by adding 816 and 750. Describe what the sum means.

Round each decimal to the place indicated. (Lesson 2-1)

1. 11.8; ones

2. 4.328; tenths

3. 0.016; hundredths

4. MULTIPLE CHOICE The population of Irving is 193,649. What is 193,649 rounded to the nearest thousands place? (Lesson 2-1)

   A 200,000   **C** 194,000

   B 190,000   **D** 193,000

5. Measurement
Estimate the amount of liquid in the sports drink bottle to the nearest ten milliliters.
(Lesson 2-1)

LIME
591 milliliters

Estimate each sum or difference. Use rounding or compatible numbers. (Lesson 2-2)

6.   89
   + 62

7.   15.9
   − 12.1

8. 371 + 1,215

9. 60.3 − 18.55

10. Measurement About how much greater is the side of the square than the side of the triangle? Show how you estimated. (Lesson 2-2)

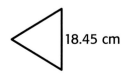

18.45 cm

21.72 cm

Use the work backward strategy to solve.
(Lesson 2-3)

11. The Mitchell Middle School basketball team won 28 more games than they lost. If they won 35 games, how many games did they play?

12. Reuben has $2 in change after buying the sweatshirt and hat shown below. How much money did Reuben have originally?

GLACIER UNIVERSITY

$25

G

$19

Add or subtract. (Lesson 2-4)

13. 315 + 120

14. 689 − 71

15. 4,678 − 1,709

16. 25,390 + 82,687

17. MULTIPLE CHOICE Algeria, a country in Africa, has an area of 919,590 square miles. The Sahara Desert is located in Algeria. It has an area of 781,651 square miles. How much of Algeria is NOT covered by the Sahara Desert? (Lesson 2-4)

   F 100,000 sq mi   **H** 173,939 sq mi

   G 137,939 sq mi   **J** 200,000 sq mi

18. WRITING IN ►MATH Explain how you would find the difference of 425 and 214. (Lesson 2-2)

MAIN IDEA I will learn to determine if a problem needs an estimate or an exact answer.

 NYSCC **5.PS.3 Interpret information correctly, identify the problem, and generate possible strategies and solutions** *Also addresses 5.RP.3, 5.CM.2.*

P.S.I. TEAM ✚

MANDAR: My family drove to my grandparents' house. We drove 58.6 miles in the first hour, 67.2 miles in the second hour, and 60.5 miles in the third hour. We followed the same route to return home.

YOUR MISSION: Find *about* how far Mandar's family traveled.

Understand	You know that the family drove 58.6 miles, 67.2 miles, and 60.5 miles. You need to find *about* how far Mandar's family traveled altogether.
Plan	Since you only need to find *about* how far they traveled, you can estimate the number of miles traveled each hour. Add the estimated miles. Then double that amount for the trip back home.
Solve	Hour One ⟶ 58.6 ⟶ 60 Hour Two ⟶ 67.2 ⟶ 70 Hour Three ⟶ + 60.5 ⟶ + 60 ⟶ 190 The one-way trip was about 190 miles. The return trip was another 190 miles. Mandar's family traveled about 190 + 190, or 380 miles.
Check	Look back. Since the trip was a total of 6 hours and they drove about 60 miles each hour, find 60 + 60 + 60 + 60 + 60 + 60. Since the sum is 360, 380 miles is reasonable.

For each problem, determine whether you need an estimate or an exact answer. Then solve.

PROBLEM-SOLVING SKILLS
• Use the four-step plan.
• Use estimation.

1. A restaurant can make 95 dinners each night. The restaurant has been sold out for 7 nights in a row. How many dinners were sold during this week?

2. Measurement A gardener has 35 feet of fencing to enclose the garden shown. About how much fencing will be left over after the garden is enclosed?

5.2 ft
4.3 ft
4.8 ft
7.6 ft
8.4 ft

3. A group goes rafting on the Guadalupe River. Each raft carries 12 people. If there are 8 rafts, how many people can go rafting?

4. A family is renting a cabin for $59.95 a day for 5 days. About how much will they pay for the cabin?

5. School raffle tickets cost $3 each. The school's goal is to raise at least $400 from the raffle. If 138 tickets were sold, did the school meet its goal?

6. Students at a high school filled out a survey. The results showed that out of 640 students, 331 speak more than one language. How many students speak only one language?

7. Estella has 9 quarters, 7 dimes, and 5 nickels. Does she have enough money to buy the box of crayons shown?

CRAYONS
$3.25

8. A library wants to buy a new painting that costs $960. So far, the library has collected $375 in donations. About how much more money does the library need to buy the painting?

9. Four friends split the cost of two pizzas. If the total cost of the pizzas was $27.80, about how much will each friend have to pay?

10. On Friday, a museum had 185 visitors. On Saturday there were twice as many visitors as Friday. On Sunday, 50 fewer people visited than Saturday. How many people visited the museum during these three days?

11. Measurement The soccer team has a game at 11:00 A.M. The game is 153 miles away. The team leaves at 8:00 A.M. and drives an average of 59 miles each hour. Will the team arrive at the game on time?

12. **WRITING IN** ►**MATH** Explain an advantage and a disadvantage of using estimation to solve a problem.

The Core Facts about Apples

Baseball, hot dogs, and apple pies are American favorites. There are about 8,000 apple orchards in the United States producing more than 100 different kinds of apples. In 2005, the value of apple crops in the United States was about $1.8 billion. Farmers harvested enough for each person in the United States to have 79 apples. That would make a lot of apple pies!

Did You Know?

One apple tree can fill 20 42-pound boxes with apples.

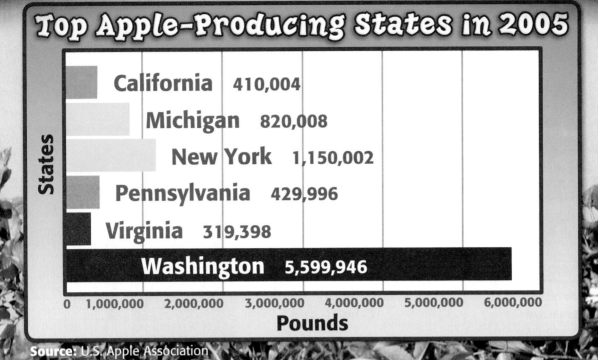

Top Apple-Producing States in 2005

States	Pounds
California	410,004
Michigan	820,008
New York	1,150,002
Pennsylvania	429,996
Virginia	319,398
Washington	5,599,946

0   1,000,000   2,000,000   3,000,000   4,000,000   5,000,000   6,000,000

Pounds

Source: U.S. Apple Association

 ## Real-World Math

Use the information on page 76 and the graph above to solve each problem.

1 Which state produced the least amount of apples? How many pounds of apples did this state produce? Round to the nearest ten thousand.

2 Which state's apple crop was closest to 1 million pounds?

3 In 2001, $1.3 billion worth of apples were grown. How much greater was the apple crop in 2005?

4 What is the difference in apple production between the top two states? Round to the nearest thousand.

5 Use compatible numbers to estimate the total amount of apples produced in Michigan, California, and Pennsylvania.

6 Find the exact sum of the apples produced in Michigan, California, and Pennsylvania. Compare this number to your answer to Exercise 5.

7 Two pounds of apples make one pie. If you want to make 6 pies, how many pounds of apples should you pick?

 **Explore**

Math Activity for 2-6
Add and Subtract Decimals

You can use grid paper to explore adding and subtracting decimals.

MAIN IDEA

I will use models to represent addition and subtraction of decimals.

NYS Core Curriculum

5.RP.2 Understand that mathematical statements can be supported, using models, facts, and relationships **to explain their thinking**

5.N.23 Use a variety of strategies to add, subtract, multiply, and divide **decimals to thousandths** *Also addresses 5.PS.13.*

You Will Need
grid paper
colored pencils

NY Math Online

macmillanmh.com
• Concepts in Motion

ACTIVITY **Use Models to Add Decimals**

Find 1.08 + 0.45.

Step 1 **Model 1.08.**

To show 1.08, shade one whole 10-by-10 grid and $\frac{8}{100}$ of a second grid.

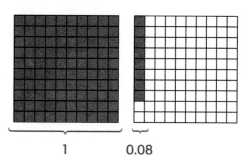

1   0.08

Step 2 **Model 0.45.**

To show 0.45, shade $\frac{45}{100}$ of the second grid using a different color.

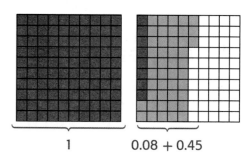

1   0.08 + 0.45

Step 3 **Add the decimals.**

Count the total number of shaded squares. Write the decimal that represents the number of shaded squares. So, 1.08 + 0.45 = 1.53.

ACTIVITY Use Models to Subtract Decimals

Find 2.4 − 1.07.

Step 1 **Model 2.4.**

To show 2.4, shade two whole grids and $\frac{40}{100}$ of a third grid.

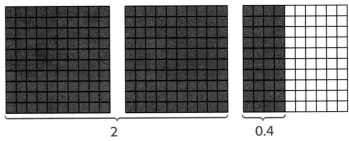

Step 2 **Subtract 1.07.**

To subtract 1.07, cross out 1 whole grid and 7 squares of the third grid. Count the number of squares that remain.

So, 2.4 − 1.07 = 1.33.

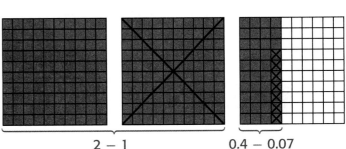

Think About It

1. Explain how using models to find 1.08 + 0.45 is similar to using models to find 108 + 45.

2. Explain how using models to find 2.4 − 1.07 is similar to using models to find 240 − 107.

CHECK What You Know

Add or subtract. Use models.

3. 2.46 + 1.13

4. 2.05 + 1.87

5. 2.91 − 1.8

6. 1.34 − 1.15

7. 0.51 + 0.63

8. 1.74 + 0.36

9. 2.05 − 1.12

10. 2.93 − 2.74

11. **WRITING IN ►MATH** Explain how to add or subtract decimals without models. Explain where to place the decimal point in the sum or difference.

2-6 Add and Subtract Decimals

GET READY **to Learn**

In Australia, each person eats an average of 44.2 pints of ice cream per year. In the United States, the average is 33.1 pints. How much ice cream is eaten on average by each person in these two countries combined?

MAIN IDEA

I will add and subtract decimals through thousandths.

NYS Core Curriculum

5.N.23 Use a variety of strategies to add, subtract, multiply, and divide **decimals to thousandths** *Also addresses 5.CN.7.*

NY Math Online

macmillanmh.com

- Extra Examples
- Personal Tutor
- Self-Check Quiz

Just as with whole numbers, you add digits in the same place-value position. To add decimals, line up the decimal points, add as with whole numbers, and bring the decimal point straight down in the sum.

Real-World EXAMPLE   Add Decimals

1 **ICE CREAM Refer to the information above. Find 44.2 + 33.1 to determine how much ice cream is eaten on average per person in Australia and the United States combined.**

Estimate $44 + 33 = 77$

Step 1	**Step 2**	**Step 3**
Line up the decimal points.	Add as with whole numbers.	Bring the decimal point straight down in the sum.
$\begin{array}{r} 44.2 \\ + 33.1 \\ \hline \end{array}$	$\begin{array}{r} 44.2 \\ + 33.1 \\ \hline 77\ 3 \end{array}$	$\begin{array}{r} 44.2 \\ + 33.1 \\ \hline 77.3 \end{array}$

So, 77.3 pints of ice cream are eaten on average per person each year in Australia and the United States combined. This is close to the estimate, so your answer is reasonable.

80   Chapter 2 Add and Subtract Whole Numbers and Decimals

If the last digits of the numbers in a subtraction problem do not have the same place value, it is helpful to annex zeros before you subtract.

EXAMPLE Annex Zeros

2 Find 19.6 − 4.31.

Estimate 20 − 4 = 16

Vocabulary Link

Annex

Everyday Use to add something, especially to a building

Math Use to annex a zero means to place a zero to the right of the decimal point without changing the value of the decimal

Step 1 Line up the decimal points. Annex a zero so that both numbers have the same place value.

$$
\begin{array}{r}
19.60 \\
-\ 4.31 \\
\end{array}
$$

Step 2 Subtract as with whole numbers, from right to left. Regroup if necessary.

$$
\begin{array}{r}
{}^{5\,10} \\
19.\cancel{6}\cancel{0} \\
-\ 4.31 \\
\hline
15\ 29 \\
\end{array}
$$

Step 3 Bring the decimal point straight down in the difference.

$$
\begin{array}{r}
19.60 \\
-\ 4.31 \\
\hline
15.29 \\
\end{array}
$$

The difference is 15.29. Since 15.29 is close to the estimate, the answer is reasonable.

✓ CHECK What You Know

Add or subtract. See Examples 1–2 (pp. 80–81)

1.
$$
\begin{array}{r}
6.32 \\
+\ 1.46 \\
\end{array}
$$

2.
$$
\begin{array}{r}
0.89 \\
-\ 0.03 \\
\end{array}
$$

3.
$$
\begin{array}{r}
0.54 \\
+\ 7.8 \\
\end{array}
$$

4.
$$
\begin{array}{r}
14.8 \\
-\ 10.26 \\
\end{array}
$$

5. 25 + 8.46

6. 6.57 − 1.2

7. 19.21 − 11.03

8. 3.008 + 1.64

9. 8.9 − 0.15

10. 42.2 + 7.169

11. Paulo bought a hand-held game version of a logic puzzle and batteries from a toy store. Use the table at the right to find the total cost of the two items, not including tax.

Item	Cost ($)
logic puzzle	14.95
batteries	10.39
carrying case	12.73

12. **Talk About It** Explain how annexing zeros might be helpful when adding decimals.

Add or subtract. See Examples 1–2 (pp. 80–81)

13. $35.08 + 11.9$

14. $0.8 - 0.22$

15. $9.14 - 2.075$

16. $5.603 + 1.22$

17. $26.768 + 2.991$

18. $12.03 - 0.145$

19. An athlete training for the Olympics swims each lap of a four-lap race in the following times: 54.73, 54.56, 54.32, and 54.54 seconds. What is the total time it takes her to swim the four laps?

20. Ethan wants to buy a basketball video game that costs $59.95, including tax. He has $45 in cash and a gift certificate for $15. Is that enough to buy the video game? Explain.

21. Terrance is biking a trail. He bikes 12.6 miles and takes a break. Then he bikes 10.7 miles. If the trail is 35 miles long, how many more miles does Terrance have left to bike?

22. A large bag of sand weighs 48.5 pounds. A small bag of sand weighs 24.6 pounds. Mrs. Waggoner needs 75 pounds. If she buys a large bag and a small bag, how much more sand does she need?

Real-World PROBLEM SOLVING

Music The table shows the frequencies of the lowest and highest notes of some musical instruments. The unit of frequency is called *hertz* (Hz). The difference between these frequencies is called the *pitch range*.

23. What is the pitch range of a bass trombone?

24. What is the pitch range of a harp?

25. Which has a greater pitch range: a concert flute or a violin? Explain.

Instrument	Frequency	
	Lowest Note (Hz)	Highest Note (Hz)
bass trombone	48.999	349.228
concert flute	246.942	2,489.02
harp	30.867	2,959.96
violin	195.998	3,951.07

Source: PSB Speakers International

H.O.T. Problems

26. OPEN ENDED Write two different pairs of decimals whose sums are 8.69. One pair should involve regrouping.

27. NUMBER SENSE Explain how you know that the sum of 2.4, 3.6, and 5.1 is greater than 10.

28. WRITING IN ►MATH Write a real-world word problem that can be solved by adding or subtracting 34.99 and 5.79. Describe what the solution means.

Find the Least Sum

Adding Decimals

Get Ready!

Players: 2 to 4 players

You will need: 10 index cards
paper

Get Set!

- Write a different digit from 0 to 9 on each index card.

- Place the cards in a pile facedown.

- Draw six boxes on a piece a paper with decimal points as shown.

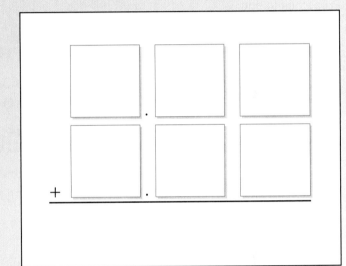

Go!

- Each player takes a turn choosing a card.

- Each time a card is chosen, each player writes the digit from the card on one of the boxes. The goal is to make up the least sum. You may not move digits after you have placed them in a box.

- When all the boxes are full, find the sum of your decimals.

- The player with the least sum is the winner.

Play again!

Addition Properties

Hannah jogs 2 miles and then walks 1 mile. The next day, she walks 1 mile and then jogs 2 miles. On which day does she go farther?

In the situation above, the order in which Hannah jogged and walked did not change the total distance. This and other properties of addition are given below.

Addition Properties   Key Concept

Commutative Property   The order in which numbers are added does not change the sum.

Examples

$7 + 11 = 11 + 7$ $2.3 + 9.5 = 9.5 + 2.3$

Associative Property   The way in which numbers are grouped does not change the sum.

Examples

$(9 + 6) + 4 = 9 + (6 + 4)$ $1.8 + (0.2 + 5) = (1.8 + 0.2) + 5$

Identity Property   The sum of any number and 0 equals the number.

Examples

$14 + 0 = 14$ $0 + 6.75 = 6.75$

EXAMPLE   Name Addition Properties

1 **Identify the addition property used to rewrite the problem below.**

$17 + (3 + 24) = (17 + 3) + 24$

The grouping of the numbers to be added changes. This is the Associative Property of Addition.

You can use properties of addition to simplify adding and to find sums of whole numbers and decimals mentally.

Remember

Sums of 10 or a multiple of 10 are compatible numbers. They help you add numbers mentally.

Real-World EXAMPLE   Use Properties to Add Whole Numbers

2 ANIMALS Hama recorded the number of birds he saw in the table. Use properties of addition to mentally find the total number of birds he saw.

Since you can easily add 5 and 15, change the order and group those numbers together.

BIRDS	NUMBER
Blue Jays	5
Robins	27
Cardinals	15

$5 + 27 + 15 = 5 + 15 + 27$ Commutative Property
$= (5 + 15) + 27$ Associative Property
$= 20 + 27$ Add 5 and 15 mentally.
$= 47$ Add 20 and 27 mentally.

EXAMPLE   Use Properties to Add Decimals

3 Use properties of addition to find $0.8 + 5.6 + 0.4$ mentally.

Since $0.6 + 0.4 = 1$, group 5.6 and 0.4 together.

$0.8 + 5.6 + 0.4 = 0.8 + (5.6 + 0.4)$ Associative Property
$= 0.8 + 6.0$ Add 5.6 and 0.4 mentally.
$= 6.8$ Add 0.8 and 6.0 mentally.

You can also form groups of 10 to make adding mentally easier.

EXAMPLE   Partial Sums of 10

4 Use properties of addition to find $18 + 26$ mentally.

$18 + 26 = (10 + 8) + (20 + 6)$ $18 = 10 + 8$ and $26 = 20 + 6$
$= 10 + 20 + 8 + 6$ Commutative Property
$= (10 + 20) + (8 + 6)$ Associative Property
$= 30 + 14$ Add inside the parentheses mentally.
$= 44$ Add 30 and 14 mentally.

Identify the addition property used to rewrite each problem. See Example 1 (p. 84)

1. $(11 + 37) + 3 = 11 + (37 + 3)$

2. $0.1 + 8 + 1.9 = 0.1 + 1.9 + 8$

Use properties of addition to find each sum mentally. Show your steps and identify the properties that you used. See Examples 2–4 (p. 85)

3. $9 + 27 + 1$

4. $3.9 + 0.5 + 2.5$

5. $69 + 22$

6. What addition property is shown below?

$$0 + 6.75 = 6.75$$

7. **Talk About It** Describe how properties of addition help to add numbers mentally.

Practice and Problem Solving

NYSCC • NYSMT

Extra Practice, p. R6.

Identify the addition property used to rewrite each problem. See Example 1 (p. 84)

8. $20 + 6 = 6 + 20$

9. $19.5 + 0 = 19.5$

10. $49 + (51 + 21) = (49 + 51) + 21$

11. $13 + 11 + 87 = 13 + 87 + 11$

Use properties of addition to find each sum mentally. Show your steps and identify the properties that you used. See Examples 2–4 (p. 85)

12. $15 + 8 + 25$

13. $7.7 + 4.3 + 11$

14. $37 + 26 + 53$

15. $10.9 + 3 + 0.1$

16. $63 + 35$

17. $57 + 48$

Algebra For Exercises 18 and 19, find the value that makes each sentence true.

18. $27 + (37 + 13) = 13 + (27 + \blacksquare)$

19. $(8 + 1.6) + 0.4 = 0.4 + (\blacksquare + 1.6)$

20. The table shows the cost of cheerleading uniforms. Use properties of addition to find the total cost of the uniform mentally. Show your steps and identify the properties that you used.

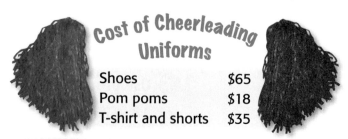

Cost of Cheerleading Uniforms

Shoes	$65
Pom poms	$18
T-shirt and shorts	$35

21. In one week, a classroom collected 43, 58, 62, 57, and 42 cans. Find the total number of cans the classroom collected using mental math. Explain how you solved it.

22. Alex spent $2.50 on a snack, $1.24 on gum, $3.76 on a comic book, and $5.50 on lunch. Use mental math to find the total amount that he spent.

H.O.T. Problems

23. OPEN ENDED Write a word problem that can be solved using the Associative Property of Addition. Explain your answer.

24. CHALLENGE Do the Associative and Commutative Properties also work for subtraction? Give examples to support your answer.

25. **WRITING IN** ▶**MATH** Jogging 2 miles and then walking 1 mile is the same as walking 1 mile and then jogging 2. This is a *commutative action*. Give another example of a commutative action. Then give an example of an action that is *not* commutative. Explain.

NYSMT Practice   5.N.23

26. SHORT RESPONSE Fina went to the grocery store and bought eggs for $1.12, milk for $2.25, butter for $0.98, and sugar for $1.65. If she gave the cashier $10, how much change in dollars did Fina receive? (Lesson 2-7)

27. Round 563.829 to the nearest hundredth. (Lesson 2-1)

   A 563.81   **C** 563.83

   B 563.828   **D** 600

28. Chloe is gluing together two pieces of wood so that their length equals the length of the board below. Which two lengths should she use? (Lesson 2-6)

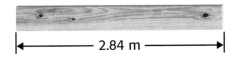

|← 2.84 m →|

   F 1.84 meters and 2.84 meters

   G 2.5 meters and 0.3 meter

   H 1.8 meters and 1.4 meters

   J 1.04 meters and 1.8 meters

Spiral Review

Add or subtract. (Lesson 2-6)

29. $5.08 + 13.7$ **30.** $12.01 - 0.23$ **31.** $24.8 - 16.095$

32. Students at a middle school filled out a survey. The survey showed that out of 1,037 students, 749 are going on a summer vacation. Find how many students are not going on a summer vacation. Is your solution an exact answer or an estimation? Explain. (Lesson 2-5)

33. Pablo Picasso's painting, *Self-Portrait,* sold for $43,500,000. Write the price of the painting in expanded form. (Lesson 1-1)

2-8 Add and Subtract Mentally

The table shows the number of dog breeds in two different categories of a dog show.

Category	Number of Breeds
Terrier	28
Toy	23

Which is easier to add: 28 + 23 or 30 + 21?

Are the sums the same?

MAIN IDEA

I will use the compensation strategy to add and subtract whole numbers and decimals mentally.

NYS Core Curriculum

5.RP.4 Make and evaluate conjectures, using a variety of strategies *Also addresses 5.RP.1.*

New Vocabulary

compensation

NY Math Online

macmillanmh.com
• Extra Examples
• Personal Tutor
• Self-Check Quiz

Sometimes you can use compensation to add mentally. To use **compensation**, add a number to one addend to make the addition easier. Then adjust by subtracting the same number from the other addend.

Real-World EXAMPLE Add Mentally

1 DOGS Refer to the table above. Use compensation to find 28 + 23, the total number of dog breeds in the two categories.

$$28 + 23$$
$$\downarrow +2 \qquad \downarrow -2 \qquad \text{Add 2 to 28. Adjust by subtracting 2 from 23.}$$
$$30 + 21 = 51$$

The total number of dog breeds in the two categories is 51.

To use compensation to subtract mentally, add or subtract the same amount from both numbers.

EXAMPLE Subtract Mentally

2 Use compensation to find 362 − 297.

$$362 - 297$$
$$\downarrow +3 \quad \downarrow +3 \qquad \text{Add 3 to 297. Adjust by adding 3 to 362.}$$
$$365 - 300 = 65$$

So, 362 − 297 is 65.

3 Use compensation to find 4.6 + 1.5.

One Way: Change 4.6 to 5.0.

4.6	+	1.5		
↓ + 0.4		↓ − 0.4		Add 0.4 to 4.6.
5.0	+	1.1	= 6.1	Adjust by subtracting 0.4 from 1.5.

Another Way: Change 1.5 to 2.

4.6	+	1.5		
↓ − 0.5		↓ + 0.5		Add 0.5 to 1.5.
4.1	+	2.0	= 6.1	Adjust by subtracting 0.5 from 4.6.

So, 4.6 + 1.5 = 6.1.

4 Use compensation to find 9.8 − 2.6.

One Way: Change 2.6 to 2.0.

9.8	−	2.6	
↓ − 0.6		↓ − 0.6	
9.2	−	2.0	= 7.2

Another Way: Change 2.6 to 3.

9.8	−	2.6	
↓ + 0.4		↓ + 0.4	
10.2	−	3.0	= 7.2

So, 9.8 − 2.6 = 7.2.

Remember

When adding or subtracting mentally, adjust either number.

Example

160 − 97
↓   ↓
+ 3   + 3
↓   ↓
163 − 100 = 63

CHECK What You Know

Add or subtract mentally. Use compensation. See Examples 1–4 (pp. 88–89)

1. 57 + 36

2. 368 + 197

3. 96 − 35

4. 410 − 318

5. 4.2 + 9.6

6. 8.7 + 3.1

7. 16.5 − 9.3

8. 39.4 − 1.7

9. A burrito costs $4.98 and a soda costs $1.75. Use compensation to find the total cost. Explain the steps you used.

10. Discuss the rules for using compensation to add or subtract mentally. When do you add to both numbers and when do you add to one number and subtract from the other number?

Practice and Problem Solving

NYSCC • NYSMT
Extra Practice, p. R7

Add or subtract mentally. Use compensation. See Examples 1–4 (pp. 88–89)

11. 98 + 64
1. 49 − 33
13. 304 − 198
14. 397 + 160

15. 188 − 27
16. 615 − 220
17. 6.7 + 2.4
18. 8.2 + 9.9

19. 30.4 − 8.6
20. 24.6 + 19.3
21. 62.3 − 45.6
22. 59.4 + 39.5

23. **Measurement** The height of a wooden pole is 56 inches. A builder attaches a birdhouse to the top of the pole. The height of the birdhouse is 18 inches. Find the total height of the pole and birdhouse.

24. You can burn 336 Calories roller skating and 380 Calories playing basketball per hour. Use mental math to find how many more Calories you can burn per hour playing basketball. Explain the steps you used.

Real-World PROBLEM SOLVING

Science Sound is measured in decibels. The higher the decibel, the louder the sound. The table shows how loud different sounds are.

25. How much louder is a conversation than a soft whisper?

26. How much louder is a blue whale than a conversation between two people?

Sound Source	Decibels
Soft whisper	30
Conversation	60
Rock concert	120
Rocket engine	180
Blue whale	180

H.O.T. Problems

27. **OPEN ENDED** Write a subtraction word problem that can be solved by using compensation. Describe the steps that you used to solve it.

28. **FIND THE ERROR** Megan and Juanita are finding 129 + 67 by using compensation. Who is correct? Explain.

Megan
129 + 67
+1   +1
↓   ↓
130 + 68 = 198

Juanita
129 + 67
+1   −1
↓   ↓
130 + 66 = 196

29. **WRITING IN ►MATH** Without using paper and pencil, how would you find the sum of 53.7 and 46.55? Explain your steps.

30. Bailey walked 23 blocks to the library. Then he walked 4 blocks to the post office and then 17 blocks home. How many blocks did he walk in all? (Lesson 2-7)

A 44

B 43

C 40

D 21

31. **SHORT RESPONSE** A video arcade in Fort Lauderdale, Florida, had 844 video arcade games when it opened. Two years later, it had 950 games. How many games did it add in two years? (Lesson 2-7)

32. Which is a true statement about the information in the table? (Lesson 2-6)

Passenger Train	Speed (miles per hour)
MagLev, China	243.0
Nozomi, Japan	162.6
TGV, France	158.0
Acela Express	150.0

F The MagLev is 81 miles per hour faster than the Nozomi.

G The MagLev is 84 miles per hour faster than the TGV.

H The Nozomi is 4.4 miles per hour faster than the TGV.

J The Nozomi is 12.6 miles per hour faster than the Acela Express.

Spiral Review

Use properties of addition to find each sum mentally. Show your steps and identify the properties that you used. (Lesson 2-7)

33. $12 + 65 + 5$

34. $39 + 17 + 1$

35. $2.6 + 1.3 + 1.7$

Add or subtract. (Lesson 2-6)

36. $0.5 + 1.1$

37. $0.95 - 0.62$

38. $0.59 + 5.6$

39. $28.3 - 10.47$

40. In a recent season, Chad Johnson of the Cincinnati Bengals had 87 receptions. Antonio Gates of the San Diego Chargers had 71 receptions. Estimate how many more receptions Johnson had than Gates. (Lesson 2-2)

41. A cougar has a mass of 102.948 kilograms. Round the mass to the nearest tenth kilogram. (Lesson 2-1)

Order each set of numbers from least to greatest. (Lesson 1-7)

42. 0.557, 0.09, 0.78, 0.67

43. 24.3, 24.08, 24.32, 23.98, 24

FOLDABLES® Study Organizer GET READY to Study

Be sure the following Big Ideas are written in your Foldable.

Key Concepts

Estimation

• When you **round** a number, you find its approximate value to a specified place value. (p. 61)

  324 rounded to the nearest ten is 320.
  6.79 rounded to the nearest tenth is 6.8.

• You can use rounding to **estimate** sums and differences. (p. 64)

426	→	400	Round each addend to
+ 385	→	+ 400	the nearest hundred.
		800	The sum is about 800.

• You can also use compatible numbers to estimate sums and differences.

Adding and Subtracting Whole Numbers and Decimals

• To add or subtract numbers, estimate first. Add or subtract digits in each place-value position. (pp. 70, 80)

2,108	36.19
+ 5,643	− 2.07
7,751	34.12

Key Vocabulary

round (p. 61)

estimate (p. 64)

compatible numbers (p. 64)

compensation (p. 88)

Vocabulary Check

Choose the correct term or number to complete each sentence.

1. When you round a number, you find its (approximate, exact) value.

2. Compatible numbers are numbers that (can, cannot) be added or subtracted mentally.

3. The difference between 10.8 and 2.05 is (8.3, 8.75).

4. To find a number that is close to the exact answer, you can (estimate, add).

5. A reasonable estimate for 619 + 285 is (900, 9,000).

6. The (Associative, Commutative) Property states that you can add numbers in any order.

7. You can use (compensation, annexing) to add numbers mentally.

Lesson-by-Lesson Review

2-1 Round Whole Numbers and Decimals (pp. 61–63)

5.N.24

Example 1
Round 4,712 to the underlined digit.

The digit in the place to be rounded is 7. The digit to the right of 7 is 1. Since 1 < 5, round down.

4,712 → 4,700

Example 2
Round 0.865 to the underlined digit.

The digit in the place to be rounded is 8. The digit to the right of 8 is 6. Since 6 > 5, round up.

0.865 → 0.9

Round each number to the place indicated.

8. 84; tens

9. 6,755; hundreds

10. 326,023; thousands

11. 0.92; tenths

12. 13.61; ones

13. 75.235; hundredths

14. **Measurement** A person set a world record by eating 14 hard boiled eggs in 14.42 seconds. Round this time to the nearest tenth of a second.

2-2 Estimate Sums and Differences (pp. 64–67)

5.N.26

Example 3
Estimate 945 + 585 using rounding.

Round 945 to 900.
Round 585 to 600.

$$
\begin{array}{rcr}
945 & \to & 900 \\
+\ 585 & \to & +\ 600 \\
\hline
 & & 1,500
\end{array}
$$

The sum is about 1,500.

Estimate each sum or difference. Use rounding or compatible numbers. Show your work.

15. 91 + 14   16. 573 − 429

17. 26.09 − 5.8   18. 3.95 + 11.76

19. 808 − 392   20. 3.162 + 0.624

21. Valeria had $78.51 in her bank at home. She adds $3.67 in change. About how much does she have now? Show your work.

2-3 **Problem-Solving Strategy:** Work Backward (pp. 68–69)

5.PS.3

Example 4
The swim team spent $385 to travel to a swim meet. The bus costs $145, and the hotel costs $30 per person. How many people went on the trip?

Subtract to undo the cost of the bus.

$$\$385 - \$145 = \$240$$

Divide to find the number of people.

$$\$240 \div \$30 = 8$$

So, 8 people went on the trip.

Solve. Use the *work backward* strategy.

22. The science club raised money to clean the beach. They spent $29 on trash bags and $74 on waterproof boots. They still have $47 left. How much did they raise?

23. Mr. Charles cut fresh roses from his garden and gave 10 roses to his neighbor. Then he gave half of what was left to his niece. He kept the remaining 14 roses. How many roses did he cut?

2-4 **Add and Subtract Whole Numbers** (pp. 70–72)

4.N.14

Example 5
Find 561 + 23.

Estimate 560 + 20 = 580

Add the ones.	Add the tens.	Add the hundreds.
561	561	561
+ 23	+ 23	+ 23
4	84	584

The sum, 584, is close to the estimate.

Example 6
Find 346 − 175.

Estimate 350 − 180 = 170

Subtract the ones and the tens.	Subtract the hundreds.
2 14	2 14
3̶4̶6	3̶4̶6
− 175	− 175
71	171

The difference, 171, is close to 170.

Add or subtract.

24. 78 + 11

25. 435 − 120

26. 3,612 + 546

27. 654 + 13

28. 6,702 − 913

29. Oklahoma and California have the highest American Indian populations, as shown in the table. What is the total American Indian population in those two states?

State	American Indian Population
Oklahoma	252,420
California	242,164

Source: U.S. Census Bureau

2-5 Problem-Solving Investigation: Estimate or an Exact Answer (pp. 74–75)

5.PS.3

Example 7

Nina's breakfast cost $2.64. She gave the cashier $5. How much change should Nina receive?

You need to find an exact answer.

Subtract $2.64 from $5.

$$
\begin{array}{r}
5.00 \\
- \ 2.64 \\
\hline
2.36
\end{array}
$$

Nina's change is $2.36.

For each problem, determine whether you need an estimate or an exact answer. Then solve.

30. A total of 8 fifth-grade teachers donated $15 each to the school's band. How much money did they donate in all?

31. A group of 5 friends are sharing the cost of renting a boat for one day. If the boat costs $144.95, about how much will they each pay for the boat?

32. The local bakery makes 85 pies each day. The bakery has sold all of the pies for 9 days in a row. About how many pies were sold during these 9 days?

2-6 Add and Subtract Decimals (pp. 80–82)

5.N.23

Example 8
Find 8.3 + 10.75.

Estimate 8 + 11 = 19

Line up the decimal points.	Annex a zero.	Add as with whole numbers.
8.3	8.30	8.30
+ 10.75	+ 10.75	+ 10.75
		19.05

The sum is 19.05. Since this is close to the estimate, the answer is reasonable.

Add or subtract.

33. 4.8   **34.** 0.64   **35.** 8.63
      + 5.7   − 0.52   + 0.19

36. 0.625 + 4.8   **37.** 7.013 − 2.21

38. The male human heart weighs an average of 11.1 ounces. This is 1.8 ounces more than the average female's heart. How much does the average female's heart weigh?

39. Measurement The Dwarf Goby is the smallest marine fish. Its average length is 0.339 inch for males and 0.35 inch for females. How much longer is the female?

2-7 Addition Properties (pp. 84–87)

5.R.9

Example 9
Identify the addition property used to rewrite the problem below.

$$28 + 5 + 62 = 28 + 62 + 5$$

The order of the numbers changed. This is the Commutative Property.

Example 10
Use properties of addition to find 1.4 + 9.7 + 8.6 mentally.

$1.4 + 9.7 + 8.6$

$= 1.4 + 8.6 + 9.7$	Commutative Property
$= (1.4 + 8.6) + 9.7$	Associative Property
$= 10 + 9.7$	Add 1.4 and 8.6 mentally.
$= 19.7$	Add 10 and 9.7 mentally.

Identify the addition property used to rewrite each problem.

40. $7 + 65 + 13 = 7 + 13 + 65$

41. $(4 + 0.7) + 0.3 = 4 + (0.7 + 0.3)$

42. $328 + 0 = 328$

Use properties of addition to find each sum mentally. Show your steps and identify the properties that you used.

43. $46 + 4 + 31$ **44.** $8.7 + 4 + 0.3$

45. Use the Associative Property to group the numbers in the table and find the total amount of money the sports team raised.

Sports Team	Donations ($)
Soccer	3,500
Football	4,250
Tennis	2,750

2-8 Add and Subtract Mentally (pp. 88–91)

5.RP.4

Example 11
Find 298 + 511. Use compensation.

```
298      +      511
↓ + 2           ↓ - 2
300      +      509     = 809
```

The sum is 809.

Example 12
Find 3.4 − 1.9. Use compensation.

```
3.4       −      1.9
↓ + 0.1          ↓ + 0.1
3.5       −      2.0     = 1.5
```

The sum is 1.5.

Add or subtract. Use compensation.

46. $27 + 45$ **47.** $62 - 19$

48. $482 + 329$ **49.** $932 - 645$

50. $4.92 - 3.74$ **51.** $12.6 + 7.5$

52. Measurement The head and body of a pygmy mouse lemur measures 2.4 inches and its tail measures 5.3 inches. How long is the animal from head to tail?

CHAPTER 2

Chapter Test

Round each number to the place indicated.

1. 785; tens

2. 120,395; thousands

3. 6.93; ones

4. 3.041; tenths

5. **MULTIPLE CHOICE** One megabyte is equal to 1,048,576 bytes. Round this to the nearest thousand.

   A 1,050,000   **C** 1,048,600

   B 1,049,000   **D** 1,000,000

Estimate each sum or difference. Use rounding or compatible numbers.

6. 653 − 81   7. 15,429 + 11,602

8. 9.16 + 2.04   9. 73.8 − 59.74

10. **MULTIPLE CHOICE** Which is the best estimate of 46,203 + 84,110?

    F 100,000   **H** 130,000

    G 120,000   **J** 140,000

11. **Measurement** The table shows the height of mountains. How much taller is Mt. McKinley than Mt. Saint Elias?

Mountain	Height (ft)
Mt. McKinley	20,320
Mt. Saint Elias	18,008

Source: *Time for Kids Almanac*

12. A helicopter flight to and from the rainforest costs $499. Supplies cost $112 for each day. How many days can the scientist study birds in the rainforest if she has a $1,283 budget?

Add or subtract.

13. 4,012 + 853   14. 8,871 − 630

15. 3.47 + 1.95   16. 260.3 − 71.8

Measurement For Exercises 17 and 18, use the table that shows the typical lengths of a Rusty Spotted cat.

Measure	Least Length (in.)	Greatest Length (in.)
body	13.7	18.8
tail	5.9	9.8

17. What is the difference between the greatest and least lengths for the cat's body?

18. How long is a rusty-spotted cat if it has the greatest lengths for its body and tail?

Use properties of addition to find each sum mentally.

19. 38 + 19 + 1   20. 0.3 + 1.2 + 0.7

21. 75 + 27 + 25   22. 1.6 + 33 + 11.4

Add or subtract. Use compensation.

23. 36 + 21   24. 14.7 + 8.5

25. **WRITING IN MATH** A speed skater's time in an event was 40.33 seconds. The same skater was 1.08 seconds faster the next time she skated in the event. What was her time in the second race? Explain how you can use compensation to solve.

PART 1   Multiple Choice

Read each question. Then fill in the correct answer on the answer sheet provided by your teacher or on a sheet of paper.

1. The times of four runners in a relay race are shown in the table. Estimate the total time of the team.

Runner	1	2	3	4
Time (s)	14.9	15.1	14.8	15.3

   A 40 sec   C 50 sec

   B 45 sec   D 60 sec

2. The cafeteria sells hamburgers for $1.19, bags of chips for $0.49, and drinks for $0.79. Which is the best estimate for the total cost of a hamburger, a bag of chips, and a drink?

   F $2.50   H $3.00

   G $2.75   J $3.25

3. Nathan received $50 for his birthday. He wants to buy the items listed below. All prices include tax. How much will Nathan have left over after paying for these items?

Item	Cost
Video game	$24.89
CD	$11.18
Poster	$7.62

   A $5.98   C $7.22

   B $6.31   D $8.56

4. Which of the following shows the decimals in order from least to greatest?

   F 0.3, 0.28, 0.279, 0.25

   G 0.25, 0.28, 0.279, 0.3

   H 0.25, 0.279, 0.28, 0.3

   J 0.3, 0.25, 0.279, 0.28

5. A football team scored 27 points in a game. These points were either 3-point field goals or 7-point touchdowns. How many field goals and touchdowns did the team score?

   A 2 field goals and 3 touchdowns

   B 2 field goals and 4 touchdowns

   C 3 field goals and 2 touchdowns

   D 3 field goals and 3 touchdowns

6. The population of Springfield is 534,694. How can you write this number in word form?

   F five-hundred thirty-four thousand, six-hundred four

   G five-hundred thirty-four thousand, six-hundred ninety-four

   H five-hundred thirty-four thousand, nine-hundred sixty-four

   J five-hundred thirty thousand, six-hundred ninety-four

7. Refer to the table that shows the prices of several items. Which is the best estimate for the cost of two notebooks, a pen, and a box of crayons?

Bookstore Prices	
pen	$0.79
notebook	$0.49
box of crayons	$3.69

A $4.00

B $4.50

C $5.00

D $5.50

8. What is 12.638 rounded to the nearest tenth?

F 10.0

G 12.6

H 12.64

J 13

9. The official weight of a college football is between 14 and 15 ounces. Which of the following weights is NOT between 14 and 15 ounces?

A 14.99 ounces

B 14.12 ounces

C 15.01 ounces

D 14.25 ounces

PART 2   Short Response

Record your answers on the sheet provided by your teacher or on a sheet of paper.

10. Tyree scored 8 points in a basketball game. This was 9 points fewer than Aura scored. Write a number sentence that shows how many points Aura scored.

PART 3   Extended Response

Record your answers on the answer sheet provided by your teacher or on a sheet of paper. Show your work.

11. The table shows the number of hours Lola worked last summer. Show how to estimate the total number of hours she worked in four months.

Month	Hours
May	78.50
June	83.25
July	81.50
August	79.75

12. Explain if an estimate or an exact answer is needed for the problem below.

You need to buy five jerseys that cost $12 each. How much money will the five jerseys cost?

NEED EXTRA HELP?												
If You Missed Question...	1	2	3	4	5	6	7	8	9	10	11	12
Go to Lesson...	2-2	2-2	2-6	1-6	2-3	1-1	2-2	2-1	1-6	2-7	2-2	2-5
NYS Core Curriculum	5.N.26	5.N.26	5.N.23	5.N.28	5.PS.3	5.N.3	5.N.26	5.N.24	5.N.28	5.N.9	5.N.26	5.PS.3

CHAPTER 3 Multiply Whole Numbers

BIG Idea **What are products and factors?**

When two or more numbers are multiplied, the result is called a **product**. The numbers that are multiplied are **factors** of the product.

Example The price of admission to an aquarium is $18. If 3 people visit the aquarium, the total cost is shown.

$$3 \times \$18 = \$54$$

factors product

What will I learn in this chapter?

- Multiply multiples of 10, 100, and 1,000 mentally.
- Estimate products of whole numbers.
- Multiply whole numbers.
- Identify and use properties of multiplication.
- Multiply whole numbers.
- Solve problems by using the *draw a picture* strategy.

Key Vocabulary

Distributive Property

factor

product

NY Math Online **Student Study Tools**
at macmillanmh.com

FOLDABLES®
Study Organizer

Make this Foldable to help you organize information about multiplying whole numbers. Begin with 3 sheets of $8\frac{1}{2}'' \times 11''$ paper.

1 **Stack** three sheets of paper $\frac{3}{4}$ inch apart.

2 **Roll** up bottom edges so that all tabs are the same size.

3 **Crease** and staple along the fold.

4 **Write** the chapter title on the front. Label each tab as shown.

ARE YOU READY for Chapter 3?

You have two ways to check prerequisite skills for this chapter.

Option 2

NY Math Online Take the Chapter Readiness Quiz at macmillanmh.com.

Option 1

Complete the Quick Check below.

QUICK Check

Multiply. (Prior Grade)

1. 6×3

2. 1×8

3. 5×4

4. 9×2

5. 7×8

6. 4×10

7. The cost of a coloring book is $2. Find the total cost of 9 coloring books.

Write a multiplication problem for each. Then find each product. (Prior Grade)

8. 8 groups of 6 pens

9. 3 rows of 7 chairs

10. 4 books at $2 each

11. There are 4 model car kits in each box. How many kits are in 5 boxes?

Add. (Lesson 2-4)

12.
$$\begin{array}{r} 1{,}125 \\ + 32{,}060 \\ \hline \end{array}$$

13.
$$\begin{array}{r} 256 \\ + 1{,}470 \\ \hline \end{array}$$

14.
$$\begin{array}{r} 438 \\ + 2{,}040 \\ \hline \end{array}$$

15. A Girl Scout troop sold 1,198 boxes of cookies last year. This year they sold 204 more boxes than last year. Next year the troop wants to sell 150 more boxes than this year's total. How many boxes of cookies does the troop want to sell next year?

3-1 Multiplication Patterns

MAIN IDEA

I will use basic facts and patterns to multiply multiples of 10, 100, and 1,000 mentally.

NYS Core Curriculum

5.N.3 Understand the place value structure of the base ten number system
Also addresses 5.CN.2, 5.A.7, 5.A.8.

New Vocabulary

product
factor

NY Math Online

macmillanmh.com
• Extra Examples
• Personal Tutor
• Self-Check Quiz

Many water parks now offer surfing rides. About 900 gallons of water flow through these rides each second.

In 1 second: $1 \times 900 = 900$ gallons
In 2 seconds: $2 \times 900 = 1,800$ gallons
In 3 seconds: $3 \times 900 = 2,700$ gallons

Do you notice a pattern?

When two or more numbers are multiplied, the result is called a **product**. The numbers that are multiplied are **factors** of the product.

$$3 \times 9 = 27$$

27 is the product of 3 and 9.

3 and 9 are factors of 27.

You can multiply some numbers mentally by using basic facts and patterns. Look at the pattern below.

$3 \times 9 = 27$	← basic fact
$3 \times 90 = 270$	THINK 3 × 9 tens = 27 tens or 270
$3 \times 900 = 2,700$	THINK 3 × 9 hundreds = 27 hundreds or 2,700
$3 \times 9,000 = 27,000$	THINK 3 × 9 thousands = 27 thousands or 27,000

EXAMPLE   Use Patterns to Multiply Mentally

1 **Use a pattern to find 6×800 mentally.**

Step 1 Write the basic fact. $6 \times 8 = 48$

Step 2 Continue the pattern. $6 \times 80 = 480$
                                                      $6 \times 800 = 4,800$

The product of 6 and 800 is 4,800.

When multiplying factors that are multiples of 10, you can find the product mentally by using basic facts and then counting zeros in the factors.

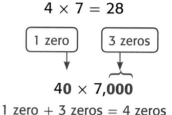

EXAMPLE Count Zeros to Multiply Mentally

2 **Find 40 × 7,000 mentally.**

Step 1 Write the basic fact. $4 \times 7 = 28$

Step 2 Count the number of zeros in each factor.

1 zero   3 zeros

$40 \times 7,000$

1 zero + 3 zeros = 4 zeros

Step 3 Write the zeros to the right of the product from Step 1.

4 zeros

280,000

So, the product is 280,000.

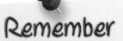

Remember

If a basic fact ends with a zero, there is an extra zero in the product. In Example 3, the first zero in 3,000 is from $5 \times 6 = 30$.

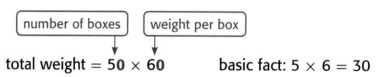

Real-World EXAMPLE

3 **SKATEBOARDS** A truck is loaded with 50 boxes of skateboards. Each box weighs 60 pounds. What is the total weight of the boxes?

number of boxes   weight per box

total weight = **50 × 60**   basic fact: $5 \times 6 = 30$

Since there are 2 zeros in the factors, write 2 zeros to the right of 30. So, $50 \times 60 = 3,000$. The boxes weigh 3,000 pounds.

CHECK What You Know

Find each product mentally. See Examples 1, 2 (pp. 103–104)

1. 2×300 **2.** 8×40 **3.** 100×13 **4.** $3 \times 9,000$

5. 70×60 **6.** 500×70 **7.** 10×120 **8.** 800×500

9. Paulita reads an average of 20 pages each day. She has 6 days to read 115 pages. Will she finish her reading in 6 days? Explain.

10. **Talk About It** Explain how many zeros are in the product *50 times 500.*

Find each product mentally. See Examples 1, 2 (pp. 103–104)

11. 7×50

12. 80×2

13. 10×19

14. 60×80

15. 200×6

16. 9×500

17. 440×10

18. 70×200

19. $22 \times 1,000$

20. $3,000 \times 20$

21. $8,000 \times 30$

22. $8 \times 4,000$

23. 900×900

24. 400×500

25. $600 \times 7,000$

26. $5,000 \times 300$

27. A group of friends bought 7 concert tickets for $30 each. How much did they spend on the tickets?

28. At a soccer tournament, there were 10 teams. If each team had 20 players, how many soccer players were there?

29. Each box contains 200 pencils. The school store has 15 boxes of pencils. How many pencils does the school store have?

30. Measurement Some glaciers in Alaska move forward 100 meters per day. At this rate, how far would these glaciers move in 6 weeks?

New York Data File

The brook trout is the official state fish of New York. Female trout lay batches of 15-60 eggs at a time. This results in a total of 400-600 eggs each mating season.

31. Suppose a female lays 9 batches with 50 eggs each. What is the total number of eggs laid?

32. Suppose 6 brook trout each lay 600 eggs. How many eggs were laid in all?

Source: Boquet River Association

H.O.T. Problems

33. OPEN ENDED Write three different pairs of factors that each have a product of 240.

CHALLENGE Find each missing factor.

34. $5 \times \blacksquare = 4,000$

35. $60 \times \blacksquare = 1,200$

36. $20,000 = \blacksquare \times 500$

37. $3 \times \blacksquare = 2,100$

38. $1,600 = 4 \times \blacksquare$

39. $28,000 = \blacksquare \times 700$

40. WRITING IN ►MATH Explain how using basic facts can help you find $10 \times 20 \times 30 \times 40$ mentally. Then explain how you would find the product.

Math Activity for 3-2
Multiply Mentally

It may be hard to find a product like 4 × 13 mentally, even if you use counters. If you separate the counters into smaller groups called *partial products*, it is easier to multiply.

MAIN IDEA

I will mentally multiply a one-digit factor by a two-digit factor.

NYS Core Curriculum

5.RP.2 Understand that mathematical statements can be supported, using models, facts, and relationships to explain their thinking *Also addresses 5.N.18.*

NY Math Online

macmillanmh.com
• Concepts in Motion

ACTIVITY

1 **Find 4 × 13 mentally using partial products.**

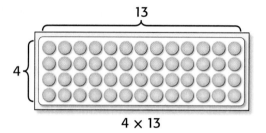

13

4 × 13

Model 4 × 13 by arranging counters in 4 rows and 13 columns.

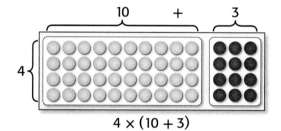

10   +   3

4 × (10 + 3)

Separate 13 into two numbers that are each easily multiplied by 4.

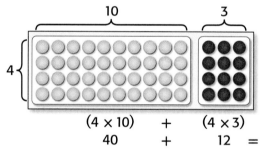

10   3

(4 × 10)   +   (4 × 3)
40   +   12   =   52

Multiply to find the number of counters in each group. Then add.

Rewrite 4 × 13 as (4 × 10) + (4 × 3). This is useful since it is easier to find (4 × 10) + (4 × 3) mentally than to find 4 × 13. So, 4 × 13 is 52.

Think About It

1. To find 4 × 13, you can also find 4 × (9 + 4). Why is it easier to find 4 × (10 + 3) mentally than it is to find 4 × (9 + 4)?

2. Which expression would you use to find 7 × 19 mentally: 7 × (13 + 6) or 7 × (10 + 9)? Explain.

ACTIVITY

2 **Find 5 × 16 mentally using partial products.**

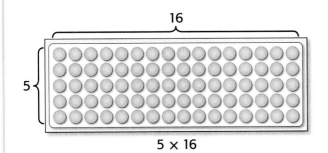

16

5 {

5 × 16

Model 5 × 16 by arranging counters in 5 rows and 16 columns.

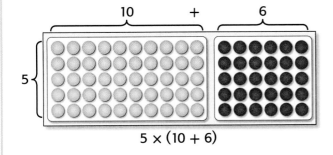

10 + 6

5 {

5 × (10 + 6)

Separate 16 into 10 + 6, since each number is easily multiplied by 5.

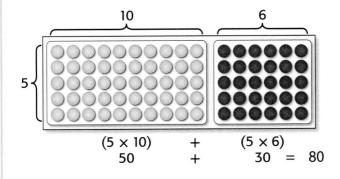

10   6

5 {

(5 × 10)   +   (5 × 6)
   50   +   30   =   80

Multiply to find the number of counters in each group. Then add 50 + 30 = 80.

So, the product of 5 and 16 is 80.

CHECK What You Know

Find each product mentally using partial products. Use counters if necessary. Show the steps you used.

3. 3 × 18   **4.** 6 × 15   **5.** 4 × 19   **6.** 5 × 24

7. 4 × 16   **8.** 3 × 17   **9.** 5 × 13   **10.** 6 × 14

11. **WRITING IN ►MATH** Write a multiplication problem with a one-digit factor and a two-digit factor. Then explain how you can find the product mentally.

3-2 The Distributive Property

MAIN IDEA

I will use the Distributive Property to multiply mentally.

NYS Core Curriculum

5.N.18 Evaluate an arithmetic expression using order of operations including multiplication, division, addition, subtraction **and parentheses** *Also addresses 5.RP.1.*

New Vocabulary

Distributive Property

NY Math Online

macmillanmh.com
• Extra Examples
• Personal Tutor
• Self-Check Quiz

GET READY to Learn

The table shows the costs for activities at a fun center. How much would it cost one person to do both activities?

Activity	Cost per Person
bumper boats	$4
laser tag	$6

How much would it cost 8 people to do both activities shown above? There are two ways to find the answer.

One Way: Multiply 8 by the cost for 1 person.

cost for 1 person

$8 \times (4 + 6) = 8 \times 10$ or $80

Another Way: Find the cost of 8 bumper boat rides and 8 laser tag games. Then add.

cost of 8 boat rides   cost of 8 games

$(8 \times 4) + (8 \times 6) = 32 + 48$ or $80

Using either method, the total cost for 8 people is $80. This shows that $8 \times (4 + 6) = (8 \times 4) + (8 \times 6)$. The **Distributive Property** combines addition and multiplication.

Distributive Property   Key Concept

To multiply a sum by a number, multiply each addend by the number. Then add.

$$3 \times (5 + 2) = (3 \times 5) + (3 \times 2)$$

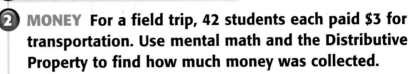

EXAMPLE   Use the Distributive Property

Vocabulary Link

Distribute to give out to each member of a group

Example: A teacher distributes a book to each student.

1 Rewrite 7 × (20 + 6) using the Distributive Property. Then evaluate.

7 × (20 + 6) = (7 × 20) + (7 × 6)   Distributive Property

$\qquad\qquad$ = 140 + 42   THINK 7 × 20 = 140 and 7 × 6 = 42

$\qquad\qquad$ = 182   Add 140 and 42 mentally.

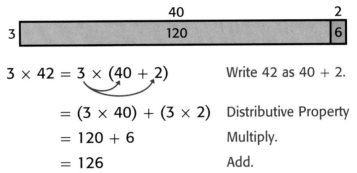

Real-World EXAMPLE   Multiply Mentally

Remember

The numbers 120 and 6 are partial products.

2 **MONEY** For a field trip, 42 students each paid $3 for transportation. Use mental math and the Distributive Property to find how much money was collected.

	40	2
3	120	6

3 × 42 = 3 × (40 + 2)   Write 42 as 40 + 2.

$\qquad\qquad$ = (3 × 40) + (3 × 2)   Distributive Property

$\qquad\qquad$ = 120 + 6   Multiply.

$\qquad\qquad$ = 126   Add.

So, $126 was collected for the field trip.

CHECK What You Know

Rewrite each expression using the Distributive Property. Then evaluate. See Example 1 (p. 109)

1. 5 × (10 + 8)   **2.** 2 × (20 + 1)   **3.** 4 × (10 + 5)

Find each product mentally using the Distributive Property. Show the steps that you used. See Examples 1, 2 (p. 109)

4. 6 × 13   **5.** 3 × 52

6. 5 × 26   **7.** 4 × 69

8. 2 × 49   **9.** 7 × 23

10. Measurement A horse is 17 *hands* tall. If 1 hand equals 4 inches, how tall is the horse in inches?

11. Explain how to use the Distributive Property to find a product mentally.

Rewrite each expression using the Distributive Property. Then evaluate. See Example 1 (p. 109)

12. $7 \times (10 + 3)$

13. $2 \times (50 + 3)$

14. $3 \times (10 + 4)$

15. $4 \times (20 + 2)$

16. $2 \times (30 + 1)$

17. $6 \times (20 + 4)$

Find each product mentally using the Distributive Property. Show the steps that you used. See Examples 1, 2 (p. 109)

18. 2×38

19. 4×61

20. 3×14

21. 5×74

22. 25×6

23. 52×3

24. 2×31

25. 3×63

26. Mr. Collins is buying 5 train tickets for $36 each. What is the total cost of the tickets? Explain your process.

27. Measurement Melanie runs 23 miles each week. Use the Distributive Property to find how many miles she runs in 9 weeks. Show the steps you used.

28. In each bag, there are 3 blueberry bagels and 3 raisin bagels. If you have 35 bags of bagels, how many bagels do you have? Show your steps.

29. Admission to a theme park is $28 and lunch costs $9. Use the Distributive Property to find the cost of 4 tickets and 4 lunches. Show your steps.

H.O.T. Problems

30. FIND THE ERROR Lars and Celeste are using the Distributive Property to simplify $6 \times (9 + 4)$. Whose expression is correct? Explain.

Celeste
$(6 \times 9) + (6 \times 4)$

Lars
$6 \times 9 + 4$

31. CHALLENGE The Distributive Property also combines subtraction and multiplication. For example, $3 \times (5 - 2) = (3 \times 5) - (3 \times 2)$. Demonstrate how you could use the Distributive Property and mental math to find 5×198.

32. **WRITING IN ►MATH** Use the Distributive Property to evaluate 8×62. Check your work using pencil and paper. Which method is easier? Explain.

33. The table shows the number of hours each week that Taran and Amelia volunteer. Which expression can be used to find the total number of hours they volunteer in 4 weeks? **(Lesson 3-2)**

Student	Number of Hours
Amelia	2
Taran	1

A $4 \times 2 \times 1$

B $4 \times (2 + 1)$

C $4 + 2 + 1$

D $4 \times (2 - 1)$

34. When you multiply two multiples of 10, which is a true statement about the product? **(Lesson 3-1)**

F It always has the same number of zeros as the factors combined.

G It always has one less zero than the factors combined.

H It never has the same number of zeros as the factors combined.

J It always has the same number of zeros or more zeros as the factors combined.

Spiral Review

Find each product mentally. **(Lesson 3-1)**

35. 40×20

36. $7 \times 3,000$

37. $1,500 \times 10$

Add or subtract mentally. Use compensation. **(Lesson 2-8)**

38. $18 + 37$

39. $7.9 + 5.5$

40. $204 - 97$

41. Measurement Refer to the table at the right. How much longer is Mammoth Cave than Lechuguilla Cave? Determine whether you need an estimate or an exact answer. Then solve. **(Lesson 2-5)**

Cave	Length (mi)
Mammoth, Kentucky	352
Lechuguilla, New Mexico	100

Estimate each sum or difference by rounding. **(Lesson 2-2)**

42. $38 + 46$

43. $214 - 105$

44. $9.6 + 8.7$

45. $5.9 - 3.4$

46. Measurement The high temperatures in degrees Fahrenheit for five days are shown below. Write the days in order from the least to greatest high temperature. **(Lesson 1-7)**

Monday	Tuesday	Wednesday	Thursday	Friday
70°	68°	67°	71°	65°

3-3 Estimate Products

GET READY to Learn

About 13 harp seal pups live in each square mile of Greenland. *About* how many pups live in a 92 square-mile area?

MAIN IDEA

I will estimate products by using rounding and compatible numbers.

NYS Core Curriculum

5.N.27 Justify the reasonableness of answers using estimation

5.M.11 Justify the reasonableness of estimates
Also addresses 5.PS.22.

NY Math Online

macmillanmh.com

• Extra Examples
• Personal Tutor
• Self-Check Quiz

When a problem asks *about* how many, you can use estimation to solve. Use strategies such as rounding and compatible numbers.

Real-World EXAMPLE

1 ANIMALS Use the information above. About how many harp seal pups live in a 92 square-mile area?

One Way: Round one factor.

THINK It is easier to compute 92 × 10 than 13 × 90.

$$
\begin{array}{rcl}
92 & \to & 92 \\
\times\,13 & \to & \underline{\times\,10} \\
& & 920 \quad \text{Find } 92 \times 10 \text{ mentally.}
\end{array}
$$

Round 13 to the nearest ten.

Another Way: Round both factors.

$$
\begin{array}{rcl}
92 & \to & 90 \\
\times\,13 & \to & \underline{\times\,10} \\
& & 900
\end{array}
$$

Round 92 to the nearest ten.
Round 13 to the nearest ten.
Find 90 × 10 mentally.

Another Way: Use compatible numbers.

$$
\begin{array}{rcl}
92 & \to & 100 \\
\times\,13 & \to & \underline{\times\,10} \\
& & 1,000
\end{array}
$$

100 and 10 are compatible numbers.
Find 100 × 10 mentally.

Depending on how you estimate, 92 × 13 is about 900, 920, or 1,000. So, there are between 900 and 1,000 pups in a 92 square-mile area.

112 Chapter 3 Multiply Whole Numbers

2 **SCHOOL** Mountain View Elementary is sending 21 boxes of magazines to a school in Paraguay. There are 154 magazines in each box. About how many magazines are they sending?

South America

Paraguay

One Way: **Round each factor to its greatest place value.**

154	→	200	Round 154 to the nearest hundred.
× 21	→	× 20	Round 21 to the nearest ten.
		4,000	Find 200 × 20 mentally.

Another Way: **Round each factor to the nearest ten.**

154	→	150	Round 154 to the nearest ten.
× 21	→	× 20	Round 21 to the nearest ten.
		3,000	Find 150 × 20 mentally.

Depending on how you round, 154 × 21 is about 3,000 or 4,000. So, they are sending 3,000 or 4,000 magazines.

You can also use compatible numbers when a factor is close to 25 or 50.

Remember

Multiplication problems can be written horizontally and vertically.

3 **BIKING** Tyson makes bike ramps. He can make 26 bike ramps in a week. About how many can he make in eight weeks?

8 × 26 → 8 × 25   Replace 26 with 25.

8 × 25 = 200   THINK Eight quarters are the same as $2.00. So, 8 × 25 is 200.

So, Tyson can make about 200 bike ramps in eight weeks.

Estimate by rounding or compatible numbers. Show your work.

See Examples 1–3 (pp. 112–113)

1. 42
   × 16

2. 32
   × 18

3. 218
   × 6

4. 131
   × 29

5. 61 × 68

6. 98 × 83

7. 392 × 46

8. 450 × 21

9. 4 × 24

10. 6 × 48

11. 12 × 27

12. **Measurement** If a heart rate is 72 beats per minute, about how many times does it beat in an hour? Show how you estimated.

13. **Talk About It** Show two different ways you could estimate 312 × 18.

Practice and Problem Solving

NYSCC • NYSMT

Extra Practice, p. R8

Estimate by rounding or compatible numbers. Show your work.

See Examples 1–3 (pp. 112–113)

14. 6
    × 33

15. 7
    × 68

16. 106
    × 52

17. 127
    × 8

18. 42
    × 89

19. 76
    × 78

20. 508
    × 27

21. 19
    × 238

22. 88 × 31

23. 64 × 91

24. 17 × 939

25. 58 × 118

26. 79 × 56

27. 33 × 84

28. 729 × 42

29. 609 × 44

30. 8 × 51

31. 8 × 24

32. 16 × 26

33. For a school assembly, students sit in chairs that are arranged in 53 rows. There are 12 chairs in each row. About how many students can be seated? Show your work.

34. **Measurement** The table shows the number of pounds of apples that were harvested each day. Estimate how many pounds of apples were harvested. Show your work.

35. In one week, a campground rented 18 cabins at $225 each. About how much did they collect in rent? Show how you estimated.

Day	Pounds of Apples
1	514
2	487
3	349
4	421
5	392

Science Sound travels through different materials at different speeds. For example, the graph shows that in 1 second, sound travels 5,971 meters through stone. However, it travels only 346 meters through air in 1 second.

For Exercises 36–39, estimate to find the distance that sound travels through each material in each given time.

36. air, 20 seconds

37. aluminum, 12 seconds

38. water, 3 seconds

39. Estimate how much farther sound travels through stone in 17 seconds than through aluminum in the same time.

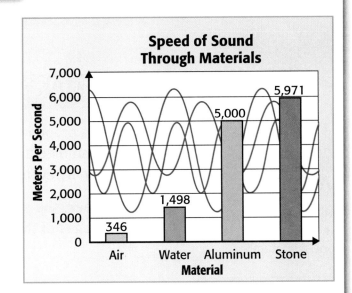

H.O.T. Problems

40. **OPEN ENDED** Use the digits 1, 3, 5, and 7 to create two whole numbers whose product is estimated to be about 600.

41. **CHALLENGE** Without calculating, which of the following methods gives a more accurate answer when estimating 42×13? Explain.

    a. increase both factors   **b.** decrease both factors

42. **FIND THE ERROR** Demont and Tran are estimating 139×18. Who is correct? Explain.

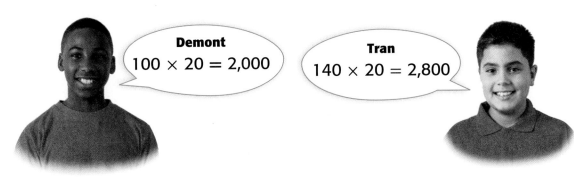

43. **NUMBER SENSE** Without calculating, predict whether 50×300 is greater than or less than 46×289. Explain your reasoning.

44. **WRITING IN ▶ MATH** Write a real-world problem in which an exact answer is not needed.

Multiply by One-Digit Numbers

MAIN IDEA

I will multiply up to a three-digit number by a one-digit number.

NYS Core Curriculum

Preparation for 5.N.16 Use a variety of strategies to multiply three-digit by three-digit numbers *Also addresses 5.CN.6.*

NY Math Online

macmillanmh.com

• Extra Examples
• Personal Tutor
• Self-Check Quiz

> **GET READY to Learn**

Karen was preparing for a spelling bee. She studied about 28 pages of the dictionary every day.

In one week, she studied about 28 × 7 pages of the dictionary.

Real-World EXAMPLES Two-Digit and Three-Digit Numbers

1 **SPELLING** **Refer to the information above. How many pages did Karen study?** Estimate 30 × 7 = 210

Step 1
Multiply the ones.

$$\begin{array}{r} \overset{5}{} \\ 28 \\ \times\ 7 \\ \hline 6 \end{array}$$ 7 × 8 = 56 ones

Step 2
Multiply the tens.

$$\begin{array}{r} \overset{5}{} \\ 28 \\ \times\ 7 \\ \hline 196 \end{array}$$ 7 × 2 tens = 14 tens
14 + 5 = 19 tens

Karen studied 196 pages.   Compare to the estimate.

2 **RIDES** **A large Ferris wheel seats 260 people. How many people can ride it in 9 rides?** Estimate 260 × 10 = 2,600

Step 1 Multiply the ones.
Regroup if necessary.

$$\begin{array}{r} 260 \\ \times\ 9 \\ \hline 0 \end{array}$$ 9 × 0 = 0 ones

Step 2 Multiply the tens.
Add any new tens.
Regroup if necessary.

$$\begin{array}{r} \overset{5}{} \\ 260 \\ \times\ 9 \\ \hline 40 \end{array}$$ 9 × 6 tens = 54 tens

Step 3 Multiply the hundreds.
Add any new hundreds.
Regroup if necessary.

$$\begin{array}{r} \overset{5}{} \\ 260 \\ \times\ 9 \\ \hline 2340 \end{array}$$ 9 × 2 hundreds = 18 hundreds
18 + 5 = 23 hundreds

So, 2,340 people can ride the Ferris wheel in 9 rides.

Multiply. See Examples 1, 2 (p. 116)

1. 42
  × 2

2. 61
  × 5

3. 314
  × 9

4. 18
  × 8

5. 5 × 31

6. 208 × 3

7. 47 × 6

8. 7 × 624

9. One 747 airplane can carry 420 passengers. Will two of these planes be able to carry 1,000 people? Explain.

10. (Talk About It) Describe each step for finding 416 × 3.

Practice and Problem Solving

NYSCC • NYSMT
Extra Practice, p. R8

Multiply. See Examples 1, 2 (p. 116)

11. 21
  × 3

12. 32
  × 6

13. 52
  × 9

14. 401
  × 7

15. 143
  × 9

16. 72
  × 4

17. 64
  × 5

18. 712
  × 3

19. 211 × 7

20. 82 × 5

21. 8 × 16

22. 67 × 8

23. 341 × 4

24. 5 × 182

25. 806 × 7

26. 6 × 97

27. Measurement The world's largest cactus is 5 times as tall as the cactus shown. How tall is the world's largest cactus?

28. Northeast Elementary School purchased 5 new computer systems. Each system cost $1,468. What was the total cost?

29. In the auditorium, there are 9 rows of seats with 18 seats in each row. There are also 6 rows of seats with 24 seats in each row. How many seats are there in the auditorium?

30. Measurement The remains of an ancient South American city are 7,710 feet above sea level. There are 5,280 feet in a mile. Are the remains closer to 1 mile or 2 miles above sea level? Explain.

31. Measurement Malcolm ran the 440-yard dash and the 220-yard dash at a track meet. There are 3 feet in one yard. How many total feet did Malcolm run?

15 ft

H.O.T. Problems

32. OPEN ENDED Write a multiplication problem involving a one-digit number in which the product is greater than 1,200 but less than 1,300.

33. WRITING IN ►MATH Write a real-world problem that can be solved by multiplying a three-digit number by 3.

NYSMT Practice 5.N.27, Preparation for 5.N.16

34. A total of 189 people visited the wildlife reserve this week. Which best represents the amount of money collected from ticket sales? (Lesson 3-3)

WILDLIFE RESERVE

Tickets $12

A Less than $200

B Between $200 and $240

C Between $2,000 and $2,400

D More than $2,400

35. Mario has 18 CDs. Amber has twice as many CDs as Mario. How many CDs does Amber have? (Lesson 3-4)

F 9

G 27

H 36

J 54

36. SHORT RESPONSE Collin bought 7 flats of flowers. Each flat contains 24 flowers. How many flowers did he buy? (Lesson 3-4)

Spiral Review

Estimate by rounding or compatible numbers. Show your work. (Lesson 3-3)

37. 8
    × 29

38. 487
     × 5

39. 63
    × 12

40. 224
     × 76

Rewrite each expression using the Distributive Property. Then evaluate. (Lesson 3-2)

41. $4 \times (10 + 1)$

42. $5 \times (30 + 6)$

43. $2 \times (50 + 1)$

44. Catalina is buying a cup of frozen yogurt for $2.29. She has a coupon for $0.50 off. What price does she pay for the frozen yogurt? (Lesson 2-6)

45. Measurement A jet ski rental company charges $9 per hour before 12 P.M., and $12 per hour after 12 P.M. Ken turned in his jet ski at 2 P.M. and paid $42 in rental fees. At what time did he rent the jet ski? (Lesson 2-3)

Find each product mentally. (Lesson 3-1)

1. 9×60 **2.** 200×40

3. 80×50 **4.** $1,000 \times 17$

5. 300×100 **6.** $70 \times 5,000$

7. Measurement The distance around a skating rink is 420 feet. If Anthony skates around the rink 10 times, how far does he skate? (Lesson 3-1)

Find each product mentally using the Distributive Property. Show the steps that you used. (Lesson 3-2)

8. 5×17 **9.** 3×71

10. 6×25 **11.** 2×37

12. 4×43 **13.** 2×31

14. MULTIPLE CHOICE A set of bleachers has 8 rows of seats. Each row can seat 25 people. If the bleachers are full, how many people are seated on the bleachers? (Lesson 3-2)

A 17

B 33

C 100

D 200

Estimate by rounding or compatible numbers. Show your work. (Lesson 3-3)

15. 39×8 **16.** 17×62

17. 114×48 **18.** 285×56

19. MULTIPLE CHOICE Which is the best estimate for the product of 502 and 423? (Lesson 3-3)

F 2,000

G 20,000

H 200,000

J 2,000,000

20. The table shows the results of a canned food drive. Estimate the total number of cans collected in all four classes. Show how you estimated. (Lesson 3-3)

Class	Number of Cans
1	415
2	402
3	380
4	426

Multiply. (Lesson 3-4)

21. 43×2 **22.** 17×9

23. 102×4 **24.** 513×6

25. WRITING IN MATH Zoe is cutting 9 pieces of wire like the one shown below for her science fair project. How much wire does she need? Estimate and then solve. Compare your estimate with the actual amount. (Lessons 3-3 and 3-4)

Problem-Solving Strategy

MAIN IDEA I will solve problems by drawing a picture.

 **5.PS.13 Model problems with pictures/diagrams** or physical objects *Also addresses 5.RP.5, 5.R.5.*

For the school carnival, the fifth grade is putting game booths in the school parking lot. Each game booth is 7 feet wide and must be 5 feet from the next booth. The booths at each end must be at least 10 feet from the end of the parking lot.

The parking lot is 82 feet long. Find the greatest number of game booths that they can have.

Understand	**What facts do you know?** • The parking lot is 82 feet long. • Information about the size and layout of the booths. **What do you need to find?** • The greatest number of game booths the carnival can have.
Plan	Draw a picture to solve.
Solve	First, mark off 10 feet from the left end and 10 feet from the right end. Then, mark 7 feet for a game booth and 5 feet of space until you have no more space remaining. 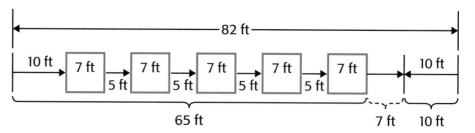 Since there is only 7 feet remaining, there is not enough space to have a sixth booth. They can have 5 booths.
Check	Look back. The space for 5 game booths is 5×7 or 35 feet. The space needed at the ends is $10 + 10$ or 20 feet. The space needed between the booths is 5×4 or 20 feet. So, $35 + 20 + 20 = 75$ feet and $75 < 82$. So, the answer makes sense.

120   Chapter 3 Multiply Whole Numbers

ANALYZE the Strategy

Refer to the problem on the previous page.

1. Explain how drawing a picture helped you solve the problem.

2. Explain whether you think drawing a picture is the best strategy to solve this problem.

3. Determine the greatest number of game booths that could be built if the parking lot was 97 feet long.

4. Describe a real-world situation in which you could use the *draw a picture* strategy.

PRACTICE the Strategy

NYSCC • NYSMT

Extra Practice, p. R8

5. A 1-mile long scenic route has signposts placed every 40 yards. There are signposts placed at the beginning and end of the mile. How many signposts are there?

6. **Measurement** A table has the dimensions shown below.

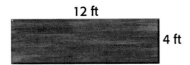

12 ft

4 ft

There are microphones on the table placed every 2 feet along the edges. There is also a microphone placed at each corner. How many microphones are on the table?

7. **Measurement** Ciara has a television stand that is 36 inches high. On the stand, she places a 24-inch high television on top of a 4-inch high DVD player. The bottom of a picture frame is 32 inches above the television stand. How many inches are between the top of the television and the bottom of the picture frame?

8. Speakers are placed every 10 yards around the walls of the school auditorium. No speakers are placed at the corners. The auditorium is 210 feet by 300 feet. How many wall speakers are placed around the school auditorium?

9. **Measurement** The picture below shows the length and width of a bookmark. Find the number of bookmarks this size that can be cut from a piece of fabric whose length is 24 inches and whose width is 36 inches.

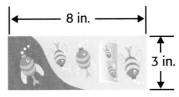

8 in.

3 in.

10. Ernie has a piece of wood that is 43 inches long. How many 13-inch pieces can he cut from the wood? Is there any wood remaining?

11. **WRITING IN ►MATH** How can words and numbers be used with the *draw a picture* strategy?

3-6 Multiply by Two-Digit Numbers

MAIN IDEA

I will multiply up to a three-digit number by a two-digit number.

NYS Core Curriculum

Preparation for 5.N.16 Use a variety of strategies to multiply three-digit by three-digit numbers *Also addresses 5.CN.6, 5.CM.1.*

NY Math Online

macmillanmh.com

• Extra Examples
• Personal Tutor
• Self-Check Quiz

GET READY to Learn

Coyotes can run up to 44 feet per second on land! At this rate, how many feet could a coyote run in 12 seconds?

Real-World EXAMPLE Multiply Two-Digit Numbers

① **COYOTES** Refer to the information above. To solve the problem, multiply 44 and 12. Estimate $44 \times 10 = 440$

Step 1	Step 2	Step 3
Multiply the ones.	Multiply the tens.	Add.

Step 1:
$$\begin{array}{r} 44 \\ \times\ 12 \\ \hline 88 \end{array}$$ $44 \times 2 = 88$

Step 2:
$$\begin{array}{r} 44 \\ \times\ 12 \\ \hline 88 \\ 440 \end{array}$$ $44 \times 10 = 440$

Step 3:
$$\begin{array}{r} 44 \\ \times\ 12 \\ \hline 88 \\ +\ 440 \\ \hline 528 \end{array}$$ $88 + 440 = 528$

So, a coyote could run 528 feet in 12 seconds.

EXAMPLE Multiply Three-Digit Numbers

② **Find 165 × 31.** Estimate $200 \times 30 = 6,000$

Step 1	Step 2	Step 3
Multiply the ones.	Multiply the tens.	Add.

Step 1:
$$\begin{array}{r} 165 \\ \times\ 31 \\ \hline 165 \end{array}$$ $165 \times 1 = 165$

Step 2:
$$\begin{array}{r} 165 \\ \times\ 31 \\ \hline 165 \\ 4950 \end{array}$$ $165 \times 30 = 4,950$

Step 3:
$$\begin{array}{r} 165 \\ \times\ 31 \\ \hline 165 \\ +\ 4950 \\ \hline 5115 \end{array}$$ $165 + 4,950 = 5,115$

So, $165 \times 31 = 5,115.$ Compare to the estimate.

Multiply. See Examples 1, 2 (p. 122)

1.   32
    × 13

2.   26
    × 45

3. 104
    × 12

4. 102
    × 56

5. 21 × 42

6. 69 × 14

7. 83 × 367

8. 534 × 67

9. A cow can eat 25 pounds of hay a day. At that rate, how many pounds of hay can a cow eat in 31 days?

10. **Talk About It** Describe how addition is used when you multiply by two-digit numbers.

Practice and Problem Solving

NYSCC • NYSMT
Extra Practice, p. R9

Multiply. See Examples 1, 2 (p. 122)

11.   24
    × 21

12.   39
    × 34

13.   13
    × 54

14.   51
    × 82

15. 141
    × 25

16. 229
    × 31

17. 470
    × 56

18. 321
    × 64

19. 19 × 15

20. 43 × 65

21. 72 × 36

22. 23 × 84

23. 48 × 101

24. 441 × 20

25. 281 × 52

26. 347 × 89

27. **Measurement** A delivery truck travels 278 miles each day. How far does it travel in 25 days?

28. Alisa earns $14 an hour. How much does she earn in 4 weeks if she works 12 hours each week?

29. Marshall's mother buys 2 boxes of granola bars each week. Each box contains 8 granola bars. If she continues buying 2 boxes each week, how many granola bars will she buy in a year?

30. Ms. Jenkins was arranging chairs for a school awards assembly. Each row contained 15 chairs. If there were 21 rows, how many chairs had to be arranged?

31. **Measurement** Alicia lives in Nashville. Last year her family drove to Atlanta each month to visit her grandmother. Find the total distance they drove for the year.

Destination City From Nashville	One-Way Distance (mi)
Atlanta	249
Raleigh	540

32. The table below shows Katrina's prices for dog walking. If she walks 5 medium-sized dogs and 8 large-sized dogs for 12 weeks, how much will she earn?

Dog Type	Cost Per Week ($)
Small	10
Medium	12
Large	14

Lesson 3-6 Multiply by Two-Digit Numbers 123

H.O.T. Problems

33. CHALLENGE Find 235 × 124. Use the same strategy for multiplying by a three-digit number that you used for multiplying by a two-digit number except include multiplying by the hundreds place.

34. **WRITING IN ►MATH** Choose four different numbers from 1 through 9 to create a multiplication problem that gives you the greatest product. Explain how you know it is the greatest.

35. Each day there are 7 tours at the glass factory. Twenty-eight people can go on a tour. How many people can tour the glass factory each day? (Lesson 3-4)

   A 156

   B 180

   C 196

   D 200

36. The table shows the average number of meals a restaurant makes each day. About how many dinners does the restaurant make in a two-week period? (Lesson 3-6)

Number of Lunches	225
Number of Dinners	425

   F 9,100   **H** 2,975

   G 5,950   **J** 850

Spiral Review

37. Measurement Leslie is making jewelry. She has a piece of wire that is 81 inches long. She uses a piece that is 3 inches long to make a pair of earrings. Find the number of 6-inch pieces she can cut from the remaining piece to make bracelets. Use the *draw a picture* strategy. (Lesson 3-5)

Multiply. (Lesson 3-4)

38.   27
    × 4

39.   48
    × 6

40.   78
    × 5

41. 208
    × 3

42. Mr. Batista was buying supplies for a picnic. He bought 6 packages of cups with 36 in each package. Use the Distributive Property to find the number of cups he bought. Show the steps you used. (Lesson 3-2)

Add or subtract. (Lesson 2-8)

43. 38 + 46   **44.** 214 − 105   **45.** 4.6 + 8.7

Game Time

What's the Difference?

Multiplying Two Numbers

Get Ready!

Players: 2 players

You will need: 0–9 spinner
paper

Get Set!

- Make a spinner as shown.

- Each player needs a sheet of paper and a pencil.

Go!

- Each player spins the spinner four times to make a multiplication problem with two two-digit factors or a one-digit and a three-digit factor.

- Each player then spins four times to make a different multiplication problem with two two-digit factors or a one-digit and a three-digit factor.

- Each player finds the product of each of his or her problems. Then the players find the difference between the two products.

- The player with the greatest difference wins the round.

- Play 5 rounds.

GET READY to Learn

Gabriela has five $2 bills and Jolon has two $5 bills.

Jolon: $5 \times \$2 = \$10$

Gabriela: $2 \times \$5 = \$10$

MAIN IDEA

I will use the associative and commutative properties to multiply mentally.

NYS Core Curriculum

5.R.9 Use mathematics to show and understand mathematical phenomena (e.g., find the missing value that makes the equation true: $(3 + 4) + 5 = 3 + (4+ \_)$ *Also addresses 5.CN.7, 5.N.18.*

NY Math Online

macmillanmh.com

• Extra Examples
• Personal Tutor
• Self-Check Quiz

As shown above, the order in which you multiply numbers does not matter. This and other properties of multiplication are given below.

Multiplication Properties   Key Concept

Associative Property   The way in which factors are grouped does not change the product.

Example $(9 \times 2) \times 5 = 9 \times (2 \times 5)$

Commutative Property   The order in which factors are multiplied does not change the product.

Example $4 \times 8 = 8 \times 4$

Identity Property   The product of any factor and 1 equals the factor.

Example $16 \times 1 = 16$

EXAMPLE   Identify Multiplication Properties

1 **Identify the multiplication property used to rewrite the problem below.**

$7 \times 11 = 11 \times 7$

The order of the factors changed.
This is the Commutative Property.

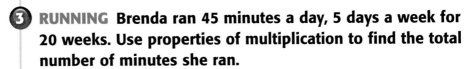 **Real-World EXAMPLES**   Use Properties to Multiply Mentally

② **SPORTS** A coach had 2 groups of 16 players in each group. Each player had to score 5 goals. Use properties of multiplication to find the total number of goals scored.

Since you can easily multiply 2 and 5, change the order and group the numbers together.

$2 \times 16 \times 5 = 2 \times 5 \times 16$	Commutative Property
$= (2 \times 5) \times 16$	Associative Property
$= 10 \times 16$	Find 2×5 mentally.
$= 160$	Find 10×16 mentally.

③ **RUNNING** Brenda ran 45 minutes a day, 5 days a week for 20 weeks. Use properties of multiplication to find the total number of minutes she ran.

$45 \times 5 \times 20 = 45 \times (5 \times 20)$	Associative Property
$= 45 \times 100$	Find 5×20 mentally.
$= 4,500$	Find 45×100 mentally.

Remember

It is easier to multiply mentally if you can find products that are multiples of 10.

 **CHECK What You Know**

Identify the multiplication property used to rewrite each problem.
See Example 1 (p. 126)

1. $6 \times 100 \times 7 = 6 \times 7 \times 100$ **2.** $(8 \times 2) \times 3 = 8 \times (2 \times 3)$

Use properties of multiplication to find each product mentally. Show your steps and identify the properties that you used.
See Examples 2, 3 (p. 127)

3. $5 \times 2 \times 34$ **4.** $2 \times 51 \times 50$ **5.** $(8 \times 4) \times 5$

6. $4 \times (25 \times 6)$ **7.** $9 \times 500 \times 2$ **8.** $200 \times 14 \times 5$

9. For a party, Shandra and James each bought 5 packages of hot dog buns, with 12 buns in each package. How many hot dog buns did they buy altogether?

10.  **Talk About It** Explain how you could use mental math and multiplication properties to find $50 \times 35 \times 2$.

Identify the multiplication property used to rewrite each problem. See Example 1 (p. 126)

11. $15 \times 2 = 2 \times 15$

12. $3 \times (9 \times 10) = (3 \times 9) \times 10$

13. $71 \times 1 = 71$

14. $4 \times 13 \times 5 = 4 \times 5 \times 13$

Use properties of multiplication to find each product mentally. Show your steps and identify the properties that you used. See Examples 2, 3 (p. 127)

15. $16 \times 2 \times 5$

16. $25 \times 4 \times 27$

17. $20 \times (5 \times 15)$

18. $40 \times (11 \times 5)$

19. $5 \times 17 \times 2$

20. $200 \times 5 \times 9$

21. $50 \times (20 \times 13)$

22. $(16 \times 25) \times 4$

23. $50 \times 38 \times 2$

24. $200 \times 5 \times 44$

25. $20 \times 56 \times 50$

26. $4 \times 23 \times 250$

Algebra Find the number that makes each sentence true.

27. $4 \times 3 \times 8 = 4 \times \blacksquare \times 3$

28. $40 \times (2 \times 11) = (40 \times \blacksquare) \times 11$

29. $(28 \times 7) \times 5 = 7 \times (28 \times \blacksquare)$

30. $12 \times 9 \times 4 = 4 \times \blacksquare \times 12$

31. Elijan and 4 of his friends are each paid $20 per afternoon for stuffing envelopes. If they work 8 afternoons, what is the total amount of their earnings?

32. Sam practiced playing his trumpet for 30 minutes a day, 6 days a week for 5 weeks. How many minutes did he practice?

33. Each package of juice contains 6 cans. Each carton of juice contains 8 packages of juice. If you have fifty cartons, how many cans of juice do you have?

34. Replace the ● in $87 \times ● \times 5$ with a number greater than 10 so that the problem is easy to solve mentally. Explain.

H.O.T. Problems

35. **OPEN ENDED** Write a multiplication sentence to show how the Associative Property can help you solve a problem mentally. Explain.

36. **CHALLENGE** Show the steps and the properties of multiplication that you could use to find $4 \times 96 \times 25 \times 50 \times 2$ mentally.

37. **WRITING IN ►MATH** Without calculating, is the statement $(7 \times 5) \times 4 = 5 \times (7 \times 4)$ true or false? Explain your reasoning.

38. A school has 13 classrooms with 28 desks in each room. All the desks in the school are being used by students. How many students are using the desks? (Lesson 3-6)

A 41

B 182

C 244

D 364

39. The Stallions basketball team has sold out their last 8 home games. Their gym has 50 rows. Each row has 20 seats. How many people altogether have attended the 8 games? (Lesson 3-7)

F 80,000   H 800

G 8,000   J 80

Spiral Review

Multiply. (Lesson 3-6)

40. 12 × 43   **41.** 80 × 76   **42.** 304 × 15   **43.** 61 × 195

44. A teacher wants to tack three rectangular pictures in a row on a bulletin board. The edges of the pictures can overlap. The teacher wants to put a tack in each corner of each picture. What is the least number of tacks that are needed? (Lesson 3-5)

45. Space camp costs $425 for one student. How much would space camp cost for 5 students? (Lesson 3-4)

Mr. Armas is ordering some items for his scrapbook store. Use the table to find the cost of each. (Lesson 3-2)

46. 300 packages of fancy stickers

47. 40 packages of scrapbook paper

Item	Cost
Fancy stickers	$2.00/package
Scrapbook paper	$3.00/package

Add or subtract. (Lesson 2-4)

48.   27
      + 41

49.   309
      + 521

50. 1,852
       − 611

51. 26,413
       − 3,750

Replace each ● with <, >, or = to make a true sentence. (Lesson 1-7)

52. 6.7 ● 7.1   **53.** 0.41 ● 0.4   **54.** 8.263 ● 8.253   **55.** 9.50 ● 9.5

Problem Solving in Health

The Bone Bank

Did you know you have between 206 and 300 bones in your body? A healthy diet makes them strong, and calcium is an important part of a healthy diet. Adults need only 1,000 milligrams of calcium each day, but fifth graders should eat or drink about 1,200 milligrams. The calcium you eat or drink is deposited in your bones. Therefore, your bones are a "bank" for calcium!

Did You Know?

Your bones grow until you are 30 years old.

Calcium Counts!

Food	Amount	Calcium
Carrots	1 cup	52 mg
Cheddar cheese	1 ounce	120 mg
Ice cream	1 cup	170 mg
Skim milk	1 cup	300 mg
Wheat bread	1 slice	20 mg
Yogurt	1 cup	490 mg

5.CN.8 Investigate the presence of mathematics in careers and areas of interest
5.R.8 Use mathematics to show and understand social phenomena (e.g., construct tables to organize data showing book sales)

 # Real-World Math

Use the information on page 130 to solve each problem.

1 If you eat 4 cups of carrots, how much calcium will you deposit in your bone bank? Solve mentally using the Distributive Property.

2 Suppose you eat one cup of yogurt each day for one week. How much calcium will you eat? Solve using the Distributive Property. Show your steps.

3 A man set a world record for drinking about 5 cups of milk in 3.2 seconds! How much calcium did he consume?

4 Suppose you make a grilled cheese sandwich with 4 ounces of cheese and 2 slices of wheat bread. Find the total amount of calcium in your sandwich. Show the steps you used.

5 You have a cup of ice cream every day for 2 weeks. How much calcium will you consume?

3-8 Extending Multiplication

GET READY to Learn

A gel pen at a craft store costs $1.05. Lucinda wants to buy three gel pens, each in a different color. She has $3.50 to spend.

Since Lucinda wants to buy three gel pens, the total cost will be 3 × $1.05. You can estimate the cost using rounding.

MAIN IDEA

I will multiply to solve problems involving money and greater numbers.

NYS Core Curriculum

5.N.26 Estimate sums, differences, **products,** and quotients **of decimals** *Also addresses 5.N.23.*

NY Math Online

macmillanmh.com

• Extra Examples
• Personal Tutor
• Self-Check Quiz

Real-World EXAMPLE   Estimate with Money

1 SHOPPING Refer to the information above. Does Lucinda have enough money to buy three gel pens?

3 × $1.05
↓   ↓
3 × $1   Round $1.05 to $1 because $1.05 is closer to $1 than $2.

3 × $1 = $3   Multiply mentally.

So, 3 × $1.05 is about $3. Since Lucinda has $3.50, she should have enough money to buy three gel pens.

You can also use rounding to estimate products of decimals that do not involve money.

Real-World EXAMPLE   Estimate with Decimals

2 GASOLINE Mrs. James buys about 15.8 gallons of gas each week for her car. About how many gallons of gas will she buy in 5 weeks?

Estimate the product of 15.8 and 5.

15.8 × 5
↓   ↓
16 × 5   Round 15.8 to 16 because 15.8 is closer to 16 than 15.

16 × 5 = 80   Multiply.

So, 16 × 5 is about 80. Mrs. James buys about 80 gallons of gas in 5 weeks.

Technology can be a useful tool for multiplying greater numbers or for performing many calculations. Always estimate first.

Real-World EXAMPLE **Greater Numbers**

3 **MEASUREMENT** **Tasha-Nicole Terani holds the world record for the most number of soccer touches in one minute at 239. If she continues at this rate, how many soccer touches would she have in one day?**

There are 60 minutes in 1 hour and 24 hours in 1 day. Find 60×239 and then multiply the product by 24.

Estimate $239 \times 60 \times 24 \approx 200 \times 60 \times 20$ or 240,000

Use the Calculator feature from your Math Tool Chest™ to find the exact answer.

Enter: **2 3 9**
Press: **x**
Enter: **6 0**
Press: **x**
Enter: **2 4**
Press: **=**
Solution: 344160

Check for Reasonableness
The estimate, 240,000 is less than 344,160. But two of the original numbers were rounded down. So, it is reasonable to expect that the estimate would be less than the exact answer. ✔

Tasha-Nicole would have 344,160 soccer touches in one day.

> **Remember**
> You can find $200 \times 60 \times 20$ mentally by counting zeros in the factors. Write 4 zeros to the right of $2 \times 6 \times 2$ or 24.

CHECK What You Know

Estimate each product. See Examples 1–2 (p. 132)

1. $2 \times \$4.10$

2. $5 \times \$12.65$

3. 18.4×10

4. 24.7×3

5. A group of five friends is going to see a movie. If one ticket costs $8.50, estimate the total price of all the tickets.

6. About 325 people have picnics at Kennywood Park each day. The park is open 165 days each year. About how many people have picnics at the park each year?

7. A cantaloupe weighs 1.8 pounds. About how much do 3 cantaloupes weigh?

8. **Talk About It** Explain how to round 18.9 to the nearest whole number.

Estimate each product. See Examples 1–2 (p. 132)

9. 4 × $4.62

10. 3 × $23.07

11. $15.50 × 6

12. $16.85 × 9

13. 7.2 × 5

14. 14.5 × 3

15. 8 × 19.7

16. 10 × 26.2

17. Measurement Turkey costs $0.89 per pound and weighs 14 pounds. Estimate the total cost.

18. A dragonfly can fly at a speed of 17.8 miles per hour. At that speed, about how far could a dragonfly fly in 5 hours?

19. An average person speaks about 5,000 words each day. There are 365 days in one year. Does the average person speak more than 2,000,000 or less than 2,000,000 words each year? Then use a calculator to find the exact answer.

20. Measurement Turtles and tortoises have long life spans. A tortoise can live as long as 150 years. There are 365 days in one year. About how many days could a tortoise live? Then use a calculator to find the exact answer.

Real-World PROBLEM SOLVING

Art *Artsonia* is the world's largest kids' online art museum, where students have their own art gallery online. Friends and family can order items like the ones shown below that display students' artwork.

$15.95

$24.95

$11.95

$5.95

For Exercises 21–24, estimate the cost of each order.

21. 4 keychains

22. 2 plush bears

23. 3 coffee mugs and 2 keychains

24. 5 mouse pads and a plush bear

25. If you have $50, how many coffee mugs can you buy? Use the *guess and check* strategy.

H.O.T. Problems

26. OPEN ENDED Write a real-world multiplication problem involving money. Describe the steps that you used to solve the problem.

CHALLENGE Find the missing digits in each factor.

27. 3■2 × ■16 = 202,272

28. 2,3■5 × 4■2 = 1,115,830

29. ● WRITING IN ►MATH Explain why it is important to make an estimate before you use a calculator to multiply.

NYSMT Practice ▷ 5.N.26

30. The speeds of two insects are shown in the table. About how much farther would the hawk moth fly than the hornet in 4 hours? **(Lesson 3-8)**

Insect	Speed (miles per hour)
Hornet	13.3
Hawk Moth	33.8

A 20 miles

B 40 miles

C 60 miles

D 80 miles

31. The table shows the cost of different types of sandwiches at Don's Deli.

Sandwich Type	Cost
Chicken salad	$3.19
Tuna salad	$2.79
Egg salad	$2.59

Joy bought 2 tuna salad sandwiches and paid with a $10 bill. About how much change should she receive? **(Lesson 3-8)**

F $7

G $6

H $5

J $4

Spiral Review

Use properties of multiplication to find each product mentally. Show your steps and identify the properties that you used. (Lesson 3-7)

32. 27 × 5 × 2

33. 4 × 30 × 25

34. 20 × 50 × 6

35. Mr. Morales bought 18 boxes of sidewalk chalk. Each box contained 12 pieces of chalk. How many pieces of chalk did Mr. Morales buy? **(Lesson 3-6)**

Estimate each sum or difference. Show your work. (Lesson 2-2)

36. 306 + 521

37. 6.85 − 1.73

38. 24.11 + 9.5

Problem-Solving Investigation

MAIN IDEA I will identify extra information or missing information to solve a problem.

 5.PS.1 Know the difference between relevant and irrelevant information when solving problems
5.PS.17 Determine what information is needed to solve problem *Also addresses 5.CN.6.*

P.S.I. TEAM +

LILIA: On Tuesday, I was put in charge of collecting book orders. The cost of each book is $3. There were 7 orders on Wednesday, 5 orders on Thursday, and more orders on Friday and Monday.

YOUR MISSION: Find how many book orders Lilia collected.

Understand	**What facts do you know?**
	You know the cost of a book. You also know the number of book orders that were collected on Wednesday and Thursday.
	What do you need to find?
	You need to find the total number of book orders.
Plan	**Is there any information that is not needed?**
	The cost of a book.
	Is there any information that is missing?
	You do not know how many book orders were collected on Friday and Monday.
Solve	Since you do not have enough information, the problem cannot be solved.
Check	Read the question again to see if you missed any information. If so, go back and rework the problem. If not, the problem cannot be solved.

Solve each problem. If there is extra information, identify it. If there is not enough information, tell what information is needed.

PROBLEM-SOLVING SKILLS
• Use the four-step plan.
• Identify extra or missing information.

1. Jayden is downloading songs onto his digital music player. The first song is 5 minutes long, the second song is 3 minutes long, and the third song is between the lengths of the first and second and songs. What is the total length of all three songs?

2. Room 220 and Room 222 are having a canned food drive. Refer to the diagram. How many more cans has Room 222 collected than Room 220?

ROOM 222
346 CANS

ROOM 220
278 cans

3. Karly is collecting money for a bowl-a-thon. Her goal is to collect $125. So far, she has collected $20 each from three people and $10 each from four people. How much more money does Karly need to collect to have $125?

4. **Measurement** Eli made pancake batter. He has $1\frac{2}{3}$ cup of batter left. How much of the batter did he use?

5. Mrs. Rollins owns a farm. She raises prize chickens. Each chicken has its own cage and eats the same amount of food. Mrs. Rollins bought 100 pounds of chicken food last week. How much food did each chicken eat?

6. Paco studied his spelling words for 4 days. How many words did he study each day if he studied the same amount of words each day?

7. What is the cost of the peaches for a peach pie?

$0.89 per lb

8. **Measurement** Rocco is slicing a loaf of Italian bread to serve with dinner. The cost of the bread was $2.99. He plans to cut the loaf into slices that are 1 inch thick. If the loaf is 18 inches long, how many pieces of bread can be cut from the loaf of bread?

9. **Measurement** The table shows the number of miles the Wong family drove each day on their vacation.

Day	Miles
Day 1	345
Day 2	50
Day 3	89
Day 4	279

How many more miles did they drive on Day 1 than on Day 4?

10. **WRITING IN ►MATH** Write a problem that has missing information. Explain how to rewrite the problem so that it can be solved.

FOLDABLES®
Study Organizer GET READY to Study

Be sure the following Big Ideas are written in your Foldable.

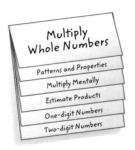

Multiply Whole Numbers
Patterns and Properties
Multiply Mentally
Estimate Products
One-digit Numbers
Two-digit Numbers

Key Concepts

Multiplying Mentally

• You can multiply multiples of 10 mentally by using basic facts and then counting zeros in the factors. **(p. 106)**

2 zeros   1 zero

$300 \times 60 = 18,000$ ← 3 zeros

Distributive Property

• To multiply a sum by a number, multiply each addend by the number. Then add. **(p. 108)**

$5 \times (10 + 2) = (5 \times 10) + (5 \times 2)$

Multiplying Whole Numbers

• The steps for multiplying by one- and two-digit numbers are similar. **(pp. 116, 122)**

```
   14          14
 × 3         × 23
 ───         ───
  42          42      14 × 3 = 42
             280      14 × 20 = 280
             ───
             322
```

Key Vocabulary

Distributive Property (p. 108)
factor (p. 103)
product (p. 103)

Vocabulary Check

State whether each sentence is *true* or *false*. If *false*, replace the underlined word or number to make a true sentence.

1. In the sentence $8 \times 2 = 16$, the numbers 8 and 2 are <u>factors</u> of 16.

2. The result when two numbers are multiplied is called a <u>difference</u>.

3. According to the <u>Distributive Property</u>, $2 \times (3 + 1) = (2 \times 3) + (2 \times 1)$.

4. To estimate 38×186, you could find <u>40 × 200</u>.

5. When you multiply 80 and 70, the result has <u>4</u> zeros.

6. The sentence $2 \times 85 = 85 \times 2$ is an example of the <u>Associative Property</u>.

7. The <u>Identity Property</u> states that a number multiplied by 1 equals the number.

Lesson-by-Lesson Review

3-1 Multiplication Patterns (pp. 103–105)

5.N.3

Example 1

Find 20 × 70 mentally.

The basic fact is 2 × 7 = 14. Now count the zeros in the factors.

$$\boxed{1 \text{ zero}} \quad \boxed{1 \text{ zero}}$$
$$20 \times 70$$

The product will have 1 + 1 or 2 zeros. Write 2 zeros to the right of 14.

20 × 70 = 1,4**00**

Find each product mentally.

8. 50 × 3   **9.** 26 × 10

10. 80 × 90   **11.** 300 × 4

12. 420 × 100   **13.** 500 × 600

14. A bank cash machine has 600 $20 bills. What is the total value of the $20 bills in the machine?

3-2 The Distributive Property (pp. 108–111)

5.N.18

Example 2

Rewrite 2 × (40 + 1) using the Distributive Property. Then evaluate.

2 × (40 + 1)

= (2 × 40) + (2 × 1)   Distributive Property

= 80 + 2   Find 2 × 40 and 2 × 1.

= 82   Add.

Example 3

Find 3 × 24 mentally.

3 × 24

= 3 × (20 + 4)   Write 24 as 20 + 4.

= (3 × 20) + (3 × 4) Distributive Property

= 60 + 12   THINK: 3 × 20 = 60 and 3 × 4 = 12

= 72   Add 60 and 12.

Rewrite each expression using the Distributive Property. Then evaluate.

15. 4 × (20 + 6)   **16.** 3 × (60 + 1)

17. 7 × (10 + 2)   **18.** 2 × (80 + 1)

Find each product mentally using the Distributive Property. Show the steps that you used.

19. 3 × 17   **20.** 2 × 28

21. 8 × 31   **22.** 3 × 65

23. Mia fills 45 pages of her photo album with photos that she took. If she puts 4 photos on each page, how many photos are in the album?

5.N.27

3-3 Estimate Products (pp. 112–115)

Example 4
Estimate 21 × 38.

Round each factor to the nearest ten.

$$
\begin{array}{rl}
21 & \rightarrow \quad 20 \quad \text{21 is rounded to 20.} \\
\times\, 38 & \rightarrow \quad \times\, 40 \quad \text{38 is rounded to 40.} \\
\hline
 & \quad\quad 800
\end{array}
$$

So, 21 × 38 is about 800.

Example 5
Estimate 46 × 107.

Round each factor to its greatest place value.

$$
\begin{array}{rl}
46 & \rightarrow \quad\quad 50 \quad \text{46 is rounded to 50.} \\
\times\, 107 & \rightarrow \quad \times\, 100 \quad \text{107 is rounded to 100.} \\
\hline
 & \quad\quad 5{,}000
\end{array}
$$

So, 46 × 107 is about 5,000.

Estimate by rounding or compatible numbers. Show your work.

24. $\begin{array}{r}42\\ \times\,16\\\hline\end{array}$	**25.** $\begin{array}{r}13\\ \times\,65\\\hline\end{array}$
26. $\begin{array}{r}791\\ \times\,9\\\hline\end{array}$	**27.** $\begin{array}{r}521\\ \times\,27\\\hline\end{array}$
28. 81 × 815	**29.** 312 × 259

30. Measurement A steamboat tour guide makes the 148-mile trip between Birmingham, Alabama, and Chattanooga, Tennessee, four times. Estimate the total number of miles she travels. Show your work.

5.N.16

3-4 Multiply by One-Digit Numbers (pp. 116–118)

Example 6
Find 7 × 54.

Estimate 7 × 50 = 350

Step 1 Multiply the ones. Regroup.

$$
\begin{array}{r}
\overset{2}{5}4\\
\times\,7\\
\hline
8
\end{array}
$$

Step 2 Multiply the tens. Add the new tens.

$$
\begin{array}{r}
\overset{2}{5}4\\
\times\,7\\
\hline
378
\end{array}
$$

So, 7 × 54 = 378. Since 378 is close to the estimate, the answer is reasonable.

Multiply.

31. $\begin{array}{r}43\\ \times\,2\\\hline\end{array}$ **32.** $\begin{array}{r}67\\ \times\,4\\\hline\end{array}$ **33.** $\begin{array}{r}112\\ \times\,5\\\hline\end{array}$

34. 6 × 32 **35.** 5 × 142 **36.** 381 × 3

37. A group uses 8 rafts on a white water rafting trip. Each raft carries 14 people. How many people go rafting?

3-5 Problem-Solving Strategy: Draw a Picture (pp. 120–121)

5.PS.13

Example 7

Tony's garden is a square 12 feet long. He wants to plant shrubs 4 feet apart around the garden. There will be a shrub in each corner. How many shrubs will he need?

Make a drawing of the garden and the shrubs.

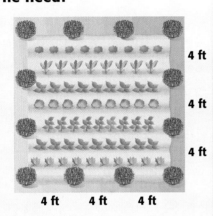

4 ft

4 ft

4 ft

4 ft   4 ft   4 ft

Tony will need 12 shrubs.

Solve by drawing a picture.

38. Cameron's bedroom wall is 13 feet wide. He wants to place two equal-size picture frames side by side along the wall so that the distance between each frame and each edge of the wall is 4 feet. If each picture frame is 2 feet wide, how many feet of space will be between the two frames?

39. A camp is putting a rope fence in a lake to mark the end of the swimming area. The rope is 60 yards long. A buoy is placed at the beginning of the rope. Another buoy is placed every 10 yards. A buoy is placed at the end of the rope. How many buoys are there?

3-6 Multiply by Two-Digit Numbers (pp. 122–124)

5.N.16

Example 8

Find 26 × 34.

Estimate $30 \times 30 = 900$

Step 1	Step 2	Step 3
Multiply the ones.	Multiply the tens.	Add.

$$\begin{array}{r} \overset{2}{26} \\ \times\, 34 \\ \hline 104 \end{array}$$

$$\begin{array}{r} \overset{1}{26} \\ \times\, 34 \\ \hline 104 \\ 780 \end{array}$$

$$\begin{array}{r} 26 \\ \times\, 34 \\ \hline 104 \\ 780 \\ \hline 884 \end{array}$$

So, $26 \times 34 = 884$.

Multiply.

40. $\begin{array}{r} 12 \\ \times\, 14 \end{array}$ **41.** $\begin{array}{r} 71 \\ \times\, 23 \end{array}$ **42.** $\begin{array}{r} 108 \\ \times\, 55 \end{array}$

43. 52×130 **44.** 42×312

45. 19×63 **46.** 761×85

47. Measurement A Chinese giant salamander weighs about 45 pounds. If 1 pound equals 16 ounces, how many ounces does a Chinese giant salamander weigh?

5.R.9

3-7 Multiplication Properties (pp. 126–129)

Example 9
Use properties of multiplication to find (14 × 2) × 5 mentally.

(14 × 2) × 5
= 14 × (2 × 5)   Associative Property
= 14 × 10   Find 2 × 5 mentally.
= 140   Find 14 × 10 mentally.

Use properties of multiplication to find each product mentally. Show your steps and identify the properties that you used.

48. 4 × 28 × 25   **49.** (19 × 20) × 5

50. Algebra What is the value of ▮ in the expression below?

(35 × 4) × 5 = 35 × (▮ × 5)

5.N.26

3-8 Extending Multiplication (pp. 132–135)

Example 10
Estimate 2 × \$6.15.
2 × \$6.15
↓
2 × \$6   Round \$6.15 to \$6.
2 × \$6 = \$12

So, 2 × \$6.15 is about \$12.

Estimate.

51. \$1.20 × 4   **52.** 42.4 × 8

53. A car travels 19.4 miles on one gallon of gas. About how far can it go with 8 gallons of gas?

5.PS.1

3-9 Problem-Solving Investigation: Extra or Missing Information
(pp. 136–137)

Example 11
Gia studied 75 spelling words over a certain number of days. How many words did she study each day if she studied the same amount of words each day?

You cannot solve this problem because you do not know how many days she studied her spelling words.

Solve the problem. If there is extra information, identify it. If there is not enough information, tell what information is needed.

54. How much higher is Mount Hayes than Mount Olympus?

Mountain	Elevation (ft)
Mount Olympus	2,429
Mount Mitchel	6,684
Mount Hayes	4,216

Chapter Test

Find each product mentally.

1. 400 × 5 **2.** 60 × 7,000

Find each product mentally using the Distributive Property. Show your work.

3. 4 × 35 **4.** 3 × 27

5. 5 × 63 **6.** 2 × 49

7. The sports center is buying new equipment. Use the table to find the cost of 7 kickballs and 5 basketballs.

Ball	Cost
Basketball	$11
Kickball	$14
Soccer ball	$19

Estimate. Show your work.

8. 92
× 31

9. 410
× 77

10. MULTIPLE CHOICE Each hour, about 88 people visit a particular tourist attraction in Florida. At this rate, about how many people will visit the attraction in four hours?

A 360 **C** 270

B 320 **D** 240

Multiply.

11. 46
× 15

12. 108
× 21

13. 53
× 30

14. 179
× 12

15. Measurement The area of a rectangle is the product of its length and width. What is the area of the rectangle below in square centimeters?

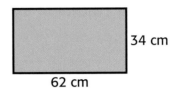

34 cm

62 cm

16. Identify the multiplication property that is shown in the sentence below.

(14 × 2) × 50 = 14 × (2 × 50)

17. A technician installed speakers around a square auditorium. She places 10 speakers on each side and one at each corner. How many speakers did she install? Use the *draw a picture* strategy.

18. Estimate 26.3 × 5.

19. MULTIPLE CHOICE Bala bought five books priced at $12.79 each. About how much was the total cost, not including tax?

F $45 **H** $65

G $55 **J** $75

20. WRITING IN MATH The tennis team is selling coupon books. The total sales are $855. How much does each coupon book cost? Explain if there is extra information to solve the problem. If there is not enough information, tell what information is needed. Rewrite the problem and solve.

PART 1   Multiple Choice

Read each question. Then fill in the correct answer on the answer sheet provided by your teacher or on a sheet of paper.

1. A souvenir shop has 51 boxes of seashells in stock. Each box contains 9 shells. Which number is the best estimate for the total number of shells?

   A 380   C 420

   B 400   D 450

2. Kenny has 250 stickers in his collection. He has 40 stickers more than Placido and 25 stickers less than Paloma. How many stickers does Paloma have?

   F 210   H 275

   G 225   J 290

3. How much larger is the area of Colorado than Utah?

State	Area (square miles)
Colorado	104,185 sq mi
Utah	84,876 sq mi

   A 16,272 sq mi   C 22,567 sq mi

   B 19,309 sq mi   D 25,006 sq mi

4. The distance from Earth to the Moon is about 400,000 kilometers. How is this number written in words?

   F forty thousand

   G four hundred thousand

   H four million

   J forty million

5. Mrs. O'Brien has 28 calculators in her classroom. If each calculator takes 4 batteries, how many batteries are used altogether?

   A 112

   B 116

   C 118

   D 124

6. The banquet hall has 42 tables with 8 seats each. If 320 seats are occupied, which of the following ways shows how to find the number of empty seats?

   F Add 320 to the product of 42 and 8.

   G Add 42 to the product of 320 and 8.

   H Subtract 320 from the product of 42 and 8.

   J Subtract 42 from the product of 320 and 8.

7. A car rental company has 29 cars on its lot. Each car has 4 wheels. How many wheels are there altogether at the car rental company lot?

A 84   **C** 116

B 108   **D** 122

8. The price of a stock over the past 4 weeks is shown in the table. If the pattern continues, what will the price be after 5 weeks?

Week	1	2	3	4	5
Price ($)	1.00	1.80	2.60	3.40	?

F $3.80   **H** $4.10

G $4.00   **J** $4.20

9. During the first week of school, Mrs. Mease asked each of her students to bring in three boxes of tissues. If there are 27 students in Mrs. Mease's classroom, how many boxes of tissues will there be?

A 71   **C** 84

B 81   **D** 92

PART 2 Short Response

Record your answers on the sheet provided by your teacher or on a sheet of paper.

10. There are 9 tables in the school cafeteria. Each table can seat 12 people. If every table is full, how many people are seated in the cafeteria at the same time? Draw a diagram to solve.

11. Show how to use the Distributive Property of Multiplication to find $4 \times (9 + 6)$.

PART 3 Extended Response

Record your answers on the answer sheet provided by your teacher or on a sheet of paper. Show your work.

12. A car wash company cleaned a total of 43 cars in one day. The price of each car wash is $14. Estimate how much money the company earned that day.

Is your estimate higher or lower than the actual amount? Explain.

NEED EXTRA HELP?												
If You Missed Question...	1	2	3	4	5	6	7	8	9	10	11	12
Go to Lesson...	2-2	1-3	2-4	1-1	3-4	3-9	3-4	2-6	3-4	3-3	3-2	3-5
NYS Core Curriculum	5.N.26	5.PS.3	4.N.14	5.N.1	5.N.16	5.PS.1	5.N.16	5.N.23	5.N.16	5.N.27	5.N.18	5.PS.13

CHAPTER 4 Divide Whole Numbers

BIG Idea — What are quotients, dividends, and divisors?

When one number is divided by another, the result is called a **quotient**. The **dividend** is the number that is divided. The **divisor** is the number used to divide another number.

Example Lions live in social communities called *prides*. The average number of lions in a pride is about 15. Suppose a nature preserve has 300 lions. There are about 300 ÷ 15, or 20 prides.

$$300 \quad \div \quad 15 \quad = \quad 20$$

dividend   divisor   quotient

What will I learn in this chapter?

- Divide multiples of 10, 100, and 1,000 mentally.
- Estimate quotients of whole numbers.
- Divide whole numbers.
- Interpret remainders in division problems.
- Solve problems by using the *act it out* strategy.

Key Vocabulary

quotient

dividend

divisor

NY Math Online ▷ **Student Study Tools** at <u>macmillanmh.com</u>

FOLDABLES®
Study Organizer

Make this Foldable to help you organize information about division. Begin with a sheet of 11″ × 17″ paper and six index cards.

1 **Fold** lengthwise about 3″ from the bottom.

2 **Fold** the paper in thirds.

3 **Open** and staple the edges on either side to form three pockets.

4 **Label** the pockets. Place two index cards in each pocket.

One-Digit Numbers Two-Digit Numbers Interpret Remainders

Chapter 4 Divide Whole Numbers **147**

ARE YOU READY for Chapter 4?

You have two ways to check prerequisite skills for this chapter.

Option 2

NY Math Online ⟩ Take the Chapter Readiness Quiz at macmillanmh.com.

Option 1

Complete the Quick Check below.

QUICK Check

Divide. (Prior Grade)

1. $8 \div 2$ **2.** $15 \div 5$ **3.** $27 \div 3$

4. $28 \div 4$ **5.** $48 \div 6$ **6.** $54 \div 9$

7. Three people spend $12 for pizza, $6 for salads, and $6 for drinks at lunch. If they divide the total cost evenly, how much does each person pay?

Write the fact family for each set of numbers.
(Prior Grade)

8. 4, 6, 24   **9.** 2, 5, 10

10. 8, 9, 72   **11.** 7, 3, 21

12. 6, 5, 30   **13.** 8, 4, 32

Tell if each number can be divided evenly by 2, 3, 5, 6, or 10. (Prior Grade)

14. 80   **15.** 90

16. 126   **17.** 203

18. 765   **19.** 1,314

20. The 82 members of the fifth grade chorus stand on a stage in rows. Can they stand in 3 equal rows? Explain.

Division Patterns

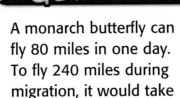 **to Learn**

A monarch butterfly can fly 80 miles in one day. To fly 240 miles during migration, it would take 240 ÷ 80, or 3 days.

MAIN IDEA

I will use basic facts and patterns to divide multiples of 10, 100, and 1,000 mentally.

NYS Core Curriculum

Preparation for 5.N.17 Use a variety of strategies to divide three-digit numbers by one and two-digit numbers
Also Addresses 5.N.3, 5.A.7, 5.A.8.

New Vocabulary

quotient
dividend
divisor

NY Math Online

macmillanmh.com
• Extra Examples
• Personal Tutor
• Self-Check Quiz

When one number is divided by another, the result is called a **quotient**. The **dividend** is the number that is divided and the **divisor** is the number used to divide another number.

$$\text{divisor} \rightarrow 80\overline{)240} \begin{array}{l} \leftarrow \text{quotient (3)} \\ \leftarrow \text{dividend} \end{array}$$

You can use basic facts and patterns to divide by multiples of 10.

$24 \div 8 = 3$	$24 \div 8 = 3$
$240 \div 8 = 30$	$240 \div 80 = 3$
$2{,}400 \div 8 = 300$	$2{,}400 \div 800 = 3$
$24{,}000 \div 8 = 3{,}000$	$24{,}000 \div 8{,}000 = 3$

← basic fact →

EXAMPLE Divide Multiples of 10

1 **Find 600 ÷ 3 mentally.**

Since 600 is a multiple of 10, you can use the basic fact and continue the pattern.

$6 \div 3 = 2$ 6 ones divided by 3 equals 2 ones.

$60 \div 3 = 20$ 6 tens divided by 3 equals 2 tens.

$600 \div 3 = 200$ 6 hundreds divided by 3 equals 2 hundreds.

So, $600 \div 3 = 200$.

Real-World EXAMPLE   Divide Multiples of 10

2 **MEASUREMENT** A cow eats 900 pounds of hay over a period of 30 days. How many pounds of hay would the cow eat each day at this rate?

You need to find 900 ÷ 30.

Remember

In multiplication, count the number of zeros in each factor. Write the zeros to the right of the product of the basic fact.

One Way: Use fact families.

3 × 3 = 9	⟷	9 ÷ 3 = 3
30 × 3 = 90	⟷	90 ÷ 30 = 3
30 × 30 = 900	⟶	900 ÷ 30 = 30

Another Way: Cross out zeros to make division easier.

90Ø ÷ 3Ø	Cross out the same number of zeros in both the dividend and divisor.
90 ÷ 3 = 30	Divide. THINK: 9 tens ÷ 3 = 3 tens.

So, 900 ÷ 30 = 30.

The cow eats 30 pounds of hay each day.

CHECK What You Know

Divide mentally. See Examples 1–2 (pp. 149–150)

1. 500 ÷ 5   **2.** 320 ÷ 8   **3.** 200 ÷ 10

4. 420 ÷ 70   **5.** 800 ÷ 2   **6.** 150 ÷ 30

7. 270 ÷ 90   **8.** 5,600 ÷ 70   **9.** 2,100 ÷ 30

10. A sailfish grabbed a fishing line and dragged it 300 feet in just 3 seconds. On average, how many feet did the fish drag the line each second?

11. **Talk About It** Explain how you know that the quotients 48 ÷ 6 and 480 ÷ 60 are equal without doing any computation.

Divide mentally. See Examples 1–2 (pp. 149–150)

12. 800 ÷ 2

13. 900 ÷ 3

14. 150 ÷ 5

15. 140 ÷ 7

16. 450 ÷ 9

17. 280 ÷ 4

18. 180 ÷ 60

19. 240 ÷ 30

20. 4,200 ÷ 70

21. 1,800 ÷ 30

22. 2,000 ÷ 400

23. 2,400 ÷ 300

24. A group of 10 people bought tickets to a reptile exhibit and paid a total of $130. What was the price of one ticket?

25. Measurement The fastest team in a wheelbarrow race traveled 100 meters in about 20 seconds. On average, how many meters did the team travel each second?

26. Measurement Daniela has a 160-ounce bag of potting soil. She puts an equal amount of soil in each pot shown. How much soil will she put in each pot?

27. A video store took in $450 in DVD rentals during one day. If DVDs rent for $9 each, how many DVDs were rented?

H.O.T. Problems

28. OPEN ENDED Write a real-world division problem. Identify the dividend, divisor, and quotient.

29. NUMBER SENSE Write two different division problems that both have a quotient of 50.

30. FIND THE ERROR Alejandro and Megan are finding 5,400 ÷ 90 mentally. Who is correct? Explain.

Alejandro

5,4$\emptyset\emptyset$ ÷ 9$\emptyset$

↓

54 ÷ 9 = 6

Megan

54 ÷ 9 = 6

540 ÷ 90 = 6

5,400 ÷ 90 = 60

31. **WRITING IN ►MATH** Describe how placing zeros at the end of basic division facts helps you divide mentally. Write an example.

GET READY to Learn

Camp Hickory Hills has 442 registered campers for the summer. If one group leader is needed for every 10 campers, about how many group leaders are needed?

$$442 \div 10$$
$$\downarrow \quad \quad \downarrow$$
$$400 \div 10 = 40$$

So, about 40 group leaders are needed.

To estimate a quotient, you can use compatible numbers, or numbers that are easy to divide mentally. Look for numbers that are part of fact families.

EXAMPLE **Find a Compatible Dividend**

1 Estimate 156 ÷ 3.

$$156 \div 3$$
$$\downarrow \quad \quad \downarrow$$
$$150 \div 3$$

Change 156 to 150 because 15 and 3 are compatible numbers.

$$150 \div 3 = 50 \quad \text{Divide mentally.}$$

So, 156 ÷ 3 is about 50.

EXAMPLE **Find a Compatible Divisor**

2 Estimate 3,200 ÷ 90.

$$3,200 \div 90$$
$$\downarrow \quad \quad \downarrow$$
$$3,200 \div 80$$

Change 90 to 80 because 32 and 8 are compatible numbers.

$$3,200 \div 80 = 40 \quad \text{Divide mentally.}$$

So, 3,200 ÷ 90 is about 40.

EXAMPLE   Use Rounding and Compatible Numbers

3 **Estimate 228 ÷ 43.**

Step 1 Round the divisor to the nearest ten.

$$228 ÷ 43$$
$$↓$$
$$228 ÷ \mathbf{40}$$

Step 2 Change the dividend to a number that is compatible with 4. Notice it is easy to divide 24 by 4.

$$228 ÷ 43$$
$$↓ \quad ↓$$
$$\mathbf{240} ÷ 40$$

Step 3 Divide mentally.

$$240 ÷ 40 = 6$$

So, 228 ÷ 43 is about 6.

Real-World EXAMPLE   Estimate to Solve Problems

4 **DOGS** Six dogs equally share a 45-pound bag of dog food each week. **About how much does each dog eat each week?**

One Way: Use compatible numbers 45 and 5.	**Another Way:** Use compatible numbers 48 and 6.
45 ÷ 6 ↓ ↓ 45 ÷ 5 = 9	45 ÷ 6 ↓ ↓ 48 ÷ 6 = 8

So, each dog eats about 8 or 9 pounds of dog food each week.

Remember

There are often different ways to estimate quotients.

✓CHECK What You Know

Estimate. Show your work. See Examples 1–4 (pp. 152–153)

1. 850 ÷ 9

2. 635 ÷ 8

3. 545 ÷ 50

4. 400 ÷ 23

5. 374 ÷ 93

6. 713 ÷ 62

7. 1,200 ÷ 380

8. 624 ÷ 314

9. A box of cereal contains 340 grams. If there are 12 servings, about how many grams are there in one serving? Show how you estimated.

10. *Talk About It* Explain how you could use compatible numbers to estimate 272 ÷ 4.

Estimate. Show your work. See Examples 1–4 (pp. 152–153)

11. 397 ÷ 4   **12.** 432 ÷ 7   **13.** 753 ÷ 90   **14.** 253 ÷ 50

15. 554 ÷ 6   **16.** 360 ÷ 7   **17.** 800 ÷ 21   **18.** 150 ÷ 48

19. 300 ÷ 59   **20.** 270 ÷ 32   **21.** 230 ÷ 73   **22.** 244 ÷ 37

23. 680 ÷ 71   **24.** 860 ÷ 318   **25.** 619 ÷ 320   **26.** 786 ÷ 189

Solve. Show your work.

27. A grocery store employee puts 8 bagels in each bag. If she has 385 bagels, about how many bags does she need?

28. **Measurement** Jani drives 232 miles in 4 hours. About how many miles does she drive each hour?

29. There are 598 goldfish divided equally among 23 fish tanks. About how many goldfish are in each tank?

30. **Measurement** Felix has 5 bags of birdseed. Each bag has about 28 ounces of birdseed. If he divides the birdseed equally into 3 containers, about how much birdseed will he put in each container?

31. The table shows how much each fifth grade room earned from a bake sale. The money is going to be given to 6 different charities. If each charity is given an equal amount, about how much will each charity receive? Show how you estimated.

Bake Sale

Room	Earnings($)
110	327
112	425
114	550
116	486

H.O.T. Problems

32. **OPEN ENDED** Write a division problem and show two different ways that you can estimate the quotient using compatible numbers.

33. **NUMBER SENSE** Without calculating, predict whether 23,510 ÷ 615 is greater than or less than 100. Explain your reasoning.

34. **WRITING IN ►MATH** Write a real-life problem in which you estimate the quotient of two numbers.

35. Paul took 144 pictures on his vacation using rolls of film like the one shown at the right. Which is the best estimate for the number of rolls of film that he used? (Lesson 4-2)

A less than 5

B between 5 and 7

C between 50 and 70

D more than 70

36. A train traveled 300 miles in 5 hours. How far did the train travel each hour on average? (Lesson 4-1)

F 60 mi

G 150 mi

H 600 mi

J 1,500 mi

37. SHORT RESPONSE Mrs. Chong bought 480 bookmarks. If each box contains 60 bookmarks, how many boxes did she buy? (Lesson 4-1)

Spiral Review

Divide mentally. (Lesson 4-1)

38. 400 ÷ 2

39. 180 ÷ 3

40. 630 ÷ 70

41. 2,500 ÷ 500

42. Miss LaHood's class is having a reading challenge. Rafe read 12 books in 7 weeks, Peter read 10 books in 7 weeks, and Misti read 11 books in 7 weeks. How many more books did Rafe read than Peter? Identify any extra or missing information. (Lesson 3-9)

43. The cost of renting a paddleboat at the lake is shown at the right. Estimate how much it will cost to rent the paddle boat for 3 hours. (Lesson 3-8)

Paddleboat Rental
$7.85 per hour

Multiply. (Lesson 3-6)

44. 14 × 11

45. 38 × 26

46. 142 × 51

47. 12 × 507

Estimate each sum or difference by rounding. Show your work.
(Lesson 2-2)

48. 58
   + 61

49. 327
   − 106

50. 19.8
   + 7.6

51. 1,402
   − 872

Explore

Math Activity for 4-3
Use Division Models

You can use base-ten blocks to help you divide.

MAIN IDEA

I will divide using models.

NYS Core Curriculum

5.RP.2 Understand that mathematical statements can be supported, using models, facts, and relationships to explain their thinking

Preparation for 5.N.17 Use a variety of strategies to divide three-digit numbers by one and two-digit numbers
Also Addresses 5.CN.6, 5.PS.13

You will need base-ten blocks

ACTIVITY

1 At the fair, you need tickets to ride the rides. Three friends share 336 tickets equally. How many tickets will each friend receive?

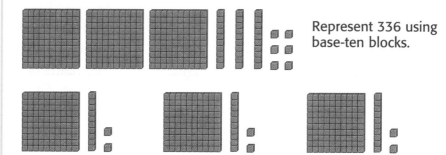

Represent 336 using base-ten blocks.

Regroup the base-ten blocks to make 3 equal groups.

When you divide 336 into three groups, there are 112 in each group.

So, $336 \div 3 = 112$.

Use multiplication to check your answer. ✔

$112 \times 3 = 336$.

ACTIVITY

2 Find $252 \div 4$.

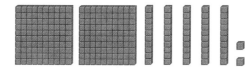

Represent 252 using base-ten blocks.

Regroup the base-ten blocks to make 4 equal groups.

When you divide 252 counters into four groups, there are 63 counters in each group.

So, 252 ÷ 4 = 63.

Use multiplication to check your answer. ✔
63 × 4 = 252.

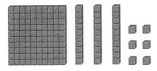 **Model Remainders**

3 **Find 136 ÷ 5.**

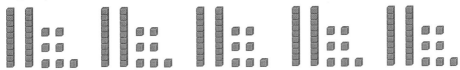

Represent 136 using base-ten blocks

Regroup the base–ten blocks to make 5 equal groups.

⬛ There is one left over.

A *remainder* is the number left after a quotient is found.

When you divide 136 counters into five groups, there are 27 counters in each group with one left over.

So, 136 ÷ 5 = 27 R1.

✔ CHECK What You Know

Use models to find each quotient.

1. 568 ÷ 4   **2.** 104 ÷ 8   **3.** 695 ÷ 5   **4.** 84 ÷ 7

5. 25 ÷ 4   **6.** 19 ÷ 4   **7.** 37 ÷ 8   **8.** 66 ÷ 5

9. **WRITING IN ►MATH** Write a real-world division problem that can be solved by using base-ten blocks.

4-3 Divide by One-Digit Numbers

MAIN IDEA

I will divide up to a four-digit number by a one-digit number.

NYS Core Curriculum

5.N.17 Use a variety of strategies to divide three-digit numbers by one and two-digit numbers *Also addresses 5.PS.5.*

New Vocabulary

remainder

NY Math Online

macmillanmh.com
• Extra Examples
• Personal Tutor
• Self-Check Quiz

GET READY to Learn

Thunder Canyon is a 1,600-foot-long ride at Cedar Point in Sandusky, Ohio. On 8 rafts, it can carry a total of 96 people. How many people can it carry on each raft?

To find the number of people *Thunder Canyon* can carry on each raft, divide 96 by 8. To divide a two-digit number by a one-digit number, first divide the tens.

Real-World EXAMPLE

1 **RIDES** **Refer to the information above. How many people can *Thunder Canyon* carry on each raft?**

To solve, divide 96 people into 8 groups. Find 96 ÷ 8.

Estimate $100 \div 10 = 10$

Step 1	**Step 2**
Divide the tens. Can 9 tens be divided among 8? Yes.	Bring down the ones. Divide the ones. Can 16 ones be divided among 8? Yes.

Step 1

$$\begin{array}{r} 1 \\ 8\overline{)96} \\ -\underline{8} \\ 1 \end{array}$$

Divide: $9 \div 8$
Multiply: 1×8
Subtract: $9 - 8$
Compare: $1 < 8$

Step 2

$$\begin{array}{r} 12 \\ 8\overline{)96} \\ -\underline{8\downarrow} \\ 16 \\ -\underline{16} \\ 0 \end{array}$$

Divide: $16 \div 8$
Multiply: 2×8
Subtract: $16 - 16$
Compare: $0 < 8$

So, *Thunder Canyon* can carry 12 people on each raft. This is close to the estimate, 10. So, the answer is reasonable.

This same process can be used to divide a three-digit number by a one-digit number. When dividing a three-digit number, the first step is to divide the hundreds.

EXAMPLE **Divide by a One-Digit Number**

2 **Find** 2)856. **Estimate** $900 \div 2 = 450$

Step 1	Step 2	Step 3
Divide the hundreds.	Bring down the tens. Divide the tens.	Bring down the ones. Divide the ones.

Step 1:
```
  4
2)856      8 ÷ 2
- 8        4 × 2
  0        8 - 8
           0 < 2
```

Step 2:
```
  42
2)856
- 8↓
  05       5 ÷ 2
- 4        2 × 2
  1        5 - 4
           1 < 2
```

Step 3:
```
  428
2)856
- 8↓|
  05 |
- 4↓
  16       16 ÷ 2
- 16       8 × 2
   0       16 - 16
           0 < 2
```

The quotient is 428.   Compare to the estimate.

If the divisor is not a factor of the dividend, then the answer will include a remainder. A **remainder** is the number left after a quotient is found. It is represented by the capital letter R.

 EXAMPLE **Division with a Remainder**

3 **Find** $137 \div 5$.   **Estimate** $150 \div 5 = 30$

Step 1	Step 2	Step 3
Divide the hundreds.	Divide the tens.	Bring down the ones. Divide the ones.

Step 1:
```
5)137
```
Can 1 hundred be divided among 5? No. So, the first digit will be in the tens place.

Step 2:
```
   2
5)137      13 ÷ 5
- 10       2 × 5
   3       13 - 10
           3 < 5
```

Step 3:
```
  27 R2
5)137
- 10↓
   37      37 ÷ 5
- 35       7 × 5
   2       37 - 35
           2 < 5
```
There are no digits left to divide, so 2 is the remainder.

The quotient is 27 R2.   Compare to the estimate.

Remember

To check division with a remainder, first multiply the quotient and the divisor. Then add the remainder.

```
  27      135
× 5     + 2
----     ----
135      137 ✔
```

Lesson 4-3 Divide by One-Digit Numbers   **159**

Divide. See Examples 1–3 (pp. 158–159)

1. 2)68   **2.** 5)95   **3.** 4)625   **4.** 3)410

5. 216 ÷ 3   **6.** 932 ÷ 6   **7.** 2,816 ÷ 5   **8.** 6,982 ÷ 7

9. An adult kangaroo is how many times heavier than a baby kangaroo?

Kangaroo	Weight (lb)
Adult	145
Baby	5

10. (Talk About It) Does the quotient of 245 and 8 have two or three digits? Explain how you know without solving.

Practice and Problem Solving

NYSCC • NYSMT
Extra Practice, p. R11

Divide. See Examples 1–3 (pp. 158–159)

11. 5)206   **12.** 6)96   **13.** 5)435   **14.** 9)837

15. 3)945   **16.** 5)630   **17.** 4)97   **18.** 2)87

19. 210 ÷ 9   **20.** 595 ÷ 4   **21.** 766 ÷ 6   **22.** 267 ÷ 8

23. 428 ÷ 3   **24.** 590 ÷ 8   **25.** 9,350 ÷ 7   **26.** 6,418 ÷ 9

27. A state park has cable cars that travel about 864 yards in 4 minutes. How many yards do the cars travel per minute?

28. Five pre-owned video games cost $185. If all the games cost the same, what is the cost of each game?

29. There were 672 people in the audience at a play. Each ticket cost $3. The audience was seated in 6 sections. If each section had the same number of people in it, how many people were in each section?

30. On Monday, a concession stand manager ordered 985 popcorn bags. If he splits the bags evenly among 5 concession stands, how many popcorn bags will each concession stand receive?

31. Mr. Harris wants to divide his 27 students into equal groups of 4 students each. How many groups of 4 students can he make? How many students will not be in a group of 4?

H.O.T. Problems

32. OPEN ENDED Write a real-world division problem with a divisor of 4 that has no remainder. Then write a real-world division problem with a divisor of 4 that has a remainder.

33. NUMBER SENSE Use the digits 2, 4, and 6 one time each in ▇ ▇ ÷ ▇. Write the division problem with the greatest quotient.

34. WRITING IN ►MATH Explain how estimation is useful when solving division problems.

NYSMT Practice 5.N.17

35. Use the table below to make a true statement. (Lesson 4-3)

Weight of Whales	
Mammal	**Weight**
Blue whale	144 tons
Gray whale	36 tons

A blue whale is _____ heavier than a gray whale.

A 3 times   **C** 6 times

B 4 times   **D** 8 times

36. Lauren poured an equal amount of the solution below in each of 8 test tubes. About how much solution is in each test tube? (Lesson 4-3)

F 30 mL   **H** 50 mL

G 40 mL   **J** 100 mL

Spiral Review

37. There are 520 baseballs that will be shipped to nine sports stores. Estimate the number of baseballs each store is to receive if they each receive about the same number. (Lesson 4-2)

Divide mentally. (Lesson 4-1)

38. 70 ÷ 2   **39.** 400 ÷ 4   **40.** 200 ÷ 5   **41.** 900 ÷ 9

Identify the multiplication property used to rewrite each problem. (Lesson 3-7)

42. 5 × 100 × 3 = 5 × 3 × 100   **43.** (7 × 5) × 2 = 7 × (5 × 2)

Estimate. Show your work. (Lesson 3-3)

44. 56 × 21   **45.** 11 × 387   **46.** 17 × 43   **47.** 29 × 88

4-4 Divide by Two-Digit Numbers

GET READY to Learn

A full sheet cake serves 76 people. To serve 152 people at a party, a bakery needs to make 152 ÷ 76, or 2 sheet cakes.

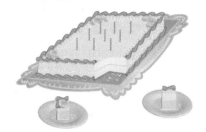

MAIN IDEA

I will divide up to a three-digit number by a two-digit number.

NYS Core Curriculum

5.N.17 Use a variety of strategies to divide three-digit numbers by one and **two-digit numbers**

NY Math Online

macmillanmh.com

- Extra Examples
- Personal Tutor
- Self-Check Quiz

In this lesson, you will learn how to divide by a two-digit number. This will help you to solve problems like the one above.

Real-World EXAMPLE — Divide by a Two-Digit Number

① **FOOD Refer to the information above. How many sheet cakes are needed to serve 836 people?**

Find $76\overline{)836}$.

Estimate $800 ÷ 80 = 10$

Step 1	Step 2
Divide the tens.	Divide the ones.

Step 1
Divide the tens.

$$
\begin{array}{r}
1 \\
76\overline{)836} \\
-76 \\
\hline
7
\end{array}
$$

Divide: 83 ÷ 76
Multiply: 76 × 1
Subtract: 83 − 76
Compare: 7 < 76

Step 2
Divide the ones.

$$
\begin{array}{r}
11 \\
76\overline{)836} \\
-76\downarrow \\
\hline
76 \\
-76 \\
\hline
0
\end{array}
$$

Bring down the ones.
Divide: 76 ÷ 76
Multiply: 1 × 76
Subtract: 76 − 76
Compare: 0 < 76

So, 11 cakes are needed to serve 836 people.

Compare to the estimate, 10. Since 11 is close to 10, the answer is reasonable.

As with division by a one-digit number, it is possible to have a remainder when you divide by a two-digit number.

EXAMPLE   **Division with a Remainder**

2 **Find 751 ÷ 30.**   Estimate 750 ÷ 30 = 25

Remember

You can check division with a remainder. Multiply the quotient and the divisor. Then add the remainder.

$$\begin{array}{r} 25 \\ \times\ 30 \\ \hline 750 \end{array} \nearrow \begin{array}{r} 750 \\ +\ 1 \\ \hline 751\ \checkmark \end{array}$$

Step 1	**Step 2**
Divide the tens.	Divide the ones.

Step 1

$$\begin{array}{r} 2 \\ 30\overline{)751} \\ -\ 60 \\ \hline 15 \end{array} \quad \begin{array}{l} 75 \div 30 \\ 2 \times 30 \\ 75 - 60 \\ 15 < 30 \end{array}$$

Step 2

$$\begin{array}{r} 25\ \text{R1} \\ 30\overline{)751} \\ -\ 60\downarrow \\ \hline 151 \\ -\ 150 \\ \hline 1 \end{array} \quad \begin{array}{l} \text{Bring down the ones.} \\ 151 \div 30 \\ 5 \times 30 \\ 151 - 150 \\ 1 < 30 \end{array}$$

So, 751 ÷ 30 is 25 R1.

Real-World EXAMPLE   **Divide by Two-Digit Numbers**

3 **MEASUREMENT** Mackenzie volunteered 208 hours last year. If she volunteered the same number of hours each week, how many hours did she volunteer each week?

To solve, find 208 ÷ 52.   1 year = 52 weeks

Estimate 200 ÷ 50 = 4

Step 1	**Step 2**
Divide the tens.	Divide the ones.

Step 1

$$52\overline{)208}$$

Since 20 tens cannot be divided by 52 ones, move to Step 2.

Step 2

$$\begin{array}{r} 4 \\ 52\overline{)208} \\ -\ 208 \\ \hline 0 \end{array} \quad \begin{array}{l} 4 \times 52 \\ 208 - 208 \end{array}$$

So, Mackenzie volunteered an average of 4 hours each week.

CHECK What You Know

Divide. See Examples 1–3 (pp. 162–163)

1. $16\overline{)176}$ **2.** $24\overline{)192}$ **3.** 375 ÷ 46   **4.** 289 ÷ 31

5. Mr. Morales buys flags for his store. Each flag costs $28. How many flags can he buy for $350?

6. **Talk About It** Explain how estimation is useful when you are dividing by two-digit numbers.

Lesson 4-4 Divide by Two-Digit Numbers   **163**

Divide. See Examples 1–3 (pp. 162–163)

7. 14)98   **8.** 32)97   **9.** 11)18   **10.** 18)216

11. 47)544   **12.** 70)359   **13.** 160 ÷ 32   **14.** 901 ÷ 18

15. A boat travels 384 miles in 24 hours. What is the average distance the boat travels in 1 hour?

16. Dreanne has 288 pictures. Her album holds 12 pictures on each page. How many pages does she need?

New York Data File

Dairy milk is New York's leading agricultural product and is produced all across the state. In the first 26 weeks, a calf gains a total of about 320 pounds. In the second 26 weeks, it gains about 370 pounds.

About how many pounds does a calf gain each week for each of the following? Round to the nearest pound.

17. during the first 26 weeks

18. during the second 26 weeks

H.O.T. Problems

19. **FIND THE ERROR** Aura and Jacob are finding 818 ÷ 21. Who is correct? Explain.

Aura

$$
\begin{array}{r}
39 \\
21\overline{)818} \\
-63 \\
\hline
188 \\
-188 \\
\hline
0
\end{array}
$$

Jacob

$$
\begin{array}{r}
38 \text{ R20} \\
21\overline{)818} \\
-63 \\
\hline
188 \\
-168 \\
\hline
20
\end{array}
$$

20. **WRITING IN ►MATH** Describe the similarities and differences when dividing by one-digit numbers and by two-digit numbers.

Mid-Chapter Check

Lessons 4-1 through 4-4

Divide mentally. (Lesson 4-1)

1. $400 \div 2$

2. $240 \div 6$

3. $3,500 \div 5$

4. $420 \div 60$

5. $4,800 \div 800$

6. $1,200 \div 300$

7. MULTIPLE CHOICE A total of 180 students went on a field trip. There were 3 buses. If each bus had the same number of students on it, how many students were on each bus? (Lesson 4-1)

A 6

B 36

C 54

D 60

Estimate. Show your work. (Lesson 4-2)

8. $232 \div 6$

9. $1,765 \div 2$

10. $5,600 \div 71$

11. $400 \div 54$

12. $756 \div 170$

13. $2,089 \div 310$

14. Measurement The length of a rectangle can be found by dividing the area by the width. Estimate the length of the rectangle below by using compatible numbers and rounding. (Lesson 4-2)

area = 621 cm² | 18 cm

Divide. (Lesson 4-3)

15. $73 \div 2$

16. $509 \div 6$

17. $874 \div 3$

18. $614 \div 5$

19. Measurement The table shows the heights of the three tallest cacti.

Cactus	Height
Saguaro	75 ft
Organ-pipe	48 ft
Opuntia	33 ft

Source: *Scholastic Book of World Records*

Find the height of each cactus in yards. (*Hint*: 1 yard = 3 feet) (Lesson 4-3)

Divide. (Lesson 4-4)

20. $109 \div 12$

21. $126 \div 18$

22. $801 \div 20$

23. $523 \div 13$

24. MULTIPLE CHOICE Suki received $864 for working 12 weeks during the summer. She earned $8 per hour and worked the same number of hours each week. How much did she earn each week? (Lesson 4-4)

F $9

G $72

H $96

J $108

25. WRITING IN ►MATH Can the remainder in a division problem ever equal the divisor? Explain. (Lesson 4-3)

Problem-Solving Strategy

 **NYSCC** **5.PS.4 Act out or model with manipulatives activities involving mathematical content** from literature
Also addresses 5.PS.2.

Annie is using a roll of plastic string to make keychains. The roll of string had 78 inches on it before she started. She has already used 12 inches for one keychain. Is Annie going to have enough plastic string for six more keychains of the same size?

Understand	**What facts do you know?** • The roll of string is 78 inches long. • Each keychain is 12 inches long. • She has already used 12 inches of string. **What do you need to find?** • Does Annie have enough string to make 6 more keychains?
Plan	Use the *act it out* strategy with a piece of string that is 78 inches long. Mark off the amount used for the first keychain, 12 inches, and continue marking off lengths of 12 inches until there are six more keychains or no more string left.
Solve	←——————— 78 in. ———————→ keychain 12 in. 12 in. 12 in. 12 in. 12 in. 12 in. 12 in. Notice that there is only enough string for 5 more keychains. So, there is not enough plastic string for 6 more keychains.
Check	Look back. Is the answer reasonable? Check by multiplying. Since $12 \times 6 = 72$ and $12 \times 7 = 84$, there is only enough string for 6 keychains in all, not 7.

Refer to the problem on the previous page.

1. If each keychain used 11 inches of string, would the roll of string be long enough for all seven keychains?

2. How does the *act it out* strategy help solve this problem?

3. Explain how the *act it out* strategy is similar to drawing a picture.

4. Give a real-world situation in which you could use the *act it out* strategy.

PRACTICE the Strategy

NYSCC • NYSMT
Extra Practice, p. R11

Solve. Use the *act it out* strategy.

5. Jesse put 15 pennies on his desk. He replaced every third penny with a nickel. Then he replaced every fourth coin with a dime. Finally, he replaced every fifth coin with a quarter. What is the value of the 15 coins that are now on his desk?

6. An aquarium at a pet store has 18 Black Neon Tetra fish in it. A customer buys 12 Black Neon Tetra fish at the same time the store clerk adds 7 more Black Neon Tetra fish to the tank. How many Black Neon Tetra fish are in the aquarium now?

7. A fifth grader takes the change from her pocket and places it on the table. The number of each coin she had in her pocket is shown below.

Coin	Number
Quarter	2
Dime	4
Nickel	3
Penny	5

How many different combinations of coins can she make with the coins she has to have $0.45?

8. During the summer Ajay wants to read 4 books. In how many different orders can he read the books?

9. Mr. Reyes baked 4 batches of muffins for his class. Each batch had 12 muffins. If Mr. Reyes has 24 students, how many muffins will each student receive?

10. Nolan, Madeline, Marco, Flor, and Julian are entered in a race. Assuming there are not any ties, how many different orders are possible for first and second place?

11. Measurement Niko has a roll of wrapping paper that had 40.5 inches on it. He has already used 4.5 inches for one gift. Does he have enough paper to wrap three gifts that require 12 inches of paper each? Explain.

12. **WRITING IN MATH** Explain a disadvantage of using the *act it out* strategy to solve Exercise 10.

Math Activity for 4-6
Interpret the Remainder

A *remainder* is the number left after a quotient is found. The following activities show you how to use remainders in different kinds of problems.

MAIN IDEA

I will interpret the remainder in a division problem.

NYS Core Curriculum

5.RP.2 Understand that mathematical statements can be supported, using models, facts, and relationships to explain their thinking

5.N.17 Use a variety of strategies to divide three-digit numbers by one and two-digit numbers *Also addresses 5.PS.13.*

NY Math Online

macmillanmh.com
• Concepts in Motion

ACTIVITY

1 **A group of fifth graders collected 46 cans of food to donate to 3 food banks. If each food bank is to get an equal number of cans, how many cans do they each receive?**

Step 1 Use 46 centimeter cubes to represent the cans of food. Use three paper plates to represent the food banks. Divide the cubes equally among the three plates.

Step 2 Interpret the remainder.

Since each food bank is to get the same number of cans of food, they will each receive 15 cans. There is one can left over.

2 **A total of 35 students are going on a field trip to NASA's Johnson Space Center in Houston. If there needs to be an adult for every 8 students, how many adults are needed?**

Use 35 centimeter cubes to represent the students. Use paper plates to represent the adults.

Place 8 cubes on as many plates as possible. Place any leftover cubes on a plate. Interpret the remainder.

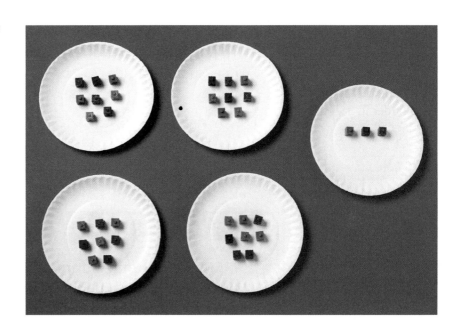

There are 4 groups of 8 students. They will each need an adult. There are 3 students who are not enough for a full group of 8. They will also need an adult.

So, 4 + 1 or 5 adults are needed.

Think About It

1. In Activity 1, the remainder was dropped. Explain why.

2. In Activity 2, the quotient was "rounded up" to 5. Explain why.

CHECK What You Know

State the solution and explain how to interpret the remainder in each division problem.

3. Each picnic table at a park seats 6 people. How many tables will 83 people at a family reunion need?

4. Mrs. Malone has $150 to buy volleyballs for Lincoln Middle School. How many can she buy at $14 each?

5. **WRITING IN** ▶**MATH** Suppose 2 friends want to share 5 cookies evenly. Interpret the remainder in two different ways.

Interpret the Remainder

MAIN IDEA

I will interpret the remainder in a division problem.

NYS Core Curriculum

5.N.17 Use a variety of strategies to divide three-digit numbers by one and two-digit numbers
Also addresses 5.CN.2, 5.CN.3.

NY Math Online

macmillanmh.com
• Extra Examples
• Personal Tutor
• Self-Check Quiz

GET READY to Learn

A state park has 257 evergreens to plant in 9 equal-sized areas. To find the number of evergreens in each area, divide 257 by 9.

Real-World EXAMPLES Interpret the Remainder

1 TREES Refer to the information above. How many evergreens are planted in each area? What does the remainder represent?

Step 1 Divide.

$$
\begin{array}{r}
28\,R5 \\
9\overline{)257} \\
-18 \\
\hline
77 \\
-72 \\
\hline
5
\end{array}
$$

Step 2 Interpret the remainder, 5.

The remainder, 5, means there are 5 evergreens left over after 28 are planted in each area.

So, the park plants 28 evergreens in each area and 5 evergreens are left over.

2 PARTY There are 174 guests invited to a dinner. Each table seats 8 guests. How many tables are needed?

Step 1 Divide.

$$
\begin{array}{r}
21\,R6 \\
8\overline{)174} \\
-16 \\
\hline
14 \\
-8 \\
\hline
6
\end{array}
$$

Step 2 Interpret the remainder, 6.

There are 6 guests left over, which is not enough for a full table of 8. But, they also need a table.

So, a total of 21 + 1, or 22 tables are needed.

Solve. Explain how you interpreted the remainder. See Examples 1, 2 (p. 170)

1. A tent is put up with 12 poles. How many tents can be put up with 200 poles?

2. There are 50 students traveling in vans on a field trip. Each van seats 8 students. How many vans are needed?

3. How many scooters shown at the right can a toy store buy for $900?

4. **Talk About It** Discuss the different ways you can interpret the remainder in a division problem.

Practice and Problem Solving

NYSCC • NYSMT

Extra Practice, p. R12

Solve. Explain how you interpreted the remainder. See Examples 1, 2 (p. 170)

5. Mrs. Washington made 144 muffins for a bake sale. She puts them into bags of 5 muffins each. How many bags of muffins can she make?

6. Students on the softball team earned $295 from a carwash. How many team jackets shown can they buy?

7. **Measurement** How many 8-foot sections of fencing are needed for 189 feet of fence?

8. Stella has 20 stuffed animals. She wants to store them in plastic bags. She estimates she can fit three stuffed animals in each bag. How many bags will she need?

9. Mrs. Luna is buying scrapbooks for her store. Her budget is $350. How many of the scrapbooks shown can she buy?

10. **Measurement** How many 6-ounce cups can be filled from 4 gallons of juice? (*Hint:* 1 gallon = 128 ounces)

11. **Measurement** Water stations will be placed every 400 meters of a five kilometer race. How many water stations are needed? (*Hint:* 1 kilometer = 1,000 meters)

12. **Measurement** Three yards of fabric will be cut into pieces so that each piece is 8 inches long. How many pieces can be cut? (*Hint:* 1 yard = 36 inches)

Real-World PROBLEM SOLVING

Money Six friends decide to pack and share an extra large submarine sandwich, which is cut into 20 equal size pieces. The cost of the submarine sandwich is $21, not including tax.

13. How much would each friend pay if each one paid the same amount? Explain how you interpreted the remainder.

14. How many pieces would each friend receive if each one receives the same amount? Explain how you interpreted the remainder.

15. Three pieces will fit into one plastic bag. How many plastic bags are needed to pack the 20 pieces? Explain how you interpreted the remainder.

H.O.T. Problems

16. OPEN ENDED Write a real-world situation that could be described by the division problem $38 \div 5 = 7$ R3 in which it makes sense to round the quotient up to 8.

17. CHALLENGE If the divisor is 30, what is the least three-digit dividend that would give a remainder of 8? Explain.

CHALLENGE For Exercises 18–20, consider each situation. In each case, decide whether you would drop the remainder, round the quotient up, or represent the quotient as a fraction to solve each problem. Explain your reasoning. Then solve each problem.

18. Greg spent $50 on four identical photo frames. How much did he spend on each frame?

19. Two friends share 3 cookies equally. How many cookies did each friend get?

20. Measurement A piece of string 50 inches long will be cut into pieces so that each piece is 4 inches long. How many full-length pieces can be cut from the string?

21. **WRITING IN** **►MATH** Write a real-world division problem that can be solved by interpreting the remainder. Does it make sense to round up or down to the next whole number? Explain.

22. Forty-six students are visiting an art museum. A tour guide is needed for each group of 6 students. How many tour guides are needed? (Lesson 4-6)

   A 7

   B 8

   C 40

   D 52

23. Ms. Meir wants to divide 135 maps as equally as possible among 4 zoo guides. Which is a true statement? (Lesson 4-6)

   F All 4 guides will get 34 maps.

   G Three guides will get 33 maps and 1 guide will get 34 maps.

   H Three guides will get 34 maps and 1 guide will get 33 maps.

   J Two guides will get 33 maps and 2 guides will get 34 maps.

Spiral Review

24. Ronada, Tori, Courtney, and Shandra went to see the class play. They sat in the four seats in the tenth row. Ronada was not on either end. Shandra was not in the last seat. Courtney was between Ronada and Tori. In what order did they sit? Use the *act it out* strategy. (Lesson 4-5)

25. A class trip costs $80 for the bus and $15 admission per student. The whole trip cost $455. How many students went on the trip? (Lesson 4-4)

Find each product mentally. (Lesson 3-1)

26. 4×600 **27.** 30×70 **28.** 10×15 **29.** 80×800

Add or subtract. (Lesson 2-6)

30. $64.2 + 3.9$ **31.** $11.65 + 18.91$ **32.** $7.8 - 4.9$ **33.** $16.2 - 12.8$

34. The library charges $0.10 for each of the first three days for overdue books. It charges $0.05 for every day after that. Janelle owed the library $1.50. How many days overdue was her book? Solve. Use the *work backward* strategy. (Lesson 2-3)

35. **Measurement** Chino is using the ribbon at the right to make spirit ribbons. He also has ribbons that measure 6.4 meters and 6.5 meters. Order the ribbons from least to greatest. (Lesson 1-7)

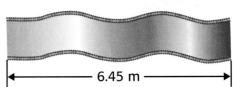

← 6.45 m →

4-7 Extending Division

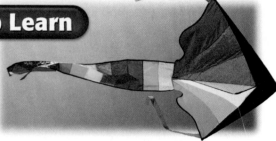

Ms. Glover buys 2 kites for a total of $15.18. If each kite costs the same, about how much did each kite cost?

MAIN IDEA

I will estimate quotients of decimals and greater numbers.

NYS Core Curriculum

5.N.17 Use a variety of strategies to divide three-digit numbers by one and two-digit numbers

5.N.23 Use a variety of strategies to add, subtract, multiply, and **divide decimals to thousandths**

NY Math Online

macmillanmh.com

- Extra Examples
- Personal Tutor
- Self-Check Quiz

To estimate $15.18 ÷ 2, you can use compatible numbers.

EXAMPLE **Divide Money**

① **MONEY Refer to the information above. About how much did each kite cost?**

$15.18 ÷ 2

↓   ↓   Change $15.18 to $16 because
$16 ÷ 2   16 and 2 are compatible numbers.

$16 ÷ 2 = $8   Divide mentally.

So, $15.18 ÷ 2 is about $8. Each kite costs about $8.

You can also use compatible numbers to estimate quotients of decimals that do not involve money.

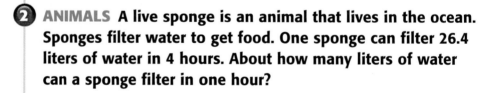

Real-World EXAMPLE **Estimate with Decimals**

② **ANIMALS A live sponge is an animal that lives in the ocean. Sponges filter water to get food. One sponge can filter 26.4 liters of water in 4 hours. About how many liters of water can a sponge filter in one hour?**

26.4 ÷ 4

↓   ↓   Change 26.4 to 28 because
28 ÷ 4   28 and 4 are compatible numbers.

28 ÷ 4 = 7   Divide mentally.

So, a sponge can filter about 7 liters of water in one hour.

Technology can be a useful tool for dividing greater numbers.

Real-World EXAMPLE   **Greater Numbers**

3 **PRESIDENTS** Theodore Roosevelt was the twenty-sixth President of the United States. One day, he shook hands with 8,513 people. If he had continued at that rate, in how many days would he have shaken hands with the one-millionth person?

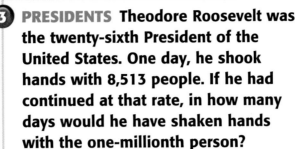

You want to find how many groups of 8,513 are in 1,000,000. So, divide 1,000,000 by 8,513.

Estimate: 1,000,000 ÷ 10,000 = 100

Use the Calculator feature from your Math Tool Chest™ to find the exact answer.

Enter:
Press: ÷
Enter: 8 5 1 3
Press: =
Solution: | 117.4674028 |

Check for Reasonableness Compare 117 to the estimate. ✓

When you use a calculator, the remainder is expressed as a decimal. It would take 117 whole days and part of one day to shake 1,000,000 hands. So, President Roosevelt would shake hands with the one-millionth person on day 118.

Remember

Always estimate first and then compare your final answer to the estimate.

CHECK What You Know

Estimate each quotient. See Examples 1, 2 (p. 174)

1. $19.50 ÷ 5

2. $47.25 ÷ 25

3. 16.8 ÷ 4

4. Jake bought 3 drawing pens for $8.07. Each pen costs the same amount. About how much did he spend for 1 pen?

5. Jupiter is about 483,879,000 miles from the Sun. Earth is about 93,000,000 miles from the Sun. About how many times as far from the Sun is Jupiter than Earth? Then use a calculator to find the exact answer rounded to the nearest whole number.

6. **Talk About It** Describe the steps for estimating dividing money by a whole number.

Estimate each quotient. See Examples 1, 2 (p. 174)

7. $28.20 ÷ 6

8. $7.92 ÷ 6

9. 88.3 ÷ 9

10. 128.9 ÷ 12

11. It costs $88.50 for 6 adults to see an exhibit on Egyptian mummies. About how much does it cost 1 adult to see the exhibit?

12. Measurement There are 74.4 grams of sugar in 3 servings of grapes. About how many grams of sugar are in a single serving?

For Exercises 13 and 14, estimate the quotient. Then use a calculator.

13. A city phone book has 152 pages. There are 46,512 names in the book. How many names are on each page?

14. Population density of a state is found by dividing the number of people by the area of the state. Refer to the table at the right. Which state has the higher population density?

State	Population	Area (square miles)
Texas	23,507,783	295,324
Virginia	7,642,884	42,745

Real-World PROBLEM SOLVING

Measurement The table shows the density of each object. *Density* describes how tightly the particles in an object are packed together. You can find density by dividing an object's mass by its volume.

Substance	Mass (g)	Volume (cm³)
Aluminum	13.5	5
Gold	56.7	3
Mercury	121.5	9

15. Estimate the density of aluminum.

16. Is the density of gold greater than the density of mercury? Explain.

17. The density of gold is about how many times greater than the density of aluminum?

H.O.T. Problems

18. OPEN ENDED Write a division problem involving money. Describe the steps that you used to estimate the quotient.

19. WRITING IN ►MATH If your heart beats 103,698 times in one day, explain how to find the number of times your heart beats per minute.

Mission: Division
Dividing Whole Numbers

Get Ready!
Players: 2, 3, or 4 players

You will need: spinner
index cards

Get Set!
- Each player makes a game sheet like the one shown at the right.

- Make a spinner as shown.

Game Sheet
—— —— ÷ ——

Go!
- The first person spins the spinner. Each player writes the number in one of the blanks on his or her game sheet. A zero cannot be placed as the divisor.

  The next person spins, and each player writes that number in a blank.

  The next player spins and each player fills in their game sheet. A player loses if he or she cannot use all the numbers.

- All players find their quotients. The player with the greatest quotient earns one point. In case of a tie, those players each earn one point.

- The first person to earn 5 points wins.

Problem Solving in Social Studies

The Statue of Liberty

The Statue of Liberty has become a symbol of freedom since its arrival in the United States. The statue stands on Liberty Island in the New York harbor. It is 151 feet tall and weighs about 448,000 pounds. There are 354 stairs from the bottom of the statue to the crown. What a hike!

When immigrants came to New York between 1886 and 1920, this statue was one of the first things they saw. Today, visitors can travel to the Statue of Liberty by a ferry or a yacht. The yacht, called the *Zephyr*, can hold up to 600 passengers at one time.

Real-World Social Studies

Use the information on pages 178–179 to solve each problem.

1. A total of 459 passengers rode the *Zephyr* to Ellis Island. If the passengers were evenly spread out on each of the ferry's three decks, how many passengers were on each deck?

2. f the *Zephyr* was completely filled, ow many people could fit evenly each deck?

3. w many adult tickets can be hased with $75? Tell how you reted the remainder.

4. How many child tickets can be purchased with $25? Tell how you interpreted the remainder.

5. How many senior tickets can be purchased with $35? Tell how you interpreted the remainder.

6. When school groups visit, one teacher must accompany each group of ten students. How many teachers should accompany a class of 25 students?

Divide Whole Numbers

NYSCC

5.CN.8 Investigate the presence of mathematics in careers and **areas of interest**
5.R.8 Use mathematics to show and understand social phenomena (e.g., construct tables to organize data showing book sales)

Did You Know?

The Statue of Liberty was completed in France. Then it was taken apart and all 350 pieces were shipped to the United States and rebuilt.

Statue of Liberty Ferry Prices ($)

Adult	10
Child (4–12 yr)	4
Senior (+62 yr)	8

Source: The National Park Service

Problem-Solving Investigation

MAIN IDEA I will choose the best strategy to solve a problem.

 NYSCC

5.PS.2 Understand that some ways of representing a problem are more efficient than others
5.PS.3 Interpret information correctly, identify the problem, and generate possible strategies and solutions
Also addresses 5.PS.5, 5.PS.8.

P.S.I. TEAM +

JAHIEM: I am helping my mother get ready for a party. I am putting 6 square tables end-to-end to make one large table. One square table can seat one person on each side.

▶

YOUR MISSION: Find the number of people that can sit around the new large table.

Understand	You know that Jahiem is putting 6 square tables end-to-end. A square table can seat one person on each side. Find the number of people that can sit around the new table.
Plan	You could act it out. But it is easier to draw a picture.
Solve	Draw the 6 tables end-to-end. Then count how many seats there are.

14 | 1 | 2 | 3 | 4 | 5 | 6 | 7
    13   12   11   10   9   8

So, Jahiem can seat 14 people around the new table.

Check	Look back. You know that 6 people can sit on one long side. There are two long sides. So, $6 \times 2 = 12$. Then add 2, the number of people that can sit on the ends. So, $12 + 2 = 14$. The answer is correct. ✔

Use any strategy shown below to solve each problem.

PROBLEM-SOLVING STRATEGIES
- Draw a picture
- Work backward
- Guess and check
- Act it out

1. On Monday, 56 DVDs were checked out at the library. This is 8 less than twice the amount of books checked out that day. How many books were checked out?

2. **Measurement** Leo takes 20 minutes to walk to practice, 30 minutes to eat dinner, and 15 minutes to warm up. If Leo needs to be ready for hockey practice at 7:15 P.M., what time does he need to leave home?

3. A ride at a theme park lasts $1\frac{1}{2}$ minutes. It takes 2 minutes to prepare the ride for each trip. How many times can the ride be completed in 30 minutes?

4. A cook needs 12 pounds of flour. He wants to spend the least amount of money. How many bags of each type of flour should he buy? What will be the total cost?

5. Kiwi bought flippers and a face mask. The face mask costs $5.96 more than the flippers. The total for the two items, before tax, was $63.94. What was the cost of the flippers?

6. Nicholas bought a camping tent. Each of the four sides of the tent needs two stakes to secure it properly. What is the least number of stakes that are needed?

7. Samantha has four coins worth $0.36. What coins does Samantha have?

8. **Measurement** Mr. Holley is adding 2 feet to the length and width of his garden shown below. Find the distance around his new garden.

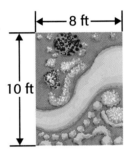

9. The farmer's market sells apples at 2 for $1. How much will 8 apples cost?

10. The fifth grade class is boxing up 85 coloring books to take to the children's hospital. If one box has 15 more books in it than the other box, how many books are in each box?

11. **WRITING IN ►MATH** A builder is putting up a fence in a backyard. The yard is 40 feet long and 50 feet wide. How much fencing will the builder need? What strategy would you use to solve this problem? Explain your reasoning and then solve.

FOLDABLES
Study Organizer

GET READY to Study

Be sure the following Big Ideas are written in your Foldable.

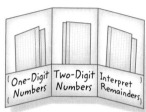

One-Digit Numbers | Two-Digit Numbers | Interpret Remainders

Key Concepts

Estimating Quotients

• You can use compatible numbers to estimate quotients. **(pp. 152–155)**

$283 \div 7$
↓   ↓
280 $\div$ **7**   28 and 7 are compatible numbers.

$280 \div 7 = 40$, so $283 \div 7$ is about 40.

Dividing Whole Numbers (pp. 158–164)

$$\begin{array}{r} 32 \\ 2\overline{)64} \\ \end{array}$$

-6 $6 \div 2$
$\overline{04}$
         3×2
-4 $4 \div 2$
$\overline{0}$ 2×2

Interpret the Remainder (pp. 170–173)

• When interpreting the remainder you can drop the remainder, use only the remainder, or add 1 to the quotient.

Key Vocabulary

dividend (p. 149)

divisor (p. 149)

quotient (p. 149)

remainder (p. 159)

Vocabulary Check

Choose the correct term or number to complete each sentence.

1. When you divide, the answer is called the (dividend, quotient).

2. When you use $450 \div 9$ to estimate $437 \div 9$, you are using (rounding, compatible numbers).

3. The (divisor, remainder) is the number left after a quotient is found.

4. The quotient $1{,}040 \div 5$ is (208, 28).

5. The value of $360 \div 90$ is (4, 40).

6. The best estimate for $6{,}217 \div 186$ is (30, 300).

7. An example of compatible numbers for division is (9 and 45, 9 and 10).

Lesson-by-Lesson Review

4-1 **Division Patterns** (pp. 149–151)

5.N.17

Example 1
Find 15,000 ÷ 5 mentally.

Step 1 Write the basic fact.
15 ÷ 5 = 3

Step 2 Continue the pattern.
150 ÷ 5 = 30
1,500 ÷ 5 = 300
15,000 ÷ 5 = 3,000

So, 15,000 ÷ 5 = 3,000.

Divide mentally.

8. 420 ÷ 7   **9.** 300 ÷ 3

10. 800 ÷ 20   **11.** 160 ÷ 8

12. 630 ÷ 10   **13.** 400 ÷ 50

14. Mara deposited a total of $240 in her account in the past 6 weeks. If she deposited the same amount each week, what was the amount of each deposit?

15. Jorge's family drove 2,700 miles during their 9-day vacation. If they drove the same distance each day, how many miles did they drive each day?

4-2 **Estimate Quotients** (pp. 152–155)

5.N.27

Example 2
Estimate 825 ÷ 20.

825 ÷ 20
↓   ↓   Change 825 to 800 because
800 ÷ 20   8 and 2 are compatible.

800 ÷ 20 = 40   Divide mentally.

So, 825 ÷ 20 is about 40.

Example 3
Estimate 356 ÷ 51.

356 ÷ 51   Change 356 to 350 and
↓   ↓   51 to 50 since 35 and 5 are
350 ÷ 50   compatible numbers.

350 ÷ 50 = 7   Divide mentally.

So, 356 ÷ 51 is about 7.

Estimate. Show your work.

16. 219 ÷ 2   **17.** 126 ÷ 4

18. 720 ÷ 91   **19.** 182 ÷ 34

20. 800 ÷ 215   **21.** 1,200 ÷ 32

22. 541 ÷ 61   **23.** 4,520 ÷ 52

24. Three plane tickets to New York cost $2,472. If each plane ticket costs the same amount, about how much does one ticket cost? Use compatible numbers to estimate the cost of one ticket.

Study Guide and Review

4-3 Divide by One-Digit Numbers (pp. 158–161)

5.N.17

Example 4

Find 79 ÷ 7.

Estimate $77 \div 7 = 11$

Step 1	**Step 2**
Divide the tens.	Bring down the ones. Divide the ones.

Step 1:
```
    1
7)79      7 ÷ 7
 - 7      1 × 7
    0     7 − 7
```

Step 2:
```
   11
7)79      
 - 7↓     
   09     9 ÷ 7
  - 7     7 × 1
    2     9 − 7
```

So, $79 \div 7 = 11$ R2. This is close to the estimate, 11, so the answer is reasonable.

Divide.

25. $3\overline{)78}$ **26.** $2\overline{)146}$

27. $756 \div 4$ **28.** $97 \div 6$

29. $412 \div 5$ **30.** $893 \div 8$

31. A cabinet with four shelves can hold 640 CDs. If the shelves each hold the same number of CDs, how many CDs does each shelf hold?

32. There are 1,250 pieces of mail to be sorted evenly into 5 bags. How many pieces of mail are in each bag?

4-4 Divide by Two-Digit Numbers (pp. 162–164)

5.N.17

Example 5

Find 632 ÷ 89.

Estimate $630 \div 90 = 7$

Step 1	**Step 2**
Divide the tens.	Divide the ones.

Step 1:
```
89)632    63 ÷ 89
          63 < 89
```

Step 2:
```
     7
89)632    632 ÷ 89
  - 623   89 × 7
      9   632 − 623
          9 < 89
```

So, $632 \div 89 = 7$ R9. This is close to the estimate, 7, so the answer is reasonable.

Divide.

33. $16\overline{)64}$ **34.** $20\overline{)451}$

35. $325 \div 23$ **36.** $741 \div 13$

37. $810 \div 75$ **38.** $586 \div 62$

39. A bakery needs 225 pounds of flour. How many 15-pound bags should the bakery buy?

40. At a football camp, 165 players are divided into 15 teams. How many players are on each team?

4-5 Problem-Solving Strategy: Act It Out (pp. 166–167)

5.PS.4

Example 6

Measurement Andre is planting seeds in a rectangular tray 10 inches by 20 inches. How many seeds will fit if each seed needs to be placed 2 inches apart and from the sides?

Use the *act it out* strategy.

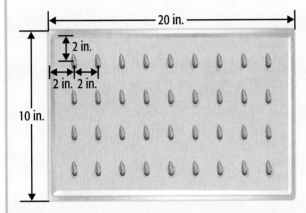

The picture shows that 36 seeds will fit in the tray.

Solve. Use the *act it out* strategy.

41. Ariana has 4 different shirts and 3 pairs of pants. If she wears a different combination of shirt and pants each day, how many days will pass before she must repeat an outfit?

42. At a business meeting, everyone shook hands with everyone else exactly once. There were a total of 15 handshakes. How many people were at the meeting?

43. How many ways are there to represent $0.77 using at least two quarters and only two pennies?

4-6 Interpret the Remainder (pp. 170–173)

5.N.17

Example 7

A florist has 86 roses. She plans to put 5 roses in each box. How many boxes can she fill?

$$
\begin{array}{r}
17\ R1 \\
5\overline{)86} \\
-\ 5 \\
\hline
36 \\
-\ 35 \\
\hline
1
\end{array}
$$

She can fill 17 boxes. The remainder 1 means that there is 1 rose left over.

Solve. Explain how you interpreted the remainder.

44. Kyle has 48 oranges. He puts 7 oranges in a bag. How many bags can he fill?

45. A factory received 1,268 sponges. Only 12 sponges fit in each box. How many boxes did the factory receive?

46. A text message has 43 words. If the text message has 8 lines, how many words are on each line?

4-7 Extending Division (pp. 174–176)

5.N.23

Example 8

Kerry bought 4 identical sweatshirts. If he spent $34 on the sweatshirts, about how much did each sweatshirt cost?

You need to find $34 ÷ 4.

$34 ÷ 4

↓   Change $34 to $36 because 36 and 4 are compatible numbers.

$36 ÷ 4

$36 ÷ 4 = $9   Divide mentally.

So, $34 ÷ 4 is about $9. Each sweatshirt costs about $9.

Check Since $9 × 4 = $36, the answer is correct. ✔

Estimate each quotient.

47. $10.80 ÷ 6   **48.** 23.9 ÷ 5.1

49. A pizza costs $14.77. If 3 people split the cost evenly, about how much will each person pay?

50. At a state forest, the rangers plant 8,000 seedlings in seedling boxes. Each box holds 164 seeds. About how many boxes are needed to plant all the seedlings?

4-8 Problem-Solving Investigation: Choose a Strategy (pp. 180–181)

5.PS.2

Example 9

Measurement It takes Santos 15 minutes to walk to school, 15 minutes to eat breakfast, and 30 minutes to get ready for school. If he needs to arrive at school at 8:45 A.M., what time does he need to set his alarm clock?

To find what time Santos should set his alarm clock start at 8:45 and work backward.

8:45 − 15 min. = 8:30
8:30 − 15 min. = 8:15
8:15 − 30 min. = 7:45

So, Santos needs to set his alarm for 7:45 A.M.

Use any strategy to solve each problem.

51. A number multiplied by itself is 256. What is the number?

52. The fifth grade class is planning a field trip. There are 472 students in the fifth grade. If each bus holds 38 people, how many buses will they need for the students?

53. Use the symbols +, −, ×, ÷ to make the following math sentence true. Use each symbol only once.

3 ▣ 6 ▣ 5 ▣ 1 = 22

CHAPTER

4

Chapter Test

Divide mentally.

1. 900 ÷ 100   **2.** 1,600 ÷ 800

3. 490 ÷ 7   **4.** 2,400 ÷ 3

5. 300 ÷ 50   **6.** 3,600 ÷ 90

7. Cedric is saving money to buy a new skateboard that costs $350. If he saves $70 each week, how many weeks will it take him to save enough money to buy the skateboard?

Estimate. Show your work.

8. 588 ÷ 2   **9.** 276 ÷ 4

10. 455 ÷ 52   **11.** 800 ÷ 34

12. 3,600 ÷ 84   **13.** 4,100 ÷ 217

14. MULTIPLE CHOICE The table shows the number of deer in a wildlife preserve and the size of the preserve in acres. Which is the best estimate for the number of deer per acre?

Number of Deer	406
Number of Acres	38

  A 1

  B 10

  C 100

  D 1,000

Divide. Write answers with remainders.

15. 3)84   **16.** 4)156

17. 5)632   **18.** 98 ÷ 7

19. 51 ÷ 20   **20.** 165 ÷ 12

21. A librarian has 88 new reference books. She puts them on 5 shelves. She puts an equal number of books on each shelf. How many books are left over?

22. MULTIPLE CHOICE Ms. Torrez bought a jar of beads that has 525 beads. If she divides the beads equally among 15 bags, how many beads will be in each bag?

  F 45   **H** 4.5

  G 35   **J** 3.5

23. Fifty-two students plan an after-school trip to a museum. There needs to be 1 adult for every 9 students. How many adults are needed? Explain how you interpreted the remainder.

24. A pizza with 10 pieces will be divided among three friends. How many pieces will each friend receive? Explain how you interpreted the remainder.

25. WRITING IN ►MATH A student group visits a butterfly exhibit. They pay $12 for each student, but receive a $34 group discount. The total cost after the discount is $242. How many students were in the group? Explain what strategy you used to solve this problem.

♦ NYSMT Practice

Cumulative, Chapters 1–4

PART 1   Multiple Choice

Read each question. Then fill in the correct answer on the answer sheet provided by your teacher or on a sheet of paper.

1. A farmer harvested 868 apples this afternoon. The apples are stored equally in 31 bushels. How many apples are there in each bushel?

   A 22   **C** 26

   B 24   **D** 28

2. A grocery store has 636 eggs on its shelves. The eggs are in cartons of 12 eggs each. How many cartons are there altogether?

   F 53   **H** 57

   G 56   **J** 59

3. There are 276 teachers in attendance at a conference. The teachers are divided into groups of 12. How many groups are there?

   A 23   **C** 27

   B 25   **D** 29

4. So far 480 people have ridden a roller coaster ride at an amusement park. The ride holds a total of 40 people each time it runs. How many times has the roller coaster run?

   F 10   **H** 12

   G 11   **J** 15

5. Mr. Smith has 15 tables in his classroom. Each table has 3 chairs around it. How many chairs are there in the classroom?

   A 5

   B 36

   C 40

   D 45

6. Miss Flores drove 360 miles. If she drove 40 miles each hour, how many hours did she drive?

   F 4 h

   G 6 h

   H 8 h

   J 9 h

7. Suppose you want to buy 3 dozen cookies for a party. How much will you save off of the regular price with today's special?

The Friendly Bakery
Cookies 50¢ each
Today's Special: One dozen cookies for only $4.00

   A $4.00

   B $6.00

   C $5.00

   D $7.00

8. Chris buys a chicken sandwich, a vegetable, and a drink. He pays with $10. How much money will he have left?

Deli Prices	
Chicken Sandwich	$3.75
Cheeseburger	$2.25
Fries	$1.25
Vegetable	$1.25
Drink	$1.35

F $2.95   H $3.65

G $3.40   J $4.20

9. Which is the best estimate for the product shown below?

$$7 \times 31.2$$

A about 280   C about 210

B about 250   D about 200

10. There are 442 people seated in the school auditorium for an assembly. There are 26 rows in the auditorium, each with the same number of seats. If the auditorium is completely filled, how many seats are there in each row?

F 16   H 18

G 17   J 19

PART 2   Short Response

Record your answers on the sheet provided by your teacher or on a sheet of paper.

11. Senon has 120 CDs in his collection. The CDs are stored in a book with 8 per page. Write a number sentence to show how many pages of CDs Senon has.

12. Oscar has $47 to buy jerseys for his basketball team. Each jersey costs $6. Oscar figures that he can buy 8 jerseys. Is he correct? Explain.

PART 3   Extended Response

Record your answers on the answer sheet provided by your teacher or on a sheet of paper. Show your work.

13. It takes Javier 720 seconds to run two miles. Explain how to find the number of minutes it takes Javier to run two miles.

14. Explain how 3 friends can share 2 pieces of cake equally. Include a drawing with your explanation.

NEED EXTRA HELP?														
If You Missed Question...	1	2	3	4	5	6	7	8	9	10	11	12	13	14
Go to Lesson...	4-4	4-4	4-4	4-1	4-3	4-1	3-6	2-6	3-8	4-4	4-3	4-6	4-1	4-7
NYS Core Curriculum	5.N.17	5.N.17	5.N.17	5.N.17	5.N.17	5.N.17	5.N.16	5.N.23	5.N.26	5.N.17	5.N.17	5.N.17	5.N.17	5.N.23

Use Algebraic Expressions

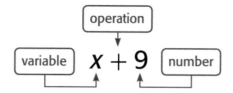

BIG Idea **What is an expression?**

An **expression** is a combination of variables, numbers, and at least one operation.

```
              operation
                 ↓
  variable    x + 9    number
```

Example The Shock Wave roller coaster is 116 feet tall. The Flashback roller coaster is *x* feet taller than the Shock Wave. You can use the expression $116 + x$ to find the height of the Flashback.

What will I learn in this chapter?

- Write and evaluate algebraic expressions.
- Illustrate functions using a function machine.
- Complete function tables.
- Solve problems by using the *solve a simpler problem* strategy.

Key Vocabulary

variable

expression

evaluate

function

order of operations

 **NY Math Online** **Student Study Tools** at macmillanmh.com

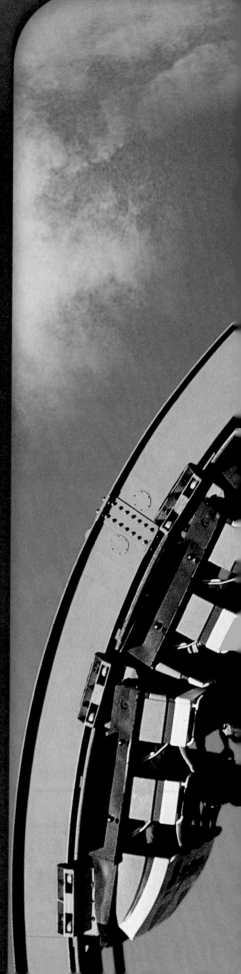

FOLDABLES®
Study Organizer

Make this Foldable to help you organize information about algebraic expressions. Begin with a sheet of $8\frac{1}{2}'' \times 11''$ paper.

① **Fold** a 2″ tab along the long side of the paper.

② **Unfold** the paper and then fold in thirds widthwise.

③ **Open** and draw lines along the folds. Label the head of each column as shown. Label the front of the folded table with the chapter title.

What I Know About Expressions	What I Need to Know	What I've Learned

ARE YOU READY for Chapter 5?

You have two ways to check prerequisite skills for this chapter.

Option 2

NY Math Online > Take the Chapter Readiness Quiz at macmillanmh.com.

Option 1

Complete the Quick Check below.

QUICK Check

Add. (Prior grade)

1. $6 + 3$

2. $9 + 8$

3. $12 + 4$

4. $19 + 2$

5. $17 + 18$

6. $24 + 35$

7. Fernando has 25 toy cars. If he buys 7 more, how many will he have?

8. Measurement Tori uses 2 cups of raisins to make one batch of granola. How many cups of raisins will she use to make 3 batches of granola?

Multiply. (Prior grade)

9. 5×2

10. 3×4

11. 7×5

12. 11×3

13. 15×2

14. 20×3

15. Greeting cards cost \$2 each. Find the cost of 6 cards.

16. Sally has 3 boxes of snack bars. She ate one snack bar. There are 7 snack bars left in that box. How many snack bars were in 3 boxes?

Write in word form. Then find the value. (Prior grade)

17. $15 - 6$

18. $6 + 4$

19. $10 \div 5$

20. 8×3

5-1 Addition Expressions

GET READY to Learn

A bag contains some apples. There are 2 apples outside the bag. The total number of apples is equal to the number of apples in the bag plus 2.

MAIN IDEA
I will write and evaluate addition expressions.

NYS Core Curriculum

5.A.1 Define and use appropriate terminology when referring to constants, variables, and algebraic expressions

5.A.2 Translate simple verbal expressions into algebraic expressions *Also addresses 5.A.3, 5.PS.13.*

New Vocabulary
variable
expression
evaluate

NY Math Online
macmillanmh.com
• Extra Examples
• Personal Tutor
• Self-Check Quiz

The unknown number of apples can be represented by a variable. A **variable** is a letter or symbol used to represent a number.

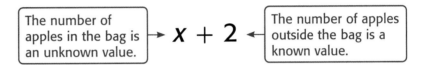

The number of apples in the bag is an unknown value. → $x + 2$ ← The number of apples outside the bag is a known value.

An **expression**, like $x + 2$, is a combination of variables, numbers, and at least one operation. When you replace a variable with a number, you can **evaluate**, or find the value of, the expression.

EXAMPLE   Evaluate Expressions

1 Evaluate the expression $x + 2$ if $x = 3$.

$x + 2$ Write the expression. Use 1 cup and 2 counters to represent $x + 2$.

$3 + 2$ Replace x with 3. Place 3 counters in the cup.

5 Add 3 and 2. There is a total of 5 counters.

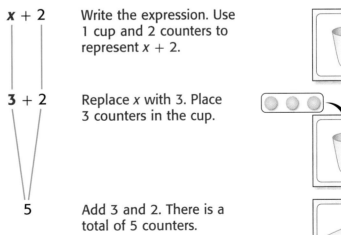

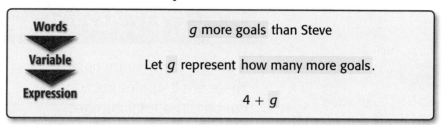

Real-World EXAMPLES · **Write and Evaluate Expressions**

② **SPORTS** Steve scored 4 goals. Theresa scored *g* more goals than Steve. Write an expression.

Words	*g* more goals than Steve
▼	
Variable	Let *g* represent how many more goals.
▼	
Expression	4 + *g*

Vocabulary Link

Variable

Everyday Use able to change

Math Use a symbol, usually a letter, to represent a number

③ **Refer to Example 2. If *g* = 7, then how many goals did Theresa score?**

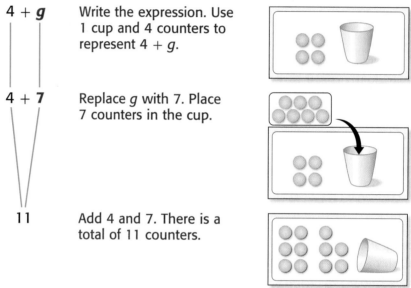

4 + **g**   Write the expression. Use 1 cup and 4 counters to represent 4 + *g*.

4 + **7**   Replace *g* with 7. Place 7 counters in the cup.

11   Add 4 and 7. There is a total of 11 counters.

So, Theresa scored 11 goals.

CHECK What You Know

Evaluate each expression if *x* = 5 and *y* = 6. See Example 1 (p. 193)

1. *x* + 6   **2.** 12 + *y*   **3.** *y* + 18   **4.** *x* + 29

Write an expression for each real-world situation. Then evaluate it.
See Examples 2, 3 (p. 194)

5. Naomi bought 12 pens. Wu bought *t* more pens than Naomi. If *t* = 9, how many pens did Wu buy?

6. Laura had *y* dollars. Her mom gave her $15. If *y* = 12, how much money does Laura have?

7. (Talk About It) Explain how to evaluate the expression *a* + 9 if *a* = 11.

Evaluate each expression if $x = 2$ and $y = 9$. See Example 1 (p. 193)

8. $x + 7$

9. $5 + y$

10. $4 + x$

11. $y + 8$

12. $15 + x$

13. $y + 12$

14. $23 + x$

15. $y + 26$

16. $x + 34$

Write an expression for each real-world situation. Then evaluate.

See Examples 2, 3 (pp. 193–194)

17. Measurement A tomato plant is t inches tall. In a month, it grows 3 inches taller. If $t = 18$, how tall is the tomato plant?

18. During one season, the Tigers lost 26 more games than they won. If the Tigers won 68 games, how many games did they lose?

19. Carmen went to a water park. She spent $15 on admission and a certain amount on food. If she spent $12 on food, how much did Carmen spend in all?

20. Josiah's grade on his last math test was 10 points higher than his first math test. On the first test, he scored p points. If $p = 23$, how many points did he score on the last test?

New York Data File

The sugar maple tree is the state tree of New York. Most sugar maple trees are 90 to 120 feet tall and can live for hundreds of years.

Write an expression. Then evaluate.

21. A sugar maple tree was 94 feet tall. In 20 years, it grew f feet. If the tree grew 21 feet, what was the new height of the tree?

22. Naima planted 34 sugar maple trees on Monday. On Tuesday, she planted y trees. If she planted 49 trees on Tuesday, how many sugar maple trees did she plant in all?

H.O.T. Problems

23. OPEN ENDED Write an expression that has a value of 15 if $m = 2$.

24. WRITING IN ►MATH Tell whether the statement below is *sometimes*, *always*, or *never* true. Justify your reasoning.

The expressions $x + 2$ and $y + 2$ represent the same value.

Problem-Solving Strategy

MAIN IDEA I will solve problems by solving a simpler problem.

 NYSCC **5.PS.17 Determine the efficiency of different representations of a problem** *Also addresses 5.RP.1, 5.PS.18.*

Emilio is one of two bakers for Brian's Bakery. Working separately, the two bakers can make a total of 2 cakes in 2 hours. The bakery wants to hire an additional 2 bakers for a large cake order. At this rate, how many cakes can 4 bakers make in 6 hours if they work separately?

Understand	**What facts do you know?** • 2 bakers can make 2 cakes in 2 hours. **What do you need to find?** • How many cakes 4 bakers can make in 6 hours.
Plan	You can solve the problem by solving a simpler problem.
Solve	**Step 1** Find how long it takes each baker to make 1 cake. $2 \div 2 = 1$ Each baker makes 1 cake in 2 hours. **Step 2** Find how many cakes each baker can make in 6 hours. Divide by 2 since it takes 2 hours to make one cake. $6 \div 2 = 3$ Each baker can make 3 cakes in 6 hours. **Step 3** Find how many cakes 4 bakers can make in 6 hours. $4 \times 3 = 12$ So, 4 bakers can make 12 cakes in 6 hours.
Check	Look back. The number of bakers doubled, so 2×2 or 4 cakes can be made in 2 hours. In 6 hours, the bakers can make 3×4 or 12 cakes. So, the answer is correct. ✔

ANALYZE the Strategy

Refer to the problem on the previous page.

1. Explain why you first found how long it takes each baker to make 1 cake.

2. If the bakers continue making cakes at the same rate, how many cakes can 6 bakers make in 8 hours?

3. Look back at Exercise 2. Check your answer. How do you know it is reasonable? Explain.

4. Explain when you would use the *solve a simpler problem* strategy to solve a problem.

PRACTICE the Strategy

NYSCC • NYSMT
Extra Practice, p. R13

Solve. Use the *solve a simpler problem* strategy.

5. **Algebra** Working separately, 3 teenagers can mow 3 lawns in 3 hours. At this rate, how many lawns can 6 teenagers mow in 9 hours?

6. **Measurement** Darby is cutting ribbons for balloons. The roll of ribbon he has is 24 feet long. Each ribbon needs to be 3 feet long. How long will it take Darby to make the cuts if each cut takes 3 seconds?

7. Find the sum of the whole numbers from 1 through 10. Explain your reasoning. Then find the sum of the whole numbers from 1 through 20.

8. Patty wants to buy a new tennis racket. So far, she has saved $25.00 and $7.25 from her two babysitting jobs. How much more money does she need to buy the tennis racket shown below?

9. **Measurement** Keith and his friend are going to the movies. The movie starts at 6:45 P.M. and lasts 1 hour and 50 minutes. If Keith's mom will be picking them up at the end of the movie, what time should she pick them up?

10. Charity and her friend each want to buy a piece of pizza, a drink, and an ice cream cone. Charity has $10 to pay for her and her friend's meal. Does she have enough money? Explain.

Menu	
Pizza	$2.75
Drink	$0.95
Ice cream cone	$1.95

11. **Algebra** At the beach, 4 children working separately made 8 sandcastles in an hour. At this rate, how many sandcastles can 12 children make in a $\frac{1}{2}$ hour?

12. **WRITING IN ▶MATH** How is the *solve a simpler problem* strategy similar to the *work backward* strategy?

Lesson 5-2 Problem-Solving Strategy: Solve a Simpler Problem **197**

Multiplication Expressions

GET READY to Learn

Lola has 2 boxes of crayons. Each box contains the same number of crayons. The total number of crayons is equal to 2 times the number of crayons in each box.

$2n$

MAIN IDEA

I will write and evaluate multiplication expressions.

NYS Core Curriculum

5.A.2 Translate simple verbal expressions into algebraic expressions

5.A.3 Substitute assigned values into variable expressions and evaluate using order of operations *Also addresses 5.A.7, 5.PS.7.*

NY Math Online

macmillanmh.com

• Extra Examples
• Personal Tutor
• Self-Check Quiz
• Concepts in Motion

The total number of crayons can be represented by the expression $2n$, which means 2 times n.

The number of boxes of crayons is a known value. → $2n$ ← The number of crayons in each box is an unknown value, or variable.

Suppose each box contains 8 crayons. To find the total number of crayons, multiply the number of crayons in each box by 2.

So, each box contains 2×8 or 16 crayons.

EXAMPLE Evaluate Expressions

① **Evaluate the expression $2n$ if $n = 5$.**

$2n$ Write the expression. Use 2 cups to represent $2n$.

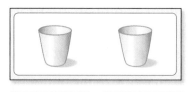

2×5 Replace n with 5. Place 5 counters in each cup.

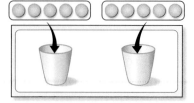

10 Multiply 2 and 5. There is a total of 10 counters.

Real-World EXAMPLES Write and Evaluate Expressions

2 **FOOD** Ivan made *x* sandwiches. He used 2 slices of bread for **each sandwich** he made. Write an expression.

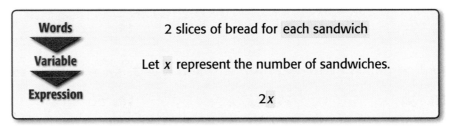

Words	2 slices of bread for each sandwich
Variable	Let *x* represent the number of sandwiches.
Expression	2*x*

3 Refer to Example 2. If *x* = 6, how many slices of bread did Ivan use?

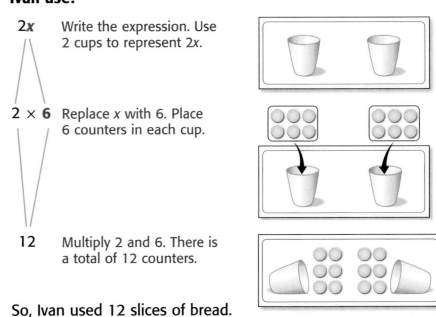

2*x*   Write the expression. Use 2 cups to represent 2*x*.

2 × **6**   Replace *x* with 6. Place 6 counters in each cup.

12   Multiply 2 and 6. There is a total of 12 counters.

So, Ivan used 12 slices of bread.

CHECK What You Know

Evaluate each expression if *x* = 4 and *y* = 7. See Example 1 (p. 198)

1. 12*y*   **2.** 9*x*   **3.** 7*y*   **4.** 12*x*

Write an expression for each real-world situation. Then evaluate.

See Examples 2, 3 (p. 199)

5. Leon has 4 sheets of stickers. Each sheet contains *t* stickers. If *t* = 8, how many stickers does Leon have?

6. Jacy bought 5 CDs. Each CD cost *c* dollars. If *c* = 10, how much did the CDs cost?

7. **Talk About It** Explain how to evaluate the expression 9*b*, if *b* = 8.

Evaluate each expression if $x = 3$ and $y = 8$. See Example 1 (p. 198)

8. $4x$ **9.** $3y$ **10.** $5x$ **11.** $6y$

12. $9x$ **13.** $8y$ **14.** $12x$ **15.** $11y$

Evaluate each expression if $a = 9$ and $b = 7$. See Example 1 (p. 198)

16. $2a$ **17.** $3b$ **18.** $5b$ **19.** $4a$

20. $8a$ **21.** $9b$ **22.** $11a$ **23.** $12b$

Write an expression for each real-world situation. Then evaluate.

See Examples 2, 3 (p. 199)

24. Cole answered 11 questions correctly on a quiz. Each question was worth q points. If $q = 3$ how many points did Cole earn?

25. Ana mowed ℓ lawns. She earned $10 for every lawn she mowed. If $\ell = 5$, how much money did Ana earn?

26. The home baseball team scored 3 times as many runs as the away team in one season. The table shows how many runs the away team scored. How many runs did the home team score?

Runs Scored	
Team	Runs
HOME	?
AWAY	62

27. A roller coaster can hold n passengers. In a half hour, the roller coaster made 6 full runs. The roller coaster can hold 28 passengers. How many passengers rode in the half hour?

H.O.T. Problems

28. OPEN ENDED Write a multiplication expression that, when evaluated, has a product of 36. Explain your reasoning.

29. NUMBER SENSE Without calculating, predict whether the value of $3n$ is greater than or less than the value of $n + n$ if $n = 8$. Explain.

30. CHALLENGE Explain whether the expressions $2n$ and $n + n$ have the same value for any value of n.

31. WRITING IN ►MATH Write a real-world problem that can be represented by a multiplication expression.

32. Ms. Pena has 28 students in her class. Mrs. Thorne has *x* more students than Ms. Pena. Which expression could be used to find the total number of students Mrs. Thorne has? (Lesson 5-1)

A 28 + *x*

B 28 − *x*

C 28*x*

D 28 ÷ *x*

33. Evaluate the expression *a* + *b* if *a* = 10 and *b* = 7. (Lesson 5-1)

F 15

G 17

H 19

J 20

34. The table shows how the ticket prices to water parks and plays have increased over the years.

Year	Water Parks	Plays
1990	$5	$27
1995	$10	$32
2000	$15	$37
2005	$20	$42

Based on the table, what is the relationship between the ticket prices? (Lesson 5-3)

A Water park ticket prices are $5 more than play ticket prices.

B Water park ticket prices are $32 less than play ticket prices.

C Play ticket prices are $22 more than water park ticket prices.

D Play ticket prices are $22 less than water park ticket prices.

Spiral Review

35. Measurement Mrs. Anderson needs to cut the piece of wood shown at the right into pieces 24 inches long. How many minutes will it take Mrs. Anderson to make the cuts if each cut takes 2 minutes? (Lesson 5-2)

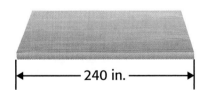

← 240 in. →

Evaluate each expression if *x* = 5 and *y* = 6. (Lesson 5-1)

36. 7 + *x*   **37.** *y* + 15   **38.** *y* + 23   **39.** *x* + *y*

40. Members of the field hockey team washed cars to raise money for new equipment. They charged $9 for large cars and $6 for small cars. They raised a total of $339. If they washed 21 large cars, how many small cars did they wash? (Lesson 4-8)

Estimate each sum or difference by rounding. Show your work.
(Lesson 2-2)

41. 2.48 + 6.61   **42.** 558 − 402   **43.** 75 + 74   **44.** 9.42 − 5.75

More Algebraic Expressions

MAIN IDEA

I will evaluate algebraic expressions.

NYS Core Curriculum

5.A.2 Translate simple verbal expressions into algebraic expressions

5.A.3 Substitute assigned values into variable expressions and evaluate using order of operations *Also addresses 5.A.1, 5.A.7, 5.PS.7.*

NY Math Online

macmillanmh.com

• Extra Examples
• Personal Tutor
• Self-Check Quiz

▶ GET READY to Learn

The Charlotte Knights are a minor league baseball team in North Carolina. The table shows the ticket prices for a Knights baseball game. The cost of a child's ticket is *d* dollars less than the cost of an adult ticket.

Charlotte Knights Tickets	
Ticket	Cost ($)
Adult	8
Senior	7
Child	?

Real-World EXAMPLE

Write and Evaluate Algebraic Expressions

① **MONEY** Refer to the above table. The cost of a child's ticket is *d* **dollars less than** $8. Write an expression.

In this case, the words *less than* mean subtraction.

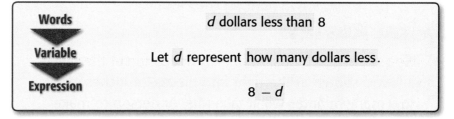

Words	*d* dollars less than 8
Variable	Let *d* represent how many dollars less.
Expression	$8 - d$

Suppose $d = 3$. Find the cost of a child's ticket.

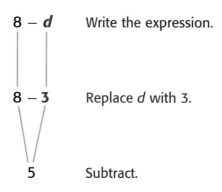

$8 - d$ Write the expression.

$8 - 3$ Replace *d* with 3.

5 Subtract.

So, the cost of a child's ticket is $5.

Write and Evaluate Algebraic Expressions

2 **SCIENCE** Adam collected half as many insects for science class as Quan. Write an expression.

In this case, half as many means to divide by 2.

Words	half as many insects as Quan
▼	
Variable	Let q represent the number of insects Quan collected
▼	
Expression	$q \div 2$

If Quan collected 12 insects, how many did Adam collect?

$q \div 2$ Write the expression.

$12 \div 2$ Replace q with 12.

6 Divide 12 by 2.

So, Adam collected 6 insects.

CHECK **What You Know**

Write an expression for each phrase. See Examples 1, 2 (pp. 202–203)

1. the sum of 11 and z **2.** p less than 22   **3.** w times 8

Evaluate each expression if $b = 3$ and $c = 4$.

4. $5 + b$ **5.** $c - 3$ **6.** $7c$ **7.** $27 \div b$

Write an expression for each real-world situation. Then evaluate.

8. Measurement The length of Kiki's room is 3 feet more than the width w of her room. The width of her room is 9 feet. What is the length of her room?

9. Franklin received $35 for his birthday. Then he bought a movie ticket for $6. How much money does he have now?

10. Curtis wants to buy some DVDs. Each DVD costs $15. If he has $60 to spend, how many DVDs can he buy?

11. (Talk About It) Describe how to evaluate the expression $x \div 5$ if $x = 15$.

Write an expression for each phrase. See Examples 1, 2 (pp. 202–203)

12. 10 more than f

13. 50 less than d

14. 25 plus a

15. 8 times p

16. half of j

17. twice k

Evaluate each expression if $r = 5$, $s = 2$, and $t = 8$.

18. $s + 19$

19. $34 + t$

20. $43 - r$

21. $r - s$

22. $4t$

23. $5r$

24. $18 \div s$

25. $25 \div r$

26. $r + t$

27. $t - s$

28. $12t$

29. $t \div s$

Write an expression for each real-world situation. Then evaluate.

30. Norman bought a hot dog and another food item. If the other item he bought was fries, what was the total cost of the food?

31. Tionna received $50 for her birthday. She spent some of the money on a board game that cost $18. How much money does Tionna have left?

32. Yolen had 84 marbles. She divided the marbles equally into a certain number of bags. If each bag had 12 marbles, how many bags did Yolen use?

Fries $3

Hamburger $4

Hot Dog $2

33. Philip planted 5 rows of sunflower seeds. Each row had s seeds. Philip had 7 seeds left over, and each row had 12 seeds. How many sunflower seeds did Philip have?

H.O.T. Problems

34. **OPEN ENDED** Write two different expressions using m and 4, one using multiplication and one using addition. Then evaluate if $m = 6$.

35. **WHICH ONE DOESN'T BELONG?** Identify the expression that does not belong with the other three. Explain your reasoning.

| $36 - a$ if $a = 9$ | $19 + b$ if $b = 8$ | $9c$ if $c = 3$ | $15 + d$ if $d = 9$ |

36. **WRITING IN ▶MATH** Explain why the expression 3 *less than* x is written as $x - 3$ and not as $3 - x$.

1. Aimee has t tickets. Dale has 7 more tickets. Write an expression for the number of tickets Dale has. (Lesson 5-1)

Evaluate each expression if $n = 3$. (Lesson 5-1)

2. $n + 7$

3. $n + 9$

4. $12 + n$

5. $n + 18$

6. Working separately, 5 carpenters can make 10 chairs in 2 days. At this rate, how many chairs can 10 carpenters make in 4 days? Solve. Use the *solve a simpler problem* strategy. (Lesson 5-2)

7. Marcy and her friend working separately can make 8 greeting cards in 32 minutes. How many greeting cards can Marcy and her friend make in 48 minutes? Solve. Use the *solve a simpler problem* strategy. (Lesson 5-2)

Evaluate each expression if $y = 4$. (Lesson 5-3)

8. $3y$

9. $5y$

10. $8y$

11. $11y$

12. **MULTIPLE CHOICE** Alonzo waited x minutes to ride the bumper cars. Pearl waited 3 times as long. Which expression could be used to find the number of minutes Pearl waited? (Lesson 5-3)

   A $3 + x$

   B $3x$

   C $x + 3$

   D $x - 3$

13. Use the table. Mr. Yu bought n new DVDs. If $n = 3$, what was the total cost of the DVDs? (Lesson 5-3)

DVD	Price ($)
New	12
Used	8

14. **MULTIPLE CHOICE** Dario is y years old. His brother Angelo is twice as old as he is. Which expression could be used to find Angelo's age? (Lesson 5-4)

   F $y + 2$ **H** $2y$

   G $y - 2$ **J** $y \div 2$

Evaluate each expression if $d = 2$ and $f = 6$. (Lesson 5-4)

15. $11 - f$

16. $24 \div d$

Measurement For Exercises 17 and 18, use the figure below. (Lesson 5-4)

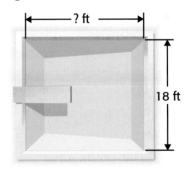

17. Write an expression to show that the length of the swimming pool is x feet more than the width.

18. If $x = 5$, what is the length of the pool?

19. **WRITING IN ►MATH** Write two different expressions using n and 2, one with division and one with subtraction. Explain how to evaluate them if $n = 6$. (Lesson 5-4)

5-5 Problem-Solving Investigation

MAIN IDEA I will choose the best strategy to solve a problem.

> NYSCC **5.PS.3 Interpret information correctly, identify the problem, and generate possible strategies and solutions**
> *Also addresses 5.PS.8, 5.CN.3.*

P.S.I. TEAM ✛

STEPHANIE: I had a lemonade stand. I sold large cups of lemonade for $0.65 and small cups of lemonade for $0.40. After one hour, I earned $6.15. How many of each size did I sell?

YOUR MISSION: Find the number of each size sold.

Understand	You know that Stephanie earned $6.15. She sold large cups for $0.65 and small cups $0.40. You need to know how many of each size Stephanie sold.
Plan	You need to think about the different combinations of large and small cups she could have sold. So, the *guess and check* strategy is a good choice.
Solve	Use a calculator. Since 10 × $0.65 = $6.50, less than 10 large cups were sold. Let's try 8.

	Large Cup	Earnings	Small Cup	Earnings	Total	
1st guess	8	$5.20	3	$1.20	$6.40	Too much.
2nd guess	6	$3.90	5	$2.00	$5.90	Too little.
3rd guess	7	$4.55	4	$1.60	$6.15	✔

So, Stephanie sold 7 large cups and 4 small cups of lemonade.

Check	Look back. Since 7 × $0.65 = $4.55 and 4 × $0.40 = $1.60, Stephanie made $4.55 + $1.60 or $6.15. So, the answer is correct. ✔

206 Chapter 5 Use Algebraic Expressions

Use any strategy shown below to solve each problem.

PROBLEM-SOLVING STRATEGIES
- Guess and check.
- Work backward.
- Draw a picture.
- Act it out.
- Solve a simpler problem.

1. Jeremy's basketball number is between 30 and 50. The sum of the digits is 4. What is Jeremy's basketball number?

2. **Algebra** Jasmine is making bookmarks. Each day she makes twice as many bookmarks as the day before. On the fifth day she makes 32 bookmarks. How many bookmarks did she make on the first day?

3. **Measurement** A plumber needs to cut the pipe shown below into 2 inch pieces. If one cut takes 3 minutes, how many minutes will it take the plumber to make the cuts?

|←——12 in.——→|

4. Some students are standing in the lunch line. Tammie is fourth. Joy is two places in front of Tammie. Eight places behind Joy is Mike. What place is Mike?

5. **Measurement** A sandbox is made of two squares side by side. Each square is 9 feet by 9 feet. What is the total distance around the sandbox?

6. Rita bought sandwiches for herself and 4 friends. She spent a total of $13.45. How many of each type of sandwich did she buy?

TURKEY $2.60   HAM $2.75

7. **Geometry** Square tables are put together end-to-end to make one long table for a birthday party. A total of 18 people attend the party. How many tables are needed if only one person can sit on each side of the square tables?

8. At the school bake sale, Kenji's mom bought 3 cookies, 1 brownie, and 2 cupcakes. She gave the cashier $2 and received $0.75 in change. Find the cost of each cupcake.

Bake Sale Prices	
Item	Price ($)
Cookie	0.15
Brownie	0.20
Cupcake	▪

9. An electronics store is selling handheld games at $27 for 3. How much will 5 handheld games cost?

10. **WRITING IN ►MATH** Write a real-world problem that you can solve using any problem-solving strategy. What strategy would you use to solve the problem? Explain your reasoning.

A *function machine* takes a number called the *input* and performs one or more operations on it to produce a new value called the *output*. A *function rule* describes the relationship between each input and output.

MAIN IDEA

I will illustrate functions using function machines.

NYS Core Curriculum

5.PS.13 Model problems with pictures/diagrams or **physical objects**

5.A.7 Create and explain patterns and algebraic relationships (e.g., 2, 4, 6, 8…) algebraically:2*n* (doubling)

ACTIVITY   Make a Function Machine

Suppose Marcus is 4 years younger than his sister Lucia. The function rule *n* − 4 can be used to find Marcus' age if you know Lucia's age. Make a function machine for the rule *n* − 4.

Step 1   Cut a sheet of paper in half lengthwise.

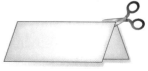

Step 2   Cut four slits into one of the halves. The slits should be at least one inch wide.

Step 3   Cut two narrow strips from the other half of the paper. These strips should be able to slide through the slits you cut on the first half sheet.

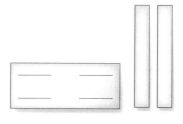

Step 4   On one of the narrow strips, write the input numbers 10 through 6 as shown. On the other strip, write the output numbers 6 through 2 as shown.

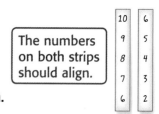

The numbers on both strips should align.

Step 5   Place the strips into the slits as shown. Then tape the ends of the strips together at the top. Write the function rule *n* − 4 as shown.

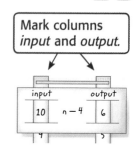

Mark columns *input* and *output*.

Step 6   Pull the strips up or down so that the input value corresponds to an output value.

Think About It

1. Use the function machine you made to find the output value for each input value. Copy and complete the function table showing the input, output, and function rule.

Lucia's Age Input	Rule: $n - 4$	Marcus' Age Output
10	■	6
9	■	■
8	■	■
7	■	■
6	■	■

2. What patterns do you notice in the function machine?

3. Use the pattern you discovered to predict how old Marcus will be when Lucia is 20 years old.

 CHECK What You Know

For Exercises 4–9, write a real-world situation for each expression. Then express the relationship using a function machine. Use the input values 3, 4, 5, and 6 for *n*. Record each input, output, and function rule in a function table.

4. $n + 4$ **5.** $n - 1$ **6.** $n + 6$

7. $n - 2$ **8.** $2n$ **9.** $3n$

Write the function rule to express the relationship between each set of input and output values. Then write a real-world situation for each function rule.

10.

Input	Rule: ■	Output
28	■	40
29	■	41
30	■	42
31	■	43

11.

Input	Rule: ■	Output
4	■	16
5	■	20
6	■	24
7	■	28

12. Create your own function machine for a real-world situation. Write pairs of inputs and outputs and have a classmate determine the rule.

13. **WRITING IN ►MATH** Why is using a function machine like finding a pattern? Explain your reasoning.

Explore Algebra Activity for 5-6: Function Machines   **209**

5-6 Function Tables

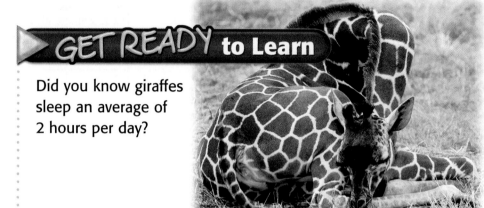

GET READY to Learn

Did you know giraffes sleep an average of 2 hours per day?

MAIN IDEA

I will complete function tables.

NYS Core Curriculum

5.A.2 Translate simple verbal expressions into algebraic expressions

5.A.3 Substitute assigned values into variable expressions and evaluate using order of operations *Also addresses 5.R.1, 5.R.5.*

New Vocabulary

function

function table

input

output

NY Math Online

macmillanmh.com

• Extra Examples
• Personal Tutor
• Self-Check Quiz

A **function** is a relationship between two variables in which one input quantity is paired with exactly one output quantity. You can use a **function table** to organize input-output values. In the Algebra Activity on page 208, you learned that the **input** is the quantity put into a function. The end amount is the **output**.

Real-World EXAMPLE Complete a Function Table

1 **ANIMALS** Refer to the above information. How many hours of sleep will a giraffe get in 5 days? Make a function table.

In words, the rule is *multiply the number of days by 2*. As an expression, the rule is 2*d*.

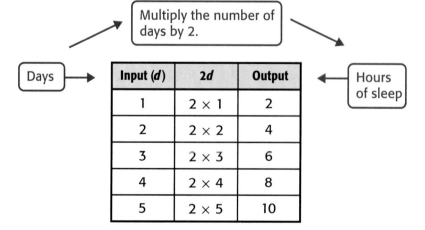

Multiply the number of days by 2.

Days →	Input (*d*)	2*d*	Output	← Hours of sleep
	1	2 × 1	2	
	2	2 × 2	4	
	3	2 × 3	6	
	4	2 × 4	8	
	5	2 × 5	10	

In 5 days, a giraffe will sleep about 10 hours.

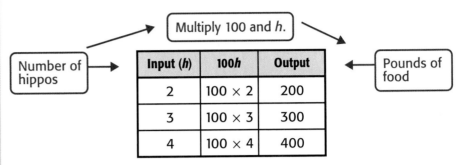

Real-World EXAMPLE Find the Function Rule

2 MEASUREMENT A zookeeper feeds each hippopotamus 100 pounds of food a day. Find the function rule. Then make a function table to find how many pounds of food the zoo will need each day for 2, 3, or 4 hippos.

The output value is 100 times the input value.

Multiply 100 and *h*.

Number of hippos →

Input (*h*)	100*h*	Output
2	100 × 2	200
3	100 × 3	300
4	100 × 4	400

← Pounds of food

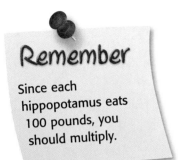

Remember

Since each hippopotamus eats 100 pounds, you should multiply.

The zoo will need 200, 300, or 400 pounds of food.

CHECK What You Know

Copy and complete each function table for each real-world situation.

See Examples 1, 2 (pp. 210–211)

1. Desmond has 9 more model airplanes than his brother.

Input (*x*)	*x* + 9	Output
6	■	■
9	■	■
12	■	■

2. Petra walked 6 less blocks than Natalie.

Input (*x*)	*x* − 6	Output
15	■	■
17	■	■
19	■	■

3. Each comic book costs $4.

Input (*x*)	4*x*	Output
5	■	■
6	■	■
7	■	■

4. Jared ate half of his pretzels.

Input (*x*)	*x* ÷ 2	Output
12	■	■
14	■	■
16	■	■

5. Hiro charges $8 for each dog he washes. Find the function rule. Then make a function table to find how much money he would make if he washes 4, 5, or 6 dogs.

6. **Talk About It** Explain what the function rule *n* − 8 means. Then find the output value if *n* = 12.

Lesson 5-6 Function Tables **211**

Copy and complete each function table for each real-world situation.

See Example 1 (p. 210)

7. Aidan scored 9 less points than Vince.

Input (x)	$x - 9$	Output
19	■	■
20	■	■
21	■	■

8. Each box weighs 10 pounds.

Input (x)	$10x$	Output
3	■	■
5	■	■
7	■	■

Find the function rule. Then make and complete a function table.

See Example 2 (p. 211)

9. Ginny had a coupon for $5 off any item at Music Mania. Find the final cost of items that cost $20, $25, and $30.

10. Measurement A textbook weighs about 6 pounds. Find the total weight of 5, 7, and 9 textbooks.

11. A certain box can hold 6 muffins. Find the number of boxes you will need if you have 24, 30 and 36 muffins. How many boxes will you need if you have 42 muffins?

12. A shop sells trail mix for $3.75 per pound. You have a coupon for $0.75 off each pound of trail mix. Find the cost of 4, 5, and 6 pounds of trail mix. What is the cost of 7 pounds of trail mix?

H.O.T. Problems

13. OPEN ENDED Write a function rule involving both addition and multiplication. Choose three input values and find the output values.

14. FIND THE ERROR Bly and Sierra are writing a function rule for the expression *5 less than y*. Who is correct? Explain.

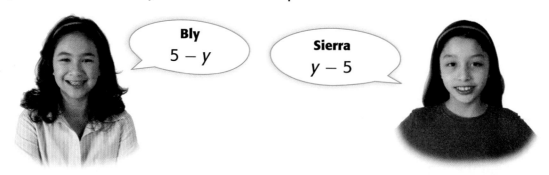

Bly

$5 - y$

Sierra

$y - 5$

15. **WRITING IN ►MATH** Write a real-life problem that can be represented by a function table.

16. Jean is buying stickers. The table shows the price of different numbers of stickers.

Number of Stickers	25	50	75	100	125
Price	$0.50	$1.00	$1.25	$2.00	$2.50

What is the relationship between the number of stickers and the price? (Lesson 5-4)

A The price is 25 more than the number of stickers.

B The number of stickers is two times the price.

C The price is two times the number of stickers.

D The number of stickers is 25 less than the price.

17. A milkshake costs $3. The function rule 3n represents the cost of buying any number of milkshakes. Which shows 3n in words? (Lesson 5-6)

F n more than 3

G 3 more than n

H 3 times n

J 3 less than n

18. Find the missing value in the function table.

Input (x)	4	5	6	7
Output	32	40	48	■

A 63   C 56

B 58   D 50

Spiral Review

19. Tickets to the museum cost $4.50 for adults and $2.50 for children. The Thorn family spent $18.50 for tickets. If they bought more adult tickets than children's tickets, how many of each type of ticket did they buy? (Lesson 5-5)

Evaluate each expression if x = 3 and y = 6. (Lesson 5-4)

20. 18 − x   21. 38 + y   22. 7y   23. 24 ÷ x

24. **Measurement** Mr. Coughlin drove 536 miles in 9 hours. About how many miles does he drive each hour on average? Show your work. (Lesson 4-2)

For Exercises 25 and 26, use the table that shows listeners' favorite types of satellite radio stations. (Lesson 2-4)

25. How many listeners favor either music or news stations?

26. How many more listeners favor sports over entertainment?

Type of Station	Number of Listeners
Music	3,897
Sports	3,160
Entertainment	2,180
News	2,054

Replace each ● with <, >, or = to make a true sentence. (Lesson 1-2)

27. 390 ● 309   28. 54 ● 45   29. 790 ● 1,669

You can use the Math Tool Chest™ to make function tables.

ACTIVITY Make a Function Table

1. **A bottlenose dolphin must rise to the surface every 6 minutes to breathe. Find the function rule. Then make a function table to find how many times a bottlenose dolphin will surface in 42, 48, and 54 minutes.**

The function rule is $x \div 6$, where x is the number of minutes and y is the number of times that the dolphin will surface.

You can use a function table from the Math Tool Chest™.

- Choose Graphs and click on level two.
- Click on Function Graph.
- Click on the link button in the bottom right-hand corner.
- Click on the formula button. Type the function rule, $x \div 6$.
- Enter the values for x (42, 48, 54) in the x column.
- Look at the values for y to solve the problem.

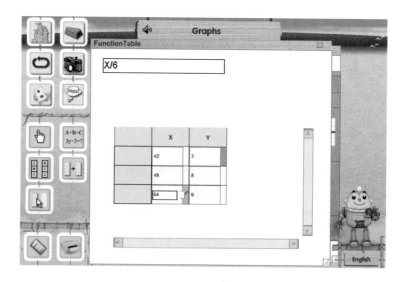

So, a bottlenose dolphin will surface every 7, 8, and 9 minutes.

CHECK What You Know

Tech Link

Find the function rule. Then use the Math Tool Chest™ to make and complete a function table.

1. Ria is 6 years younger than her brother. How old will Ria be when her brother is 12, 17, and 23 years old?

2. The fastest fish is the sailfish. A sailfish can swim 68 miles per hour. How many miles can a sailfish swim in 3, 5, or 7 hours?

3. The width of a flower pot is 4 inches longer than its height. Find the width of the pot if its height is 5, 8, or 12 inches.

4. Each student will receive the same number of pizza rolls. There are 48 pizza rolls. How many rolls will each student receive if there are 6, 12, or 24 students?

5. **WRITING IN ►MATH** Explain the advantages of using Math Tool Chest™ to make and complete function tables.

For Exercises 6–12, use the function table at the right to solve.

6. Analyze the numbers in the *x* and *y* values to find the function rule for the table.

7. If $x = 20$, what is the value of *y*?

8. If $x = 100$, what is the value of *y*?

9. If $y = 14$, what is the value of *x*?

10. If $y = 29$, what is the value of *x*?

11. An odd number is placed in the *x* column. What will always be true for the value of *y*?

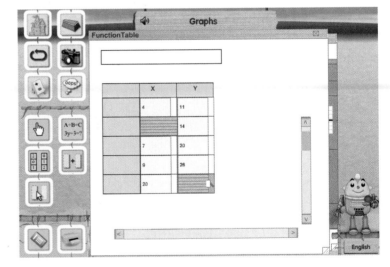

12. If an even number is placed in the *x* column, then what will always be true for the value of *y*?

13. **WRITING IN ►MATH** Write a real-world problem that could be solved using a function table.

Extend Technology Activity for 5-6: Function Tables **215**

Problem Solving in Science

UNDERWATER MAPS

Oceans cover $\frac{7}{10}$ of Earth's surface. Just as there are maps of land, there are maps of the ocean's floor. Oceanographers use sonar to measure the depths of different places in the ocean. The average depth of Earth's oceans is 12,200 feet.

Oceanographers send out sound waves from a sonar device on a ship. They measure how long it takes for sound waves to reach the bottom of the ocean and return. They use the fact that sound waves travel through sea water at about 5,000 feet per second. That's about 3,400 miles per hour!

Did You Know? The deepest part of the ocean floor has been recorded at 36,198 feet. This distance is 7,163 feet greater than the height of Mount Everest, the highest mountain on Earth.

Real-World Math

Use the information from page 216 and the table below to solve each problem. Use a calculator.

1. Make a function table to find the number of feet sound travels through sea water for 1, 2, 3, 4, and 5 seconds.

2. Use your table to estimate how long it will take a sound wave to reach the average depth of Earth's oceans.

3. Suppose your ship sends out a sound wave and it returns to the ship in 8 seconds. About how deep is the ocean where you are?

4. Suppose a thunderstorm is about 1 mile away from where you are standing. About how long will it take before you hear the thunder? (*Hint:* 1 mile = 5,280 feet)

5. WRITING IN ►MATH Explain how to write an expression that gives the number of feet that sound travels through steel for any number of seconds. How would you vary your expression if the sound was traveling through diamond?

SPEED OF SOUND THROUGH DIFFERENT MEDIA (FEET PER SECOND)	
Air (20°C)	1,121
Pure Water	4,882
Sea Water	5,012
Steel	16,000
Diamond	39,240

Order of Operations

MAIN IDEA

I will use order of operations to evaluate expressions.

NYS Core Curriculum

5.N.18 Evaluate an arithmetic expression using order of operations including multiplication, division, addition, subtraction and parentheses

5.A.3 Substitute assigned values into variable expressions and evaluate using order of operations
Also addresses 5.A.1, 5.A.2.

New Vocabulary

order of operations

NY Math Online

macmillanmh.com
• Extra Examples
• Personal Tutor
• Self-Check Quiz

GET READY to Learn

The table shows the number of Calories burned in one minute for two different activities. If you swim for 4 minutes, you will burn 12 × 4 Calories. If you run for 8 minutes, you will burn 10 × 8 Calories.

Activity	Calories Burned per Minute
Swimming	12
Running	10

If you do both activities, you need to find the value of the expression 12 × 4 + 10 × 8.

The expression 12 × 4 + 10 × 8 has more than one operation. The **order of operations** tells you which operation to do first, so that everyone finds the same value for the expression.

Order of Operations   Key Concept

1. Perform operations in parentheses.

2. Multiply and divide in order from left to right.

3. Add and subtract in order from left to right.

Real-World EXAMPLE   Evaluate Expressions

1   **HEALTH Refer to the information above. How many Calories would you burn doing both activities?**

$c = 12 \times 4 + 10 \times 8$

$c = \quad 48 \quad + \quad 80$ Multiply 12 and 4. Multiply 10 and 8.

$c = \quad\quad\quad 128$ Add 48 and 80.

So, you would burn 128 Calories.

Real-World EXAMPLE — Write and Evaluate Expressions

2 MEASUREMENT The table shows the number of minutes Roberto spent playing baseball at camp. Find the total number of minutes he spent playing baseball.

Baseball Time	
Day	**Time (minutes)**
Monday	60
Tuesday	90
Wednesday	60
Thursday	90
Friday	60

On three days, he played for 60 minutes. On two days, he played for 90 minutes.

$$60 \times 3 + 90 \times 2$$

number   number   number   number
of   of   of   of
minutes   days   minutes   days

Now evaluate.

$m = 60 \times 3 + 90 \times 2$

$m = \quad 180 \quad + \quad 180$ Multiply 60 by 3. Multiply 90 by 2.

$m = \qquad\quad 360$ Add 180 and 180.

So, Roberto played 360 minutes of baseball.

Real-World EXAMPLE — Use a Function Table

3 MONEY The cost of renting a popcorn machine is $8 per hour plus $30. Find the function rule. Then make a function table to find the cost of renting the popcorn machine for 4, 5, and 6 hours.

First multiply 8 by the input value. Then, add 30. The function rule is $8x + 30$.

Remember

The expression 8x means 8 times the value of x.

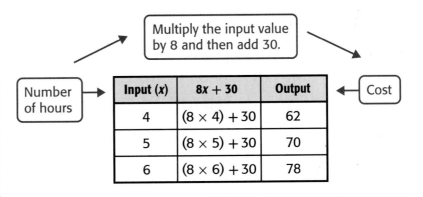

Multiply the input value by 8 and then add 30.

Number of hours →

Input (x)	8x + 30	Output
4	$(8 \times 4) + 30$	62
5	$(8 \times 5) + 30$	70
6	$(8 \times 6) + 30$	78

← Cost

CHECK What You Know

Find the value of each expression. See Examples 1–3 (pp. 218–219)

1. $12 - 2 \times 5$ **2.** $15 - 3 \times 4$ **3.** $(15 - 3) \times 4$

4. Giselle bought three DVDs that each cost $12. She also had a coupon for $10 off her total purchase. Write an expression to find her final cost. Then evaluate the expression.

5. The table shows the number of minutes Percy read in five days. How many minutes did he read? Write an expression. Then evaluate the expression.

Percy's Reading Time	
Day	**Time (minutes)**
Monday	25
Tuesday	20
Wednesday	25
Thursday	25
Friday	20

6. The cost of shipping books bought on the Internet is $3 plus $1 for each book purchased. Find the function rule. Then make a function table to find the cost of shipping 3, 4, and 5 books.

7. **Talk About It** Explain why Exercises 2 and 3 have different answers even though the numbers are the same.

Practice and Problem Solving

NYSCC • NYSMT

Extra Practice, p. R15

Evaluate each expression. See Examples 1–3 (pp. 218–219)

8. $(15 - 5) \times (3 + 3)$ **9.** $58 - 6 \times 7$ **10.** $32 + 4 \times 8$

11. **Measurement** The total distance around the garden shown below is 2 times the length plus 2 times the width. What is the total distance around the garden?

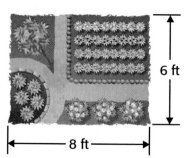

6 ft

8 ft

12. Vikram counted the number of cans turned in on Monday morning.

His results are shown. Each 𝍩 represents 5 cans.

𝍩 𝍩 𝍩 𝍩 𝍩 𝍩 𝍩 |||

How many cans did Vikram count? Write an expression. Then evaluate the expression.

For Exercises 13 and 14, find the function rule. Then make and complete a function table.

13. **Measurement** A fish tank has 100 gallons of water in it. The water is draining at a rate of 4 gallons per minute. Find how much water is left in the tank after 11, 14, and 17 minutes.

14. Tarie is planning on reading 15 pages of her book each night. She has already read 12 pages. Find the number of pages she has read after 2, 3, and 4 nights. How many pages has she read after 5 nights?

Real-World PROBLEM SOLVING

Algebra Temperature can be measured in degrees Fahrenheit (°F) or in degrees Celsius (°C). When you know a temperature in degrees Fahrenheit, you can find the temperature in degrees Celsius by using the expression $5 \times (F - 32) \div 9$.

15. Find each temperature in degrees Celsius. Copy and complete the table. (*Hint:* If an expression has both multiplication and division, evaluate them in order from left to right.)

Temperature (°F)	$5 \times (F - 32) \div 9$	Temperature (°C)
41	▪	▪
68	▪	▪
95	▪	▪

16. If the temperature of a cup of hot chocolate is 104°F, what is the temperature of the cup of hot chocolate in degrees Celsius?

17. Guess and check to find the temperature in degrees Fahrenheit that would equal 0°C.

H.O.T. Problems

18. **OPEN ENDED** Write an expression using only multiplication and subtraction so that its value is 25.

19. **CHALLENGE** Use each of the numbers 2, 3, 4, and 5 exactly once to write an expression that equals 5.

20. **WRITING IN ▶MATH** Should you ever add or subtract before you multiply in an expression? Explain your reasoning.

21. Each of Marie's 4 photo albums holds 24 vertical photos and 24 horizontal photos. Which shows one way to find the total number of photos Marie's photo albums can hold? (Lesson 5-7)

A $24 + 24 + 4$

B $24 \times 24 + 4$

C $24 \times 24 \times 4$

D $24 + 24 \times 4$

22. A seating area has 8 rows, with 15 chairs in each row. If 47 seats are occupied, which of the following shows how to find the number of empty chairs? (Lesson 5-6)

F Add 47 to the product of 15 and 8.

G Add 15 to the product of 47 and 8.

H Subtract 47 from the product of 15 and 8.

J Subtract 15 from the product of 47 and 8.

Spiral Review

23. Basketballs cost $18 each. Find a function rule for the cost of b balls. Then make a function table to find the cost of 2, 3, and 4 basketballs. What is the cost of 5 basketballs? (Lesson 5-6)

24. Measurement For a concert, Elvio must set up the speakers for a sound system around a square room. Speakers are set up in the corners of the room and 10 yards apart. The room is 60 yards long. How many speakers will Elvio set up? (Lesson 5-5)

Identify the multiplication property used to rewrite each expression. (Lesson 3-7)

25. $25 \times 3 \times 14 = 14 \times 25 \times 3$

26. $4 \times (6 \times 2) = (4 \times 6) \times 2$

27. Measurement The table shows the average weight of leopard seals. What is the difference between the weight of an adult leopard seal and a leopard seal pup? (Lesson 2-4)

Leopard Seal Weight (lb)

Adult	992
Pup	66

Replace each ● with <, >, or = to make a true sentence. (Lesson 1-6)

28. 0.41 ● 0.40

29. 3.9 ● 3.7

30. 0.45 ● 0.54

31. 14.3 ● 8.9

Write each fraction as a decimal. (Lesson 1-4)

32. sixty hundredths

33. nine thousandths

34. five tenths

Order Matters
Evaluating Expressions

Get Ready!
Players: 2 players

Get Set!
Label the index cards with the expressions as shown.

You will need: a number cube
10 index cards

$2n$	$5n$
$n + 3$	$10n$
$n + 6$	$n + 12$
$2n + 1$	$3n + 2$
$4n + 5$	$20 - 2n$

Go!
- Shuffle the cards. Then spread the cards facedown on the table.

- Player 1 turns over a card and rolls the number cube.

- Player 1 replaces n on his or her card with the number rolled and then evaluates the expression.

- If player 1 correctly evaluates the expression, he or she receives the value of the expression in points. The player can double their points if they correctly provide a real-world example for their expression.

- If player 1 incorrectly evaluates the expression, the card is returned facedown on the table.

- Player 2 takes a turn.

- Continue taking turns until all the cards have been played correctly. Each player adds up their points. The player with the most points wins.

FOLDABLES Study Organizer GET READY to Study

Be sure the following Big Ideas are written in your Foldable.

What I Know About Expressions | What I Need to Know | What I've Learned

Key Concepts

- A **variable** is a letter or symbol used to represent a number. (p. 193)

- An **expression** is a combination of variables, numbers, and at least one operation. (p. 193)

Evaluating Expressions (p. 193)

- To **evaluate** an expression means to find the value of the expression.

  $x + 4$ if $x = 3$
  ↓
  $3 + 4$ or 7

Functions (p. 210)

- A **function** is a relationship between two variables in which one input quantity is paired with one output quantity.

Order of Operations (p. 218)

- The **order of operations** is a set of rules that tell you which operation to do first when evaluating an expression.

Key Vocabulary

evaluate (p. 193)

expression (p. 193)

function (p. 210)

function table (p. 210)

order of operations (p. 218)

variable (p. 193)

Vocabulary Check

State whether each sentence is *true* or *false*. If *false*, replace the underlined word or number to make a true sentence.

1. A <u>function</u> is a relationship in which one input quantity is paired with exactly one output quantity.

2. An expression is a combination of variables, numbers, and at least <u>two</u> operations.

3. A variable represents the <u>known</u> value.

4. A <u>function table</u> can be used to organize input and output values.

5. To <u>evaluate</u> an expression means to find its value.

6. When evaluating $15 - 3 \times 4$, the order of operations tells you to evaluate $15 - 3$ <u>first</u>.

Lesson-by-Lesson Review

Addition Expressions (pp. 193–195)

5.A.1,
5.A.2

Example 1
Evaluate 8 + *a* if *a* = 4.

$8 + a$ Write the expression.

$8 + 4$ Replace *a* with 4.

12 Add 8 and 4.

Evaluate each expression if *x* = 3 and *y* = 6.

7. $y + 6$ **8.** $4 + x$

9. $18 + x$ **10.** $y + 14$

11. TJ had *m* marbles. Alvin gave him 7 more marbles. Write an expression to find the total number of marbles. If *m* = 45, how many marbles does TJ have now?

Problem-Solving Strategy: Solve a Simpler Problem (pp. 196–197)

5.PS.17

Example 2
There are 16 teams in a basketball tournament. If a team loses, it is out of the tournament. How many games must be played to determine the winner?

Use the *solve a simpler problem* strategy.

Two teams would play one game.

Team 1
Team 2 ⟩ Game 1

Four teams would play three games.

Team 1
Team 2 ⟩ Game 1
Team 3
Team 4 ⟩ Game 2 ⟩ Game 3

The number of games is equal to the number of teams minus 1. So, 16 − 1 is 15. Fifteen games would be played.

Solve. Use the *solve a simpler problem* strategy.

12. Use the table below. Ms. Villialta needs to buy 3 children's tickets and 1 adult ticket. If she has $20, does she have enough money to buy all the tickets? Explain.

MOVIE PRICES
Adult: $6.65
Child: $3.80

13. Measurement Justin and Max working separately can pick a total of 4 baskets of apples in an hour. At this rate, how many baskets of apples can 10 people pick in $\frac{1}{2}$ hour?

CHAPTER 5 · Study Guide and Review

5-3 · **Multiplication Expressions** (pp. 198–201)

5.A.2,
5.A.3

Example 3
Evaluate the expression 4w if w = 7.

$4w$ — Write the expression.

4×7 — Replace w with 7.

28 — Multiply 4 and 7.

Evaluate each expression if $b = 2$ and $c = 5$.

14. $3c$ **15.** $5b$

16. $12b$ **17.** $10c$

18. Measurement A single brick weighs 4 pounds. Mr. Badilla has b bricks. Write an expression to find the total weight of the bricks. If $b = 9$, find the total weight of the bricks.

5-4 · **More Algebraic Expressions** (pp. 202–204)

5.A.2,
5.A.3

Example 4

Measurement The length of the garden is 5 more feet than the width w of a garden. Write an expression.

In this case, the words *more than* mean addition.

w — Start with w.
$w + 5$ — Then add 5.

So, $w + 5$ represents 5 *more than the width*.

Then, find the length of the garden if the width is 3 feet.

$w + 5$ — Write the expression.

$3 + 5$ — Replace w with 3.

8 — Add.

The length of the garden is 8 feet.

Write an expression for each phrase.

19. n less than 8   **20.** multiply 7 by c

21. 12 plus a **22.** h divided by 7

Evaluate each expression if $y = 4$ and $z = 8$.

23. $12 - y$ **24.** $z \div 2$

25. $4y$ **26.** $23 + z$

27. $8y$ **28.** $z \div y$

29. Ms. Washer has 42 bottles of water. Each package contains n bottles of water. Write an expression to find the number of packages if each package contains 6 bottles of water. How many packages of water did Ms. Washer buy?

5-5 Problem-Solving Investigation: Choose a Strategy (pp. 206–207)

5.PS.3

Example 5

Dee is running for president of student council. Last week she gave half of her buttons away. This week she gave 7 buttons away. There are 16 buttons remaining. How many buttons did Dee have to begin with?

Understand

- 16 buttons are left.

- 7 buttons were given away this week.

- Half of the buttons were given away last week.

Plan   To solve this problem, work backward.

Solve   Dee gave out 7 buttons. Add 7 to the remaining buttons.

$$16 + 7 = 23$$

There were 23 buttons before Dee handed out any this week. Last week she handed out half of the original amount. So, multiply 23 by 2.

$$23 \times 2 = 46$$

Dee had 46 buttons at the beginning.

Check   Look back. Solve it by working forward. First, $46 \div 2 = 23$. Then, $23 - 7 = 16$. The answer is correct.

Use any strategy to solve each problem.

30. At a snack bar, Urick was served before Mirna, but after Mallory. Terrel was the first of the four friends to be served. Which friend was served last?

31. Measurement Softball practice begins at 5:00 P.M. It takes Mandy 15 minutes to get ready and 30 minutes to get to the field. What time must Mandy leave to get to softball practice on time?

32. Macario can buy rolls of film in 18 or 24 exposures. He buys 5 rolls of film and gets 108 exposures. How many rolls of each film did Macario buy?

33. Selena has $150 to spend on skateboarding equipment. Does she have enough money to buy all the equipment listed below? Explain.

Gloves	$14.95
Helmet	$34.50
Skateboard	$84.50
Mouth guard	$9.95

34. Sean is thinking of a number. It has 3 ones. It has twice as many hundreds as ones and 3 times as many tens as ones. It has 2 more thousands than hundreds. What is the number?

Chapter 5 Study Guide and Review   **227**

5.A.2,
5.A.3

5-6 Function Tables (pp. 210–213)

Example 6

Sofia jumped rope for 2 minutes less than her sister. Find the function rule. Then make a function table to find the number of minutes Sofia jumped if her sister jumped for 6, 8, and 10 minutes. How many minutes did Sofia jump if her sister jumped for 10 minutes?

Subtract 2 from each input. The function rule is $x - 2$.

Input (x)	$x - 2$	Output
6	6 − 2	4
8	8 − 2	6
10	10 − 2	8

She jumped for 8 minutes.

35. Dino has 3 more pets than his friend. Copy and complete the table.

Input (x)	$x + 3$	Output
5	■	■
3	■	■
1	■	■

36. Paperback books cost $5 each at Book Smart. Find the function rule. Then make a function table to find the cost of buying 3, 4, and 5 books at Book Smart. What is the cost of 5 books?

5-7 Order of Operations (pp. 218–222)

5.N.18,
5.A.2,
5.A.3

Example 7

Find the value of $3 \times (4 + 5)$.

$3 \times (4 + 5)$

3×9 Add 4 and 5.

27   Multiply 3 and 9.

So, $3 \times (4 + 5) = 27$.

Find the value of each expression.

37. $(12 + 6) \times 2$

38. $26 - 3 \times 6$

39. Marisol bought 3 pairs of running shorts that cost $15 each from an internet store. Shipping costs an additional $5. Write an expression to find the total cost. Then evaluate the expression.

40. Lonnie has 3 pencils. He buys b boxes of pencils. Each box contains 12 pencils. Use the expression $12b + 3$ to find how many pencils he has if he buys 4 boxes of pencils.

Evaluate each expression if $x = 7$ and $y = 5$.

1. $x + 7$ **2.** $12 - y$

3. $21 \div x$ **4.** $12y$

5. $x + y$ **6.** xy

7. Della is typing survey questions. She can type 5 words in 10 seconds. At this rate, how many words can she type in 5 minutes? Use the *solve a simpler problem* strategy.

8. Kara made 48 brownies for the bake sale. She packs b brownies in each box. If $b = 12$, write an expression to find how many boxes Kara needs.

Write an expression for each phrase.

9. 4 less than z **10.** h times 5

11. MULTIPLE CHOICE Mr. Diaz is buying gumballs. The table shows the price of different amounts of gumballs.

Number of Gumballs	20	40	60	80	100
Price	$2	$4	$6	$8	$10

What is the relationship between the number of gumballs and the price?

A The price is two times the number of gumballs.

B The price is ten times the number of gumballs.

C The price is half the number of gumballs.

D The number of gumballs is ten times the price.

12. Martin's fish tank has 5 less goldfish than Bill's fish tank. Copy and complete the function table.

Input (x)	x − 5	Output
6	■	■
12	■	■
18	■	■

13. Shante can make 4 keychains in an hour. Find a function rule. Then make a function table to find how many keychains Shante can make in 2, 3, and 4 hours. How many keychains can she make in 5 hours?

Find the value of each expression.

14. $5 \times 6 + 2 \times 3$

15. $26 + 7 \times 2$

16. $(4 + z) - 13$ if $z = 28$

17. MULTIPLE CHOICE A room has 3 rows of desks. Each row has 8 desks. In addition, there are 4 desks at the back of the room. Which expression could be used to find how many desks there are in all?

F $(8 \times 3) + (8 \times 4)$

G $(3 + 8) + 4$

H $(3 \times 8) + (3 \times 4)$

J $(3 \times 8) + 4$

18. WRITING IN ►MATH Write an expression whose value is 5 and contains at least two operations.

◄ NYSMT Practice
Cumulative, Chapters 1–5

PART 1   Multiple Choice

Read each question. Then fill in the correct answer on the answer sheet provided by your teacher or on a sheet of paper.

1. Mrs. Grey bought 5 boxes of fruit snacks. Each box contains 12 packages of fruit snacks. In addition, she had 4 packages of fruit snacks at home. Which expression could be used to find the total number of fruit snack packages Mrs. Grey has?

A $5 \times 12 + 12 \times 4$

B $4 \times 12 + 5$

C $5 \times 4 + 12$

D $5 \times 12 + 4$

2. Marita is 6 years old. Pablo is 2 years older than Marita. Alita is twice as old as Pablo. Which expression could be used to find Alita's age?

F $2 + (6 \times 2)$ **H** $6 + (2 \times 2)$

G $2 \times (6 + 2)$ **J** $6 \times (2 + 2)$

3. The gym teacher bought 8 dodge balls for $32. If each dodge ball costs the same amount, what it the cost of one dodge ball?

A $4

B $6

C $8

D $128

4. There are 120 players at a soccer camp. The players are divided into groups of 15 for warm-ups. How many groups of players are there?

F 6   **H** 10

G 8   **J** 15

5. Maryanne has $10 to spend on art supplies. All prices include tax. Which of the following combinations does she NOT have enough money to buy?

Item	Price
Pencils	$4.79
Paper	$5.38
Paintbrush	$2.35
Markers	$4.21
Clay	$2.15

A paper, paintbrush, and clay

B pencils, paintbrush, and clay

C pencils, markers, and clay

D paper and markers

6. The manager of a park keeps track of the number of people who visit the park each day. The table shows part of these records. Which is *not* a way to find the number of people who visit the park each day?

Day	Visitors
3	300
4	400
5	500
6	600
7	700

F Divide 500 by 5.

G Divide 700 by 7.

H Subtract 500 from 600.

J Subtract 500 from 700.

7. What is the missing value in the table?

Input	2	4	6	8	10
Ouput	0	■	4	6	8

A 2

B 3

C 5

D 7

8. Tyler tells Nate to choose a number, add 5, and multiply by 8. The answer is 64. Which number did Nate choose?

F 6

G 4

H 3

J 2

9. A store parking lot has 30 rows with 15 spaces in each row. In addition, there are 8 spaces near the front of the store. Which expression can be used to find the total number of parking spaces?

A $(30 \times 15) + 8$

B $(30 \times 15) + (30 \times 8)$

C $(30 + 8) \times 15$

D $(30 + 8) \times (8 + 15)$

10. Evaluate the expression $12x$ if $x = 7$.

F 19

G 52

H 74

J 84

PART 2   Short Response

Record your answers on the answer sheet provided by your teacher or on a sheet of paper.

11. Thomas purchased 60 baseball cards this week and 15 baseball cards last week. If there are 5 cards in each pack, write a number sentence to show how many packs of cards he bought.

12. Name two decimals that are larger than 3.1, but smaller than 3.2.

PART 3   Extended Response

Record your answers on the answer sheet provided by your teacher or on a sheet of paper.

13. Explain the steps to find the value of the expression $150 - (10 \times 7)$. What is the value of the expression?

14. Conner is 8 years younger than Eva. Create a function table to show Eva's age when Conner is 8, 12, and 16 years old. Explain how you can use the function table to find Eva's age when Conner is 30 years old.

NEED EXTRA HELP?														
If You Missed Question...	1	2	3	4	5	6	7	8	9	10	11	12	13	14
Go to Lesson...	5-7	5-7	4-3	4-4	2-6	5-5	5-6	5-5	5-7	5-3	5-7	1-6	5-7	5-6
NYS Core Curriculum	5.N.18	5.A.3	5.N.17	5.N.17	5.N.23	5.PS.3	5.A.3	5.PS.3	5.A.3	5.A.3	5.R.9	5.A.3	5.A.3	5.A.3

Use Equations and Function Tables

BIG Idea **What is an equation?**

The number sentence $7x = 35$ is an example of an equation. An **equation** is a number sentence that contains an equals sign (=), showing that two expressions are equal.

Example Each day for 7 days, a sea otter ate the same number of pounds of food. The otter ate 35 pounds of food in all.

$$7x = 35$$

7 days → $7x = 35$ ← 35 pounds in all

x pounds each day

What will I learn in this chapter?

- Write and solve equations for problem situations.
- Name and locate points on a coordinate grid.
- Use function tables.
- Solve problems by using the *make a table* strategy.

Key Vocabulary

equation

solve

coordinate grid

ordered pair

graph

NY Math Online > **Student Study Tools** at macmillanmh.com

FOLDABLES®
Study Organizer

Make this Foldable to help you organize information about equations and functions. Begin with a sheet of $8\frac{1}{2}"$ by $11"$ paper.

① **Fold** the short sides toward the middle.

② **Fold** the top to the bottom.

③ **Open.** Cut along the second fold to make four tabs.

④ **Label** each of the tabs as shown.

+Equations   −Equations

×Equations   Functions/Equations/Ordered Pairs

Chapter 6 Use Equations and Function Tables   **233**

ARE YOU READY for Chapter 6?

You have two ways to check prerequisite skills for this chapter.

Option 2

NY Math Online Take the Chapter Readiness Quiz at macmillanmh.com.

Option 1

Complete the Quick Check below.

QUICK Check

Find the missing number in each fact family. (Prior Grade)

1. $5 + \blacksquare = 7$

2. $\blacksquare + 6 = 9$

3. $\blacksquare + 3 = 15$

4. $9 + \blacksquare = 15$

5. $6 + \blacksquare = 14$

6. $\blacksquare + 5 = 7$

7. $4 \times \blacksquare = 28$

8. $\blacksquare \times 9 = 81$

9. $\blacksquare \times 3 = 30$

10. $7 \times \blacksquare = 56$

11. $8 \times \blacksquare = 48$

12. $\blacksquare \times 5 = 30$

13. Anderson added 4 more seashells to his collection. Now he has 16 seashells. How many seashells did he have at first?

Write an expression for each situation. (Lessons 5-1 and 5-3)

14. 7 plus d

15. 5 less than t

16. the sum of 14 and s

17. the product of y and 7

18. 6 less than x

19. f increased by 2

20. the product of 8 and n

21. the sum of 3 and z

22. Hugo has $4 less than Eloy. If m stands for the amount of money Eloy has, write an expression to show how much money Hugo has. If m is $16, how much money does Hugo have?

Model Addition Equations

An **equation** is a number sentence that contains an equals sign, (=), showing that two expressions are equal. To **solve** an equation means to find the value of the variable so the sentence is true. You can use diagrams like cups and counters to represent problem situations.

ACTIVITY

Jack had some goldfish, and then he bought 2 more. Now he has 8 goldfish. Solve the equation $x + 2 = 8$ to find how many goldfish Jack had at first.

Step 1 **Model the equation.**

Place the cup on the left side to show x and two counters to show 2. Place 8 counters on the right side to show 8.

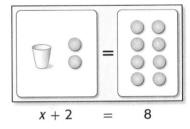

$$x + 2 \quad = \quad 8$$

Step 2 **Solve the equation.**

THINK How many counters need to be in the cup so there is an equal number of counters on each side of the mat?

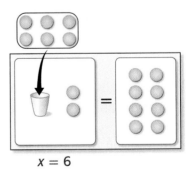

$$x = 6$$

When you found the number of counters in the cup, you found the solution of the equation. A **solution** is the value of the variable that makes the sentence true.

So, $x = 6$.

Jack had 6 goldfish at first.

Explore Algebra Activity for 6-1: Model Addition Equations 235

Think About It

1. Refer to the opening Activity. What does x represent?

2. How did you know that 6 was the solution to the equation?

3. Describe how you would model $x + 4 = 6$.

4. What is the value of x so that $x + 4 = 6$ is true?

✓ CHECK What You Know

Write an equation for each model. Then solve.

5.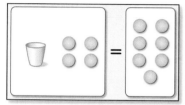

6.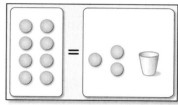

Solve each equation using cups, counters, and an algebra mat.

7. Calvin added 3 model cars to his collection. Now he has 12 model cars. Use the equation $x + 3 = 12$ to find how many model cars he started with.

8. Mrs. Jones planted 5 rose bushes. Then she planted some more rose bushes. If she planted a total of 11 rose bushes, how many more rose bushes did Mrs. Jones plant? Use the equation $5 + x = 11$.

Write an equation for each problem situation. Then solve each equation using cups, counters, and an algebra mat.

9. Melissa had x dollars in her wallet. Her mother gave her $5 more. Melissa now has $20. How much money did Melissa start with?

10. A bakery sold a total of 14 pies on Wednesday and Thursday. If the bakery sold 6 pies on Wednesday, how many pies did the bakery sell on Thursday?

11. **WRITING IN ▶MATH** Explain why it does not matter on which side of the equals sign the variable is located.

Addition and Subtraction Equations

MAIN IDEA

I will write and solve addition and subtraction equations.

NYS Core Curriculum

5.A.4 Solve simple one-step equations using basic whole-number facts *Also addresses 5.A.5.*

New Vocabulary

defining the variable

NY Math Online

macmillanmh.com

• Extra Examples
• Personal Tutor
• Self-Check Quiz

> ### GET READY to Learn
>
> On Monday and Tuesday, Audrey walked a total of 7 blocks. If she walked 3 blocks on Tuesday, how many blocks did she walk on Monday?
>
>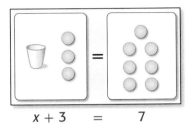
>
> $x + 3 = 7$

The equation $x + 3 = 7$ represents this situation. You can solve this equation using mental math.

EXAMPLE   Addition Equations

① **Solve $x + 3 = 7$.**

$x + 3 = 7$

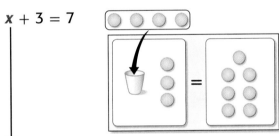

$4 + 3 = 7$ You know that 4 plus 3 is equal to 7.

So, $x = 4$. Audrey walked 4 blocks on Monday.

You can also find solutions using mental math.

EXAMPLE   Subtraction Equations

② **Solve $y - 6 = 8$.**

$y - 6 = 8$ Write the equation.

THINK What number minus 6 is equal to 8?

$14 - 6 = 8$ You know that 14 minus 6 is 8.

So, $y = 14$. The solution is 14.

Lesson 6-1 Addition and Subtraction Equations 237

Choosing a variable to represent an unknown value is called **defining the variable**.

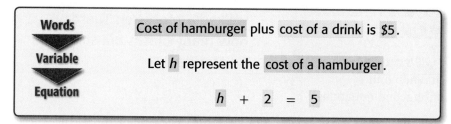

Real-World EXAMPLE Write and Solve Equations

3 FOOD At the school festival, the total cost of a hamburger and a soft drink is $5. If the drink costs $2, what is the cost of the hamburger?

Words	Cost of hamburger plus cost of a drink is $5.
Variable	Let h represent the cost of a hamburger.
Equation	$h + 2 = 5$

Remember

You can use the first letter of the word you are defining as a variable. For example: h is for the cost of the hamburger.

$h + 2 = 5$ Write the equation.

THINK What number plus 2 is equal to 5?

$3 + 2 = 5$ Replace h with 3 to make the equation true.

So, $h = 3$. The cost of the hamburger is $3.

To check your solution, replace the variable with 3. Does this make the right side of the equation equal to the left side?

Check $h + 2 = 5$ Write the equation.

$3 + 2 \overset{?}{=} 5$ Replace h with 3.

$5 = 5$ ✓   Simplify. The solution is correct.

CHECK What You Know

Solve each equation. Check your solution. See Examples 1, 2 (p. 237)

1. $h + 4 = 8$ **2.** $2 + x = 9$ **3.** $p - 7 = 1$ **4.** $r - 5 = 4$

5. $3 + g = 10$ **6.** $b + 6 = 12$ **7.** $x - 9 = 8$ **8.** $s - 8 = 7$

9. Monya led her softball team in stolen bases. At Wednesday's game, she stole 2 bases giving her a total of 8 stolen bases. Write and solve an equation to find how many stolen bases Monya had before Wednesday's game. See Example 3 (p. 238)

10. **Talk About It** Explain what it means to solve an equation.

Solve each equation. Check your solution. See Examples 1, 2 (p. 237)

11. $x + 1 = 5$　　**12.** $3 + a = 6$　　**13.** $y - 8 = 1$　　**14.** $n - 4 = 2$

15. $b - 13 = 1$　　**16.** $t - 12 = 4$　　**17.** $z + 2 = 11$　　**18.** $5 + k = 13$

19. $d - 2 = 18$　　**20.** $7 + x = 16$　　**21.** $c + 13 = 19$　　**22.** $m - 5 = 15$

Write an equation and then solve. Check your solution. See Example 3 (p. 238)

23. A box contained some snack bars. Tyrese ate 4 snack bars. Now there are 8 snack bars left. How many snack bars were there at the beginning?

24. Leroy bought 2 comic books. Now he has 11 comic books in all. How many comic books did Leroy start with?

25. Mrs. Oxley had some glue sticks. She used 8 glue sticks on an art project. Now she has 6 glue sticks left. How many glue sticks did she have at first?

26. In one season, the girl's volleyball team won 16 games. If they played a total of 30 games that season, how many games did they lose?

27. Eugene's team scored 34 points in a game. He scored 12 of the points. How many points did the rest of the team score?

H.O.T. Problems

28. **REASONING** If $x + 3 = 5$ and $5 = y + 2$, then is it true that $x + 3 = y + 2$? Explain.

29. **FIND THE ERROR** Daniel and Juliana each solved the equation $a - 5 = 10$. Who is correct? Explain your answer.

Daniel
$a = 5$

Juliana
$a = 15$

30. **WRITING IN ►MATH** Explain why the equation $n + 7 = 15$ has the same solution as $15 - n = 7$.

Extend

Algebra Activity for 6-1
Inequalities

Recall that an *inequality* is a mathematical sentence stating that two quantities are *not* equal. The expression $x < 2$ means that the value of x *is less than* 2. To solve an inequality, find the values of the variables so the inequality is true.

MAIN IDEA

Use models to represent and solve simple addition and subtraction inequalities.

NYS Core Curriculum

5.PS.13 Model problems with pictures/diagrams or **physical objects**

5.A.4 Solve simple one-step equations using basic whole-number facts

ACTIVITIES Solve Inequalities

1 **Solve $x < 2$ using a model.**

The scale below contains a cup and two positive counters. Note that the left side weighs *less than* the right side. Copy and complete the table.

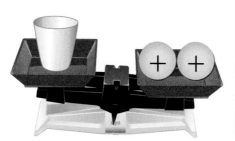

$x < 2$

x	Is $x < 2$?	True or False
0	$0 \overset{?}{<} 2$	true
1	$1 \overset{?}{<} 2$	
2	$2 \overset{?}{<} 2$	
3	$3 \overset{?}{<} 2$	
4	$4 \overset{?}{<} 2$	

So, the solution of $x < 2$ is 0 or 1.

2 **Solve $x + 1 < 3$ using a model.**

Copy and complete the table.

$x + 1 < 3$

x	Is $x+1 < 3$?	True or False
0	$0+1 \overset{?}{<} 3$	true
1	$1+1 \overset{?}{<} 3$	
2	$2+1 \overset{?}{<} 3$	
3	$3+1 \overset{?}{<} 3$	
4	$4+1 \overset{?}{<} 3$	

The solution does not change when one counter is added to each side. Possible values of x include 0 and 1 but do not include 2, 3, or 4. So, the solution of the inequality $x + 1 < 3$ is any number less than 2. This is written $x < 2$.

You can also solve inequalities using models or tables.

ACTIVITY   Solve an Addition Inequality

Remember

Check your solution by substituting any number greater than 3. For example, substitute 6.

$6 + 2 > 5 = 8 > 5.$

This is true.

③ Solve $x + 2 > 5$ using mental math.

The model shows one cup and two positive counters on the left side and five positive counters on the right side.

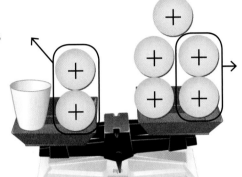

Remove two positive counters from each side of the scale. There are three positive counters remaining on the right scale.

The solution is any number greater than 3. So, $x > 3$.

ACTIVITY   Solve a Subtraction Inequality

④ Solve $x - 3 < 7$ using a table.

Check possible values of x. The table suggests that the solution is any number less than 10.

So, $x < 10$.

x	Is $x - 3 \overset{?}{<} 7$?	True or False
8	$8 - 3 \overset{?}{<} 7$	true
9	$9 - 3 \overset{?}{<} 7$	
10	$10 - 3 \overset{?}{<} 7$	
11	$11 - 3 \overset{?}{<} 7$	

Check the solution with other values of x.

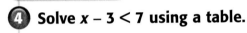
CHECK What You Know

Solve each inequality by using a model or mental math.

1. $x + 1 < 6$ **2.** $x - 3 > 1$ **3.** $x + 4 > 8$

4. Write two different inequalities, one involving addition and one involving subtraction, both with the solution $x < 3$.

5. **WRITING IN ►MATH** Explain how you could solve the inequality $x + 13 < 18$.

Extend Algebra Activity for 6-1: Addition and Subtraction Inequalities   **241**

Algebra Activity for 6-2
Model Multiplication Equations

You can use cups and counters to represent problem situations involving multiplication.

ACTIVITY

Two friends split the cost of a pizza evenly. If the cost of the pizza is $8, how much did each friend spend? Solve the equation $2x = 8$ to find how much each friend spent.

Step 1 Model the equation.

Place 2 cups on the left side to show $2x$. Place 8 counters on the right side to show 8.

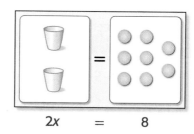

$$2x \quad = \quad 8$$

Step 2 Solve the equation.

THINK How many counters need to be in each cup so there is an equal number of counters in each cup and an equal number of counters on each side of the mat?

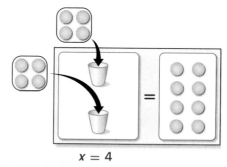

$$x = 4$$

So, $x = 4$. Each friend paid $4.

Check $2x = 8$ Write the equation.

      $2 \cdot 4 \stackrel{?}{=} 8$ Replace x with 4.

        $8 = 8$ ✓   Simplify.

Think About It

1. Describe how you would model $8x = 16$ using cups, counters, and an algebra mat.

2. What is the value of x so that $8x = 16$ is true?

3. Refer to Exercise 2. How would you check your solution?

CHECK What You Know

Write an equation for each model and then solve. Check your solution.

4.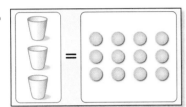

5.

Solve each equation using cups, counters, and an algebra mat. Check your solution.

6. Jerome bought 3 paperback books from the local bookstore. The total cost of the books was $15. Each book costs the same amount. Use the equation $3c = 15$ to find the cost of one book.

7. Josephina bought 2 boxes of pencils. Each box contained the same amount of pencils. If she had a total of 14 pencils, how many were in one box? Use the equation $2n = 14$.

Write an equation and then solve each equation using cups, counters, and an algebra mat. Check your solution.

8. Mr. Tyznik wants to walk 16 miles in the next 4 days. If he walks the same amount each day, how many miles will he walk each day?

9. Matt and two friends bought tickets to a hockey game. The total cost of the tickets was $24. If each ticket costs the same amount, what was the cost of one ticket?

10. **WRITING IN ►MATH** Explain why you place an equal number of counters in each cup when you solve a multiplication equation using cups, counters, and an algebra mat.

Multiplication Equations

Carlota bought 2 tickets to the school play for a total of $6. If each ticket costs the same amount, what is the cost of one ticket to the school play?

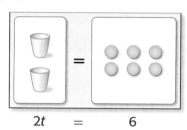

$$2t \quad = \quad 6$$

MAIN IDEA

I will write and solve multiplication equations.

NYS Core Curriculum

5.A.4 Solve simple one-step equations using basic whole-number facts

5.A.5 Solve and explain simple one-step equations using inverse operations involving whole numbers

NY Math Online

macmillanmh.com
• Extra Examples
• Personal Tutor
• Self-Check Quiz

To find the cost of one ticket to the school play, solve the multiplication equation $2t = 6$.

EXAMPLES Multiplication Equations

① **Solve $2t = 6$.**

$$2t = 6$$

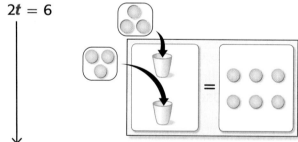

$2 \times \mathbf{3} = 6$ You know that 2 times 3 is equal to 6.

So, $t = 3$. One ticket to the play costs $3.

② **Solve $20 = 5z$.**

$20 = 5z$ Write the equation.

THINK What number times 5 is equal to 20?

$20 = 5 \times \mathbf{4}$ You know that 20 is equal to 5 times 4.

So, $z = 4$.

Real-World EXAMPLE   Write and Solve Equations

③ **FOOTBALL** In one game, the Carolina Panthers scored **3 times as many** points as their opponent. If the Panthers scored **21 points**, **how many points did their opponent score**?

Remember

The word *times* means multiplication.

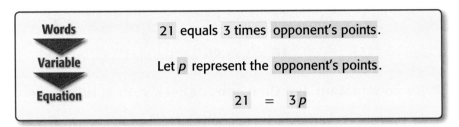

Words	21 equals 3 times opponent's points.
Variable	Let p represent the opponent's points.
Equation	$21 = 3p$

$21 = 3p$ Write the equation.

THINK 21 is equal to 3 times what number?

$3 \times 7 = 21$ Replace p with 7.

So, $p = 7$.

The opponent scored 7 points.

To check your solution, replace the variable with 7.

Check: $3p = 21$ Write the equation.

$3 \times 7 \stackrel{?}{=} 21$ Replace p with 7.

$21 = 21$ ✓   Simplify. The solution is correct.

CHECK What You Know

Solve each equation. Check your solution. See Examples 1, 2 (p. 244)

1. $2b = 8$ **2.** $18 = 3t$ **3.** $21 = 7x$ **4.** $6x = 24$

Write an equation and then solve. Check your solution. See Example 3 (p. 244)

5. Irena is twice as old as Yoko. If Irena is 20, how old is Yoko?

6. Five friends earned $30 for doing yard work. If the friends split the money evenly, how much money would each friend receive?

7. To paint a classroom, you need 3 gallons of paint. If you have 27 gallons of paint, how many classrooms can you paint if they are all identical?

8. **Talk About It** Describe how to find the solution of $8x = 72$.

Solve each equation. Check your solution. See Examples 1, 2 (p. 244)

9. $4b = 16$ **10.** $18 = 2d$ **11.** $30 = 5h$ **12.** $3z = 27$

13. $7r = 49$ **14.** $8c = 64$ **15.** $55 = 5p$ **16.** $60 = 10g$

17. $33 = 11t$ **18.** $3y = 45$ **19.** $12s = 84$ **20.** $72 = 6x$

Write an equation and then solve. Check your solution. See Example 3 (p. 245)

21. Seven fifth-grade students spent a total of 35 hours cleaning a park. Each student spent an equal amount of time. Find how many hours each student spent cleaning the park.

22. A Girl Scout troop collected 54 cans for the food drive. There are 6 members in the troop, and each member collected the same number of cans. How many cans did each member collect?

For Exercises 23 and 24, use the graphic that shows the number of bottles of water for two different sized boxes.

23. Bert and 3 friends evenly divide a large box of water bottles. How many bottles of water does each friend receive?

24. A coach buys one small and one large box of bottled water. She divides the bottles evenly among 8 players. How many bottles will each player receive?

Box Size	Number of Bottles of Water
Small	32
Large	64

 New York Data File

The Staten Island Zoo is located in Staten Island, New York. The zoo features a large reptile collection and a children's center where kids can feed the animals.

Write an equation. Then solve.

25. Mr. Patel bought 2 adult tickets and y youth tickets. If the total cost of the tickets was $30, how many youth tickets did Mr. Patel buy?

26. The McCauley family bought 4 adult tickets, 3 youth tickets, and s senior tickets. The cost of all the tickets was $55. How many senior tickets did the family buy?

Admission Prices	
Ticket	Price ($)
Adult	7
Senior (60+)	5
Youth (3–14)	4

Source: *Staten Island Zoo*

H.O.T. Problems

27. OPEN ENDED Write two different multiplication equations that each have a solution of 9.

28. WHICH ONE DOESN'T BELONG? Identify which equation doesn't belong with the other three. Explain your reasoning.

| $35 - n = 28$ | $21 = 3n$ | $n + 49 = 56$ | $7n = 63$ |

29. **WRITING IN** ►**MATH** Write a real-world problem that can be solved using a multiplication equation.

NYSMT Practice   5.A.4

30. Felipa is twice as old as Juan. If Felipa is 12 years old, which equation could be used to find a, Juan's age? (Lesson 6–2)

A $12 \times 2 = a$

B $12a = 2$

C $2 \times a = 12$

D $a + 2 = 12$

31. A full basket contained 27 apples. There are 9 apples left in the basket now. Which equation could be used to find how many apples were taken from the basket? (Lesson 6–1)

F $27 + x = 9$

G $27 - x = 9$

H $27 + 9 = x$

J $x - 9 = 21$

Spiral Review

Algebra Solve each equation. Check your solution. (Lesson 6-1)

32. $z + 4 = 20$ **33.** $y - 7 = 9$ **34.** $7 + q = 11$ **35.** $w - 5 = 8$

Algebra Evaluate each expression. (Lesson 5–7)

36. $10 - 2 \times 4$ **37.** $10 \times 3 - 2 \times 5$ **38.** $3 + 6 \times 9$

39. The soccer team has $150 to spend on new soccer balls. Soccer balls cost $29 each. How many soccer balls can the team buy? Tell how you interpret the remainder. (Lesson 4–6)

40. The sum of two numbers is 28. Their product is 195. What are the two numbers? Use the *guess and check* strategy to solve. (Lesson 1–8)

Write each fraction as a decimal. (Lesson 1–4)

41. $\dfrac{7}{10}$ **42.** $\dfrac{90}{100}$ **43.** $\dfrac{53}{100}$ **44.** $\dfrac{23}{1,000}$

Problem-Solving Strategy

MAIN IDEA I will solve problems by making a table.

 **NYSCC** **5.CM.4 Share organized mathematical ideas through the manipulation of** objects, numerical tables, drawings, pictures, charts, graphs, **tables,** diagrams, models, and symbols in written and verbal form

Julio is saving money to buy a new camping tent. Each week he doubles the amount he saved the previous week. If he saves $1 the first week, how much money will Julio save in 7 weeks?

Understand	**What facts do you know?**
	• Each week he doubles the amount he saved the previous week.
	• The first week he saved $1.
	What do you need to find?
	• How much money he will have saved in 7 weeks.
Plan	You can make a table to solve the problem.
Solve	Draw a table with two rows as shown. In the first row, list each week. Then complete the table by doubling the amount he saved the previous week.

Week	1	2	3	4	5	6	7
Amount Saved	$1	$2	$4	$8	$16	$32	$64

×2 ×2 ×2 ×2 ×2 ×2

Next, add the amount of money he saved each week.
$1 + $2 + $4 + $8 + $16 + $32 + $64 = $127
So, Julio will save $127 in 7 weeks.

Check	Look back. Check to see if the amount saved doubled each week. Use estimation to check for reasonableness. Round each two-digit number to the nearest $10.

$1 + $2 + $4 + $8 + $20 + $30 + $60 = $125 ✓

ANALYZE the Strategy

Refer to the problem on the previous page.

1. Explain why you multiplied each week's savings by 2 to solve the problem.

2. Explain why making a table made this problem easier to solve.

3. Find the amount of money Julio will save in 9 weeks.

4. Suppose Julio tripled the amount of money he saved each week. How many weeks will it take him to save $120?

PRACTICE the Strategy

NYSCC • NYSMT
Extra Practice, p. R16

Solve. Use the *make a table* strategy.

5. **Algebra** Betsy is saving to buy a new sound system. She saves $1 the first week, $3 the second week, $9 the third week, and so on. How much money will she save in 5 weeks?

6. Kendall is planning to buy the laptop shown below. Each month she doubles the amount she saved the previous month. If she saves $20 the first month, in how many months will Kendall have enough money to buy the laptop?

$1,200

7. **Measurement** Muna is 3 years old. Her mother is 35 years old. How old will Muna be when her mother is exactly five times as old as she is?

8. Devon bought packages of pencils for $3 each. Each package of pencils contains 12 pencils. If he spent $15 on pencils, how many pencils did he buy?

9. **Measurement** A recipe for cupcakes calls for 3 cups of flour for every 2 cups of sugar. How many cups of sugar are needed for 18 cups of flour?

10. Mrs. Piant's yearly salary is $42,000 and increases $2,000 per year. Mr. Piant's yearly salary is $37,000 and increases $3,000 per year. In how many years will Mr. and Mrs. Piant make the same salary?

11. **Geometry** Mr. Ortega is making a model of a staircase he is going to build. Use the picture below to find how many blocks Mr. Ortega will need if the staircase has 12 steps.

12. **WRITING IN MATH** Write a real-world problem that you can solve using the *make a table* strategy. Explain why making a table is the best strategy to use when solving your problem.

Geometry: Ordered Pairs

GET READY to Learn

The map at the right shows Amy's neighborhood. When she walks home from school, she walks right to 3 and up to 5. How could she walk from school to the library? How could she walk to the park?

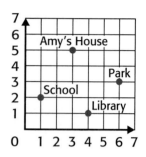

MAIN IDEA

I will name points on a coordinate grid.

NYS Core Curriculum

5.G.12 Identify and plot points in the first quadrant
Also addresses 5.G.13.

New Vocabulary

coordinate grid
origin
ordered pair
***x*-coordinate**
***y*-coordinate**

NY Math Online

macmillanmh.com

• Extra Examples
• Personal Tutor
• Self-Check Quiz

In mathematics, points are located on a coordinate grid.

A **coordinate grid** is formed when two number lines intersect. One number line has numbers along the horizontal axis (across) and the other has numbers along the vertical axis (up). The point where the two axes meet is the **origin**.

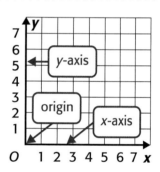

An **ordered pair** is a pair of numbers that is used to name a point on the coordinate grid.

The first number is the ***x*-coordinate** and corresponds to a number on the *x*-axis.

(3, 2)

The second number is the ***y*-coordinate** and corresponds to a number on the *y*-axis.

EXAMPLE   Name Points Using Ordered Pairs

1 Name the ordered pair for point *A*.

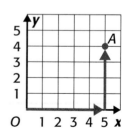

Step 1 Start at the origin (0, 0). Move right along the *x*-axis until you are under point *A*. The *x*-coordinate of the ordered pair is 5.

Step 2 Move up until you reach point *A*. The *y*-coordinate is 4.

So, point *A* is named by the ordered pair (5, 4).

Name Points Using Ordered Pairs

2 **Name the point for the ordered pair (2, 3).**

Vocabulary Link
Origin
Everyday Use the beginning

Step 1 Start at the origin (0, 0). Move right along the *x*-axis until you reach 2, the *x*-coordinate.

Step 2 Move up until you reach 3, the *y*-coordinate.

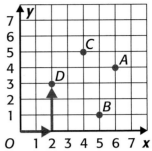

So, point *D* is named by (2, 3).

Real-World EXAMPLE

3 **SCIENCE** An archaeologist recorded the location of objects she found at a dig. Use the coordinate grid to name the location of the necklace.

Step 1 Start at the origin (0, 0). Move right along the *x*-axis until you are under the necklace. The *x*-coordinate is 3.

Step 2 Move up until you reach the necklace. The *y*-coordinate is 5.

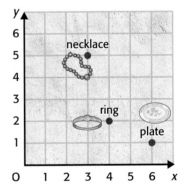

So, the necklace is located at (3, 5).

CHECK What You Know

Locate and name the ordered pair. See Example 1 (p. 250)

1. *A*   **2.** *C*   **3.** *D*

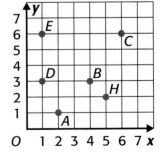

Locate and name the point. See Example 2 (p. 251)

4. (4, 3)   **5.** (1, 6)   **6.** (5, 2)

7. Refer to Example 3. Write the ordered pair that names the ring on the grid.

8. **Talk About It** Are the points at (3, 8) and (8, 3) in the same location? Explain your reasoning.

Locate and name the ordered pair. See Example 1 (p. 250)

9. *A* **10.** *J* **11.** *Q*

12. *R* **13.** *E* **14.** *N*

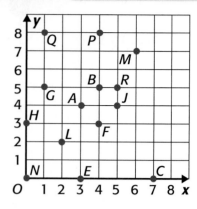

Locate and name the point. See Example 2 (p. 251)

15. (2, 2) **16.** (1, 5) **17.** (4, 8)

18. (0, 3) **19.** (6, 7) **20.** (7, 0)

For Exercises 21–24, use the map of the playground at the right. See Example 3 (p. 251)

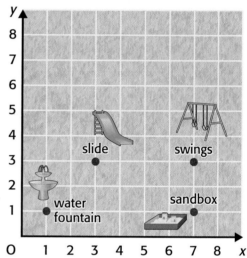

21. What is located at (7, 3)?

22. Write the ordered pair for the sandbox.

23. Suppose the *x*-coordinate of the water fountain was moved to the right 1 unit. What would be the new ordered pair of the water fountain?

24. If the *y*-coordinate of the slide was moved up 2 units, what would be the ordered pair of the slide?

25. Cam identified a point that was 4 units above the origin and 8 units to the right of the origin. What was the ordered pair?

26. Suppose point (6, 5) was moved 3 units to the left and moved 2 units down. Write the new ordered pair.

H.O.T. Problems

27. OPEN ENDED Create a map of a zoo using a coordinate grid. Locate five animals on the map. Include the ordered pairs for the location of the five animals.

28. CHALLENGE Name the ordered pair whose *x*-coordinate and *y*-coordinate are each located on an axis.

29. CHALLENGE Give the coordinates of the point located halfway between (3, 3) and (3, 4).

30. WRITING IN ►MATH Describe the steps to locate point (7, 4).

Solve each equation. Check your solution. (Lesson 6-1)

1. $s + 16 = 30$ **2.** $m - 6 = 51$

3. A bike path is a certain number of miles. Jody has already biked 16 miles and has 9 miles left to bike. How many miles is the bike trail? (Lesson 6-1)

4. MULTIPLE CHOICE Carrie's softball team scored 9 runs. Carrie scored 5 of the runs. Which equation could you use to find how many runs the rest of the team scored? (Lesson 6-1)

A $9 = x + 5$ **C** $9 - x = 14$

B $14 = x + 5$ **D** $x - 5 = 14$

Solve each equation. Check your solution. (Lesson 6-2)

5. $72 = 8y$ **6.** $5g = 40$

7. Measurement It took Mrs. Cook 4 hours to make 60 bookmarks. She made an equal amount of bookmarks each hour. Write and solve an equation to find how many bookmarks she made each hour. (Lesson 6-2)

8. MULTIPLE CHOICE Xavier wants to buy a new video game that costs $45. He saves $5 each week. Which equation shows how many weeks it will take until he has enough money for the game? (Lesson 6-2)

F $w = 45 \times 5$ **H** $w = 9 \times 5$

G $45 = w \div 5$ **J** $5w = 45$

9. A gardener is planting flowers in rows. The first row has 28 flowers. Each additional row has 6 fewer flowers than the previous row. If there is a total of 5 rows in the garden, how many flowers will the gardener have to plant? Solve. Use the *make a table* strategy. (Lesson 6-3)

10. Measurement Rakim is training for a bike marathon. He bikes 7.25 miles on the first day. He plans to bike 2.5 more miles each day than he did on the previous day. How many total miles will Rakim have biked after 5 days? Solve. Use the *make a table* strategy. (Lesson 6-3)

For Exercises 11–16, use the map shown.

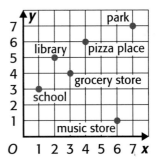

Locate and name the ordered pair for each place on the map. (Lesson 6-4)

11. park   **12.** school   **13.** library

Locate and name the place on the map for each ordered pair. (Lesson 6-4)

14. (4, 6)   **15.** (6, 1)   **16.** (3, 4)

17. **WRITING IN** ►**MATH** Explain what it means to *define a variable*.

Algebra and Geometry: Graph Functions

GET READY to Learn

Bailey was making a treasure map for a game he was playing with his friend. From the starting point, he wanted his treasure to be buried 3 places to the right and up 6 units. He marked the spot with an X.

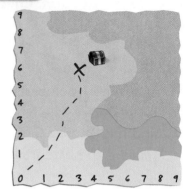

MAIN IDEA

I will graph points on a coordinate grid.

NYS Core Curriculum

5.G.12 Identify and plot points in the first quadrant
Also addresses 5.G.13.

New Vocabulary

graph

NY Math Online

macmillanmh.com

• Extra Examples
• Personal Tutor
• Self-Check Quiz

To **graph** a point in mathematics means to place a dot at the point named by an ordered pair.

EXAMPLES Graphing Ordered Pairs

① **Graph and label point *X*(3, 6) on the coordinate grid.**

   Step 1 Start at the origin (0, 0).

   Step 2 Move 3 units to the right on the *x*-axis.

   Step 3 Then move up 6 units to locate the point.

   Step 4 Draw a dot and label the point *X*.

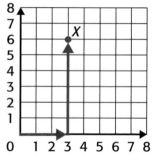

② **Graph and label point *M*(2, 4) on the coordinate grid.**

   Step 1 Start at the origin (0, 0).

   Step 2 Move 2 units to the right on the *x*-axis.

   Step 3 Then move up 4 units to locate the point.

   Step 4 Draw a dot and label the point *M*.

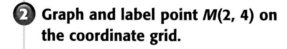

Review Vocabulary

input the value you put into a function (Lesson 5–6)

output the resulting value of a function (Lesson 5–6)

In Chapter 5, you learned about functions. The input and output values from a function table can be written as ordered pairs.

Real-World EXAMPLE Graphing Functions

3 **BASKETBALL** **For every shot a basketball player makes from outside the 3-point line, the player scores 3 points. Given the function rule 3n, find the total number of points for 1, 2, 3, and 4 of these shots. Make a function table and then graph the ordered pairs.**

The function rule is $3n$. Multiply the number of 3-point shots made by 3 to find the total points.

3-Point Shots Made (n)	Total Points (3n)	Ordered Pairs
1	3	(1, 3)
2	6	(2, 6)
3	9	(3, 9)
4	12	(4, 12)

Now graph the ordered pairs.

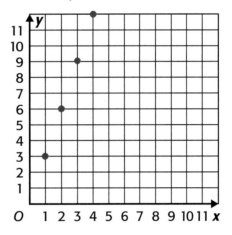

CHECK What You Know

Graph and label each point on a coordinate grid.

See Examples 1, 2 (p. 254)

1. $Z(2, 2)$

2. $D(4, 0)$

3. $Y(5, 6)$

4. $W(7, 6)$

5. $C(0, 4)$

6. $B(3, 7)$

7. A bag of birdseed weighs 5 pounds. Given the function rule $5b$, find the total weight for 0, 1, 2, and 3 bags of birdseed. Make a function table and then graph the ordered pairs. See Example 3 (p. 255)

8. **Talk About It** Explain how you would graph the point $S(10, 7)$.

Lesson 6-5 Algebra and Geometry: Graph Functions **255**

Graph and label each point on a coordinate grid. See Examples 1, 2 (p. 254)

9. J(1, 1) **10.** K(7, 0) **11.** L(2, 5) **12.** M(0, 6)

13. N(4, 1) **14.** P(8, 2) **15.** Q(3, 4) **16.** R(6, 3)

For Exercises 17–20, make a function table and then graph the ordered pairs on a coordinate grid. See Example 3 (p. 255)

17. Miss Henderson has a coupon for $2 off any item at Sport Inc. Find the new cost of items if they originally cost $4, $6, $8, and $10, given the function rule $c - 2$.

18. Measurement Amado's book bag weighs 1 pound. Each book that he puts in his book bag weighs 3 pounds. Given the function rule $3n + 1$, find the total weight of the book bag if Amado has 0, 1, 2, and 3 books in his book bag.

19. Reiko works in an electronics store. Every day he earns a flat rate of $10 plus $5 per hour. Given the function rule $5h + 10$, find how much Reiko would earn if he worked 2, 3, 4, and 5 hours.

20. Gaspar and Kendra agreed to split the cost of a DVD. Given the function rule $\frac{c}{2}$, find how much each friend would pay if the DVD cost $8, $10, $12, and $14.

Real-World PROBLEM SOLVING

Science The growth rate of a baby blue whale is one of the fastest in the animal kingdom. The table shows the age in months and length in feet of a baby blue whale.

21. Use the table to write the ordered pairs.

22. Graph the ordered pairs.

23. What is the length of a baby blue whale when it is 2 months old?

24. How old is a baby blue whale that is 37 feet long?

25. Estimate the length of a baby blue whale that is $2\frac{1}{2}$ months old.

Growth of Blue Whale	
Age (months)	Length (ft)
0	23
1	27
2	31
3	35
4	39

H.O.T. Problems

26. OPEN ENDED Write an ordered pair for a point that would be graphed on the *y*-axis.

27. **WRITING IN ▸MATH** Write a real-world problem about a situation that would be represented by the function 15*x*.

28. Ashley made the grid below to show the location of objects in her backyard. Which ordered pair represents the point on the grid labeled tree house? (Lesson 6–4)

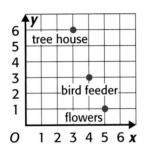

    A (5, 1)   **C** (3, 6)

    B (6, 3)   **D** (4, 3)

29. Which of the following points is located at (4, 0)? (Lesson 6-5)

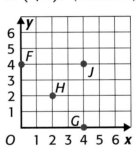

    F Point *F*

    G Point *G*

    H Point *H*

    J Point *J*

Spiral Review

Algebra Solve each equation. Check your solution. (Lesson 6-4)

30. $3y = 33$ **31.** $9h = 45$ **32.** $75 = 5g$ **33.** $84 = 7w$

34. Jacque is 12 years old. His father is 44 years old. How old will Jacque be when his father is exactly three times as old as he is? Use the *make a table* strategy. (Lesson 6-3)

35. At a bus stop, 7 students got on the bus so that there were a total of 23 students on the bus. Write and solve an equation to find how many students were already on the bus. (Lesson 6-1)

Algebra Evaluate each expression if *x* = 7 and *y* = 8. (Lessons 5-1 and 5-3)

36. $6x$ **37.** $y + x$ **38.** $y \div 4$ **39.** $y - x$

Problem Solving in Geography

What's Your Latitude?

Think of your street address. You use this to describe the location of your home. How can you describe this location on Earth? Latitude and longitude are used to describe the position of any place on Earth. They are measured in degrees (°), minutes ('), and seconds ("). For example, San Diego is located at 32°42'55"N, 117°9'23"W. That is 32 degrees, 42 minutes, and 55 seconds north of the equator and 117 degrees, 9 minutes, and 23 seconds west of the Prime Meridian.

Is there a relationship between latitude and temperature? Complete the exercises on page 259 to help you decide.

Did You Know?
The longest latitude line is the equator, whose latitude is zero degrees.

City	Latitude (nearest degree)	High Temperature, 2004 (°F)	Low Temperature, 2004 (°F)
Atlanta, GA	34	95	16
Honolulu, HI	21	92	60
Nashville, TN	36	94	11
New York, NY	41	91	1
San Diego, CA	33	96	41
Seattle, WA	48	96	20

Source: *The World Almanac*

 # Real-World Math

Use the table above to solve each problem.

1. Which cities had the highest temperature? the lowest temperature?

2. The higher the latitude number is, the farther the location is from the equator. Which city is closest to the equator? Which city is farthest from the equator?

3. Make a table listing the cities from least to greatest latitude. Include latitude and low temperatures. What do you notice about the relationship between latitudes and low temperatures?

4. Write the latitude and the low temperature of each city as an ordered pair. Graph and label the ordered pairs on a coordinate grid.

5. Find the difference between the high and low temperatures for each city. Write the latitude and the temperature difference of each city as an ordered pair.

6. Refer to Exercise 5. Graph and label the ordered pairs on a coordinate grid. Let the *x*-axis represent the latitude and the *y*-axis represent the temperature difference. Then describe the graph.

Functions and Equations

MAIN IDEA

I will find a function rule.

NYS Core Curriculum

5.CM.4 Share organized mathematical ideas through the manipulation of objects, numerical tables, drawings, pictures, charts, graphs, **tables,** diagrams, models, and symbols in written and verbal form

5.A.4 Solve simple one-step equations using basic whole-number facts

NY Math Online

macmillanmh.com
• Extra Examples
• Personal Tutor
• Self-Check Quiz

GET READY to Learn

Brady's neighbor pays him $8 each week to walk her dog. How much money will Brady earn in 5 weeks?

There are two ways to describe the relationship between the number of weeks and money earned.

Real-World EXAMPLE Describe Relationships

① **DOGS** The amount Brady earns depends on the number of weeks he works. The amount earned is 8 times the number of weeks.

One Way: Use a function table.

Number of Weeks	1	2	3	4	5
Amount Earned ($)	8	16	24	32	40

Another Way: Use an equation to represent the function.

Step 1   Define each variable.

Let w = number of weeks
Let m = amount of money earned

Step 2   Write the equation.

$m = 8w$

Step 3   Replace the variable.

$m = 8w$ Write the equation.
$m = 8 \times 5$ Replace w with 5.
$m = 40$ Multiply 8 by 5.

So, Brady earns $40 in 5 weeks.

Real-World EXAMPLE — Use Functions and Equations

2 **TRANSPORTATION** The cost of a taxi ride is $3 plus $2 for each mile. What is the total cost of a 7-mile taxi ride?

Remember

See Lesson 5-6 for a review of function tables.

One Way: Use a function table.

Number of Miles	1	2	3	4	5	6	7
Cost ($)	5	7	9	11	13	15	17

Another Way: Write an equation.

Step 1 Define each variable.

Let m = number of miles.
Let c = the cost.

Step 2 Write the equation.

$c = 3 + 2m$ The cost equals $3 plus $2 for each mile.

Step 3 Replace the variable.

$c = 3 + 2m$	Write the equation.
$c = 3 + (2 \times 7)$	Replace m with 7.
$c = 3 + 14$	Multiply 2 by 7.
$c = 17$	Add 3 and 14.

So, the cost of a 7-mile taxi ride is $17.

CHECK What You Know

Describe each relationship using a function table or equation.
See Examples 1, 2 (pp. 260–261)

1. The cost c of shipping mittens purchased online is $2 plus $6 for each of p pair of mittens. What is the total cost c of buying 5 pairs?

2. Tia collected $10 for a walk-a-thon and $5 from each of n friends. What is the total amount of donations d she collected from 4 friends?

3. Renee saves $3 a week from her babysitting job. If she saves for 7 weeks, how much money will Renee have?

4. **Talk About It** What information can you find in a function table that is not found in the equation?

Describe each relationship using a function table or equation. See Example 1, 2 (pp. 260–261)

5. Corrine bought 5 tickets to the skating rink. If she had a coupon for $4 off a total purchase, how much did the tickets cost?

SKATING $4

6. Dwayne receives 3 points for every game he wins. He already has 9 points. How many points will he have after winning 7 more games?

7. **Measurement** The width of a garden is equal to one-half of the length. If the length of the garden is 12 feet, what is the width?

8. A three-point shot in basketball counts 3 points. A regular field goal is 2 points. Lina scored 19 points. If she made three 3-point shots, how many 2-point shots did she make?

9. **Measurement** The distance around a sandbox is 4 times the length of one of the sides. If the length of one side is 7 feet, what is the distance around the sandbox?

10. Each box contains 12 mini muffins. Three friends decide to split 4 boxes of mini muffins evenly. How many mini muffins will each friend receive?

11. To rent a bus for a field trip, it costs $50 plus $3 for each person. If a total of 16 students and 4 parents went on the field trip, how much did it cost to rent the bus?

H.O.T. Problems

12. **FIND THE ERROR** Trevor and Toshi translated the phrase *10 is 5 less than a number* into an equation. Who is correct? Explain.

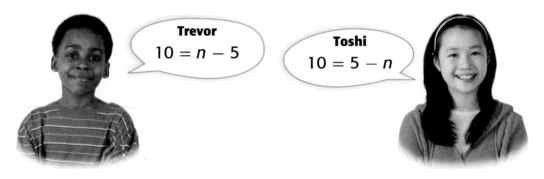

Trevor
$10 = n - 5$

Toshi
$10 = 5 - n$

13. **WRITING IN MATH** Which method is easier to use to solve a real-world problem, a function rule or an equation? Explain.

Where's My Line?

Naming and Locating Points

Get Ready!

Players: 2 players

You will need: graph paper

Get Set!

- Players should sit so they cannot see each others' papers.

- Each player draws a coordinate grid on graph paper and labels each axis from 0 to 10.

- Then each player draws a straight line on the graph paper. The line should pass through at least three points that are named by ordered pairs of whole numbers.

- Players choose who will go first.

Go!

- Each player begins by naming the ordered pair of one point on his or her line.

- Player 1 calls out a whole number ordered pair. Player 2 calls out "Hit!" if the ordered pair describes a point on his or her line, or "Miss!" if it does not.

- If Player 1 scores a hit, he or she takes another turn. If not, Player 2 takes a turn.

- The first player to locate two additional points on the other player's line wins.

Extend

Functions and Equations

Tech Link

You can use Math Tool Chest™ to graph functions.

ACTIVITY Graphing Ordered Pairs

MAIN IDEA

I will use technology to create function tables and graph ordered pairs.

NYS Core Curriculum

5.R.1 Use physical objects, drawings, charts, **tables, graphs, symbols, equations, or objects using technology as representations**

5.G.12 Identify and plot points in the first quadrant

1. **Hector saves $2 each week. This can be described by $y = 2x$, where x represents the number of weeks and y represents the amount Hector has saved. Graph this equation.**

First create a function table for $y = 2x$.

Number of weeks (x)	Amount saved (y)
1	2
2	4
3	6
4	8
5	10

Now use the graph feature from the Math Tool Chest™.

- Click on level two. Then choose Coordinate Graph.
- Click on Setup. Choose the graph that goes from 0 to 10 on both axes. Click on Show Ordered Pairs and Connect Points.
- Place the points in your function table on the coordinate grid by clicking the appropriate location.

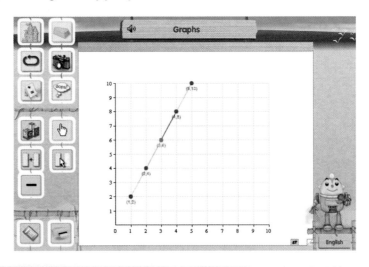

Think About It

1. Suppose Hector decides to save either $3 each week or $4 each week. Write an equation for each situation and graph them. How are the graphs the same? How are they different?

ACTIVITY

2 **Misty has already saved $3 and wants to save $2 more each week. This can be described by $y = 2x + 3$, where x is the number of weeks and y is the amount that Misty has saved. Graph this equation.**

First create a function table for $y = 2x + 3$. Then use the graph feature from the Math Tool Chest™.

- Click on Setup. Choose a coordinate grid that goes from 0 to 20.
- Place points on the coordinate grid by clicking the appropriate location.

Number of weeks (x)	Amount saved (y)
1	5
2	7
3	9
4	11
5	13
6	15
7	17

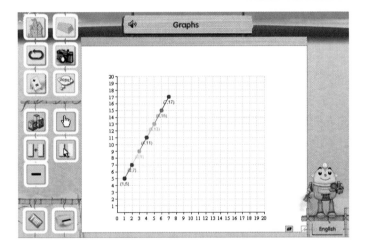

Think About It

2. Suppose Misty had already saved $10 but still wants to save $2 more each week. How does this graph differ from the one in Activity 2?

✓ CHECK What You Know

Write an equation, and create a function table. Then graph.

3. Kimbra is paying her sister $3 a day. If she has already paid $12, how many days until she will have paid her sister $21?

4. Josh has to write an 18 page report. He has 6 pages written. He writes 2 more pages per day. How many days will it take him to finish?

5. **WRITING IN ▶MATH** Write your own real-world problem and create a function table. Graph the equation.

Problem-Solving Investigation

<u>**MAIN IDEA**</u> I will choose the best strategy to solve a problem.

 NYSCC **5.PS.2** Understand that some ways of representing a problem are more efficient than others
5.PS.3 Interpret information correctly, identify the problem, and generate possible strategies and solutions
Also addresses 5.PS.5, 5.A.8.

P.S.I. TEAM ✛

VICTOR: I bought a small pizza at Pizza Palace. The price of an extra large pizza is equal to 2 times the price of a small pizza plus $3. If the price of an extra large pizza is $17, how much did I pay for the small pizza?

YOUR MISSION: Find the price of a small pizza.

Understand	You know that the price of an extra large pizza is $17. It is equal to 2 times the price of a small pizza plus $3. You need to find the price of a small pizza.
Plan	To solve this problem, you can work backward.
Solve	Since subtraction is the opposite of addition, take the price of the extra large pizza and subtract $3. $$\$17 - \$3 = \$14$$ Since division is the opposite of multiplication, divide $14 by 2. $$\$14 \div 2 = \$7$$ The cost of a small pizza is $7.
Check	Look back. Start with the price of a small pizza and multiply by 2. Then add $3. Since $(\$7 \times 2) + \$3 = \$17$, the answer is correct. ✔

Use any strategy shown below to solve each problem.

PROBLEM-SOLVING STRATEGIES
• Guess and check.
• Work backward.
• Draw a picture.
• Make a table.

1. At a bird sanctuary, Ricky counted 88 birds. Of the birds he counted, 16 were baby birds. If he counted an equal number of adult males and females, how many adult female birds did Ricky count?

2. Mrs. Vallez spent $19.90 on sand toys. How many of each type of sand toy below did Mrs. Vallez buy?

$2.95 $3.50

3. Sue has four DVDs and Terry has six DVDs. They put all their DVDs together and sold them for $10 for two. How much money will they earn if they sell all of their DVDs?

4. **Measurement** Jacinda is decorating cookies for a class party. She can decorate five cookies in ten minutes. At this rate, how many cookies can she decorate in an hour?

5. Pia, Evan, and Jonas each prefer a different type of music. They listen to rock, rap, and country. Pia does not like country. Evan does not like country or rap. Which type of music does each person like best?

6. **Algebra** If this pattern continues, how many blocks are in the bottom row of the fifth figure?

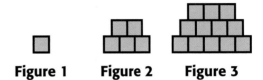

Figure 1   **Figure 2**   **Figure 3**

7. The number of new health club members in May was half as many as the number of new members in June. In July, there were 18 more new members than in June. If there were 76 new members in July, how many new members were there altogether during the three months?

8. **Measurement** To make four apple pies you need about two pounds of apples. How many pounds of apples will you need to make 20 apple pies?

9. Mi-Ling sets up tables for visitors at the art museum. Each square table can seat two people on each side. How many people can be seated if 8 square tables are pushed together in a row?

10. **WRITING IN ►MATH** A number multiplied by itself is 441. What is the number? Is the *guess and check* strategy a reasonable strategy to find the number? Explain.

FOLDABLES
Study Organizer
GET READY to Study

Be sure the following Key Vocabulary words and Big Ideas are written in your Foldable.

Key Concepts

Solving Equations (p. 235)

• An **equation** is a number sentence that contains an equals sign.

• Check your answer by replacing the variable with your answer to see whether it results in a true sentence.

Ordered Pairs (p. 250)

• A location on a coordinate grid can be described by using an ordered pair.

• An example of an **ordered pair** is (7, 4).

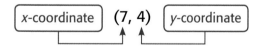

x-coordinate | (7, 4) | y-coordinate

Graph Functions (p. 254)

• To **graph** a point means to place a dot at the point named by the ordered pair.

Functions and Equations (p. 260)

• An equation can represent a function.

Key Vocabulary

coordinate grid (p. 250)

equation (p. 235)

graph (p. 254)

ordered pair (p. 250)

solve (p. 235)

Vocabulary Check

Choose the correct term or number to complete each sentence.

1. An (expression, equation) is a number sentence that contains an equals sign.

2. Points on a coordinate grid are found using (ordered pairs, distance).

3. When you find the value of a variable, you (solve, check) an equation.

4. The ordered pair (0, 0) represents the (coordinate grid, origin).

5. The first number in an ordered pair is the (x-coordinate, y-coordinate).

Lesson-by-Lesson Review

6-1 **Addition and Subtraction Equations** (pp. 237–239)

5.A.4

Example 1
Solve $x + 4 = 10$.

$x + 4 = 10$ THINK What number
$\downarrow$ plus 4 is 10?
$6 + 4 = 10$ You know that $6 + 4$ is 10.
   $x = 6$ The solution is 6.

Check $x + 4 = 10$
        $6 + 4 \overset{?}{=} 10$
             $10 = 10$ ✓

Example 2
Solve $m - 2 = 8$.

  $m - 2 = 8$ THINK What number take
                away 2 is 8?
$10 - 2 = 8$ You know that $10 - 2$ is 8.
     $m = 10$ The solution is 10.

Solve each equation. Check your solution.

6. $p + 5 = 13$ **7.** $14 = x - 6$

8. $r - 5 = 3$ **9.** $22 = 11 + n$

Write an equation and then solve. Check your solution.

10. Jason gave 4 baseball cards to his brother. He now has 16 baseball cards left. How many baseball cards did Jason have at first?

11. Sonia is 10 years old. If the sum of Sonia's and Alberto's ages equals 21, how old is Alberto?

6-2 **Multiplication Equations** (pp. 244–247)

5.A.5

Example 3
Solve $4s = 32$.

    $4s = 32$ THINK 4 times what
    $\downarrow$ number is 32?
$4 \times 8 = 32$ You know that 4 times
               8 is 32.
     $s = 8$ The solution is 8.

Check $4s = 32$
       $4 \times 8 \overset{?}{=} 32$
          $32 = 32$ ✓

Solve each equation. Check your solution.

12. $40 = 10c$ **13.** $2z = 16$

14. $3k = 27$ **15.** $56 = 7v$

Write an equation and then solve. Check your solution.

16. Twenty students in Mrs. Lytle's class raised $120 for charity. Each raised the same amount. How much money did each student raise?

17. You have 150 CDs to place in storage boxes. Each box holds 25 CDs. How many boxes will you need? Write and solve an equation.

5.CM.4

6-3 **Problem-Solving Strategy: Make a Table** (pp. 248–249)

Example 4

One marching band formation calls for 9 band members in the front row. Each row in the formation has 3 more band members than the row in front of it. If there are 5 rows, how many band members are there?

Use the *make a table* strategy.

Row	1	2	3	4	5
Members	9	12	15	18	21

+3 +3 +3 +3

Add the number of band members in each row. $9 + 12 + 15 + 18 + 21 = 75$. So, there are 75 band members.

Solve. Use the *make a table* strategy.

18. Sabrina is saving money for a vacation. She plans to increase her savings by $3.50 each week until she is saving $20 each week. If she saves $2.50 the first week, how many weeks will it take Sabrina until she is saving $20 each week?

19. Jay is arranging rows of chairs in the gymnasium. In the last row, there are 54 chairs. Each row has 4 fewer chairs than the previous row. If there is a total of 5 rows, how many chairs will Jay have to arrange?

5.G.12

6-4 **Geometry: Ordered Pairs** (pp. 250–252)

Example 5

Locate and write the ordered pair that names point *T*.

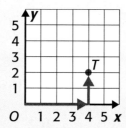

Step 1 Start at the origin (0, 0). Move right along the *x*-axis until you are under point *T*. The *x*-coordinate of the ordered pair is 4.

Step 2 Move up until you reach point *T*. The *y*-coordinate is 2.

So, the point *T* is located at (4, 2).

For Exercises 20–22, use the coordinate grid below.

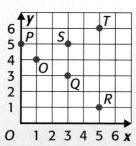

Locate and write the point for each ordered pair.

20. (3, 5) 21. (5, 6) 22. (1, 4)

23. Min identified a point that was 5 units above the origin and 2 units to the right of the origin. What was the ordered pair?

6-5 Algebra and Geometry: Graph Functions (pp. 254–257)

5.G.12

Example 6
Graphing Ordered Pairs

Graph and label point Q(2, 4).

Step 1 Start at the origin (0, 0).

Step 2 Move 2 units to the right on the *x*-axis.

Step 3 Then move up 4 units to locate the point.

Step 4 Draw a dot and label the point Q.

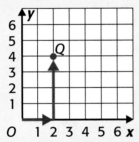

Graph and label each point on a coordinate grid.

24. A(4, 1) **25.** B(2, 1) **26.** C(6, 5)

27. D(4, 4) **28.** E(2, 7) **29.** F(2, 3)

30. A breath mint has 10 calories. Given the function rule 10x, find the total number of calories for 1, 2, 3, and 4 breath mints. Make a function table and then graph the ordered pairs.

31. Measurement There are 3 feet in one yard. Given the function rule $x \div 3$, find the total number of yards for 3, 6, 9, and 12 feet. Make a function table and then graph the ordered pairs.

6-6 Functions and Equations (pp. 260–262)

5.R.1

Example 7
The cost of renting a canoe is $5 per hour. Find how much it would cost to rent a canoe for 6 hours. Write an equation and then solve.

Step 1 Define each variable.
Let h = number of hours.
Let c = cost.

Step 2 Write the equation.
$c = 5h$

Step 3 Replace the variable.

$c = 5h$	Write the equation.
$c = 5 \times 6$	Replace h with 6.
$c = 30$	Multiply 5 by 6.

The cost is $30.

Describe each relationship using a function table or equation.

32. Yvonne bought a car wash pass that allows her to purchase any number of car washes in advance for $8 per wash. If she bought a pass for 6 washes, how much will it cost?

33. A dog groomer pays her assistant $10 a day plus $5 for each dog she washes. If the assistant washes 12 dogs in one day, how much money will she make?

Problem-Solving Investigation: Choose a Strategy (pp. 266–267)

5.PS.2

Example 8

A gardener wants to enclose his garden that is 15 feet long and 12 feet wide, by placing fence posts every 3 feet including the corners of the garden. Find the number of fence posts the gardener will need to enclose the garden.

Understand
- The garden is 15 feet wide and 12 feet long.
- Set a fence post every 3 feet.
- Posts are to be set at the corners.

Plan
Draw a picture.

Solve
Draw a 15 by 12 rectangle. Starting from one corner, draw a dot. Continue drawing dots 3 units apart around the rectangle.

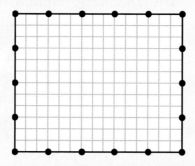

Count the number of dots. The gardener will need 18 posts.

Check
Look back.
$5 + 4 + 4 + 5 = 18$.
The answer is correct. ✔

Use any strategy to solve each problem.

34. Marti can bike 4 miles in 24 minutes. At this rate, how many miles can Marti bike in 120 minutes?

35. The pictures below show the prices of hamburgers and cheeseburgers at a fast food restaurant. Pedro bought a total of 5 burgers for $4.08. How many of each type of burger did he buy?

$0.86 $0.75

36. A soccer coach is enclosing a square practice soccer field. She places a cone every 8 feet including the corners. If each side of the field is 32 feet long, how many cones will the coach need?

37. Elan spent $8.50 at the school store. He spent $2.40 on paper, $0.88 on pencils, and $2.65 on markers. He spent the rest on a notebook. What was the price of the notebook?

38. Edrick took a bus to visit his grandparents. The bus left at 9:45 A.M. and traveled 325 miles at a rate of 65 miles per hour. What time did the bus arrive?

Chapter Test

Solve each equation. Check your solution.

1. $x + 5 = 8$ **2.** $y - 2 = 11$

3. $6z = 42$ **4.** $9d = 36$

5. $t - 4 = 16$ **6.** $3n = 33$

7. MULTIPLE CHOICE The daily cost
of renting a boat is $50 plus $6 for
each hour. Which equation represents
c, the cost in dollars for boating for
h hours?

   A $c = 50h + 6$ **C** $50 = 6h + c$

   B $c = 6h + 50$ **D** $50 = 6c + h$

**For Exercises 8–13, use the coordinate
grid below.**

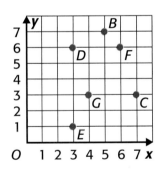

Name the ordered pair for each point.

   8. B **9.** C **10.** D

Name the point for each ordered pair.

11. $(3, 1)$ **12.** $(4, 3)$ **13.** $(6, 6)$

14. A grocery store clerk is stacking soup
cans. The bottom row has 21 soup
cans. Each additional row has 2 fewer
soup cans than the previous row. If
there are 8 rows, how many soup cans
will the clerk have to stack?

**Graph and label each point on a
coordinate grid.**

15. $(2, 7)$ **16.** $(4, 5)$ **17.** $(1, 6)$

18. MULTIPLE CHOICE Alyssa made the
graph below to show how much she
makes babysitting. The equation
$m = 5h$ describes how much money
m she earns babysitting.

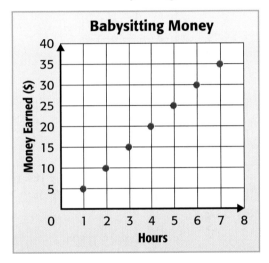

Which ordered pair represents how
much money she earns for 4 hours?

   F $(20, 4)$ **H** $(5, 25)$

   G $(15, 3)$ **J** $(4, 20)$

19. The sum of two whole numbers
between 20 and 40 is 58. The
difference of the two numbers is 12.
What are the two numbers? Tell
what strategy you used to find the
numbers.

20. WRITING IN ►MATH Explain why
the variable x can have any value in
$x + 3$, but in $x + 3 = 7$, the variable x
can have only one value.

PART 1 Multiple Choice

Read each question. Then fill in the correct answer on the answer sheet provided by your teacher or on a sheet of paper.

1. Which point is located at (2, 4)?

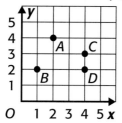

A Point *A*   **C** Point *C*

B Point *B*   **D** Point *D*

---

2. Which of the following is greater than 5.023?

F 5.0   **H** 5.022

G 5.02   **J** 5.03

---

3. Tomas records how much money he has saved. The table shows part of his records. Which is NOT a way to find the amount he saves each week?

Week	Total Saved
2	$30
3	$45
4	$60
5	$75
6	$90

A Divide $60 by 4.

B Divide $90 by 6.

C Subtract $45 from $75.

D Subtract $60 from $75.

---

4. An auditorium has 24 rows with 20 seats in each row. If 305 seats are occupied, which of the following shows a way to find the number of empty seats in the auditorium?

F Subtract 24 from the product of 305 and 20.

G Subtract 305 from the product of 24 and 20.

H Add 305 to the product of 24 and 20.

J Add 24 to the product of 305 and 20.

---

5. Gregory rode his bike 12 miles around a bicycle track. He wants to find his biking time per mile in minutes. What additional information does he need?

A The number of minutes that he rode.

B The number of feet in 12 miles.

C The number of laps in one mile.

D The number of laps that he rode.

---

6. There are 640 cans of coffee at a distributon warehouse. The cans will be packed into boxes that hold 40 cans each. How many boxes are needed?

F 12

G 15

H 16

J 18

7. Claudio bought 4 cans of green beans priced at $1.45 each. He used a coupon for $0.75 off the total cost. Which number sentence can be used to show how much money Claudio needed to buy the beans?

A $(4 + 1.45) - 0.75 = 4.70$

B $(4 \times 1.45) - 0.75 = 5.05$

C $(4 - 1.45) + 0.75 = 3.30$

D $(4 \times 1.45) + 0.75 = 6.55$

8. The sum of two numbers is 18. Their product is 72. What are the two numbers?

F 8, 9

G 9, 9

H 6, 12

J 4, 14

9. Martin is 12 years old. His father is three times as old as he is. How old will Martin be when his father is 40?

A 15

B 16

C 18

D 20

Record your answers on the answer sheet provided by your teacher or on a sheet of paper.

10. The numbers below form a pattern. What are the next two numbers in the pattern?

7, 15, 23, 31, 39, ...

11. Show how you would use the Distributive Property to evaluate the expression $6 \times (9 + 2)$.

Record your answers on the answer sheet provided by your teacher or on a sheet of paper.

12. The graph shows the number of inches of rain during a tropical storm. Create a function table to represent the data. Explain the pattern.

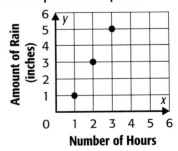

NEED EXTRA HELP?												
If You Missed Question...	1	2	3	4	5	6	7	8	9	10	11	12
Go to Lesson...	6-4	1-6	6-3	6-7	4-3	4-1	5-7	6-7	6-2	6-1	5-7	5-6
NYS Core Curriculum	5.G.12	5.N.8	5.CM.4	5.PS.2	5.N.17	5.N.17	5.N.18	5.PS.2	5.A.5	5.A.4	5.N.18	5.A.3

Display and Interpret Data

BIG Idea What is data?

Data are pieces of information that are often numerical. There are many ways to organize data.

Example The table below shows data about the world's largest balloon festivals.

The World's Largest Balloon Festivals	
Location	Number of Balloons
Albuquerque, New Mexico	1,000
Gallup, New Mexico	200
Greenville, South Carolina	150
Gatineau, Canada	150
Scottsdale, Arizona	150

Source: *Scholastic Book of World Records*

What will I learn in this chapter?

- Find the median, mode, and range of a set of data.
- Make and interpret line plots and frequency tables.
- Make and interpret bar graphs and line graphs.
- Choose and make an appropriate graph for presenting data.
- Solve problems by using the *make a graph* strategy.

Key Vocabulary

line graph

median

mode

range

 NY Math Online

Student Study Tools
at macmillanmh.com

FOLDABLES®
Study Organizer

Make this Foldable to help you organize information about data and graphs. Begin with four sheets of $8\frac{1}{2}'' \times 11''$ graph paper.

1 **Stack** the pages, placing the sheets of paper $\frac{3}{4}$ inch apart.

2 **Roll** up bottom edges so all tabs are the same size.

3 **Crease** and staple along the fold.

4 **Label** each tab as shown.

Data and Graphs

Median and Mode
Line Plots
Frequency Tables
Scales and Intervals
Bar Graphs
Line Graphs

You have two ways to check prerequisite skills for this chapter.

Option 2

NY Math Online ⟩ Take the Chapter Readiness Quiz at macmillanmh.com.

Option 1

Complete the Quick Check below.

QUICK Check

Order each set of numbers from least to greatest. (Lesson 1-7)

1. 3, 16, 2, 9, 13

2. 18, 11, 22, 19, 14

3. 36, 45, 40, 21, 39, 60

4. 87, 30, 55, 15, 12, 71, 77

5. 1.4, 0.5, 3.2, 1.8, 2.6

6. 3.18, 3.08, 3.2, 3.96, 3.05, 3.68

7. The table shows the costs of disposable cameras. Order the costs from least to greatest. (Lesson 1-7)

Cost of Disposable Cameras			
$5.99	$8.50	$12.95	$9.95
$8.95	$9.05	$14.99	$6.75

Subtract. (Lesson 2-4)

8. 24 − 13

9. 36 − 22

10. 32 − 19

11. 65 − 43

12. 80 − 26

13. 112 − 37

14. The original price of a sweater was $42. It is on sale for $15 off. Katsu has a coupon for an additional $10 off. What is the final price of the sweater? (Lesson 2-4)

Write the ordered pair for each point.
(Lesson 6-4)

15. A

16. B

17. C

18. D

19. E

20. F

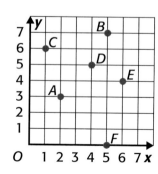

7-1 Median and Mode

GET READY to Learn

Zachary Taylor, the 12th President of the United States, had six letters in his last name. The table shows the number of letters in the last names of the first twelve presidents.

Letters in the Last Names of United States Presidents			
10	5	9	7
6	5	7	8
8	5	4	6

MAIN IDEA

I will find the median and mode of a set of data.

NYS Core Curriculum

5.S.1 Collect and record data from a variety of sources (e.g., newspapers, magazines, polls, charts, and surveys)

New Vocabulary

data

median

mode

NY Math Online

macmillanmh.com

• Extra Examples
• Personal Tutor
• Self-Check Quiz

Data are pieces of information that are often numerical. The numbers in the table above are data. One way to describe data is to use the median. One half of the data are greater than the median, and one half of the data are less than the median.

Median   Key Concept

Words	The **median** of a set of data is the middle number of the data that has been written in order.
Example	data: 2, 4, ⑤, 7, 11 → **median:** 5
Words	If there is an even number of data, the median is the number exactly halfway between the two middle numbers.
Example	data: 2, 4, ⑤, ⑦, 11, 16 → **median:** $(5 + 7) \div 2$ or 6

Real-World EXAMPLE   Find the Median

① **PRESIDENTS** Refer to the table above. Find the median of the data. Then describe the data.

Step 1 Order the numbers from least to greatest.

4, 5, 5, 5, 6, ⑥, 7, 7, 8, 8, 9, 10

Step 2 The middle two numbers are 6 and 7.
The median is the number half way between them, 6.5.

So, half of these United States Presidents had 6.5 or fewer letters in their last name. Half had 6.5 or more letters in their last name.

Another way to describe a set of data is to use the mode.

Mode

Key Concept

Words   The **mode** of a set of data is the number that occurs most often.

Examples   **data:** 1, 6, 8, (10, 10) → **mode:** 10

There may be more than one mode.

data: 1, (6, 6,) 8, (10, 10) → **modes:** 6 and 10

There may not be a mode.

data: 1, 6, 8, 10 → **mode:** none

Real-World EXAMPLE   **Find the Mode**

 MONEY The cost of a movie ticket in different theaters is shown below. Find the mode of the data. Then describe the data.

$6.00, ($7.50, $7.50,) ($8.00, $8.00,) $8.50, $9.75, $10.50

The prices $7.50 and $8.00 each occur twice. So, the modes are $7.50 and $8.00. More theaters charge $7.50 or $8.00 than any other price.

 ## CHECK What You Know

Find the median and mode of each set of data. See Examples 1, 2 (pp. 279–280)

1. cost of lunches: $5, $8, $5, $6, $9

2. ages of students: 12, 10, 13, 14, 11, 13, 11

3. inches of rain: 7.3, 8.1, 4.2, 7.2, 8.1, 7.3

4. The scores of the top eight finishers in a golf tournament are shown. Find the median and mode. Then describe the data.

Golf Scores			
70	72	68	72
83	71	74	72

5. **Talk About It**   Describe the steps for finding the median of a set of data.

Find the median and mode of each set of data. See Examples 1, 2 (pp. 279–280)

6. bowling scores: 85, 106, 106, 74, 95

7. length of wire in meters: 0.27, 0.15, 1.19, 0.52, 0.50, 0.20, 0.04

8. gallons of water: 207, 198, 187, 201, 178, 200, 196, 201, 197, 204

9. letters in spelling words: 9, 8, 7, 7, 9, 7, 6, 7, 10, 9, 7, 6, 9, 9, 11

10.

Weight of Students (lb)			
70	72	68	72
83	71	74	76

11.

Number of Pets				
2	1	1	2	3
3	1	0	1	0

12.

Visits to the Alamo this Year					
0	3	1	0	2	3
5	2	3	7	0	0

13.

Test Scores			
93	88	85	98
90	96	79	85
92	86	88	90

14. The table shows the number of shirts sold each day for three weeks. Find the median and mode. Then explain which value you could use to predict how many shirts could be sold each day.

Number of Shirts Sold						
32	5	5	38	35	40	29
30	31	45	43	36	44	42
39	33	41	50	46	37	34

15. The table shows the number of weeks on The Billboard Hot 100 chart for each of the top 25 hits. Find the median and mode. Then describe the data.

Weeks on Hot 100

14	14	13	19	6
11	12	14	25	17
11	3	6	27	19
6	8	9	29	7
11	19	10	16	24

H.O.T. Problems

16. **COLLECT THE DATA** Use the newspaper to collect a set of real-world data. Find the median and mode and explain what they mean.

17. **OPEN ENDED** Write a set of data that has a median of 14 and a mode of 2.

18. **WRITING IN ►MATH** Suppose the median height of the students in your class is 50 inches. What can you conclude about the heights of your classmates? Explain how you know.

7-2 Problem-Solving Investigation

MAIN IDEA I will choose the best strategy to solve a problem.

 NYSCC **5.PS.3 Interpret information correctly, identify the problem, and generate possible strategies and solutions** *Also addresses 5.PS.5, 5.PS.8*

P.S.I. TEAM +

MAI: I noticed that there were more dogs than cats in the veterinarian's waiting room. The vet said that for about every 3 dogs he sees, he sees 2 cats. If 20 animals were brought in, I wonder how many would be dogs?

YOUR MISSION: Find about how many dogs the vet will see if 20 animals come into the office.

Understand	You know that for every 3 dogs, there are 2 cats. You need to find the number of dogs.
Plan	To solve this problem, you can use red and yellow counters to act out how many dogs and cats the vet will see.
Solve	Use red counters to represent the dogs and yellow counters to represent the cats. Place 3 red counters and 2 yellow counters in a group. Make groups of 5 counters until you have 20 counters. Add the number of red counters to find about how many dogs the vet will see. $$3 + 3 + 3 + 3 = 12$$ So, about 12 of the animals will be dogs.
Check	Work backward. Start with 12 red counters and 8 yellow counters. Remove groups of 3 red and 2 yellow counters until none remain.

Use any strategy shown below to solve each problem.

PROBLEM-SOLVING STRATEGIES
• Guess and check.
• Act it out.
• Make a table.

1. Zach purchases two books. The total cost is $32. One book costs $8 more than the other. How much does each book cost?

2. Four friends ran a race. Benny finished after Diego and before Alana. Marcia finished after Benny but before Alana. Who won the race?

3. **Measurement** A recipe for banana nut muffins calls for 1 cup bananas and 2 cups of flour. Eboni wants to make more muffins than the recipe yields. In Eboni's batter, there are 6 cups of flour. If she is using the recipe as a guide, how many cups of bananas will she need?

4. The table shows the number of submarine sandwiches sold by members of a hockey club. One number is missing. If the median of the data is 20 and there is more than one mode, find a possible value for the missing number.

Number of Subs Sold

22	18	26	10	11
14	20	18	23	24

5. Mr. Hoy plants 7 more flowers in his garden than his neighbor. If they plant 37 flowers in all, how many flowers does each person plant?

6. Cameron has $40 in his bank account and his brother, Caden, has $35. Caden saves $5 per week and Cameron saves $4 per week. In how many weeks will they both have the same amount in their accounts?

7. **Algebra** A certain type of bacterial cell doubles every 10 minutes. Use the table to determine how many cells there will be after 60 minutes.

Minutes	Number of Cells
0	1
10	2
20	4
30	8
60	■

8. Erica is saving money to buy a new hamster cage. In the first week, she saved $24.80. Each week after the first, she saves $6.50. How much money will Erica have saved in six weeks?

9. Haley is having a birthday party with 7 people. She asks the guests to introduce themselves and shake hands with each of the other guests. How many handshakes will there be?

10. **WRITING IN MATH** What strategy did you use to solve Exercise 9? Explain why your strategy makes sense.

7-3 Line Plots

GET READY to Learn

Students in Mr. Cotter's fifth grade class were asked how many after-school activities they have. Their responses are shown in the table.

Number of After-School Activities

0	2	1	3	3	1
1	1	4	4	0	2
2	1	4	1	3	1
2	3	0	1	2	1

MAIN IDEA

I will make and interpret line plots.

NYS Core Curriculum

5.S.1 Collect and record data from a variety of sources (e.g., newspapers, magazines, polls, charts, and surveys)

5.S.4 Formulate conclusions and make predictions **from graphs**
Also addresses 5.CM.4.

New Vocabulary

line plot
range
outlier

NY Math Online

macmillanmh.com

• Extra Examples
• Personal Tutor
• Self-Check Quiz

One way to give a picture of the data is to make a line plot. A **line plot** is a graph that uses Xs above a number line to show the number of times values in a set of data occur.

Real-World EXAMPLE Make a Line Plot

① **ACTIVITIES** Refer to the table above. Make a line plot of the data. Then describe the data presented in the graph.

Step 1 Draw and label a number line.

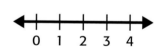

Step 2 Place as many Xs above each number as there are responses for that number.

Step 3 Describe the data.

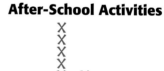

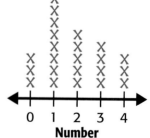

• 24 students responded to the question.
• No one is involved in more than 4 after-school activities.
• Three students are involved in no after-school activities.
• The response given most is 1 after-school activity. This represents the mode.

284 Chapter 7 Display and Interpret Data

Vocabulary Link

range

Everyday Use the highest to lowest notes that a person can sing

Math Use the difference between the greatest and least values in a data set

Another way to describe a set of data is to use the range and any outliers.

Range and Outliers

Key Concepts

Words The **range** of a set of data is the difference between the greatest and least values in a data set.

Example **data:** 2, 4, 5, 7, 12 → **range:** 12 − 2 or 10

Words An **outlier** is a data value that is not close to the other values in a data set.

Example **data:** 5, 8, 10, 14, 63 → **outlier:** 63

Real-World EXAMPLES Analyze Line Plots

HATS The line plot shows the prices of cowboy hats.

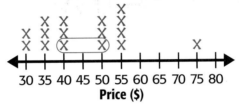

Prices of Cowboy Hats

② **Find the median and mode of the data. Then describe the data using them.**

There are 16 numbers represented in the line plot. The median is between the 8th and 9th pieces of data.

The two middle numbers, shown on the line plot, are 40 and 50. So, the median is 45. This means that half of the cowboy hats cost more than $45 and half cost less than $45.

The number that appears most often is 55. So, the mode of the data is 55. This means that more cowboy hats cost $55 than any other price.

③ **Find the range and any outliers of the data. Then describe the data using them.**

range = greatest value − least value
      = 75 − 30, or 45

The range of the prices is $45. The price $75 is much higher than the rest of the prices. So, $75 is an outlier.

Remember

You can find the median by counting the Xs on the graph. You do not have to list all of the data values. Cross off a least and a greatest value until you reach the middle.

CHECK What You Know

Draw a line plot for each set of data. Find the median, mode, range, and any outliers of the data shown in the line plot.

See Examples 1–3 (pp. 284–285)

1.

Number of Stories of 15 Tallest Buildings		
101	88	88
110	88	88
80	69	102
78	70	54
85	80	73

2.

Calories in Serving of Peanut Butter			
190	160	210	210
200	188	190	190
188	200	190	210
190	188	200	200

3.

Sum of Two Number Cubes				
10	3	11	5	5
7	5	6	7	6
7	7	12	5	7
9	8	8	8	9
5	9	3	3	11

4. Refer to the line plot in Exercise 3. Write a sentence or two to describe the data.

5. **Talk About It** What are the advantages of representing data in a line plot rather than in a table?

Practice and Problem Solving

NYSCC • NYSMT

Extra Practice, p. R18

Draw a line plot for each set of data. Find the median, mode, range, and any outliers of the data shown in the line plot.

See Examples 1–3 (pp. 284–285)

6. Length of summer camps in days: 7, 7, 14, 10, 5, 10, 5, 7, 10, 9, 7, 9, 6, 10, 5, 8, 7, and 8

7. Daily high temperatures in degrees Fahrenheit: 71, 72, 74, 72, 72, 68, 71, 67, 68, 71, 68, 72, 76, 75, 72, 73, 68, 69, 69, 73, 74, 76, 72, and 74

8.

Students' Estimates of Room Length (m)				
10	11	12	12	13
13	13	14	14	14
15	15	15	15	15
16	16	16	17	17
17	17	18	18	25

9.

Number of Songs on MP3 Players				
25	50	40	40	42
50	39	39	42	36
38	42	40	45	38

10.

Hours Spent Watching TV					
3	3	5	2	2	1
2	0	1	1	5	2
0	2	2	3	1	0
2	1	3	2	3	5

11.

Number of Tornadoes				
0	1	1	1	6
0	0	0	0	0
2	1	3	0	0

12. The line plot shows students' favorite pizza toppings. Which can you find using the line plot: the median, mode, range, or outlier(s)? Explain. Then write a sentence or two to describe the data set.

Favorite Pizza Toppings

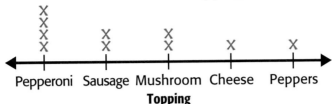

A softball team scored 14, 9, 6, 11, and 9 runs in their last five games. How many runs would the team need to score in the next game so that each statement is true?

13. The range is 10.

14. The mode is 11.

15. The median is $9\frac{1}{2}$.

Real-World PROBLEM SOLVING

Social Studies The table shows the years in which different machines were invented.

16. What is the range of the years of the inventions?

17. Which invention represents the median year?

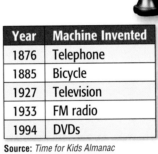

Year	Machine Invented
1876	Telephone
1885	Bicycle
1927	Television
1933	FM radio
1994	DVDs

Source: *Time for Kids Almanac*

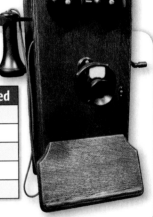

H.O.T. Problems

18. COLLECT THE DATA Write a survey question that has a numerical answer. Some examples are "How many CDs do you have?" or "How many feet long is your bedroom?" Ask your friends and family the question. Record the results and organize the data in a line plot. Use the line plot to make conclusions about your data. For example, describe the data using the median, mode, or range.

19. CHALLENGE There are several sizes of flying disks in a collection. The range is 8 centimeters. The median is 22 centimeters. The smallest size is 16 centimeters. What is the largest disk in the collection?

20. WRITING IN ►MATH Suppose two sets of data have the same median but different ranges. What can you conclude about the sets?

21. The table shows the speeds of the world's fastest roller coasters. Which roller coaster in the table represents the median speed? (Lesson 7-1)

Roller coaster	Speed (mi per h)
Dodonpa, Japan	107
Kingda Ka, USA	128
Superman the Escape, USA	100
Top Thrill Dragster, USA	120
Tower of Terror, Australia	100

A Dodonpa

B Kingda

C Top Thrill Dragster

D Tower of Terror

22. The line plot shows the number of weekly chores that fifth graders have.

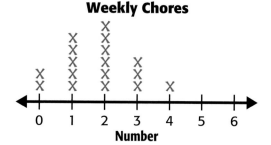

Which represents the range of the data? (Lesson 7-3)

F 0

G 2

H 4

J 6

Spiral Review

For Exercises 23 and 24, use the information below. Gia and her three friends went to the movie theater. They each spent $6 on snacks and $8 on a movie ticket. (Lesson 7-2)

23. If the total amount the four friends have now is $12, how much money did they have altogether originally?

24. If they each had the same amount of money originally, how much did each friend have?

25. The table shows the number of students who visited the National Wildlife Refuge every day for two weeks. Find the median and mode. (Lesson 7-1)

Number of Student Visitors						
68	65	56	62	68	56	56
58	56	63	62	60	65	64

Graph and label each point on a coordinate grid. (Lesson 6-5)

26. $J(0, 6)$ **27.** $K(5, 7)$ **28.** $L(4, 0)$ **29.** $M(3, 3)$

Algebra Solve each equation. (Lesson 6-2)

30. $4x = 8$ **31.** $6n = 24$ **32.** $15 = 5a$ **33.** $60 = 12r$

7-4 Frequency Tables

MAIN IDEA

I will make and interpret frequency graphs.

NYS Core Curriculum

5.S.1 Collect and record data from a variety of sources (e.g., newspapers, magazines, polls, charts, and surveys) *Also addresses 5.CM.4.*

New Vocabulary

frequency table

NY Math Online

macmillanmh.com
• Extra Examples
• Personal Tutor
• Self-Check Quiz

GET READY to Learn

The table shows the number of days that Middletown had thunderstorms each month in a recent year.

Thunderstorm Days			
2	2	1	1
7	5	7	7
6	6	0	0

We can use a **frequency table** to organize data in a table that shows the number of times each data value appears.

Real-World EXAMPLE   Make a Frequency Table

1 **THUNDERSTORMS Refer to the table above. Make a frequency table of the data. Then describe the data.**

Step 1 Make a table with three columns. Label the columns *Number*, *Tally*, and *Frequency* as shown.

Step 2 Use tally marks to record each data value. The last column provides a count, or *frequency*, of the data.

Step 3 Describe the data.

Thunderstorm Days		
Number	**Tally**	**Frequency**
0				2
1				2
2				2
3		0
4		0
5			1
6				2
7					3

• The median is $3\frac{1}{2}$. Half of the data are above $3\frac{1}{2}$ and half of the data are below $3\frac{1}{2}$.

• The mode is 7. More months had 7 days of thunderstorms than any other number.

• The range of the data is 7 − 0 or 7. There are no outliers.

Lesson 7-4 Frequency Tables   **289**

Real-World EXAMPLE **Make and Interpret a Frequency Table**

2 **TEXT MESSAGES** **The number of text messages that Sonja sent each day for 25 days is shown. Make a frequency table. Find the, median mode, range, and any outliers. Then describe the data.**

Number of Text Messages				
3	5	2	1	1
4	4	3	3	2
3	1	2	0	4
1	3	2	4	2
3	2	1	3	0

The least number of text messages is 0, and the greatest number is 5. So, in the first column, write the numbers 0 to 5. Tally the data and add the tallies.

Number of Messages	Tally	Frequency
0	||	2
1	|||||	5
2	||||| |	6
3	||||| ||	7
4	||||	4
5	|	1

The median is the 13th number, or 2 messages. Half of the data are above 2 and half are below 2.

The mode is 3 messages, since 3 appears more often than any other number.

The range is 5 − 0, or 5 messages. There are no outliers.

For a frequency table without numbers, you can find the mode of the data, but not the median nor the range.

 Real-World EXAMPLE **Non-Numerical Data**

3 **PETS** **The table shows the kinds of pets that students have. Make a frequency table of the data. Then describe the mode.**

Pets						
F	D	D	D	C	H	F
D	C	D	D	F	H	C
H	D	C	D	C	C	F

D = dog, C = cat, F = fish, H = hamster

Pet	Tally	Frequency
dog	||||| |||	8
cat	||||| |	6
fish	||||	4
hamster	|||	3

Since more students have dogs than any other pet, the mode is dog.

> **Remember**
>
> The first column in the frequency table should always include the least value, the greatest value, and all the values in between.

CHECK What You Know

Lamar counted the number of children with each adult who entered a grocery store in one hour. His results are shown at the right. See Examples 1, 2 (pp. 289–290)

1. Make a frequency table of the data.

2. Find the median, mode, and range of the data. Identify any outliers. Then describe the data.

Number of Children with Each Adult				
1	2	1	4	0
5	2	2	0	2
0	1	0	5	6
1	2	1	3	4

The table shows a geography vocabulary list.

See Examples 1, 2 (pp. 289–290)

3. Make a frequency table to show the number of letters in each word.

4. Find the median, mode, and range of the data. Identify any outliers in the data. Then describe the data.

Vocabulary List		
bay	island	source
hill	dam	range
peninsula	mouth	canal
tributary	ocean	coast
plain	river	valleys
mountain	glacier	

5. The table shows the political parties of the 43 United States Presidents as of 2008. What is the mode? What does the mode mean? See Example 3 (p. 290)

6. **Talk About It** Explain how a line plot is similar to a frequency table.

Political Party	Frequency
Federalist	2
Democratic-Republican	6
Whig	4
Democrat	13
Republican	18

Practice and Problem Solving

Extra Practice, p. R18

The table shows the record low May daily temperatures in the city of Lakeview. See Examples 1, 2 (pp. 289–290)

7. Make a frequency table of the data.

8. Find the median, mode, and range of the data. Identify any outliers. Then describe the data.

Temperatures (°F)			
42	42	43	43
45	43	46	45
40	44	43	43
43	46	46	46
45	46	46	46

The table shows the heights of 15 different Collie dogs.

See Examples 1, 2 (pp. 289–290)

9. Make a frequency table of the data.

10. Find the median, mode, and range of the data. Identify any outliers. Then describe the data.

Height of Collies (in.)				
24	26	22	22	23
24	25	24	23	23
18	26	25	22	24

Lesson 7-4 Frequency Tables **291**

Gerri surveyed her classmates to determine their favorite colors. See Example 3 (p. 290)

11. Make a frequency table for these data.

12. Describe the mode of the data.

13. Can you determine the median, range, and outliers for these data? Explain.

Favorite Colors Gerri's Classmates				
K	R	P	G	V
R	V	R	P	P
G	P	G	B	K
B	R	K	G	B
G	B	V	P	R

B: Blue Y: Yellow R: Red G: Green
V: Purple P: Pink K: Black

The table shows the number of each size of T-shirt sold.
See Example 3 (p. 290)

14. Make a frequency table for these data.

15. Describe the mode of the data.

T-shirts Sold					
S	S	L	M	S	XL
L	M	M	L	S	M
XL	M	S	L	M	XL
S	L	M	M	L	S
M	S	M	XL	S	M

S = small, M = medium, L = large,
XL = extra large

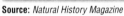
Real-World PROBLEM SOLVING

Science The table shows the top speeds of animals over short distances.

Animal	Speed (miles per hour)	Animal	Speed (miles per hour)
Lion	50	Rabbit	35
Gazelle	50	Cat	30
Wildebeest	50	White-tailed deer	30
Cape hunting dog	45	Grizzly bear	30
Elk	45	Wart hog	30
Ostrich	40	Kangaroo	30
Zebra	40	Elephant	25
Jackal	35	Black mamba snake	20

Source: *Natural History Magazine*

16. Make a frequency table of the speeds.

17. Describe the data. Include the median, mode, and range of the data.

H.O.T. Problems

18. **COLLECT THE DATA** With a classmate, create a survey about weekend activities. Gather data and make a frequency table to show your results. Report the median, mode, and range of your data. Identify any outliers.

19. **WRITING IN ►MATH** Explain how frequency tables help to organize data.

Find the median and mode of each set of data. (Lesson 7-1)

1. daily high temperature in degrees Fahrenheit: 79, 72, 80, 76, 80

2. price of coffee: $2.99, $3.50, $1.20, $3.50, $1.50, $0.99, $1.50

3. **MULTIPLE CHOICE** The table below shows the miles of shoreline of five different lakes.

Lake	Shoreline (mi)
Camille Creek	320
Trout	233
Clearwater	450
Bay Point	600
Yellow Springs	245

Which lake in the table represents the median miles of shoreline? (Lesson 7-1)

A Camille Creek   C Clearwater

B Trout   D Bay Point

4. Mika buys a fishing rod and a hat. His total bill is $140. The rod is 9 times the cost of the hat. How much does each item cost? (Lesson 7-2)

5. How many more students have blue backpacks than red? (Lesson 7-4)

Students' Backpacks

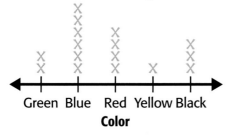

Color

6. Draw a line plot for the data set shown. Then find the median, mode, range, and any outliers. Then describe the data. (Lesson 7-3)

Weight of Apples (oz)					
7	5	5	6	8	7
6	7	8	5	5	5

7. **MULTIPLE CHOICE** Which set of data is shown in the table? (Lesson 7-4)

Price ($)	Tally	Frequency
15	||	2
16	|	1
17		0
18	|	1
19	|||	3

F $15, $15, $16, $18, $19, $19, $19

G $15, $16, $17, $18, $19, $19, $19

H $15, $15, $16, $16, $18, $18, $19

J $15, $16, $16, $17, $18, $19, $19

8. **WRITING IN ▶MATH** The table shows the ages of students in a classroom.

Ages of Students						
10	10	11	12	11	11	10
11	10	10	11	11	10	11

Suppose the age of the teacher was added to the data set. Would the median, mode, or range of the data change the most? Explain. (Lesson 7-3)

Scales and Intervals

7-5

GET READY to Learn

There are thirty teams in the NBA. The number of 3-point shots made by each team in the 2006-2007 season have been grouped into six equal intervals. The data are shown at the right.

NBA Teams 3-Point Statistics		
Number Made	Tally	Frequency
200–299	I	1
300–399	IIII	5
400–499	IIII IIII	10
500–599	IIII IIII	9
600–699	II	2
700–799	III	3

Source: National Basketball Association

MAIN IDEA

I will choose appropriate scales and intervals for frequency tables.

NYS Core Curriculum

5.S.1 Collect and record data from a variety of sources (e.g., newspapers, magazines, polls, charts, and surveys) *Also addresses 5.CM.4.*

New Vocabulary

scale

interval

NY Math Online

macmillanmh.com

• Extra Examples
• Personal Tutor
• Self-Check Quiz

The frequency table has a scale from 200 to 799. The **scale** includes the least and greatest values in the data set. The scale is separated into equal **intervals**. In this case, the interval is 100.

Real-World EXAMPLE   Make a Frequency Table

① **HATS** Choose an appropriate scale and interval size for the data shown below. Then make a frequency table.

Price of Baseball Caps ($)									
18	19	12	24	16	26	16	23	22	25
24	14	18	17	27	22	20	25	20	15

The data are from 12 to 27. Make the scale from 12 to 27 and the interval size 4. The categories are 12–15, 16–19, 20–23, and 24–27.

In the tally column, record the number of caps in each category. Write the total number of tallies in the frequency column.

Price ($)	Tally	Frequency
12–15	III	3
16–19	IIII I	6
20–23	IIII	5
24–27	IIII I	6

Real-World EXAMPLE Make a Frequency Table

2 **FOOD** The table shows concession stand sales for one hour. Make a frequency table of the data. Then write a sentence or two to describe how the data are distributed among the intervals.

Concession Stand Sales ($)			
9.19	6.10	6.40	1.20
3.25	9.80	3.50	8.75
6.40	8.30	1.80	7.00
9.50	3.10	8.80	7.20

The sales range from $1.20 to $9.50. You could make the scale from $0.01 to $10.00 with an interval size of $1.99.

Sales ($)	Tally	Frequency
0.01–2.00	||	2
2.01–4.00	|||	3
4.01–6.00		0
6.01–8.00	̶H̶H̶	5
8.01–10.00	̶H̶H̶ |	6

Most sales were in the $8.01–$10.00 interval. No sales were in the $4.01–$6.00 interval.

CHECK What You Know

The *United States Specialty Sports Association* (USSSA) ranks sports teams based on tournament wins. The table shows the USSSA points for the top 25 boys 12-and-under baseball teams in a recent season. See Examples 1, 2 (pp. 294–295)

USSSA Points				
850	725	715	695	450
445	425	390	365	340
330	330	320	305	300
300	300	295	280	275
265	260	255	255	245

1. Choose an appropriate scale and interval size for a frequency table that will represent the data. Describe the intervals.

2. Create a frequency table using the scale and interval size you described.

3. Write a sentence or two to describe how the points are distributed among the intervals.

4. **Talk About It** Explain how to choose an appropriate scale and interval size when making a frequency table of a set of data.

Practice and Problem Solving

The table shows the millions of cookies sold for the top 15 cookie brands in a recent year. See Examples 1, 2 (pp. 294–295)

Cookie Sales (millions)		
75	50	39
31	29	33
48	56	21
35	20	17
16	14	14

5. Choose an appropriate scale and interval size for a frequency table that will represent the sales. Describe the intervals.

6. Create a frequency table using the scale and interval size you described.

7. Write a sentence or two to describe how the sales information is distributed among the intervals.

Building model rockets is a popular hobby. The table shows the bid prices for a certain model rocket kit at an auction.

See Examples 1, 2 (pp. 294–295)

Bid Prices	
Price ($)	Number
30	9
28	1
2	1
21	11
13	15
6	2
9	5
23	4
10	2
16	5

8. Choose an appropriate scale and interval size for a frequency table that will represent the bid prices. Describe the intervals.

9. Create a frequency table using the scale and interval size you described.

10. Write a sentence or two to describe how the bid prices are distributed among the intervals.

The table shows the prices of 11 dog books for children.

See Examples 1, 2 (pp. 294–295)

Title	Price ($)	Title	Price ($)
Pepper's Snow Day	8.99	Danger at Snow Hill	4.99
Wind-wild Dog	16.95	A Puppy for Annie	15.99
Snowball	3.99	Helpful Puppy	5.99
Adam of the Road	6.99	The Inside Tree	14.99
Polo: The Runaway Book	16.95	Sassie: The True Confessions of a Poodle Princess	15.99
Dogabet	16.95		

11. Choose an appropriate scale and interval size for a frequency table that will represent the list prices of these books. Describe the intervals.

12. Create a frequency table using the scale and interval size you described.

13. Write a sentence or two to describe how the list prices are distributed among the intervals.

The table shows race results to the nearest tenth for the top 25 junior finishers in a recent bicycle race.

See Examples 1, 2 (pp. 294–295)

Time (min)				
37.4	37.8	38.2	39.2	40.9
37.4	37.8	39.2	42.1	37.8
37.4	37.8	39.5	39.5	38.2
37.8	37.8	39.7	39.5	40.2
37.8	37.9	40.1	37.8	37.9

14. Choose an appropriate scale and interval size for a frequency table that will represent the race result times. Describe the intervals.

15. Create a frequency table using the scale and interval size you described.

16. Write a sentence or two to describe how the race result times are distributed among the intervals.

 New York Data File

The New York Red Bulls is a Major League Soccer team. The number of goal attempts per player in a recent season is recorded in the table.

New York Red Bulls Goal Attempts					
56	65	24	7	30	23
32	19	59	8	3	2
2	0	2	19	3	1
0	7	6	6	4	10

Source: New York Red Bulls

17. Choose an appropriate scale and interval size for a frequency table that will represent the data. Describe the intervals.

18. Create a frequency table using the scale and interval size you described.

19. Write a sentence or two to describe how the data is distributed among the intervals.

H.O.T. Problems

20. COLLECT THE DATA Find a list of real-world data in an almanac. Describe the scale and interval that you would use to make a frequency table of the data. Then make a frequency table.

21. CHALLENGE Refer to the frequency table at the beginning of the lesson that shows the number of 3-point shots made by NBA teams. Is it possible to find the median, mode, or range of the data? Explain.

22. WRITING IN ►MATH Describe when it is better to use intervals rather than individual values when making a frequency table of data.

23. The data below describes the average weights of popular breeds of dogs. Which scale and interval would be most appropriate in a frequency table representing the data? (Lesson 7-5)

Average Weights (lb) of Popular Dog Breeds					
70	6	100	20	4	26
30	65	80	70	75	15

A scale: 1–100; interval size: 5

B scale: 1–100; interval size: 10

C scale: 1–50; interval size: 1

D scale: 1–200; interval size: 10

24. Which is a true statement about the data represented by the frequency table below? (Lesson 7-4)

Cost ($)	Tally	Frequency
0–4	ⵑⵑⵑ	5
5–9	ⵑⵑⵑ ⵏ	6
10–14	ⵏⵏ	2
15–19	ⵏ	1

F None of the values are $0.

H None of the values are $20.

G The greatest number of values is between $0 and $4.

J The greatest value is $19.

Spiral Review

The table shows the number of hours 15 students practiced their musical instruments one week. (Lesson 7-4)

Practice Time (h)				
1	4	4	2	6
3	2	4	5	5
2	5	4	6	1

25. Make a frequency table of the data. Then find the median, mode, range, and any outliers.

For Exercises 26 and 27, use the table that shows the lengths of twelve different lizards. (Lesson 7-3)

Length (cm)			
14	12	14	14
19	18	11	16
30	12	19	15

26. Make a line plot of the data.

27. Find the median, mode, range, and any outliers of the data shown in the line plot.

28. For every $5 that Wesley earns, he saves $3. How much does he save if he earns $25? Use the *make a table* strategy to solve. (Lesson 6-3)

Solve each equation. Check your solution. (Lesson 6-1)

29. $c + 7 = 13$ **30.** $y - 4 = 5$ **31.** $r - 3 = 2$ **32.** $9 + k = 11$

Algebra Evaluate each expression if $a = 5$ and $b = 8$. (Lesson 5-3)

33. $2b$ **34.** $4a$ **35.** $9a$ **36.** $7b$

Bar Graphs

MAIN IDEA

I will make and interpret bar graphs and double bar graphs.

NYS Core Curriculum

5.S.1 Collect and record data from a variety of sources (e.g., newspapers, magazines, polls, charts, and surveys)

5.S.4 Formulate conclusions and make predictions **from graphs** *Also addresses 5.CM.4.*

New Vocabulary

bar graph

double bar graph

NY Math Online

macmillanmh.com

• Extra Examples
• Personal Tutor
• Self-Check Quiz

GET READY to Learn

The table shows students' favorite exhibits at the zoo.

Exhibit	Number of Students
Reptiles	10
Pachyderms	9
Islands of Southeast Asia	8
Herbivores/Carnivores	5
African Forest	15

Another way to organize data is to use a bar graph. A **bar graph** uses bars to display the number of items in each group.

Real-World EXAMPLE | **Make and Interpret a Bar Graph**

1 ZOO **Make a bar graph of the data in the table above.**

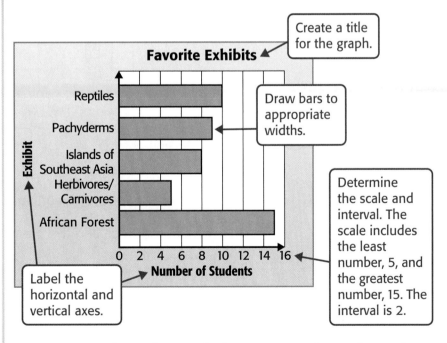

Create a title for the graph.

Draw bars to appropriate widths.

Determine the scale and interval. The scale includes the least number, 5, and the greatest number, 15. The interval is 2.

Label the horizontal and vertical axes.

You can see from the graph that more students chose the African Forest exhibit as their favorite exhibit than any other.

A **double bar graph** can be used to display two sets of data dealing with the same subject. You can use a double bar graph to make conclusions about the data.

Remember

Always include a key to describe what each bar in a double bar graph represents.

Real-World EXAMPLE
Make and Interpret a Double Bar Graph

② **MASCOTS** The fifth and sixth graders are voting for a new school mascot. The results are shown in the table below.

Mascot	Fifth Grade Votes	Sixth Grade Votes
Cardinals	42	26
Jaguars	21	18
Cougars	33	36
Patriots	12	21
Colts	14	19

Make a double bar graph of the data. Then use the graph to make conclusions about the data.

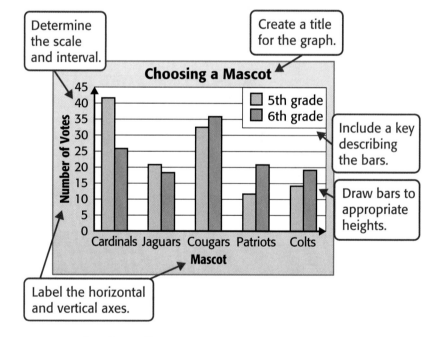

Determine the scale and interval.

Create a title for the graph.

Include a key describing the bars.

Draw bars to appropriate heights.

Label the horizontal and vertical axes.

Vocabulary Link

horizontal
Everyday Use flat or level

vertical
Everyday Use up and down

You can make the following conclusions from the graph.

• The mascot that received the greatest number of fifth grade votes was Cardinals.

• The mascot that received the greatest number of sixth grade votes was Cougars.

• The range of fifth grade votes is 42 − 12 or 30. The range of sixth grade votes is 36 − 18 or 18. So, the fifth grade votes were more spread out.

CHECK What You Know

The five longest rivers in the United States are shown in the table. See Examples 1, 2 (pp. 299–300)

1. Make a bar graph of the data. Describe the scale and interval that you used.

2. How much longer is the Missouri than the Yukon?

3. Which river represents the median length? Explain your reasoning.

U.S. Rivers	
River	**Length (mi)**
Missouri	2,540
Mississippi	2,340
Yukon	1,980
Rio Grande	1,900
St. Lawrence	1,900

The 10- and 11-year olds on a soccer team voted on a new name. See Examples 1, 2 (pp. 299–300)

4. Which name received the most votes from 10-year olds?

5. Which name received the most votes from 11-year olds?

6. Which name received the fewest votes overall?

7. How many votes were cast in all?

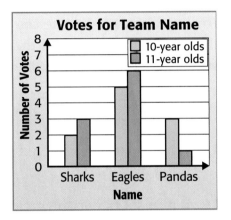

For Exercises 8 and 9, use the table that shows the number of student absences for one week. See Examples 1, 2 (pp. 299–300)

Student Absences for One Week					
Grade	**Monday**	**Tuesday**	**Wednesday**	**Thursday**	**Friday**
Fourth	7	3	4	6	10
Fifth	5	4	4	5	3

8. Make a bar graph for each of the two data sets.

9. Combine the data sets to create a double bar graph. Then write one or two sentences describing the data in the double bar graph.

10. It is estimated that there were about 100,000 cheetahs in the wild in 1900; about 30,000 in 1950; and about 12,500 in 2006. Make a bar graph to show how the population of the cheetah has declined.

11. **Talk About It** Summarize the steps you take to make a double bar graph.

Practice and Problem Solving

For Exercises 12 and 13, use the table that shows the number of scoops of five flavors of ice cream sold one day at Mom's Shoppe. See Examples 1, 2 (pp. 299–300)

Ice Cream Scoops Sold	
Flavor	**Number**
Chocolate	96
Vanilla	82
Rocky road	43
Strawberry	25
Mint chip	20

12. Make a bar graph of the data. Describe the scale and interval size that you used.

13. Which flavor had the greatest number of scoops?

Stanislaus surveyed students in his school about their favorite snack. For Exercises 14–17, use the graph that shows the results of the survey. See Examples 1, 2 (pp. 299–300)

14. Which snack was favored most often by boys?

15. Which snack was favored most often by girls?

16. Which snack had the greatest difference in boys' and girls' favorites?

17. Estimate the range of responses given by the girls.

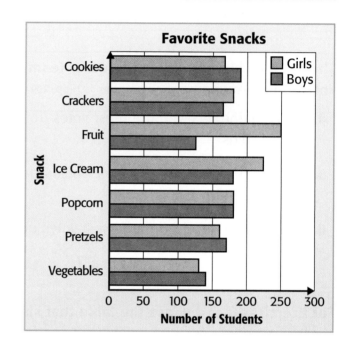

For Exercises 18–20, use the tables that show the record high daily temperatures in November for two cities.

18. Create a bar graph of the temperatures for each city.

19. Find the median, mode, and range of the temperatures for Jonesville. Then describe the data using them.

20. Combine the bar graphs from Exercise 18 to create a double bar graph. Then write one or two sentences summarizing the data in the double bar graph.

Record High Daily Temperatures for each day in November (°F)				
Jonesville				
85	85	85	84	81
82	82	82	87	82
81	84	84	80	82
80	85	84	77	81
86	80	82	80	79
81	79	82	84	79
Orchard City				
88	88	87	89	88
89	89	88	88	91
87	89	91	89	90
87	86	85	87	83
83	86	87	87	85
86	85	89	84	82

For Exercises 21–23, use the table that shows the ages of first-year teachers for two school districts.

Age of First-Year Teachers (yr)								
District A					District B			
25	23	24	21	24	25	24	22	24
22	22	24	24	23	25	23	23	23
23	22	22	21	26	25	26	23	21
23	23	22	24		26	22		

21. Create a bar graph of the ages of first-year teachers for each district.

22. Find the median, mode, and range of the ages of first-year teachers for District A. Then describe the data using them.

23. Combine the bar graphs from Exercise 21 to create a double bar graph. Then write one or two sentences summarizing the data in the double bar graph.

H.O.T. Problems

24. FIND THE ERROR The graph at the right shows the number of students in the Spanish club in its first three years. Kamila and James are analyzing the data in the graph. Who is correct? Explain.

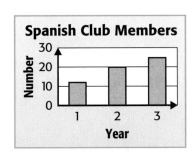

Kamila
The number of members from Year 1 to Year 2 more than doubled.

James
The number of members from Year 1 to Year 3 more than doubled.

25. OPEN ENDED Write a set of four data values. When the data are displayed in a bar graph, two bars have the same height. One of the bars is 10 units taller than the two equal bars.

26. ✎ WRITING IN ▸MATH Write a real-world problem that can be represented by using a bar graph. Create a bar graph and write two questions about the graph. Ask another student to use your graph to answer the questions.

Problem Solving in Art

Art Work

Artists hold about 290,000 jobs in the United States. Some are cartoonists, sketch artists for law enforcement, or illustrators for medical and scientific publications. Many artists are involved in movie-making and theater productions. Graphic designers and animators help create videos.

About 63% of artists in the United States are self-employed. Some self-employed artists have contracts to work on individual projects for different clients. Fine artists usually sell their work when it is finished, including painters, sculptors, craft artists, and printmakers.

Art Careers Chosen by Students in a Survey

Career	Frequency
Art Museum Director	10
Book Illustrator	14
Cartoonist	16
Computer Graphic Artist	9
Craft Artist	14
Fine Art Restorer	2
Scientific Sketch Artist	12

Average Annual Salary

Profession	Salary ($)
Dancers	27,390
Fashion Designers	60,160
Film and Video Editors	44,540
Fine Artists	43,750
Graphic Designers	41,380
Interior Designers	43,770
Photographers	28,810

A **double line graph** shows two different data sets, each represented by a line graph. The two line graphs share a common scale.

Real-World EXAMPLE Make and Interpret a Double Line Graph

② **TECHNOLOGY** The table below shows the changes in television viewing and Internet use, not including the use of E-mail, from 2000 to 2006.

Year	Average Daily Hours	
	Television Viewing	Internet Use
2000	4.1	2.0
2001	4.3	2.1
2002	4.3	2.3
2003	4.4	2.4
2004	4.4	2.6
2005	4.5	2.7
2006	4.6	2.9

Source: Nielsen Media Research, The Harris Poll

Make a double line graph of the data. Then use the graph to describe the changes in television viewing and Internet use from 2000 to 2006.

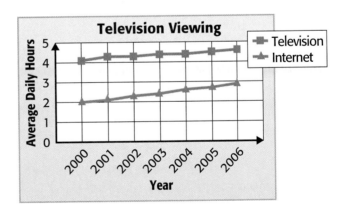

Remember

When making a double line graph, make each set of points different, as in Example 2. Another method is to use different colors for the two lines.

- Both the hours of television viewing and Internet use steadily increased from 2000 to 2006.

- The hours of Internet use appear to be increasing slightly more quickly than the hours of television viewing.

- People still spend more time watching television than using the Internet.

For Exercises 1–4, refer to the line graph at the right. It shows the weight gain of a kitten. See Example 1 (p. 306)

1. What is the scale of the vertical axis?

2. What is the size of each interval on the vertical axis?

3. About how many ounces did the kitten gain per month?

4. Why is a line graph used in this example instead of a bar graph?

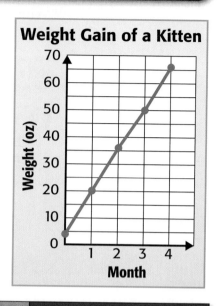

Weight Gain of a Kitten

The table shows population data for two counties. See Example 2 (p. 307)

5. Create a double line graph to show the populations from 1900 to 2000.

6. Write a few sentences to describe each county's population change and how the two counties' populations compare over time.

7. Predict each county's population for the 2010 U.S. Census. Explain.

8. **Talk About It** Explain when you would use a line graph to show data.

Year	County Population	
	County A	County B
1900	1,716	1,641
1910	2,106	2,814
1920	2,064	4,050
1930	2,219	7,691
1940	3,469	10,383
1950	4,252	10,113
1960	7,006	10,975
1970	8,902	9,494
1980	14,260	9,289
1990	17,892	7,976
2000	22,497	7,828

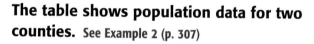
Practice and Problem Solving

NYSCC • NYSMT

Extra Practice, p. R20

For Exercises 9–11, refer to the line graph at the right that shows total water use for a town. See Example 1 (p. 306)

9. What is the scale of each axis?

10. What is the size of each interval on each axis?

11. Describe water use patterns for the town from 1990 to 2008.

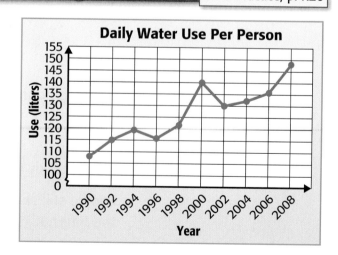

Daily Water Use Per Person

The table shows the number of baseball cards that Julian had in his collection. See Example 1 (p. 306)

Year	Total Number of Baseball Cards
2006	35
2007	62
2008	88
2009	110

12. Make a line graph of the data.

13. Write a sentence or two describing the changes from 2006 to 2009.

For Exercises 14–17, refer to the double line graph at the right that shows the number of two different types of first class mail from 1995 to 2005. See Example 2 (p. 307)

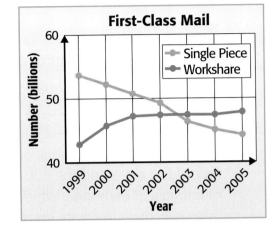

14. What is the scale of each axis?

15. What is the size of each interval on each axis?

16. Describe the patterns the line graphs show about the volume of these two types of first class mail.

17. Predict the volume for single piece first class mail in the year 2010. Explain your reasoning.

For Exercises 18–20, refer to the table at the right. It shows the distance ran by two marathon runners over a one-hour period. See Example 2 (p. 307)

Marathon Running		
Time (minutes)	Runner 1 (miles)	Runner 2 (miles)
10	1.8	1.0
20	3.0	1.9
30	4.1	2.7
40	4.7	4.0
50	5.1	4.8
60	5.4	5.7

18. Create a double line graph to show the distance traveled by the two runners in one hour.

19. Write a few sentences describing the distance traveled by each runner.

20. If both runners continued for another hour, predict which runner would be leading the race.

H.O.T. Problems

21. OPEN ENDED The line graph at the right has several parts missing. Create a story and a context to go along with the graph. Create axes labels and a title for the graph.

22. WRITING IN ►MATH Write a problem that can be solved by making a line graph. Then make the line graph. Solve. Exchange problems and graphs with another person to solve.

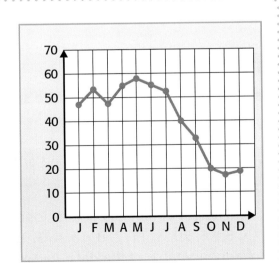

23. Tyson made a graph of the high temperatures for a week. Which statement is true about the graph? (Lesson 7-7)

   A No temperature was greater than 65°C.

   B No temperature was less than 57°C.

   C The lowest temperature was at 5 minutes.

   D The temperature increased each minute.

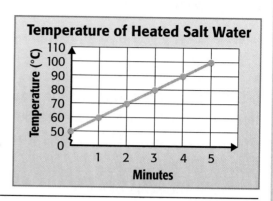

24. A wildlife refuge is divided into different areas. The graph shows four of the areas and the number of animals in each area. Which table was used to create the graph?

(Lesson 7-6)

F

Area	Number of Animals
Africa	1
Australia	2
North America	3
Southeast Asia	4

H

Area	Number of Animals
Africa	19
Australia	24
North America	27
Southeast Asia	8

G

Area	Number of Animals
Africa	20
Australia	25
North America	25
Southeast Asia	10

J

Area	Number of Animals
Africa	27
Australia	24
North America	19
Southeast Asia	8

Spiral Review

The table shows students' favorite seasons. (Lesson 7-6)

25. Make a bar graph of the data.

26. Use the bar graph to write one or two sentences describing the data.

Season	Number of Votes
Fall	8
Spring	10
Summer	25
Winter	5

27. The length in minutes of Mrs. Jones' most recent phone calls are: 5, 8, 16, 20, 3, 11, 2, 8, 13, 4, 3, 15, 6, 4, and 17. Create a frequency table of the data. (Lesson 7-5)

Four in a Row

Making a Line Graph

Get Ready!

Players: 2 or more

You will need: 2 number cubes labeled 0–5
paper
grid paper
counters in two different colors

Get Set!

Make a 6 × 6 coordinate grid as shown.
Graphs should be big enough for the counters.

Create a record sheet for each game
listing the names of each player.

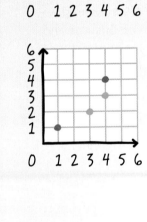

Go!

- A player tosses the number cubes to make
  an ordered pair. For example, if the number
  cubes show 3 and 2, the player could choose
  to use (3, 2) or (2, 3).

- The player uses a counter to graph the ordered
  pair on the grid. If both possible ordered pairs
  are already covered, the player loses a turn. Use
  different color counters to cover the points.

- Repeat until one player
  graphs four ordered
  pairs in a row, column,
  or diagonal.

Use an Appropriate Graph

MAIN IDEA

I will select and make an appropriate graph for presenting data.

NYS Core Curriculum

5.S.1 Collect and record data from a variety of sources (e.g., newspapers, magazines, polls, charts, and surveys)

5.S.4 Formulate conclusions and **make predictions from graphs**
Also addresses 5.CN.4.

New Vocabulary

pictograph

NY Math Online

macmillanmh.com
• Extra Examples
• Personal Tutor
• Self-Check Quiz
• Concepts in Motion

GET READY to Learn

The number of pounds of cans recycled by the fifth grade class are shown in the table.

Recycling Cans	
Week	Number of Pounds
1	10
2	14
3	9
4	12

You have learned to represent data using different types of graphs: line plots, bar graphs, double bar graphs, line graphs, and double line graphs. Another type of graph called a **pictograph**, compares data by using picture symbols.

You can use a pictograph to represent the data in the table above.

Step 1 Choose a picture that is related to the data and is easy to draw. For this pictograph, let a can represent the data.

Step 2 Decide how much data each symbol will represent in whole and half symbols. For this situation, you can let one can represent 2 pounds. Then a half-can will represent 1 pound.

Step 3 Draw the pictograph. Include a key showing what each picture symbol represents.

Recycling Cans	
Week	Number of Pounds
1	🥫🥫🥫🥫🥫
2	🥫🥫🥫🥫🥫🥫🥫
3	🥫🥫🥫🥫
4	🥫🥫🥫🥫🥫🥫
🥫 = 2 pounds	

Each type of graph has a different purpose.

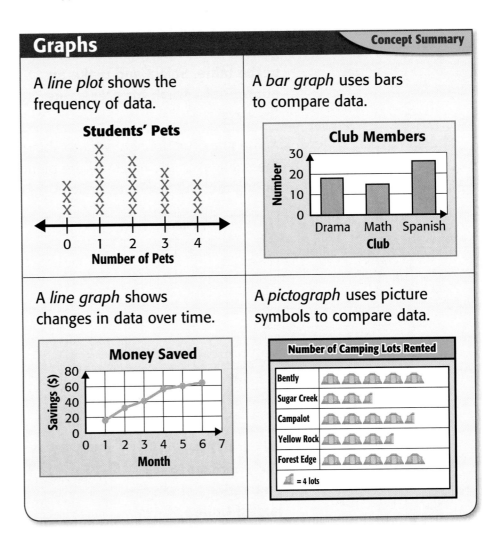

Graphs

A *line plot* shows the frequency of data.

Students' Pets

Number of Pets

A *bar graph* uses bars to compare data.

Club Members

A *line graph* shows changes in data over time.

Money Saved

Month

A *pictograph* uses picture symbols to compare data.

Number of Camping Lots Rented

Bently	
Sugar Creek	
Campalot	
Yellow Rock	
Forest Edge	

= 4 lots

Remember

There is more than one way to graph data correctly. The data in Example 1 could have also been displayed in a bar graph. The bars could represent the number of songs downloaded.

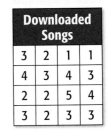

Real-World EXAMPLE   **Use an Appropriate Graph**

1 MUSIC **The table shows the number of songs that were downloaded one day by 16 students. Select and make an appropriate graph for presenting the data.**

A line plot could be used to show the frequency of the data.

Downloaded Songs

3	2	1	1
4	3	4	3
2	2	5	4
3	2	3	3

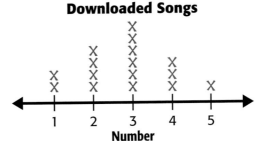

Downloaded Songs

Number

② **PLANTS** Carmita was tracking the growth rate of her plant as shown in the table. Select and make an appropriate graph for presenting the data.

Plant Growth	
Week	**Height (in.)**
1	1.5
2	2
3	3.5
4	4
5	6

A line graph would be useful to show the changes in the height of the plant throughout the five week period.

Plant Growth

③ **POPULATIONS**

The approximate populations of the five largest United States cities from two different years are shown. Select and make an appropriate graph for presenting the data.

Population of the Five Largest United States Cities		
City	**1990 Census**	**2000 Census**
New York City	7,322,564	8,008,278
Los Angeles	3,485,398	3,694,820
Chicago	2,783,726	2,896,016
Houston	1,630,553	1,953,631
Philadelphia	1,585,577	1,517,550

Remember

When there are two sets of data, use a double bar graph or a double line graph.

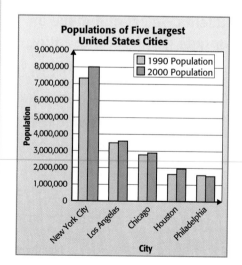

There are two sets of data: the 1990 and 2000 populations. To compare the populations of all five United States cities, use a double bar graph. It allows you to compare both sets of data at a glance.

Which type of graph would you use to display the data in each table? Write *line plot, bar graph, double bar graph, line graph, double line graph,* or *pictograph*. Explain why. Then make the graph. See Examples 1–3 (pp. 313–314)

1.

Tallest Roller Coasters in the World	
Roller Coaster	**Height (ft)**
Kingda Ka	456
Top Thrill Dragster	420
Superman: The Escape	415
Tower of Terror	377
Steel Dragon 2000	318
Millennium Force	310

Source: Coaster Grotto

2.

Car's Acceleration Rate	
Time (sec)	**Speed (mph)**
2	22
4	44
6	60

3.

Smallest Countries	
Country	**Land Area (sq km)**
Vatican City	1
Monaco	2
Nauru	21
Tuvalu	26
San Marino	61

4.

Students' Favorite Movies	
Movie	**Number of Students**
A	30
B	50
C	40
D	20
E	60

5. **Talk About It** Explain why it is necessary to choose a certain type of graph to represent a set of data. Give an example.

Practice and Problem Solving

NYSCC • NYSMT
Extra Practice, p. R20

Which type of graph would you use to display the data in each table? Write *line plot, bar graph, double bar graph, line graph, double line graph,* or *pictograph*. Explain why. Then make the graph.

See Examples 1–3 (pp. 313–314)

6.

Continent	Number of Countries
Africa	53
Asia	44
Europe	46
North America	23
Oceania	14
South America	12
Antarctica	0

7.

Movies Owned by Molly	
Type of Movie	**Number of Movies**
Musical	3
Drama	1
Adventure	2
Comedy	6
Western	2

Which type of graph would you use to display the data in each table? Write *line plot, bar graph, double bar graph, line graph, double line graph,* or *pictograph.* Explain why. Then make the graph.

See Examples 1–3 (pp. 313–314)

8.

Money Earned by the End of Each Hour	
Hour	Dollars Earned from Video Rentals
1:00	$23
2:00	$45
3:00	$120
4:00	$164
5:00	$210

9.

2005 Touchdowns		
Team	Number by Running	Number by Receiving
Seattle	29	25
Indianapolis	18	31
New York	17	24
Cincinnati	15	32
San Diego	22	27

Source: National Football League

10.

Number of Text Messages per Day				
8	3	4	10	5
5	7	6	9	8
6	5	4	8	10

11.

Patrick's Growth Rate	
Age (yr)	Height (in.)
3	34
6	51
9	53
12	59

12. Malina conducted a survey at her school to determine students' favorite fruits. She recorded her results in the table below. Graph the data to show the results. Explain why you chose the graph that you did.

Fruit	Tally	Number of People
Apples	$\cancel{||||}$ $\cancel{||||}$ $\cancel{||||}$ $\cancel{||||}$ $\cancel{||||}$ $|$	26
Bananas	$\cancel{||||}$ $\cancel{||||}$ $||$	12
Grapes	$\cancel{||||}$ $\cancel{||||}$ $\cancel{||||}$ $\cancel{||||}$ $|$	21
Oranges	$\cancel{||||}$ $\cancel{||||}$ $\cancel{||||}$ $|$	16
Peaches	$\cancel{||||}$ $|$	6
Pineapple	$\cancel{||||}$	5
Raspberries	$||||$	4
Strawberries	$\cancel{||||}$ $\cancel{||||}$ $||$	12

13. Examine the pictograph. If the person who created it was sitting next to you, what question(s) would you ask him or her to help understand the graph?

Weekly Sales	
Week 1	💵 💵 💵 💵
Week 2	💵 💵 💵 💵 💵
Week 3	💵 💵 💵

H.O.T. Problems

14. COLLECT THE DATA Take a survey of your class to see what activity they prefer to do on the weekend. Record your results in a table like the one shown below.

Activity	Tally	Frequency
Bicycling		
Skateboarding		
In-line Skating		
Swimming		

Graph the data. Explain what type of graph you used.

15. CHALLENGE The two line graphs show the same data about the amount of money in Trong's savings account for a 5-month period. For what purposes might each version of these graphs be useful?

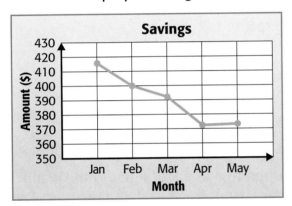
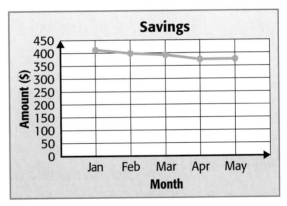

16. FIND THE ERROR Four frogs have masses of 91 grams, 95 grams, 105 grams, and 100 grams. Isabella and Eric are choosing which type of graph to use to display the data. Who is correct? Explain.

Isabella
I think the data would be best displayed using a bar graph.

Eric
I think the data would be best displayed using a line graph.

17. **WRITING IN ▸MATH** Describe some of the things you look for in a set of data when you are deciding on the type of graph to use.

Extend

Tech Link

You can use Math Tool Chest™ to display data in bar graphs and line graphs.

MAIN IDEA

I will use technology to select and create graphs.

NYS Core Curriculum

5.S.1 Collect and record data from a variety of sources (e.g., newspapers, magazines, polls, charts, and surveys)

5.S.4 Formulate conclusions and make predictions **from graphs** *Also addresses 5.S.2, 5.R.1*

ACTIVITY **Choose an Appropriate Graph**

1. **Morgan is writing a paper about why the Boston Celtics are the most successful NBA team in history. She wants to include a graph of the information at the right.**

NBA Championships Won	
Lakers	14
Celtics	16
76ers	3
Bulls	6

A bar graph would be the most appropriate graph to display the data. It would allow Morgan to compare the team's championships.

- Choose Graphs, and click on level two.
- Click on Bar Graph.
- Click on the up arrow next to the ten to increase the *y*-axis to 20.
- Click on the add bar button to add a fourth bar to the graph.
- Input the correct labels for the *x*-axis, *y*-axis, and title.
- Drag each team's bar up to match their total number of championships won.

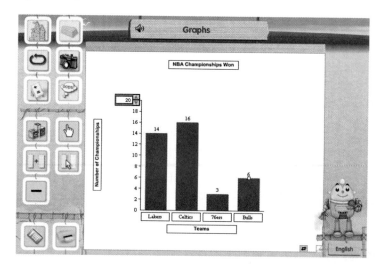

2 Owen started a bike race at 10:00 A.M. and finished at 12:00 P.M. He tracked how far he traveled every 30 minutes. Based on Owen's data, select and make an appropriate graph.

Biking	
Time	**Distance (mi)**
10:30	8
11:00	8
11:30	6
12:00	5

A line graph would be the most appropriate graph to display Owen's data.

- Choose Graphs, and click level two.
- Click Line Graphs.
- Click the add bar button to add a fourth section.
- Input the labels for the title, times, x-axis and y-axis.
- Drag the line above each day up to match the number of miles that Owen traveled.

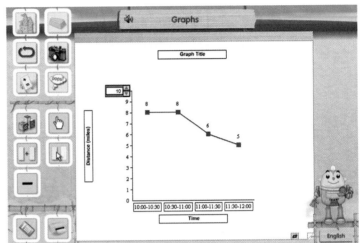

CHECK What You Know

Which type of graph would you use to display the data in each table? Write *bar graph, double bar graph, line graph,* or *double line graph*. Then create the graph using Math Tool Chest™.

1.

Basketball Scoring	
Student	**Points**
Becky	20
Jeff	12
Simeon	15
Pete	8

2.

Puppy's Growth	
Month	**Weight (lb)**
January	8
February	8
March	11
April	10
May	13

3.

Olympic Medals Won	
Type of Medal	**Number of Medals Received**
Bronze	15
Silver	9
Gold	1

4. COLLECT THE DATA Collect three different data sets. One set should be appropriate for a line graph, and one for a pictograph. Graph the data.

5. WRITING IN ►MATH Write a sentence or two about each of the graphs you made in Exercise 4. Explain why you chose each type of graph and analyze the data.

7-9 Problem-Solving Strategy

MAIN IDEA I will solve problems by making a graph.

The table shows the number of gallons of lemonade that were needed at the school picnic in recent years. It also shows the temperature the day of the picnic.

Temperature (°F)	Lemonade (gallons)
91	36
80	15
86	22
95	40
87	25

This year, the temperature is expected to be 93°F. About how many gallons of lemonade will be needed?

Understand	**What facts do you know?** • You know the temperature and gallons of lemonade. **What do you need to find?** • How much lemonade will be needed if it is 93°F.
Plan	One way to solve the problem is to graph the ordered pairs on a coordinate grid and look for patterns in the data. Making a graph is like drawing a picture of the data.
Solve	**Use your plan to solve the problem.** As the temperature increases, the number of gallons of lemonade increases. Place a dot midway between (91, 36) and (95, 40). The graph shows (93, 38). So, about 38 gallons of lemonade should be needed. 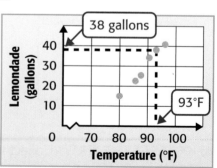
Check	Look back. List the temperatures from least to greatest. When the temperature is between 91°F and 93°F, the gallons of lemonade needed is between 36 and 40. The answer makes sense. ✔

Refer to the problem on the previous page.

1. What are some advantages and disadvantages of showing the data in a graph?

2. What are some advantages and disadvantages of showing the data in a table?

3. Suppose the temperature was expected to be 85°F. How much lemonade would be needed? Explain.

4. One year, the picnic needed 45 gallons of lemonade. Estimate the temperature that day. Explain.

PRACTICE the Strategy

NYSCC • NYSMT

Extra Practice, p. R21

Solve by *using a graph*.

5. The table lists the number of wins by the teams in the American Football Conference (AFC) and the National Football Conference (NFC) for a recent season.

Number of Wins	
AFC	12, 10, 7, 6, 13, 8, 8, 4, 12, 8, 8, 6, 14, 9, 9, 2
NFC	10, 9, 8, 5, 13, 8, 6, 3, 10, 8, 7, 4, 9, 8, 7, 5

Graph the data on line plots. Which conference seemed to have the better record? Explain your reasoning using the graph and the term *median*.

6. Company A and Company B make flashlight batteries. Ten batteries from each company were selected and tested to see how many hours they would last. The results are shown below.

Hours of Life from Flashlight Batteries	
Company A	19, 11, 14, 15, 8, 16, 14, 16, 15, 24, 10
Company B	18, 12, 15, 16, 17, 18, 16, 17, 20, 14, 9

Graph the data on line plots. From which company would you purchase batteries? Use the line plots and the term *median* to help explain your reasoning.

For Exercises 7–10, use the table. It gives the number of chirps per minute made by crickets at a given temperature.

Cricket Chirps	
Temperature (°F)	Number
72	136
84	165
68	98
75	110
80	150
94	210
60	84
75	158
92	221
89	178

7. Graph the ordered pairs on a coordinate grid.

8. What appears to happen to the number of chirps as the temperature increases?

9. Suppose the temperature is 65°F. How many times per minute would you expect a cricket to chirp?

10. Suppose you hear a cricket chirp 200 times per minute. About what would you expect the temperature to be?

11. **WRITING IN ►MATH** Find two different sets of data in the newspaper or from the Internet. Write a real-world problem about the data. Ask a classmate to solve your problem.

FOLDABLES®
Study Organizer **GET READY to Study**

Be sure the following Big Ideas are written in your Foldable.

Data and Graphs

Key Concepts

Median and Mode

- The **median** of a set of data is the middle number of the data that has been written in order. **(p. 279)**

- The **mode** of a set of data is the number that occurs most often. **(p. 280)**

Displaying Data

- A **line plot** uses Xs above a number line to show the number of times values in a set of data occur. **(p. 284)**

- A **frequency table** shows the number of times each data value or each value within an interval appears. **(p. 289)**

- A **bar graph** uses bars to compare data. **(p. 299)**

- A **line graph** has plotted points that are connected to show how a quantity changes over time. **(p. 306)**

- A **pictograph** shows data by using picture symbols. **(p. 313)**

Key Vocabulary

bar graph (p. 299)

line graph (p. 306)

median (p. 279)

mode (p. 280)

range (p. 285)

Vocabulary Check

Complete. Use a word from the Key Vocabulary list.

1. The middle number in a set of ordered numbers is the ___?___.

2. To show the change in temperature over a period of time, use a(n) ___?___.

3. The difference between the greatest and least values in a set of data is the ___?___.

4. The ___?___ in the set of data {4, 6, 2, 3, 3, 5, 7} is 3.

5. A(n) ___?___ is a graph that uses bars to compare data.

6. The ___?___ of a set of data is the number that occurs most often.

Lesson-by-Lesson Review

7-1 **Median and Mode** (pp. 279–281)

5.S.1

Example 1
The fat grams of eleven different food items are shown below. Find the median and the mode.

6, 10, 10, 15, 10, 11, 4, 6, 8, 9, 2

First, order the numbers.

2, 4, 6, 6, 8, ⑨, 10, 10, 10, 11, 15

median: 9   the middle number

mode: 10   the number that occurs most often

Find the median and mode of each set of data.

7. number of CDs owned: 11, 8, 6, 9, 15, 15, 12

8. distance from school in miles: 2, 1, 3, 2, 4, 1, 5

9. quiz scores: 90, 88, 82, 97, 100, 88

10. The cost of a fruit smoothie at eight different restaurants is shown below. Find the median and mode.
$1.50, $2.85, $1.75, $1.95, $2.25, $2.30, $1.85, $1.65

7-2 **Problem-Solving Investigation:** **Choose a Strategy** (pp. 282–283)

5.PS.3

Example 2
Algebra For a science experiment, Miss Washington added 6 drops of salt water to a solution on Day 1. She added 11 drops on Day 2, and 16 drops on Day 3. If the pattern continues, how many drops of salt water will she add on Day 5?

Make a table.

Day	1	2	3	4	5
Drops	6	11	16	21	26

+5   +5   +5   +5

So, on Day 5, she will add 26 drops of salt water.

Solve each problem.

11. Find five consecutive odd numbers that have a sum of 65.

12. Marina brought 3 sweaters and 2 pairs of pants. If she wears only her new clothes, how many days will pass before she must repeat an outfit?

13. There are four rabbits. Fluffy is larger than Max but smaller than Cotton. Max is larger than Pepper. Which rabbit is the smallest?

CHAPTER 7 Study Guide and Review

 7-3 **Line Plots** (pp. 284–288)

5.S.1

Example 3

The number of days each month in a non-leap year are shown in the line plot. Find the median, mode, range, and any outliers.

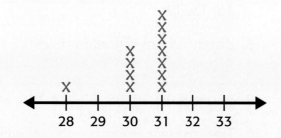

median: 31 days   **mode:** 31 days
range: 3 days   **outliers:** none

14. Draw a line plot for the set of data. Then find the median, mode, range, and any outliers of the data.

number of volunteers: 8, 11, 7, 10, 16, 12, 8, 9, 7, 6, 7, 8, 12

15. The table below shows the number of flavors of ice cream at different ice cream stands.

Flavors of Ice Cream					
11	12	10	8	3	12
12	10	12	9	9	10

Make a line plot of the data. Then write one or two sentences describing the data.

 7-4 **Frequency Tables** (pp. 289–292)

5.S.1

Example 4

The frequency table shows the ages of students' pets. Find the median, mode, range, and any outliers.

Age	Tally	Frequency
1	⦀⦀ ‖	7
2	⦀⦀	5
3	‖	2
4	‖	2

median: 2   **mode:** 1
range: 3   **outliers:** none

Measurement The table below shows the heights of bean plants from science class.

Heights of Bean Plants (cm)				
2	8	8	9	11
7	10	8	11	8
9	11	9	8	8

16. Make a frequency table of the data.

17. Find the median, mode, and range of the data. Identify any outliers.

7-5 Scales and Intervals (pp. 294–298)

Example 5

Number	Tally	Frequency
11–15	||	2
16–20	|||	3
21–25	|||| |	6

scale: 11 to 25   **interval size:** 5

The table shows the number of dogs entered in a dog show for each of the past 12 years.

Number of Dogs					
34	22	38	41	20	36
35	29	45	42	50	48

18. Create a frequency table of the data.

7-6 Bar Graphs (pp. 299–303)

Example 6

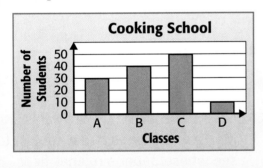

19. Make a double bar graph of the data below.

Minutes of Fireworks		
Town	Last Year	This Year
Milton	32	25
Oak Park	30	24
Fallsworth	25	25
Coryville	27	30

7-7 Line Graphs (pp. 306–310)

Example 7

Baby Panda's Weight

20. Make a line graph of the data below that shows the amount of water left during a science experiment.

Water (mL)	Time (days)
50	1
45	2
33	3
26	4
20	5

CHAPTER 7 Study Guide and Review

7-8 Use an Appropriate Graph (pp. 312–317)

Example 8
Which would be best to show the growth of a elm tree over the last 50 years: a line plot, bar graph, line graph, or pictograph? Explain.

Since a line graph shows change over time, it would be the most appropriate graph to display this data.

The table shows the heights of four waterfalls in the United States.

Waterfall	Height (ft)
Bridalveil	620
Illilouette	370
Inspiration	350
Snoquera	400

21. Which graph would be best to display the data: line plot, bar graph, line graph, or pictograph? Explain.

22. Graph the data.

7-9 Problem-Solving Strategy: Make a Graph (pp. 320–321)

Example 9
The graph shows the attendance at four festivals for two different years. Which town had the greatest increase in attendance?

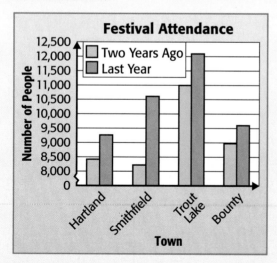

Smithville had the greatest increase in attendance.

Solve by making a graph.

23. Measurement Mr. Sullivan's and Ms. Fazio's classes had a contest to see whose paper airplanes flew farther. The table shows the distances of each airplane.

Paper Airplane Contest	
Class	Distance (ft)
Mr. Sullivan	5, 2, 4, 5, 6, 10, 6, 3, 5, 7
Ms. Fazio	1, 3, 6, 7, 4, 5, 7, 6, 7, 8

Which class would you pick as the winner? Use line plots and the term *median* to explain your reasoning.

Chapter Test

Find the median and mode.

1. cost of breakfast: $2, $4, $3, $3, $2, $3, $4, $5, $4

2. number of movies at theaters: 7, 10, 13, 15, 13, 14, 19, 7, 16, 14, 6, 5

The table shows the time students spent playing video games during one weekend.

Hours Playing Video Games				
2	4	4	3	0
2	1	3	5	3
8	3	0	2	2

3. Draw a line plot of the data.

4. Find the median, mode, range, and any outliers.

5. **MULTIPLE CHOICE** The results of a survey about methods of transportation for vacation are shown in the graph below.

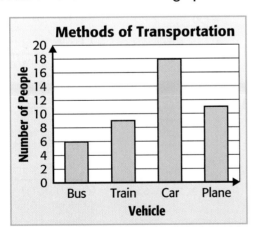

Which statement about the data shown on the graph is NOT true?

  A 44 people were surveyed.

  B The median is 9 people.

  C There were 5 more people who used a plane than a bus.

  D The range of the data is 12.

The table shows the number of students who bought lunch on 12 school days.

Number of Students					
84	76	77	80	71	70
64	92	88	65	79	80

6. Choose an appropriate scale and interval size for a frequency table of the data.

7. Make a frequency table. Describe how the data are distributed among the intervals.

8. **MULTIPLE CHOICE** The frequency table shows the number of laps Allie swam. Which is a true statement?

Laps	Tally	Frequency
26	ⅢⅢ	5
27	‖	2
28	ⅢⅢ Ⅰ	6

  F The mode is 6 laps.

  G The mode is 28 laps.

  H The median is 2 laps.

  J The median is 26 laps.

9. Make a line graph of the data shown below.

Daily Temperature Change in Columbus						
Time	12:00 A.M.	4:00 A.M.	8:00 A.M.	12:00 P.M.	4:00 P.M.	8:00 P.M.
Temperature (°F)	65	60	67	75	84	77

10. **WRITING IN ►MATH** Refer to the table in Exercises 6 and 7. Choose an appropriate graph to display the data. Then graph the data.

PART 1   Multiple Choice

Read each question. Then fill in the correct answer on the answer sheet provided by your teacher or on a sheet of paper.

1. The heights, in inches, of the players on Jordan's volleyball team are 64, 66, 59, 60, 63, 62, 68, 66, and 67. What is the median height?

A 62 in.

C 66 in.

B 64 in.

D 67 in.

2. The table shows the weight of Trina's puppy during its first several months. Which graph would best show the growth of the puppy?

Month	Weight (lb)
1	4
2	5
3	7
4	10
5	12

F line graph

H circle graph

G bar graph

J picture graph

3. The table shows the number of miles Isaiah jogs over a certain number of days. If the pattern continues, how many miles will he jog in 10 days?

Days	Miles Jogged
2	8
4	16
6	24
8	32

A 33 mi

C 38 mi

B 35 mi

D 40 mi

4. Which rule best describes the pattern?

12, 16, 15, 19, 18, 22, 21, …

F Add 4, subtract 1

G Add 5, subtract 2

H Add 5, subtract 2

J Add 10, subtract 5

5. The table below shows the coordinates of three points. Which graph shows the line containing these three points?

Point	H	J	K
x	1	3	5
y	2	4	6

A 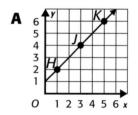   **C**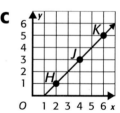

B 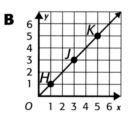   **D**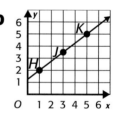

6. Rick's mom is baking 90 brownies for a bake sale. She will put 15 brownies on each plate. Which sentence can be used to find the number of plates, p, she will need?

F $p = 90 \times 15$ **H** $p = 90 - 15$

G $p = 90 \div 15$ **J** $p = 90 + 15$

7. The line graph shows the growth of a plant in a science experiment. Which statement about the data is NOT true?

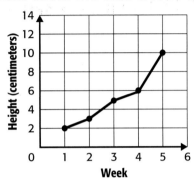

A The range of the data is 8.

B The plant grew the most between weeks 2 and 3.

C The plant grew the same amount between weeks 1 and 2 and weeks 3 and 4.

D The plant grew 2 centimeters between weeks 2 and 3.

---

8. Sugar maple trees can reach heights up to 100 feet. The table below shows the heights of nine different sugar maple trees. What is the median height?

Sugar Maple Heights (ft)		
72	80	89
84	74	81
88	83	74

F 74 ft   **H** 82 ft

G 81 ft   **J** 89 ft

PART 2   Short Response

Record your answers on the sheet provided by your teacher or on a sheet of paper.

9. The heights of the players on a high school basketball team are listed. Order the heights from least to greatest.

Position	Height (cm)
Center	193.45
Point Guard	165.1
Shooting Guard	172.63
Small Forward	182.50
Power Forward	182.92

PART 3   Extended Response

Record your answers on the answer sheet provided by your teacher or on a sheet of paper. Show your work.

10. Explain the mistake in this problem.

$$
\begin{array}{r}
136 \\
\times\ 47 \\
\hline
952 \\
+\ 5{,}440 \\
\hline
5{,}392
\end{array}
$$

---

11. Explain how to multiply 4 and 8,000 mentally.

NEED EXTRA HELP?											
If You Missed Question...	1	2	3	4	5	6	7	8	9	10	11
Go to Lesson...	7-1	7-8	7-3	6-1	6-1	6-6	7-3	7-1	1-6	3-6	3-8
NYS Core Curriculum	5.S.1	5.S.1	5.S.1	5.A.4	5.A.4	5.CM.4	5.S.1	5.S.1	5.N.8	5.N.16	5.N.26

CHAPTER 8 Develop Fraction Concepts

BIG Idea What are fractions?

A **fraction** is a number that names equal parts of a whole or set. Fractions can also represent division situations.

Example At the Watermelon Festival in Lahaska, Pennsylvania, four people are sharing three slices of watermelon.

Each person gets $\frac{3}{4}$ of a slice. In the drawing, each color represents the portion of watermelon shared by each person.

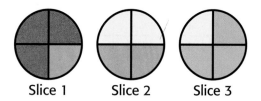

Slice 1   Slice 2   Slice 3

What will I learn in this chapter?

- Represent division situations using fractions.
- Generate an improper fraction equivalent to a mixed number and generate a mixed number equivalent to an improper fraction.
- Compare fractions and mixed numbers and estimate fractions using a number line.
- Solve problems by using logical reasoning.

Key Vocabulary

fraction

mixed number

improper fraction

 **NY Math Online** **Student Study Tools** at macmillanmh.com

FOLDABLES
Study Organizer

Make this Foldable to help you organize information about fractions. Begin with 4 sheets of $8\frac{1}{2}"\times 11"$ paper.

1 Stack four sheets of paper $\frac{3}{4}$ inch apart.

2 Roll up bottom edges so that all tabs are the same size.

3 Crease and staple along the fold.

4 Write the chapter title on the front. Label each tab with the title.

You have two ways to check prerequisite skills for this chapter.

Option 2

NY Math Online > Take the Chapter Readiness Quiz at macmillanmh.com.

Option 1

Complete the Quick Check below.

QUICK Check

Write the fraction that names the shaded part of the whole or set. (Prior Grade)

1.

2.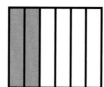

3.

4.

5.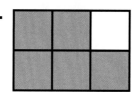

6.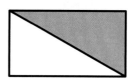

Divide. (Lesson 4-3)

7. $15 \div 2$

8. $22 \div 4$

9. $38 \div 6$

10. $31 \div 7$

11. $42 \div 5$

12. $57 \div 9$

13. There are 51 golf balls to be packaged 6 to a box. How many boxes will be full? Interpret the remainder.

For Exercises 14–16, use the number line below.
Replace each ● with < or > to make a true statement. (Lesson 1-2)

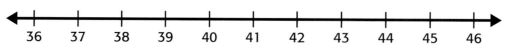

14. 39 ● 36

15. 40 ● 46

16. 38 ● 44

17. Kanya has 45 photos in her album. Lago has 46 photos in his album. Who has more photos in their album?

8-1 Fractions and Division

MAIN IDEA

I will represent division situations using fractions.

NYS Core Curriculum

Reinforcement of 4.N.7 Develop an understanding of fractions as locations on number lines and as divisions of whole numbers

Preparation for 5.N.20 Convert improper fractions to mixed numbers, and mixed numbers to improper fractions

New Vocabulary

fraction
numerator
denominator

NY Math Online

macmillanmh.com
• Extra Examples
• Personal Tutor
• Self-Check Quiz

GET READY to Learn

Kayla feeds 1 cup of cat food to her 3 cats. You can divide to find the amount of food that each cat eats.

1 cup divided among 3 cats
1 ÷ 3

A **fraction** is a number that names equal parts of a whole or parts of a set. A fraction represents division. So, if 1 cup of cat food is divided into 3 equal parts, each cat eats $\frac{1}{3}$ cup of food.

$$\frac{1}{3} \quad \begin{array}{l} \longleftarrow \text{ numerator} \\ \longleftarrow \text{ denominator} \end{array}$$

The **numerator**, or the top number in a fraction, is the number of parts you have. The **denominator**, or the bottom number in a fraction, represents the number of parts in the whole.

Real-World EXAMPLE   Use Fractions

① **FOOD** Dylan, Drake, and Jade are sharing 2 small pizzas equally. How much does each person get?

Two pizzas are divided among three people.

2 ÷ 3

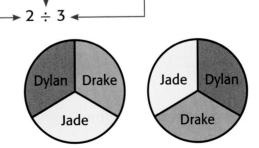

Each person gets $\frac{2}{3}$ of a pizza.

Sometimes it is helpful to interpret the remainder.

Remember

With fractions, objects or quantities being divided are always divided into equal parts.

Real-World EXAMPLE   Interpret the Remainder

2 **FOOD** **Ray and Bailey are sharing 3 brownies equally. How much does each person get?**

Three brownies are divided between two people.

$3 \div 2$

Each person gets $\frac{3}{2}$ of a brownie. The models below show that each person gets 1 whole brownie. There is one brownie remaining, which can be divided equally between the two people. So, each person gets $1\frac{1}{2}$ brownies.

Ray	Bailey —— Ray	Bailey

CHECK What You Know

Represent each situation using a fraction and a model. Then solve.

See Examples 1, 2 (pp. 333–334)

1. Two bags of bird seed are used to fill three bird feeders. How much bird seed does each feeder use?

2. In art class, there are three pounds of clay for four students. Each student receives the same amount. How many pounds of clay will each student receive?

3. Four families equally share the pies below. How much pie will each family receive?

4. Six bags of soil are used to fill 5 flower pots. How much soil does each flower pot use?

5. **Talk About It** Discuss how fractions represent division situations in real life. Give an example.

Represent each situation using a fraction and a model. Then solve.

See Examples 1, 2 (pp. 333–334)

6. One yard of fabric is used to make two school banners. How many yards of fabric does each banner use?

7. One large submarine sandwich is divided equally among four people. How much of the sandwich did each person receive?

8. Measurement Three pounds of potatoes make eight equal size servings of mashed potatoes. How many pounds of potatoes are in each serving?

9. Two truckloads of mulch are used to cover seven playground areas. Each playground receives the same amount of mulch. How much mulch does each playground receive?

10. Demont used the gasoline shown below in three days driving to work. Each day he used the same amount of gasoline. How many gallons of gasoline did he use each day?

11. The loaves of banana bread below are sliced to be placed in five storage containers. If each slice is the same size, how much of a loaf of banana bread is in each container?

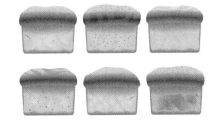

12. Four gallons of paint are used to paint 25 chairs. If each chair used the amount of paint, how many chairs be painted from each gallon?

13. Measurement Mrs. Larsen made seven pillows from nine yards of same fabric. How much fabric was used to can make each pillow?

H.O.T. Problems

14. OPEN ENDED Write a real-world division problem involving four objects that are being divided equally. Then solve.

15. REASONING Five pounds of trail mix are divided equally among a group of Girl Scouts.

   a. If the number of Girl Scouts increases, what happens to the amount of trail mix that each girl gets? Explain.

   b. If the number of pounds of trail mix increases, what happens to the amount of trail mix that each girl gets? Explain.

16. WRITING IN ►MATH Write a real-world problem that has a solution of $\frac{2}{15}$. Describe what the fraction represents.

Math Activity for 8-2
Model Mixed Numbers and Improper Fractions

MAIN IDEA

I will use models to represent mixed numbers and improper fractions.

NYS Core Curriculum

Preparation for 5.N.20 Convert improper fractions to mixed numbers, and mixed numbers to improper fractions

New Vocabulary

mixed number
improper fraction

You can use rectangles to model whole numbers.

  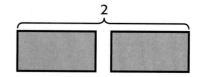

Rectangles can be divided into equal parts to model fractions.

The rectangle is divided into 2 equal parts.

The rectangles are divided into 3 equal parts.

A **mixed number** has a whole number and a fraction. It is a number greater than one.

ACTIVITY

1) **Use a model to represent $2\frac{1}{3}$. How many thirds are there?**

Step 1 Draw and shade two rectangles to represent 2.

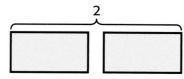

Step 2 Draw another rectangle and shade $\frac{1}{3}$ of it to represent the fraction $\frac{1}{3}$.

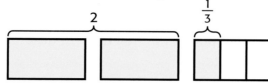

Step 3 Divide each rectangle into thirds.

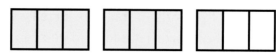

There are 7 thirds. So, $2\frac{1}{3} = \frac{7}{3}$.

Improper fractions are fractions that have a numerator greater than or equal to the denominator.

ACTIVITY

2 Use a model to represent $\frac{7}{4}$. Then write it as a mixed number.

Step 1 Since the denominator is 4, draw rectangles that are divided into 4 equal parts.

Draw enough rectangles so that you can shade 7 parts. In this case, two rectangles are needed.

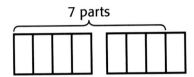

7 parts

Step 2 Since the numerator is 7, shade 7 of the parts.

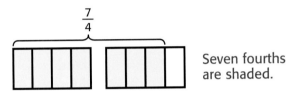

$\frac{7}{4}$

Seven fourths are shaded.

Step 3 There is one whole and three fourths. So, $\frac{7}{4} = 1\frac{3}{4}$.

Think About It

1. How can you tell if a fraction can be written as a mixed number?

✓ CHECK What You Know

Use a model to represent each mixed number. Then write it as an improper fraction.

2. $1\frac{1}{2}$ **3.** $2\frac{3}{4}$ **4.** $2\frac{1}{5}$ **5.** $1\frac{5}{8}$

Use a model to represent each improper fraction. Then write it as a mixed number.

6. $\frac{5}{3}$ **7.** $\frac{7}{2}$ **8.** $\frac{9}{4}$ **9.** $\frac{10}{6}$

10. **WRITING IN ►MATH** What do the improper fractions $\frac{2}{2}$, $\frac{6}{3}$, and $\frac{12}{4}$ have in common? Explain your reasoning.

8-2

GET READY to Learn

Mrs. Danko divided cakes into thirds for a school bake sale. At the end of the sale, she had 5 thirds left.

$$\frac{5}{3}$$ ← has 5 parts
← divided into thirds

MAIN IDEA

I will write improper fractions as mixed numbers.

NYS Core Curriculum

5.N.20 Convert improper fractions to mixed numbers, and mixed numbers to improper fractions

NY Math Online

macmillanmh.com
• Extra Examples
• Personal Tutor
• Self-Check Quiz

In the Explore Activity for 8-2, you learned about improper fractions and mixed numbers. Some examples are shown below.

Improper Fractions	**Mixed Numbers**
$\frac{5}{3}$ $\frac{9}{8}$ $\frac{12}{12}$	$1\frac{4}{5}$ $8\frac{1}{2}$

Since a fraction represents division, $\frac{5}{3}$ means $5 \div 3$. To write an improper fraction that is equivalent to a mixed number, perform the division. Then, express the remainder as a fraction.

EXAMPLE **Rename an Improper Fraction**

1 Write $\frac{5}{3}$ as an equivalent mixed number.

Step 1 Divide the numerator by the denominator.

$$\begin{array}{r} 1\ R2 \\ 3\overline{)5} \\ -3 \\ \hline 2 \end{array}$$ ← number of thirds left

Step 2 Write the remainder as a fraction with the divisor as the denominator.

$$1\frac{2}{3}$$
↑
Write the quotient as the whole number.

So, $\frac{5}{3} = 1\frac{2}{3}$. The model above shows that this makes sense.

EXAMPLE **Rename an Improper Fraction**

2 Write $\frac{20}{10}$ as an equivalent mixed number.

Divide the numerator by
the denominator.

$$\begin{array}{r} 2 \\ 10\overline{)20} \\ -20 \\ \hline 0 \end{array}$$
← there is no remainder

Since 10 divides evenly into 20, $\frac{20}{10}$ can be written as 2.

Real-World EXAMPLE

Remember

It is important to think about what the fractional part of the mixed number means in real-life situations.

3 ROLLER COASTERS Each train on a roller coaster can hold 24 passengers. If there are 55 people, then the number of trains needed to hold them is $\frac{55}{24}$. Write $\frac{55}{24}$ with a remainder. Then write it as an equivalent mixed number. Explain what both numbers mean.

Find 55 ÷ 24.

$$\begin{array}{r} 2\;R7 \\ 24\overline{)55} \\ -48 \\ \hline 7 \end{array} \Rightarrow 2\frac{7}{24}$$
← number of passengers left of the 24 total passengers

So, $\frac{55}{24}$ = 2 R7. This means that 2 trains are completely full and a third train has 7 people on it. Also, $\frac{55}{24} = 2\frac{7}{24}$. This means that $2\frac{7}{24}$ trains are full.

Improper Fractions	Key Concept

Words   To write an improper fraction as a mixed number, divide the numerator by the denominator. Write the remainder as a fraction of the divisor.

Numbers

$$\begin{array}{r} 1\;R2 \\ 3\overline{)5} \\ -3 \\ \hline 2 \end{array} \Rightarrow 1\frac{2}{3}$$

Write each improper fraction as an equivalent mixed number. See Examples 1–3 (pp. 338–339)

1. $\frac{5}{2}$

2. $\frac{8}{3}$

3. $\frac{9}{5}$

4. $\frac{11}{10}$

5. $\frac{18}{2}$

6. $\frac{29}{8}$

7. $\frac{25}{12}$

8. $\frac{36}{6}$

9. Miss Kim divides 12 ounces of granola among 5 children. How much granola does each child get? Write the answer with a remainder. Then write as a mixed number. Explain what both numbers mean.

10. **Talk About It** Explain how to write an improper fraction as a mixed number. Give an example and show each step.

Practice and Problem Solving

> NYSCC • NYSMT
> Extra Practice, p. R21

Write each improper fraction as an equivalent mixed number. See Examples 1–3 (pp. 338–339)

11. $\frac{9}{2}$

12. $\frac{8}{5}$

13. $\frac{7}{5}$

14. $\frac{16}{8}$

15. $\frac{11}{4}$

16. $\frac{19}{5}$

17. $\frac{18}{9}$

18. $\frac{17}{3}$

19. $\frac{24}{8}$

20. $\frac{19}{4}$

21. $\frac{13}{10}$

22. $\frac{23}{5}$

23. $\frac{29}{2}$

24. $\frac{30}{3}$

25. $\frac{37}{12}$

26. $\frac{35}{6}$

27. **Measurement** A delivery truck travels 36 miles in 7 hours. Write the number of miles driven each hour as a mixed number.

28. In a recent year, $\frac{26}{5}$ million football video games were sold. Write the number in millions as a mixed number.

Measurement For Exercises 29–31, use the graphic that shows the length of various dirt bike courses.

29. Write the length of course A as a mixed number.

30. Write the length of course B as a mixed number.

31. Which course is longer, course A or course C?

32. Mrs. Blair has 35 pencil top erasers to divide equally among her 16 students. How many erasers does each student receive? Write the answer with a remainder. Then write as a mixed number. Explain what the remainder means.

DIRT BIKE COURSES

COURSE	LENGTH (MI)
A	$\frac{5}{4}$
B	$\frac{7}{4}$
C	$\frac{9}{4}$

Real-World PROBLEM SOLVING

Science The birds listed in the table lay the largest eggs in the world—up to 4 pounds each for an ostrich and about $1\frac{1}{2}$ pounds each for emus and kiwis.

Write the height of each bird as a mixed number.

33. emu

34. kiwi

35. ostrich

Bird	Height
Emu	$\frac{47}{8}$ ft
Kiwi	$\frac{55}{4}$ in.
Ostrich	$\frac{32}{5}$ ft

H.O.T. Problems

36. OPEN ENDED Give an example of an improper fraction that is greater than 5 and less than 8.

37. FIND THE ERROR Sophia and Oliver are writing $\frac{35}{12}$ as a mixed number. Who is correct? Explain.

Sophia
$\frac{35}{12} = 3\frac{5}{12}$

Oliver
$\frac{35}{12} = 2\frac{11}{12}$

38. Algebra If $\frac{x}{y}$ is an improper fraction, which is a true statement? Explain.

- $x < y$
- $x > y$ or $x = y$
- $x \neq y$

39. CHALLENGE Write $1\frac{10}{3}$ so that it does not contain an improper fraction.

40. WRITING IN ►MATH Write a real-world problem that can be solved by changing an improper fraction to a mixed number. First find the remainder. Then write it as a mixed number. Include an explanation of what both numbers mean.

41. Jerome recorded the colors of trucks that he saw while traveling. The table shows the data he collected.

Truck Colors				
Color	black	blue	red	other
Number of Trucks	5	3	6	3

Which fraction represents the number of red trucks that he saw? (Lesson 8-1)

A $\frac{1}{6}$

C $\frac{6}{11}$

B $\frac{6}{17}$

D $\frac{6}{9}$

42. Five people equally share the apples.

How many apples does each person get? (Lesson 8-2)

F 2 apples

H $\frac{5}{8}$ of an apple

G $1\frac{3}{5}$ apples

J 1 apple

Spiral Review

43. Two sticks of butter are used to make 3 batches of cookies. How much butter does each batch of cookies need? (Lesson 8-1)

44. Kishi's science quiz scores are 86, 88, 90, 84, 92, 80, 92, 88, 86, 84, and 86. Domingo's science quiz scores are 90, 84, 88, 92, 90, 80, 94, 88, 90, 92, and 84. Which student has the higher median quiz score? Use line plots. (Lesson 7-9)

45. The table shows the number of cans each classroom recycled. Which would be best to display the data: a bar graph, double bar graph, line graph, or double line graph? Explain. (Lesson 7-8)

Classroom	1	2	3	4	5	6	7	8
Recycled Cans (lb)	15	22	17	23	28	35	37	40

Algebra Solve each equation. (Lesson 6-1)

46. $x + 2 = 9$

47. $t - 8 = 4$

48. $15 = 5 + r$

49. $n - 7 = 1$

50. Mariko makes and sells ceramic mugs for $6 each. She pays $24 to enter a festival. She sells 29 mugs. How much money does Mariko earn after paying to enter the festival? (Lesson 3-4)

Write each number in standard form. (Lesson 1-5)

51. 4 and 22 hundredths

52. $30 + 5 + 0.8 + 0.02$

That's Not Proper

Converting Improper Fractions to Mixed Numbers

You will need: Spinners

Get Ready!

Players: 3 players

Get Set!

- Label equal sections of one spinner with the numbers 13, 17, 23, 29, 37, 41, 57. The numbers on this spinner stand for the numerators of improper fractions.

- Label equal sections of a second spinner with the numbers 3, 4, 5, 6, 7, 8, 9, 11. These numbers stand for the denominators of improper fractions.

Go!

- One student spins both spinners.

- The first of the other two students to express the resulting improper fraction as an equivalent mixed number wins the round.

- Play several rounds, trading roles each time.

Problem-Solving Strategy

MAIN IDEA I will solve problems by using logical reasoning.

NYSCC **5.PS.9 Understand the basic language of logic in mathematical situations** *Also addresses 5.PS.21.*

Of the students in a fifth grade class, 15 play basketball and 18 play soccer. Three of those students play both sports. How many students play only basketball? only soccer?

Understand	**What facts do you know?** • We know how many students play basketball, play soccer, and play both sports. **What do you need to find?** • The number of students that play only basketball and only soccer.
Plan	One way to solve the problem is to make a Venn diagram. A **Venn diagram** uses overlapping circles to show how common elements among sets of objects are related. The overlapping section shows the objects that are in both groups.
Solve	Draw two overlapping circles to represent the two different sports. Since 3 students are involved in both sports, place a 3 in the overlapping section. Use subtraction to determine the number for each of the other sections. only basketball: $15 - 3 = 12$ only soccer: $18 - 3 = 15$ 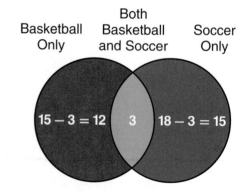
Check	Look back. Check each circle to make sure that the correct number of students is represented. ✔

ANALYZE the Strategy

Refer to the problem on the previous page.

1. If there were 39 students in the fifth grade class, how many students did not play either soccer or basketball?

2. Two of the students that played neither sport began playing both basketball and soccer. How many students now play soccer? Basketball? Both?

3. How would the Venn diagram change if some students in the class began playing baseball?

4. Explain how drawing a Venn diagram can help you solve problems.

PRACTICE the Strategy

NYSCC • NYSMT
Extra Practice, p. R22

Solve by *using logical reasoning*.

5. Elisa's family is choosing pizza toppings for their pizza. Five people like pepperoni, 6 people like extra cheese, and 3 people like both. How many people like pepperoni only?

6. Refer to Exercise 5. Can you tell how many people are in Elisa's family? Explain.

7. Mr. Lewis surveyed 20 students in his class about their favorite ice cream. If all students surveyed liked at least one of the two flavors, how many students liked both flavors?

Favorite Ice Cream	
Flavor	Number of Students
Chocolate	11
Strawberry	13

8. In an art club meeting, 30 people want to use paint on a mural. Twenty-seven people want to use transfers. Twelve people want to use both. How many people want to use only paint?

9. There are 15 kittens in a pet shelter and 9 of them are brown. Eight kittens have long fur, and four of the kittens are both brown and have long fur. How many kittens do not have long fur or are not brown?

10. In the school orchestra, 43 students play string instruments, 15 students play woodwind instruments, and 30 students play brass instruments. Five students play all three, 3 students play both strings and brass, 1 student plays string and woodwind and no students play woodwind and brass. How many students play only brass?

11. **WRITING IN MATH** A survey of 100 people found that 67 people like skiing, 58 people like skating, and 25 people like both sports. Describe the steps you would take to find how many people like only skiing.

Lesson 8-3 Problem-Solving Strategy: Use Logical Reasoning 345

Mixed Numbers

GET READY to Learn

One of the smallest dogs in the world is a long-haired Chihuahua. It is only $5\frac{1}{3}$ inches tall.

The model shows $5\frac{1}{3}$ divided into thirds. You can write $5\frac{1}{3}$ as an equivalent improper fraction by counting the number of thirds.

You can also use multiplication and addition to write mixed numbers as improper fractions.

Real-World EXAMPLE — Write a Mixed Number as an Improper Fraction

1 **MEASUREMENT** Refer to the information above. Write $5\frac{1}{3}$ inches as an equivalent improper fraction.

Step 1 To find how many thirds are in 5, multiply the whole number, 5, by the denominator, 3.

$5 \times 3 = 15$

Step 2 There is one more third. Add the numerator.

$(5 \times 3) + 1 = 16$

Step 3 Write the sum over the original denominator, 3.

$\frac{(5 \times 3) + 1}{3} = \frac{16}{3}$

So, $5\frac{1}{3}$ inches $= \frac{16}{3}$ inches.

EXAMPLE   **Rename a Mixed Number**

2 **Write $2\frac{7}{8}$ as an equivalent improper fraction.**

> **Remember**
>
> There are two wholes, each with eight parts, plus seven parts.

Step 1 Multiply the whole number by the denominator.

$$2 \times 8 = 16$$

Step 2 Add the numerator.

$$(2 \times 8) + 7 = 23$$

Step 3 Write the sum over the original denominator.

$$\frac{(2 \times 8) + 7}{8} = \frac{23}{8}$$

So, $2\frac{7}{8} = \frac{23}{8}$. You can use models to check.

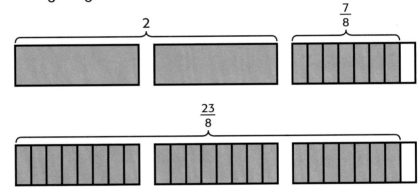

CHECK What You Know

Write each mixed number as an equivalent improper fraction. Check using models. See Examples 1, 2 (pp. 346–347)

1. $1\frac{2}{5}$ **2.** $3\frac{1}{4}$ **3.** $5\frac{2}{3}$ **4.** $7\frac{3}{5}$

5. $4\frac{1}{8}$ **6.** $5\frac{9}{10}$ **7.** $2\frac{4}{7}$ **8.** $10\frac{3}{4}$

9. Measurement The camel shown at the right is $6\frac{1}{2}$ feet tall. Write the camel's height as an improper fraction.

10. **Talk About It** Describe each step that you would take to write $5\frac{1}{9}$ as an improper fraction.

Write each mixed number as an equivalent improper fraction.
Check using models. See Examples 1, 2 (pp. 346–347)

11. $2\frac{1}{3}$ **12.** $1\frac{1}{8}$ **13.** $6\frac{1}{2}$ **14.** $3\frac{2}{7}$

15. $9\frac{1}{2}$ **16.** $6\frac{1}{5}$ **17.** $8\frac{2}{5}$ **18.** $3\frac{4}{9}$

19. $4\frac{3}{8}$ **20.** $5\frac{3}{10}$ **21.** $7\frac{3}{4}$ **22.** $1\frac{5}{6}$

23. $5\frac{7}{8}$ **24.** $6\frac{2}{9}$ **25.** $2\frac{3}{11}$ **26.** $12\frac{4}{5}$

27. A maze in England has a path made of hedges that is $2\frac{3}{16}$ miles long. Write the length as an improper fraction.

28. The longest tournament chess game ever played lasted $20\frac{1}{4}$ hours. What is the time written as an improper fraction?

New York Data File

The Eurypterus Remipes, or "sea scorpion," is the state fossil of New York. One such fossil has a length of $17\frac{1}{2}$ centimeters and a width of $9\frac{2}{10}$ centimeters.

Write each measure as an improper fraction.

29. the fossil's length

30. the fossil's width

Source: Virtual Fossil Museum

H.O.T. Problems

CHALLENGE **If $y = 4$, find a value for x that satisfies each situation.**

31. $\frac{x}{y}$ is equal to an improper fraction beween 1 and 2.

32. $\frac{x}{y}$ is equal to an improper fraction between 2 and 3.

33. $\frac{x}{y}$ is equal to an improper fraction between 3 and 4.

34. **WRITING IN ►MATH** Choose a whole number and write it as an improper fraction in three different ways. Explain.

For Exercises 1 and 2, represent each situation using a fraction. Describe what the fraction means. (Lesson 8-1)

1. Eight people equally share 5 quarts of strawberries. How many quarts of strawberries does each person receive?

2. Jonathon, Luke, Delmar, and Kelsey share a bag of pretzels equally. What fraction of the bag does each person receive?

3. **MULTIPLE CHOICE** Three bags of popcorn are used to fill the bowls below. Which is a true statement? (Lesson 8-1)

C08-057A-105939

A Each bowl gets 1 bag of popcorn.

B Each bowl gets $\frac{1}{3}$ bag of popcorn.

C Each bowl gets $\frac{1}{5}$ bag of popcorn.

D Each bowl gets $\frac{3}{5}$ bag of popcorn.

Write each improper fraction as an equivalent mixed number. (Lesson 8-2)

4. $\frac{9}{5}$

5. $\frac{10}{7}$

6. $\frac{16}{3}$

7. $\frac{30}{10}$

8. There are 35 life jackets. Each canoe must have 4 life jackets. How many canoes have the required number of life jackets? How many life jackets are left? (Lesson 8-3)

9. In a survey, 28 students said they go to the roller skating rink, and 14 said they go to the ice skating rink. Seven students said they go to both rinks. How many students go to the ice skating rink but not the roller skating rink? (Lesson 8-3)

10. **MULTIPLE CHOICE** The largest yo-yo measures $10\frac{1}{3}$ feet across. Which is another way of writing this measure? (Lesson 8-4)

F $\frac{33}{3}$ ft   H $\frac{11}{3}$ ft

G $\frac{31}{3}$ ft   J $\frac{10}{3}$ ft

Write each mixed number as an equivalent improper fraction. (Lesson 8-4)

11. $1\frac{3}{8}$

12. $2\frac{5}{9}$

13. $5\frac{2}{3}$

14. $3\frac{1}{7}$

15. **Measurement** The dog bone is $2\frac{7}{8}$ inches long. Write the length as an improper fraction. (Lesson 8-4)

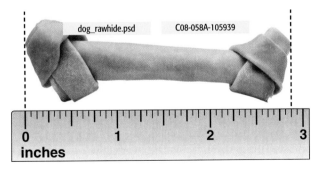

dog_rawhide.psd   C08-058A-105939

16. **WRITING IN ►MATH** Explain how you know whether a fraction is less than 1 or greater than 1. (Lesson 8-3)

8-5 Fractions on a Number Line

GET READY to Learn

A recipe for chili calls for $\frac{1}{8}$ teaspoon of cayenne pepper and $\frac{7}{8}$ teaspoon of salt. Does the chili have more cayenne pepper or salt? You can see from the models that $\frac{1}{8} < \frac{7}{8}$.

$\frac{1}{8}$

$\frac{7}{8}$

MAIN IDEA

I will compare fractions and mixed numbers using a number line.

NYS Core Curriculum

5.N.9 Compare fractions using <, >, or = *Also addresses 5.N.5.*

NY Math Online

macmillanmh.com
• Extra Examples
• Personal Tutor
• Self-Check Quiz
• Concepts in Motion

Real-World EXAMPLE Compare Fractions

1 **MEASUREMENT** Is $\frac{5}{8}$ yard of fabric enough for a pattern that needs $\frac{7}{8}$ yard of fabric? Use a number line.

There are 8 equal sections between 0 and 1.

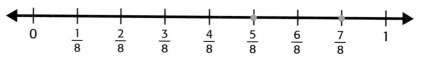

Since $\frac{7}{8}$ is to the right of $\frac{5}{8}$ on the number line, $\frac{7}{8} > \frac{5}{8}$.
So, $\frac{5}{8}$ yard of fabric is not enough.

EXAMPLE Compare Fractions and Mixed Numbers

2 Replace ● with < or > to make $2\frac{3}{5}$ ● $\frac{7}{5}$ a true statement.

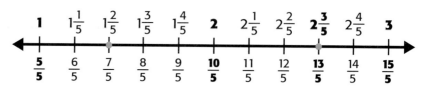

Since $\frac{7}{5} = 1\frac{2}{5}$, and $2\frac{3}{5}$ is to the right of $1\frac{2}{5}$, $2\frac{3}{5} > \frac{7}{5}$.

350 **Chapter 8** Develop Fraction Concepts

EXAMPLE

Fractions and Mixed Numbers on a Number Line

3 Write the fraction or mixed number that is represented by points *A* and *B* below.

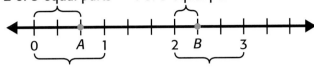

2 of 3 equal parts   1 of 3 equal parts

3 equal parts   3 equal parts

Point *A* represents 2 of 3 parts or $\frac{2}{3}$. Point *B* represents

2 whole units plus 1 of 3 parts or $2\frac{1}{3}$.

CHECK What You Know

For Exercises 1–3 use the number line. Replace each ● with < or > to make a true statement. See Examples 1, 2 (p. 350)

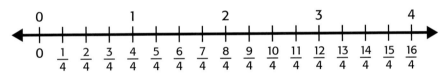

1. $\frac{3}{4}$ ● $\frac{1}{4}$

2. $\frac{5}{4}$ ● $\frac{11}{4}$

3. $3\frac{1}{4}$ ● $\frac{9}{4}$

Replace each ● with < or > to make a true statement. Use a number line if needed. See Examples 1, 2 (p. 350)

4. $\frac{4}{7}$ ● $\frac{6}{7}$

5. $1\frac{1}{3}$ ● $1\frac{2}{3}$

6. $2\frac{1}{9}$ ● $\frac{15}{9}$

Write the fraction or mixed number that is represented by each point.

See Example 3 (p. 351)

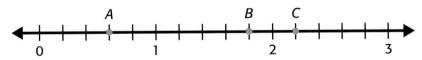

7. *A*

8. *B*

9. *C*

10. Measurement Jan's recipe for cookies uses $\frac{1}{3}$ cup of peanut butter and $\frac{2}{3}$ cup of sugar. Does the recipe call for more peanut butter or sugar? Support your answer with a model.

11. **Talk About It** Explain how to compare $4\frac{8}{10}$ and $5\frac{7}{10}$ without using a number line.

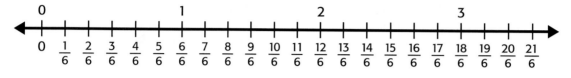

Practice and Problem Solving

NYSCC • NYSMT

Extra Practice, p. R22

For Exercises 12–17 use the number line. Replace each ⬤ with < or > to make a true statement. See Examples 1, 2 (p. 350)

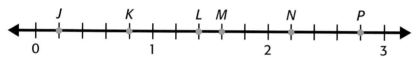

12. $\frac{5}{6}$ ⬤ $\frac{2}{6}$

13. $\frac{4}{6}$ ⬤ $\frac{9}{6}$

14. $\frac{11}{6}$ ⬤ $\frac{19}{6}$

15. $\frac{10}{6}$ ⬤ $1\frac{3}{6}$

16. $1\frac{5}{6}$ ⬤ $\frac{15}{6}$

17. $3\frac{2}{6}$ ⬤ $3\frac{1}{6}$

Replace each ⬤ with < or > to make a true statement.

See Examples 1, 2 (p. 350)

18. $\frac{3}{8}$ ⬤ $\frac{6}{8}$

19. $\frac{5}{9}$ ⬤ $\frac{11}{9}$

20. $2\frac{5}{6}$ ⬤ $2\frac{4}{6}$

21. $\frac{16}{7}$ ⬤ $2\frac{1}{7}$

22. $\frac{14}{5}$ ⬤ $3\frac{2}{5}$

23. $1\frac{3}{10}$ ⬤ $\frac{15}{10}$

Write the fraction or mixed number that is represented by each point. See Example 3 (p. 351)

24. *J*

25. *K*

26. *L*

27. *M*

28. *N*

29. *P*

30. **Measurement** Sherita lives $2\frac{4}{5}$ miles from school and $\frac{12}{5}$ miles from the gym where she takes gymnastics. Is Sherita's home closer to school or to the gym? Explain.

31. **Measurement** Gustavo's pumpkin weighs $3\frac{7}{8}$ pounds. Shelby's pumpkin weighs $\frac{32}{8}$ pounds. Whose pumpkin weighs more? Explain. Support your answer with a model.

32. **Measurement** A recipe for banana bread calls for $2\frac{3}{4}$ cups of flour. Sam's mom has measured out nine $\frac{1}{4}$ cup scoops of flour. Has she measured enough flour? Explain.

33. Emmett rode his bike 25 miles in 2 hours. Lauren rode her bike $14\frac{1}{5}$ miles in 1 hour. Who rode faster in miles per hour? Explain.

352 Chapter 8 Develop Fraction Concepts

H.O.T. Problems

34. OPEN ENDED Write two improper fractions that would be graphed between points *A* and *B* on the number line.

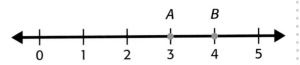

35. FIND THE ERROR Kedar and Ashley are comparing $3\frac{5}{6}$ and $\frac{19}{6}$. Who is correct? Explain.

Kedar

$3\frac{5}{6} = \frac{(3 + 6 + 5)}{6}$

$\frac{14}{6} \, \bullet \, \frac{19}{6}$

$\frac{14}{6} < \frac{19}{6}$

Ashley

$3\frac{5}{6} = \frac{(3 \times 6) + 5}{6}$

$\frac{23}{6} \, \bullet \, \frac{19}{6}$

$\frac{23}{6} > \frac{19}{6}$

36. **WRITING IN ►MATH** Explain how you can use a number line to compare a fraction and a mixed number.

NYSMT Practice 5.N.20, 5.PS.9

37. Which shows the correct relationship between the numbers in the table below? (Lesson 8-5)

Day	Rainfall (in.)
Monday	$\frac{7}{10}$
Tuesday	$1\frac{3}{10}$

A $\frac{7}{10} > 1\frac{3}{10}$ **C** $1\frac{3}{10} > \frac{7}{10}$

B $\frac{7}{10} = 1\frac{3}{10}$ **D** $1\frac{3}{10} < \frac{7}{10}$

38. A song is $4\frac{3}{10}$ minutes long. Which is another way of writing $4\frac{3}{10}$? (Lesson 8-4)

F $\frac{7}{10}$

G $\frac{12}{10}$

H $\frac{40}{10}$

J $\frac{43}{10}$

Spiral Review

Write each mixed number as an improper fraction. (Lesson 8-4)

39. $3\frac{1}{5}$ **40.** $1\frac{7}{8}$ **41.** $4\frac{2}{11}$ **42.** $6\frac{5}{9}$

Write each improper fraction as a mixed number. (Lesson 8-2)

43. $\frac{11}{8}$ **44.** $\frac{17}{6}$ **45.** $\frac{37}{5}$ **46.** $\frac{21}{4}$

Problem Solving in Geography

The Great United States

How big is the United States? In total land area, the United States is about three times as large as India and about one and one-third times as large as Australia. However, the United States is only about two-thirds the size of Russia and only accounts for about one-fifteenth of the world's land area.

Largest Countries in the World

Russia $\frac{1}{10}$

Canada $\frac{1}{15}$

United States $\frac{1}{15}$

China $\frac{1}{15}$

Brazil $\frac{3}{50}$

India $\frac{1}{50}$

Argentina $\frac{1}{50}$

Australia $\frac{1}{20}$

Countries and Their Approximate Fractions of World's Land Area

Source: World Atlas

Did You Know?

About one-fifth of the area of the United States is water.

 ## Real-World Math

Use the information on page 354 to solve each problem.

1. The land size of the United States is about how many times as large as Australia? Write this number as an improper fraction.

2. The land size of Russia is about $2\frac{1}{5}$ times the land size of Australia. Write this mixed number as an improper fraction.

3. The land size of the United States is about $\frac{37}{11}$ times the land size of Argentina. Write this improper fraction as a mixed number.

4. Does Russia or Canada account for a greater fraction of the world's land area?

5. Does Brazil or India account for a lesser fraction of the world's land area?

6. Name two countries that account for the same fraction of the world's land area.

8-6 Round Fractions

MAIN IDEA

I will round fractions to 0, $\frac{1}{2}$, and 1 using a number line.

NYS Core Curriculum

Preparation for 5.N.25 Estimate sums and differences of fractions with like denominators

NY Math Online

macmillanmh.com
- Extra Examples
- Personal Tutor
- Self-Check Quiz

GET READY to Learn

A poison dart frog is 2 inches long. This is equal to $\frac{2}{12}$ of a foot.

One way to round a fraction is to use a number line.

Real-World EXAMPLE Round Fractions

1 **ANIMALS** Refer to the information above. Is the length of a poison dart frog closest to 0 foot, $\frac{1}{2}$ foot, or 1 foot?

Graph $\frac{2}{12}$ on a number line.

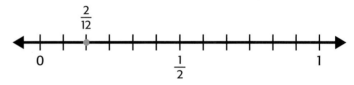

On the number line, $\frac{2}{12}$ is closer to 0 than to $\frac{1}{2}$ or 1. So, the length of a poison dart frog is closest to 0 feet.

You can also round fractions mentally.

Rounding Fractions		Key Concept
Round Down	**Round to $\frac{1}{2}$**	**Round Up**
If the numerator is much smaller than the denominator, round the number down to the previous whole number.	If the numerator is about half of the denominator, round the fraction to $\frac{1}{2}$.	If the numerator is almost as large as the denominator, round the number up to the next whole number.
Example	**Example**	**Example**
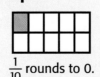	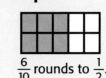	
$\frac{1}{10}$ rounds to 0.	$\frac{6}{10}$ rounds to $\frac{1}{2}$.	$\frac{9}{10}$ rounds to 1.

Remember

The numerator is the top number in a fraction. The denominator is the bottom number. In the fraction $\frac{4}{9}$, 4 is the numerator and 9 is the denominator.

2 Round $\frac{4}{9}$ to 0, $\frac{1}{2}$, or 1.

Since 4 is about half of 9, $\frac{4}{9}$ is closest to $\frac{1}{2}$. You can see from the number line that $\frac{4}{9}$ is closer to $\frac{1}{2}$ than it is to 0 or 1.

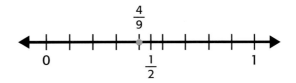

3 Round $\frac{10}{11}$ to 0, $\frac{1}{2}$, or 1.

Since 10 is close to 11, $\frac{10}{11}$ is closest to 1.

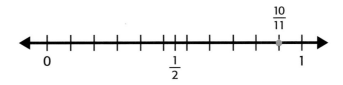

CHECK What You Know

State whether each fraction is closest to 0, $\frac{1}{2}$, or 1.

See Example 1 (p. 356)

1. $\frac{5}{6}$

2. $\frac{5}{8}$

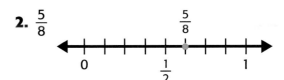

Round each fraction to 0, $\frac{1}{2}$, or 1. See Examples 2, 3 (p. 357)

3. $\frac{1}{8}$ **4.** $\frac{5}{9}$ **5.** $\frac{7}{8}$ **6.** $\frac{3}{7}$

7. $\frac{3}{11}$ **8.** $\frac{4}{5}$ **9.** $\frac{8}{16}$ **10.** $\frac{1}{9}$

11. Measurement Round the length of the ribbon to the nearest half inch.

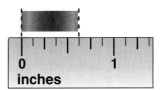

12. Tell how to round fractions in your own words.

State whether each fraction is closest to 0, $\frac{1}{2}$, or 1. See Example 1 (p. 356)

13. $\frac{6}{7}$

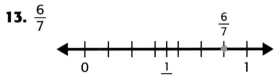

14. $\frac{2}{5}$

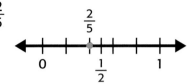

15. $\frac{3}{8}$

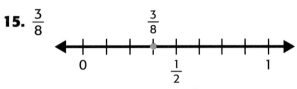

16. $\frac{1}{6}$

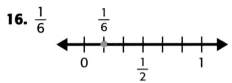

Round each fraction to 0, $\frac{1}{2}$, or 1. See Examples 2–3 (p. 357)

17. $\frac{1}{5}$　　　　18. $\frac{1}{14}$　　　　19. $\frac{12}{15}$　　　　20. $\frac{8}{14}$

21. $\frac{6}{7}$　　　　22. $\frac{2}{7}$　　　　23. $\frac{6}{11}$　　　　24. $\frac{2}{13}$

25. $\frac{9}{17}$　　　　26. $\frac{2}{10}$　　　　27. $\frac{6}{13}$　　　　28. $\frac{14}{16}$

29. Kevin ate $\frac{5}{12}$ of a pizza. Which is a better estimate for the amount of pizza that he ate: about half of the pizza or about all of the pizza?

30. **Measurement** Savannah is using $\frac{15}{16}$ foot squares in a quilt she is making. Are the squares closer to $\frac{1}{2}$ foot or 1 foot long?

31. Peter has read about $\frac{12}{15}$ of his book. Has he read half of his book or almost all of his book?

32. Darius has mowed $\frac{2}{10}$ of his backyard. Which is a better estimate for how much of the lawn he has left to mow: all of the lawn or half of the lawn?

H.O.T. Problems

33. **OPEN ENDED** Write a fraction with a denominator of 15 that you could round to $\frac{1}{2}$.

34. **WHICH ONE DOESN'T BELONG?** Identify the fraction that does not belong with the other three. Explain your reasoning.

$$\frac{2}{11} \qquad \frac{8}{15} \qquad \frac{7}{13} \qquad \frac{5}{12}$$

35. **CHALLENGE** Write two fractions in which the difference between the numerator and the denominator is 2. One fraction can be rounded to 1 and the other fraction can be rounded to $\frac{1}{2}$.

36. **WRITING IN ▶MATH** Describe two different ways of rounding fractions. When is the best time to use each method?

37. Samantha shaded $\frac{3}{7}$ of her design.

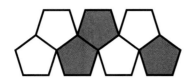

Which number is the best estimate for the shaded part of her design?
(Lesson 8-6)

A 0

B $\frac{1}{7}$

C $\frac{1}{2}$

D 1

38. The table shows the lengths of two different races. Which correctly shows the relationship between the lengths?
(Lesson 8-5)

Race	Length
1	$\frac{7}{16}$ mile
2	$\frac{9}{16}$ mile

F $\frac{7}{16} < \frac{9}{16}$

G $\frac{7}{16} > \frac{9}{16}$

H $\frac{9}{16} \geq \frac{7}{16}$

J $\frac{9}{16} = \frac{7}{16}$

Spiral Review

Replace each ● with < or > to make a true statement. (Lesson 8-5)

39. $\frac{9}{4}$ ● $\frac{2}{4}$

40. $\frac{12}{5}$ ● $3\frac{1}{5}$

41. $\frac{13}{9}$ ● $1\frac{2}{9}$

42. Measurement A bike path is $6\frac{3}{4}$ miles long. Write the length of the bike trail as an improper fraction. (Lesson 8-4)

43. Allison surveyed her classmates and found that 17 own a cat and 14 own a dog. Six of those surveyed own both a cat and a dog. How many of her classmates own only a cat? Only a dog?
(Lesson 8-3)

The bar graph shows students' favorite colors. (Lesson 7-6)

44. What colors were chosen by more than 8 students?

45. How many more students chose yellow as their favorite color than purple?

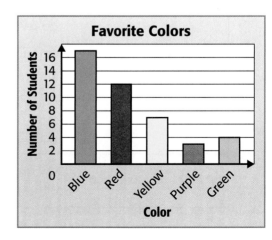

Algebra Evaluate each expression if $x = 7$.
(Lesson 5-7)

46. $5x + 2$

47. $3x - 1$

Problem-Solving Investigation

MAIN IDEA I will choose the best strategy to solve a problem.

 NYSCC **5.PS.3 Interpret information correctly, identify the problem, and generate possible strategies and solutions**
Also addresses 5.PS.2, 5.PS.23.

P.S.I. TEAM +

Christian wants to buy a new skateboard. So far, he has saved $31.26 and $45.50 from his two lawn mowing jobs. How much more money does he need to buy the skateboard if it costs $131.99?

YOUR MISSION: Find how much more money Christian needs to buy the skateboard.

Understand	You know that Christian has saved $31.26 and $45.50. The skateboard costs $131.99. You need to know how much more money Christian needs.
Plan	You need to find how much money Christian has now and how much money he still needs. So, breaking the problem down by using the *solve a simpler problem* strategy is a good choice.
Solve	First, find how much money Christian has. $31.26 + $45.50 $76.76 Christian has $76.76. Then, find how much money he still needs. Subtract $76.76 from $131.99. $131.99 − $76.76 $55.23 Christian needs $55.23.
Check	Look back. $55.23 + $31.26 + $45.50 = $131.99. So, the answer is correct. ✔

Use any strategy shown below to solve each problem.

PROBLEM-SOLVING STRATEGIES
- Guess and check.
- Work backward.
- Make a table.
- Solve a simpler problem.
- Use logical reasoning.

1. **Measurement** A movie starts at 7:10 P.M. and lasts 1 hour and 45 minutes. At what time does the movie end?

2. How many ways can you make change for a $50 bill using only $5, $10, and $20 bills?

3. What two numbers have a sum of 12 and a product of 32?

4. Sports Inc. sells two different sized packages of trading cards. Thomas bought 7 packages of trading cards and spent a total of $16.75. How many of each type of package did he buy?

$1.75 TRADING CARDS

$3.25 TRADING CARDS

5. A pipe 10 feet long needs to be cut into pieces 10 inches long. How many minutes will it take if each cut takes two minutes?

6. Gracia has $1.85 in quarters and in dimes only. She has a total of 11 coins. How many of each coin does she have?

7. Joy tells her mother that she scored 4 less than 3 times as many points in Tuesday's game as she scored on Monday. If Joy scored 5 points on Monday, how many points did she score on Tuesday?

8. Rey picks tomatoes. Each day he picks twice as many as the day before. On the fourth day he picks 48 tomatoes. How many does he pick the first day?

9. Mr. Arturo makes two square pans of gelatin. He cuts one pan into 39 more squares than the other pan. How many squares of gelatin does he cut in each pan?

10. Silvia has a paper route. Each week she earns $20 plus $0.10 for each paper she delivers. Last week she earned $32. How many papers did she deliver?

11. The grocery store is having a sale on juice cartons. How much will 10 cartons cost?

ORANGE JUICE   ORANGE JUICE

4 for $5

12. **WRITING IN MATH** Of the 50 people surveyed at a fitness center, 32 said that they use the treadmills and 24 said that they use the bikes. Six of the people said that they use both. How many people said that they use the bikes, but not the treadmills? What strategy would you use to solve this problem? Explain.

FOLDABLES Study Organizer GET READY to Study

Be sure the following Big Ideas are written in your Foldable.

Fractions
Fractions and Division
Improper Fractions
Mixed Numbers
Fractions on a Number Line
Round Fractions
Problem Solving
Vocabulary and Examples

Key Concepts

Improper Fractions and Mixed Numbers

- To write an improper fraction as a mixed number, divide the numerator by the denominator. Write the remainder as a fraction of the divisor. (p. 337)

$$\frac{14}{5} \rightarrow 14 \div 5 = 2\frac{4}{5}$$

- To write a mixed number as an improper fraction, multiply the whole number by the denominator. Then add the numerator. Write the sum over the denominator. (p. 346)

$$6\frac{1}{3} \rightarrow \frac{(6 \times 3) + 1}{3} = \frac{19}{3}$$

Compare Fractions and Mixed Numbers

- Use a number line to compare fractions and mixed numbers. (p. 350)

0   $\frac{1}{3}$ $\frac{2}{3}$ 1 $\frac{4}{3}$ $\frac{5}{3}$ $\frac{6}{3}$ $\frac{7}{3}$

$$\frac{2}{3} < \frac{5}{3}$$

Key Vocabulary

denominator (p. 333)
fraction (p. 333)
improper fraction (p. 337)
mixed number (p. 336)
numerator (p. 333)

Vocabulary Check

State whether each sentence is *true* or *false*. If *false*, replace the underlined word or number to make a true sentence.

1. The top number in a fraction is called the <u>numerator</u>.

2. The number $1\frac{3}{4}$ is an example of an <u>improper fraction</u>.

3. The fraction $\frac{12}{13}$ should be rounded to <u>1</u>.

4. An improper fraction is a fraction that is <u>greater than or equal to 1</u>.

5. A fraction whose numerator is much smaller than the denominator can be rounded to <u>0</u>.

6. On a number line, $\frac{8}{7}$ is to the <u>right</u> of $\frac{9}{7}$.

7. The number $\frac{9}{5}$ equals $1\underline{\frac{4}{5}}$.

Lesson-by-Lesson Review

8-1 **Fractions and Division** (pp. 333–335)

5.N.20

Example 1
Three people share 2 appetizers. What fraction of an appetizer does each person get?

Words: 2 appetizers divided by 3 people

Symbols: 2 ÷ 3

Fraction: $\frac{2}{3}$ ← appetizers ← people

Each person gets $\frac{2}{3}$ of an appetizer.

Represent each situation using a fraction. Describe what the fraction means.

8. **Measurement** Five gallons of water are used to fill 6 pitchers. How much water did each pitcher use?

9. Three bags of gravel are used to cover the bottom of 4 fish tanks. How much gravel did each fish tank use?

10. Three students share 4 cookies. How many cookies did each person receive?

8-2 **Improper Fractions** (pp. 338–342)

5.N.20

Example 2
Write $\frac{17}{6}$ as a mixed number.

Find 17 ÷ 6. Write the remainder as a fraction.

$$\begin{array}{r} 2 \text{ R5} \\ 6\overline{)17} \\ -12 \\ \hline 5 \end{array} \Rightarrow 2\frac{5}{6}$$

Example 3
Write $\frac{7}{5}$ as a mixed number.

Find 7 ÷ 5. Write the remainder as a fraction.

$$\begin{array}{r} 1 \text{ R2} \\ 5\overline{)7} \\ -5 \\ \hline 2 \end{array} \Rightarrow 1\frac{2}{5}$$

Write each improper fraction as a mixed number.

11. $\frac{5}{4}$

12. $\frac{9}{7}$

13. $\frac{16}{8}$

14. $\frac{15}{4}$

15. $\frac{38}{5}$

16. $\frac{26}{11}$

17. Mrs. Vu walked 5 blocks in 2 minutes. Write the number of blocks walked each minute as a mixed number.

18. Adelina cuts 49 inches of ribbon into eight pieces of equal length. How long is each piece? Write the answer with a remainder. Then write as a mixed number. Explain what both numbers mean.

8-3 **Problem-Solving Strategy:** **Use Logical Reasoning** (pp. 344–345)

5.PS.9

Example 4
Out of a group of fifth graders, 19 like to go to the park and 16 like to go to the zoo. Nine like to go to both places. How many fifth graders like to go to the zoo but not the park?

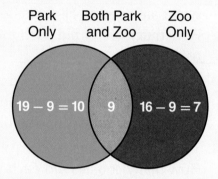

Park Only   Both Park and Zoo   Zoo Only

$19 - 9 = 10$ 9 $16 - 9 = 7$

So, 7 fifth graders like the zoo only.

Solve. Use logical reasoning.

19. In Devon's family three people listen to pop music only, and two people listen to both pop and jazz. There are eight people in her family, and everyone listens to music. How many listen to jazz music only?

20. Julio surveyed his friends and found that nine will eat scrambled eggs, five will eat fried eggs, three will not eat eggs at all, and two will eat both scrambled and fried eggs. How many will eat only fried eggs?

8-4 **Mixed Numbers** (pp. 346–348)

5.N.20

Example 5
Write $5\frac{3}{7}$ as an equivalent improper fraction.

$$5\frac{3}{7} = \frac{(5 \times 7) + 3}{7}$$ Multiply the whole number and denominator. Add the numerator.

$$= \frac{35 + 3}{7}$$

$$= \frac{38}{7}$$

Example 6
Write $6\frac{1}{4}$ as an equivalent improper fraction.

$$6\frac{1}{4} = \frac{(6 \times 4) + 1}{4}$$ Multiply the whole number and denominator. Add the numerator.

$$= \frac{24 + 1}{4}$$

$$= \frac{25}{4}$$

Write each mixed number as an equivalent improper fraction.

21. $4\frac{1}{7}$ **22.** $9\frac{1}{2}$

23. $1\frac{5}{12}$ **24.** $8\frac{2}{3}$

25. $5\frac{5}{6}$ **26.** $3\frac{4}{9}$

27. A Siberian tiger is $10\frac{1}{4}$ feet long. Write this length as an equivalent improper fraction.

28. A school bus is $18\frac{2}{3}$ feet long. Write this length as an equivalent improper fraction.

8-5 Fractions on a Number Line (pp. 350–353)

5.N.9

Example 7

Replace ● with < or > to make $\frac{5}{4}$ ● $1\frac{3}{4}$ a true statement.

```
        0   1/4  2/4  3/4   1  1 1/4 1 2/4 1 3/4  2
        |----|----|----|----|----|----|----|----|
        0   1/4  2/4  3/4  4/4  5/4  6/4  7/4  8/4
```

$\frac{5}{4} = 1\frac{1}{4}$. Since $1\frac{3}{4}$ is to the right of $\frac{5}{4}$ on the number line, $\frac{5}{4} < 1\frac{3}{4}$.

Replace each ● with < or > to make a true statement.

29. $\frac{5}{7}$ ● $\frac{3}{7}$ **30.** $\frac{1}{6}$ ● $\frac{5}{6}$

31. $\frac{6}{8}$ ● $\frac{9}{8}$ **32.** 2 ● $\frac{10}{3}$

33. $\frac{5}{2}$ ● $1\frac{1}{2}$ **34.** $3\frac{1}{9}$ ● $3\frac{2}{9}$

35. Measurement On Friday, Danielle walked $1\frac{1}{4}$ miles. On Saturday, she walked $\frac{7}{4}$ miles. On which day did she walk farther? Explain.

36. In May, Kina volunteered for $\frac{55}{6}$ hours. In June, she volunteered for $9\frac{5}{6}$ hours. In which month did Kina volunteer more hours? Explain.

8-6 Round Fractions (pp. 356–359)

5.N.25

Example 8

Round $\frac{6}{13}$ to 0, $\frac{1}{2}$, or 1.

Since 6 is about half of 13, $\frac{6}{13}$ is rounded to $\frac{1}{2}$.

Example 9

Round $\frac{2}{18}$ to 0, $\frac{1}{2}$, or 1.

Since 2 is much smaller than 18, $\frac{2}{18}$ is rounded to 0.

Round each fraction to 0, $\frac{1}{2}$, or 1.

37. $\frac{6}{11}$ **38.** $\frac{16}{17}$

39. $\frac{1}{12}$ **40.** $\frac{7}{9}$

41. Measurement A seedling is $\frac{10}{12}$ inch tall. Round $\frac{10}{12}$ to 0 inch, $\frac{1}{2}$ inch, or 1 inch.

42. Ernesto chewed $\frac{6}{10}$ of a pack of gum. Which is a better estimate for the amount of gum that he chewed: about half of the pack or about all of the pack?

8-7 **Problem-Solving Investigation: Choose a Strategy** (pp. 360–361)

5.PS.3

Example 10

Jarvis and 2 of his friends can shovel snow from 12 driveways in 2 hours. At this rate, how many driveways can Jarvis and his friends shovel in 3 hours?

You can solve the problem by solving a simpler problem.

First, find how many driveways each boy shovels.

$12 \div 3 = 4$ Each boy shovels 4 driveways in 2 hours.

Then, find how many driveways each boy can shovel in 1 hour.

$4 \div 2 = 2$ Each boy shovels 2 driveways in 1 hour.

Then, find how many driveways 3 people can shovel in 1 hour.

$3 \times 2 = 6$ Three boys shovel 6 driveways in 1 hour.

Finally, find how many driveways 3 boys can shovel in 3 hours.

$6 \times 3 = 18$

So, Jarvis and 2 of his friends can shovel 18 driveways in 3 hours.

Use any strategy to solve each problem.

43. **Algebra** Three times some number, plus 3, divided by 2 is equal to 18. Find the number.

44. Find the sum of the first ten even numbers.

45. The admission prices to the local fair are shown. The total cost for 15 people to attend the fair was $148. How many adults and children attended the fair?

Fair Admission Prices	
Ticket	**Price**
Adult	$12
Child	$8

46. **Measurement** Denise has started an exercise program in which she walks daily. She plans to increase the distance that she walks by 0.25 mile each week. If she walks 2.25 miles each day the first week, how many miles will she be walking each day during the fifth week?

47. What two positive integers have a product of 48 and a sum of 14?

48. Kato increases the number of sit-ups he does each week by 8. The first week he did 10 sit-ups. He is now doing 74 sit-ups. How many weeks has he been doing sit-ups?

Represent each situation using a fraction. Describe what the fraction means.

1. Five people share 3 bags of trail mix. How much trail mix did each person have?

2. Four gallons of water are used to water 3 trees. How much water did each tree use?

3. MULTIPLE CHOICE Which fraction is represented by the model below?

A $\frac{1}{2}$ **C** $\frac{3}{2}$

B $1\frac{1}{3}$ **D** $2\frac{1}{2}$

Write each improper fraction as a mixed number.

4. $\frac{20}{3}$ **5.** $\frac{16}{9}$ **6.** $\frac{26}{5}$

7. MULTIPLE CHOICE A river is $20\frac{1}{3}$ miles long. Which is another way to express this distance?

F $\frac{21}{3}$ mi   **H** $\frac{61}{3}$ mi

G $\frac{20}{3}$ mi   **J** $\frac{60}{3}$ mi

8. Martina surveyed her class and found that her classmates had 28 pets with long tails and 36 pets with short ears. Of these pets, 20 have both long tails and short ears. How many pets have long tails but do not have short ears?

Write each mixed number as an improper fraction.

9. $1\frac{3}{7}$ **10.** $4\frac{1}{10}$ **11.** $2\frac{5}{9}$

Replace each ● with < or > to make a true statement.

12. $\frac{5}{9}$ ● $\frac{11}{9}$ **13.** $2\frac{1}{6}$ ● $\frac{8}{6}$

14. Measurement Does the bag of peaches or the bag of oranges weigh more? Explain.

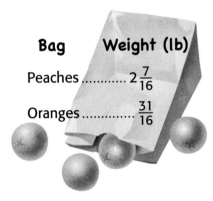

Bag	Weight (lb)
Peaches	$2\frac{7}{16}$
Oranges	$\frac{31}{16}$

15. Measurement The table shows the lengths of two pens. Which is longer?

Pen	Length (in.)
1	$4\frac{5}{8}$
2	$\frac{46}{8}$

Round each fraction to 0, $\frac{1}{2}$, or 1.

16. $\frac{1}{10}$ **17.** $\frac{4}{7}$ **18.** $\frac{5}{11}$

19. A number is divided by 2. Next, 6 is subtracted from the quotient. Then 4 is added to the difference. If the result is 18, what is the number?

20. **WRITING IN ▶MATH** How do you know when to round a fraction to 0, $\frac{1}{2}$, or 1?

Read each question. Then fill in the correct answer on the answer sheet provided by your teacher or on a sheet of paper.

1. The table below shows the colors of the cars parked on Jillian's street and the fraction of total number of cars for each color. Which correctly shows the relationship between the fractions?

Cars on Jillian's Street	
Color	**Fraction**
Silver	$\frac{7}{12}$
Black	$\frac{9}{12}$

A $\frac{7}{12} < \frac{9}{12}$

C $\frac{9}{12} \leq \frac{7}{12}$

B $\frac{7}{12} > \frac{9}{12}$

D $\frac{7}{12} \geq \frac{9}{12}$

2. A deep-sea fishing boat spent 126 hours on fishing trips. If the boat made 1 trip per day for 21 days, how long did each trip take?

F 4 h

H 6 h

G 5 h

J 8 h

3. Larry has spent $\frac{9}{16}$ of his birthday money. Which of the following fractions is NOT greater than $\frac{9}{16}$

A $\frac{14}{16}$

C $\frac{10}{16}$

B $\frac{12}{16}$

D $\frac{8}{16}$

4. Benito has 80 books in his room. The books are organized on shelves with 16 books on each shelf. How many shelves does Benito have?

F 5

H 7

G 6

J 8

5. The bar graph shows the results of a survey of 38 fifth graders on their favorite school subject. Which statement about the data shown on the graph is true?

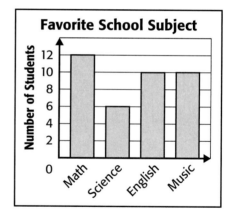

A The range of the data is 20.

B Music was twice as popular as science.

C The same number of students voted for English and math.

D Two more students voted for math than English.

6. What digit is in millions place in the number 7,521,423,201?

F 1

H 5

G 2

J 7

7. Ralph recorded the colors of the shirts of the first 36 people that came through the doors at school.

Color	Number
White	18
Black	5
Blue	9
Red	4

Which number represents the fraction of black shirts recorded?

A $\frac{18}{36}$ **C** $\frac{5}{36}$

B $\frac{9}{36}$ **D** $\frac{4}{36}$

8. Which is the solution of the equation $x + 4 = 24$?

F 28   **H** 8

G 20   **J** 6

9. The table shows the number of text messages Fredricka sent each day for 12 days.

Number of Text Messages			
10	3	8	4
2	5	7	8
0	11	0	6

What graph(s) can be used to display this information?

A bar graph only

B line graph and bar graph

C pictograph only

D bar graph and line plot

PART 2   Short Response

Record your answers on the answer sheet provided by your teacher or on a sheet of paper.

10. The table shows the number of volunteer hours worked by five students. What is the median number of hours?

Student	1	2	3	4	5
Hours	61	70	65	77	99

11. Nina's cheerleading practice lasted $1\frac{2}{3}$ hours on Friday. Write this mixed number as an improper fraction.

PART 3   Extended Response

Record your answers on the answer sheet provided by your teacher or on a sheet of paper.

12. The lengths of four insects in Tommy's insect collection are $1\frac{1}{6}$ inches, $2\frac{3}{8}$ inches, $1\frac{5}{6}$ inches, and $2\frac{7}{8}$ inches. Draw a model for each insect and order the fractions from least to greatest.

NEED EXTRA HELP?												
If You Missed Question...	1	2	3	4	5	6	7	8	9	10	11	12
Go to Lesson...	8-5	4-4	8-5	4-4	7-6	1-1	8-2	6-1	7-8	7-1	8-4	8-5
NYS Core Curriculum	5.N.9	5.N.17	5.N.9	5.N.17	5.S.1	5.N.1	5.N.20	5.A.4	5.S.1	5.S.1	5.N.20	5.N.9

CHAPTER 9
Use Factors and Multiples

BIG Idea What are multiples?

A **multiple** of a number is the product of that number and any whole number.

Example It costs $6 for a fifth grade student to enter the Frederik Meijer Gardens and Sculpture Park in Grand Rapids, Michigan. If two fifth grade students enter the park, the cost would be 6 × 2, or 12. So, 12 is a multiple of 6.

What will I learn in this chapter?

- Identify common factors and common multiples of a set of whole numbers.
- Identify prime and composite numbers.
- Find equivalent fractions and simplify fractions.
- Relate decimals to fractions.
- Compare fractions using a variety of methods, including common denominators.
- Solve problems by using the *look for a pattern* strategy.

Key Vocabulary

common factor

composite number

equivalent fractions

prime number

simplest form

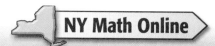 **NY Math Online** > **Student Study Tools**
at macmillanmh.com

FOLDABLES
Study Organizer

Make this Foldable to help you organize information about factors and multiples. Begin with nine sheets of notebook paper.

1 **Fold** 9 sheets of paper in half along the width.

2 **Cut** a 1" tab along the left edge through one thickness.

3 **Glue** the 1" tab down. Write the lesson number and title on the front tab.

Chapter 9
Use Factors
and Multiples

4 **Repeat** Steps 2 and 3 for the remaining sheets. Staple them together on the glued tabs to form a booklet.

Chapter 9
Use Factors
and Multiples

ARE YOU READY for Chapter 9?

You have two ways to check prerequisite skills for this chapter.

Option 2

NY Math Online Take the Chapter Readiness Quiz at macmillanmh.com.

Option 1

Complete the Quick Check below.

QUICK Check

Write all of the factors of each number. (Prior Grade)

1. 8 **2.** 11 **3.** 6

4. 15 **5.** 32 **6.** 24

Identify the number of rows and columns in each figure. (Prior Grade)

7. **8.**

9. **10.**

Write each decimal in words. (Lesson 1-4)

11. 0.3 **12.** 0.8 **13.** 0.1

14. 0.45 **15.** 0.06 **16.** 0.04

17. Measurement A rock has a mass of 0.925 kilogram. Write this measure in words.

18. Measurement A bottle of water contains 0.85 pint. Write this amount in words.

Common Factors

GET READY to Learn

A pet store has 6 dog bones and 18 dog biscuits to give away as samples. They put an equal number of bones and an equal number of biscuits in each sample bag. What is the greatest number of sample bags they can give away?

MAIN IDEA

I will identify common factors of a set of whole numbers.

NYS Core Curriculum

5.N.15 Find the common factors and the greatest common factor of two numbers *Also addresses 5.N.14, 5.N.12.*

New Vocabulary

common factor

greatest common factor (GCF)

NY Math Online

macmillanmh.com
• Extra Examples
• Personal Tutor
• Self-Check Quiz

The factors of 6 and 18 are listed below.

Product	Factors
6	1 × 6
6	2 × 3

Product	Factors
18	1 × 18
18	2 × 9
18	3 × 6

factors of 6: **1, 2, 3, 6**

factors of 18: **1, 2, 3, 6**, 9, 18

A **common factor** is a number that is a factor of two or more numbers. So, 1, 2, 3, and 6 are common factors of 6 and 18. Since 6 is the greatest of these common factors, the greatest number of sample bags that can be made is 6.

EXAMPLE   Find Common Factors

1 **Find the common factors of 16 and 20.**

Step 1 List all the factors of each number.

$16 = 1 \times 16$ $16 = 2 \times 8$ $16 = 4 \times 4$
factors of 16: 1, 2, 4, 8, 16

$20 = 1 \times 20$ $20 = 2 \times 10$ $20 = 4 \times 5$
factors of 20: 1, 2, 4, 5, 10, 20

Step 2 Find the common factors.

factors of 16: **1, 2, 4**, 8, 16
factors of 20: **1, 2, 4**, 5, 10, 20

The common factors of 16 and 20 are 1, 2, and 4.

EXAMPLE   **Numbers with One Common Factor**

② **Find the common factors of 4, 8, and 15.**

factors of 4: **1**, 2, 4
factors of 8: **1**, 2, 4, 8
factors of 15: **1**, 3, 5, 15

The only factor common to all three numbers is 1.

The greatest of the common factors of two or more numbers is called the **greatest common factor (GCF)**.

EXAMPLE   **Find the Greatest Common Factor**

③ **Find the greatest common factor of 10, 15, and 20.**

List all the factors of 10, 15, and 20 to find the common factors.

factors of 10: 1, 2, **5**, 10
factors of 15: 1, 3, **5**, 15
factors of 20: 1, 2, 4, **5**, 10, 20

The common factors are 1 and 5. The greatest of these is 5. So, the greatest common factor, or GCF, of 10, 15, and 20 is 5.

 **Real-World EXAMPLE**   **Use the Greatest Common Factor**

④ **FOOD A chef made 24 baked cheese sticks and 36 egg rolls to arrange on plates. Each plate will have an equal number of cheese sticks and an equal number of egg rolls. What is the greatest number of plates he can arrange?**

First, find the common factors of each number.

factors of 24: **1**, **2**, **3**, **4**, **6**, 8, **12**, 24
factors of 36: **1**, **2**, **3**, **4**, **6**, 9, **12**, 18, 36

common factors of 24 and 36: 1, 2, 3, 4, 6, 12

The chef can arrange 1, 2, 3, 4, 6, or 12 plates with each plate having an equal number of cheese sticks and an equal number of egg rolls. Since 12 is the GCF, the greatest number of plates the chef can arrange is 12.

Check There will be $24 \div 12$, or 2 cheese sticks and $36 \div 12$, or 3 egg rolls on each plate. ✔

CHECK What You Know

Find the common factors of each set of numbers. See Examples 1, 2 (pp. 373–374)

1. 9, 12   **2.** 13, 15   **3.** 24, 28, 32   **4.** 10, 30, 50

Find the GCF of each set of numbers. See Examples 3, 4 (p. 374)

5. 8, 14   **6.** 15, 20   **7.** 21, 24, 27   **8.** 30, 48, 60

9. Fourteen boys and 21 girls will be divided into equal groups. Find the greatest number of children that can be in each group if no one is left out.

10. **Talk About It** Explain the steps for finding the GCF of two numbers. Give an example.

Practice and Problem Solving

NYSCC • NYSMT

Extra Practice, p. R23

Find the common factors of each set of numbers. See Examples 1, 2 (pp. 373–374)

11. 5, 20   **12.** 6, 15   **13.** 8, 9   **14.** 14, 25

15. 12, 18, 30   **16.** 27, 36, 45   **17.** 21, 28, 35   **18.** 18, 36, 54

Find the GCF of each set of numbers. See Examples 3, 4 (p. 374)

19. 4, 10   **20.** 15, 18   **21.** 18, 42   **22.** 20, 35

23. 21, 35, 49   **24.** 24, 30, 42   **25.** 12, 18, 26   **26.** 24, 40, 56

27. A grocery store clerk has 16 oranges, 20 apples, and 24 pears. The clerk needs to put an equal number of apples, oranges, and pears into each basket. What is the greatest number of apples that can be in each basket?

28. A gardener has 27 pansies and 36 daisies. If the gardener plants an equal number of each type of flower in each row, what is the greatest number of pansies in each row?

H.O.T. Problems

29. **OPEN ENDED** Write two numbers that have common factors of 1, 3, and 5. Explain how you found the numbers.

30. **NUMBER SENSE** Three numbers have a GCF of 4. The largest number is 12. Explain how to find the other numbers.

31. **WRITING IN ►MATH** Can the GCF of two numbers ever be 1? Explain your answer. Give an example to support it.

Lesson 9-1 Common Factors **375**

Explore

Math Activity for 9-2
Prime and Composite Numbers

MAIN IDEA

I will use models to identify prime and composite numbers.

NYS Core Curriculum

5.N.12 Recognize that some numbers are only divisible by one and themselves (prime) and others have multiple divisors (composite)
Also addresses 5.R.1

New Vocabulary

prime
composite

Three bass drums may be stored on shelves in only two different arrangements.

These rectangular arrangements show that the only factors of 3 are 1 and 3.

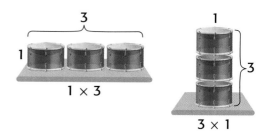

When a number, like 3, has exactly two factors, the number is **prime**.

You can store 4 drums in any of the three ways shown at the right. What are the factors of 4?

When a number, like 4, has more than two factors, the number is **composite**.

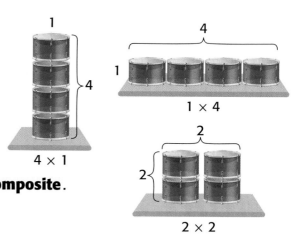

ACTIVITY

1 **Use models to determine whether 6 is *prime* or *composite*.**

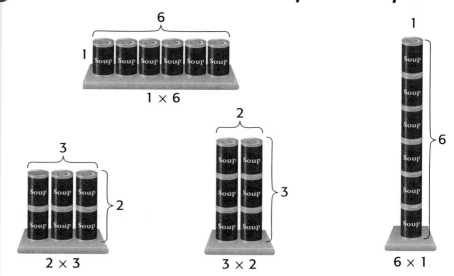

You can arrange the 6 soup cans in four different ways. So, 6 is a composite number.

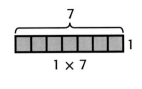

2 **Use models to determine whether 7 is *prime* or *composite*.**

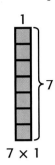

7

1 × 7

1

7

7 × 1

You can arrange the 7 tiles in only 2 ways: 7 × 1 and 1 × 7.
So, 7 is a prime number.

Think About It

1. Are all even numbers composite? Use a drawing in your explanation.

2. Are all odd numbers prime? Support your explanation with a drawing.

CHECK **What You Know**

Use objects or pictures to determine whether each number is *prime* or *composite*. Describe the models that you used.

3. 13   **4.** 10   **5.** 11

6. 8   **7.** 17   **8.** 9

9. Caleb made 12 dinner rolls. He placed the rolls in 3 rows of 4 on a table. In what other ways could he have arranged the rolls in equal rows?

10. Write a number between 20 and 30. Then use objects or pictures to show whether the number is prime or composite.

11. **WRITING IN ►MATH** Is there a connection between the number of rectangular arrangements that are possible when modeling a number and the number of factors the number has? Explain your reasoning.

Explore Math Activity for 9-2: Prime and Composite Numbers   **377**

Prime and Composite Numbers

MAIN IDEA

I will identify prime and composite numbers.

NYS Core Curriculum

5.N.12 Recognize that some numbers are only divisible by one and themselves (prime) and others have multiple divisors (composite)

New Vocabulary

prime factorization

NY Math Online

macmillanmh.com
• Extra Examples
• Personal Tutor
• Self-Check Quiz

GET READY to Learn

Stella makes and sells jewelry at craft shows. She has 12 rings that she wants to display in equal rows.

OOOOOOOOOOOO
1 row of 12 rings

OOOOOO
OOOOOO
2 rows of 6 rings

OOOO
OOOO
OOOO
3 rows of 4 rings

In the Math Activity, you learned that a *composite* number has more than two factors. So, 12 is a composite number because its factors are 1, 2, 3, 4, 6, and 12.

The number 5 has only two factors: 1 and 5. So, 5 is a *prime* number.

The numbers 1 and 0 are neither prime nor composite.

• 1 has only one factor: 1
• 0 has a never ending number of factors: 0×1, 0×2, 0×3, ...

EXAMPLE Use Models

1 **Tell whether the number 10 represented by the model at the right is *prime* or *composite*.**

The model shows 2 rows of 5 squares. The squares could also be arranged in 5 rows of 2 squares, 10 rows of 1 square, or 1 row of 10 squares.

So, the number 10 is a composite number because it has more than 2 factors.

Prime and composite numbers can help you solve real-world situations.

Real-World EXAMPLE Use Factor Pairs

2 GEOMETRY A banquet hall has 24 square tables that are to be placed together to form a rectangle. Is 24 prime or composite? What does this mean in the problem? What would happen if the banquet hall had only 23 tables?

factors of 24: 1, 2, 3, 4, 6, 8, 12, 24

Since 24 has more than two factors, it is a composite number. This means that there are more than two ways to arrange the 24 tables. Some of the ways are listed below.

- 1 row of 24 tables
- 2 rows of 12 tables
- 3 rows of 8 tables
- 4 rows of 6 tables

If the banquet hall had only 23 tables, there could be only two possible arrangements, since 23 has only two factors. This is because 23 is a prime number.

- 1 row of 23 tables
- 23 rows of 1 table

Remember

You can use models to identify 24 as prime or composite. Twenty-four counters can be arranged in equal rows in more than two ways. So, 24 is composite.

You can write every composite number as a product of prime numbers. This is called the **prime factorization** of a number. A *factor tree* can be used to find the prime factorization of a number.

EXAMPLE Find the Prime Factorization of a Number

3 Find the prime factorization of 36.

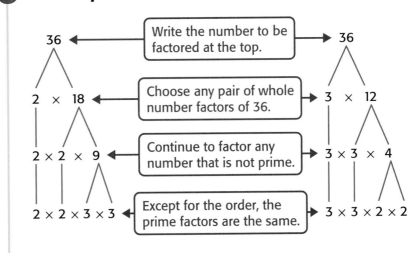

In order, the prime factorization of 36 is 2 × 2 × 3 × 3.

Tell whether the number represented by each model is *prime* or *composite*. See Example 1 (p. 378)

1. ▢▢▢▢▢

2. (grid model)

Tell whether each number is *prime* or *composite*. Use objects or models to justify your answer. See Examples 1, 2 (pp. 378–379)

3. 9

4. 24

5. 17

6. 31

Find the prime factorization of each number. See Example 3 (p. 379)

7. 18

8. 20

9. 24

10. 45

11. Is there more than one way for Mark to display 21 model cars if each row has the same number of cars? Explain.

12. **Talk About It** Is 33 prime or composite? Explain how you know.

Practice and Problem Solving

NYSCC • NYSMT
Extra Practice, p. R24

Tell whether the number represented by each model is *prime* or *composite*. See Example 1 (p. 378)

13. 2 ▢▢

14. 8 (grid model)

15. 7 ▢▢▢▢▢▢▢

16. 4 ▢▢▢▢

Tell whether each number is *prime* or *composite*. Use objects or models to justify your answer. See Examples 1, 2 (pp. 378–379)

17. 18

18. 29

19. 15

20. 26

21. 13

22. 16

23. 37

24. 53

Find the prime factorization of each number. See Example 3 (p. 379)

25. 16

26. 22

27. 30

28. 42

29. 63

30. 70

31. 50

32. 88

33. A mountain range has 90 mountains that are one mile or more tall. Is 90 a prime or composite number?

34. Alex's birthday is February 29. Is 29 a prime or composite number?

H.O.T. Problems

35. NUMBER SENSE Find the least prime number that is greater than 100. Explain.

36. CHALLENGE Two prime numbers that have a difference of 2 are called *twin primes*. For example, 5 and 7 are twin primes. Find all pairs of twin primes less than 50.

37. WRITING IN ►MATH Explain how you can use objects or models to tell if a number is prime or composite.

NYSMT Practice 5.N.12

38. The table shows how many Calories you can burn in 10 minutes for certain activities.

Activity	Number of Calories
Basketball	64
Dancing	35
Hiking	47
Roller skating	57

For which activity is the number of Calories a prime number? (Lesson 9-2)

A basketball   **C** hiking

B dancing   **D** roller skating

39. Which group names all the common factors of 27 and 54? (Lesson 9-1)

F 1, 3, 9

G 1, 3, 9, 18

H 1, 3, 9, 27

J 1, 3, 9, 27, 54

40. What is the missing number in the prime factorization of 156?

$$2 \times 2 \times 3 \times \blacksquare$$

A 3   **C** 13

B 5   **D** 17

Spiral Review

Find the GCF of each set of numbers. (Lesson 9-1)

41. 6, 15   **42.** 18, 24   **43.** 14, 28   **44.** 10, 25

45. Jackie bought 5 papayas for $1.99 each and 3 yogurts for $0.75 each. The cashier gave her $8 change. What is the least number of coins she could have given the cashier? What would they have been? (Lesson 8-7)

46. The Jackson family went swimming $2\frac{5}{6}$ hours on Saturday and $1\frac{3}{6}$ hours on Sunday. On which day did they spend more time swimming? (Lesson 8-5)

Equivalent Fractions

MAIN IDEA

I will write a fraction that is equivalent to a given fraction.

NYS Core Curriculum

5.N.4 Create equivalent fractions, given a fraction
Also addresses 5.N.12.

New Vocabulary

equivalent fractions

NY Math Online

macmillanmh.com

• Extra Examples
• Personal Tutor
• Self-Check Quiz

GET READY to Learn

Mrs. Bahn is dividing her garden into thirds. One third of her garden will be used for tomatoes. If her garden is 9 feet wide, she figures that she needs to save a width of 3 feet of the garden for tomatoes. Did she figure correctly?

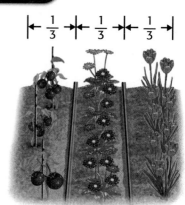

Equivalent fractions are fractions that have the same value. The fractions $\frac{1}{3}$ and $\frac{3}{9}$ name the same part of the whole. So, they are equivalent fractions. Mrs. Bahn figured correctly.

Multiplying the numerator and denominator each by 3 gives $\frac{3}{9}$.

$$\frac{1}{3} \times \frac{3}{3} = \frac{1 \times 3}{3 \times 3} = \frac{3}{9}$$

Recall that $\frac{3}{3}$ is an equivalent form of 1. To find equivalent fractions, you can multiply a fraction by an equivalent form of 1, such as $\frac{2}{2}$, $\frac{3}{3}$, or $\frac{4}{4}$.

EXAMPLE   Find Equivalent Fractions by Multiplying

① **Find two fractions that are equivalent to $\frac{1}{4}$.**

Multiply $\frac{1}{4}$ by equivalent forms of one, such as $\frac{2}{2}$ and $\frac{3}{3}$.

Multiply $\frac{1}{4}$ by $\frac{2}{2}$.   Multiply $\frac{1}{4}$ by $\frac{3}{3}$.

$$\frac{1}{4} \times \frac{2}{2} = \frac{1 \times 2}{4 \times 2} = \frac{2}{8} \qquad\qquad \frac{1}{4} \times \frac{3}{3} = \frac{1 \times 3}{4 \times 3} = \frac{3}{12}$$

So, $\frac{2}{8}$ and $\frac{3}{12}$ are both equivalent to $\frac{1}{4}$.

Remember

There are many different fractions that are equivalent to a given fraction.

2 **SCIENCE** Ethan measured the length of an insect to be $\frac{7}{8}$ inch. Find two equivalent measurements for the length of the insect, in inches.

Multiply $\frac{7}{8}$ by equivalent forms of one, such as $\frac{2}{2}$ and $\frac{3}{3}$.

Multiply $\frac{7}{8}$ by $\frac{2}{2}$.

Multiply $\frac{7}{8}$ by $\frac{3}{3}$.

$$\frac{7}{8} \times \frac{2}{2} = \frac{7 \times 2}{8 \times 2} = \frac{14}{16}$$

$$\frac{7}{8} \times \frac{3}{3} = \frac{7 \times 3}{8 \times 3} = \frac{21}{24}$$

So, the insect's length is equivalent to $\frac{14}{16}$ inch and $\frac{21}{24}$ inch.

EXAMPLE **Find a Missing Number**

3 **ALGEBRA** Find the number for ▪ that makes the fractions in $\frac{2}{7} = \frac{▪}{21}$ equivalent.

$$\frac{2}{7} = \frac{2 \times ?}{7 \times ?} = \frac{▪}{21}$$ THINK What number times 7 equals 21?

$$\frac{2}{7} = \frac{2 \times 3}{7 \times 3} = \frac{6}{21}$$ $7 \times 3 = 21$, so multiply the numerator by 3.

The missing number is 6. So, $\frac{2}{7} = \frac{6}{21}$.

CHECK What You Know

Find two fractions that are equivalent to each fraction. Check your answer using fraction tiles or number lines. See Examples 1, 2 (pp. 382–383)

1. $\frac{2}{5}$

2. $\frac{3}{4}$

3. $\frac{6}{10}$

4. $\frac{2}{8}$

5. $\frac{1}{3}$

6. $\frac{5}{6}$

Algebra Find the number for ▪ that makes the fractions equivalent. See Example 3 (p. 383)

7. $\frac{1}{2} = \frac{▪}{4}$

8. $\frac{2}{5} = \frac{10}{▪}$

9. $\frac{4}{18} = \frac{12}{▪}$

10. Measurement How many sixteenths of an inch are equal to $\frac{5}{8}$ inch?

11.  Explain how to find an equivalent fraction for $\frac{4}{9}$.

Find two fractions that are equivalent to each fraction. Check your answer using fraction tiles or number lines. See Examples 1, 2 (pp. 382–383)

12. $\frac{2}{3}$ **13.** $\frac{1}{2}$ **14.** $\frac{2}{6}$ **15.** $\frac{1}{5}$

16. $\frac{2}{12}$ **17.** $\frac{3}{6}$ **18.** $\frac{3}{5}$ **19.** $\frac{6}{8}$

20. $\frac{4}{16}$ **21.** $\frac{2}{7}$ **22.** $\frac{5}{10}$ **23.** $\frac{6}{14}$

Algebra Find the number for ▇ that makes the fractions equivalent.
See Example 3 (p. 383)

24. $\frac{1}{3} = \frac{▇}{9}$ **25.** $\frac{8}{16} = \frac{16}{▇}$ **26.** $\frac{6}{9} = \frac{18}{▇}$ **27.** $\frac{3}{5} = \frac{9}{▇}$

28. Fatima read $\frac{2}{5}$ of a book. Gary read $\frac{4}{10}$ of the same book. Did Gary read more than, less than, or the same amount as Fatima?

29. Measurement Mr. Bixler ran $\frac{5}{6}$ mile. How many twelfths and how many eighteenths of a mile are equal to $\frac{5}{6}$ mile?

30. Rodolfo ate $\frac{1}{4}$ of a cantaloupe. Aida ate the same amount from another cantaloupe, cut into eighths. How many pieces did Aida eat?

31. In 1 minute, 10 people can slide down a water slide. Complete the following. Explain what the equivalent fractions mean.

$$\frac{1}{10} = \frac{5}{▇} \qquad \frac{1}{10} = \frac{▇}{300}$$

H.O.T. Problems

32. OPEN ENDED Using fraction tiles or a number line, show 3 fractions that are equivalent to each other.

33. FIND THE ERROR Jeremy and Antwon are finding an equivalent fraction for $\frac{3}{7}$. Who is correct? Explain.

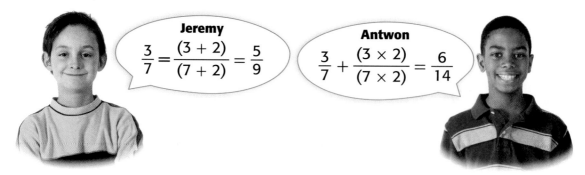

Jeremy
$$\frac{3}{7} = \frac{(3+2)}{(7+2)} = \frac{5}{9}$$

Antwon
$$\frac{3}{7} + \frac{(3 \times 2)}{(7 \times 2)} = \frac{6}{14}$$

34. **WRITING IN ►MATH** Write about a real-world situation that can be represented by $\frac{3}{4}$. Then write an equivalent fraction and describe the meaning of the equivalent fraction.

Match Up

Equivalent Fractions

Get Ready!

Players: 2 players

You will need: 32 index cards

Get Set!

Label each index card with one fraction as shown.

$\frac{1}{2}$	$\frac{1}{3}$	$\frac{2}{3}$	$\frac{1}{4}$	$\frac{2}{4}$	$\frac{3}{4}$	$\frac{2}{5}$	$\frac{3}{5}$
$\frac{4}{5}$	$\frac{1}{6}$	$\frac{5}{6}$	$\frac{2}{7}$	$\frac{1}{8}$	$\frac{2}{8}$	$\frac{3}{8}$	$\frac{2}{9}$
$\frac{6}{9}$	$\frac{4}{10}$	$\frac{5}{10}$	$\frac{8}{10}$	$\frac{2}{12}$	$\frac{4}{12}$	$\frac{2}{16}$	$\frac{4}{16}$
$\frac{4}{18}$	$\frac{6}{18}$	$\frac{15}{18}$	$\frac{12}{20}$	$\frac{15}{20}$	$\frac{6}{21}$	$\frac{3}{24}$	$\frac{9}{24}$

Go!

- Shuffle the cards. Then one player deals 5 cards to each player. The remaining cards are placed in a pile facedown on the table.

- Players place any pairs of cards that are equivalent fractions on the table. If 3 cards are equivalent, the player must choose a pair.

- Player 1 chooses a card from the pile and tries to form an equivalent fraction pair. He or she then discards any other card facedown on a discard pile of cards.

- Player 2 takes a turn choosing a card, forming pairs of equivalent fractions, and placing a card facedown on the discard pile.

- Continue playing until there are no more cards in the pile or until neither player can make an equivalent fraction pair. The player with the most pairs of equivalent fractions wins.

9-4 Simplest Form

MAIN IDEA

I will write a fraction in simplest form.

NYS Core Curriculum

5.N.15 Find the common factors and the greatest common factor of two numbers

5.N.19 Simplify fractions to lowest terms *Also addresses 5.N.12.*

New Vocabulary

simplest form

NY Math Online

macmillanmh.com
• Extra Examples
• Personal Tutor
• Self-Check Quiz

GET READY to Learn

A praying mantis is 12 centimeters long, and a walking stick is 22 centimeters long. So, a praying mantis is $\frac{12}{22}$ the length of a stick insect. Is this the simplest way to write this fraction?

A fraction is written in **simplest form** when the GCF of the numerator and the denominator is 1. The simplest form of a fraction is one of its many equivalent fractions.

Real-World EXAMPLE   Simplest Form

1 **MEASUREMENT Refer to the information above. What fraction of a walking stick's length is the length of a praying mantis? Write the fraction in simplest form.**

Step 1 Find the GCF of the numerator and the denominator.

> factors of 12: 1, **2**, 3, 4, 6, 12
> factors of 22: 1, **2**, 11, 22   The GCF of 12 and 22 is 2.

Step 2 Divide both the numerator and the denominator by the GCF. Dividing both the numerator and the denominator by the same number is equivalent to dividing by one. The appearance of the fraction changes, not its value.

$$\frac{12}{22} = \frac{12 \div 2}{22 \div 2} = \frac{6}{11} \quad \text{The GCF of 6 and 11 is 1.}$$

So, a walking stick's length is $\frac{6}{11}$ the length of a praying mantis.

You can see from the models at the right that $\frac{12}{22} = \frac{6}{11}$.

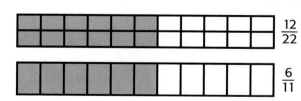

$\frac{12}{22}$

$\frac{6}{11}$

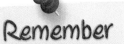

Remember

The divisibility rules are useful for finding common factors.

EXAMPLE Simplest Form

② Write $\frac{18}{30}$ in simplest form.

One Way: Divide by Common Factors

$\frac{18}{30} = \frac{18 \div 2}{30 \div 2} = \frac{9}{15}$ Divide 18 and 30 by the common factor 2.

$\frac{9}{15} = \frac{9 \div 3}{15 \div 3} = \frac{3}{5}$ Divide 9 and 15 by the common factor 3.

Since 3 and 5 have no common factors other than 1, stop dividing.

Another Way: Divide by the GCF

factors of 18: 1, 2, 3, 6, 9, 18
factors of 30: 1, 2, 3, 5, 6, 10, 15, 30
The GCF of 18 and 30 is 6.

$\frac{18}{30} = \frac{18 \div 6}{30 \div 6} = \frac{3}{5}$ Divide by the GCF 6.

Using either method, $\frac{18}{30}$ written in simplest form is $\frac{3}{5}$.

Check
You can see from the models at the right that $\frac{18}{30} = \frac{3}{5}$. ✔

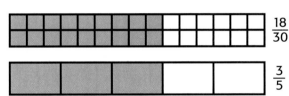

CHECK What You Know

Write each fraction in simplest form. If the fraction is already in simplest form, write *simplified*. See Examples 1, 2 (pp. 386–387)

1. $\frac{4}{6}$

2. $\frac{2}{12}$

3. $\frac{8}{24}$

4. $\frac{8}{9}$

5. $\frac{9}{18}$

6. $\frac{4}{14}$

7. $\frac{15}{20}$

8. $\frac{21}{35}$

9. Kara buys 24 bagels. Ten are whole wheat. What fraction of the bagels are whole wheat, in simplest form?

10. **Talk About It** Use at least 2 sentences to explain how to find the simplest form of any fraction.

Write each fraction in simplest form. If the fraction is already in simplest form, write *simplified*. See Examples 1, 2 (pp. 386–387)

11. $\frac{6}{8}$ 12. $\frac{6}{10}$ 13. $\frac{3}{18}$ 14. $\frac{2}{15}$

15. $\frac{4}{16}$ 16. $\frac{12}{24}$ 17. $\frac{6}{25}$ 18. $\frac{21}{30}$

19. $\frac{12}{40}$ 20. $\frac{4}{11}$ 21. $\frac{8}{28}$ 22. $\frac{9}{24}$

23. $\frac{3}{36}$ 24. $\frac{25}{30}$ 25. $\frac{18}{45}$ 26. $\frac{36}{48}$

27. A basket of fruit has 10 oranges, 12 apples, and 18 peaches. Express in simplest form the fraction of fruit that are oranges.

28. **Measurement** Andeana is 4 feet tall. Her brother Berto is 38 inches tall. What fractional part of Andeana's height is Berto's height?

New York Data File

The Statue of Liberty was a gift from the people of France in 1886 to celebrate the friendship of the United States and France.

• The Statue of Liberty is 305 feet tall. It is more than half of the size of the Washington Monument in Washington D.C., which is 555 feet tall.

• There are 354 steps to the crown.

Write each as a fraction in simplest form.

29. You have climbed 177 out of 354 steps.

30. The statue is $\frac{305}{555}$ as tall as the Washington Monument.

Source: National Park Service

H.O.T. Problems

31. **OPEN ENDED** Write a real-world problem that uses $\frac{14}{18}$ in the problem. Write the fraction in simplest form.

32. **WHICH ONE DOESN'T BELONG?** Identify the fraction that does not belong with the other three. Explain your reasoning.

$$\frac{3}{12} \qquad \frac{4}{16} \qquad \frac{5}{25} \qquad \frac{6}{24}$$

33. **WRITING IN ►MATH** Explain how you would write $\frac{24}{36}$ in simplest form.

34. Gil's aunt cut his birthday cake into 32 equal pieces, as shown below. Eighteen pieces were eaten at his birthday party. What fraction of the cake was left? (Lesson 9-4)

A $\frac{7}{16}$ **C** $\frac{7}{12}$

B $\frac{9}{16}$ **D** $\frac{9}{14}$

35. The fractions $\frac{2}{8}$, $\frac{3}{12}$, $\frac{4}{16}$, and $\frac{5}{20}$ are each equivalent to $\frac{1}{4}$. What is the relationship between the numerator and denominator in each fraction that is equivalent to $\frac{1}{4}$? (Lesson 9-3)

F The numerator is 4 times the denominator.

G The denominator is 4 times the numerator.

H The numerator is 4 more than the denominator.

J The denominator is 4 more than the numerator.

Spiral Review

Write two fractions that are equivalent to each fraction. (Lesson 9-3)

36. $\frac{4}{7}$ **37.** $\frac{2}{9}$ **38.** $\frac{4}{8}$ **39.** $\frac{1}{6}$

40. A tangerine has about 37 Calories. Is 37 *prime* or *composite*? (Lesson 9-2)

41. Thirty-six fourth graders, 48 fifth graders, and 24 sixth graders will attend a play. An equal number of students must sit in each row, and only students from the same grade can sit in a row. What is the greatest number of fifth graders that can sit in each row? (Lesson 9-1)

Write each mixed number as an improper fraction. Check using models. (Lesson 8-4)

42. $1\frac{2}{5}$ **43.** $3\frac{1}{8}$ **44.** $5\frac{2}{3}$

45. The table shows the distances that Terrell threw a flying disk. Find the median and mode of the data. (Lesson 7-1)

Throw	Distance (ft)
1	30
2	26
3	26
4	37

46. Swimming lessons cost $62 per swimmer. A total of $806 was collected for swimming lessons. How many people took swimming lessons? (Lesson 4-4)

Find the common factors of each set of numbers. (Lesson 9-1)

1. 5, 15   **2.** 12, 30

3. 24, 32, 40   **4.** 10, 22, 30

5. MULTIPLE CHOICE Which group shows all the numbers that are common factors of 24 and 40? (Lesson 9-1)

A 1, 2, 4

B 1, 2, 4, 6

C 1, 2, 4, 8

D 1, 2, 4, 6, 8, 12

Find the GCF of each set of numbers.
(Lesson 9-1)

6. 9, 21   **7.** 12, 26

8. 20, 30, 40   **9.** 8, 24, 32

Tell whether each number is *prime* or *composite*. (Lesson 9-2)

10. 20   **11.** 36

12. 19   **13.** 28

14. MULTIPLE CHOICE Which model does NOT represent a composite number? (Lesson 9-2)

F

G

H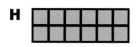

J

Find two fractions that are equivalent to each fraction. (Lesson 9-3)

15. $\frac{2}{7}$ **16.** $\frac{1}{5}$ **17.** $\frac{4}{10}$ **18.** $\frac{3}{8}$

19. Algebra What number makes $\frac{4}{9} = \frac{16}{\blacksquare}$ a true statement? (Lesson 9-3)

20. MULTIPLE CHOICE Devin recorded the shirt color of the 30 students who rode his bus on Monday. The results are shown below.

Shirt Color	Number of Students
Blue	12
White	9
Red	5
Green	3
Other	1

Which fraction of shirts were red?
(Lesson 9-4)

A $\frac{1}{3}$ **B** $\frac{1}{4}$ **C** $\frac{1}{5}$ **D** $\frac{1}{6}$

Write each fraction in simplest form. If the fraction is already in simplest form, write *simplified*. (Lesson 9-4)

21. $\frac{8}{24}$ **22.** $\frac{6}{14}$

23. $\frac{9}{20}$ **24.** $\frac{25}{30}$

25. **WRITING IN MATH** Explain how you would find two fractions that are equivalent to $\frac{6}{10}$. (Lesson 9-3)

Decimals and Fractions

A cashier weighs two peaches. The scale reads 0.75 pound. What fraction of a pound do the peaches weigh?

0.75 lb

You can use models to write any decimal that names tenths, hundredths, or thousandths as a fraction. Use the place value of the right most digit in the decimal to name the denominator of the fraction.

MAIN IDEA

I will relate decimals to fractions.

NYS Core Curriculum

Reinforcement of 4.N.24 Express decimals as an equivalent form of fractions to tenths and hundredths
Also addresses 5.N.3.

NY Math Online

macmillanmh.com

• Extra Examples
• Personal Tutor
• Self-Check Quiz

Real-World EXAMPLE   **Write a Decimal as a Fraction**

1 **FOOD** Refer to the information above. Write the weight of the peaches as a fraction in simplest form.

Step 1 Shade a model of 0.75.

THINK 0.75 is 75 hundredths.

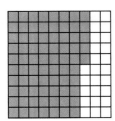

Step 2 Write a fraction with 100 as the denominator.

$$0.75 = \frac{75}{100}$$

Step 3 If necessary, simplify the fraction.

$$\frac{75}{100} = \frac{75 \div 25}{100 \div 25} \quad \text{Divide by the GCF, 25.}$$
$$= \frac{3}{4} \quad \text{Simplify.}$$

So, the peaches weigh $\frac{3}{4}$ pound.

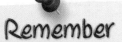

Remember

Use the place value of the right most digit in the decimal as the denominator.

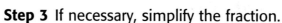

EXAMPLE   Write a Decimal as a Fraction

2 **Write 0.8 as a fraction in simplest form.**

Step 1 Shade a model of 0.8.

Step 2 Write a fraction with 10 as the denominator.

$$0.8 = \frac{8}{10}$$

Step 3 If necessary, simplify the fraction.

$$\frac{8}{10} = \frac{8 \div 2}{10 \div 2} \quad \text{Divide by the GCF, 2.}$$

$$= \frac{4}{5} \qquad \text{Simplify.}$$

EXAMPLE   Write a Decimal as a Fraction

3 **Write 0.009 as a fraction in simplest form.**

Shade a model of 0.009.

Write a fraction with 1,000 as the denominator.

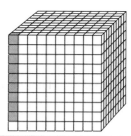

$$0.009 = \frac{9}{1,000} \quad \frac{9}{1,000} \text{ is in simplest form.}$$

✓ CHECK What You Know

Write each decimal or decimal model as a fraction in simplest form. See Examples 1–3 (pp. 391–392)

1.

2.
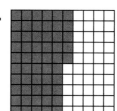

3.
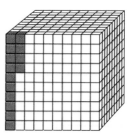

4. 0.6

5. 0.17

6. 0.125

7. It rained 0.68 inch last night. What fraction of an inch did it rain? Write in simplest form.

8. **Talk About It** How would you write a decimal as a fraction? Provide an example.

Write each decimal or decimal model as a fraction in simplest form.

See Examples 1–3 (pp. 391–392)

9.

10.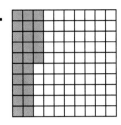

11.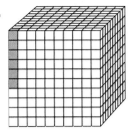

12. 0.9	**13.** 0.2	**14.** 0.5	**15.** 0.1
16. 0.65	**17.** 0.87	**18.** 0.45	**19.** 0.06
20. 0.875	**21.** 0.255	**22.** 0.045	**23.** 0.008

24. A three-toed sloth can travel at a rate of 0.07 mile per hour. Write 0.07 as a fraction in simplest form.

25. What fraction of a dollar is a penny, a nickel, a dime, a quarter, and a half dollar? Write each in simplest form.

Real-World PROBLEM SOLVING

Science The *radius* of a planet is the distance from the planet's center to its surface. The table compares the radius of three planets in the solar system to the radius of Earth.

What fraction times Earth's radius is the radius of each planet? Write in simplest form.

26. Mercury

27. Venus

28. Mars

Comparing a Planet's Radius with Earth's	
Planet	**Radius (in Earth radii)**
Mercury	0.38 × Earth
Venus	0.95 × Earth
Earth	1 × Earth
Mars	0.53 × Earth

H.O.T. Problems

29. OPEN ENDED Write a real-world problem that relates a decimal to a fraction between $\frac{30}{100}$ and $\frac{40}{100}$.

30. **WRITING IN ►MATH** Explain why 0.08 is not equal to $\frac{8}{10}$.

Problem-Solving Strategy

MAIN IDEA I will solve problems by looking for a pattern.

 **NYSCC** **5.PS.14 Analyze problems by observing patterns**

Shawna is training to run in a half-marathon. A half-marathon is about 13 miles. On her first day of training, she ran 1.25 miles. Then she increased her distance each day according to a pattern. Here are the number of miles Shawna ran the first five days of training.

1.25, 1.85, 2.45, 3.05, 3.65

Based on her pattern, how many miles will Shawna run on the sixth day?

Understand	**What facts do you know?**
	• We know how many miles Shawna ran each day for five days.
	• She increased the distance she ran each day according to a pattern.
	What do you need to find?
	• The number of miles Shawna will run on the sixth day.
Plan	One way to solve the problem is by looking for a pattern among the number of miles she ran each day for five days. Then extend the pattern to find the number of miles she will run on the sixth day.
Solve	**Use your plan to solve the problem.** Find the amounts by which Shawna increased her distances. 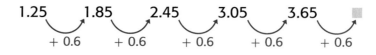 1.25 1.85 2.45 3.05 3.65 + 0.6 + 0.6 + 0.6 + 0.6 + 0.6 Shawna increases her distance by 0.6 mile each day. Add 0.6 to 3.65 to find the number of miles Shawna will run on the sixth day. $3.65 + 0.6 = 4.25$ So, on the sixth day, she will run 4.25 miles.
Check	Look back. $4.25 - 0.6 = 3.65$. So, the answer is correct. ✓

Refer to the problem on the previous page.

1. How many miles will Shawna run on day seven if she wants to double her normal increase?

2. Explain why Shawna cannot continue her pattern forever.

3. Explain when to use the *look for a pattern* strategy to solve a problem.

4. Can you always use the *look for a pattern* strategy when solving a problem?

PRACTICE the Strategy

NYSCC • NYSMT
Extra Practice, p. R25

Solve. Use the *look for a pattern* strategy.

5. Draw the next two figures in the pattern.

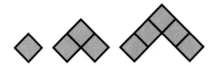

6. Stefano is buying a few pencils. The table shows the price of different numbers of pencils.

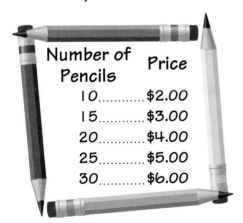

Number of Pencils	Price
10	$2.00
15	$3.00
20	$4.00
25	$5.00
30	$6.00

What is the relationship between the number of pencils and price?

7. **Measurement** Cheryl is filling a pool. She measures the depth in feet every 5 minutes. Her measurements are 2.5, 3.6, 4.7, and 5.8. If this pattern continues, how deep will the water be the next time she measures?

For Exercises 8–10, use the following information.

Gavin rode his bike for a longer distance each day while training. Here is his record of the number of miles he rode.

Mon	Tues	Wed	Thurs	Fri
3.5 mi	4.2 mi	5.0 mi		6.9 mi

8. Based on Gavin's pattern, how long did he ride on Thursday?

9. **Algebra** If the pattern continues, how far will Gavin ride on Saturday?

10. Explain how to find the number of miles Gavin will ride on Sunday, if the pattern continues.

11. The Fibonacci sequence is a famous pattern of numbers. The first seven numbers in the Fibonacci sequence are 1, 1, 2, 3, 5, 8, and 13. Find the next three numbers. Explain the pattern.

12. **WRITING IN ►MATH** Write a real-world problem that uses the *look for a pattern* strategy. Use the pattern below.

2.45, 2.8, 3.15, 3.5, . . .

MAIN IDEA

I will identify common multiples of a set of whole numbers.

NYS Core Curriculum

5.N.13 Calculate multiples of a whole number and the least common multiple of two numbers

New Vocabulary

multiple

common multiple

least common multiple (LCM)

NY Math Online

macmillanmh.com

• Extra Examples
• Personal Tutor
• Self-Check Quiz

GET READY to Learn

 Hands-On Mini Activity

A **multiple** of a number is the product of the number and any whole number. The first few multiples of 4 are 4, 8, 12, and 16.

1. Use a hundreds chart to place a colored cube on the multiples of 4. Part of a hundreds chart is shown.

×	1	2	3	4	5	6	7	8	9	10
1	1	2	3	4	5	6	7	8	9	10
2	2	4	6	8	10	12	14	16	18	20
3	3	6	9	12	15	18	21	24	27	30
4	4	8	12	16	20	24	28	32	36	40

2. On the same chart, place a different colored cube on the multiples of 6.

3. List all the numbers that have two cubes.

4. What is the least number that has two cubes?

In the Mini Activity, you found common multiples of 4 and 6. A whole number that is a multiple of two or more whole numbers is a **common multiple**.

EXAMPLE Find Common Multiples

1 List multiples to find the first two common multiples of 8 and 12.

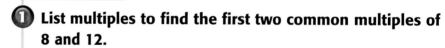

multiples of 8: 8, 16, **24**, 32, 40, **48**, … 8 × 1, 8 × 2, 8 × 3, 8 × 4, 8 × 5, 8 × 6…

multiples of 12: 12, **24**, 36, **48**, 60, … 12 × 1, 12 × 2, 12 × 3, 12 × 4, 12 × 5, 12 × 6, …

The first two common multiples of 8 and 12 are 24 and 48.

The **least common multiple (LCM)** is the least multiple, other than 0, common to sets of multiples. In the Mini Activity, the LCM of 4 and 6 is 12.

Remember

You can always find a common multiple by finding the product of the numbers. This does not always give the LCM. In Example 2, $2 \times 3 \times 4 = 24$ which is a multiple of all three numbers. But the LCM of 2, 3, and 4 is 12.

Real-World EXAMPLE   Find and Use the LCM

② **FOOD** Ben's Burgers gives away a free order of fries every 2 days, a free milkshake every 3 days, and a free hamburger every 4 days. If they gave away all three items today, in how many days will they give away all three items again?

To solve, find the LCM of 2, 3 and 4.

multiples of 2: 2, 4, 6, 8, 10, **12** ... $2 \times 1, 2 \times 2, 2 \times 3, 2 \times 4, \dots$
multiples of 3: 3, 6, 9, **12**, 15, 18... $3 \times 1, 3 \times 2, 3 \times 3, 3 \times 4, \dots$
multiples of 4: 4, 8, **12**, 16, 20... $4 \times 1, 4 \times 2, 4 \times 3, 4 \times 4, \dots$

Notice that 12 is the least common multiple of 2, 3, and 4. So, Ben's Burgers will give away all three items again in 12 days.

Draw a number line to check. Use F for fries, M for milkshake, and H for hamburger. You can see that the first day that all three items appear again, after today, is day 12. So, the answer is correct.

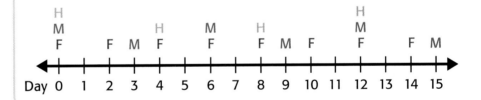

CHECK What You Know

List multiples to find the first two common multiples of each set of numbers. See Example 1 (p. 396)

1. 2 and 6
2. 4 and 10
3. 5, 6, and 10
4. 3, 4, and 6

Find the LCM of each set of numbers. Make a table or a number line.
See Example 2 (p. 397)

5. 3 and 4
6. 2 and 7
7. 4, 5, and 10
8. 3, 6, and 7

9. Inez waters her plants every two days. She trims them every 15 days. She did both today. When will she do both again?

10. **Talk About It** When is the LCM of two numbers one of the numbers? Give an example.

Practice and Problem Solving

List multiples to find the first two common multiples of each set of numbers. See Example 1 (p. 396)

11. 2 and 4

12. 8 and 12

13. 3 and 12

14. 4 and 8

15. 2, 5, and 10

16. 3, 4, and 8

17. 2, 3, and 9

18. 6, 10, and 15

Find the LCM of each set of numbers. Make a table or a number line.
See Example 2 (p. 397)

19. 5 and 6

20. 3 and 5

21. 6 and 9

22. 12 and 18

23. 6, 12, and 15

24. 5, 10, and 15

25. 3, 9, and 15

26. 9, 12, and 18

27. Macy is painting a design that contains two repeating patterns. One pattern repeats every 8 inches. The other pattern repeats every 12 inches. In how many inches will the two patterns begin at the same place?

28. The science department buys the following equipment. They bought all three items this year. In how many years will they again have to buy all three items?

Item	Time Bought
Microscopes	every 5 years
Safety goggles	every 4 years
Test tubes	every 2 years

Real-World PROBLEM SOLVING

Music A trumpet player plays a note on the fourth beat and every 4 beats after that. A saxophone player plays a note on the eighth beat and every 8 beats after that.

29. On which beat will the musicians play a note together?

30. Suppose a clarinet player joins them. He plays a note on the sixth beat and every 6 beats after that. On which beat will all three musicians play a note together?

H.O.T. Problems

31. OPEN ENDED Write a real-world problem that involves two numbers between 9 and 21. Find the LCM of the numbers and describe what it means in the problem.

32. FIND THE ERROR Carrie and Bryant are finding the least common multiple of 18 and 24. Who is correct? Explain.

Carrie

$$\begin{array}{r} 18 \\ \times\ 24 \\ \hline 72 \\ 360 \\ \hline 432 \end{array}$$

The LCM is 432.

Bryant

multiples of 18:
18, 36, 54 0, …
multiples of 24:
24, 48, 72, 96, …
The LCM is 72.

33. CHALLENGE Consider the numbers from 2 to 10. For which two numbers is the LCM the greatest? Explain.

34. **WRITING IN ▶MATH** How is the GCF of 36 and 45 different from their LCM?

NYSMT Practice ▷ 4.N.24, 5.N.13

35. A tree grew 0.85 inch in the first year. What fraction of an inch did it grow in the first year? **(Lesson 9-5)**

A $\frac{4}{5}$ **C** $\frac{21}{25}$

B $\frac{17}{20}$ **D** $\frac{17}{50}$

36. Look for the pattern in the sequence of numbers below. Each sequence is an example of which kind of numbers? **(Lesson 9-7)**

3, 6, 12, 24, 48
5, 10, 20, 40, 80
8, 16, 32, 64, 128

F even numbers   **H** multiples

G odd numbers   **J** prime numbers

Spiral Review

37. The table shows the heights of different sizes of bleachers. If the pattern continues, what would be the height of bleachers that have 7 rows? **(Lesson 9-6)**

Number of Rows	Height of Bleachers (ft)
1	2
2	4
3	6

Write each decimal as a fraction in simplest form. **(Lesson 9-5)**

38. 0.2   **39.** 0.12   **40.** 0.08

Problem-Solving Investigation

MAIN IDEA I will choose the best strategy to solve a problem.

 5.PS.2 Understand that some ways of representing a problem are more efficient than others
5.PS.3 Interpret information correctly, identify the problem, and generate possible strategies and solutions
Also addresses 5.CM.2.

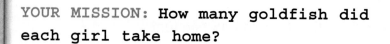 **P.S.I. TEAM +**

MYKAELA: My science teacher is giving goldfish to some of my classmates to take care of during the summer. He gave some of them to Gisela. Then he gave twice as many to Liseta. He gave twice as many to Clara as he gave to Liseta. He gave out all 28 goldfish.

YOUR MISSION: How many goldfish did each girl take home?

Understand	There are 28 goldfish. He gave some to Gisela. He gave twice as many to Liseta as to Gisela. He gave twice as many to Clara as to Liseta. You need to determine how many goldfish each girl took home.
Plan	You can use the *guess and check* strategy to find how many goldfish each girl took home.
Solve	Make a guess as to how many goldfish the teacher gave Gisela. See if it is correct. Then adjust the guess, if necessary.

<table>
<tr><th colspan="4">Number of Goldfish</th><th></th></tr>
<tr><th>Gisela</th><th>Liseta</th><th>Clara</th><th>Total</th><th></th></tr>
<tr><td>5</td><td>2 × 5 = 10</td><td>2 × 10 = 20</td><td>35</td><td>35 > 28; too many</td></tr>
<tr><td>3</td><td>2 × 3 = 6</td><td>2 × 6 = 12</td><td>21</td><td>21 < 28; too few</td></tr>
<tr><td>4</td><td>2 × 4 = 8</td><td>2 × 8 = 16</td><td>28</td><td>28 = 28; correct</td></tr>
</table>

So, the teacher gave 4 goldfish to Gisela, 8 goldfish to Liseta, and 16 goldfish to Clara.

Check	Look back. 4 + 8 + 16 = 28. So, the answer is correct. ✔

Use any strategy shown below to solve each problem.

PROBLEM-SOLVING STRATEGIES
- Guess and check.
- Look for a pattern.
- Solve a simpler problem.

1. Lorraine and Yori have 12 plants between them. Yori has 4 more than Lorraine. How many does each girl have?

2. **Algebra** When Cesar's Pizza Parlor makes a pizza, they use the following amount of cheese on each pizza:

Number of Pizzas	Amount of Cheese (ounces)
1	4
2	8
3	12
5	20
7	▨
8	▨

Complete the table and find how much cheese Cesar's uses to make 8 pizzas.

3. Annette put $5 in her bank account each week for 14 weeks. Isabel put $7 in her bank account each week for 11 weeks. Who saved more money? How much more?

4. During the World Series, one pitcher used a pattern when he pitched. The pattern was two fastballs followed by two sliders followed by a change-up. If the pattern continues, what kind of pitch will the eleventh pitch be?

5. Mr. Whitmore bought tickets for a movie. Adult tickets cost $5 each and children's tickets cost $3 each. He spent a total of $22 for the tickets. How many adult tickets and how many children's tickets did he buy?

6. Liu has $53 in his bank account. Each week for 5 weeks, he adds $2.50 to the account. How much does he now have in his bank account?

7. Maggie and her younger brother, Ty, went to lunch. Ty had a sandwich and soft drink. Maggie had a hamburger and milkshake. How much more did Maggie's lunch cost than Ty's?

Menu			
Item	**Cost**	**Item**	**Cost**
Sandwich	$2.25	Milkshake	$3.00
Hamburger	$4.50	Soft drink	$0.75

8. A total of 48 students joined the math team. There were 12 more girls than boys who joined. How many boys and how many girls joined the math team?

9. Oscar makes leather belts. If he continues his pattern below, what will be the design of the seventeenth link in the belt?

10. **WRITING IN ►MATH** Explain how you use the *guess and check* strategy.

Technology Activity for 9-9
Compare Fractions

MAIN IDEA

I will use technology to compare fractions.

NYS Core Curriculum

5.R.1 Use physical objects, drawings, charts, tables, graphs, symbols, equations, **or objects created using technology as representations**

5.N.5 Compare and order fractions including unlike denominators (with and without the use of a number line) **Note: Commonly used fractions such as those that might be indicated on ruler, measuring cup, etc.**

ACTIVITY

1. Jeffrey studied for $\frac{3}{4}$ hour and Estella studied for $\frac{5}{6}$ hour. **Who studied longer?**

You can use the Fractions option from the Math Tool Chest™.

• Choose Fractions. Click on Level 2.

• Click on Math Type. Select the 2 Sections option.

• At the bottom of the first section, stamp out three of the $\frac{1}{4}$ stamps in a horizontal line to represent $\frac{3}{4}$.

• Directly under the $\frac{1}{4}$ stamps and lined up with the left edge, place five of the $\frac{1}{6}$ stamps. This represents $\frac{5}{6}$.

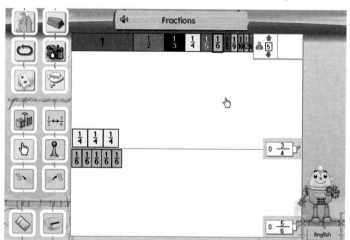

The model shows that $\frac{5}{6} > \frac{3}{4}$. So, Estella studied longer.

CHECK What You Know

Use the Fraction Option from Math Tools Chest™ to compare fractions. Then name the fraction that is greater.

1. $\frac{2}{3}$ and $\frac{3}{4}$

2. $\frac{2}{5}$ and $\frac{1}{4}$

3. $\frac{5}{8}$ and $\frac{7}{9}$

4. $\frac{11}{12}$ and $\frac{9}{10}$

5. $\frac{7}{8}$ and $\frac{5}{6}$

6. $\frac{2}{9}$ and $\frac{3}{10}$

7. $\frac{7}{12}$ and $\frac{1}{2}$

8. $\frac{3}{12}$ and $\frac{3}{8}$

ACTIVITY

2 Terrence, Yasmin, and Delsin were kicking soccer balls into a net. Terrence made $\frac{6}{10}$ of his shots, Yasmin made $\frac{3}{8}$ of her shots, and Delsin made $\frac{7}{9}$ of his shots. Compare the fractions and arrange them in order from least to greatest.

Follow the same steps as in Activity 1, with the following exceptions.

• Select the 3 Sections option from Mat Type.

• Align the stamps with the left most edge of the screen to ensure accuracy when comparing fractions.

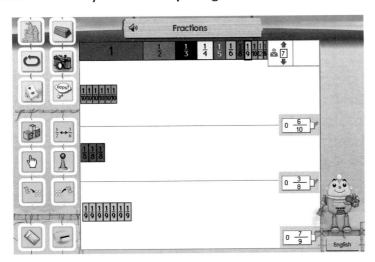

The model shows that $\frac{3}{8} < \frac{6}{10} < \frac{7}{9}$.

CHECK What You Know

Use Math Tool Chest™ to order the fractions from least to greatest.

9. $\frac{2}{5}$, $\frac{3}{16}$, and $\frac{3}{4}$

10. $\frac{8}{9}$, $\frac{3}{4}$, and $\frac{1}{2}$

11. $\frac{4}{12}$, $\frac{2}{5}$, and $\frac{4}{5}$

Solve. Use Math Tool Chest™.

12. Francisca lives $\frac{7}{10}$ mile from the park and Sereeta lives $\frac{3}{4}$ mile from the park. Who lives closer to the park?

13. Keith and Ines are sharing a pizza. Keith ate $\frac{5}{12}$ of the pizza and Ines ate $\frac{1}{3}$ of the pizza. Who ate more pizza?

Compare Fractions

MAIN IDEA

I will compare fractions using common denominators.

NYS Core Curriculum

5.N.2 Compare and order numbers to millions

5.N.5 Compare and order fractions including unlike denominators (with and without the use of a number line) **Note: Commonly used fractions such as those that might be indicated on ruler, measuring cup, etc.**

New Vocabulary

common denominator

least common denominator (LCD)

NY Math Online

macmillanmh.com
• Extra Examples
• Personal Tutor
• Self-Check Quiz
• Concepts in Motion

> **GET READY to Learn**

A class survey showed that $\frac{5}{8}$ of the class favored apple pie, $\frac{1}{4}$ favored peach pie, and $\frac{1}{8}$ of class liked pumpkin pie. Which type of pie was favored most?

| $\frac{1}{8}$ | $\frac{1}{8}$ | $\frac{1}{8}$ | $\frac{1}{8}$ | $\frac{1}{8}$ | $\frac{1}{8}$ | $\frac{1}{8}$ | $\frac{1}{8}$ |

| $\frac{1}{4}$ | $\frac{1}{4}$ | $\frac{1}{4}$ | $\frac{1}{4}$ |

| $\frac{1}{8}$ | $\frac{1}{8}$ | $\frac{1}{8}$ | $\frac{1}{8}$ | $\frac{1}{8}$ | $\frac{1}{8}$ | $\frac{1}{8}$ | $\frac{1}{8}$ |

You can use models to compare fractions. If fractions have the same denominators, compare the numerators. If the fractions have different denominators, first write equivalent fractions with a common denominator. A **common denominator** of two or more fractions is a number that is a multiple of the denominators of the fractions.

Use the **least common denominator (LCD)**, or the least common multiple of the denominators, to compare fractions.

EXAMPLE Compare Fractions

1 Compare $\frac{3}{5}$ and $\frac{1}{2}$ using models and the least common denominator.

The models show that $\frac{3}{5} > \frac{1}{2}$.

Step 1 Find the LCM of the denominators. The LCM of 5 and 2 is 10.

Step 2 Find equivalent fractions with a denominator of 10.

$\frac{3}{5} = \frac{6}{10}$ THINK $5 \times 2 = 10, 3 \times 2 = 6$

$\frac{1}{2} = \frac{5}{10}$ THINK $2 \times 5 = 10, 1 \times 5 = 5$

Step 3 Compare the numerators. Since $6 > 5$, then $\frac{6}{10} > \frac{5}{10}$.
So, $\frac{3}{5} > \frac{1}{2}$.

In Example 1, the LCD of $\frac{3}{5}$ and $\frac{1}{2}$ is 10, which can also be found by multiplying 5 and 2. You can always multiply the denominators of two fractions to find a common denominator. This method does not always give the LCD.

EXAMPLE   Compare Fractions Using the LCD

2 Compare $\frac{5}{6}$ and $\frac{7}{9}$ using the least common denominator.

Step 1 Find the LCM of the denominators. The LCM of 6 and 9 is 18. Note that multiplying 6 by 9 gives a common denominator of 54, which is not the LCD, 18.

Step 2 Find an equivalent fraction with a denominator of 18 for each fraction.

$\frac{5}{6} = \frac{15}{18}$ THINK $6 \times 3 = 18, 5 \times 3 = 15$

$\frac{7}{9} = \frac{14}{18}$ THINK $9 \times 2 = 18, 7 \times 2 = 14$

Step 3 Compare the numerators. Since $15 > 14$, then $\frac{15}{18} > \frac{14}{18}$. So, $\frac{5}{6} > \frac{7}{9}$.

Real-World EXAMPLE

3 **SPORTS** Trevor made 2 out of 3 field goals and Tyler made 5 out of 6. Who made a greater fraction of field goals?

The models show $\frac{5}{6} > \frac{2}{3}$.

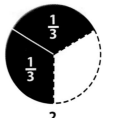

Step 1 Find the LCM of the denominators. The LCM of 3 and 6 is 6.

Step 2 Find an equivalent fraction with a denominator of 6 for each fraction.

$\frac{2}{3} = \frac{4}{6}$ THINK $3 \times 2 = 6, 2 \times 2 = 4$

$\frac{5}{6} = \frac{5}{6}$ THINK $6 \times 1 = 6, 5 \times 1 = 5$

Step 3 Compare the numerators. Since $5 > 4$, then $\frac{5}{6} > \frac{4}{6}$.

So, $\frac{5}{6} > \frac{2}{3}$. Tyler made a greater fraction of field goals.

Compare each pair of fractions using models or the LCD.
See Examples 1–3 (pp. 404–405)

1. $\frac{1}{5}$ and $\frac{1}{3}$

2. $\frac{1}{2}$ and $\frac{1}{6}$

3. $\frac{3}{4}$ and $\frac{7}{8}$

4. $\frac{2}{3}$ and $\frac{7}{10}$

Algebra Replace each ● with <, >, or = to make a true statement. See Examples 1–3 (pp. 404–405)

5. $\frac{1}{3}$ ● $\frac{5}{9}$

6. $\frac{2}{3}$ ● $\frac{7}{12}$

7. $\frac{1}{4}$ ● $\frac{1}{6}$

8. $\frac{2}{5}$ ● $\frac{6}{15}$

9. A recipe calls for $\frac{5}{8}$ cup of brown sugar and $\frac{2}{3}$ cup of flour. Which ingredient is greater?

10.  Talk About It — Explain how the LCM and the LCD are alike. How are they different?

Practice and Problem Solving

NYSCC • NYSMT
Extra Practice, p. R26

Compare each pair of fractions using models or the LCD.
See Examples 1–3 (pp. 404–405)

11. $\frac{2}{3}$ and $\frac{3}{4}$

12. $\frac{1}{5}$ and $\frac{3}{15}$

13. $\frac{1}{6}$ and $\frac{1}{3}$

14. $\frac{2}{5}$ and $\frac{3}{4}$

15. $\frac{4}{5}$ and $\frac{5}{6}$

16. $\frac{7}{8}$ and $\frac{2}{3}$

17. $\frac{3}{10}$ and $\frac{1}{12}$

18. $\frac{5}{6}$ and $\frac{4}{9}$

Algebra Replace each ● with <, >, or = to make a true statement. See Examples 1–3 (pp. 404–405)

19. $\frac{2}{5}$ ● $\frac{3}{10}$

20. $\frac{3}{4}$ ● $\frac{3}{7}$

21. $\frac{1}{5}$ ● $\frac{1}{4}$

22. $\frac{1}{2}$ ● $\frac{6}{12}$

23. $\frac{2}{6}$ ● $\frac{3}{7}$

24. $\frac{11}{12}$ ● $\frac{5}{8}$

25. $\frac{3}{8}$ ● $\frac{5}{6}$

26. $\frac{15}{16}$ ● $\frac{3}{8}$

27. A trail mix has $\frac{1}{2}$ cup of raisins, $\frac{1}{4}$ cup of almonds, and $\frac{2}{3}$ cup of peanuts. Which ingredient is greater?

28. A class survey showed that $\frac{7}{15}$ of the class liked soccer, $\frac{3}{10}$ liked tennis, and $\frac{2}{5}$ liked basketball. Which sport was liked the least?

29. The amounts of water four runners drank are shown at the right. Who drank the most?

30. The fifth graders were given sandwiches for lunch during their field trip. Nathan ate $\frac{5}{6}$ of his sandwich, Leroy ate $\frac{7}{8}$ of his sandwich, and Sofia ate $\frac{5}{8}$ of her sandwich. Who had the least amount of sandwich left to eat?

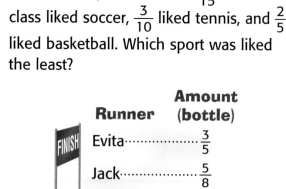

Runner	Amount (bottle)
Evita	$\frac{3}{5}$
Jack	$\frac{5}{8}$
Keisha	$\frac{3}{4}$
Sirjo	$\frac{5}{10}$

H.O.T. Problems

31. OPEN ENDED Replace ■ with a number to make $\frac{■}{24} > \frac{1}{4}$ a true statement.

32. NUMBER SENSE Suppose two fractions have the same numerator and different denominators. How can you decide which fraction is greater without finding the LCD?

33. WRITING IN ►MATH Write a real-world problem that can be solved by comparing two fractions with different denominators. Then solve. Support your answer with a model.

NYSMT Practice 5.N.13, 5.N.5

34. The table shows the cost of renting a bicycle. If the pattern continues, how much will it cost to rent a bicycle for 6 hours? (Lesson 9-7)

Number of Hours	Cost ($)
2	12
3	18
4	24
5	30

A $6   **C** $36

B $32   **D** $42

35. Eighteen out of 24 of Emil's CDs are country music. Five out of 8 of Imani's CDs are country music. Which is a true statement? (Lesson 9-9)

F Both of their CD collections are half country music.

G Both of their CD collections are less than half country music.

H Emil's collection is closer to half country than Imani's collection.

J Imani's collection is closer to half country than Emil's collection.

Spiral Review

36. Find the missing number in the pattern 1, 2, 4, 7, ■, 16, ... (Lesson 9-8)

Find the first two common multiples of each pair of numbers. (Lesson 9-7)

37. 4 and 6   **38.** 3, 9   **39.** 2, 5   **40.** 8, 20

41. The table shows the number of games won and lost by the girls' basketball team. What fraction of the games did the team win? Write the fraction in simplest form. (Lesson 9-4)

Number of Wins	Number of Losses
12	4

Problem Solving in Social Studies

SWEET DREAMS

Dreamcatchers were first made by the Chippewa people, who hung them over the beds of children to trap bad dreams. The Chippewa are one of the largest Native American groups in North America. In 1990, around 106,000 Chippewa were living throughout their original territories.

Each dreamcatcher is made with many beads and feathers. A simple dreamcatcher has 28 pony beads and is made with 7 yards of string. Today, Native Americans continue to make dreamcatchers on more than 300 reservations.

Did You Know?

The Chippewa people have signed 51 treaties with the United States government, the most of any Native American tribe.

NYSCC > **5.CN.8** Investigate the presence of mathematics in careers and **areas of interest**
5.R.8 **Use mathematics to show and understand social phenomena** (e.g., construct tables to organize data showing book sales)

Real-World Math

Use the information on page 408 to solve each problem.

1. In a simple dreamcatcher, how many beads do you use for each yard of string?

2. For each dreamcatcher you made, you used 12 beads. If you had 144 beads, how many dreamcatchers did you make?

3. Each time you add a feather to a dreamcatcher, you add 3 turquoise beads. Use a function table to find out how many beads you will need if you have 2, 5, 8, or 13 feathers in your dreamcatcher.

4. Find the rule for the function table you created in Exercise 3.

5. You are making dreamcatchers that require 6 beads for every 1 feather. Let *f* represent the number of feathers. Then write a function rule that relates the total number of beads to the number of feathers.

6. Use the function rule from Exercise 5 to find the number of beads you would use if you made a dreamcatcher with 17 feathers.

7. Suppose you use 12 feathers and a certain amount of beads to make a dreamcatcher. If you had 48 feathers and beads, how many beads did you use?

FOLDABLES®
Study Organizer
GET READY to Study

Be sure the following Big Ideas are written in your Foldable.

Chapter 9
Use Factors
and Multiples

Key Concepts

Prime and Composite Numbers

• A prime number has exactly two factors, 1 and itself. A composite number has more than two factors. **(p. 376)**

   prime numbers: 2, 3, 11, 29
   composite numbers: 4, 8, 12, 20

Equivalent Fractions and Fractions in Simplest Form

• Fractions that have the same value are **equivalent fractions**. **(p. 382)**

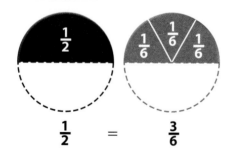

$$\frac{1}{2} = \frac{3}{6}$$

• A fraction is in **simplest form** when the GCF of the numerator and denominator is 1. **(p. 386)**

Compare Fractions

• To compare fractions with different denominators, rename the fractions using common denominators.

Key Vocabulary

common factor (p. 373)
composite number (p. 376)
equivalent fractions (p. 382)
prime number (p. 376)
simplest form (p. 386)

Vocabulary Check

Complete. Use a word from the Key Vocabulary list.

1. A whole number greater than 1 that has exactly two factors, 1 and itself, is called a(n) __?__.

2. $\frac{3}{5}$ and $\frac{6}{10}$ are called __?__.

3. A whole number that has more than two factors is called a(n) __?__.

4. A fraction is written in __?__ when the numerator and denominator have no common factor greater than 1.

5. A whole number that is a factor of two or more numbers is called a(n) __?__.

6. The fraction $\frac{5}{12}$ is written in __?__.

Lesson-by-Lesson Review

9-1 **Common Factors** (pp. 373–375)

5.N.15

Example 1
Find the greatest common factor of 6 and 21.

First, list the factors of 6 and 21.

factors of 6: **1, 2, 3, 6**

factors of 21: **1, 3, 7, 21**

The common factors are 1 and 3. The greatest of these is 3. So, the greatest common factor of 6 and 21 is 3.

Find the common factors of each set of numbers.

7. 6, 8   **8.** 9, 21, and 24

Find the GCF of each set of numbers.

9. 12, 30   **10.** 18, 45

11. Twelve pens and 16 pencils will be placed in bags with an equal number of each item. What is the most number of bags that can be made?

9-2 **Prime and Composite Numbers** (pp. 378–381)

5.N.12

Example 2
Tell whether 51 is *prime* or *composite*.

$51 = 1 \times 51$ $51 = 3 \times 17$

factors of 51: 1, 3, 17, 51

Since 51 has more than two factors, it is a composite number.

Tell whether each number is *prime* or *composite*.

12. 23   **13.** 48   **14.** 34

15. A goliath birdeater is a spider that can grow up to 28 centimeters. Find the prime factorization of 28.

9-3 **Equivalent Fractions** (pp. 382–384)

Example 3
Find two fractions that are equivalent to $\frac{2}{9}$.

Multiply $\frac{2}{9}$ by $\frac{2}{2}$. $\frac{2}{9} = \frac{2 \times 2}{9 \times 2} = \frac{4}{18}$

Multiply $\frac{2}{9}$ by $\frac{3}{3}$. $\frac{2}{9} = \frac{2 \times 3}{9 \times 3} = \frac{6}{27}$

So, $\frac{2}{9} = \frac{4}{18}$ and $\frac{2}{9} = \frac{6}{27}$.

Find two fractions that are equivalent to each fraction.

16. $\frac{1}{6}$ **17.** $\frac{4}{5}$ **18.** $\frac{2}{7}$

19. Lucinda cut her birthday cake into 16 slices. If Lucinda and her friends ate $\frac{1}{4}$ of the cake, how many pieces of cake did they eat? Support your answer with a model.

9-4 Simplest Form (pp. 386–389)

5.N.19

Example 4

Write $\frac{4}{20}$ in simplest form.

factors of 4: 1, 2, **4**

factors of 20: 1, 2, **4**, 5, 10, 20

The GCF of 4 and 20 is 4.

$\frac{4}{20} = \frac{4 \div 4}{20 \div 4} = \frac{1}{5}$ Divide the numerator and denominator by 4.

So, $\frac{4}{20}$ in simplest form is $\frac{1}{5}$.

Write each fraction in simplest form. If the fraction is already in simplest form, write *simplified*.

20. $\frac{2}{10}$ **21.** $\frac{4}{18}$

22. $\frac{6}{21}$ **23.** $\frac{8}{24}$

24. $\frac{12}{25}$ **25.** $\frac{20}{32}$

26. What fraction is represented by the model shown below? Write the fraction in simplest form.

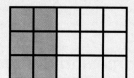

9-5 Decimals and Fractions (pp. 391–393)

4.N.24

Example 5

Write 0.45 as a fraction in simplest form.

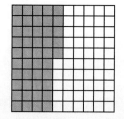

Step 1
Write a fraction with 100 as the denominator.

$0.45 = \frac{45}{100}$ 0.45 is 45 hundredths.

Step 2
Simplify the fraction.

$\frac{45}{100} = \frac{45 \div 5}{100 \div 5}$ Divide by the GCF, 5.

$= \frac{9}{20}$ Simplify.

So, $0.45 = \frac{9}{20}$.

Write each decimal as a fraction in simplest form.

27. 0.9   **28.** 0.4

29. 0.13   **30.** 0.88

31. 0.28   **32.** 0.06

33. A model train is 0.025 the length of an actual train. What fraction of the actual train length is the model? Write the fraction in simplest form.

34. A small black-legged tick is 0.125 inch long. What fraction of an inch is the black-legged tick? Write the fraction in simplest form.

9-6 Problem-Solving Strategy: Look for a Pattern (pp. 394–395)

5.PS.14

Example 6

This stairway is made of cubes. How many cubes would be needed to make it 7 steps high?

Understand   You know how many cubes are 1, 2, and 3 steps.

Plan   Look for a pattern.

Solve   2 steps: 2 + 1, or 3
3 steps: 3 + (2 + 1), or 6
4 steps: 4 + (3 + 2 + 1), or 10
7 steps: 7 + (6 + 5 + 4 + 3 + 2 + 1), or 28

Check   Draw a picture and count the cubes. There are 28 cubes, so the answer is correct. ✔

35. Find the next three numbers.
3, 7, 12, 18, 25,...

36. Bena makes bracelets. She uses red, white, and gray beads. If she continues her pattern, what color is the 15th bead?

37. Draw the next two figures in the pattern.

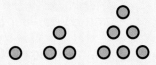

38. Jackson wrote the following fractions on the board.

$$\frac{1}{2}, \frac{2}{5}, \frac{3}{8}, \frac{4}{11}, \frac{5}{14}$$

If he continues writing fractions according to the pattern, what will be the next three fractions?

9-7 Multiples (pp. 396–399)

5.N.13

Example 7
Find the LCM of 12 and 16.

List multiples of each number to find the least common multiple.

multiples of 12: 12, 24, 36, **48**, 60 ...

multiples of 16: 16, 32, **48**, 64, 80...

The LCM of 12 and 16 is 48.

Find the LCM of each set of numbers. Make a table or a graph.

39. 5 and 9   **40.** 4, 7, and 14

41. Every 7 days, a video store gives free popcorn with movie rentals. Every 5 days, they offer a free movie. If they gave away popcorn and a movie today, when will they give away both again?

Chapter 9 Study Guide and Review   **413**

9-8 Problem-Solving Investigation: Choose a Strategy (pp. 400–401)

5.PS.2

Example 8

Pilar has $69 to spend on presents. CDs cost $13, and DVDs cost $15. How many CDs and DVDs can she buy?

Understand   You know how much money Pilar has. You know how much CDs and DVDs cost.

Plan   Use can guess and check to find how many CDs and DVDs Pilar can buy.

Solve   Pilar can buy 3 CDs and 2 DVDs with $69.

Check   Look back.
$13 + $13 + $13 + $15 + $15 = $69
So, Pilar is correct. ✓

Solve. Use any strategy.

42. Charlotte has two hamster cages. When she cleans them, she uses $\frac{3}{8}$ bag of hamster bedding for one cage and $\frac{1}{4}$ bag for the other cage. Does she need 1 bag or 2 bags when she cleans the cages?

43. Hot dogs are sold in packages of 10. Hot dog buns are sold in packages of 8. What are the fewest packages of hot dogs and packages of buns needed so the number of hot dogs matches the number of buns?

44. The table shows the number of tickets sold for the school play. If adult tickets were $3.50 and student tickets were $2, what were the total sales?

Ticket	Number Sold
Adult	126
Student	205

9-9 Compare Fractions (pp. 402–405)

5.N.5

Example 9

Replace ● with <, >, or = to make $\frac{2}{5}$ ● $\frac{3}{4}$ a true statement.

The LCM of 5 and 4 is 20. So, 20 is the LCD of $\frac{2}{5}$ and $\frac{3}{4}$.

$\frac{2}{5} = \frac{8}{20}$ THINK $5 \times 4 = 20$, $2 \times 4 = 8$

$\frac{3}{4} = \frac{15}{20}$ THINK $4 \times 5 = 20$, $3 \times 5 = 15$

Since $8 < 15$, $\frac{8}{20} < \frac{15}{20}$. So, $\frac{2}{5} < \frac{3}{4}$.

Replace each ● with <, >, or = to make a true statement.

45. $\frac{1}{4}$ ● $\frac{6}{8}$ 46. $\frac{2}{3}$ ● $\frac{3}{5}$

47. $\frac{2}{3}$ ● $\frac{7}{12}$ 48. $\frac{5}{8}$ ● $\frac{7}{12}$

49. Christine worked on social studies homework $\frac{3}{4}$ of an hour. She worked on math for $\frac{5}{6}$ of an hour. On which subject did she spend more time?

Find the common factors of each set of numbers.

1. 15, 45

2. 24, 32, and 40

Find the GCF of each set of numbers.

3. 8, 28

4. 21, 24, and 27

5. MULTIPLE CHOICE Which is a prime factor of the composite number 24?

A 3   **C** 5

B 4   **D** 12

6. The table shows the countries with the most wins for the Tour De France cycling race. Tell whether each number in the table is *prime* or *composite*.

Country	Number of Wins
Belgium	18
France	36
Netherlands	2
Spain	8
United States	7

7. Which fractions below are equivalent?

$$\frac{4}{5} \quad \frac{6}{10} \quad \frac{24}{30} \quad \frac{2}{5} \quad \frac{16}{25}$$

Write each fraction in simplest form. If the fraction is already in simplest form, write *simplified*.

8. $\frac{9}{18}$

9. $\frac{15}{16}$

10. $\frac{28}{32}$

11. $\frac{6}{27}$

12. The table shows when customers at Maltey's Burgers receive items free with the purchase of a burger deal.

Free Item	When
Milkshake	every 4 days
Tater tots	every 10 days

If they gave away both items today, in how many days will a customer be able to get both a milkshake and tater tots free again?

Write each decimal as a fraction in simplest form.

13. 0.7

14. 0.24

15. 0.875

16. 0.02

17. What is the least common multiple of 12 and 20?

18. Measurement Grasshoppers can jump 40 times the length of their body. If one foot equals 12 inches, how many feet could a 3-inch grasshopper jump?

19. MULTIPLE CHOICE Amber went to the library after school 3 of the 5 school days this week. Which fraction is less than $\frac{3}{5}$?

F $\frac{1}{2}$ **H** $\frac{4}{5}$

G $\frac{3}{4}$ **J** $\frac{5}{6}$

20. WRITING IN MATH Explain the steps you would take to make the following a true statement.

$$\frac{3}{10} \bullet \frac{9}{20}$$

PART 1   **Multiple Choice**

Read each question. Then fill in the correct answer on the answer sheet provided by your teacher or on a sheet of paper.

---

1. Sancho picked up a handful of coins from a jar without looking. He got 7 pennies, 5 nickels, 3 dimes, and 2 quarters. What fraction of the coins that he picked were nickels?

   A $\frac{2}{17}$ **C** $\frac{5}{17}$

   B $\frac{3}{17}$ **D** $\frac{7}{17}$

---

2. Paige cut a cake into 20 pieces. If 14 pieces have been eaten, what fraction of the cake remains?

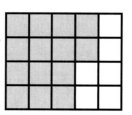

   F $\frac{1}{10}$ **H** $\frac{3}{10}$

   G $\frac{1}{5}$ **J** $\frac{2}{5}$

---

3. Natalie has washed the dishes 8 out of the last 12 nights. Which fraction shows the portion of time spent washing dishes?

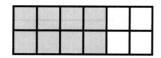

   A $\frac{1}{3}$ **C** $\frac{2}{3}$

   B $\frac{1}{2}$ **D** $\frac{5}{6}$

---

4. Emilia used 4 of her 8 stamps to mail letters. Which fraction is less than $\frac{4}{8}$?

   F $\frac{5}{8}$ **H** $\frac{1}{2}$

   G $\frac{3}{4}$ **J** $\frac{3}{7}$

---

5. Which is a prime factor of the composite number 32?

   A 2   **C** 4

   B 3   **D** 5

---

6. The table shows the number of bills of each value that Bree received for her birthday. In all, what fraction of the number of bills that Bree received for her birthday were $10 or $20 bills?

Birthday Money	
Value of Bill	**Number of bills**
$5	5
$10	3
$20	2
$50	1

   F $\frac{5}{22}$ **H** $\frac{5}{11}$

   G $\frac{3}{11}$ **J** $\frac{8}{11}$

---

7. Clarence bought a 3-pound can of mixed nuts for a party. One-fourth of the can is made up of walnuts, and two-fifths of the can is made up of peanuts. Which of the following shows the correct relationship between $\frac{1}{4}$ and $\frac{2}{5}$?

   A $\frac{1}{4} = \frac{2}{5}$ **C** $\frac{1}{4} < \frac{2}{5}$

   B $\frac{1}{4} > \frac{2}{5}$ **D** $\frac{1}{5} < \frac{3}{10}$

Preparing for NYSMT
For test-taking strategies and
practice, see pages R42–R55.

8. An assembly hall was set up with 20 rows of chairs. Each row had 16 chairs. In addition, there were 15 chairs on stage. Which expression can be used to find how many chairs there were in all?

F $(20 \times 16) + 15$

G $(20 + 16) + 15$

H $(20 \times 15) + 16$

J $(20 + 15) \times 16$

9. Which group shows the prime factorization of the number 252?

A $2 \times 3 \times 3 \times 7$

B $2 \times 2 \times 2 \times 3 \times 5$

C $2 \times 2 \times 3 \times 3 \times 7$

D $2 \times 2 \times 2 \times 3 \times 3 \times 7$

10. A florist sells vases of roses for $35 each. If the florist sold 62 vases last weekend, how much money did she collect?

F $1,855

G $1,930

H $2,170

J $2,310

PART 2 Short Response

Record your answers on the answer sheet provided by your teacher or on a sheet of paper.

11. List all of the factors of 68.

12. A pizza was divided into eighths. You ate $\frac{3}{4}$ of the pizza. How many slices did you eat?

PART 3 Extended Response

Record your answers on the answer sheet provided by your teacher or on a sheet of paper. Show your work.

13. Explain the difference between a prime number and a composite number. Be sure to include examples of each.

14. Determine if $\frac{1}{3}$ and $\frac{3}{9}$ are equivalent fractions by using a drawing.

NEED EXTRA HELP?														
If You Missed Question...	1	2	3	4	5	6	7	8	9	10	11	12	13	14
Go to Lesson...	9–4	9–4	9–4	9–9	9–2	9–9	9–9	6–6	9–2	9–4	9–1	9–3	9–2	9–3
NYS Core Curriculum	5.N.19	5.N.19	5.N.19	5.N.5	5.N.12	5.N.5	5.N.5	5.A.4	5.N.12	5.N.19	5.N.15	5.N.12	5.N.12	5.N.12

CHAPTER 10 Add and Subtract Fractions

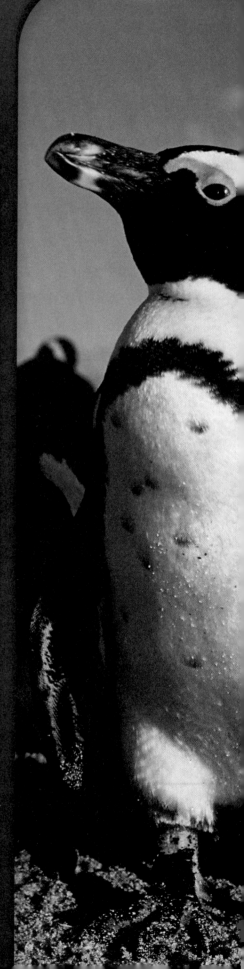

BIG Idea What are like fractions?

Fractions that have the same denominator are **like fractions**.

$$\frac{1}{8} \qquad \frac{3}{8} \qquad 2\frac{5}{8} \qquad 5\frac{7}{8}$$

You can add and subtract like fractions.

Example The average height of an African penguin is $26\frac{1}{2}$ inches. The average height of an Emperor penguin is $36\frac{1}{2}$ inches. You can subtract $26\frac{1}{2}$ from $36\frac{1}{2}$ to find the difference in height between the two penguins.

What will I learn in this chapter?

- Add and subtract like and unlike fractions.
- Estimate sums and differences of mixed numbers.
- Add and subtract mixed numbers.
- Solve problems by determining reasonable answers.

Key Vocabulary

like fractions

unlike fractions

NY Math Online **Student Study Tools**
at macmillanmh.com

FOLDABLES®
Study Organizer

Make this Foldable to organize information about like and unlike fractions. Begin with a sheet of $8\frac{1}{2}'' \times 11''$ paper, four index cards, and glue.

① **Fold** the paper in half widthwise.

② **Open** and fold along the length about $2\frac{1}{2}''$ from the bottom.

③ **Glue** the edges on either side to form two pockets.

④ **Label** the pockets *Like Fractions* and *Unlike Fractions*. Place two index cards in each pocket.

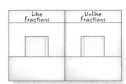

Chapter 10 Add and Subtract Fractions **419**

ARE YOU READY for Chapter 10?

You have two ways to check prerequisite skills for this chapter.

Option 2

NY Math Online Take the Chapter Readiness Quiz at macmillanmh.com.

Option 1

Complete the Quick Check below.

QUICK Check

Write each fraction in simplest form.

(Lesson 9-4)

1. $\frac{4}{8}$

2. $\frac{4}{12}$

3. $\frac{15}{20}$

4. $\frac{4}{24}$

5. Monica made 4 out of 16 free throws. Write the fraction of free throws she made in simplest form.

Write each improper fraction as a mixed number.

(Lesson 8-2)

6. $\frac{10}{7}$

7. $\frac{3}{2}$

8. $\frac{14}{6}$

9. $\frac{22}{4}$

10. A recipe for potato casserole calls for $\frac{7}{4}$ cups of cheese. Write the fraction as a mixed number.

Estimate each sum or difference by rounding. Show your work. (Lesson 2-1)

11. $10.5 - 7.1$

12. $6.2 + 4.7$

13. $5.2 + 2.1$

14. $12.7 - 6.6$

15. Sierra bought the two items shown at the right. About how much did she spend? Round to the nearest dollar.

$9.65
$3.25

16. Two classes are recycling. One class earns $17.69, and the other earns $31.15. About how much more did the second class earn? Round to the nearest dollar.

You can use fraction tiles to add fractions with the same denominator. Fractions with the same denominator are called **like fractions**. For example, $\frac{3}{5}$ and $\frac{1}{5}$ are like fractions because they both have a denominator of 5.

MAIN IDEA

I will use models to add fractions with like denominators.

NYS Core Curriculum

5.N.21 Use a variety of strategies to add and subtract **fractions with like denominators**

New Vocabulary

like fractions

NY Math Online

macmillanmh.com
• Concepts in Motion

ACTIVITY

1. **Lauren sliced an apple to eat as a snack. She ate $\frac{3}{5}$ of the apple and gave $\frac{1}{5}$ of the apple to her sister. How much of the apple did they eat?**

Step 1 **Model $\frac{3}{5}$.**

Use three $\frac{1}{5}$-fraction tiles to show $\frac{3}{5}$.

Step 2 **Model $\frac{1}{5}$.**

Add one $\frac{1}{5}$-fraction tile to show $\frac{1}{5}$.

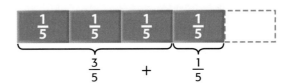

Step 3 **Add.**

Count the total number of $\frac{1}{5}$-fraction tiles.

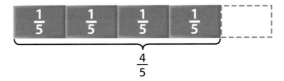

Since $\frac{3}{5} + \frac{1}{5} = \frac{4}{5}$, you can say that Lauren and her sister ate $\frac{4}{5}$ or *four fifths* of the apple.

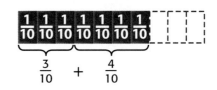

2 Theo asked his class what type of pet they like the best. Of the class, $\frac{3}{10}$ said they like dogs, and $\frac{4}{10}$ said they like cats. What fraction of the class likes dogs or cats?

Step 1 Model $\frac{3}{10}$.

Use three $\frac{1}{10}$-fraction tiles to show $\frac{3}{10}$.

Step 2 Model $\frac{4}{10}$.

Use four $\frac{1}{10}$-fraction tiles to show $\frac{4}{10}$.

Step 3 Add.

Count the total number of $\frac{1}{10}$-fraction tiles.

$\frac{3}{10} + \frac{4}{10} = \frac{7}{10}$. So, $\frac{7}{10}$ or *seven tenths* of the class likes dogs or cats.

Think About It

1. Describe how you would model $\frac{1}{8} + \frac{6}{8}$.

2. Explain how to find $\frac{1}{8} + \frac{6}{8}$. Then find and write the sum in words.

CHECK What You Know

Model each sum using fraction tiles. Then find the sum and write it in words.

3.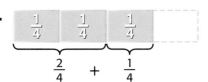

4.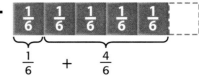

5. $\frac{3}{8} + \frac{4}{8}$

6. $\frac{5}{10} + \frac{4}{10}$

Find each sum. Use fraction tiles if needed.

7. $\frac{1}{3} + \frac{1}{3}$

8. $\frac{2}{8} + \frac{5}{8}$

9. $\frac{5}{12} + \frac{6}{12}$

10. **WRITING IN ►MATH** Look at the numerators and denominators in each exercise. Do you notice a pattern? Explain how you could find the sum of $\frac{1}{5} + \frac{1}{5}$ without using fraction tiles.

10-1 Add Like Fractions

MAIN IDEA

I will add fractions with like denominators.

NYS Core Curriculum

5.N.21 Use a variety of strategies to add and subtract **fractions with like denominators**

NY Math Online

macmillanmh.com
• Extra Examples
• Personal Tutor
• Self-Check Quiz

▶ **GET READY to Learn**

At the county fair, Lorena and her father decided to share a foot-long sub sandwich. Lorena ate $\frac{2}{6}$ of the sandwich, and her father ate $\frac{3}{6}$ of the sandwich. How much of the sandwich did they eat?

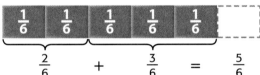

To find how much of the sub sandwich Lorena and her father ate, you can add the like fractions. When you add like fractions, the denominator names the units.

EXAMPLE Add Like Fractions

① Find $\frac{2}{6} + \frac{3}{6}$. Use models to check.

$$\frac{2}{6} + \frac{3}{6} = \frac{2+3}{6}$$

$$= \frac{5}{6} \quad \text{Add.}$$

So, $\frac{2}{6} + \frac{3}{6} = \frac{5}{6}$.

| $\frac{1}{6}$ | $\frac{1}{6}$ | $\frac{1}{6}$ | $\frac{1}{6}$ | $\frac{1}{6}$ |

$$\underbrace{\frac{2}{6}}_{} + \underbrace{\frac{3}{6}}_{} = \frac{5}{6}$$

Add Like Fractions   Key Concept

Words   To add fractions with the same denominator, add the numerators and use the same denominator.

Examples

Numbers

$$\frac{1}{4} + \frac{2}{4} = \frac{1+2}{4}$$

$$= \frac{3}{4}$$

Model

| $\frac{1}{4}$ | $\frac{1}{4}$ | $\frac{1}{4}$ |

$$\underbrace{\frac{1}{4}}_{} + \underbrace{\frac{2}{4}}_{} = \frac{3}{4}$$

Words
One fourth plus two fourths equals three fourths.

Lesson 10-1 Add Like Fractions   **423**

Real-World EXAMPLE Add Like Fractions

2 **READING** The table shows how much of a book Cleveland read each day. What fraction of the book did Cleveland read on Monday and Wednesday?

Day	Fraction
Monday	$\frac{1}{10}$
Tuesday	$\frac{4}{10}$
Wednesday	$\frac{3}{10}$
Thursday	$\frac{2}{10}$

Add $\frac{1}{10}$ and $\frac{3}{10}$.

$$\frac{1}{10} + \frac{3}{10} = \frac{1+3}{10} \quad \text{Add the numerators.}$$

$$= \frac{4}{10} \quad \text{Simplify.}$$

$$= \frac{4 \div 2}{10 \div 2} \quad \text{Divide the numerator and denominator by the GCF, 2.}$$

$$= \frac{2}{5} \quad \text{Simplify. Check by drawing a picture.}$$

So, Cleveland read $\frac{2}{5}$ of the book on Monday and Wednesday.

EXAMPLE Add Like Fractions

3 Find $\frac{2}{5} + \frac{4}{5}$. Use models to check.

$$\frac{2}{5} + \frac{4}{5} = \frac{2+4}{5} \quad \text{Add the numerators.}$$

$$= \frac{6}{5} \quad \text{Simplify.}$$

$$= 1\frac{1}{5} \quad \text{Write as a mixed number.}$$

So, $\frac{2}{5} + \frac{4}{5} = 1\frac{1}{5}$.

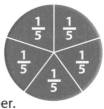

Remember

To review writing an improper fraction as a mixed number, see Lesson 8-2 on pages 338–342.

✓ CHECK What You Know

Add. Write each sum in simplest form. Use models to check.

See Examples 1–3 (pp. 423–424)

1. $\frac{1}{7} + \frac{3}{7}$

2. $\frac{2}{9} + \frac{3}{9}$

3. $\frac{1}{4} + \frac{1}{4}$

4. $\frac{1}{6} + \frac{1}{6}$

5. $\frac{5}{8} + \frac{3}{8}$

6. $\frac{2}{9} + \frac{8}{9}$

7. Tia painted $\frac{5}{12}$ of a fence. Rey painted $\frac{4}{12}$ of the fence. How much of the fence did they paint?

8. Write two sentences to explain how you solved Exercise 7.

Add. Write each sum in simplest form. Use models to check. See Examples 1–3 (pp. 423–424)

9. $\frac{4}{7} + \frac{2}{7}$
10. $\frac{2}{10} + \frac{5}{10}$
11. $\frac{2}{6} + \frac{2}{6}$
12. $\frac{3}{8} + \frac{1}{8}$

13. $\frac{3}{4} + \frac{1}{4}$
14. $\frac{4}{9} + \frac{5}{9}$
15. $\frac{3}{5} + \frac{4}{5}$
16. $\frac{2}{3} + \frac{2}{3}$

17. What is the sum of *two fifths and one fifth*? Write your answer in words.

18. What is the sum of *six ninths and three ninths*? Write your answer in words.

19. Mia walked $\frac{9}{10}$ of a mile to the park. She walked the same distance home. How much did she walk altogether?

20. It rained $\frac{2}{8}$ of an inch in one hour. It rained twice as much in the next hour. Find the total amount of rain.

For Exercises 21 and 22, refer to the table.

21. What fraction of the floats were from either a dance group or a radio station?

22. What fraction of the floats were *not* from a sports team?

Type of Parade Float	Number
Sports Team	6
Radio Station	5
High School	3
Dance Group	4

Algebra Find the value of *x* that makes a true sentence.

23. $\frac{3}{8} + \frac{x}{8} = \frac{7}{8}$
24. $\frac{x}{9} + \frac{5}{9} = \frac{7}{9}$
25. $\frac{5}{12} + \frac{x}{12} = 1$

 New York Data File

A recipe for Long Island scallops is shown.

26. If you double the recipe, how many pounds of scallops will you need?

27. Miss Kleiner triples the recipe. For what ingredient will she need $1\frac{1}{2}$ tablespoons?

Recipe for Long Island Scallops

$1\frac{1}{4}$ lb scallops
$\frac{1}{2}$ tsp salt
$\frac{1}{8}$ tsp pepper
3 Tbsp flour (about)
$\frac{1}{4}$ cup olive oil
$\frac{1}{2}$ tsp lemon juice
1 tsp parsley, minced

H.O.T. Problems

28. OPEN ENDED Select two fractions whose sum is $\frac{3}{4}$ and whose denominators are the same, but not 4. Justify your selection.

29. **WRITING IN ►MATH** Write a real-world problem that can be solved by adding like fractions. Then solve.

You can use fraction tiles to subtract fractions with like denominators.

MAIN IDEA

I will use models to subtract fractions with like denominators.

NYS Core Curriculum

5.N.21 Use a variety of strategies to add and **subtract fractions with like denominators**

ACTIVITY

① **Miguel has a bag of marbles. Of the marbles, $\frac{5}{8}$ are blue, and $\frac{2}{8}$ are red. How many more blue marbles than red marbles are in the bag?**

Step 1 Model $\frac{5}{8}$.

Use five $\frac{1}{8}$-fraction tiles to show $\frac{5}{8}$.

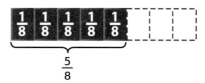

Step 2 Subtract $\frac{2}{8}$.

Remove two $\frac{1}{8}$-fraction tiles to show the subtraction of $\frac{2}{8}$.

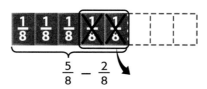

Step 3 Count the total number of $\frac{1}{8}$-fraction tiles that are left.

$\frac{5}{8} - \frac{2}{8} = \frac{3}{8}$. So, there are $\frac{3}{8}$ or *three eighths* more blue marbles.

ACTIVITY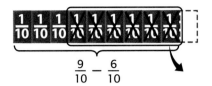

2 Abbi bought $\frac{9}{10}$ pound of Swiss cheese and $\frac{6}{10}$ pound of cheddar cheese. How much more Swiss cheese did she buy?

Step 1 Model $\frac{9}{10}$.

Use nine $\frac{1}{10}$-fraction tiles to show $\frac{9}{10}$.

Step 2 Subtract $\frac{6}{10}$.

Remove six $\frac{1}{10}$-fraction tiles.

Step 3 Count the total number of $\frac{1}{10}$-fraction tiles that are left.

$\frac{9}{10} - \frac{6}{10} = \frac{3}{10}$. So, Abbi bought $\frac{3}{10}$ or *three tenths* pound more Swiss cheese.

Think About It

1. Describe how you would model $\frac{4}{5} - \frac{3}{5}$.

2. Describe how you would find the difference $\frac{4}{5} - \frac{3}{5}$. Then find the difference.

CHECK What You Know

Model each difference using fraction tiles. Then find the difference and write in words.

3.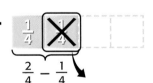

$\frac{2}{4} - \frac{1}{4}$

4.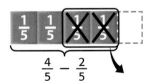

$\frac{4}{5} - \frac{2}{5}$

Find each difference. Use fraction tiles if needed.

5. $\frac{6}{7} - \frac{4}{7}$

6. $\frac{2}{3} - \frac{1}{3}$

7. $\frac{4}{6} - \frac{3}{6}$

8. $\frac{5}{9} - \frac{3}{9}$

9. $\frac{7}{10} - \frac{4}{10}$

10. $\frac{11}{12} - \frac{6}{12}$

11. **WRITING IN MATH** Look at the numerators and denominators in each exercise. Explain how you could find $\frac{9}{12} - \frac{4}{12}$ without using fraction tiles.

GET READY to Learn

Frankie is walking on a nature trail that is $\frac{7}{8}$-mile long. He has already walked $\frac{4}{8}$ mile. How much farther does Frankie have to walk?

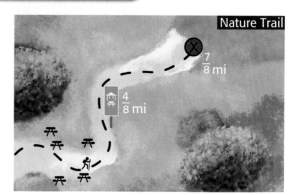

Nature Trail
$\frac{7}{8}$ mi
$\frac{4}{8}$ mi

To find how much farther, subtract $\frac{4}{8}$ from $\frac{7}{8}$.

EXAMPLE Subtract Like Fractions

1 Find $\frac{7}{8} - \frac{4}{8}$. Use models to check.

$$\frac{7}{8} - \frac{4}{8} = \frac{7 - 4}{8}$$

$$= \frac{3}{8} \qquad \text{Subtract.}$$

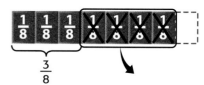

$\frac{3}{8}$

So, $\frac{7}{8} - \frac{4}{8} = \frac{3}{8}$.

Subtracting like fractions is similar to adding like fractions.

Subtract Like Fractions Key Concept

Words To subtract fractions with the same denominator, subtract the numerators and use the same denominator.

Examples **Numbers** **Model**

$$\frac{4}{5} - \frac{2}{5} = \frac{4 - 2}{5}$$

$$= \frac{2}{5}$$

$\frac{2}{5}$

Words

Four fifths minus two fifths equals two fifths.

WEATHER The table shows the amount of rainfall several cities received in a recent month.

RAINFALL

City	Rainfall (in.)
Spring Valley	$\frac{1}{10}$
Clarksburg	$\frac{6}{10}$
Centerville	$\frac{9}{10}$
Brushton	$\frac{3}{10}$

2 **How much more rain did Centerville receive than Brushton? Write in simplest form. Use models to check.**

Subtract the amount of rain that fell in Brushton from the amount of rain that fell in Centerville.

Remember

Divide both the numerator and denominator by the greatest common factor.

$$\frac{9}{10} - \frac{3}{10} = \frac{9-3}{10} \quad \text{Subtract the numerators.}$$

$$= \frac{6}{10} \quad \text{Simplify.}$$

$$= \frac{6 \div 2}{10 \div 2} \quad \text{Divide by the GCF, 2.}$$

$$= \frac{3}{5} \quad \text{Simplify.}$$

Use models to check.

$$\frac{9}{10} - \frac{3}{10}$$

So, $\frac{3}{5}$ inch more rain fell in Centerville than in Brushton.

3 **How many fewer inches of rain did Spring Valley receive than Clarksburg? Write in simplest form. Use models to check.**

Subtract the amount of rain that fell in Spring Valley from the amount of rain that fell in Clarksburg.

$$\frac{6}{10} - \frac{1}{10} = \frac{6-1}{10} \quad \text{Subtract the numerators.}$$

$$= \frac{5}{10} \quad \text{Simplify.}$$

$$= \frac{5 \div 5}{10 \div 5} \quad \text{Divide by the GCF, 5.}$$

$$= \frac{1}{2} \quad \text{Simplify.}$$

Use models to check.

$$\frac{6}{10} - \frac{1}{10}$$

So, it rained $\frac{1}{2}$ inch less in Spring Valley than in Clarksburg.

Subtract. Write each difference in simplest form. Use models to check. See Examples 1–3 (pp. 428–429)

1. $\frac{5}{7} - \frac{3}{7}$

2. $\frac{3}{5} - \frac{2}{5}$

3. $\frac{6}{9} - \frac{3}{9}$

4. $\frac{5}{6} - \frac{3}{6}$

5. Ciro spent $\frac{5}{6}$ hour drawing and $\frac{2}{6}$ hour reading. How much more time did he spend drawing than reading?

6. **Talk About It** Explain how you solved Exercise 5 using words.

Practice and Problem Solving

NYSCC • NYSMT Extra Practice, p. R27

Subtract. Write each difference in simplest form. Use models to check. See Examples 1–3 (pp. 428–429)

7. $\frac{2}{3} - \frac{1}{3}$

8. $\frac{3}{5} - \frac{1}{5}$

9. $\frac{6}{7} - \frac{5}{7}$

10. $\frac{3}{6} - \frac{1}{6}$

11. $\frac{5}{9} - \frac{2}{9}$

12. $\frac{6}{8} - \frac{4}{8}$

13. $\frac{3}{4} - \frac{1}{4}$

14. $\frac{9}{12} - \frac{3}{12}$

15. Find the difference between *seven ninths and four ninths.* Write your answer in words.

16. What is the difference between *six sevenths and five sevenths?* Write your answer in words.

17. **Measurement** Roshanda bought $\frac{5}{8}$ pound of ham and $\frac{7}{8}$ pound of roast beef. How much more roast beef than ham did she buy?

18. A bucket was $\frac{7}{10}$ full with water. After Vick washed the car, the bucket was only $\frac{3}{10}$ full. What part did Vick use to wash the car?

For Exercises 19 and 20, use the results of a survey of 28 students and their favorite tourist attractions.

19. What fraction of students prefer Mt. Rushmore over the Grand Canyon?

20. Suppose 4 students change their minds and choose the Statue of Liberty instead of the Grand Canyon. What part of the class now prefers Mt. Rushmore over the Statue of Liberty?

Favorite Tourist Attactions

Place	Number of Students
Mt. Rushmore	14
Grand Canyon	8
Statue of Liberty	6

Algebra Find the value of *x* that makes a true sentence.

21. $\frac{6}{9} - \frac{x}{9} = \frac{1}{9}$

22. $\frac{x}{8} - \frac{3}{8} = \frac{1}{8}$

23. $\frac{8}{12} - \frac{x}{12} = \frac{1}{4}$

H.O.T. Problems

24. OPEN ENDED Choose two like fractions whose difference is $\frac{1}{6}$ and whose denominators are not 6.

CHALLENGE Compare. Write $>$, $<$, or $=$ to make a true sentence.

25. $\frac{5}{6} - \frac{1}{6} \bullet \frac{3}{6} - \frac{2}{6}$

26. $\frac{8}{8} - \frac{8}{8} \bullet \frac{2}{9} - \frac{2}{9}$

27. $\frac{3}{4} - \frac{2}{4} \bullet \frac{5}{5} - \frac{1}{5}$

28. WRITING IN ▶MATH Write a problem about a real-world situation in which you would find $\frac{3}{4} - \frac{1}{4}$. Then solve.

NYSMT Practice ▷ 5.N.21

29. Measurement Paul is making dinner. He uses $\frac{1}{4}$ cup of cheese for a salad and $\frac{2}{4}$ cup of cheese for a casserole. How many cups of cheese does Paul use altogether? **(Lesson 10-1)**

A $\frac{1}{8}$ c   **C** $\frac{3}{8}$ c

B $\frac{1}{4}$ c   **D** $\frac{3}{4}$ c

30. The pictures below show how much sausage and pepperoni pizza was left over at the end of one day.

Sausage   Pepperoni

Which fraction represents how much more sausage pizza was left over than pepperoni pizza? **(Lesson 10-2)**

F $\frac{3}{16}$ **H** $\frac{11}{16}$

G $\frac{3}{8}$ **J** $\frac{11}{8}$

Spiral Review

Add. Write each sum using words in simplest form. **(Lesson 10-1)**

31. $\frac{7}{11} + \frac{2}{11}$ **32.** $\frac{2}{13} + \frac{5}{13}$ **33.** $\frac{5}{14} + \frac{2}{14}$ **34.** $\frac{8}{15} + \frac{4}{15}$

35. Measurement A recipe for trail mix calls for $\frac{2}{3}$ cup of marshmallows, $\frac{7}{8}$ cup of pretzels, and $\frac{3}{4}$ cup of raisins. Which ingredient is the greatest amount? Which ingredient is the least amount? **(Lesson 9-9)**

Write each improper fraction as a mixed number. **(Lesson 8-2)**

36. $\frac{45}{6}$ **37.** $\frac{68}{8}$ **38.** $\frac{62}{12}$ **39.** $\frac{80}{15}$

Math Activity for 10-3
Add Unlike Fractions

In Lesson 10-1, you learned that like fractions are fractions with the same denominator. Fractions with different denominators are called *unlike fractions*.

Like Fractions	Unlike Fractions
$\frac{3}{8}, \frac{4}{8}$	$\frac{1}{2}, \frac{5}{6}$

You can add fractions that have different denominators using fraction tiles.

MAIN IDEA

I will use models to add unlike fractions.

NYS Core Curriculum

Preparation for 6.N.16 Add and subtract fractions with unlike denominators.

1. **To finish building a birdhouse, Jordan uses two boards. One is $\frac{1}{2}$ foot long and the other is $\frac{1}{3}$ foot long. What is the total length of the boards?**

Step 1 Model each fraction using fraction tiles and place them side by side.

$\frac{1}{2}$	$\frac{1}{3}$

Step 2 Find fraction tiles that will match the length of the combined fractions above. Line them up below the model.

$\frac{1}{2}$		$\frac{1}{3}$	

$\frac{1}{6}$	$\frac{1}{6}$	$\frac{1}{6}$	$\frac{1}{6}$	$\frac{1}{6}$

Step 3 Add. There are five of the $\frac{1}{6}$-fraction tiles in all. So, $\frac{1}{2} + \frac{1}{3} = \frac{5}{6}$.

The total length of the boards is $\frac{5}{6}$ foot.

Hands-On Activity

ACTIVITY

2 Muna bought $\frac{3}{4}$ pound of grapes and $\frac{5}{8}$ pound of cherries. What is the combined weight of the fruit?

Step 1 Model each fraction using fraction tiles.

| $\frac{1}{4}$ | $\frac{1}{4}$ | $\frac{1}{4}$ | $\frac{1}{8}$ | $\frac{1}{8}$ | $\frac{1}{8}$ | $\frac{1}{8}$ | $\frac{1}{8}$ |

Step 2 Find fraction tiles that will match the length of the combined fractions above. Line them up below the model.

| $\frac{1}{4}$ | $\frac{1}{4}$ | $\frac{1}{4}$ | $\frac{1}{8}$ | $\frac{1}{8}$ | $\frac{1}{8}$ | $\frac{1}{8}$ | $\frac{1}{8}$ |

| $\frac{1}{8}$ | $\frac{1}{8}$ | $\frac{1}{8}$ | $\frac{1}{8}$ | $\frac{1}{8}$ | $\frac{1}{8}$ | $\frac{1}{8}$ | $\frac{1}{8}$ | $\frac{1}{8}$ | $\frac{1}{8}$ |

Step 3 Add. There are eleven of the $\frac{1}{8}$-fraction tiles.

So, $\frac{3}{4} + \frac{5}{8} = \frac{11}{8}$ or $1\frac{3}{8}$.

The combined weight of the fruit is $1\frac{3}{8}$ pounds.

Think About It

1. How can finding the multiples of 4 and 12 help you find $\frac{3}{4} + \frac{7}{12}$?

2. Describe how you could use fraction tiles to find the sum of $\frac{2}{5}$ and $\frac{1}{10}$.

✓ CHECK What You Know

Find the sum using fraction tiles.

3. $\frac{2}{3} + \frac{1}{6}$ 4. $\frac{3}{4} + \frac{1}{3}$ 5. $\frac{3}{8} + \frac{1}{4}$ 6. $\frac{1}{2} + \frac{5}{6}$

7. $\frac{3}{10} + \frac{1}{5}$ 8. $\frac{5}{8} + \frac{1}{4}$ 9. $\frac{1}{2} + \frac{1}{4}$ 10. $\frac{3}{4} + \frac{2}{3}$

11. **WRITING IN MATH** Write a real-world problem that can be solved by adding unlike fractions.

Explore Math Activity 10-3 Add Unlike Fractions   433

10-3 Add Unlike Fractions

GET READY to Learn

Gene spent $\frac{1}{3}$ hour writing an article for the school paper, and $\frac{1}{4}$ hour proofreading it. How long did Gene spend writing and proofreading his article?

MAIN IDEA

I will add fractions with unlike denominators.

NYS Core Curriculum

Preparation for 6.N.16 Add and subtract fractions with unlike denominators.

New Vocabulary

unlike fractions

NY Math Online

macmillanmh.com
• Extra Examples
• Personal Tutor
• Self-Check Quiz

Before you can add two **unlike fractions**, one or both of the fractions must be renamed so that they have a common denominator.

Adding Unlike Fractions	Key Concept

To add unlike fractions, perform the following steps:

• Rename the fractions using the least common denominator (LCD).

• Add as with like fractions.

• If necessary, simplify the sum.

EXAMPLE Add Unlike Fractions

1 Refer to the information above. Find $\frac{1}{3}$ hour $+ \frac{1}{4}$ hour.

The least common denominator of $\frac{1}{3}$ and $\frac{1}{4}$ is 12.

Step 1
Write the problem.

Step 2
Rename using the LCD.

Step 3
Add the like fractions.

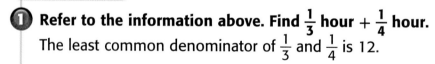

$$\frac{1}{3} \quad \rightarrow \quad \frac{1 \times 4}{3 \times 4} = \frac{4}{12} \quad \rightarrow \quad \frac{4}{12}$$

$$+\frac{1}{4} \quad \rightarrow \quad \frac{1 \times 3}{4 \times 3} = \frac{3}{12} \quad \rightarrow \quad +\frac{3}{12}$$

$$\frac{7}{12}$$

So, Gene spent $\frac{7}{12}$ hour writing and proofreading his article.

Real-World EXAMPLE

2 MUSIC Catalina spent $\frac{1}{6}$ of her free time reading and $\frac{5}{12}$ of her free time practicing her flute. What fraction of her free time did she spend reading and practicing her flute?

Add $\frac{1}{6}$ and $\frac{5}{12}$.

The least common denominator of $\frac{1}{6}$ and $\frac{5}{12}$ is 12.

Remember
You can rename unlike fractions as like fractions by using the LCD.

Step 1	**Step 2**	**Step 3**
Write the problem.	Rename using the LCD.	Add the like fractions.

$$\frac{1}{6} \quad \rightarrow \quad \frac{1 \times 2}{6 \times 2} = \frac{2}{12} \quad \rightarrow \quad \frac{2}{12}$$
$$+\frac{5}{12} \quad \rightarrow \quad \frac{5 \times 5}{12 \times 1} = \frac{5}{12} \quad \rightarrow \quad +\frac{5}{12}$$
$$\overline{\qquad\qquad} \quad \frac{7}{12}$$

So, Catalina spent $\frac{7}{12}$ of her free time reading and practicing her flute.

CHECK What You Know

Add. Write in simplest form. See Examples 1, 2 (p. 434–435)

1. $\frac{3}{4} + \frac{1}{8}$ **2.** $\frac{2}{3} + \frac{1}{9}$ **3.** $\frac{2}{5} + \frac{1}{2}$ **4.** $\frac{5}{7} + \frac{2}{14}$

5. $\frac{2}{5} + \frac{3}{10}$ **6.** $\frac{1}{2} + \frac{3}{7}$ **7.** $\frac{5}{6} + \frac{3}{4}$ **8.** $\frac{2}{5} + \frac{7}{10}$

9. $\frac{4}{9} + \frac{2}{3}$ **10.** $\frac{5}{12} + \frac{1}{4}$ **11.** $\frac{4}{7} + \frac{1}{2}$ **12.** $\frac{5}{8} + \frac{2}{3}$

13. A farmer harvested $\frac{3}{8}$ of a pecan crop on Friday and $\frac{1}{3}$ of the crop on Saturday. What fraction of the pecan crop was harvested in the two days?

14. (Talk About It) Describe the steps for adding the fractions $\frac{5}{12}$ and $\frac{5}{6}$. What is the solution?

Add. Write in simplest form. See Examples 1,2 (pp. 434–435)

15. $\frac{2}{3} + \frac{1}{6}$ 16. $\frac{1}{2} + \frac{1}{4}$ 17. $\frac{1}{6} + \frac{7}{12}$ 18. $\frac{5}{8} + \frac{1}{16}$

19. $\frac{1}{3} + \frac{1}{4}$ 20. $\frac{1}{2} + \frac{4}{5}$ 21. $\frac{3}{5} + \frac{3}{10}$ 22. $\frac{3}{5} + \frac{3}{6}$

23. $\frac{2}{16} + \frac{3}{4}$ 24. $\frac{7}{8} + \frac{1}{2}$ 25. $\frac{3}{4} + \frac{7}{20}$ 26. $\frac{1}{4} + \frac{3}{8}$

27. Angel has two chores after school. She rakes leaves for $\frac{3}{4}$ hour and spends $\frac{1}{2}$ hour washing the car. How long does Angel spend on her chores?

28. **Measurement** One craft project requires $\frac{3}{8}$ yard of ribbon, and another requires $\frac{1}{4}$ yard of ribbon. How much ribbon is needed for both projects?

29. Leon walked $\frac{5}{6}$ mile to the store and $\frac{1}{3}$ mile more to the theater. How far did he walk in all?

30. Tashia ate $\frac{1}{3}$ of the pizza and Jay ate $\frac{3}{7}$ of the pizza. What fraction of the pizza did they eat?

H.O.T. Problems

31. **OPEN ENDED** Write an addition problem involving two unlike fractions. One fraction should have a denominator of 12 and the other fraction should have a denominator of 9. Then, find the sum.

32. **FIND THE ERROR** Kate and Josh are finding the sum of $\frac{3}{4}$ and $\frac{9}{10}$. Who is correct? Explain your reasoning.

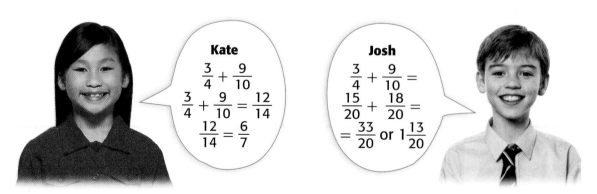

Kate
$\frac{3}{4} + \frac{9}{10}$
$\frac{3}{4} + \frac{9}{10} = \frac{12}{14}$
$\frac{12}{14} = \frac{6}{7}$

Josh
$\frac{3}{4} + \frac{9}{10} =$
$\frac{15}{20} + \frac{18}{20} =$
$= \frac{33}{20}$ or $1\frac{13}{20}$

33. **WRITING IN MATH** Write a real-world problem that can be solved by adding two fractions. Then solve the problem.

Math Activity for 10-4
Subtract Unlike Fractions

You can use fraction tiles to subtract fractions with unlike denominators.

ACTIVITY

1 Akio lives $\frac{3}{4}$ mile from school. Bianca lives $\frac{1}{6}$ mile from school. How much farther from school does Akio live than Bianca?

Step 1 Model each fraction using fraction tiles. Place the $\frac{1}{6}$-tiles underneath the $\frac{1}{4}$-tiles.

Step 2 Find which fraction will fill in the area of the dotted box.

Two of the $\frac{1}{3}$-tiles are too large to fit. Try a different fraction tile.

✔ Seven of the $\frac{1}{12}$-tiles fit.

Step 3 Since $\frac{7}{12}$ fills in the area of the dotted box, $\frac{3}{4} - \frac{1}{6} = \frac{7}{12}$.

So, Akio lives $\frac{7}{12}$ mile farther from school than Bianca.

MAIN IDEA

I will use models to subtract unlike fractions.

NYS Core Curriculum

Preparation for 6.N.16 Add and subtract fractions with unlike denominators.

2 Lisa and Kofi each bought a small tub of popcorn. Lisa ate $\frac{4}{5}$ of her popcorn and Kofi ate $\frac{3}{10}$ of her popcorn. **What fraction more did Lisa eat than Kofi?**

Step 1 Model each fraction using fraction tiles. Place the $\frac{1}{10}$-fraction tiles underneath the $\frac{1}{5}$-fraction tiles.

Step 2 Find which fraction will fill in the area of the dotted box.

The $\frac{1}{2}$-fraction tile fits. ✔

Step 3 Since $\frac{1}{2}$ fills in the area of the dotted box, $\frac{4}{5} - \frac{3}{10} = \frac{1}{2}$.

So, Lisa ate $\frac{1}{2}$ tub more popcorn than Kofi.

Think About It

1. Would any of the other fraction tiles fit inside the dotted box for Activity 2?

2. Describe how you would use fraction tiles to find $\frac{1}{2} - \frac{1}{3}$.

CHECK What You Know

Find each difference using fraction tiles.

3. $\frac{2}{3} - \frac{1}{6} =$ **4.** $\frac{5}{6} - \frac{1}{4} =$ **5.** $\frac{5}{8} - \frac{1}{4} =$ **6.** $\frac{4}{5} - \frac{1}{2} =$

7. **WRITING IN ▶MATH** Write a real-world problem that can be solved by subtracting unlike fractions.

Subtract Unlike Fractions

MAIN IDEA

I will subtract fractions with unlike denominators.

NYS Core Curriculum

**Preparation for
6.N.16** Add and
subtract fractions with
unlike denominators.

NY Math Online

macmillanmh.com
• Extra Examples
• Personal Tutor
• Self-Check Quiz

GET READY to Learn

A female Cuban tree frog can be up to $\frac{5}{12}$ foot long. A male Cuban tree frog can be up to $\frac{1}{4}$ foot long. How much longer is the female Cuban tree frog than the male?

Subtracting unlike fractions is similar to adding unlike fractions.

Subtract Unlike Fractions   **Key Concept**

To subtract unlike fractions, perform the following steps:

• Rename the fractions using the LCD.

• Subtract as with like fractions.

• If necessary, simplify the answer.

EXAMPLE   Subtract Unlike Fractions

① **FROGS** How much longer is the female Cuban tree frog than the male Cuban tree frog?

Find $\frac{5}{12} - \frac{1}{4}$.

The least common denominator of $\frac{5}{12}$ and $\frac{1}{4}$ is 12.

Step 1	Step 2	Step 3
Write the problem.	Rename using the LCD.	Add the like fractions.

$$
\begin{array}{ccccc}
\dfrac{5}{12} & \rightarrow & \dfrac{5 \times 1}{12 \times 1} = \dfrac{5}{12} & \rightarrow & \dfrac{5}{12} \\[2mm]
-\dfrac{1}{4} & \rightarrow & \dfrac{1 \times 3}{4 \times 3} = \dfrac{3}{12} & \rightarrow & -\dfrac{3}{12} \\
\end{array}
$$

$$\frac{2}{12} = \frac{1}{6} \text{ Simplify.}$$

A female Cuban tree frog is $\frac{1}{6}$ foot longer than the male.

2️⃣ **HOMEWORK** Jessie finished $\frac{1}{2}$ of her homework. Lakshani finished $\frac{4}{5}$ of her homework. What fraction more of her homework did Lakshani finish than Jessie?

Subtract $\frac{4}{5} - \frac{1}{2}$.

The least common denominator of $\frac{4}{5}$ and $\frac{1}{2}$ is 10.

Step 1	**Step 2**	**Step 3**
Write the problem.	Rename using the LCD.	Add the like fractions.

$$\frac{4}{5} \quad \rightarrow \quad \frac{4 \times 2}{5 \times 2} = \frac{8}{10} \quad \rightarrow \quad \frac{8}{10}$$

$$-\frac{1}{2} \quad \rightarrow \quad \frac{1 \times 5}{2 \times 5} = \frac{5}{10} \quad \rightarrow \quad -\frac{5}{10}$$

$$\overline{\qquad\qquad\qquad\qquad\qquad \frac{3}{10}}$$

Lakshani finished $\frac{3}{10}$ more of her homework than Jessie.

✓CHECK What You Know

Subtract. Write in simplest form. See Examples 1, 2 (pp. 439–440)

1. $\frac{3}{8} - \frac{1}{4} =$

2. $\frac{5}{6} - \frac{1}{2} =$

3. $\frac{2}{5} - \frac{1}{4} =$

4. $\frac{4}{5} - \frac{1}{6} =$

5. $\frac{7}{8} - \frac{1}{2} =$

6. $\frac{7}{12} - \frac{1}{3} =$

7. $\frac{5}{6} - \frac{1}{3} =$

8. $\frac{2}{3} - \frac{3}{10} =$

9. **Measurement** Danielle poured $\frac{3}{4}$ gallon of water from the full bucket shown at the right. How much water is left in the bucket?

$\frac{7}{8}$ gallon

10. **Talk About It** Describe the steps you can use to find $\frac{3}{4} - \frac{1}{12}$.

Subtract. Write in simplest form. See Examples 1,2 (pp. 439–440)

11. $\frac{5}{8} - \frac{1}{2}$ **12.** $\frac{2}{5} - \frac{1}{10}$ **13.** $\frac{1}{2} - \frac{1}{4}$ **14.** $\frac{4}{5} - \frac{2}{15}$

15. $\frac{5}{12} - \frac{1}{6}$ **16.** $\frac{7}{10} - \frac{1}{4}$ **17.** $\frac{5}{6} - \frac{3}{4}$ **18.** $\frac{2}{3} - \frac{3}{5}$

19. $\frac{7}{8} - \frac{1}{4}$ **20.** $\frac{7}{10} - \frac{1}{2}$ **21.** $\frac{5}{8} - \frac{1}{6}$ **22.** $\frac{7}{12} - \frac{1}{3}$

23. Denelle rides her bicycle $\frac{2}{3}$ mile to school. On Friday, she took a shortcut so that the ride to school was $\frac{1}{9}$ mile shorter. How long was Denelle's bicycle ride on Friday?

24. Measurement The average snowfall in April and October for Springfield is shown in the table at the right. How much more snow falls on average in April than in October?

Average Snowfall for Springfield	
Month	**Snowfall (in.)**
April	$\frac{4}{5}$
October	$\frac{3}{10}$

25. Wyatt is hiking a trail that is $\frac{11}{12}$ mile long. After hiking $\frac{1}{4}$ mile, he stops for water. How much farther must he hike to finish the trail?

26. Lavell has $\frac{7}{10}$ of his homework finished. Jaclyn has $\frac{4}{9}$ of her homework finished. How much more of his homework does Lavell have finished than Jaclyn?

27. A mosaic design is $\frac{7}{15}$ red, $\frac{1}{5}$ blue, and $\frac{1}{3}$ yellow. What fraction more of the mosaic is blue and yellow than red?

H.O.T. Problems

28. OPEN ENDED Write a subtraction problem involving fractions with the denominators 8 and 24. Then find the difference. Include the steps you used.

29. CHALLENGE Evaluate $x - y$ if $x = \frac{5}{6}$ and $y = \frac{7}{10}$.

30. WRITING IN MATH Describe the difference between subtracting fractions with like denominators and subtracting fractions with unlike denominators.

MAIN IDEA I will solve problems by determining reasonable answers.

NYSCC **5.PS.19 Determine between valid and invalid answers**
Also addresses 5.RP.8.

Leandra feeds her pet rabbit Bounce the same amount of food each day. Bounce eats three times a day. *About* how much food does Leandra feed Bounce in a week?

Time	Food (cups)
Morning	$\frac{3}{4}$
Afternoon	$\frac{3}{4}$
Evening	$\frac{1}{4}$

Understand	**What facts do you know?** • Leandra feeds the rabbit the same amount every day. **What do you need to find?** • About how much food she feeds her rabbit each week.
Plan	You can use estimation to find a reasonable answer.
Solve	Round each amount of food to the nearest whole number. Morning　　　Afternoon　　　Evening $\frac{3}{4} \rightarrow 1$　　$\frac{3}{4} \rightarrow 1$　　$\frac{1}{4} \rightarrow 0$ In one day, she feeds Bounce about $1 + 1 + 0$ or 2 cups of food. Multiply by the number of days in a week. days in 1 week ⌐　⌐ cups of food each day 　　　　$7 \times 2 = 14$ ← cups of food in 7 days or 1 week Leandra feeds Bounce about 14 cups of food in a week.
Check	Look back. Since there are 7 days in a week, multiply each amount by 7. $(7 \times 1) + (7 \times 1) + (7 \times 0) = 14$ So, the answer is reasonable.

Refer to the problem on the previous page.

1. Explain why estimation is often the best way to find reasonable answers.

2. What other methods of computation could you use to solve the problem? Explain.

3. Find how much more food Leandra feeds her rabbit in the morning than in the evening.

4. What method of computation did you use to solve Exercise 3? Explain your reasoning.

▶ PRACTICE the Strategy

NYSCC • NYSMT
Extra Practice, p. R28

Solve. Determine which answer is reasonable.

5. Thirty students from the Netherlands set up a record 1,500,000 dominoes. Of these, 1,138,101 were toppled by one push. Which is a more reasonable estimate for how many dominoes remained standing after that push: 350,000 or 400,000?

6. Use the graph below. Is 20 inches, 23 inches, or 215 inches a reasonable total amount of rain that fell in May, June, and July?

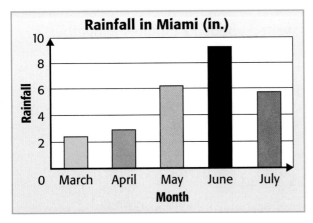

Rainfall in Miami (in.)

7. A puzzle book costs $4.25. A novel costs $9.70 more than the puzzle book. Which is a more reasonable estimate for the total cost of both items: $14, $16, or $18?

8. Use the table to determine whether 245 pounds, 260 pounds, or 263 pounds is a reasonable estimate for how much more the ostrich weighs than the flamingo. Explain.

Bird	Weight (lb)
Flamingo	$9\frac{1}{10}$
Ostrich	$253\frac{1}{2}$

9. **Measurement** A grocer sells 12 pounds of apples. Of those, $5\frac{3}{4}$ pounds are green and $3\frac{1}{4}$ pounds are golden. The rest are red. Which is a more reasonable estimate for how many pounds of red apples the grocer sold: 3 pounds or 5 pounds? Explain.

10. **WRITING IN ►MATH** Write an addition or subtraction problem involving fractions with like denominators. Ask a classmate to determine a reasonable answer for the problem.

Estimate Sums and Differences

MAIN IDEA

I will estimate sums and differences of mixed numbers.

NYS Core Curriculum

5.N.25 Estimate sums and differences of fractions with like denominators *Also addresses 6.N.16.*

NY Math Online

macmillanmh.com

• Extra Examples
• Personal Tutor
• Self-Check Quiz

▶ **GET READY to Learn**

Lucita and Alexis waited in line for the bumper cars for $7\frac{1}{6}$ minutes. Then they waited in line for the Ferris wheel for $4\frac{5}{6}$ minutes. About how long did they wait for the bumper cars and the Ferris wheel altogether?

To estimate the sum of $7\frac{1}{6}$ and $4\frac{5}{6}$, round each mixed number to the nearest whole number. Then add.

EXAMPLE   Estimate Sums

① **Estimate $7\frac{1}{6} + 4\frac{5}{6}$ to answer the problem above.**

THINK: $\frac{1}{6}$ is less than $\frac{1}{2}$.
So, round $7\frac{1}{6}$ down to 7.

$7\frac{1}{6} + 4\frac{5}{6}$

THINK: $\frac{5}{6}$ is greater than $\frac{1}{2}$.
So, $4\frac{5}{6}$ rounds up to 5.

Estimate $7 + 5 = 12$

So, Lucita and Alexis waited about 12 minutes altogether.

EXAMPLE   Estimate Differences

② **Estimate $3\frac{5}{8} - 1\frac{1}{8}$.**

THINK: $\frac{5}{8} > \frac{1}{2}$.
Round $3\frac{5}{8}$ up to 4.

$3\frac{5}{8} - 1\frac{1}{8}$

THINK: $\frac{1}{8} < \frac{1}{2}$.
Round $1\frac{1}{8}$ down to 1.

Estimate $4 - 1 = 3$

So, $3\frac{5}{8} - 1\frac{1}{8}$ is about 3.

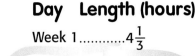

Real-World EXAMPLE

 ③ SWIMMING The table shows how many hours Alfie swam in two weeks. About how many hours did he swim altogether?

Day	Length (hours)
Week 1	$4\frac{1}{3}$
Week 2	$2\frac{5}{6}$

Round each mixed number to the nearest whole number. Then add.

THINK: $\frac{1}{3} < \frac{1}{2}$. Round down.	$4\frac{1}{3} + 2\frac{5}{6}$	THINK: $\frac{5}{6} > \frac{1}{2}$. Round up.

Estimate $4 + 3 = 7$

So, Alfie swam for about 7 hours.

Real-World EXAMPLE

 ④ MEASUREMENT A fish tank can hold $10\frac{2}{5}$ gallons of water. Suppose the tank has $6\frac{1}{10}$ gallons of water. About how much more water is needed to fill the tank?

Round $10\frac{2}{5}$ to 10 and $6\frac{1}{10}$ to 6.

Estimate $10 - 6 = 4$

So, about 4 more gallons are needed to fill the tank.

CHECK What You Know

Estimate by rounding each mixed number to the nearest whole number. See Examples 1–4 (pp. 444–445)

1. $2\frac{1}{8} + 3\frac{5}{8}$ **2.** $3\frac{3}{5} + 1\frac{1}{5}$ **3.** $5\frac{2}{9} - 3\frac{2}{3}$ **4.** $7\frac{4}{6} - 4\frac{3}{12}$

5. Liam spent $1\frac{3}{4}$ hours playing board games and $2\frac{1}{4}$ hours watching a movie. About how much time did Liam spend on these two activities?

6. Write at least two sentences to explain how you would estimate $8\frac{4}{7} - 4\frac{2}{7}$.

Lesson 10-6 Estimate Sums and Differences **445**

Estimate. See Examples 1–4 (pp. 444–445)

7. $9\frac{1}{7} - 5\frac{6}{7}$

8. $6\frac{7}{10} - 1\frac{2}{10}$

9. $5\frac{3}{9} + 3\frac{7}{9}$

10. $8\frac{11}{12} + 4\frac{4}{12}$

11. $10\frac{2}{7} + 7\frac{5}{7}$

12. $12\frac{5}{10} + 9\frac{6}{10}$

13. $15\frac{6}{14} - 3\frac{4}{7}$

14. $13\frac{4}{11} - 4\frac{1}{4}$

15. $7\frac{7}{9} - \frac{15}{18}$

16. $8\frac{9}{15} - \frac{4}{5}$

17. $19\frac{3}{7} + \frac{13}{14}$

18. $\frac{9}{16} + 16\frac{5}{8}$

19. Polly has played soccer for $3\frac{5}{6}$ years. Gen has played soccer for $6\frac{1}{12}$ years. Estimate how many more years Gen has played soccer than Polly.

20. To clean a large painting, you need $3\frac{1}{4}$ ounces of cleaner. A small painting requires only $2\frac{3}{4}$ ounces. You have 8 ounces of cleaner. About how many ounces of cleaner will you have left if you clean a large and a small painting?

Measurement For Exercises 21 and 22, use the picture shown.

21. About how much taller is the birdhouse than the tree house?

22. Find the height difference between the birdhouse and the tree house. Is it greater than or less than the difference in height between the swing set and the tree house? Use estimation.

$14\frac{8}{16}$ ft $11\frac{13}{16}$ ft $8\frac{4}{16}$ ft

Algebra Estimate the value of each expression if $n = 2\frac{7}{8}$.

23. $n + 2\frac{5}{8}$

24. $n - \frac{6}{8}$

25. $15 - n$

26. $n + 18$

H.O.T. Problems

27. OPEN ENDED Select two mixed numbers whose estimated difference is 1. Justify your selection.

CHALLENGE Without calculating, replace ● with < or > to make a true sentence. Explain your reasoning.

28. $3\frac{7}{8} + 4\frac{1}{8}$ ● 9

29. $6\frac{7}{9} - 5\frac{3}{9}$ ● 1

30. 3 ● $4\frac{8}{10} - 3\frac{1}{10}$

31. **WRITING IN** ►MATH Describe a real-world situation where it makes sense to round two numbers up even though one number could be rounded down.

Add. Write each sum in simplest form. (Lesson 10-1)

1. $\frac{4}{11} + \frac{5}{11}$ 2. $\frac{9}{13} + \frac{3}{13}$

3. **MULTIPLE CHOICE** A family bought two pizzas and ate only part of each pizza. The pictures show how much of the pizzas were left. How much of one whole pizza was left over? (Lesson 10-1)

A $\frac{7}{8}$ C $\frac{1}{5}$

B $\frac{5}{8}$ D $\frac{1}{8}$

Subtract. Write each difference in simplest form. (Lesson 10-2)

4. $\frac{6}{7} - \frac{4}{7}$ 5. $\frac{7}{11} - \frac{6}{11}$

Add. Write in simplest form. (Lesson 10-3)

6. $\frac{2}{3} + \frac{1}{6}$ 7. $\frac{2}{7} + \frac{1}{2}$

8. Sasha ran $\frac{2}{4}$ mile on Monday and $\frac{5}{12}$ mile on Tuesday. What is the total distance Sasha ran?

Subtract. Write in simplest form. (Lesson 10-4)

9. $\frac{6}{7} - \frac{1}{3}$ 10. $\frac{2}{3} - \frac{1}{2}$

Algebra Find the value of x that makes a true sentence. (Lesson 10-4)

11. $\frac{x}{12} - \frac{5}{12} = \frac{1}{12}$ 12. $\frac{3}{16} + \frac{x}{4} = \frac{7}{16}$

13. An $156.99 electric scooter has been discounted by $19.99. Which is a more reasonable estimate for the discounted price: $130, $137, or $140? Explain. (Lesson 10-5)

14. **Measurement** Mr. Nair bought $3\frac{1}{4}$ pounds of oranges. He bought $\frac{3}{4}$ pound more of bananas than oranges. *About* how many pounds of oranges and bananas did he buy? (Lesson 10-6)

Estimate by rounding each mixed number to the nearest whole number. (Lesson 10-6)

15. $11\frac{1}{6} - 2\frac{5}{6}$ 16. $9\frac{7}{10} + 3\frac{6}{10}$

17. $7\frac{2}{7} + 6\frac{5}{7}$ 18. $14\frac{3}{16} - 11\frac{9}{16}$

19. **MULTIPLE CHOICE** Mrs. Orta used $5\frac{3}{4}$ gallons of blue paint and $2\frac{1}{4}$ gallons of yellow paint. About how many gallons of paint did she use? (Lesson 10-6)

F 2 gal   H 6 gal

G 4 gal   J 8 gal

20. **WRITING IN ►MATH** Write an addition problem using words for the following model. Then find the sum. (Lesson 10-1)

| $\frac{1}{6}$ | $\frac{1}{6}$ | $\frac{1}{6}$ | $\frac{1}{6}$ | $\frac{1}{6}$ | |

10-7 Add Mixed Numbers

MAIN IDEA

I will add mixed numbers.

NYS Core Curriculum

5.N.22 Add and subtract **mixed numbers with like denominators** *Also addresses 6.N.16.*

NY Math Online

macmillanmh.com

- Extra Examples
- Personal Tutor
- Self-Check Quiz

GET READY to Learn

One day Emma gathered $2\frac{1}{4}$ dozen eggs. The next day, she gathered $1\frac{1}{4}$ dozen eggs. How many dozen eggs did she gather in all?

You can find an exact answer by adding the mixed numbers.

Real-World EXAMPLE   Add Mixed Numbers

1 **FOOD** **Refer to the information above. How many dozen eggs did Emma gather?**

Find $2\frac{1}{4} + 1\frac{1}{4}$.   **Estimate** $2 + 1 = 3$

Step 1 Add the fractions.

$$\begin{array}{r} 2\frac{1}{4} \\ + 1\frac{1}{4} \\ \hline \frac{2}{4} \end{array}$$

$\frac{1}{4} + \frac{1}{4} = \frac{2}{4}$

Step 2 Add the whole numbers.

$$\begin{array}{r} 2\frac{1}{4} \\ + 1\frac{1}{4} \\ \hline 3\frac{2}{4} \end{array}$$

$2 + 1 = 3$

Step 3 Simplify.

$3\frac{2}{4} = 3\frac{1}{2}$ Divide the numerator and denominator by the GCF, 2.

Check for Reasonableness $3\frac{1}{2} \approx 3$ ✔

So, Emma gathered $3\frac{1}{2}$ dozen eggs.

Real-World EXAMPLE

2 **REPTILES** The diagram shows the length of a sea turtle. What is the total length of the sea turtle?

Find $\frac{7}{8} + 3\frac{1}{4} + 1\frac{1}{8}$.

$\frac{7}{8}$ ft ← $3\frac{1}{4}$ ft → $1\frac{1}{8}$ ft

Remember

Estimate first. Then compare your answer with the estimate.

Step 1

Write the problem.

$$\frac{7}{8}$$
$$3\frac{1}{4}$$
$$+1\frac{1}{8}$$

Step 2

Rename the fractions using the LCD.

$$\frac{7}{8} = \frac{7}{8}$$
$$3\frac{1 \times 2}{4 \times 2} = 3\frac{2}{8}$$
$$+1\frac{1}{8} = 1\frac{1}{8}$$

Step 3

Add the fractions and whole numbers.

$$\frac{7}{8}$$
$$3\frac{2}{8}$$
$$+1\frac{1}{8}$$
$$\overline{4\frac{10}{8}}$$

Step 4 Simplify.

$$4\frac{10}{8} = 4 + 1\frac{2}{8} = 5\frac{2}{8} = 5\frac{1}{4}$$

The total length of the sea turtle is $5\frac{1}{4}$ feet.

Add Mixed Numbers

Key Concepts

- Rename the fraction using the LCD.
- Add the fractions and then the whole numbers.
- Simplify if needed.

CHECK What You Know

Add. Write each sum in simplest form. See Examples 1, 2 (pp. 448–449)

1. $3\frac{3}{8} + 2\frac{4}{8}$

2. $4\frac{4}{6} + 2\frac{1}{6}$

3. $5\frac{1}{10} + 5\frac{3}{10}$

4. $3\frac{4}{9} + 4\frac{2}{3}$

5. $6\frac{3}{4} + 3\frac{1}{8}$

6. $4\frac{3}{7} + 7\frac{1}{2}$

7. Yushua worked $5\frac{1}{2}$ hours on Monday, $7\frac{1}{2}$ hours on Tuesday, and $6\frac{1}{2}$ hours on Wednesday. How many hours did he work in all?

8. **Talk About It** Explain how to simplify $3\frac{6}{4}$.

Add. Write each sum in simplest form. See Examples 1, 2 (pp. 448–449)

9. $4\frac{3}{5} + 3\frac{1}{5}$

10. $7\frac{4}{11} + 2\frac{6}{11}$

11. $5\frac{1}{12} + 6\frac{3}{12}$

12. $8\frac{4}{15} + 3\frac{2}{15}$

13. $6\frac{1}{9} + 2\frac{1}{3}$

14. $5\frac{3}{9} + 6\frac{1}{2}$

15. $9\frac{9}{10} + 7\frac{3}{5}$

16. $14\frac{19}{20} + 8\frac{1}{4}$

17. Find *five and two eighths plus three and six eighths*. Write in words.

18. Find *ten and three sevenths plus eighteen and two sevenths*. Write in words.

19. **Measurement** Zita made $1\frac{5}{8}$ quarts of punch. Then she made $1\frac{7}{8}$ more quarts. How much punch did she make in all?

20. A flower is $9\frac{3}{4}$ inches tall. In one week, it grew $1\frac{1}{8}$ inches. How tall is the flower at the end of the week?

21. Pati made fruit salad using the recipe. How many cups of fruit are needed?

Fruit Salad

$3\frac{2}{4}$ c Apple
$1\frac{1}{4}$ c Grapefruit
$1\frac{3}{4}$ c Orange
$2\frac{1}{4}$ c Pear

22. **Measurement** Connor is filling a 15-gallon wading pool. On his first trip, he carried $3\frac{1}{12}$ gallons of water. He carried $3\frac{5}{6}$ gallons on his second trip and $3\frac{1}{2}$ gallons on his third trip. Suppose he carries 5 gallons on his next trip. Will the pool be filled? Explain.

H.O.T. Problems

23. **OPEN ENDED** Write a real-world problem involving the addition of two mixed numbers whose sum is $5\frac{1}{4}$. Then solve the problem.

24. **FIND THE ERROR** Urbano and Brandy are finding $4\frac{1}{5} + 2\frac{3}{5}$. Who is correct? Explain your reasoning.

Urbano
$4\frac{1}{5} + 2\frac{3}{5} = 6\frac{4}{5}$

Brandy
$4\frac{1}{5} + 2\frac{3}{5} = 6\frac{4}{10}$

25. **WRITING IN MATH** Is the sum of two mixed numbers *always*, *sometimes*, or *never* a mixed number? Use an example to explain.

26. Marie bought $4\frac{1}{2}$ pints of ice cream for her birthday party. Her mother also bought $2\frac{1}{4}$ pints of ice cream for the party. How many pints of ice cream did Marie have for her birthday party? (Lesson 10-5)

A $2\frac{1}{4}$ pt

B $2\frac{3}{4}$ pt

C $6\frac{3}{8}$ pt

D $6\frac{3}{4}$ pt

27. The length and the width of Samson's swimming pool is shown.

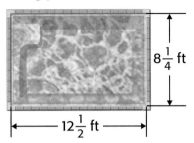

$8\frac{1}{4}$ ft

$12\frac{1}{2}$ ft

About how much longer is the length of the pool than the width of the pool? (Lesson 10-4)

F 3 ft   **H** 20 ft

G 5 ft   **J** 21 ft

Spiral Review

28. Nestor and Tanya rode two different rides at the fair. Nestor rode the Roller Express. The ride lasted about $1\frac{1}{3}$ minutes. Tanya rode the Rattler, which lasted about $2\frac{2}{3}$ minutes. About how much longer did the Rattler last than the Roller Express? (Lesson 10-6)

29. Measurement The distance around Saturn is 235,298 miles. The distance around Jupiter is 279,118 miles. Is 45,000 miles or 55,000 miles a more reasonable estimate for the difference between the distance around Jupiter and the distance around Saturn? Explain. (Lesson 10-5)

Write each decimal as a fraction in simplest form. (Lesson 9-5)

30. 0.8   **31.** 0.9   **32.** 0.29   **33.** 0.11

Write each mixed number as an improper fraction. (Lesson 8-4)

34. $3\frac{5}{6}$ **35.** $6\frac{1}{4}$ **36.** $4\frac{1}{3}$ **37.** $5\frac{2}{5}$

38. Ginny's basketball team scored 44 points in one game. If Ginny scored 16 points, how many points did the rest of team score? Write and solve an addition equation. (Lesson 6-2)

Divide. (Lesson 4-3)

39. 48 ÷ 5   **40.** 48 ÷ 3   **41.** 172 ÷ 4   **42.** 264 ÷ 6

MAIN IDEA

I will subtract mixed numbers.

NYS Core Curriculum

5.N.22 Add and subtract mixed numbers with like denominators *Also addresses 6.N.16.*

NY Math Online

macmillanmh.com
• Extra Examples
• Personal Tutor
• Self-Check Quiz

GET READY to Learn

Payat has a $2\frac{3}{4}$ cup package of cheese. He uses $1\frac{1}{4}$ cups to make a pizza. How much cheese is left?

You can find an exact answer by subtracting $1\frac{1}{4}$ from $2\frac{3}{4}$.

Real-World EXAMPLE Subtract Mixed Numbers

1 **FOOD Refer to the information above. How many cups of cheese are left? Check by using fraction tiles.**

Find $2\frac{3}{4} - 1\frac{1}{4}$.   **Estimate** $3 - 1 = 2$

Step 1 Subtract the fractions.

$$\begin{array}{r} 2\frac{3}{4} \\ -1\frac{1}{4} \\ \hline \frac{2}{4} \end{array}$$

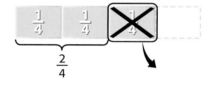

Step 2 Subtract the whole numbers.

$$\begin{array}{r} 2\frac{3}{4} \\ -1\frac{1}{4} \\ \hline 1\frac{2}{4} \end{array}$$

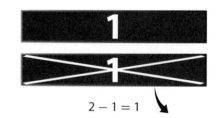

$2 - 1 = 1$

Step 3 Simplify $1\frac{2}{4}$.

$1\frac{2}{4} = 1\frac{1}{2}$ Divide the numerator and denominator by the GCF, 2.

Check for reasonableness $1\frac{1}{2} \approx 2$ ✔

So, $1\frac{1}{2}$ cups of cheese were left.

2 **FISH** A Pigfish and a Shiner are shown below. How much longer is the Pigfish than the Shiner?

 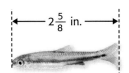

Find $6\frac{11}{16} - 2\frac{5}{8}$ **Estimate** $7 - 3 = 4$

Step 1
Write the problem.

$$6\frac{11}{16}$$
$$-\ 2\frac{5}{8}$$

$\rightarrow$

Step 2
Rename the fractions using the LCD.

$$6\frac{11}{16} = 6\frac{11}{16}$$
$$-\ 2\frac{5 \times 2}{8 \times 2} = 2\frac{10}{16}$$

$\rightarrow$

Step 3
Subtract the fractions and mixed numbers.

$$6\frac{11}{16}$$
$$-\ 2\frac{10}{16}$$
$$\overline{\ \ \ 4\frac{1}{16}}$$

So, the Pigfish is $4\frac{1}{16}$ inches longer than the Shiner.

> **Remember**
>
> Always check for reasonableness.
>
> $4\frac{1}{16} \approx 4$ ✔

Subtract Mixed Numbers
Key Concept

- If needed, rename the fractions using the LCD.
- Subtract the fractions.
- Then subtract the whole numbers.
- Simplify if needed.

✓ CHECK What You Know

Subtract. Write each difference in simplest form. See Examples 1, 2 (pp. 452–453)

1. $4\frac{2}{3} - 2\frac{1}{3}$

2. $5\frac{4}{5} - 3\frac{2}{5}$

3. $6\frac{5}{6} - 5\frac{2}{6}$

4. $7\frac{7}{8} - 4\frac{1}{2}$

5. $12\frac{7}{10} - 7\frac{2}{5}$

6. $15\frac{11}{12} - 4\frac{1}{3}$

7. Bella is $10\frac{5}{12}$ years old. Franco is $12\frac{7}{12}$ years old. What is the difference in their ages?

8. Describe the steps you would take to find $3\frac{5}{8} - 2\frac{3}{8}$.

Subtract. Write each difference in simplest form. See Examples 1, 2 (pp. 452–453)

9. $5\frac{3}{4} - 2\frac{2}{4}$ **10.** $6\frac{5}{7} - 3\frac{3}{7}$ **11.** $7\frac{8}{9} - 5\frac{3}{9}$ **12.** $8\frac{3}{8} - 2\frac{2}{8}$

13. $13\frac{9}{10} - 4\frac{4}{10}$ **14.** $12\frac{5}{6} - 7\frac{2}{6}$ **15.** $11\frac{11}{12} - 2\frac{1}{6}$ **16.** $14\frac{9}{14} - 5\frac{2}{7}$

17. $18\frac{11}{15} - 9\frac{2}{5}$ **18.** $17\frac{15}{16} - 9\frac{3}{4}$ **19.** $35\frac{7}{8} - 18\frac{5}{12}$ **20.** $44\frac{6}{7} - 21\frac{3}{4}$

21. Find *ten and seven tenths minus three and four tenths*. Write in words.

22. Find *twelve and five ninths minus five and two ninths*. Write in words.

23. Measurement The length of Mr. Cho's garden is $8\frac{5}{6}$ feet. Find the width of Mr. Cho's garden if it is $3\frac{1}{6}$ feet less than the length.

24. Mrs. Gabel bought $7\frac{5}{6}$ gallons of punch for the class party. The students drank $4\frac{3}{6}$ gallons of punch. How much punch was left at the end of the party?

25. Warner lives $9\frac{2}{3}$ blocks away from school. Shelly lives $12\frac{7}{8}$ blocks away from school. How many more blocks does Shelly live away from school than Warner?

26. A snack mix recipe calls for $5\frac{3}{4}$ cups of cereal and $3\frac{5}{12}$ cups less raisins. How many cups of raisins are needed?

H.O.T. Problems

27. OPEN ENDED Write a real-world problem involving the subtraction of two mixed numbers whose difference is less than $2\frac{1}{2}$. Then solve.

CHALLENGE Find the value of each variable that makes a true sentence.

28. $n + 2\frac{1}{2} = 6\frac{3}{10}$ **29.** $k + 3\frac{2}{8} = 7\frac{5}{8}$ **30.** $4\frac{1}{6} + t = 13\frac{5}{6}$

31. WHICH ONE DOESN'T BELONG? Identify the expression that does not belong with the other three. Explain your reasoning.

| $5\frac{7}{10} - 3\frac{2}{10}$ | $11\frac{6}{8} - 9\frac{2}{8}$ | $8\frac{5}{6} - 6\frac{2}{6}$ | $7\frac{3}{4} - 5\frac{2}{4}$ |

32. WRITING IN ►MATH Write a real-word problem involving subtraction of mixed numbers with unlike denominators. Then solve. Use fraction tiles to justify your solution.

Fraction Subtraction

Subtract Mixed Numbers

Get Ready!

Players: 2 players

Get Set!

Copy one problem shown on each index card.

Go!

- Shuffle the cards. Then spread out the cards face down on the table.

- Player 1 turns over any two cards.

- If the answers to the problems are equivalent, Player 1 keeps the cards and receives one point. Player 1 continues his or her turn.

- If the solutions are *not* equivalent, the cards are turned over and Player 2 takes a turn.

- Play continues until all matches are made. The player with most points wins.

You will need: 12 index cards

$2\frac{1}{2} - 1\frac{1}{2}$	$5\frac{3}{4} - 4\frac{3}{4}$	$6\frac{2}{3} - 3\frac{1}{3}$
$3\frac{9}{10} - \frac{2}{5}$	$4\frac{7}{8} - 2\frac{1}{8}$	$13\frac{3}{4} - 10\frac{5}{12}$
$5\frac{15}{16} - 3\frac{3}{16}$	$10\frac{5}{6} - 7\frac{1}{3}$	$10\frac{4}{5} - 8\frac{3}{5}$
$8\frac{3}{5} - 6\frac{2}{5}$	$8\frac{6}{7} - 3\frac{2}{7}$	$7\frac{5}{7} - 2\frac{1}{7}$

10-9 Problem-Solving Investigation

MAIN IDEA I will choose the best strategy to solve a problem.

NYSCC 5.PS.2 Understand that some ways of representing a problem are more efficient than others
5.PS.3 Interpret information correctly, identify the problem, and generate possible strategies and solutions
Also addresses 5.PS.21.

P.S.I. TEAM +

JACOBO: I have a bolt of material that has $6\frac{1}{4}$ yards of material on it. I have used $1\frac{3}{8}$ yards to make a large pillow. Do I have enough material to make four more pillows just like the first one?

YOUR MISSION: Find out whether Jacobo has enough material for four more pillows.

Understand	You know the bolt has $6\frac{1}{4}$ yards on it and $1\frac{3}{8}$ yards were used. You need to see if he can make four more pillows.
Plan	Use the *act it out* strategy to measure the material.
Solve	Start by marking the floor to show a length of $6\frac{1}{4}$ yards. Then mark off the amount used to make the first pillow. Then continue to mark 4 more pillows.

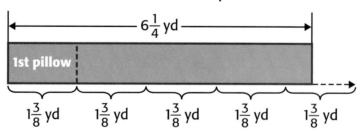

There is not enough material to make 4 more pillows.

Check	Look back. You can estimate. Round $1\frac{3}{8}$ to $1\frac{1}{2}$. $1\frac{1}{2} + 1\frac{1}{2} + 1\frac{1}{2} + 1\frac{1}{2} + 1\frac{1}{2} = 7\frac{1}{2}$ Since $7\frac{1}{2} > 6\frac{1}{4}$, the answer is correct.

Use any strategy shown below to solve each problem.

PROBLEM-SOLVING STRATEGIES
• Act it out.
• Make a graph.
• Look for a pattern.
• Use logical reasoning.

1. Alyssa needs $7\frac{5}{8}$ inches of ribbon for one project and $4\frac{7}{8}$ inches of ribbon for another project. If she has 12 inches of ribbon, will she have enough to complete both projects? Explain.

2. Berto surveyed his classmates about their favorite type of movie. He used C for comedy, A for Action, and S for scary. How many more people favored comedies than action movies?

FAVORITE MOVIES

S	C	A	C	C
A	C	S	A	A
C	A	C	C	S
A	C	S	A	C
C	S	A	C	C

3. **Measurement** A high jumper starts the bar at 48 inches and raises the bar $\frac{1}{2}$ inch after each jump. How high will the bar be on the seventh jump?

4. Max, Aleta, Digna, and Tom won the first four prizes in the spelling bee. Max placed second. Aleta did not place third. Tom placed fourth. What did Digna place?

5. Shanté has eight coins in her pocket that total $1.32. What are the eight coins that she has in her pocket?

6. Gift boxes come in five different sizes. The length of the gift boxes decreases by $2\frac{1}{2}$ inches. For each $2\frac{1}{2}$-inch decrease, the price decreases by $0.75. The length of the largest box is 22 inches and costs $3.75. Find the length and cost of the smallest box.

7. What is the next figure in the pattern?

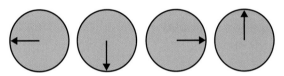

8. **Measurement** Josiah has a piece of wood that measures $9\frac{3}{8}$ feet. He wants to make 5 shelves. If each shelf is $1\frac{3}{4}$ feet long, does he have enough to make 5 shelves?

9. Franklin leaves home at 10:00 A.M. He rides his bike an average of 14 miles each hour. By 2:00 P.M., how many miles will Franklin have biked?

10. The number of siblings each student in Ms. Kennedy's class has is shown below. How many more students have two or more siblings than students who have only one sibling?

Number of Siblings					
2	1	4	2	1	0
3	2	1	1	2	3
1	1	2	0	3	1

11. **WRITING IN MATH** Refer to Exercise 4. Which strategy did you use to solve this problem? Why?

10-10 Subtraction with Renaming

MAIN IDEA

I will subtract mixed numbers.

NYS Core Curriculum

5.N.22 Add and **subtract mixed numbers with like denominators** *Also addresses 6.N.16.*

NY Math Online

macmillanmh.com

• Extra Examples
• Personal Tutor
• Self-Check Quiz

GET READY to Learn

The black-tailed jackrabbit and the swamp rabbit are two mammals common to the Southern United States. A black-tailed jackrabbit weighs about $2\frac{1}{3}$ pounds. A swamp rabbit weighs about $1\frac{2}{3}$ pounds.

Sometimes the fraction in the first mixed number is less than the fraction in the second mixed number. In this case, the first mixed number needs to be renamed.

Real-World EXAMPLE Rename Mixed Numbers to Subtract

① **ANIMALS** How much more does the black-tailed jackrabbit weigh than the swamp rabbit?

You need to find $2\frac{1}{3} - 1\frac{2}{3}$.

Since $\frac{1}{3}$ is less than $\frac{2}{3}$, rename $2\frac{1}{3}$ before subtracting.

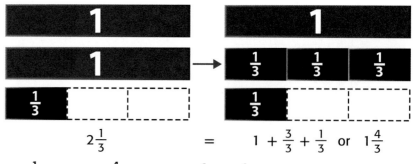

$$2\frac{1}{3} \qquad = \qquad 1 + \frac{3}{3} + \frac{1}{3} \text{ or } 1\frac{4}{3}$$

$$\begin{aligned} 2\frac{1}{3} &\rightarrow 1\frac{4}{3} \qquad \text{Rename } 2\frac{1}{3} \text{ as } 1\frac{4}{3}. \\ -1\frac{2}{3} &\rightarrow -1\frac{2}{3} \\ \hline & \qquad\quad \frac{2}{3} \qquad \text{Subtract the fractions and then the whole numbers.} \end{aligned}$$

So, a black-tailed jackrabbit weighs about $\frac{2}{3}$ pound more than a swamp rabbit.

EXAMPLE **Rename Mixed Numbers to Subtract**

2 Find $4\frac{1}{4} - 2\frac{5}{8}$.

Remember

You can always check by using fraction tiles or drawing a picture.

Rename $4\frac{1}{4}$ as $4\frac{2}{8}$ to make like fractions.

Since $\frac{2}{8}$ is less than $\frac{5}{8}$, rename $4\frac{2}{8}$ before subtracting.

THINK $4\frac{2}{8} = 3 + 1 + \frac{2}{8}$

$\qquad\quad = 3 + \frac{8}{8} + \frac{2}{8}$ or $3\frac{10}{8}$ Rename 1 as $\frac{8}{8}$.

$$4\frac{2}{8} \quad \rightarrow \quad 3\frac{10}{8} \quad \text{Rename } 4\frac{2}{8} \text{ as } 3\frac{10}{8}.$$
$$-2\frac{5}{8} \quad \rightarrow \quad -2\frac{5}{8}$$
$$\overline{\qquad\qquad\qquad 1\frac{5}{8}}$$

Subtract the fractions and then the whole numbers.

So, $4\frac{2}{8} - 2\frac{5}{8} = 1\frac{5}{8}$. Check your answer by drawing a picture.

Real-World EXAMPLE **Rename Mixed Numbers to Subtract**

3 **Measurement** **Sally is making a flag. She has 2 yards of fabric. The sewing pattern calls for $1\frac{1}{4}$ yards. How much fabric will be left?**

Rename 2 as a mixed number before subtracting.

1	**1**
1	$\frac{1}{4}$ $\frac{1}{4}$ $\frac{1}{4}$ $\frac{1}{4}$

$\qquad\qquad 2 \qquad\qquad = \qquad 1 + \frac{1}{4}$ or $1\frac{4}{4}$

$$2 \quad \rightarrow \quad 1\frac{4}{4} \quad \text{Rename 2 as } 1\frac{4}{4}.$$
$$-1\frac{1}{4} \quad \rightarrow \quad -1\frac{1}{4}$$
$$\overline{\qquad\qquad\qquad \frac{3}{4}} \quad \text{Subtract the fractions and then the whole numbers.}$$

So, Sally will have $\frac{3}{4}$ yard of fabric left.

Subtract. Write each difference in simplest form. See Examples 1–3 (pp. 458–459)

1. $3\frac{1}{6} - 1\frac{1}{3}$

2. $5\frac{2}{5} - 3\frac{4}{5}$

3. $6\frac{2}{9} - 2\frac{8}{9}$

4. **Measurement** Arlo had 5 gallons of paint. He used $2\frac{10}{16}$ gallons. How much paint does he have left?

5. **Talk About It** Describe the steps you would use to solve $3\frac{2}{7} - 1\frac{4}{7}$. Then solve.

Practice and Problem Solving

NYSCC • NYSMT
Extra Practice, p. R29

Subtract. Write each difference in simplest form. See Examples 1–3 (pp. 458–459)

6. $4\frac{3}{8} - 1\frac{5}{8}$

7. $5\frac{1}{4} - 4\frac{1}{2}$

8. $7\frac{2}{7} - 6\frac{4}{7}$

9. $9\frac{3}{10} - 5\frac{7}{10}$

10. $10\frac{1}{3} - 3\frac{6}{9}$

11. $13 - 4\frac{1}{3}$

12. $12 - 5\frac{1}{6}$

13. $18 - 9\frac{2}{8}$

14. $17 - 7\frac{3}{12}$

15. Find *ten and one fourth minus three and two fourths*. Write in words.

16. Find *nine minus four and six tenths*. Write in words.

17. Sherman's backpack weighs $6\frac{1}{4}$ pounds. Brie's backpack weighs $5\frac{3}{4}$ pounds. How much heavier is Sherman's backpack than Brie's backpack?

18. Rosa jogged $10\frac{3}{16}$ miles in one week. The next week she jogged $8\frac{7}{16}$ miles. How many more miles did she jog the first week?

Real-World PROBLEM SOLVING

Science The table shows the average lengths of common United States insects.

19. Find the difference in length between a walking stick and a bumble bee.

20. Is the difference in length between a monarch butterfly and a bumble bee greater or less than the difference in length between a walking stick and grasshopper? Explain your reasoning.

Insect	Length (in.)
Monarch Butterfly	$3\frac{4}{8}$
Walking Stick	4
Grasshopper	$1\frac{6}{8}$
Bumble Bee	$\frac{5}{8}$

Source: Natural Wildlife Federation

H.O.T. Problems

21. OPEN ENDED Write a subtraction problem in which you have to rename a fraction and whose solution is between 3 and 4.

22. FIND THE ERROR Rachel and Brandon are finding $3\frac{1}{5} - 2\frac{3}{5}$. Who is correct? Explain.

Rachel

$3\frac{1}{5} - 2\frac{3}{5} = \frac{3}{5}$

Brandon

$3\frac{1}{5} - 2\frac{3}{5} = 1\frac{2}{5}$

23. WRITING IN ►MATH Write a real-world problem involving subtraction in which you have to rename a fraction.

NYSMT Practice   5.N.22

24. Ross has 6 yards of material. He uses $2\frac{1}{3}$ yards. How many yards of material does he have left?
(Lesson 10-8)

   A $2\frac{2}{3}$ yd   **C** $3\frac{2}{3}$ yd

   B $3\frac{1}{3}$ yd   **D** $8\frac{1}{3}$ yd

25. Careta swam $7\frac{5}{8}$ miles. Joey swam $5\frac{1}{8}$ miles. How many more miles did Careta swim than Joey?
(Lesson 10-8)

   F $13\frac{3}{4}$ mi   **H** $2\frac{1}{2}$ mi

   G $2\frac{6}{8}$ mi   **J** $2\frac{1}{4}$ mi

Spiral Review

26. Kendra buys a sandwich for $2.79, a carton of milk for $0.65, and a bag of pretzels for $0.99. How much more can she spend without going over $6? (Lesson 10-9)

Subtract. Write each difference in simplest form. (Lesson 10-8)

27. $5\frac{3}{10} - 2\frac{2}{10}$ **28.** $6\frac{9}{11} - 5\frac{2}{11}$ **29.** $14\frac{7}{9} - 12\frac{1}{9}$ **30.** $15\frac{6}{8} - 12\frac{1}{4}$

31. Kira and Justin are sharing a pizza. Kira eats $\frac{2}{6}$ of the pizza, and Justin eats $\frac{1}{6}$ of the pizza. What part of the pizza did they eat in all? Support your answer with a model. (Lesson 10-1)

Problem Solving in Science

Making Mixtures

Mixtures are all around you. Rocks, air, and ocean water are all mixtures. So are paints, clay, and chalk. The substances in mixtures are combined physically, not chemically. Although some substances seem to dissolve in others, each substance in a mixture keeps its own physical properties. This means that the substances in mixtures can be physically separated.

You can make some fun mixtures by using specific amounts of substances. For example, to make one type of invisible ink, you use $\frac{1}{2}$ as much baking soda as water. If you use $\frac{1}{2}$ of a cup of water, you use $\frac{1}{4}$ of a cup of baking soda. You can use other recipes to make mixtures such as sculpting clay and bubble-blowing liquid.

 Real-World Math

Use the information on page 463 to solve each problem.

1. How much water do you need to make a batch of clay?

2. How much more salt than cornstarch do you need to make a batch of clay?

3. What amount of solid ingredients do you need to make a batch of clay?

4. How much liquid do you need to make bubble-blowing liquid? (*Hint:* Glycerin is a liquid.)

5. If you make three batches of clay, how much food coloring will you need?

6. If you make two batches of bubble-blowing liquid, how much water will you need?

7. If you make two batches of bubble-blowing liquid, how much soap will you need?

8. How many teaspoons of oil and food coloring do you need to make one batch of clay?

Did You Know?

Hundreds of different colors of paint can be made by mixing different amounts of just three colors: yellow, magenta, and cyan.

Clay

$2\frac{1}{3}$ cups of salt

$\frac{3}{4}$ cup of cold water

$1\frac{2}{3}$ cups cornstarch

$\frac{1}{2}$ cup boiling water

$1\frac{2}{3}$ teaspoons of oil

$\frac{2}{3}$ teaspoon food coloring

Bubble-Blowing Liquid

$4\frac{1}{4}$ cups of water

$\frac{1}{4}$ cup glycerin

$1\frac{3}{4}$ ounces grated soap

Problem Solving in Science   463

FOLDABLES® Study Organizer GET READY to Study

Be sure the following Big Ideas are written in your Foldable.

Like Fractions	Unlike Fractions

Key Concepts

Add and Subtract Like Fractions
(pp. 423, 424)

• Add or subtract the numerators. Use the same denominator.

$$\frac{1}{4} + \frac{2}{4} = \frac{3}{4} \qquad \frac{5}{8} - \frac{2}{8} = \frac{3}{8}$$

Add and Subtract Unlike Fractions
(pp. 434, 437)

• Rename the fraction using the LCD. Then add or subtract as with **like fractions**.

Estimation (p. 444)

• Estimate sums and differences of mixed numbers by rounding to the nearest whole number.

Add and Subtract Mixed Fractions
(pp. 448, 452)

• Add or subtract the fractions. Then add or subtract the whole numbers.

Key Vocabulary

like fractions (p. 421)
unlike fractions (p. 432)

Vocabulary Check

Choose the correct word or number that completes each sentence.

1. A number formed by a whole number and a fraction is a (mixed number, like fraction).

2. When the greatest common factor (GCF) of the numerator and denominator is 1, a fraction is written in (improper form, simplest form).

3. Fractions with the same (numerator, denominator) are called like fractions.

4. Fractions with different (numerators, denominators) are called unlike fractions.

5. When you add fractions with like denominators, you add the (numerators, denominators).

6. An improper fraction is a fraction that has a numerator that is (greater than, less than) or equal to its denominator.

Lesson-by-Lesson Review

Add Like Fractions (pp. 423–425)

5.N.21

Example 1

Find $\dfrac{4}{10} + \dfrac{4}{10}$.   Estimate $\dfrac{1}{2} + \dfrac{1}{2} = 1$

$\dfrac{4}{10} + \dfrac{4}{10} = \dfrac{4+4}{10}$ Add the numerators.

$= \dfrac{8}{10}$ Simplify.

$= \dfrac{8 \div 2}{10 \div 2}$ Divide by the GCF, 2.

$= \dfrac{4}{5}$ Simplify.

Add. Write each sum in simplest form. Check your answer by using models.

7. $\dfrac{3}{9} + \dfrac{6}{9}$ 8. $\dfrac{1}{6} + \dfrac{4}{6}$

9. What fraction of flowers in the table are either pansies or tulips?

Flower	Number
Mums	3
Pansies	7
Tulips	8

Subtract Like Fractions (pp. 428–431)

5.N.21

Example 2

Find $\dfrac{11}{12} - \dfrac{5}{12}$.   Estimate $1 - \dfrac{1}{2} = \dfrac{1}{2}$

$\dfrac{11}{12} - \dfrac{5}{12} = \dfrac{11-5}{12}$ Subtract the numerators.

$= \dfrac{6}{12}$ Simplify.

$= \dfrac{6 \div 6}{12 \div 6}$ Divide by the GCF, 6.

$= \dfrac{1}{2}$ Simplify.

Subtract. Write each difference in simplest form. Check your answer by using models.

10. $\dfrac{2}{9} - \dfrac{1}{9}$ 11. $\dfrac{11}{14} - \dfrac{4}{14}$

12. A class is surveyed to find out their favorite color. Of the class, $\dfrac{7}{24}$ prefers red, $\dfrac{4}{24}$ prefers green, and $\dfrac{13}{24}$ prefers blue. What fraction of the class prefers blue over red?

Add Unlike Fractions (pp. 434–436)

6.N.16

Example 3

Find $\dfrac{2}{3} + \dfrac{1}{2}$.

$\dfrac{2 \times 2}{3 \times 2} = \dfrac{4}{6}$ Rename the fractions using the LCD.

$+ \dfrac{1 \times 3}{2 \times 3} = \dfrac{3}{6}$ Add as with like fractions.

$= \dfrac{7}{6} = 1\dfrac{1}{6}$ Simplify.

Add. Write each sum in simplest form.

13. $\dfrac{1}{4} + \dfrac{3}{8}$ 14. $\dfrac{1}{2} + \dfrac{2}{7}$

15. On Monday, Matt ran $\dfrac{4}{9}$ mile. On Tuesday, he ran $\dfrac{1}{3}$ mile. How far did he run in all?

Subtract Unlike Fractions (pp. 439–441)

6.N.16

Example 4

Find $\frac{4}{5} - \frac{1}{4}$.

$\frac{4 \times 4}{5 \times 4} = \frac{16}{20}$ Rename the fractions using the LCD.

$-\frac{1 \times 5}{4 \times 5} = \frac{5}{20}$ Add as with like fractions.

$= \frac{11}{20}$

Subtract. Write each difference in simplest form.

16. $\frac{4}{6} - \frac{1}{2}$ **17.** $\frac{11}{12} - \frac{2}{3}$

18. Jada cleaned $\frac{7}{9}$ of her room. Trent cleaned $\frac{1}{2}$ of his room. How much more of her room did Jada clean?

  Problem-Solving Skill: Determine Reasonable Answers
(pp. 442–443)

5.PS.19

Example 5

Ted Hoz has the world's largest collection of golf balls. He has 74,849 golf balls. He estimates that he has room for 95,000 golf balls. Is 20,000 or 25,000 a more reasonable estimate for how many more golf balls he can collect?

Estimate 95,000–74,849.

Step 1 Round 74,849 to the nearest thousand.

$$74,849 \rightarrow 75,000$$

Step 2 Subtract.

$$
\begin{array}{r}
95,000 \\
- 75,000 \\
\hline
20,000
\end{array}
$$

So, Ted Hoz can collect about 20,000 more golf balls.

Solve. Determine which answer is reasonable. Explain your answer.

19. A footbag is a small bean bag controlled by the feet. The table shows how many times the male and female world record holders kicked a footbag.

Record Holder	Number of Times Kicking Footbag
Constance Constable	24,713
Ted Martin	63,326

Which is a more reasonable estimate for how many more times Ted Martin kicked the footbag than Constance Constable: 38,000 or 45,000?

20. Measurement Susan is $5\frac{5}{6}$ feet tall and her brother Nick is $4\frac{1}{6}$ feet tall. Which is a more reasonable estimate for how much taller Susan is than her brother: $1\frac{1}{2}$ feet, 2 feet, or 3 feet?

10-6 Estimate Sums and Differences (pp. 444–446)

5.N.25

Example 6

Estimate $8\frac{7}{9} - 5\frac{1}{9}$.

$$8\frac{7}{9} - 5\frac{1}{9}$$

$$\downarrow \qquad \downarrow$$

Estimate $9 - 5 = 4$

So, $8\frac{7}{9} - 5\frac{1}{9}$ is about 4.

Estimate by rounding the mixed number to a whole number.

21. $4\frac{1}{3} + 3\frac{5}{6}$ 22. $8\frac{2}{3} - 3\frac{7}{9}$

23. $14\frac{5}{12} - 8\frac{7}{12}$ 24. $12\frac{8}{15} + 9\frac{4}{15}$

25. Darnell is $13\frac{3}{4}$ years old. His younger sister is $9\frac{1}{4}$ years old. About how many years older is Darnell?

10-7 Add Mixed Numbers (pp. 448–451)

5.N.22

Example 7

Find $5\frac{3}{6} + 2\frac{2}{6}$.

Step 1 Add the fractions.

$$5\frac{3}{6}$$
$$+ 2\frac{2}{6}$$
$$\overline{\quad \frac{5}{6}}$$

Step 2 Add the whole numbers.

$$5\frac{3}{6}$$
$$+ 2\frac{2}{6}$$
$$\overline{7\frac{5}{6}}$$

Add. Write each sum in simplest form.

26. $1\frac{1}{5} + 2\frac{3}{5}$ 27. $2\frac{3}{9} + 6\frac{1}{3}$

28. $3\frac{3}{10} + 7\frac{7}{10}$ 29. $8\frac{7}{12} + 7\frac{2}{3}$

30. Vera and Sonia went canoeing. They traveled $5\frac{3}{8}$ miles in the morning and $4\frac{1}{8}$ miles in the afternoon. How many miles did they canoe altogether?

10-8 Subtract Mixed Numbers (pp. 452–454)

5.N.22

Example 8

Find $4\frac{5}{6} - 3\frac{2}{6}$.

Step 1 Subtract the fractions.

$$4\frac{5}{6}$$
$$- 3\frac{2}{6}$$
$$\overline{\quad \frac{3}{6}}$$

Step 2 Subtract the whole numbers.

$$4\frac{5}{6}$$
$$- 3\frac{2}{6}$$
$$\overline{1\frac{3}{6} = 1\frac{1}{2}}$$

Subtract. Write each difference in simplest form.

31. $3\frac{4}{5} - 1\frac{3}{5}$ 32. $5\frac{8}{9} - 3\frac{5}{9}$

33. $14\frac{11}{12} - 8\frac{7}{12}$ 34. $19\frac{14}{15} - 12\frac{1}{5}$

35. In one week, the fifth grade class recycled $9\frac{2}{3}$ pounds of glass, and $12\frac{3}{4}$ pounds of newspaper. How many more pounds of newspaper than glass did the class recycle?

Problem-Solving Investigation: **Choose a Strategy** (pp. 456–457)

5.PS.3

Example 9

After one month, Migina had saved $25. After 2 months, she had saved $40. After 3 months, she had saved $55. Suppose she continues saving at this rate. How long will it take Migina to save enough money to buy a satellite radio that costs $90?

To solve the problem, you can use the *look for a pattern* strategy.

$25 $40 $55 $70 $85 $100
　　+15　　+15　　+15　　+15　　+15

She will have saved enough money in 6 months.

Solve.

36. **Measurement** Frank is building steps for a porch. He has $12\frac{5}{6}$ feet of wood. He needs to build 4 steps. If each step uses $3\frac{1}{3}$ feet of wood, does he have enough to make 4 steps? Explain.

37. Mrs. Orta is making candles for the school craft show. The supplies needed to make a dozen candles cost $5.25. How much profit will Mrs. Orta make if she sells all the candles for $4.25 each?

10-10 **Subtraction with Renaming** (pp. 458–461)

5.N.22

Example 10

Find $7\frac{1}{5} - 2\frac{4}{5}$.　　**Estimate** $7 - 3 = 4$

Since $\frac{1}{5}$ is less than $\frac{4}{5}$, rename $7\frac{1}{5}$.

THINK $7\frac{1}{5} = 6 + \frac{5}{5} + \frac{1}{5} = 6\frac{6}{5}$

$$
\begin{array}{ccl}
7\frac{1}{5} & \rightarrow & 6\frac{6}{5} \quad \text{Rename } 7\frac{1}{5} \text{ as } 6\frac{6}{5}. \\
-2\frac{4}{5} & \rightarrow & -2\frac{4}{5} \quad \text{Subtract.} \\
\hline
& & 4\frac{2}{5}
\end{array}
$$

So, $7\frac{1}{5} - 2\frac{4}{5} = 4\frac{2}{5}$.

Subtract. Write each difference in simplest form. Check your answer by using models.

38. $5\frac{1}{8} - 2\frac{6}{8}$　　39. $8\frac{3}{7} - 3\frac{6}{7}$

40. $9\frac{4}{9} - 8\frac{7}{9}$　　41. $15\frac{6}{10} - 8\frac{4}{5}$

42. Jin lives 10 miles from the beach. Her friend lives $6\frac{1}{3}$ miles from the beach. How much farther does Jin live from the beach than her friend?

CHAPTER 10 Chapter Test

Add or subtract. Write each sum or difference in simplest form.

1. $\frac{9}{11} + \frac{1}{11}$

2. $\frac{9}{13} - \frac{7}{13}$

3. $\frac{4}{7} - \frac{1}{3}$

4. $\frac{4}{15} + \frac{3}{5}$

5. MULTIPLE CHOICE Zacharias has $\frac{2}{3}$ cup of pasta. He uses $\frac{1}{3}$ cup for a salad as shown in the measuring cups below.

How much pasta does he have left?

A 1 c

C $\frac{1}{3}$ c

B $\frac{1}{2}$ c

D 0 c

6. Measurement On a recent trip around Kentucky, Mr. Chavez drove 83 miles from Newport to Lexington and then 77 miles from Lexington to Louisville. Which is a reasonable estimate for the total number of miles he drove: 100 miles, 160 miles, or 180 miles?

7. A sea otter remained underwater for $\frac{6}{8}$ minute. Then it came back to the surface for air. It dove a second time and stayed underwater for $\frac{3}{4}$ minute. About how long was the sea otter underwater altogether?

Estimate by rounding the mixed number to a whole number.

8. $6\frac{1}{5} - 4\frac{3}{5}$

9. $9\frac{4}{5} + 1\frac{3}{10}$

10. $8\frac{3}{11} + 3\frac{6}{11}$

11. $12\frac{8}{15} - 7\frac{1}{3}$

Add or subtract. Write each sum or difference in simplest form.

12. $9\frac{4}{6} - 5\frac{1}{2}$

13. $3\frac{1}{9} + 7\frac{6}{9}$

14. $14\frac{9}{12} - 8\frac{1}{4}$

15. $9\frac{5}{16} + 11\frac{7}{16}$

16. MULTIPLE CHOICE On Saturday, Phoebe biked $5\frac{2}{10}$ miles. Then she biked $6\frac{6}{10}$ miles on Sunday. How many miles did she bike altogether?

F $12\frac{8}{10}$ mi

H $11\frac{8}{20}$ mi

G $11\frac{4}{5}$ mi

J $1\frac{2}{5}$ mi

17. Algebra What is the next figure in the pattern?

Subtract. Write each difference in simplest form.

18. $16\frac{1}{10} - 7\frac{3}{10}$

19. $20\frac{1}{3} - 5\frac{5}{6}$

20. WRITING IN ►MATH Explain how you would find $4 - 3\frac{5}{6}$. Justify your steps by using a model.

PART 1   Multiple Choice

Read each question. Then fill in the correct answer on the answer sheet provided by your teacher or on a sheet of paper.

1. Hakeem ate $\frac{1}{4}$ of a pie. His two brothers each ate $\frac{1}{8}$ of the pie. How much of the pie did Hakeem and his brothers eat altogether?

   A $\frac{1}{3}$

   B $\frac{2}{8}$

   C $\frac{1}{2}$

   D $\frac{5}{8}$

2. Last school week, it rained 2 out of 5 days. Which fraction is greater than $\frac{2}{5}$?

   F $\frac{1}{2}$ H $\frac{1}{4}$

   G $\frac{1}{3}$ J $\frac{3}{16}$

3. Javier made a pan of brownies to share with his classmates. The pan was divided evenly into 30 brownies. Javier gave away 20 brownies. What fraction of the brownies did he have left?

   A $\frac{1}{4}$ C $\frac{2}{3}$

   B $\frac{1}{3}$ D $\frac{3}{4}$

4. The graph shows some areas around Anica's home town.

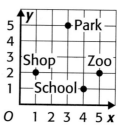

   Which ordered pair best represents the point on the graph labeled "School"?

   F (1, 2)   H (5, 2)

   G (4, 1)   J (1, 4)

5. Enrique and Sydney are making oatmeal raisin cookies. Enrique's recipe calls for $\frac{1}{2}$ cup of raisins per dozen, and Sydney's recipe calls for $\frac{5}{8}$ cup of raisins per dozen. How many raisins do they need in all?

   A 1

   B $1\frac{1}{8}$

   C $1\frac{1}{2}$

   D 2

6. Malak's family bought a bag of apples at a farmer's market. If they ate $\frac{7}{12}$ of the apples, what fraction of the apples remained?

   F $\frac{1}{3}$ H $\frac{1}{2}$

   G $\frac{5}{12}$ J $\frac{2}{3}$

7. Agustin has completed $\frac{5}{12}$ of his project, and Evelina has completed $\frac{2}{6}$ of her project. How much more of the project does Agustin have finished than Evelina?

A $\frac{1}{12}$ **C** $\frac{3}{4}$

B $\frac{2}{6}$ **D** $\frac{11}{12}$

---

8. Myron gives his cat $\frac{2}{5}$ cup of dry food in the morning and $\frac{1}{5}$ cup of dry food in the afternoon, as shown below. How much dry food does he give his cat each day?

Morning

Afternoon

F $\frac{2}{5}$ cup   **H** $\frac{4}{5}$ cup

G $\frac{3}{5}$ cup   **J** 1 cup

---

9. Which fraction is greater than $\frac{3}{4}$?

A $\frac{1}{2}$ **C** $\frac{1}{3}$

B $\frac{6}{7}$ **D** $\frac{3}{8}$

PART 2   Short Response

Record your answers on the sheet provided by your teacher or on a sheet of paper.

10. Explain how to find the x-coordinate of point P shown below.

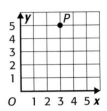

11. Malcom delivered $\frac{1}{3}$ of the newspapers. Angela delivered $\frac{2}{3}$ of the newspapers. Are there any newspapers that still need to be delivered? Explain.

PART 3   Extended Response

Record your answers on the answer sheet provided by your teacher or on a sheet of paper. Show your work.

12. Compare $\frac{2}{3}$ and $\frac{1}{8}$ using a drawing.

---

13. Explain how to find $5\frac{1}{8} + 6\frac{2}{4}$.

NEED EXTRA HELP?													
If You Missed Question...	1	2	3	4	5	6	7	8	9	10	11	12	13
Go to Lesson...	10–3	9–9	10–2	6–4	10–7	10–2	10–8	10–1	9–9	6–4	10–3	9–9	10–7
NYS Core Curriculum	6.N.16	5.N.5	5.N.21	5.G.12	5.N.22	5.N.21	5.N.22	5.N.21	5.N.5	5.G.12	6.N.16	5.N.21	5.N.22

CHAPTER 11 Use Measures in the Customary System

BIG Idea · How do you convert among customary units?

You can use multiplication or division to convert among customary units.

Example The Manhattan Bridge in New York City connects Manhattan to Brooklyn. The bridge is 1,470 feet long. This is 1,470 ÷ 3, or 490 yards.

What will I learn in this chapter?

- Choose appropriate customary units for measuring length.
- Convert customary units of length, weight, and capacity.
- Convert units of time.
- Solve problems involving elapsed time.
- Solve problems by using the *draw a diagram* strategy.

Key Vocabulary

length

customary units

weight

capacity

elapsed time

NY Math Online > Student Study Tools
at macmillanmh.com

FOLDABLES®
Study Organizer

Make this Foldable to help you organize information about the customary system. Begin with a sheet of $8\frac{1}{2}"$ by $11"$ paper.

① **Fold** the short sides toward the middle.

② **Fold** the top to the bottom.

③ **Open.** Cut along the second fold to make four tabs.

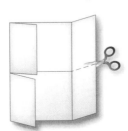

④ **Label** each of the tabs as shown.

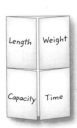

Chapter 11 Use Measures in the Customary System **473**

You have two ways to check prerequisite skills for this chapter.

Option 2

NY Math Online > Take the Chapter Readiness Quiz at macmillanmh.com.

Option 1

Complete the Quick Check below.

QUICK Check

Multiply. (Lesson 3-6)

1. 14×3

2. 36×5

3. 760×2

4. 15×12

5. 16×14

6. 280×4

7. A musical was sold out for three straight shows. If 825 tickets were sold at each performance, how many tickets were sold in all?

Divide. Write any remainders as fractions in simplest form. (Lessons 4-4 and 8-1)

8. $45 \div 3$

9. $112 \div 16$

10. $39 \div 4$

11. $52 \div 12$

12. $950 \div 20$

13. $220 \div 8$

14. A box has 144 ounces of grapes. How many 16-ounce packages of grapes can be made?

Find how much time has passed. (Prior Grade)

15.

8:10 A.M.   8:30 A.M.

16.

7:35 P.M.   7:50 P.M.

17. 6:05 A.M. to 6:45 A.M.

18. 12:25 A.M. to 12:50 A.M.

19. April walked her dog from 11:05 A.M. to 11:25 A.M. For how many minutes did she walk her dog?

Measurement Activity for 11-1
Measure with a Ruler

MAIN IDEA

I will measure length to the nearest half inch and quarter inch.

NYS Core Curriculum

5.M.1 Use a ruler to measure to the nearest inch, $\frac{1}{2}$, $\frac{1}{4}$, and $\frac{1}{8}$ inch

You Will Need
a ruler

NY Math Online

macmillanmh.com
• Concepts in Motion

Length is the measurement of distance between two points. You can use a ruler like the one at the right to measure the length of objects to the nearest half inch or quarter inch.

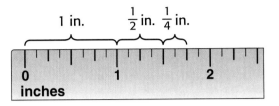

ACTIVITY

1 **Find the length of the button to the nearest half inch and quarter inch.**

Step 1 Place the ruler against one edge of the object. Line up the zero on the ruler with the end of the object.

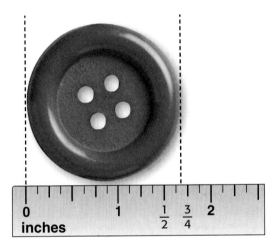

Step 2 Find the half inch mark that is closest to the other end. Repeat for the quarter inch mark.

To the nearest half inch, the button is $1\frac{1}{2}$ inches long. To the nearest quarter inch, it is $1\frac{3}{4}$ inches long.

Think About It

1. Explain how you can tell the difference between the half inch and quarter inch marks when measuring an object with a ruler.

2. Will you ever have the same answer when measuring to the nearest half inch and measuring to the nearest quarter inch? Explain your reasoning.

Measure the length of each of the following to the nearest half inch and quarter inch.

3.

4.

5.

6.

Inches are used to measure small objects. You can measure the length of larger objects using *feet* or *yards*. *Miles* are used to measure very great lengths. Select an appropriate unit to measure each of the following.

7. distance from your home to school   **8.** length of your classroom

9. width of a cell phone   **10.** height of a classmate

11. Copy the table below. Then complete the table using ten objects found in your classroom. The first one is done for you.

Object	Unit of Measure	Estimate	Actual Length
Height of classroom door	feet	6 feet	8 feet

Name an object that you would measure using each unit.

12. inch   **13.** yard   **14.** foot   **15.** mile

16. Draw a line that is between 4 and 5 inches long. Measure the length to the nearest quarter inch.

17. Draw a line that is $2\frac{1}{2}$ inches long when measured to the nearest half inch and nearest quarter inch.

18. **WRITING IN ▶MATH** Suppose you know that a line is 3 inches long when measured to the nearest inch. What do you know about the actual length of the line?

Units of Length

GET READY to Learn

For many of the thrill rides at amusement parks, riders must be at least 48 inches tall.

MAIN IDEA

I will choose an appropriate customary unit for measuring length and convert customary units of length.

NYS Core Curriculum

5.M.2 Identify customary equivalent units of length

5.M.5 Convert measurement within a given system
Also addresses 5.M.9, 5.M.1.

New Vocabulary

length
customary units
foot
inch
yard
mile
convert

NY Math Online

macmillanmh.com

• Extra Examples
• Personal Tutor
• Self-Check Quiz

The units of **length** most often used in the United States are the inch, foot, yard, and mile. These units are called **customary units**.

Customary Units of Length	Key Concepts

1 **foot** (ft) = 12 **inches** (in.)
1 **yard** (yd) = 3 ft or 36 in.
1 **mile** (mi) = 5,280 ft or 1,760 yd

When you **convert** measurements, you change from one unit to another. To convert a larger unit to a smaller unit, *multiply*.

Real-World EXAMPLE

Convert Larger Units to Smaller Units

1 **RIDES** Refer to the information above. Cheng is 4 feet tall. Is he tall enough to ride a thrill ride at an amusement park?

4 ft = ▇ in.   Larger units (feet) are being converted to smaller units (inches).

Since 1 foot = 12 inches, multiply 4 by 12.

4 × 12 = 48

So, 4 ft = 48 in. Since 4 feet equals 48 inches, Cheng is tall enough to ride the thrill rides.

```
┌────────┐
│ 12 in. │
├────────┤
│ 12 in. │  ⎫
├────────┤  ⎬ 4 ft
│ 12 in. │  ⎭
├────────┤
│ 12 in. │
└────────┘
```

To convert a smaller unit to a larger unit, *divide*.

Real-World EXAMPLE — **Convert Smaller Units to Larger Units**

2 **SPORTS A basketball court is 84 feet long. How many yards long is it?**

84 ft = ■ yd   Smaller units (feet) are being converted to larger units (yards).

Since 3 feet = 1 yard, divide 84 by 3.

84 ÷ 3 = 28
So, 84 ft = 28 yd. The basketball court is 28 yards long.

Vocabulary Link

Customary

Everyday Use
commonly practiced, used, or observed

Math Use system of measurement

Units of length in the customary system can also be expressed using different units of measure or as fractions.

EXAMPLE — **Parts of Units**

3 **Convert 42 inches to feet.**

One Way: Use feet and inches.

Since you are changing a smaller unit to a larger unit, divide.
42 ÷ 12 = 3 R6   12 in. = 1 ft
The remainder 6 means there are 6 inches left over.
42 in. = 3 ft 6 in.

Remember

All measurements are approximations. However, if you use smaller units, you will get a more *precise* measure, or a measure that is closer to the exact measure.

Another Way: Use fractions.

42 ÷ 12 = 3 R6   3 R6 means 42 inches = 3 feet 6 inches.

The remainder 6 means there are 6 inches out of a foot left over.

The fraction of a foot is $\frac{6}{12}$ or $\frac{1}{2}$.

42 in. = $3\frac{1}{2}$ ft

| 12 in. |
| 12 in. |
| 12 in. |
| 6 in. |

$3\frac{1}{2}$ ft

So, 42 inches is equal to 3 feet 6 inches or $3\frac{1}{2}$ feet.

CHECK What You Know

Complete. See Examples 1–3 (pp. 477–478)

1. 60 in. = ▓ ft

2. 5,280 ft = ▓ mi

3. 9 ft = ▓ in.

4. 6 yd = ▓ in.

5. 22 ft = ▓ yd ▓ ft

6. 40 in. = ▓ ft

7. Carlos is 63 inches tall. What is his height in feet?

8. *Talk About It* Explain how to convert units from feet to inches.

Practice and Problem Solving

NYSCC • NYSMT
Extra Practice, p. R29

Complete. See Examples 1–3 (pp. 477–478)

9. 19 yd = ▓ in.

10. 26,400 ft = ▓ mi

11. 5 mi = ▓ yd

12. 105 in. = ▓ yd ▓ in.

13. 15 ft 8 in. = ▓ in.

14. 150 in. = ▓ yd

15. Measurement A bull had horns that measured 98 inches across. What is this length in feet and inches? in feet?

16. Ty has two pieces of wood. Which piece of wood is longer?

Piece	Length
1	1 yd 9 in.
2	44 in.

17. The *U.S.S. Harry Truman* is an aircraft carrier that is 1,092 feet long. Find the length in yards.

18. Dana ran $\frac{1}{4}$ mile. Trish ran 445 yards. Who ran the greater distance? Explain.

Choose an appropriate unit to measure each of the following.

19. length of a cellular phone

20. length of a kitchen

21. width of a television

22. length of community swimming pool

23. distance between two cities

24. height of soccer goal posts

Real-World PROBLEM SOLVING

Social Studies Around 3000 B.C., the Egyptians developed units of length based on parts of the body.

Choose the appropriate measure to find each distance.

25. width of your desk

26. width of a sheet of paper

27. your height

28. width of the classroom

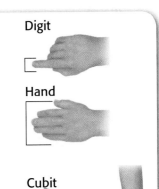
Digit
Hand
Cubit

H.O.T. Problems

29. OPEN ENDED Estimate the width of a window in your school. Then measure the width in feet and inches.

30. CHALLENGE There are 320 *rods* in a mile. Find the length of a *rod* in feet.

31. **WRITING IN ►MATH** Write a real-world problem that can be solved by converting yards to feet. Then solve.

NYSMT Practice 5.M.2

32. Which relationship between units of length is correct? (Lesson 11-1)

A One foot is $\frac{1}{12}$ of one yard.

B One yard is $\frac{1}{4}$ of one mile.

C One foot is $\frac{1}{3}$ of one yard.

D One inch is $\frac{1}{3}$ of one foot.

33. The picture shows the height of a statue. What is the height of the statue in inches? (Lesson 11-1)

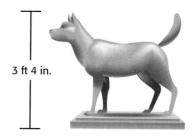

3 ft 4 in.

F 13 inches   **H** 36 inches

G 22 inches   **J** 40 inches

Spiral Review

34. A full bag contains $7\frac{2}{4}$ cups of flour. There are $1\frac{3}{4}$ cups left in a bag. How many cups have been used? (Lesson 10-8)

35. The softball team has ten players. Suppose each player shakes hands with every other player. How many handshakes take place? (Lesson 10-7)

Add or subtract. (Lessons 10-1 and 10-2)

36. $\frac{3}{5} - \frac{1}{5}$ **37.** $\frac{1}{10} + \frac{3}{10}$ **38.** $\frac{2}{9} + \frac{8}{9}$ **39.** $\frac{7}{9} - \frac{4}{9}$

40. The model at the right shows 0.004. Write 0.004 as a fraction in simplest form. (Lesson 9-5)

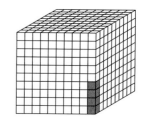

41. Four friends share three brownies equally. How many brownies does each friend get? (Lesson 8-1)

Mystery Measurements

Using Customary Measures

Get Ready!

Players: 2

You will need: 2 yardsticks, 24 index cards, scissors

Get Set!

- Working alone, each player secretly measures the length or width of six objects in the classroom and records them on a piece of paper. The measures may be in inches or feet. This will serve as the answer sheet at the end of the game.

- Each player takes 12 index cards.

- For each object, the measurement is recorded on one card. A description of what was measured is recorded on another card. Make sure each measurement is different.

Width of
Math Book

1 in.

Go!

- Each player shuffles his or her cards.

- Keeping the cards facedown, players exchange cards.

- At the same time, players turn over all the cards given to them.

- Each player attempts to match each object with its measure.

- The player with more correct matches after 1 minute is the winner.

11-2 Problem-Solving Strategy

MAIN IDEA I will solve problems by drawing a diagram.

 NYSCC **5.PS.13** Model problems with pictures/diagrams or physical objects *Also addresses 5.RP.5, 5.R.6.*

A frog and a cricket start at the same place and jump in the same direction. The table shows the distance they jump each time.

Animal	Length of Jump
frog	5 feet
cricket	3 feet

If the frog jumps 15 times and the cricket jumps 25 times, how many times will they land in the same place?

Understand	**What facts do you know?** • The distance each animal jumps. **What do you need to find?** • The number of jumps each animal will make before landing in the same place.
Plan	Solve the problem by drawing a diagram.
Solve	**Use your plan to solve the problem.** Draw a diagram to show how many jumps each animal makes. 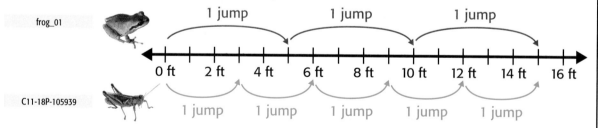 The animals meet after every 3 jumps by the frog and every 5 jumps by the cricket. The animals will land in the same place after the frog jumps three, six, nine, twelve, and fifteen times. So, the animals will land in the same place 5 times.
Check	Look back. Divide the total number of feet jumped by the LCM of 3 and 5 to find how many times the animals are in the same place. Since $75 \div 15$ is 5, the answer is correct.

ANALYZE the Strategy

Refer to the problem on the previous page.

1. If the frog jumped 4 feet each time and the cricket jumped 3 feet each time, after how many jumps would they meet?

2. Why did it help to draw a diagram of the situation to solve the problem?

3. Can you think of a time when drawing a diagram was helpful to you?

4. Is there another strategy you could use to solve this problem?

PRACTICE the Strategy

NYSCC • NYSMT
Extra Practice, p. R30

Solve. Use the *draw a diagram* strategy.

5. On her way home from school, Becky walked 2 blocks south to the corner store, 3 blocks east to visit a friend, and then 5 blocks north to go home. What direction is her home from the school?

6. Measurement Mr. Blackmon is building a fence around his garden. He wants to put fence posts every 3 feet, including each corner. How many total posts will be around the outside of the garden?

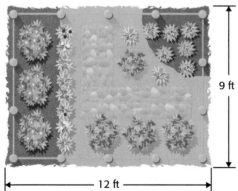

9 ft

12 ft

7. There are four booths in a row at the school carnival: face painting, ring toss, the dunk tank, and a cupcake walk. The dunk tank is on the far left. The ring toss is in between the face painting booth and the cupcake walk. The cupcake walk has only one neighbor. List the order of the booths from left to right.

8. For a school lunch, students must choose one entrée, one side dish, and one drink from the table shown. How many different school lunches can be purchased?

Entrée	Side dish	Drink
spaghetti	potatoes	milk
chicken	fruit cup	juice
hamburger	salad	

9. To score a touchdown, a football team needed to gain 35 yards. On their next five plays, the team gained 10 yards, lost 5 yards, lost 3 yards, gained 15 yards, and gained 10 yards. Did they score a touchdown? If not, how many more yards did they need to gain?

10. Kylie has 5 pictures to display on a shelf. She wants the picture of her family on the right end and the picture of her dog on the left end. How many ways can she arrange the pictures?

11. **WRITING IN ►MATH** Refer to Exercise 7. How did you use the *draw a diagram* strategy to solve this problem?

Units of Weight

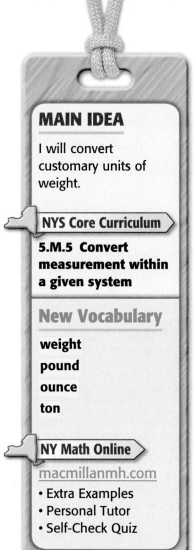

MAIN IDEA

I will convert customary units of weight.

NYS Core Curriculum

5.M.5 Convert measurement within a given system

New Vocabulary

weight

pound

ounce

ton

NY Math Online

macmillanmh.com

• Extra Examples
• Personal Tutor
• Self-Check Quiz

GET READY to Learn

A newborn lion cub weighs about 5 pounds. How many ounces is this?

Weight is a measure of how heavy an object is. Customary units of weight are ounce, pound, and ton.

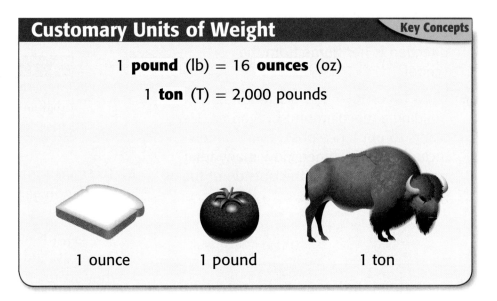

Customary Units of Weight   Key Concepts

1 **pound** (lb) = 16 **ounces** (oz)

1 **ton** (T) = 2,000 pounds

1 ounce   1 pound   1 ton

To convert a larger unit of weight to a smaller unit, *multiply*.

Real-World EXAMPLE   **Convert Larger Units to Smaller Units**

1 **ANIMALS Refer to the information above. How many ounces does a newborn lion cub weigh?**

5 lb = ■ oz   Larger units (pounds) are being converted to smaller units (ounces).

Since 1 pound = 16 ounces, multiply 5 by 16.

A newborn lion weighs about 5 × 16 or 80 ounces.

Real-World EXAMPLE Parts of Units

2 FOOD Lindsay's mother bought $1\frac{1}{2}$ pounds of hamburger. How many ounces of hamburger did she buy?

Since $1\frac{1}{2}$ pounds means 1 pound + $\frac{1}{2}$ pound, convert each to ounces. Then add.

1 lb = 16 oz, $\frac{1}{2}$ lb = 8 oz

So, $1\frac{1}{2}$ pound = 16 + 8 or 24 ounces.

$\left. \begin{array}{c} \boxed{16\ oz} \\ \boxed{8\ oz} \end{array} \right\} 1\frac{1}{2}\ lb$

Lindsay's mother bought 24 ounces of hamburger.

To convert a smaller unit to a larger unit, *divide.*

EXAMPLE Convert Smaller Units to Larger Units

3 Convert 6,000 pounds to tons.

6,000 lb = ▇ T   Smaller units (pounds) are being converted to larger units (tons).

Since 2,000 pounds = 1 ton, divide 6,000 by 2,000.

$6,000 \div 2,000 = 3$

So, 6,000 pounds = 3 tons.

$\left. \begin{array}{c} \boxed{2,000\ lb} \\ \boxed{2,000\ lb} \\ \boxed{2,000\ lb} \end{array} \right\} 3\ T$

As with units of length, units of weight in the customary system can also be expressed using different units or as fractions.

EXAMPLE Parts of Units

4 Complete: 56 oz = ▇ lb

Since you are converting a smaller unit to a larger unit, divide.

$56 \div 16 = 3\ R8$

The remainder 8 means there are 8 ounces out of a pound left over. The fraction of a pound is $\frac{8}{16}$ or $\frac{1}{2}$.

So, 56 oz = 3 lb 8 oz or $3\frac{1}{2}$ lb.

$\left. \begin{array}{c} \boxed{16\ oz} \\ \boxed{16\ oz} \\ \boxed{16\ oz} \\ \boxed{8\ oz} \end{array} \right\} 3\frac{1}{2}\ lb$

Remember

When converting measures, there will be more smaller units than larger units.

smaller units	larger units
6,000 lb	= 3 T
56 oz	= $3\frac{1}{2}$ lb

Complete. See Examples 1–4 (pp. 484–485)

1. 3 lb = ■ oz

2. 32 oz = ■ lb

3. 8,000 lb = ■ T

4. $2\frac{1}{2}$ lb = ■ oz

5. 45 oz = ■ lb ■ oz

6. 52 oz = ■ lb

7. A restaurant serves a 20-ounce steak. How much does the steak weigh in pounds and ounces?

8. (Talk About It) Explain how to convert from ounces to pounds.

Practice and Problem Solving

NYSCC • NYSMT
Extra Practice, p. R30

Complete. See Examples 1–4 (pp. 484–485)

9. 96 oz = ■ lb

10. 7 T = ■ lb

11. 10,000 lb = ■ T

12. $2\frac{1}{2}$ T = ■ lb

13. 50 oz = ■ lb ■ oz

14. $1\frac{1}{4}$ lb = ■ oz

15. 7,000 lb = ■ T ■ lb

16. 104 oz = ■ lb

17. 1,500 lb = ■ T

Replace ● with <, >, or = to make a true statement. See Examples 1–4 (pp. 484–485)

18. 16 lb ● 246 oz

19. 7,500 lb ● 4 T

20. $\frac{1}{2}$ T ● 1,000 lb

21. 1,200 oz ● 72 lb

22. 7 T 500 lb ● 7,300 oz

23. 6 lb 11 oz ● 117 oz

24. Mia combines the items in the table to make potting soil. Order the items according to amount, from least to greatest.

25. How many $\frac{1}{4}$-pound bags of peanuts can be filled from a 5-pound bag of peanuts?

26. A puppy weighs 12 ounces. What fractional part of a pound is this?

Item	Amount
Topsoil	3 lb
Fertilizer	2 lb 9 oz
Bone meal	43 oz

H.O.T. Problems

27. **CHALLENGE** A baby weighs 8 pounds 10 ounces. If her weight doubles in 6 months, how much will she weigh?

28. **WRITING IN ►MATH** Tell which units of weight you would use to measure the following: a bag of oranges, a fork, and a submarine. Explain your reasoning.

29. Ladonna is placing blocks side-by-side on a shelf, as shown below. Measure the width in inches of one block.

width

If the shelf is 1 foot long, what is the greatest number of blocks that Ladonna can stack on the shelf? (Lesson 11-1)

A 6   C 24

B 12   D 30

30. A rabbit weighs 4 pounds and 6 ounces. How many ounces does the rabbit weigh? (Lesson 11-3)

1 pound = 16 ounces

F 70 oz

G 64 oz

H 16 oz

J   6 oz

31. SHORT RESPONSE A cabin is 450 yards away from the lake. What is this distance in feet? (Lesson 11-1)

Spiral Review

32. A tennis ball is dropped from a height of 12 feet. It hits the ground and bounces up half as high as it fell. This is true for each additional bounce. What height does the ball reach on the fourth bounce? Use the *draw a diagram* strategy. (Lesson 11-2)

33. Measurement Vultures have been known to fly 37,000 feet above sea level. About how many miles high is this? (Lesson 11-1)

Estimate. (Lesson 10-6)

34. $3\frac{12}{16} + 8\frac{5}{8}$ **35.** $7\frac{5}{12} + 2\frac{7}{12}$ **36.** $8\frac{7}{10} - 6\frac{3}{10}$ **37.** $12\frac{2}{4} - 5\frac{6}{8}$

Replace each ● with <, >, or = to make a true statement. (Lesson 9-9)

38. $\frac{5}{8}$ ● $\frac{1}{2}$ **39.** $\frac{1}{3}$ ● $\frac{3}{12}$ **40.** $\frac{3}{18}$ ● $\frac{1}{6}$ **41.** $\frac{7}{10}$ ● $\frac{4}{5}$

42. Is $\frac{3}{10}$ closest to 0, $\frac{1}{2}$, or 1? Explain.

(Lesson 8-6)

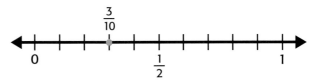

43. A CD display has 128 boxes on the bottom row. Each row has half the number of boxes as the row below. If there is one box on top, how many rows are there? (Lesson 6-7)

Units of Capacity

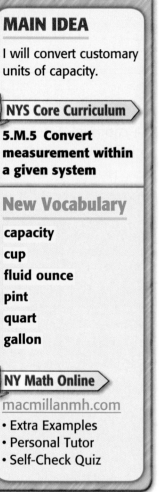

MAIN IDEA

I will convert customary units of capacity.

NYS Core Curriculum

5.M.5 Convert measurement within a given system

New Vocabulary

capacity

cup

fluid ounce

pint

quart

gallon

NY Math Online

macmillanmh.com

• Extra Examples
• Personal Tutor
• Self-Check Quiz

GET READY to Learn

Sondra tries to drink 9 cups of water each day. How many fluid ounces of water is 9 cups?

Capacity is the measure of how much a container can hold.

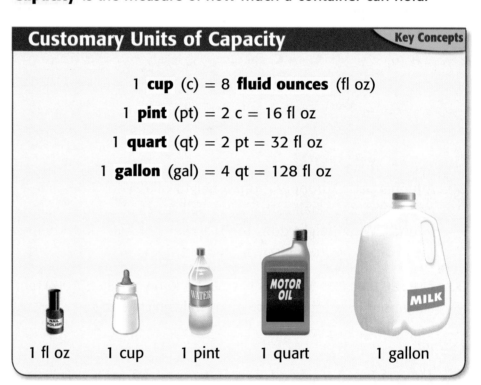

Customary Units of Capacity   Key Concepts

1 **cup** (c) = 8 **fluid ounces** (fl oz)

1 **pint** (pt) = 2 c = 16 fl oz

1 **quart** (qt) = 2 pt = 32 fl oz

1 **gallon** (gal) = 4 qt = 128 fl oz

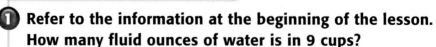

1 fl oz   1 cup   1 pint   1 quart   1 gallon

Real-World EXAMPLE   Convert Units of Capacity

① **Refer to the information at the beginning of the lesson. How many fluid ounces of water is in 9 cups?**

9 c = ▉ fl oz   Larger units (cups) are being converted to smaller units (fluid ounces).

Since 1 cup = 8 fluid ounces, multiply 9 by 8.

So, 9 cups of water is equal to 9 × 8 or 72 fluid ounces.

Remember

Any substance that takes on the shape of its container, such as liquids, some solids, and air can be measured in units of capacity.

EXAMPLE Convert Units of Capacity

2 **Paco has 3 pints of juice plus 1 cup of juice. How many cups of juice does he have in all?**

First, convert 3 pints 1 cup to cups.

Since 1 pint = 2 cups, multiply 3 by 2.

$3 \times 2 = 6$

Then add the remaining 1 cup.

So, Paco has $6 + 1$ or 7 cups of juice.

As with units of length and units of weight, units of capacity in the customary system can also be expressed as fractions.

EXAMPLE Parts of Units

3 **How many quarts are in 7 pints?**

$7 \text{ pt} = \blacksquare \text{ qt}$

To convert a smaller unit to a larger unit, divide. Since 2 pints = 1 quart, divide 7 by 2.

$7 \div 2 = 3 \text{ R1, or } 3\frac{1}{2}$

2 pt
2 pt
2 pt
1 pt

$\} 3\frac{1}{2}$ qt

So, there are 3 quarts 1 pint or $3\frac{1}{2}$ quarts in 7 pints.

CHECK What You Know

Complete. See Examples 1–3 (pp. 488–489)

1. $3 \text{ c} = \blacksquare \text{ fl oz}$

2. $4 \text{ qt} = \blacksquare \text{ c}$

3. $18 \text{ pt} = \blacksquare \text{ qt}$

4. $50 \text{ gal} = \blacksquare \text{ qt}$

5. $16 \text{ pt } 1 \text{ c} = \blacksquare \text{ c}$

6. $68 \text{ fl oz} = \blacksquare \text{ c}$

7. $5 \text{ qt} = \blacksquare \text{ gal } \blacksquare \text{ qt}$

8. $75 \text{ fl oz} = \blacksquare \text{ c } \blacksquare \text{ fl oz}$

9. The cafeteria sells lemonade in glasses that hold 12 fluid ounces. How many glasses can be filled with 3 gallons of lemonade?

10. **Talk About It** Explain how to convert from fluid ounces to pints.

Lesson 11-4 Units of Capacity **489**

Complete. See Examples 1–3 (pp. 488–489)

11. 5 c = ■ fl oz

12. 2 gal = ■ fl oz

13. 16 fl oz = ■ c

14. 25 gal = ■ qt

15. 19 c = ■ fl oz

16. 50 c = ■ pt

17. 2 gal 3 qt = ■ qt

18. 2 qt 3 c = ■ c

19. 5 c = ■ pt ■ c

20. 17 fl oz = ■ c ■ fl oz

21. 19 qt = ■ gal ■ qt

22. 18 qt = ■ gal

23. 7 c = ■ pt

24. Zach had 1 quart of milk. He used 1 pint to make pancakes and 1 cup to make scrambled eggs. How many cups of milk were left?

25. The average person drinks 1 pint of milk a day. At this rate, how many gallons will a person drink in a leap year (366 days)?

26. The table shows the amount of paint left in each jar. Which jar contains the greatest amount of paint? the least?

27. Measurement A bucket has $1\frac{1}{2}$ gallons of water. Is this amount *greater, than less than,* or *equal to* 6 quarts? Explain.

Jar	Amount
blue	2 pt 4 oz
purple	5 cups
green	39 fl oz

H.O.T. Problems

28. FIND THE ERROR Jasmine and Pablo are converting 32 cups to quarts. Who is correct? Explain.

Jasmine
32 c = ■ qt
32 ÷ 2 = 16
32 c = 16 qt

Pablo
32 c = ■ qt
32 ÷ 4 = 8
32 c = 8 qt

29. CHALLENGE Convert the following to the greatest whole number units of capacity.

200 fl oz = ■ gal ■ qt ■ pt ■ c ■ fl oz

30. **WRITING IN ►MATH** Write about a real-world situation that can be solved by converting between customary units of capacity. Then solve.

Chapter 11 Mid-Chapter Check

Lessons 11-1 through 11-4

NYS Core Curriculum
5.M.2, 5.M.5

Complete. (Lesson 11-1)

1. 84 in. = ■ ft **2.** 2 mi = ■ ft

3. 41 in. = ■ ft ■ in. **4.** 25 ft = ■ yd

Choose an appropriate unit to measure the length of each. (Lesson 11-1)

5. height of giraffe

6. length of soccer field

7. **MULTIPLE CHOICE** Alexander is 32 inches tall. His brother Josh is 4 feet tall. What fractional part of Josh's height is Alexander's height? (Lesson 11-1)

A $\frac{1}{8}$ **C** $\frac{1}{2}$

B $\frac{1}{4}$ **D** $\frac{2}{3}$

8. Five toy remote cars are in a race. Car 2 is just ahead of Car 3. Car 3 is two places behind Car 4. Car 4 is a few seconds behind the leader, Car 1. Car 5 is in last place. Order the cars from first to last place. Use the *draw a diagram* strategy.

Complete. (Lesson 11-3)

9. $2\frac{1}{2}$ lb = ■ oz **10.** 80 oz = ■ lb

11. 35 oz = ■ lb ■ oz **12.** 7,500 lb = ■ T

13. Refer to the sign at the right. What is the weight limit in pounds? (Lesson 11-3)

14. A motorcycle weighs 500 pounds. What fractional part of a ton is this? (Lesson 11-3)

Complete. (Lesson 11-4)

15. 10 gal = ■ pt

16. 7 qt = ■ gal ■ qt

17. 28 fl oz = ■ c

18. The table below shows the bottles of cleaning products that Lucas bought. Which cleaner contains the greatest amount? the least? (Lesson 11-4)

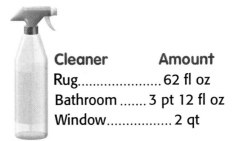

Cleaner	Amount
Rug	62 fl oz
Bathroom	3 pt 12 fl oz
Window	2 qt

19. **MULTIPLE CHOICE** What is the total number of cups in 7 quarts? (Lesson 11-4)

1 pint	= 2 cups
1 quart	= 4 cups

F 6 cups

G 8 cups

H 14 cups

J 28 cups

20. **WRITING IN MATH** What is the difference between weight and capacity? Use objects to explain your answer. (Lessons 11-3 and 11-4)

Units of Time

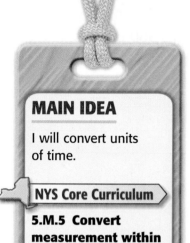

MAIN IDEA

I will convert units of time.

NYS Core Curriculum

5.M.5 Convert measurement within a given system

NY Math Online

macmillanmh.com

• Extra Examples
• Personal Tutor
• Self-Check Quiz

GET READY to Learn

Joe spends 1 hour a day doing his chores. He washes dishes, takes out the trash, and walks the dog.

Units of Time	Key Concepts

1 minute (min) = 60 seconds (s)

1 hour (h) = 60 min

1 day (d) = 24 h

1 week (wk) = 7 d

1 year (y) = 52 wk = 12 months (mo)

The steps that you use to convert units of length, weight, and capacity can be used to convert units of time.

 Real-World EXAMPLE   Convert Units of Time

1 **MEASUREMENT Joe walked his dog for 15 minutes before he went to school. How many seconds did he walk his dog?**

15 min = ■ s

To convert larger units of time to smaller units, multiply. Since 1 minute = 60 seconds, multiply 15 by 60.

15 × 60 = 900

So, Joe walked his dog for 900 seconds.

Use mental math to check the answer.
10 min = 10 × 60 or 600 s   20 min = 20 × 60 or 1,200 s

Since 900 seconds is between 600 and 1,200 seconds, the answer is reasonable.

To convert smaller units of time to larger units, divide.

EXAMPLE Use Different Units of Measure

2 **Complete: 56 hours = ▇ days ▇ hours.**

Since 24 hours = 1 day, divide 56 by 24 to find the number of days.

56 ÷ 24 = 2 R8

2 R8 means 2 whole days and 8 hours of another day. So, 56 hours = 2 days 8 hours.

As with other units of measure, units of time can also be expressed using fractions.

EXAMPLE Use Fractions in Measures

3 **How many hours are 150 minutes?**

150 min = ▇ h

To convert a smaller unit to a larger unit, divide. Since 60 minutes = 1 hour, divide 150 by 60 to find the number of hours.

150 ÷ 60 = 2 R30

2 R30 means 2 whole hours and 30 minutes of another hour. So, 150 minutes = 2 hours 30 minutes or $2\frac{1}{2}$ hours.

CHECK What You Know

Complete. See Examples 1–3 (pp. 492–493)

1. 3 h = ▇ min

2. 7 d = ▇ h

3. 420 s = ▇ min

4. 5 h = ▇ s

5. 30 mo = ▇ y

6. 84 h = ▇ d

7. 500 s = ▇ min ▇ s

8. 42 mo = ▇ y ▇ mo

9. Some lungfish can live up to 4 years without water by forming a cocoon around their bodies. How many months can they live without water?

10. **Talk About It** Would you multiply or divide to find the number of seconds in 3 minutes? Explain.

Practice and Problem Solving

Complete. See Examples 1–3 (pp. 492–493)

11. 840 s = ■ min

12. 3 mo = ■ y

13. 8 wk = ■ d

14. 12 min = ■ s

15. 72 h = ■ d

16. 252 d = ■ wk

17. 24 h = ■ min

18. 1,095 d = ■ y

19. 270 min = ■ h

20. 156 h = ■ d

21. 36,000 s = ■ h

22. 28 mo = ■ y

23. 135 min = ■ h ■ min

24. 200 s = ■ min ■ s

25. 423 d = ■ y ■ d

26. 50 d = ■ wk ■ d

27. 1 d 2 h = ■ min

28. 8 wk 2 d = ■ d

29. **Measurement** Katija spent 40 minutes raking leaves. What fraction of an hour did she spend raking leaves?

30. Jasper recorded 1 hour and 14 minutes on a CD. The CD can hold 80 minutes of music. How many seconds of recording time are left?

31. Lamar and Jesse are running in a race. Lamar's time was 90 seconds. Jesse finished 15 seconds later. What were their times in minutes?

32. Kari and her friend were comparing their number of days off for summer break. Kari has 85 days off and her friend has 7 weeks and 2 days off. Is there a difference between the number of days off? Explain.

 New York Data File

The New York Marathon is a 26-mile race. More than 90,000 runners compete. The shortest time it has taken a person to complete a marathon is 2 hours 10 minutes and 30 seconds.

33. Suppose it takes a marathon runner 115 minutes to run half of the marathon. How many hours and minutes will it take the runner to complete the marathon at this rate?

34. Mr. Adams completed a marathon in 328 minutes. Mrs. Adams completed the marathon in 255 minutes. How much faster did Mrs. Adams complete the marathon in hours and minutes?

H.O.T. Problems

35. **OPEN ENDED** Write a word problem that includes a length of time that is between 4 hours and 5 hours. Then convert the time to minutes.

36. **WHICH ONE DOESN'T BELONG?** Identify the time that does not belong with the other three. Explain your reasoning.

| 2 h 104 min | 2 h 114 min | 3 h 54 min | 234 min |

37. **WRITING IN ►MATH** Explain the steps you take to convert hours to seconds.

NYSMT Practice 5.M.2, 5.M.5

38. Mrs. Westin bought 3 gallons of apple cider for her class. What is the total number of pints in 3 gallons? (Lesson 11-4)

   | 1 quart = 2 pints |
   | 1 gallon = 8 pints |

   A 8 pints   **C** 16 pints

   B 10 pints   **D** 24 pints

39. Which relationship between the units of time is correct? (Lesson 11-5)

   F One day is $\frac{1}{24}$ of one hour.

   G One hour is $\frac{1}{24}$ of one day.

   H One second is $\frac{1}{60}$ of one hour.

   J One hour is $\frac{1}{60}$ of one second.

Spiral Review

40. Thomas is making a cake. The liquids that he uses are shown at the right. One cup is equal to 8 fluid ounces. What is the total number of cups of liquids? (Lesson 11-4)

Liquid   Amount (fl oz)
Milk.....................12
Vegetable Oil.........4

Complete. (Lessons 11-3 and 11-4)

41. 28 c = ▦ pt

42. 9 qt = ▦ c

43. 6 lb = ▦ oz

44. 7 T = ▦ lb

45. Tell whether the number represented by the model is prime or composite. Explain. (Lesson 9-2)

Problem-Solving Investigation

MAIN IDEA I will choose the best strategy to solve a problem.

 **NYSCC** 5.PS.2 Understand that some ways of representing a problem are more efficient than others
5.PS.3 Interpret information correctly, identify the problem, and generate possible strategies and solutions
Also addresses 5.CM.2.

P.S.I. TEAM +

BETHANY: They are giving away prizes at the grand opening of the CD Music Shop. At 7:00, there were two people in the line. At 7:15 when two more people arrived, there were 4 people in line. At 7:30, 4 more people arrived so there were 8 people in line. Every 15 minutes as many people as were already in line arrived.

YOUR MISSION: Find how many people were in line when the store opened at 8:00.

Understand	You know how many people arrived every 15 minutes. You need to know how many people were in line when the store opened at 8:00.
Plan	Make a table to show how many people are in line.
Solve	

Time (A.M.)	Number Who Arrive	Number in Line
7:00	2	2
7:15	2	4
7:30	4	8
7:45	8	16
8:00	16	32

There were 32 people in line at 8:00.

Check	Look back. Add the number of people who arrive. 2 + 2 + 4 + 8 + 16 = 32 So, the answer is correct.

Mixed Problem Solving

Use any strategy shown below to solve each problem.

PROBLEM-SOLVING STRATEGIES
• Look for a pattern.
• Draw a picture.
• Work backward.
• Draw a diagram.

1. The table shows the choices for ordering a sundae at the Ice Cream Shop. How many different sundaes could be made using one choice from ice cream and one choice from sauce?

Ice Cream Shop	
Ice cream	vanilla, chocolate, strawberry
Sauce	chocolate, caramel, strawberry
Toppings	sprinkles, nuts, cherries
Cones	sugar, waffle

2. Tamika left her house and rode 3 miles east and then 2 miles south to the library. From there she rode 1 mile west and 4 miles north to Jodi's house. Jodi and Tamika rode 1 mile south and 2 miles west to the park. How far north was Tamika from her house?

3. A number is divided by 6. Next the quotient is multiplied by 2. Then 4 is added to the product. If the result is 12, what is the number?

4. Alana is 4 years older than her brother Ernie. Ernie is 2 years older than their sister Amelia. Amelia is 10 years younger than their brother Mazo. If Mazo is 17 years old, how old is Alana?

5. Deidre is making a necklace by alternating long and short beads. The long beads are 0.5 inch long, and the short beads are 0.25 inch long. She starts and ends with a long bead, and the necklace is 14 inches long. How many of each size bead does she use?

6. Lake Superior is 531 feet deeper than Lake Ontario. Lake Ontario is 592 feet deeper than Lake Erie. Lake Erie is 210 feet deep. How deep is Lake Superior?

7. Annie and Max are putting roses into vases. For every 4 red roses, they put half as many white roses. If they put 18 roses in the vase altogether, how many are white?

8. **Algebra** Austin took the same amount of time each day to walk his dog last week. The table shows the time he left his house and the time he arrived home on four days. If the pattern continues, what time will he arrive home on Friday?

Day	Time Left Home	Time Arrived Back Home
Monday	4:32 P.M.	5:00 P.M.
Tuesday	6:05 P.M.	6:33 P.M.
Wednesday	7:15 P.M.	7:43 P.M.
Thursday	5:20 P.M.	5:48 P.M.
Friday	6:12 P.M.	■

9. **WRITING IN MATH** Gino has $3.75 after spending $4.75 on lunch and $1.50 on bus fare. How much money did Gino have originally? Which strategy would you use to solve this problem? Explain your reasoning. Then solve.

Soccer Rules!

Soccer is the most popular sport in the world, although it's called football in every country except the United States. The men's World Cup has been played every four years since 1930. The women's World Cup has been played every four years since 1991. Teams from all over the world compete to win the most exciting sports tournament on Earth.

If you're serious about playing soccer, who knows—maybe you'll be on a World Cup team!

Did You Know?

In 2006, about 5 billion people watched the World Cup.

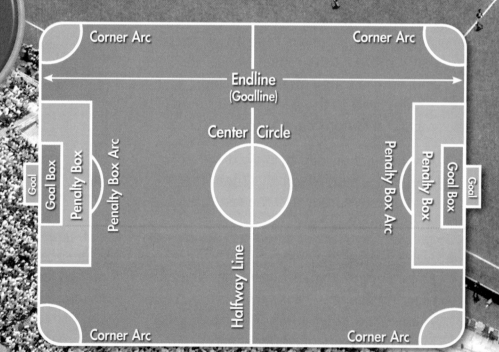

NYSCC **5.CN.8** Investigate the presence of mathematics in careers and **areas of interest**
5.R.8 **Use mathematics to show and understand social phenomena** (e.g., construct tables to organize data showing book sales)   *Also addresses 5.CN.9.*

⚽ Youth Soccer Guidelines ⚽

Age (years)	Field Size (yards)	Weight of Ball (ounces)	Length of Game
14	60 x 100	15	two 45-minute halves
12	50 x 80	12	two 30-minute halves
10	40 x 70	12	two 25-minute halves
8	25 x 50	11	four 12-minute quarters
6	15 x 30	11	four 8-minute quarters

Source: U.S. Youth Soccer

 ## Real-World Math

Use the information in the above table to solve each problem.

1 How many feet longer is the field used by 14-year-olds than the field used by 10-year-olds?

2 Suppose on one Sunday, a referee officiated three 8-year-old soccer games. How much time did the official spend refereeing, not including breaks?

3 A soccer game with 14-year-old players began at 9:30 A.M. on a Saturday. If the players rested at half-time for 15 minutes, how long was the game?

4 There are 16 players on a youth soccer team. Each player had a water bottle with $1\frac{1}{2}$ quarts of water for the game. How many gallons of water did the players have altogether?

5 A coach of a team of 10-year-olds has a bag of 6 soccer balls. What is the weight in pounds of the 6 soccer balls?

Elapsed Time

MAIN IDEA

I will add and subtract measures of time.

NYS Core Curriculum

5.M.7 Calculate elapsed time in hours and minutes

New Vocabulary

elapsed time

NY Math Online

macmillanmh.com
• Extra Examples
• Personal Tutor
• Self-Check Quiz

GET READY to Learn

Belinda started babysitting at 6:45 P.M. She finished at 10:55 P.M. How long did Belinda babysit?

6:45

10:55

Elapsed time is the difference in time between the start and the end of an event.

Real-World EXAMPLE   Elapsed Time

① MEASUREMENT Refer to the information above. How long did Belinda babysit?

Step 1 Write the times in units of hours and minutes.

Ending time: 10:55 P.M. →   10 hours 55 minutes
Starting time: 6:45 P.M. →   6 hours 45 minutes

Step 2 Subtract the starting time from the ending time. Make sure you subtract hours from hours and minutes from minutes.

$$
\begin{array}{r}
10 \text{ hours } 55 \text{ minutes} \\
- 6 \text{ hours } 45 \text{ minutes} \\
\hline
\end{array}
$$
Elapsed time: 4 hours 10 minutes

So, Belinda babysat 4 hours and 10 minutes.

Check
$$
\begin{array}{r}
4 \text{ hours } 10 \text{ minutes} \\
+ 6 \text{ hours } 45 \text{ minutes} \\
\hline
10 \text{ hours } 55 \text{ minutes}
\end{array}
$$

Sometimes it is necessary to rename the units before subtracting.

Real-World EXAMPLE Rename Units of Time

2 **Ben started to do his homework at 7:30 P.M. He finished at 9:05 P.M. How long did Ben study?**

$$\begin{array}{r} \overset{8}{\cancel{9}} \text{ hours } \overset{60}{\cancel{5}} \text{ minutes} \\ -\ 7 \text{ hours } 30 \text{ minutes} \end{array} \rightarrow \begin{array}{r} 8 \text{ hours } 65 \text{ minutes} \\ -\ 7 \text{ hours } 30 \text{ minutes} \\ \hline 1 \text{ hour } 35 \text{ minutes} \end{array}$$

Ben studied for 1 hour 35 minutes.

Remember

To find elapsed time from P.M. to A.M., remember to count through midnight.

Real-World EXAMPLE From P.M. to A.M.

3 **Dr. Sedaca arrived at work at 10:03 P.M. and went home at 7:27 A.M. How long was her shift?**

$$\begin{array}{ll} 10{:}03 \text{ P.M. } + & 57 \text{ min} \rightarrow 11{:}00 \text{ P.M.} \\ 11{:}00 \text{ P.M. } + 1 \text{ h} & \rightarrow 12{:}00 \text{ A.M.} \\ \underline{12{:}00 \text{ A.M. } + 7 \text{ h } 27 \text{ min}} \rightarrow \ 7{:}27 \text{ A.M.} \\ \quad\quad\quad 8 \text{ h } 84 \text{ min} \end{array}$$

Count 1 hour and 57 minutes until 12 A.M.

Count 7 hours and 27 minutes until 7:27 A.M.

8 h + 84 min = 9 h 24 min   84 min = 60 min + 24 min
                                          = 1 h 24 min

So, Dr. Sedaca's shift was 9 hours 24 minutes long.

CHECK What You Know

Find the elapsed time. See Examples 1–3 (pp. 500–501)

1. 6:14 A.M. to 10:30 A.M.

2. 8:18 P.M. to 9:22 P.M.

3. 11:50 A.M. to 2:04 P.M.

4. 7:22 A.M. to 9:20 A.M.

5. 11:30 P.M. to 2:14 A.M.

6. 3:40 P.M. to 6:09 P.M.

7. Kevin finished walking a trail at 11:44 A.M., and Rogelio finished at 12:16 P.M. How many minutes faster was Kevin than Rogelio?

8. Quan leaves for school at 7:15 A.M. He gets back home from school at 3:45 P.M. How long is he away from his house on a school day?

9. Measurement An all night movie marathon begins at 9:30 P.M. The last movie ends at 5:27 A.M. How long is the movie marathon?

10. **Talk About It** Compare how to find the elapsed time from 8:30 A.M. to 11:30 A.M. and from 10:30 P.M. to 1:30 A.M.

Find the elapsed time. See Examples 1–3 (pp. 500–501)

11. 4:00 A.M. to 10:23 A.M.

12. 9:20 A.M. to 11:58 A.M.

13. 1:27 P.M. to 5:30 P.M.

14. 8:15 P.M. to 1:11 A.M.

15. 3:15 A.M. to 11:00 A.M.

16. 10:58 A.M. to 5:29 P.M.

17. 9:15 A.M. to 3:20 P.M.

18. 10:30 P.M. to 7:15 A.M.

19. Tyson starts talking on the phone at 6:29 P.M. He finishes 55 minutes later. At what time did he finish talking on the phone?

20. Sed left his house at 4:58 P.M. to be at band practice at 5:45 P.M. How much time does he have to get to practice?

21. Alejandra was selling cookies at a bake sale. She started at 8:13 A.M. and finished at 5:47 P.M. How long did Alejandra sell cookies?

22. Baltimore, Maryland, is two hours ahead of Cheyenne, Wyoming. Griselda left at 3:42 P.M. She arrived in Cheyenne at 9:58 P.M. How long was her flight?

23. Part of a bus schedule is shown below. Which trip from Springdale to Cheswick takes the most time?

Bus Schedule				
Leave Springdale	6:52 A.M.	7:45 A.M.	8:43 A.M.	9:58 A.M.
Arrive in Cheswick	7:16 A.M.	8:20 A.M.	9:13 A.M.	10:23 A.M.

H.O.T. Problems

24. OPEN ENDED Write a beginning time and an ending time so that the elapsed time is 2 hours 16 minutes.

25. FIND THE ERROR Megan and Anita are finding the elapsed time from 2:30 P.M. to 5:46 P.M. Who is correct? Explain.

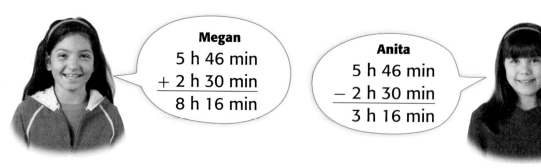

Megan
5 h 46 min
+ 2 h 30 min
8 h 16 min

Anita
5 h 46 min
− 2 h 30 min
3 h 16 min

26. WRITING IN MATH Write a story that takes place all in one day, using the times 6:45 A.M., 1:07 P.M., and 8:39 P.M. Include the elapsed times in your story.

27. The Williams family spent 4 hours at a theme park. What fractional part of a day is 4 hours? (Lesson 11-5)

   A $\frac{1}{12}$

   B $\frac{1}{6}$

   C $\frac{1}{4}$

   D $\frac{1}{3}$

28. Jordan went to the pool from 11:20 A.M. to 3:45 P.M., as shown on the clocks below.

   Arrive   **Leave**

How many hours and minutes was Jordan at the pool? (Lesson 11-7)

   F 4 h 5 min   H 4 h 20 min

   G 4 h 15 min   J 4 h 25 min

Spiral Review

29. Mrs. Spring needs to buy 2 dozen muffins for a family brunch. According to the sign, how much will she save by buying the muffins by the dozen instead of individually? (Lesson 11-6)

BLUEBERRY MUFFINS
$1 each or
$8 per dozen

Complete. (Lesson 11-5)

30. 360 s = ▨ min

31. 7 wk = ▨ d

32. 12 h = ▨ min

33. 135 min = ▨ h ▨ min

34. Emily has a 4-foot long board to make some shelves for her desk. Her father cuts two shelves, each 19 inches long, from the board. How long is the piece of the board that is left? (Lesson 11-1)

Add. Write each sum in simplest form. Check your answer by drawing a picture. (Lesson 10-1)

35. $\frac{1}{3} + \frac{1}{3}$

36. $\frac{2}{5} + \frac{1}{5}$

37. $\frac{5}{16} + \frac{7}{16}$

38. $\frac{9}{10} + \frac{3}{10}$

Write each improper fraction as a mixed number. (Lesson 8-2)

39. $\frac{9}{2}$

40. $\frac{13}{4}$

41. $\frac{20}{3}$

42. $\frac{27}{5}$

FOLDABLES® Study Organizer GET READY to Study

Be sure the following Big Ideas are written in your Foldable.

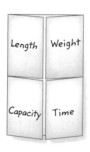

Length Weight

Capacity Time

Key Concepts

Customary Units of Length (p. 477)

1 foot (ft) = 12 inches (in.)

1 yard (yd) = 3 ft or 36 in.

1 mile (mi) = 5,280 ft or 1,760 yd

Customary Units of Weight (p. 484)

1 pound (lb) = 16 ounces (oz)

1 ton (T) = 2,000 pounds

Customary Units of Capacity (p. 488)

1 cup (c) = 8 fluid ounces (fl oz)

1 pint (pt) = 2 c = 16 fl oz

1 quart (qt) = 2 pt = 32 fl oz

1 gallon (gal) = 4 qt = 128 fl oz

Units of Time (p. 492)

1 minute (min) = 60 seconds (s)

1 hour (h) = 60 min

1 day (d) = 24 h

1 week (wk) = 7 d

1 year (y) = 52 wk = 12 months (mo)

Key Vocabulary

capacity (p. 488)

customary units (p. 477)

elapsed time (p. 500)

length (p. 475)

weight (p. 484)

Vocabulary Check

State whether each sentence is *true* or *false*. If *false*, replace the underlined word or number to make a true sentence.

1. <u>Capacity</u> is the amount that a container can hold.

2. The inch, foot, yard, and mile are called <u>metric</u> units.

3. Three feet equals 1 <u>yard</u>.

4. One gallon equals 4 <u>pints</u>.

5. Fluid ounce is a customary measure of <u>weight</u>.

6. To convert from feet to inches, <u>divide</u> by 12.

7. A reasonable estimate for the height of an oak tree is 30 <u>feet</u>.

8. <u>Elapsed time</u> is the amount of time that passes between two events.

9. To change 3 days to hours, multiply 3 by <u>60</u>.

Lesson-by-Lesson Review

 11-1 **Units of Length** (pp. 477–480)

5.M.2

Example 1
Convert 54 inches to feet.

To change a smaller unit to a larger unit, divide.

Since 12 in. = 1 ft, divide 54 by 12.

54 ÷ 12 = 4 R6

4 R6 means 4 feet and 6 inches of another foot.

So, 54 inches = 4 feet 6 inches or $4\frac{1}{2}$ feet.

Complete.

10. 8 ft = ▦ in.

11. 7 yd = ▦ ft

12. 32 in. = ▦ ft ▦ in.

13. 7,920 ft = ▦ mi

14. Which unit of length would you use to measure the distance between two fire stations?

15. The bill of an Australian pelican can be as long as 18 inches. Write this measure in feet and inches.

11-2 **Problem-Solving Strategy: Draw a Diagram** (pp. 482–483)

5.PS.13

Example 2
Mrs. Juarez left her house and drove 5 miles north to the bank, 6 miles west to the post office, 3 miles south to the store, 2 miles east to the cleaners, and 2 miles south to the school. How many miles is she from her house?

Solve by drawing a diagram.

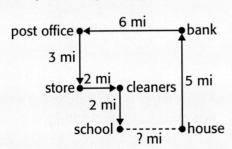

Mrs. Juarez is 4 miles from her house.

16. Mr. Muhammad rented a 5-gallon smoothie machine for a carnival. The smoothies will be sold in two sizes: 12 fluid ounces and 20 fluid ounces. Find two different combinations of both drink sizes that equal 5 gallons.

17. At a bakery, a tray of cookies is taken out of the oven every 10 minutes, and a pan of brownies is taken out every 25 minutes. At 1:00 P.M., both are taken out of the oven. How many trays of cookies will be taken out before both are taken out of the oven at the same time? What time will it be?

11-3 Units of Weight (pp. 484–487)

5.M.5

Example 3

In two weeks, Teresa feeds her cat 56 ounces of cat food. How many pounds of cat food does she feed her cat?

To change a smaller unit to a larger unit, divide. Since 16 oz = 1 lb, divide 56 by 16.

56 ÷ 16 = 3 R8

3 R8 means 3 pounds and 8 ounces of another pound.

So, 56 ounces = 3 pounds 8 ounces or $3\frac{1}{2}$ pounds.

Teresa feeds her cat $3\frac{1}{2}$ pounds of cat food.

Complete.

18. 112 oz = ■ lb

19. 12,000 lb = ■ T

20. 36 oz = ■ lb ■ oz

21. 7,000 lb = ■ T

22. A 1-pound package of butter has four sticks. How many ounces does each stick weigh?

11-4 Units of Capacity (pp. 488–490)

5.M.5

Example 4

How many pints are in 3 gallons?

3 gal = ■ pt

To convert a larger unit to a smaller unit, multiply. Since 1 gal = 8 pt, multiply 3 by 8.

3 × 8 = 24

So, there are 24 pints in 3 gallons.

Complete.

23. 14 qt = ■ pt

24. 5 c = ■ fl oz

25. 90 fl oz = ■ c ■ fl oz

26. 19 qt = ■ gal

27. A container has 24 fluid ounces of hot chocolate. Is 24 fluid ounces *greater than*, *less than*, or *equal to* $1\frac{1}{2}$ pints? Explain.

11-5 Units of Time (pp. 492–495)

5.M.5

Example 5

Complete: 200 minutes = ▪ hours.

To change from a smaller unit to a larger unit, divide. Since 1 min = 60 s, divide 200 by 60.

$200 \div 60 = 3$ R20

3 R20 means 3 whole hours and 20 minutes of another hour. So,

200 minutes = 3 hours 20 minutes or $3\frac{1}{3}$ hours.

Complete.

28. 5 h = ▪ min

29. 420 s = ▪ min

30. 2 wk = ▪ d

31. 580 min = ▪ h ▪ min

32. Laura practices the piano 30 minutes every day. How many hours a week is this?

11-6 Problem-Solving Investigation: Choose a Strategy (pp. 496–497)

5.PS.2, 5.PS.3

Example 6

An electronics store is having a grand opening in which every 15th customer receives a free CD and every 25th customer receives a free DVD. Which customer will be first one to receive a CD and a DVD?

Make a table to solve.

Multiples of 15	15	30	45	60	75
Multiples of 25	25	50	75	100	125

So, the 75th customer receives a CD and a DVD.

33. A forest fire covered 51 square miles by Friday. This is 3 less than 3 times the number of square miles it covered on Wednesday. How many square miles did it cover on Wednesday?

34. A new train glides along a magnetic field. The train takes 5 hours to travel 1,200 miles. How far can it travel in 2 hours?

35. The Eagles won 13 games and lost 5 games. The Gators won 12 games and lost 4 games. Which team won a greater fraction of their games?

11-7 **Elapsed Time** (pp. 500–503)

5.M.7

Example 7
Delmar started washing his bike at 4:16 P.M. He finished at 4:57 P.M. How long did it take Delmar to wash his bike?

Step 1 Write the times in units of hours and minutes.

   End: 4:57 P.M. → 4 h 57 min

   Start: 4:16 P.M. → 4 h 16 min

Step 2 Subtract the time starting from the ending time.

              4 hours 57 minutes
          − 4 hours 16 minutes
Elapsed time: 0 hours 41 minutes

So, Delmar spent 41 minutes washing his bike.

Example 8
Find the elapsed time from 2:20 P.M. to 9:15 P.M.

Step 1 Write the times in units of hours and minutes.

   End: 9:15 P.M. → 9 h 15 min

   Start: 2:20 P.M. → 2 h 20 min

Step 2 Subtract the starting time from the ending time.

     9 h 15 min →   8 h 75 min
   − 2 h 20 min   − 2 h 20 min
                        6 h 55 min

The elapsed time is 6 hours 55 minutes.

Find each elapsed time.

36. 4:15 P.M. to 5:40 P.M.

37. 4:45 A.M. to 8:05 A.M.

38. 12:17 A.M. to 1:57 A.M.

39. 8:34 P.M. to 3:08 A.M.

40. 3:16 P.M. to 9:26 A.M.

41. A turkey is put into the oven at 11:25 A.M. The turkey was done at 4:10 P.M. How long did it take the turkey to cook?

42. Erica arrived at school at 8:15 A.M. She left the house at 7:48 A.M. How long did it take Erica to get to school?

43. Mr. Torre makes some bread for dinner using his bread machine. If he starts his bread at 2:45 P.M. and it is done at 5:30 P.M., how long did it take to make the bread?

Complete.

1. 132 in. = ▧ ft   2. 4 mi = ▧ yd

3. 64 in. = ▧ ft   4. 500 ft = ▧ yd ▧ ft

5. Mariah is filling a wading pool with water. Every two minutes, the water level increases by $1\frac{1}{2}$ inches. If the pool is 9 inches deep, how long will it take to fill the pool to its capacity?

Complete.

6. 96 oz = ▧ lb

7. 60 oz = ▧ lb ▧ oz

8. 1,500 lb = ▧ T

9. 22 qt = ▧ gal ▧ qt

10. **MULTIPLE CHOICE** A recipe for punch is shown below.

Ingredient	Amount
fruit juice	1 gal
lemon-lime soda	3 qt

Suppose you want to double the recipe. How many gallons of punch will the recipe make?

A $1\frac{3}{4}$ gal   C $3\frac{1}{2}$ gal

B 3 gal   D 14 qt

11. Mr. Roland fences in a 20-foot by 25-foot section of his yard for his dog. He puts fence posts every 5 feet and at the corners. How many posts are there?

12. Manny bought $2\frac{1}{2}$ pounds of coleslaw and 42 ounces of potato salad. Which food item weighed more?

Complete.

13. 12 wk = ▧ d

14. 585 min = ▧ h

15. 84 h = ▧ d ▧ h

16. Michelle leaves for school at 7:50 A.M. She gets home at 4:10 P.M. How long is Michelle gone from home?

Find each elapsed time.

17. 7:39 A.M. to 11:50 A.M.

18. 10:30 P.M. to 5:08 A.M.

19. **MULTIPLE CHOICE** Elijah leaves his house in the morning at the time shown on the clock.

He walks for 15 minutes to his friend's house. They play two video games for 25 minutes each game. Then they go outside. At what time do they go outside?

F 10:10 A.M.   H 10:30 A.M.

G 10:25 A.M.   J 10:35 A.M.

20. **WRITING IN ►MATH** When you are finding the elapsed time between two events, why is it important to note whether the times are A.M. or P.M.?

PART 1 **Multiple Choice**

Read each question. Then fill in the correct answer on the answer sheet provided by your teacher or on a sheet of paper.

1. Use a ruler to measure the line segment along the route from the lake to the archery field to the nearest inch. What is the actual distance in yards?

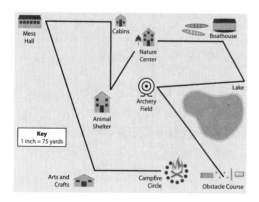

A 2 yd

B 6 yd

C 75 yd

D 150 yd

2. Refer to the map in Exercise 1. Use a ruler to measure the line segments along the route from the campfire circle to the cabins to the nearest $\frac{1}{4}$ inch. What is the total distance in yards?

F 100 yd   **H** 300 yd

G 225 yd   **J** 400 yd

3. The fractions $\frac{2}{6}$, $\frac{3}{9}$, $\frac{4}{12}$, $\frac{5}{15}$, and $\frac{6}{18}$ are each equivalent to $\frac{1}{3}$. What is the relationship between the numerator and denominator in each fraction that is equivalent to $\frac{1}{3}$?

A The denominator is three more than the numerator.

B The numerator is three more than the denominator.

C The denominator is three times the numerator.

D The numerator is three times the denominator.

4. Which group shows all the numbers that are common factors of 24 and 36?

F 1, 2, 4, 6, 12

G 1, 2, 3, 4, 6, 12

H 1, 2, 3, 4, 6, 8, 12

J 1, 2, 3, 4, 6, 8, 9, 12

5. Harada wants to watch a television special. The program starts at 8:00 P.M. and is 105 minutes long. What time will the television special end?

A 9:00 P.M.

B 9:15 P.M.

C 9:30 P.M.

D 9:45 P.M.

6. Tori needs a string that is 2 inches long for a bracelet. Use the ruler on the Mathematics Chart to measure the line segment under each string. Which string is 2 inches long?

F ━━━

G ━━━━━━━━

H ━━━━━━━

J ━━━━━━━

7. A new action movie is 134 minutes long. What is this time in hours and minutes?

A 1 hour 14 minutes

B 1 hour 34 minutes

C 2 hours 14 minutes

D 2 hours 34 minutes

8. Five friends share three sandwiches equally. How much does each friend get?

F $\frac{3}{5}$ sandwich

G $1\frac{1}{3}$ sandwich

H $1\frac{3}{5}$ sandwich

J $1\frac{2}{3}$ sandwich

Record your answers on the sheet provided by your teacher or on a sheet of paper.

9. Mykia weighed 7 pounds 5 ounces when she was born. How many ounces did she weigh when she was born?

10. Name two unlike fractions that have a sum of $3\frac{5}{6}$.

11. Write any four digit number that has a 3 in the hundreds place and a 7 in the tens place.

Record your answers on the answer sheet provided by your teacher or on a sheet of paper. Show your work.

12. For each item below, choose an appropriate unit. Choose from inches, feet, yards, or miles. Explain your choice.

- the length of a football field
- the distance around Earth
- the length of a toothbrush
- the height of a rollercoaster

NEED EXTRA HELP?												
If You Missed Question...	1	2	3	4	5	6	7	8	9	10	11	12
Go to Lesson...	11–1	11–1	9–3	9–1	11–5	11–1	11–5	8–1	11–3	10–3	1–1	11–1
NYS Core Curriculum	5.M.2	5.M.2	5.N.12	5.N.15	5.M.5	5.M.2	5.M.5	4.N.7	5.M.5	6.N.16	5.N.1	5.M.2

CHAPTER 12
Use Measures in the Metric System

 **BIG Idea** What is the metric system?

The **metric system** is a decimal system of measurement.

Example Speed skating at the Olympic Games consists of the events listed in the table.

Speed Skating Events	
• 500 meter	• 1,500 meter
• 1,000 meter	• 5,000 meter

In the metric system, a meter is a unit of length.

What will I learn in this chapter?

- Choose appropriate metric units for measuring length.
- Convert metric units of length, mass, and capacity.
- Use integers to represent real-world situations.
- Solve problems involving changes in temperature.
- Solve problems by determining reasonable answers.

 **Key Vocabulary**

metric system

mass

negative number

positive number

integer

 **NY Math Online** **Student Study Tools**
at macmillanmh.com

FOLDABLES®
Study Organizer

Make this Foldable to help you organize information about the metric system. Begin with a sheet of 11″ by 17″ paper.

① **Fold** the short sides toward the middle.

② **Fold** the top to the bottom.

③ **Open.** Cut along the second fold to make four tabs.

④ **Label** each tab as shown.

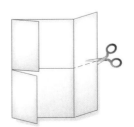

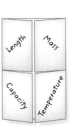

Chapter 12 Use Measures in the Metric System **513**

ARE YOU READY for Chapter 12?

You have two ways to check prerequisite skills for this chapter.

Option 2

NY Math Online > Take the Chapter Readiness Quiz at macmillanmh.com.

Option 1

Complete the Quick Check below.

QUICK Check

Multiply. (Lessons 3-1 and 3-8)

1. $6 \times 1,000$

2. 15×100

3. 180×10

4. 947×100

5. 36×10

6. $24 \times 1,000$

7. A bean bag chair costs $16. How much do one hundred bean bag chairs cost?

Divide. (Lessons 4-1 and 4-7)

8. $150 \div 10$

9. $500 \div 100$

10. $140 \div 10$

11. $64,000 \div 1,000$

12. $7,900 \div 100$

13. $3,120 \div 10$

14. Roz has $480 to spend on her 10-day trip. If she wants to spend the same amount daily, how much can she spend each day?

Write the temperature shown on each thermometer. (Prior Grade)

15.

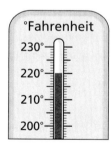

16.

17.

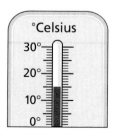

18.

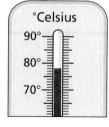

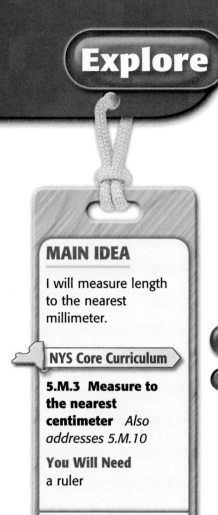

Explore

Measurement Activity for 12-1
Metric Rulers

MAIN IDEA

I will measure length to the nearest millimeter.

NYS Core Curriculum

5.M.3 Measure to the nearest centimeter *Also addresses 5.M.10*

You Will Need
a ruler

NY Math Online

macmillanmh.com
• Concepts in Motion

In the customary system, you measure length using inches, feet, or yards. In the metric system, you use meters, centimeters, or millimeters.

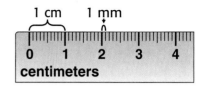

Use a ruler like the one above to measure objects to the nearest centimeter or to the nearest millimeter.

ACTIVITY

① **Find the length of the piece of chalk to the nearest centimeter.**

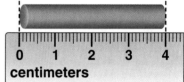

Step 1 Place the ruler against the piece of chalk. Line up the zero on the ruler with the end of the piece of chalk.

Step 2 Find the centimeter mark that is closest to the other end.

To the nearest centimeter, the length of the piece of chalk is 4 centimeters long.

ACTIVITY

② **Find the length of the toy car to the nearest millimeter.**

To the nearest millimeter, the toy car is 73 millimeters long.

Explore Measurement Activity for 12-1: Metric Rulers **515**

Think About It

1. Is it easier to measure objects to the nearest centimeter or to the nearest millimeter? Explain.

2. Will you get a more exact measurement if you measure an object to the nearest centimeter or to the nearest millimeter? Explain your reasoning.

 CHECK **What You Know**

Use a metric ruler to find the length of each object to the nearest centimeter and to the nearest millimeter.

3.

4.

5.

Millimeters and *centimeters* are used to measure small objects. You can measure the length of larger objects using *meters*. One meter is a little longer than one yard. Select an appropriate unit to measure the length of each object.

6. width of your textbook

7. height of a classmate

8. length of classroom

9. length of an ant

10. Copy the table below. Then complete the table using ten objects found in your classroom. The first one is done for you.

Object	Unit of Measure	Estimate	Actual Length
Pencil	centimeter	15 centimeters	17 centimeters

Name an object that you would measure using each unit.

11. millimeter

12. centimeter

13. meter

14. **OPEN ENDED** Draw a line that is between 5 and 6 centimeters long. Then measure the length of the line to the nearest millimeter.

15. **WRITING IN ►MATH** Would you measure the length of a bicycle in centimeters or millimeters? Explain your reasoning.

12-1 Units of Length

MAIN IDEA

I will choose an appropriate metric unit for measuring length and convert metric units of length.

NYS Core Curriculum

5.M.4 Identify equivalent metric units of length

5.M.10 Determine personal references for metric units of length *Also addresses 5.M.5, 5.R.4.*

New Vocabulary

metric system

centimeter

millimeter

meter

kilometer

NY Math Online

macmillanmh.com

• Extra Examples
• Personal Tutor
• Self-Check Quiz

GET READY to Learn

The tree shown at the right is estimated to be 150 years old and 45 meters or 150 feet tall. The tallest tree in the world is over 370 feet tall.

The **metric system** is a decimal system of measurement. The common units of length in the metric system are millimeter, centimeter, meter, and kilometer.

Metric Units of Length   Key Concepts

1 **centimeter** (cm) = 10 **millimeters** (mm)

1 **meter** (m) = 100 cm or 1,000 mm

1 **kilometer** (km) = 1,000 m

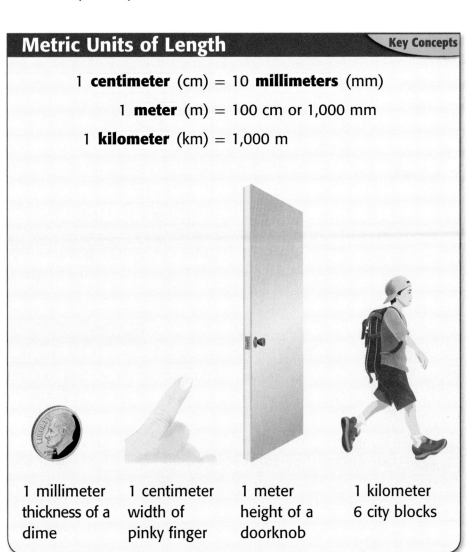

1 millimeter
thickness of a dime

1 centimeter
width of pinky finger

1 meter
height of a doorknob

1 kilometer
6 city blocks

Lesson 12-1 Units of Length   **517**

Real-World EXAMPLE   Select an Appropriate Unit

① **SCIENCE Which unit would you use to measure the length of a river: *millimeter, centimeter, meter,* or *kilometer*?**

The length of a river is much greater than the height of a doorknob. So, *kilometer* is an appropriate unit of measure.

Remember

To convert a larger unit to a smaller unit, *multiply.*

To convert a smaller unit to a larger unit, *divide.*

In the chart below, each place value is 10 times the place value to its right. To convert metric units, multiply or divide by a multiple of 10, such as 10, 100, or 1,000.

Thousands	Hundreds	Tens	Ones	Tenths	Hundredths	Thousandths
		4	5.			
kilo	hecto	deca	meter	deci	centi	milli

1,000   100   10

Real-World EXAMPLE   Convert Larger Units to Smaller Units

② **ART Cynthia cut a piece of ribbon that is 5 meters long. How many centimeters long is the ribbon?**

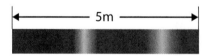

You need to convert 5 meters to centimeters.

5 m = ▦ cm   A larger unit (m) is being converted to a smaller unit (cm), so you will multiply.

5 × 100 = 500   Since 1 m = 100 cm, multiply 5 by 100.

So, 5 m = 500 cm.

The piece of ribbon is 500 centimeters long.

Remember

To multiply by 10, 100, or 1,000, use basic facts and count the number of zeros in the factors.

Convert Smaller Units to Larger Units

3 **GAMES** Roshonda has 50 dominoes. Each domino is 4 centimeters long. She lines them up end to end as shown. How many meters long is the line of dominoes?

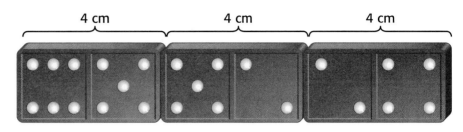

4 cm   4 cm   4 cm

Step 1 Find the length in centimeters.

$$\underbrace{50}_{\text{number of dominoes}} \times \underbrace{4 \text{ cm}}_{\text{length of each domino}} = \underbrace{200 \text{ cm}}_{\text{total length}}$$

Step 2 Convert 200 centimeters to meters.

200 cm = ▨ m   A smaller unit (cm) is being converted to a larger unit (m), so divide.

200 ÷ 100 = 2   Since 100 cm = 1 m, divide 200 by 100.

So, 200 cm = 2 m.

The line of 50 dominoes is 2 meters long.

Remember
To divide by 10, 100, or 1,000, cross out the same number of zeros in both the dividend and divisor.

CHECK What You Know

Select an appropriate unit to measure each length. Write *millimeter*, *centimeter*, *meter*, or *kilometer*. See Example 1 (p. 518)

1. soccer field   **2.** necklace   **3.** distance between two cities

Complete. See Examples 2, 3 (pp. 518–519)

4. 5 m = ▨ cm   **5.** 9 km = ▨ m   **6.** 700 cm = ▨ m

7. 20 mm = ▨ cm   **8.** 6,000 m = ▨ km   **9.** 45 cm = ▨ mm

10. Which is the most reasonable estimate for the depth of a pond: 6 millimeters, 6 centimeters, or 6 meters? Explain.

11. (Talk About It) Find three items in your classroom: one that is about 3 meters long, one that is about 3 centimeters long, and one that is about 3 millimeters long. Check by measuring each item.

Select an appropriate unit to measure each length. Write *millimeter*, *centimeter*, *meter*, or *kilometer*. See Example 1 (p. 518)

12. height of oak tree

13. cell phone

14. water slide

15. ladybug

16. train route

17. book

Complete. See Examples 2, 3 (pp. 518–519)

18. 2 m = ■ mm

19. 73,000 m = ■ km

20. 3 cm = ■ mm

21. 170 mm = ■ cm

22. 15 km = ■ m

23. 8,000 mm = ■ m

24. 9 m = ■ cm

25. 300 cm = ■ m

26. 6 cm = ■ mm

27. A spider is 6 millimeters long. What fractional part of 1 centimeter is 6 millimeters?

28. Which is the most reasonable estimate for the length of a piano: 170 millimeters, 170 centimeters, or 170 meters? Explain.

29. Two lizards are shown below. How many millimeters longer is the larger lizard than the smaller lizard?

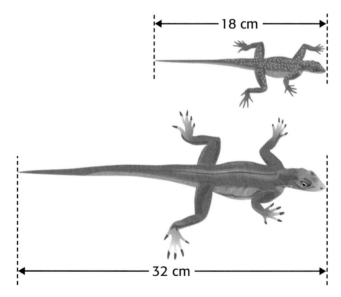

18 cm

32 cm

30. Measure the distance across the sunflower shown. What is this measurement to the nearest centimeter? How many centimeters smaller than 1 meter is the width of the sunflower?

31. A hiking trail is 1 kilometer long. Ronan just passed the 250-meter marker. What fractional part of the trail does he still have to hike?

32. The table shows the lengths of Julian's backpack and notebook binder. How much longer is the backpack than the binder?

Object	Length
Backpack	60 cm
Notebook binder	430 mm

Real-World PROBLEM SOLVING

Science The largest active volcano in the world is Mauna Loa in Hawaii.

- Its crater is 180 meters deep.
- Its dome is 120 kilometers long and 50 kilometers wide.
- Its summit is 17 kilometers above its base.

33. What is the depth of the crater in centimeters?

34. How many centimeters above the base is the summit?

35. How many meters greater is the length of the dome than the width?

H.O.T. Problems

36. OPEN ENDED Estimate the length of three objects in your classroom. Then measure and compare the measurements to your estimates. Tell what metric units you used.

37. REASONING Explain how you decide which metric unit to use when measuring the length of an object. Provide examples to explain your reasoning.

38. WHICH ONE DOESN'T BELONG? Identify the measure that does not belong with the other three. Explain your reasoning.

| 3,500 Km | 35 m | 350 cm | 3,500 mm |

39. CHALLENGE Explain how to find 30 cm + 1 m + 4,000 mm. Then solve.

40. **WRITING IN ►MATH** Compare and contrast converting customary units of length and converting metric units of length. Which type of conversion is easier? Explain.

Problem-Solving Skill

MAIN IDEA I will solve problems by determining reasonable answers.

 NYSCC **5.PS.22 Discuss whether a solution is reasonable in the context of the original problem.** *Also addresses 5.RP.3, 5.RP.6*

Juanita is trimming hedges. They are 37 meters from an electrical outlet. Her extension cord is 3,500 centimeters long. Juanita estimates that the extension cord is long enough to reach the hedges. Is she correct? If not, how much longer does an extension cord need to be to reach the hedges?

Understand	**What facts do you know?** • The distance from the hedges to the electrical outlet. • The length of the extension cord in centimeters. **What do you need to find?** • Does Juanita have a long enough extension cord?
Plan	Convert 3,500 centimeters to meters. Then compare.
Solve	First, convert 3,500 centimeters to meters. 3,500 centimeters = ■ meters 3,500 ÷ 100 = 35 So, 3,500 centimeters = 35 meters. Since 35 < 37 meters, Juanita's extension cord will not be long enough to reach the hedges. To find how much longer the extension cord needs to be, subtract. 37 − 35 = 2 So, Juanita will need an extension cord that is 2 meters or 200 centimeters longer to reach the hedges.
Check	Look back. Since 3,700 > 3,500 and 3,700 − 3,500 = 200. The answer is reasonable. ✔

Refer to the problem on the previous page.

1. Would Juanita be able to reach the hedges using one extension cord that is 4,000 centimeters long? Explain.

2. Juanita wants to trim a tree that is 75 meters from the outlet. How many 3,500-centimeter extension cords will she need?

3. Describe another method you could use to check if an estimate is reasonable.

4. Explain why it is always a good idea to check if your answers are reasonable.

NYSCC • NYSMT
Extra Practice, p. R32

Solve. Determine reasonable answers.

5. Estella needs 4 pints of vegetable broth to make soup. She has only a 1-cup measuring cup. Will Estella need 4 cups, 8 cups, or 16 cups of broth? Explain.

6. Dylan is making bookmarks. It takes him 15 minutes to make one bookmark. Dylan estimates that he can make 14 bookmarks in 3 hours. Is he correct? If not, how many bookmarks can he make in 3 hours?

7. For a small art project, Mr. Adams estimates that each student will need the amount of clay shown below. Does this seem reasonable? Explain.

1 lb   1 lb   1 lb   1 lb

8. To make one cup of hot chocolate you need 8 ounces of water. Elsu's mother is making 12 cups of hot chocolate. Will she need 2 quarts, 3 quarts, or 4 quarts of water? Explain.

9. Ahmik buys a carpet that is 7,300 centimeters long in order to cover the hallway shown below. Is the carpet long enough to cover the hallway? If not, how much of the hallway will not be covered by the carpet?

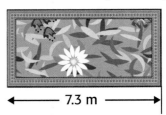

← 7.3 m →

10. Tonya needs to buy a cable that is at least 12 yards long. At the store, all of the cables are marked in feet. Tonya estimates that a 40-foot cable will be long enough. Is her estimate reasonable? Explain.

11. Tommy estimates that his skateboard is about 90 millimeters long. Is this a reasonable estimate? Explain.

12. **WRITING IN ►MATH** Write a real-world problem that has an unreasonable answer. Explain why the answer is unreasonable.

GET READY to Learn

The goliath beetle is the heaviest insect in the world. At 100 grams, it has about the same *mass* as a can of sardines.

MAIN IDEA

I will convert metric units of mass.

NYS Core Curriculum

Reinforcement of 4.M.5 Measure mass, using grams

5.M.5 Convert measurement within a given system

New Vocabulary

mass

gram

milligram

kilogram

NY Math Online

macmillanmh.com
• Extra Examples
• Personal Tutor
• Self-Check Quiz

Mass is a measure of the amount of matter in an object. Metric units of mass are milligram, gram, and kilogram.

Metric Units of Mass   **Key Concepts**

1 **gram** (g) = 1,000 **milligrams** (mg)

1 **kilogram** (kg) = 1,000 g

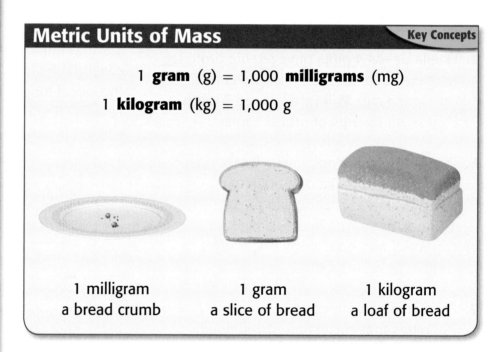

1 milligram   1 gram   1 kilogram
a bread crumb   a slice of bread   a loaf of bread

Real-World EXAMPLE   **Convert Larger Units to Smaller Units**

① **SCIENCE** In 1876, pieces of a meteorite were found in Tennessee. The largest single piece of meteorite had a mass of 136 kilograms. What was the mass of this piece in grams?

136 kg = ▓ g   A kilogram is a larger unit than a gram.

136 × 1,000 = 136,000   1 kg = 1,000 g, so multiply 136 by 1,000.

So, 136 kg = 136,000 g.

The mass of the meteorite was 136,000 grams.

Remember

Mass and weight are different measures. If you were flying in the space shuttle, you would have the same mass as on Earth, but a different weight.

Real-World EXAMPLE

Convert Smaller Units to Larger Units

2 **FOOD** Mr. Benavides bakes muffins that have a mass of about 2,000 milligrams. What is the mass in grams?

2,000 mg = ▨ g   A milligram is smaller than a gram.

2,000 ÷ 1,000 = 2   1,000 mg = 1 g, so divide 2,000 by 1,000.

So, 2,000 mg = 2 g.

Each muffin has a mass of 2 grams.

Real-World EXAMPLE   Compare Mass

3 **MAIL** Luke is shipping a box that has a mass of 4,300 grams. If the mass of the box is greater than 5 kilograms, shipping will cost extra. Will shipping cost extra? Explain.

5 kg = ▨ g   Convert a larger unit to a smaller unit.

5 × 1,000 = 5,000   1 kg = 1,000 g, so multiply 5 by 1,000.

So, 5 kg = 5,000 g.

The mass of the box is 4.3 kilograms. Since 4,300 grams < 5,000 grams, shipping will not cost extra.

CHECK What You Know

Complete. See Examples 1, 2 (pp. 524–525)

1. 5,000 mg = ▨ g

2. 9 g = ▨ mg

3. 230 mg = ▨ g

4. 8,000 g = ▨ mg

5. 4 kg = ▨ g

6. 5,000 g = ▨ kg

Replace ● with <, >, or = to make a true statement. See Example 3 (p. 525)

7. 2,300 mg ● 2 g

8. 3 kg ● 3,000 g

9. 75 g ● 800 mg

10. One highlighter has a mass of 11 grams. Another highlighter has a mass of 108 milligrams. Which highlighter has the greater mass?

11.  Which is a more reasonable estimate for the mass of a baseball: 140 milligrams, 140 grams, or 140 kilograms? Explain.

Complete. See Examples 1, 2 (pp. 524–525)

12. 2 g = ■ mg

13. 6 kg = ■ g

14. 3,000 g = ■ kg

15. 1,000 mg = ■ g

16. 4,000 g = ■ kg

17. 7 g = ■ mg

Replace ● with <, >, or = to make a true statement. See Example 3 (p. 525)

18. 1.9 kg ● 1,900 g

19. 3,500 mg ● 0.35 g

20. 814 g ● 8.14 kg

21. 0.7 g ● 700 mg

22. 690 g ● 6,900 mg

23. 2.2 g ● 22,000 mg

For Exercises 24–26, use the table at the right.

24. Which macaw has a mass closest to 1 kilogram?

25. How many yellow-colored macaws would have a combined mass of 1 kilogram?

26. Is the combined mass of two red-footed macaws and three blue and gold macaws closer to 3 kilograms or 4 kilograms? Explain.

Macaws	
Species	**Mass (grams)**
Blue and Gold	800
Green-winged	900
Red-footed	525
Yellow-collared	250

27. One computer has a mass of 0.8 kilogram and another has a mass of 800 grams. Compare the masses of the computers.

H.O.T. Problems

28. OPEN ENDED Estimate how many paper clips have a mass of 10 grams. Then use a balance to check your estimate.

29. FIND THE ERROR Terrez and Ella are converting 3,000 grams to kilograms. Who is correct? Explain.

Ella
3,000 g ÷ 100 = 30 kg

Terrez
3,000 g ÷ 1,000 = 3 kg

30. WRITING IN ►MATH Explain which units of mass you would use to measure the following: a grain of salt, a bowl of cereal, a football player, and a tube of toothpaste.

12-4 Units of Capacity

GET READY to Learn

The pitcher of orange juice at the right holds 1 liter. This is a little more than a quart.

MAIN IDEA

I will convert metric units of capacity.

NYS Core Curriculum

Reinforcement of 4.M.7 Measure capacity, using milliliters and liters

5.M.5 Convert measurement within a given system

New Vocabulary

liter

milliliter

NY Math Online

macmillanmh.com
• Extra Examples
• Personal Tutor
• Self-Check Quiz

In the metric system, the common units of capacity are liter and milliliter.

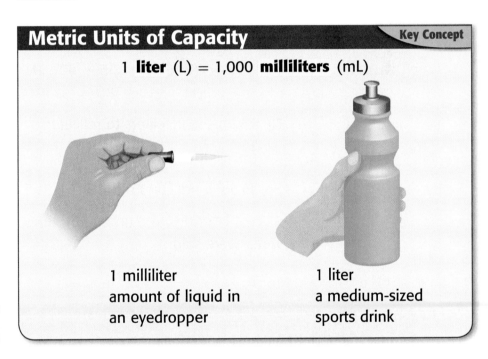

Metric Units of Capacity   Key Concept

1 **liter** (L) = 1,000 **milliliters** (mL)

1 milliliter
amount of liquid in
an eyedropper

1 liter
a medium-sized
sports drink

Convert units of capacity just as you convert units of length.

Real-World EXAMPLE   Convert Larger Units to Smaller Units

① **WATER** A faucet that is constantly dripping wastes about **90 liters of water every week. How many milliliters of water is this?**

90 L = ■ mL   A liter is larger than a milliliter, so multiply.

90 × 1,000 = 90,000   1 L = 1,000 mL, so multiply 90 by 1,000.

90 L = 90,000 mL   So, 90,000 milliliters of water are wasted.

Lesson 12-4 Units of Capacity   **527**

Remember

In everyday life, customary units of capacity such as gallons and pints are often compared to the metric units liters and milliliters.

2 JUICE **A container of orange juice holds 580 milliliters. How many liters is 580 milliliters?**

Estimate 580 mL < 1,000 mL, so the number of liters is less than 1.

580 mL = ■ L   580 mL is what part of 1,000 mL?

580 mL = $\frac{580}{1,000}$ L or 0.58 L   Write $\frac{580}{1,000}$ as a decimal.

So, 580 mL = 0.58 L.   0.58 liter is less than a whole liter.
                             So, the answer is reasonable.

3 ALGEBRA **The table shows the number of water bottles sold on a recent day. Were more than 100,000 milliliters sold?**

Bottle	Number Sold
1-liter	55
2-liter	30

First, find the total number of liters sold.

$(1 \times 55) + (2 \times 30) = 55 + 60$ Multiply.
$\qquad\qquad\qquad\qquad = 115$ L   Add.

Next, convert 115 liters to milliliters.

$115 \times 1,000 = 115,000$ 1 L = 1,000 mL, so multiply 115 by 1,000.

So, 115 L = 115,000 mL.

Since 115,000 > 100,000, more than 100,000 milliliters of water were sold.

 **What You Know**

Complete. See Examples 1, 2 (pp. 527–528)

1. 6 L = ■ mL

2. 7,000 mL = ■ L

3. 4 L = ■ mL

4. 325 mL = ■ L

5. 42 mL = ■ L

6. 1.5 L = ■ mL

Replace each ● with <, >, or = to make a true statement. See Example 3 (p. 528)

7. 1.7 L ● 1,000 mL

8. 390 mL ● 0.39 L

9. A detergent bottle holds 700 milliliters. Find the capacity in liters.

10. (Talk About It) Which unit would you use to measure the capacity of a glass of milk? Explain.

Complete. See Examples 1, 2 (pp. 527–528)

11. 70 L = ▓ mL

12. 4 L = ▓ mL

13. 3,000 mL = ▓ L

14. 230 mL = ▓ L

15. 6 L = ▓ mL

16. 10 mL = ▓ L

17. 5,000 mL = ▓ L

18. 0.5 L = ▓ mL

19. 1.5 L = ▓ mL

Replace each ● with <, >, or = to make a true statement. See Example 3 (p. 528)

20. 82.5 L ● 825 mL

21. 0.07 L ● 70 mL

22. 834 mL ● 8.34 L

23. To prepare for his camping trip, Emanuel filled his canteen with water. Is 15,000 milliliters or 1,500 milliliters a more reasonable estimate for the amount of water in the canteen? Explain.

24. One serving of punch is 250 milliliters. Will ten servings fit in a 2-liter bowl? Explain.

25. Yesterday, Audrey drank the liquids shown. How many liters of liquids did she drink in all?

26. The Nail Shop purchases nail polish in 13-milliliter bottles. Find the total capacity of 1,000 bottles in liters.

Liquid	Amount
Juice	210 mL
Milk	480 mL
Water	1.2 L

H.O.T. Problems

27. **OPEN ENDED** Name three things that have a capacity greater than 10 liters.

28. **FIND THE ERROR** Joseph and Kendra are converting 14 milliliters to liters. Who is correct? Explain.

Kendra
$14 \div 1,000 = \frac{14}{1,000}$
14 mL = 0.014 L

Joseph
$14 \times 1,000 = 1,400$
14 mL = 1,400 L

29. **WRITING IN ►MATH** Write a real-world problem that can be solved by converting milliliters to liters. Then solve.

30. How many milligrams are equivalent to 900 grams? (Lesson 12-3)

    A 0.9 mg

    B 9 mg

    C 90 mg

    D Not here

31. Claudio's fish tank has 3 liters of water in it. How many milliliters of water are in the fish tank? (Lesson 12-4)

    F 30 mL

    G 300 mL

    H 3,000 mL

    J 30,000 mL

Spiral Review

Complete. (Lessons 12-1 and 12-3)

32. 12 km = ▦ m

33. 400 cm = ▦ m

34. 8,000 cm = ▦ mm

35. 34 g = ▦ mg

36. 9 kg = ▦ g

37. 2,000 mg = ▦ g

38. Mara wants to put 90 CDs on the shelf shown below. Each CD is 1 centimeter wide. Is it reasonable for her to expect to fit all the CDs on the shelf? Explain. (Lesson 12-2)

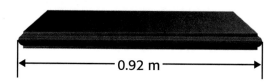

← 0.92 m →

Find each elapsed time. (Lesson 11-7)

39. 3:10 A.M. to 5:20 A.M.

40. 1:08 P.M. to 7:39 P.M.

41. 10:30 A.M. to 2:14 P.M.

Subtract. (Lessons 10-8 and 10-10)

42. $8\frac{5}{6} - 6\frac{2}{6}$

43. $10\frac{2}{5} - 3\frac{1}{5}$

44. $8\frac{3}{12} - 5\frac{1}{12}$

45. $3\frac{1}{4} - 1\frac{3}{4}$

46. $6\frac{1}{5} - 1\frac{3}{5}$

47. $7\frac{4}{8} - 4\frac{5}{8}$

48. The model represents 0.014. Write 0.014 as a fraction in simplest form. (Lesson 9-5)

49. Mrs. Rexroad's cell phone bill for one month was $48.70. The next month it was $56.04. Estimate the total cost of the two bills using compatible numbers. (Lesson 2-2)

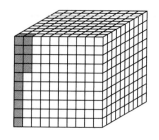

Metric Pairs!

Identifying Equivalent Metric Units

Get Ready!

Players: 2

Get Set!

Write each measure shown at the right on a separate index card.

Go!

- Shuffle the index cards.

- Place the cards facedown in five rows and four columns.

- The first player chooses two cards. If the measurements are equal, the player keeps the cards and chooses two more. If the measurements are not equal, the cards are placed back facedown.

- The next player takes a turn choosing two cards.

- The game continues until all of the cards have been paired up correctly.

- The player with more pairs wins.

You will need: 20 index cards

1 km	1,000 m
10 cm	100 mm
10 m	0.01 km
100 cm	1,000 mm
10 g	10,000 mg
10,000 g	10 kg
1,000 mg	1 g
1 L	1,000 mL
0.1 L	100 mL
10 mL	0.01 L

Choose an appropriate unit to measure each length. Write *millimeter*, *centimeter*, *meter*, or *kilometer*. (Lesson 12-1)

1. pencil

2. house

3. distance from Earth to the moon

4. Measure the length and width of the rectangle to the nearest millimeter.
(Lesson 12-1)

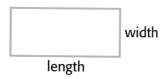

width

length

5. MULTIPLE CHOICE Choose the most reasonable measurement for the height of a classroom door. (Lesson 12-1)

A 20 cm

B 20 m

C 200 mm

D 200 cm

Complete. (Lesson 12-1)

6. 4 m = ■ cm

7. 750 mm = ■ cm

8. 1,000 m = ■ km

9. 63 cm = ■ mm

10. Which of the following is a reasonable estimate for the height of a fifth grade student: 75 cm, 125 cm, or 175 cm? Explain. (Lesson 12-2)

11. The table shows the average brain mass of a human and of an African elephant. How many grams greater is the mass of an African elephant brain than the mass of a human brain? (Lesson 12-3)

Brain	Average Mass (kg)
African elephant	5.4
Human	1.4

Complete. (Lesson 12-3)

12. 7 kg = ■ g

13. 10,000 g = ■ kg

14. 2,000 mg = ■ g

15. Tamara has a bag of dog food that weighs 4 kilograms. How many grams are in the bag? (Lesson 12-3)

16. MULTIPLE CHOICE Which unit is $\frac{1}{1,000}$ of a kilogram? (Lesson 12-3)

F milligram   **H** centigram

G gram   **J** Not Here

Complete. (Lesson 12-4)

17. 6 L = ■ mL

18. 280 mL = ■ L

19. 3,000 mL = ■ L

20. **WRITING IN ►MATH** Which metric unit would you use to measure the capacity of a bathtub? Explain. (Lesson 12-4)

GET READY to Learn

The top of an underwater mountain is about 2 kilometers above sea level. The base of the mountain is 6 kilometers below sea level. You can represent the distance *2 km above sea level* as +2 or 2, and the distance *6 km below sea level* as −6.

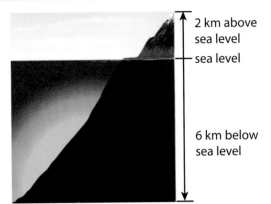

2 km above sea level
sea level

6 km below sea level

MAIN IDEA

I will use integers to represent real-life situations and graph them on a number line.

NYS Core Curriculum

Preparation for 6.N.14 Locate rational numbers on a number line (including positive and negative)

New Vocabulary

positive number
negative number
integer
negative integers
positive integers
opposite integers

NY Math Online

macmillanmh.com

• Extra Examples
• Personal Tutor
• Self-Check Quiz

The number 2 is a **positive number**, or a number greater than 0. The number −6 is a **negative number**, or a number less than 0. Negative and positive whole numbers and zero are called **integers**.

Negative integers are integers less than zero. They are written with a − sign.

Positive integers are integers greater than zero. They can be written with or without a + sign.

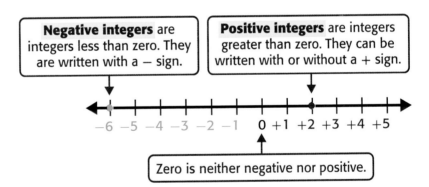

−6 −5 −4 −3 −2 −1 0 +1 +2 +3 +4 +5

Zero is neither negative nor positive.

Real-World EXAMPLE   Number Line

① **TEMPERATURE** Yesterday, the temperature was 4 degrees below zero. Today, it is 4 degrees above zero. Use integers to represent these situations. Then graph the integers on a number line.

4° below: −4   4° above: +4 or 4

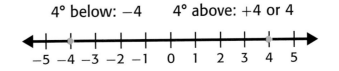

−5 −4 −3 −2 −1 0 1 2 3 4 5

Opposite integers are integers that are the same distance from 0 on the number line, but on opposite sides of 0. The integers −4 and 4 are opposite integers.

- The opposite of 4 is −4.
- The opposite of −4 is 4.

Real-World EXAMPLES Opposites

2 **TEMPERATURE** One winter day, the temperature in Rapid City, South Dakota, was 5° below zero. Write an integer to represent this situation. Then write its opposite.

5° below zero: −5
The opposite of −5 is +5 or 5.

So, −5 represents this situation. The integer +5 or 5 is its opposite.

3 **MONEY** Demont deposited $75 into his bank account. Write an integer to represent this situation. Then write its opposite.

deposited $75: +75 or 75

The opposite of 75 is −75. It represents withdrawing $75 from the account.

✓ CHECK What You Know

Write an integer to represent each situation. Then graph the integer on a number line. See Example 1 (p. 533)

1. lost $2

2. 20 degrees above 0

3. 5 points deducted from a grade

4. 6 yards gained in football

Write an integer to represent each situation. Then write its opposite. See Examples 2, 3 (p. 534)

5. Meagan spent $35.

6. Geraldo gained 9 yards on the play.

7. The temperature is 14° below zero.

8. Mai earned $28 babysitting.

9. Death Valley National Park in California is 282 feet below sea level. Write an integer to represent this situation.

10. Talk About It Explain how to find the opposite of an integer using a number line.

Write an integer to represent each situation. Then graph the integer on a number line. See Example 1 (pp. 533–534)

11. spent $3

12. profit of $8

13. 40° above zero

14. loss of 15 yards in football

15. 25 feet below sea level

16. 200 feet above ground

For Exercises 17–22, write an integer to represent each situation. Then write its opposite. See Examples 2, 3 (p. 534)

17. Sandi had to backtrack 32 meters.

18. The lake was 42 feet deep.

19. The temperature was 11° below zero.

20. The cliff was 140 feet above sea level.

21. A Ferris wheel goes up 212 feet.

22. The elevation of Daytona Beach is 7 feet above sea level.

Real-World PROBLEM SOLVING

Science The table shows the deepest dives of birds.

23. Represent the dive of each bird using an integer.

24. Which bird is able to dive deeper? Explain how you know.

Bird	Deepest Dive (m)
Flying: thick-billed murre	210
Non-flying: Emperor penguin	534

H.O.T. Problems

25. **OPEN ENDED** Write an integer to represent an outside temperature today. Then write the opposite.

26. **WHICH ONE DOESN'T BELONG?** Identify the situation that does not belong with the other three. Explain your reasoning.

17 feet below sea level	17 degrees	spending $17.00	17 points subtracted from a perfect score

27. **WRITING IN ►MATH** Write about a real-world situation that can be described using the integers −18 and 10.

Mrs. Rodriguez did a science experiment for her class that measured how fast a cup of hot water cooled. She measured its temperature every two minutes. The line graph shows her data.

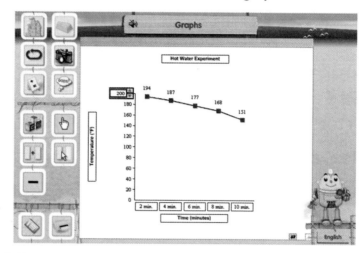

In the following Activity, you will make a similar line graph.

MAIN IDEA

I will use technology to make and explain line graphs.

NYS Core Curriculum

5.R.1 Use physical objects, drawings, charts, tables, **graphs,** symbols, equations, **or objects created using technology as representations**

5.S.2 Display data in a line graph to show an increase or decrease over time

ACTIVITY **Graphing Temperature Change**

① **Step 1** Pour 1 cup of cold water into a glass.

Step 2 Measure the temperature of the water every two minutes for ten minutes.

Step 3 Use the Graph feature from the Math Tool Chest™ to make a line graph of the data.

Think About It

1. Compare and contrast your graph with the graph above.

2. After 10 minutes, what was the change in temperature of your water?

3. Predict what the temperature will be if 5 more minutes pass.

4. Room temperature is about 65°F. Predict how long it will be until the temperature of the water reaches room temperature. Check your prediction by continuing to measure the temperature of the water every five minutes.

Units of Temperature

MAIN IDEA

I will choose appropriate temperatures in degrees Fahrenheit and Celsius.

NYS Core Curriculum

5.M.5 Convert measurement within a given system
Also addresses 5.S.1

New Vocabulary

degrees
Celsius (°C)
Fahrenheit (°F)

NY Math Online

macmillanmh.com
• Extra Examples
• Personal Tutor
• Self-Check Quiz

> **GET READY to Learn**

Animals that are cold-blooded take on the temperature of their surroundings. So, if the outside temperature is 70°F, the body temperature of a snake will also be 70°F.

Degrees are the units of measurement used to describe temperature. Temperature can be measured in degrees **Celsius (°C)** and in degrees **Fahrenheit (°F)**.

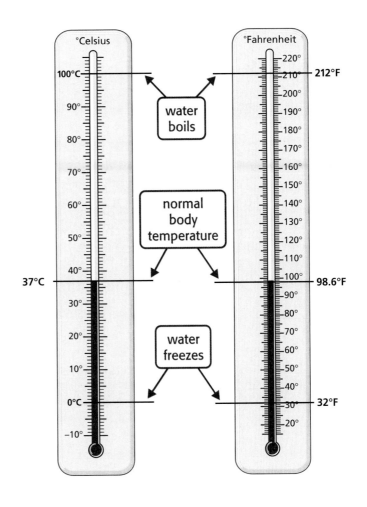

°Celsius   °Fahrenheit

100°C — — 212°F

water boils

37°C — — 98.6°F

normal body temperature

water freezes

0°C — — 32°F

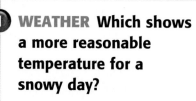

Choose Reasonable Temperatures

1 **WEATHER** Which shows a more reasonable temperature for a snowy day?

The freezing point of water is 32°F. 20°F is below the freezing point of water. 40°F is too warm for snow. So, the more reasonable temperature is 20°F.

2 **Which is a more reasonable temperature for warm water: 23°C or 43°C? Use the thermometers on page 537 to help you decide.**

23°C is cooler than body temperature. Water that is 23°C would feel cool to the touch. So, the more reasonable estimate is 43°C.

You can find changes in temperature by using subtraction.

EXAMPLE Subtract Temperature

3 **TEMPERATURE** The temperature this afternoon was 48°F. By evening, the temperature was 30°F. Find the change in temperature. Use an integer to represent the change.

change in temperature

= higher temperature − lower temperature

= 48° − 30°   Substitute the temperatures.

= 18°   Subtract.

The temperature decreased 18 degrees.

The change can be represented by the integer −18.

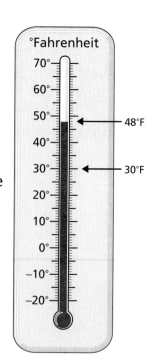

Choose the more reasonable temperature for each situation. Use the thermometers on page 537. See Examples 1, 2 (p. 538)

1. a cold day: 5°C or 32°C

2. hot water: 65°F or 190°F

3. a snow cone: 30°C or 30°F

4. warm bowl of soup: 82°C or 82°F

5. The thermometer at the right shows the temperature outside. Could it snow today? Explain.

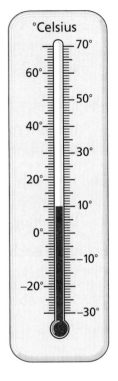

Find each change in temperature. Use an integer to represent the change. See Example 3 (p. 538)

6. 0°C to 12°C

7. 65°F to 59°F

8. Yesterday, the temperature of the water in a swimming pool was 82°F. Today, the temperature of the water is 78°F. Describe the change in temperature with an integer.

9. **Talk About It** Describe how you can estimate the temperature in degrees Celsius when you know the temperature in degrees Fahrenheit. Give an example.

Practice and Problem Solving

NYSCC • NYSMT

Extra Practice, p. R33

Choose the more reasonable temperature for each situation. Use the thermometers on page 537. See Examples 1, 2 (p. 538)

10. person with a fever: 38°C or 98°C

11. glass of lemonade: 46°F or 10°F

12. bicycling: 130°F or 75°F

13. swimming: 30°C or 10°C

14. a summer day: 82°C or 82°F

15. boiling water: 100°F or 100°C

16. frozen yogurt: 20°F or 20°C

17. melting ice: 1°C or 1°F

Find each change in temperature. Use an integer to represent the change. See Example 3 (p. 538)

18. 55°F to 65°F

19. 16°C to 0°C

20. 36°C to 12°C

21. 8°C to 11°C

22. 94°F to 61°F

23. 49°F to 77°F

For Exercises 24–26, use the table at the right. It shows the high and low temperatures for several cities for a certain day in January.

City	High Temperature (°F)	Low Temperature (°F)
Boston	37	22
Detroit	31	18
Omaha	32	12
Pittsburgh	35	20
Seattle	43	36

24. Which city had the greatest temperature change? What was the temperature change?

25. Which city had the least temperature change? What was the temperature change?

26. On the same day, Denver's high temperature was 43°F and low temperature was 15°F. Does this change your answer to Exercise 24 or 25? If so, how?

27. Normal body temperature for a human is 98.6°F. Lilly's little brother had a temperature of 101.3°F. How much greater is his temperature than normal body temperature?

28. The body temperature of a snake is the same as its environment. Suppose it was 25°C outside, and the temperature is now 21.5°C. How much did the snake's body temperature decrease?

Estimate each temperature in degrees Celsius or degrees Fahrenheit. Use the thermometers on page 537.

29. 1°C is about ▒ °F

30. 212°F is about ▒ °C

31. 68°F is about ▒ °C

32. 30°F is about ▒ °C

33. 15°C is about ▒ °F

34. 44°F is about ▒ °C

35. The preferred temperature for the inside of a refrigerator is about 35°F. Estimate this temperature in degrees Celsius.

36. If you wanted to go to a water park, describe a good outside temperature in degrees Celsius.

New York Data File

In Albany, New York, it is not uncommon for summer day temperatures to reach 90°F. The average temperature in July is 72°F.

Estimate each temperature in degrees Celsius.

37. 72°F

38. 90°F

Use an integer to represent each change in temperature.

39. 72°F to 90°F

40. 87°F to 71°F

H.O.T. Problems

41. OPEN ENDED Describe two real-world situations in which the temperatures 21°C and 210°F would be appropriate.

42. CHALLENGE Cora was in a place where the temperature was about 10°C. When she walked to a different place, the temperature was about 26°C. Describe a situation in which these temperatures are reasonable.

43. **WRITING IN ►MATH** Write a problem that requires you to find the change in temperature. Then exchange problems with a classmate and solve.

NYSMT Practice ⟩ 6.N.14, 5.M.5

44. Which situation is best represented by the integer graphed below?
(Lesson 12-5)

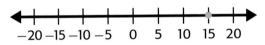

A 15° below zero

B giving away $15

C 15 feet above sea level

D 15 meters deep

45. The temperature at 10:15 A.M. in Chicago was 57°F. By 3:45 P.M., the temperature was 78°F. How many degrees Fahrenheit did the temperature rise? (Lesson 12-6)

F 5°F

G 21°F

H 23°F

J 30°F

Spiral Review

Write an integer to represent each situation. Then write its opposite. (Lesson 12-5)

46. An altitude is 139 feet below sea level.

47. A baby gained 12 ounces.

48. The temperature is 58° above zero.

49. Hai spent $4.

Complete. (Lesson 12-4)

50. 2 L = ▇ mL

51. 5,000 mL = ▇ L

52. 750 mL = ▇ L

53. One can of soup is 12 fluid ounces and makes two servings. If 8 fluid ounces of water are added, what is the capacity of one serving? (Lesson 11-4)

The *Wright* Measurements

The Wright brothers were self-trained engineers from Ohio who designed, built, and piloted the first engine-powered airplane. On December 17, 1903, the Wright brothers completed the world's first successful controlled flight. They later named the flyer the *Kitty Hawk*, after the location in North Carolina near where they made this historic flight.

The temperature at Kitty Hawk on this day was 34°F, but because of the wind chill factor, the temperature felt like 8°F. These might not have been the most comfortable weather conditions, but the winds definitely helped the Wright Brothers' flyer to stay in the air!

On that cold December day, the Wright brothers made four flights in their flyer. On the first flight, which was piloted by Orville Wright, the flyer traveled 39 meters in 12 seconds. On the fourth flight, Wilbur flew 279 meters in 59 seconds.

Wright Brothers' 1903 Flyer Data	
Wingspan	12.3 m
Length	6.4 m
Height	2.8 m
Wing Droop	25.4 cm
Mass	229 kg
Speed	17 km/h

Did You Know?

Before their experiments with airplanes, the Wright brothers were successful bicycle manufacturers.

Orville and Wilbur Wright

 # Real-World Math

Use the information and the table on page 542 to solve each problem.

1 What was the wingspan of the *Kitty Hawk* flyer in centimeters?

2 What was the mass of the flyer in grams?

3 What was the wing droop of the flyer in millimeters?

4 What was the air speed of the flyer in meters per hour?

5 How many more meters did Wilbur fly on the fourth flight than Orville flew on the first flight?

6 What was the difference between the wingspan and the length of the flyer?

7 If Orville Wright's mass was 81 kilograms at the time of the flight, what was the combined mass of the flyer and Orville Wright?

Problem-Solving Investigation

<u>**MAIN IDEA**</u> I will choose the best strategy to solve a problem.

5.PS.2 Understand that some ways of representing a problem are more efficient than others
5.PS.3 Interpret information correctly, identify the problem, and generate possible strategies and solutions

P.S.I. TEAM +

ARIANA: I checked the temperature this morning, and according to the thermometer, it was −3°F. This afternoon, the temperature was 7°F. I know it got warmer outside, but by how much?

YOUR MISSION: Find the change in temperature.

Understand	The morning temperature was −3°F. The afternoon temperature was 7°F. You need to find how many degrees the temperature increased.
Plan	You can use a model such as a number line to find the change in temperature. Graph the morning and afternoon temperatures on the number line and find the distance between them.
Solve	Draw a number line that includes −3 and 7. morning afternoon −4 −3 −2 −1 0 1 2 3 4 5 6 7 8 10 Since the distance between −3 and 7 is 10, the temperature rose 10° from the morning to the afternoon.
Check	The increase in temperature from −3°F to 0°F is 3 degrees. The increase in temperature from 0°F to 7°F is 7 degrees. Since 3 + 7 = 10, the answer is reasonable.

Use any strategy shown below to solve each problem.

PROBLEM-SOLVING STRATEGIES
- Work backward.
- Look for a pattern.
- Use a model.
- Solve a simpler problem.

1. **Measurement** Charlene is putting up a border along both sides of a path. Between each stake, she will use 0.61 meter of rope. She will need 48 stakes for each side of the path. There is a stake at the beginning and at the end of the path. Which is the best estimate for the number of centimeters of rope she will need; 280 cm, 2,800 cm, or 28,000 cm? Explain.

2. Gabriella is cutting out stars. First she cuts a 5-centimeter star. Then she cuts a 4.5-centimeter star, followed by a 4-centimeter star. The last star she cuts is a 2-centimeter star. If she followed the pattern, how many stars did she make?

3. Two students make 14 party bags in 20 minutes. How many party bags can 4 students make at the same rate in 40 minutes?

4. **Measurement** It takes Jasmine 40 minutes to paint a bookshelf with one coat of paint. After each coat, she waits 50 minutes for the paint to dry. How long will it take Jasmine to apply three coats of paint to the bookshelf?

5. The greatest temperature change on Earth in a 24-hour period was in Loma, Montana, on January 15, 1972. The temperature rose from −54°F to 49°F. How much did the temperature increase?

6. Brady planted vegetables in his garden. The table shows the height of a plant during a 2-week period. If the plant grows at the same rate, estimate its height on June 15th.

Vegetable Heights	
Date	**Height (cm)**
May 18	48.5
May 25	54.9
June 1	61.3

7. **Algebra** Describe the pattern below. Then find the next three numbers in the pattern.

2, 4, 7, 11, 16, 22, ■, ■, ■ . . .

8. **Algebra** A number is divided by 3. Next, the quotient is multiplied by 5. Then 5 is added to the product. If the result is 25, what is the number?

9. **WRITING IN ►MATH** The temperature in Calgary rose from −17°C to 13°C in four hours on January 11, 1983. Explain how to use a number line to find the change in temperature.

FOLDABLES Study Organizer **GET READY** to Study

Be sure the following Big Ideas are written in your Foldable.

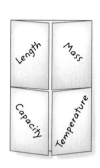

Key Concepts

Metric Units of Length (p. 517)

• 1 centimeter (cm) = 10 millimeters (mm)

• 1 meter (m) = 100 cm or 1,000 mm

• 1 kilometer (km) = 1,000 m

Metric Units of Mass (p. 524)

• 1 gram (g) = 1,000 milligrams (mg)

• 1 kilogram (kg) = 1,000 g

Metric Units of Capacity (p. 527)

• 1 liter (L) = 1,000 mL

Integers (p. 533)

• **Negative numbers** are less than 0.

• **Positive numbers** are greater than 0.

• **Integers** are negative and positive whole numbers and zero.

Units of Temperature (p. 537)

• Temperature can be measured in degrees **Fahrenheit** (°F) or degrees **Celsius** (°C).

Key Vocabulary

integer (p. 533)

mass (p. 524)

metric system (p. 517)

negative number (p. 533)

positive number (p. 533)

Vocabulary Check

Choose the correct word or number that completes each sentence.

1. One (liter, kiloliter) equals 1,000 milliliters.

2. A (centimeter, kilometer) is one hundredth of a meter.

3. One thousand grams equals 1 (milligram, kilogram).

4. Gram is a metric measure of (mass, length).

5. Temperature is measured in (grams, degrees).

6. A good outside temperature for water sports is 30 degrees (Celsius, Fahrenheit).

7. A reasonable estimate for the capacity of a soup can is (360, 36) milliliters.

8. To change meters to millimeters, multiply by (1,000, 100).

Lesson-by-Lesson Review

12-1 Units of Length (pp. 517–521)

5.M.4

Example 1
Complete: 7 m = ▨ cm.

$7 \times 100 = 700$ 1 m = 100 cm

So, 7 meters = 700 centimeters.

Example 2
Complete: 6,000 m = ▨ km.

$6,000 \div 1,000 = 6$ 1,000 m = 1 km

So, 6,000 meters = 6 kilometers.

Complete.

9. 4,000 m = ▨ km

10. 5 m = ▨ mm

11. 30 mm = ▨ cm

12. 12 cm = ▨ mm

13. A giant squid that was found in the 1800s had a body 6 meters long and a tentacle 11 meters long. How many centimeters longer was the tentacle than the body?

12-2 Problem-Solving Skill: Determine Reasonable Answers
(pp. 522–523)

5.PS.22

Example 3
A marathon race is about 42 kilometers long. The length of the average person's stride is 1 meter. Is it reasonable to say that a person takes about 4,200 strides in a marathon race?

$42 \times 1,000 = 42,000$ 1 km = 1,000 m

A marathon is about 42,000 meters long.

Since a person runs about 1 meter for each stride, the average person takes about 42,000 strides in a marathon race. So, 4,200 strides is not a reasonable estimate.

Solve. Determine reasonable answers.

14. A cube of small self-stick notes is 5.2 centimeters long. Will it fit in a square container that is 50 millimeters long? Explain.

15. A doorway is 0.95 meter wide, and a desk is 120 centimeters wide. Will the desk fit through the doorway without having to tilt it? Explain.

16. Leroy estimates that his kite flew 2,000 centimeters high. Does this seem reasonable? Explain.

12-3 **Units of Mass** (pp. 524–526)

5.M.5

Example 4

A bag of flour has a mass of 2,000 grams. What is the mass of the bag of flour in kilograms?

To convert a smaller unit to a larger unit, divide.

$2,000 \div 1,000 = 2$ $1,000 \text{ g} = 1 \text{ kg}$

So, 2,000 grams equals 2 kilograms.

The mass of the bag of flour is 2 kg.

Complete.

17. 8 kg = ■ g

18. 24,000 g = ■ kg

19. 9 g = ■ mg

20. 165 mg = ■ g

21. 75 kg = ■ g

22. Mrs. Mathews bought the cheese shown in the table. How many grams of cheese did she buy altogether?

Cheese	Amount
American	8,000 mg
Swiss	7,000 mg

12-4 **Units of Capacity** (pp. 527–530)

5.M.5

Example 5

Mr. Rueben bought 15 liters of orange juice for a class party. How many milliliters of orange juice did he buy?

To convert a larger unit to a smaller unit, multiply.

$15 \times 1,000 = 15,000$ $1 \text{ L} = 1,000 \text{ mL}$

15 liters = 15,000 milliliters

So, Mr. Rueben bought 15,000 milliliters of orange juice.

Complete.

23. 3 L = ■ mL

24. 6,000 mL = ■ L

25. 4,000 mL = ■ L

26. 250 mL = ■ L

27. 1 L = ■ mL

28. A 2-liter bottle of fruit juice is used to fill 3 glasses. Each glass holds 300 milliliters. How many milliliters are left in the bottle?

12-5 Integers and Graphing on Number Lines (pp. 533–535)

6.N.14

Example 6
A swimmer dove 6 feet below the surface of the water. Write an integer to represent this situation. Then graph the integer on a number line.

6 feet below: −6

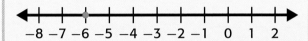

$$-8 \quad -7 \quad -6 \quad -5 \quad -4 \quad -3 \quad -2 \quad -1 \quad 0 \quad 1 \quad 2$$

Example 7
A plant grew to a height of 8 inches. Write an integer to represent this situation. Then write its opposite.

grew 8 inches: +8 or 8

The opposite of 8 is −8.

Write an integer to represent each situation. Then graph the integer on a number line.

29. a golf score of 3 under par

30. stock value up $1

Write an integer to represent each situation. Then write its opposite.

31. gaining 12 points

32. 10 miles below the surface

33. An airport control tower is 18 meters above the ground. The subway is 6 meters below the ground. Write two integers to represent these situations.

12-6 Units of Temperature (pp. 537–541)

5.M.5

Example 8
Which is the more reasonable temperature for a chilly room: 60°C or 60°F?

• 60°C is warmer than body temperature.

• 60°F is cooler than body temperature.

The more reasonable temperature is 60°F.

Example 9
The temperature changed from 77°F to 70°F in one day. Use an integer to represent the change in temperature.

77° − 70° = 7°   decrease in temperature

The change in temperature is −7.

Choose the more reasonable temperature for each situation.

34. hot sandwich: 40°F or 160°F

35. inside a refrigerator: 5°C or 50°C

Find each change in temperature. Use an integer to represent the change.

36. 29°C to 31°C   **37.** 14°F to 0°F

38. The temperature at 6:30 P.M. was 43°F. By 10:00 P.M. it was 28°F. Find the change in temperature. Use an integer to represent the change.

CHAPTER 12 — Study Guide and Review

12-7 Problem-Solving Investigation: Choose a Strategy (pp. 544–545)

5.PS.2

Example 10

Selena has $80. She wants to buy 2 shirts, a pair of jeans, and a belt. The belt costs $8. Each shirt costs twice this amount. Together, both shirts cost $10 less than the jeans. Does Selena have enough money to buy all the items?

To solve the problem, you can use the *work backward* strategy.

One shirt costs twice what the belt costs. So, multiply the cost of the belt by 2.

$8 × 2 = $16

Since she bought 2 shirts, multiply the cost of one shirt by 2.

2 × $16 or $32

The cost of the jeans is $10 more than the cost of both shirts. So, add 10 to the cost of the 2 shirts.

$32 + $10 = $42

Next, find the total cost of all the items.

belt + 2 shirts + jeans = total cost

$8 + $32 + $42 = $82

Since $82 > $80, Selena does not have enough money to buy all the items.

Use any strategy to solve each problem.

39. Dominique made party invitations on her computer. She gave out half of the invitations, while her friend gave out 11. There are 5 more invitations that need to be delivered. How many invitations did Dominique make?

40. An antique desk is 1.5 meters wide. Will it fit in a space that is 2,000 centimeters wide? Explain.

41. **Algebra** Describe the change in temperature from 1:00 to 3:00.

Time	Temperature (°F)
1:00 P.M.	59
3:00 P.M.	65

42. On Day 1, Troy swam 350 meters. On Day 2, he swam 500 meters, and on Day 3 he swam 650 meters. If he continues this pattern, how many meters will he have swum in 5 days?

43. Andrew and 2 friends can blow up 15 balloons in 10 minutes. How many balloons can Andrew and 5 friends blow up at the same rate in 20 minutes?

Complete.

1. 150 mm = ▨ cm 2. 4 km = ▨ m

3. 3,000 m = ▨ km 4. 8 m = ▨ cm

5. **MULTIPLE CHOICE** Lance needs to draw line segment *PL* to complete the figure. Use a metric ruler to measure the distance from point *P* to point *L*.

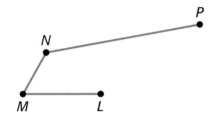

To the nearest centimeter, what is the length of line segment *PL*?

A 2 cm   C 4 cm

B 3 cm   D 5 cm

6. Is 20 kilometers a reasonable estimate for the length of an Olympic-sized swimming pool? Explain.

Complete.

7. 21,000 g = ▨ kg 8. 390 mg = ▨ g

9. 4,000 mL = ▨ L 10. 74 L = ▨ mL

11. A loaf of bread has 20 slices. Each slice has a mass of 24 grams. Find the mass of the loaf in kilograms.

12. A nickel has a mass of 5 grams. Find the total mass of the roll of nickels shown in grams.

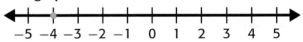
$2.00

Find each change in temperature. Use an integer to represent the change.

13. 20°C to 11°C   14. 43°F to 58°F

15. 35°C to 48°C   16. 92°F to 74°F

17. **MULTIPLE CHOICE** Which is the best estimate for the capacity of a trash can?

F 2 mL   H 2 L

G 20 mL   J 20 L

Write an integer to represent each situation. Then write its opposite.

18. 11° below zero

19. a hole 3 feet deep

20. 5 points added to a grade

21. **Algebra** Write a real-world situation that can be represented by the integer graphed.

$$\overset{\textstyle\longleftrightarrow}{\underset{\substack{-5\ -4\ -3\ -2\ -1\ \ \ 0\ \ \ 1\ \ \ 2\ \ \ 3\ \ \ 4\ \ \ 5}}{\rule{0pt}{0pt}}}$$

Choose the more reasonable temperature for each situation.

22. hot tea: 300°F or 200°F

23. cold water: 5°C or 25°C

24. Jayden has a tropical fish tank. Is 40° Fahrenheit or 75° Fahrenheit a more reasonable temperature for the water in the tank? Explain.

25. **WRITING IN ►MATH** Explain how you can use integers to represent changes in temperature.

PART 1 Multiple Choice

Read each question. Then fill in the correct answer on the answer sheet provided by your teacher or on a sheet of paper.

1. A bag of dog food has a mass of 96 kilograms. The food is divided equally into 2 containers. How many grams of dog food are in each container?

   A 48,000 grams   C 480 grams

   B 4,800 grams   D Not Here

2. Xavier used the lemon juice shown to make lemonade. What fraction of a liter did he use?

   F $\frac{1}{4}$ H $\frac{1}{12}$

   G $\frac{1}{8}$ J $\frac{1}{16}$

3. Eduardo says that the next term in the sequence below is 35. Which shows that his solution is not reasonable?

   55, 47, 39, 31, …

   A The terms are increasing.

   B The terms are decreasing.

   C The terms are multiples of 5.

   D The terms are odd numbers.

4. An advertisement is shown below. Which word problem matches this advertisement?

   F The regular price is $25. The television is on sale for 24.5% off. What is the sale price?

   G The regular price is $245. The television is on sale for 25% off. What is the sale price?

   H The sale price is $245 at 25% off. What is the regular price of a television?

   J The regular price is $245. If you buy two televisions, the second one is priced at 25% off the regular price. What is the total cost of two televisions?

5. Dion and his brother bought a bag of roasted nuts at the fair. If they ate $\frac{5}{6}$ of the roasted nuts, what fraction of the nuts remained?

   A $\frac{1}{2}$ C $\frac{1}{5}$

   B $\frac{1}{4}$ D $\frac{1}{6}$

6. Hunter has four old stamps. Stamp A is worth $3. Stamp B is worth 4 times the value of stamp A. Stamp C is worth 5 times the value of Stamp A. The stamps are worth $45 altogether. What is the value of stamp D?

F $12   **H** $18

G $15   **J** $27

7. What fraction of their games did the soccer team win?

Soccer Team's Games	
Played	**Won**
20	15

A $\frac{1}{5}$ **C** $\frac{3}{4}$

B $\frac{1}{4}$ **D** $\frac{4}{5}$

8. Larry ran a 5-kilometer race. When he was halfway to the finish line, how many meters did he have left to run?

F 5,000 meters

G 2,500 meters

H 500 meters

J 250 meters

PART 2   Short Response

Record your answers on the answer sheet provided by your teacher or on a sheet of paper.

9. The table shows the number of cars washed during the 3 days of a fundraiser car wash. Estimate how many cars were washed in all. Is your estimate greater or less than the exact number?

Day	Cars Washed
Friday	62
Saturday	83
Sunday	78

PART 3   Extended Response

Record your answers on the answer sheet provided by your teacher or on a sheet of paper.

10. Write an example where the temperature drops 10°F and an example where the temperature rises 10°F.

---

11. A fence is placed around a playground in the shape of a rectangle. The length of the fence is 32 meters. The width of the fence is 1,200 centimeters. How much fence is needed for the playground? Explain.

NEED EXTRA HELP?											
If You Missed Question...	1	2	3	4	5	6	7	8	9	10	11
Go to Lesson...	12–3	12–4	6–6	5–3	10–4	6–2	9–3	12–1	2–4	12–6	12–1
NYS Core Curriculum	5.M.5	5.M.5	5.A.4	5.A.2	5.M.5	5.A.4	5.N.4	5.M.4	4.N.14	5.M.5	5.M.4

CHAPTER 13
Identify, Compare, and Classify Geometric Figures

BIG Idea What is geometry?

Geometry is the study of lines and shapes.

Example Every year, a sandcastle building competition is held along the Outer Banks of North Carolina. Sandcastles are composed of many geometric figures. Geometric figures include triangles, squares, and rectangles.

What will I learn in this chapter?

- Identify and label basic geometric terms.
- Identify characteristics of triangles and quadrilaterals.
- Sketch translations, rotations, and reflections on a coordinate grid.
- Identify transformations.
- Solve problems by using *logical reasoning*.

Key Vocabulary

parallel lines

perpendicular lines

translation

reflection

rotation

 **NY Math Online** — **Student Study Tools**
at macmillanmh.com

FOLDABLES
Study Organizer

Make this Foldable to help you organize information about geometric figures. Begin with a sheet of $8\frac{1}{2}'' \times 11''$ paper.

1 **Fold** lengthwise to the holes.

2 **Cut** along the top line. Then make equal cuts to form 10 tabs.

3 **Label** each tab as shown.

You have two ways to check prerequisite skills for this chapter.

Option 2

NY Math Online ⟩ Take the Chapter Readiness Quiz at macmillanmh.com.

Option 1

Complete the Quick Check below.

QUICK Check

Describe the number of sides and the number of angles in each figure. (Prior Grade)

1.

2.

3.

Use the figure below for Exercises 4 and 5. (Prior Grade)

4. Which side appears to have the same length as side *AB*?

5. At which point do sides *BC* and *DC* meet?

6. Anthony is drawing a triangle that has two sides that are equal. Draw a sketch of this triangle.

Graph each point on a coordinate grid. (Lesson 6-5)

7. *J*(1, 7)

8. *K*(6, 0)

9. *L*(5, 6)

10. *M*(3, 3)

Geometry Vocabulary

MAIN IDEA

I will identify and label basic geometric terms.

 NYS Core Curriculum

Reinforcement of 4.G.2 Identify points and line segments when drawing a plane figure

5.G.11 Identify and draw lines of symmetry of basic geometric shapes *Also addresses 5.CM.9, 5.CM.10, 5.CM.11.*

New Vocabulary

point
line
ray
line segment
plane
intersecting lines
perpendicular lines
parallel lines
congruent line segments

NY Math Online

macmillanmh.com
• Extra Examples
• Personal Tutor
• Self-Check Quiz

GET READY to Learn

The butterfly kite at the right is made up of different geometric figures. Can you identify a point and a line segment on the kite?

The table shows basic geometric figures.

Geometric Figures	Key Concepts
Definition	**Model**
A **point** is an exact location in space, represented by a dot.	• A **Words** point A
A **line** is a set of points that form a straight path that goes in opposite directions without ending.	C D **Words** line CD or line DC **Symbols** $\overleftrightarrow{CD}$ or $\overleftrightarrow{DC}$
A **ray** is a line that has an endpoint and goes on forever in one direction.	S T **Words** ray ST **Symbols** $\overrightarrow{ST}$
A **line segment** is part of a line between two endpoints.	G H **Words** line segment GH or line segment HG **Symbols** $\overline{GH}$ or $\overline{HG}$
A **plane** is a flat surface that goes on forever in all directions.	M O N **Words** plane MNO

EXAMPLE   Identify a Figure

1 **Identify the figure at the right. Then name it using symbols.**

The figure has one endpoint. The arrow indicates that it goes on forever in one direction. So, it is a ray.

symbol: $\overrightarrow{JK}$

K

J

Remember

The endpoint is named first in a ray. The ray in Example 1 cannot be named $\overrightarrow{KJ}$.

Two lines in a plane can be related in three ways. They can be intersecting, perpendicular, or parallel.

Pairs of Lines	Key Concepts
Definition	**Model**
Intersecting lines are lines that meet or cross at a point.	
Perpendicular lines are lines that meet or cross each other to make a square corner.	
Parallel lines are lines that are the same distance apart and do not intersect.	

Vocabulary Link

Perpendicular
Everyday Use vertical or meeting at a corner

EXAMPLE   Describe a Pair of Lines

2 **Describe the lines at the right as** *intersecting, perpendicular,* **or** *parallel.* **Choose the most specific term.**

The lines cross at one point, so they are intersecting. Since they do not form a square corner, they are not perpendicular lines.

Congruent Segments

Line segments that have the same length are called **congruent line segments**.

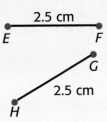
2.5 cm
E · F
G
2.5 cm
H

Words $\overline{EF}$ is congruent to $\overline{HG}$.

Symbols $\overline{EF} \cong \overline{HG}$

EXAMPLE Identify Congruent Line Segments

3 **MEASUREMENT** Determine whether the line segments at the right are congruent.

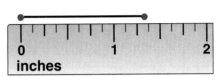

The segments do not have the same length. So, they are not congruent.

CHECK What You Know

Identify each figure. Then name it using symbols. See Example 1 (p. 558)

1.
W   X

2. R
Q

3. • T

Describe each pair of lines as *intersecting, perpendicular,* or *parallel*. Choose the most specific term. See Example 2 (p. 558)

4.

5.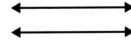

Measure each segment. Then determine whether each pair of line segments are congruent. Write *yes* or *no*. See Example 3 (p. 559)

6.

7.

8. What type of lines are the double yellow lines on the road at the right? Explain.

9. **Talk About It** Describe the difference between a ray and a line.

Identify each figure. Then name it using symbols. See Example 1 (p. 558)

10. E ———— F

11.

12.

13. •P

14.

15.

Describe each pair of lines as *intersecting,* *perpendicular,* **or** *parallel.*
Choose the most specific term. See Example 2 (p. 558)

16.

17.

18.

**Measure each line segment. Then determine whether each pair of
line segments are congruent. Write** *yes* **or** *no.* See Example 3 (p. 559)

19.

20.

21.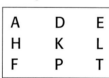

22. Name the letters shown at the right that appear to contain
parallel line segments.

A	D	E
H	K	L
F	P	T

23. Describe an object in your room that contains parallel lines.
Then describe an object that contains lines that are perpendicular.

24. In gymnastics, the floor exercises are done on a mat that is 40 feet
long and 40 feet wide. Is the mat an example of a point, a line, a
line segment, or part of a plane? Explain.

H.O.T. Problems

25. **OPEN ENDED** Name three objects in your classroom that are a part
of a plane.

26. **CHALLENGE** Are the lines at the right *intersecting,* *parallel,* or
neither? Explain your reasoning.

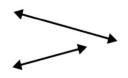

27. **WRITING IN ►MATH** Compare perpendicular lines and
parallel lines.

Geometry Concentration

Identifying Geometry Attributes

Get Ready!

Players: 2 or more

You will need: 20 index cards

Get Set!

Make ten index cards like the ones shown at the right. Then make two sets of each of the following symbols:

P, $\overrightarrow{PR}$, $\overleftrightarrow{PR}$, $\overline{PR}$, plane MNO

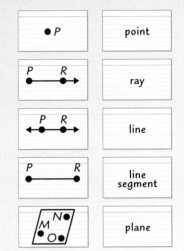

Go!

- Shuffle all the index cards.

- Place the cards facedown.

- Player 1 turns over two cards. The player tries to match a geometric symbol with the correct term or drawing for the symbol.

- If the cards match, Player 1 keeps the cards and turns over two more. If no match is made, turn the cards facedown again.

- Player 2 then takes a turn choosing two cards.

- The game continues until all of the cards have been paired up.

- The player with the most pairs wins.

Problem-Solving Strategy

MAIN IDEA I will solve problems by using logical reasoning.

 **5.PS.9 Understand the basic language of logic in mathematical situations**
Also addresses 5.RP.8, 5.CN.1.

Maggie, Sam, Aisha, and Nicolás each have a different colored notebook:
blue, red, purple, and green. Use the clues to determine which person
has each notebook.

1. Sam and the girl with the green notebook
   are in the same class.

2. A girl has the purple notebook.

3. Nicolás and the person with the red
   notebook eat lunch together.

4. Maggie is not in the same class as Sam.

Understand	**What facts do you know?**
	• The four clues that are listed above.
	What do you need to find?
	• Which person has each notebook.

Plan	You can use logical reasoning to find which person has each notebook. Make a table to help organize the information.

Solve	Place an "X" in each box that cannot be true.

	Blue	Red	Purple	Green
Maggie	X	X	yes	X
Sam	X	yes	X	X
Aisha	X	X	X	yes
Nicolás	yes	X	X	X

• Clue 3 shows that Nicolás does not have the red notebook.

• Clues 1 and 2 show that girls have the green and purple notebooks and the boys have the blue and red notebooks.

• Clue 4 shows that Maggie is not in the same class as Sam, so she does not have the green notebook.

So, Maggie has a purple notebook, Sam has a red notebook, Aisha has a green notebook, and Nicolás has a blue notebook.

Check	Look back. Since all of the answers match the clues, the solution is reasonable.

Refer to the problem on the previous page.

1. If you did not know that a girl had the purple notebook, would it be possible to determine who had each notebook? Explain your reasoning.

2. Suppose Aisha is not in the same class as Sam. Who has which notebook?

3. The area of a garden is 16 square feet. If the length and width are whole numbers, is the garden definitely a square? Explain.

4. Explain when to use the *logical reasoning* strategy to solve a problem.

PRACTICE the Strategy

NYSCC • NYSMT
Extra Practice, p. R34

Solve the problem. Use *logical reasoning.*

5. Main Street and Park Street do not meet. They are always the same distance apart. Central Avenue crosses both streets to form square corners. Central Avenue and Fletcher Avenue also do not meet. Which streets are perpendicular?

6. **Algebra** If the pattern below continues, how many pennies will be in the fifth figure?

Figure 1   Figure 2   Figure 3

7. Charlotte, Ramon, and Nora have different professions: scientist, athlete, and teacher. Charlotte does not like sports. Ramon is not a teacher nor an athlete. Nora likes to run. Who is the teacher?

8. Three dogs are sitting in a line. Rocky is not last. Coco is in front of the tallest dog. Marley is sitting behind Rocky. List the dogs in order from first to last.

9. Ethan has $1.25 in change. He has twice as many dimes as pennies, and the number of nickels is one less than the number of pennies. How many dimes, nickels, and pennies does he have?

10. There are 4 more girls in Mrs. Pitt's class than Mr. Brown's class. Five girls moved from Mrs. Pitt's class to Mr. Brown's class. Now there are twice as many girls in Mr. Brown's class as there are in Mrs. Pitt's. How many girls were in Mr. Brown's class to begin with?

11. **Geometry** Set up 12 toothpicks as shown below. Move three toothpicks so that you form four squares.

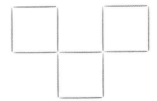

12. **WRITING IN ►MATH** How did you use logical reasoning to determine that Nora is not the teacher in Exercise 7?

An **angle** is formed by two rays with a common endpoint. The point where the two rays meet is called a **vertex**. The plural form of vertex is *vertices.*

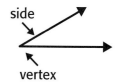

The unit used to measure an angle is called a **degree** (°). A circle contains 360°. So, a full turn on a circle is 360°.

1 full turn = 360°

$1° = \frac{1}{360}$ of a turn

When a turn on a circle is less than full, the angle formed is less than 360°.

1 quarter turn

less than
1 quarter turn

more than
1 quarter turn

Angles can be identified according to whether they measure 90°, less than 90°, or greater than 90°.

Angles

Key Concepts

Right Angle	Acute Angle	Obtuse Angle
This symbol means right angle.		
A **right angle** measures 90°.	An **acute angle** measures between 0° and 90°.	An **obtuse angle** measures between 90° and 180°.

It is easy to identify acute and obtuse angles because they are less than or greater than 90°. You can use a protractor.

ACTIVITY

1 **Identify the angle as *acute*, *right*, or *obtuse*.**

The angle appears to be a right angle. Use a protractor to measure the angle.

So, the measure of the angle is 90°. It is a right angle.

Step 3: Read the measure on the protractor where the other ray crosses the protractor.

Step 2: Make sure one ray of the angle passes through zero on the protractor.

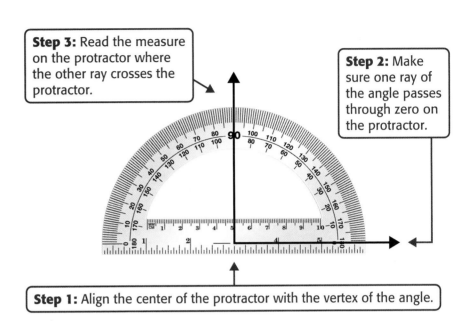

Step 1: Align the center of the protractor with the vertex of the angle.

CHECK What You Know

Use a protractor to identify each angle as *acute*, *right*, or *obtuse*.

1.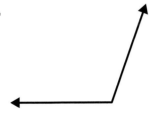

2.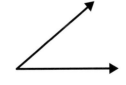

3.

4.

5.

6.

7. **OPEN ENDED** Draw an obtuse angle.

8. **WRITING IN ►MATH** Write a definition for perpendicular lines that includes the words *right angle*.

GET READY to Learn

MAIN IDEA

I will identify characteristics of triangles.

NYS Core Curriculum

5.G.6 Classify triangles by properties of their angles and sides

New Vocabulary

isosceles triangle

equilateral triangle

scalene triangle

acute triangle

right triangle

obtuse triangle

NY Math Online

macmillanmh.com

• Extra Examples
• Personal Tutor
• Self-Check Quiz

There is a large pyramid standing in front of the Louvre (loo-vrah) museum in Paris, France. The sides of the pyramid are shaped like triangles.

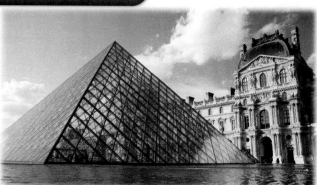

You can classify triangles by the lengths of their sides.

Classify Triangles by Angles		Key Concepts
Isosceles Triangle	**Equilateral Triangle**	**Scalene Triangle**
2 in. 2 in. $1\frac{1}{2}$ in.	3 in. 3 in. 3 in.	3 in. 2 in. 4 in.
at least two sides congruent	all sides congruent	no sides congruent

Real-World EXAMPLE   Identify Sides

1 MEASUREMENT **Measure each side of the triangle. Then find the number of congruent sides. State whether any of the sides appear to be perpendicular. Write *yes* or *no*.**

None of the sides of the triangle have the same length. So, no sides are congruent.

Yes; two sides of the triangle appear to be perpendicular.

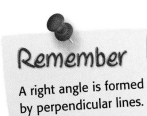

Remember

A right angle is formed by perpendicular lines.

Hands-On Mini Activity

Step 1 Draw and cut out three different triangles that each have one right angle. Draw and cut out three different triangles that do not have any right angles.

Right Triangles   **Not Right Triangles**

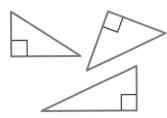   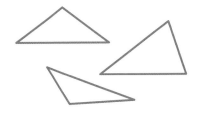

Step 2 Draw and cut out three different triangles that each have one obtuse angle.

Step 3 Draw and cut out three different triangles that do not have either a right angle or an obtuse angle.

Step 4 Separate your triangles into three different groups, based on the measures of the angles.

In the Hands-On Mini Activity, you classified triangles by the measures of their angles.

Classify Triangles by Angles		Key Concepts
Acute Triangle	**Right Triangle**	**Obtuse Triangle**
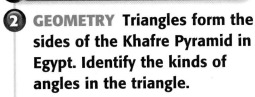		
3 acute angles	1 right angle, 2 acute angles	1 obtuse angle, 2 acute angles

Real-World EXAMPLE   **Identify Angles**

2 GEOMETRY Triangles form the sides of the Khafre Pyramid in Egypt. Identify the kinds of angles in the triangle.

All three angles are acute.

Measure the sides of each triangle. Then find the number of congruent sides. State whether any of the sides appear to be perpendicular. Write *yes* or *no*. See Example 1 (p. 566)

1.

2.

Identify the kinds of angles in each triangle. See Example 2 (p. 567)

3.

4.

5. A triangle is formed by the racked pool balls shown in the photograph. Find the number of congruent sides in the triangle.

6. **Talk About It** Write a description of an isosceles right triangle.

Practice and Problem Solving

NYSCC • NYSMT
Extra Practice, p. R35

Measure the sides of each triangle. Then find the number of congruent sides. State whether any of the sides appear to be perpendicular. Write *yes* or *no*. See Example 1 (p. 566)

7.

8.

9.

10.

Identify the kinds of angles in each triangle. See Example 2 (p. 567)

11.

12.

13.

14.

15. the triangles in the bridge

16. half of a square sandwich

17. Look at the triangle on the top of the White House on a twenty dollar bill. Describe the sides and angles of the triangle.

18. The sum of the measures of the angles of a triangle is 180°. In a right triangle, what is the sum of the measures of the two acute angles?

 Real-World PROBLEM SOLVING

Art The image shown at the right contains many triangles.

19. Describe the different types of triangles found in the image.

20. Look at the purple triangle. State whether any sides appear to be perpendicular. Then identify the triangle.

H.O.T. Problems

21. OPEN ENDED Draw a triangle that has all acute angles and two congruent sides. Then classify the triangle by its side lengths and by its angle measures.

22. WHICH ONE DOESN'T BELONG? Identify the triangle that does not belong with the other three. Explain your reasoning.

A   **B**   **C**   **D**

23. CHALLENGE Emma, Gabriel, Jorge, and Makayla each have a different triangle. Use the clues below to describe each person's triangle as isosceles, equilateral, or scalene and as acute, right, or obtuse. Explain your process.

- Gabriel and Jorge each have a 90° angle in their triangles.
- Gabriel's triangle does not have any congruent sides.
- One of Emma's angles measures greater than 90°.
- Each side of Makayla's triangle and two sides of Emma's and Jorge's triangles are four centimeters long.

24. **WRITING IN ►MATH** A triangle has two sides that are perpendicular. Could the triangle be isosceles, equilateral, or scalene? Explain.

MAIN IDEA

I will identify characteristics of quadrilaterals.

NYS Core Curriculum

5.G.4 Classify quadrilaterals by properties of their angles and sides
Also addresses 5.CM.9.

New Vocabulary

quadrilateral
rectangle
square
parallelogram
rhombus
trapezoid

NY Math Online

macmillanmh.com
• Extra Examples
• Personal Tutor
• Self-Check Quiz

GET READY to Learn

The image shown at the right includes squares and rectangles. These are two different types of *quadrilaterals*.

A **quadrilateral** is a polygon with four sides and four angles.

Hands-On Mini Activity

Draw and cut out three different parallelograms like the ones shown. Then draw and cut out three different quadrilaterals that are *not* parallelograms.

Parallelograms   **Not Parallelograms**

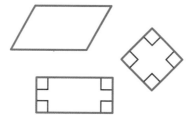   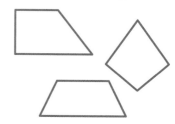

a. What attribute do all the parallelograms have that the other quadrilaterals do not?

b. Use the figures above and your figures to write a definition for *parallelogram*.

You can classify quadrilaterals using one or more of the attributes listed below.

• congruent sides   • parallel sides   • perpendicular sides

Classifying Quadrilaterals

Quadrilateral	Example	Attributes
Rectangle		• Opposite sides congruent • All angles are right angles • Opposite sides parallel
Square		• All sides congruent • All angles are right angles • Opposite sides parallel
Parallelogram		• Opposite sides congruent • Opposite sides parallel
Rhombus		• All sides congruent • Opposite sides parallel
Trapezoid		• Exactly one pair of opposite sides parallel

Remember

The square corners on the angles indicate which angles are right angles.

EXAMPLES   Describe Sides and Angles

Vocabulary Link

Prefixes

The prefix *quad-* means four. A **quadruped** is an animal that has four feet.

1 **Describe the congruent sides in the quadrilateral shown at the right. Then state whether any sides appear to be parallel or perpendicular.**

Opposite sides are congruent and parallel. Adjacent sides are perpendicular.

2 **The design below is made up of repeating quadrilaterals. Find the number of acute and obtuse angles in each quadrilateral.**

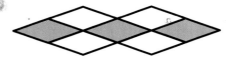

Each quadrilateral has two acute angles and two obtuse angles.

Describe the sides that appear to be congruent in each quadrilateral. Then state whether any sides appear to be parallel or perpendicular.
See Example 1 (p. 571)

1.

2.

Find the number of acute angles in each quadrilateral. See Example 2 (p. 571)

3.

4.

5.

6. Many aircraft display the shape of the American flag as shown below to indicate motion. Find the number of obtuse angles in each figure.

7. Talk About It — Tell the difference between a rhombus and a trapezoid.

Practice and Problem Solving

NYSCC • NYSMT
Extra Practice, p. R35

Describe the sides that appear to be congruent in each quadrilateral. Then state whether any sides appear to be parallel or perpendicular.
See Example 1 (p. 571)

8.

9.

10.

11.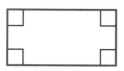

Find the number of acute angles in each quadrilateral.
See Example 2 (p. 571)

12.

13.

14.

15.

Determine whether each statement is *true* or *false*. Explain.

16. All squares are parallelograms.

17. Some rhombi are squares.

18. All rectangles are squares.

19. Some rectangles are parallelograms.

Real-World PROBLEM SOLVING

Art **For Exercises 20 and 21, use the photo of the New York Knicks basketball court.**

20. What kind of quadrilateral does the basketball court resemble most?

21. Describe two more quadrilaterals that are shown in the photo.

22. Traci has a piece of wood that is 1 inch wide and 1 foot long. She cuts the wood into four 3-inch strips. What type of quadrilateral can the strips be classified as?

Name the quadrilaterals that have the given attributes.

23. two pairs of parallel sides

24. all adjacent sides are perpendicular

25. exactly one pair of parallel sides

26. four congruent sides

H.O.T. Problems

27. **OPEN ENDED** Draw a parallelogram that is not a square, rhombus, or rectangle.

28. **FIND THE ERROR** Aliane and Levon are discussing the relationship between quadrilaterals. Who is correct? Explain your reasoning.

Aliane
Some trapezoids are rectangles.

Levon
No trapezoids are rectangles.

29. **WRITING IN ►MATH** Write a real-world problem that involves quadrilaterals. Solve and explain your reasoning.

30. Which statement about the figures shown below is true?
(Lessons 13-3 and 13-4)

A Figures *K* and *L* are congruent.

B Figures *L* and *N* have all acute angles.

C Figures *M* and *N* each have at least two obtuse angles.

D Figures *M* and *N* are congruent.

31. Which is NOT a true statement?
(Lesson 13-4)

F All parallelograms have opposite sides parallel.

G Squares have four congruent angles and sides.

H All trapezoids have exactly one pair of parallel sides.

J Parallelograms have exactly one pair of parallel sides.

Spiral Review

Identify the kinds of angles in each triangle. (Lesson 13-3)

32.

33.

34.

35. Can a triangle be both right and obtuse? Explain your reasoning.
(Lesson 13-2)

Complete. (Lesson 12-4)

36. 3 L = ▧ mL

37. 900 mL = ▧ L

38. 7,000 mL = ▧ L

39. Algebra A bag contained 16 balloons. Rama's mom used 9 balloons to decorate her bedroom. Which of the following equations can be used to find the number of balloons left in the bag: $y = 16 + 9$, $y = 16 - 9$, or $y = 16 \times 9$? Then find the number of balloons. (Lesson 6-1)

40. Algebra Some bamboo plants can grow 3 feet in one day. Write an expression to show the number of feet a bamboo plant can grow in *x* days. (Lesson 5-3)

Identify each figure. Then name it using symbols. (Lesson 13-1)

1.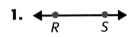

2.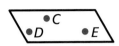

Describe each pair of lines as *intersecting*, *perpendicular*, or *parallel*. (Lesson 13-1)

3.

4.

5. On Monday, Gavin bought some apples. He bought twice as many on Tuesday as he did on Monday. On Wednesday, he bought 5 more than he did on Monday. He bought a total of 21 apples. How many apples did he buy on Tuesday? (Lesson 13-2)

6. The sum of the measures of the angles in the figure below is 540°.

If all the angles have equal measure, what is the measure of each angle? (Lesson 13-2)

Measure the sides of each triangle. Then find the number of congruent sides. State whether any of the sides appear to be perpendicular. Write *yes* or *no*. (Lesson 13-3)

7.

8.

Identify the kinds of angles in each triangle. (Lesson 13-3)

9.

10.

11. MULTIPLE CHOICE Which shape could never have parallel sides?
(Lessons 13-3 and 13-4)

  A rectangle   **C** trapezoid

  B rhombus   **D** triangle

Find the number of acute angles in each quadrilateral. (Lesson 13-4)

12.

13.

14. MULTIPLE CHOICE Which statement about the trapezoid shown at the right is true? (Lesson 13-4)

  F The trapezoid has two right angles.

  G The trapezoid has two acute angles.

  H The trapezoid has two pairs of parallel sides.

  J The trapezoid has three obtuse angles.

15. WRITING IN ►MATH Is every parallelogram a quadrilateral? Explain. (Lesson 13-4)

Problem-Solving Investigation

MAIN IDEA I will choose the best strategy to solve a problem.

 5.PS.3 Interpret information correctly, identify the problem, and generate possible strategies and solutions
Also addresses 5.PS.21.

P.S.I. TEAM +

EMILIO: To make a quilt pattern, I pieced together triangles to make squares of different sizes. The first square has 2 triangles, the second square has 8 triangles, and the third square has 18 triangles. The quilt will have squares of five different sizes.

YOUR MISSION: Find how many triangles are in the fifth square.

Understand	You know how many triangles are in the first, second, and third squares. You need to find how many triangles are in the fifth square.
Plan	Look for a pattern to find the number of triangles.
Solve	Each square has twice as many triangles as small squares. First square 2 × 1 or 2 triangles Second square 2 × 4 or 8 triangles Third square 2 × 9 or 18 triangles Continuing the pattern, the fourth square has 2 × 16 or 32 triangles. The fifth square has 2 × 25 or 50 triangles.
Check	Draw the fifth square and count the number of triangles. Since there are 50 triangles in the fifth square, the answer is correct. ✔

Use any strategy shown below to solve each problem.

PROBLEM-SOLVING STRATEGIES

• Draw a diagram.

• Look for a pattern.

• Use logical reasoning.

1. Mr. Toshi's fifth grade class sold containers of popcorn and peanuts. If each day they sold 25 less containers of peanuts than popcorn, how many containers of popcorn and peanuts did they sell in all?

	Day 1	Day 2	Day 3	Day 4
Popcorn	225	200	150	300
Peanuts	▦	▦	▦	▦

2. Algebra Find the fifteenth term in the pattern shown below.

$$5, 4, 7, 6, 9, 8, 11, \ldots$$

3. Selma is taller than Motega and shorter than Cheye. If Cheye is shorter than Dominic, who is the shortest person?

4. There are 8 girls for every 7 boys on a field trip. If there are 56 girls on the trip, how many students are on the trip?

5. Measurement When Cheryl goes mountain climbing, she rests 5 minutes for every 15 minutes that she climbs. If Cheryl climbs for 2 hours, how many minutes does she rest?

6. The fraction $\frac{a}{b}$ is equivalent to $\frac{5}{20}$, and $b - a = 3$. Find the values of a and b.

7. A family has four cats. Fluffy is 8 years old and is 4 years younger than Tiger. Tiger is 2 years older than Max, and Max is 3 years older than Patches. List the cats from oldest to youngest.

8. The number of fifth grade students who helped clean the park this year was 5 less than twice as many as last year. If 39 fifth graders helped clean up the park this year, how many cleaned the park last year?

9. Five friends go to a batting cage. Andrea bats after Daniel and before Jessica. Juwan bats after Andrea and before Jessica and Filipe. Jessica always bats immediately after Juwan. Who bats last?

10. Madeline has 2 times the number of games as Paulo. Paulo has 4 more games than Tyler. If Tyler has 9 games, how many games are there between the 3 friends?

11. Algebra The first three *triangular numbers* are shown below. How many dots will be in the sixth triangular number?

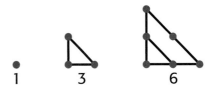

12. **WRITING IN ►MATH** In addition to logical reasoning, what is another strategy that you could use to solve Exercise 11?

13-6 Translations and Graphs

GET READY to Learn

Helena slid her desk from one side of her room to the other. This movement is an example of a translation.

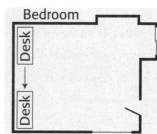

Bedroom

Desk

Desk

A **transformation** is a movement of a geometric figure. The resulting figure is called the **image**. One type of transformation is a translation.

MAIN IDEA

I will sketch translations on a coordinate grid.

NYS Core Curriculum

5.G.13 Plot points to form **basic geometric shapes** (identify and classify)

New Vocabulary

transformation

image

translation

NY Math Online

macmillanmh.com
• Extra Examples
• Personal Tutor
• Self-Check Quiz

Translation   Key Concept

Sliding a figure without turning it is called a **translation**. A translation does not change the size or shape of a figure.

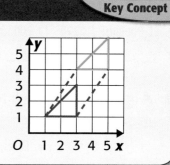

To translate a figure, move all of the vertices the same distance and in the same direction.

Hands-On Mini Activity

A triangle has vertices at *A*(3, 6), *B*(4, 9), and *C*(7, 6). Draw a coordinate grid on graph paper. Copy the triangle.

a. With a different colored pencil, graph points *A*, *B*, and *C* after they are moved down 4 units.

b. Connect the points.

c. What are the vertices of the image?

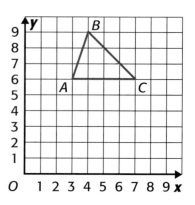

EXAMPLE Sketch a Translation

① **A triangle has vertices F(1, 5), G(5, 7), and H(3, 4). Graph the triangle. Then graph its translation image 2 units right and 3 units down. Graph and then write the ordered pairs for the new vertices.**

Remember

In a translation, you slide a figure from one position to another without turning it.

Step 1 Graph the original triangle.

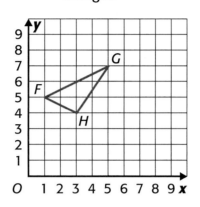

Step 2 Graph the translated image.

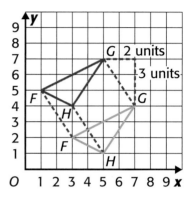

The new vertices are F(3, 2), G(7, 4), and H(5, 1).

CHECK What You Know

Graph the triangle after each translation. Then write the ordered pairs for the vertices of the image. See Example 1 (p. 579)

1. 3 units left

2. 4 units up

3. 5 units left, 2 units down

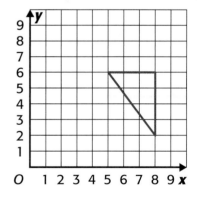

For Exercises 4 and 5, graph each figure and the translation image described. Write the ordered pairs for the vertices of the image. See Example 1 (p. 579)

4. quadrilateral with vertices J(1, 5), K(2, 8), L(4, 8), M(3, 5); translated 5 units right

5. triangle with vertices W(7, 2), X(8, 6), Y(9, 3); translated 6 units left, 1 unit up

6. Jerome walks 2 blocks west and then 4 blocks north. Describe this transformation.

7. Explain why a translation is sometimes called a slide.

Graph the triangle after each translation image. Then write the ordered pairs for the vertices of the image.

See Example 1 (p. 579)

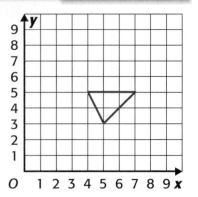

8. 2 units right   **9.** 1 unit down

10. 5 units up   **11.** 1 unit right, 1 unit up

12. 3 units left, 4 units up   **13.** 2 units left, 3 units down

For Exercises 14 and 15, graph each figure and the translation image described. Write the ordered pairs for the vertices of the image. See Example 1 (p. 579)

14. quadrilateral with vertices $N(6, 1)$, $P(7, 4)$, $Q(9, 4)$, $R(9, 1)$; translated 5 units up

15. triangle with vertices $D(1, 3)$, $E(4, 5)$, $F(3, 0)$; translated 3 units right, 4 units up

16. A triangular picture with vertices described in the table is being moved. The new coordinates for two of the vertices are (6, 5) and (6, 7). What are the new coordinates for the third vertex?

Vertex	1	2	3
Coordinates	(1, 2)	(1, 4)	(4, 4)

17. A swing set has posts at (10, 2), (6, 6), (14, 14), and (18, 10). It is being moved 4 units up. What are the new coordinates? Draw a sketch of the translation.

18. A table tennis table has coordinates (0, 0), (0, 5), (9, 5), and (9, 0). Each unit represents 1 foot. If the table is moved 6 feet to the right and 2 feet up, what are the new coordinates of the table?

19. Anne wants to move a right-triangular table from one corner of a room to another. If both corners have 90° angles, will the translated figure fit in the new corner? Explain.

H.O.T. Problems

20. OPEN ENDED Draw a triangle on a coordinate grid with one vertex at (5, 1). Then translate the triangle so the same vertex is at (6, 5). Describe the translation.

21. **WRITING IN ►MATH** Explain how to translate a figure in a diagonal direction.

22. Which statement about trapezoid *ABCD* appears to be true? (Lesson 13-4)

A ─────────── B
  ╱   │
 ╱   │
C ─────────── D

A $\overline{AC}$ and $\overline{CD}$ form a right angle.

B $\overline{AB}$ and $\overline{CD}$ are parallel.

C $\overline{AB}$ and $\overline{BD}$ are parallel.

D $\overline{AC}$ and $\overline{AB}$ form an acute angle.

23. Which diagram shows only a translation of the figure? (Lesson 13-6)

F 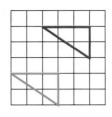   H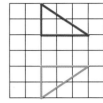

G 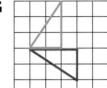   J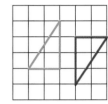

Spiral Review

24. The number of chairs in each row in an amphitheater is shown in the table. If this pattern continues, how many chairs will be in the tenth row? Explain. (Lesson 13-5)

Row	Number of Chairs
1	68
2	72
3	76
4	80

Describe the sides that appear to be congruent in each quadrilateral. Then state whether any sides appear to be parallel or perpendicular.
(Lesson 13-4)

25.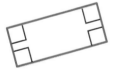

26.

27.

Find each change in temperature. Use an integer to represent the change. (Lesson 12-6)

28. 57°F to 60°F

29. 110°F to 102°F

30. 22°C to 0°C

31. Carlota walked her dog from 10:47 A.M. to 11:23 A.M. How long did she walk her dog? (Lesson 11-7)

32. Yesterday, Oscar drank 3 cups of water, 2 cups of milk, and 3 cups of juice. How many quarts of liquid did he drink? (Lesson 11-4)

GET READY to Learn

Cartoonists sometimes use transformations to change characters. The figures at the right are *reflections* of each other.

Another transformation that does not change the size or shape of a figure is a reflection.

Reflection   Key Concepts

Flipping a figure over a line to create a mirror image of the figure is called a **reflection**. The line is called a **line of reflection**.

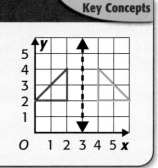

When a figure is reflected across a line, corresponding vertices are the same distance from the line of reflection.

Hands-On Mini Activity

A parallelogram has vertices A(0, 4), B(4, 8), C(5, 5), and D(1, 1). Draw a coordinate grid on graph paper. Copy the parallelogram.

a. With a different colored pencil, graph points *A*, *B*, *C*, and *D* after they are reflected across the line.

b. Connect the points.

c. What are the vertices of the image?

EXAMPLE Reflect Across a Horizontal Line

① Graph the triangle after it is reflected across the line. Then write the ordered pairs for the new vertices.

Remember

In a reflection, a figure is flipped from one position to another without being turned. Reflections are sometimes called *flips*.

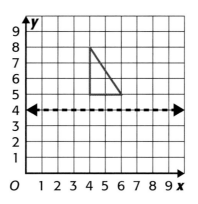 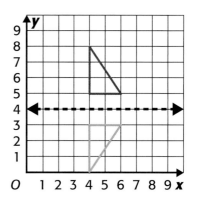

The ordered pairs for the new vertices are (4, 0), (4, 3), and (6, 3).

You can check the reasonableness of the vertices by drawing the triangles on grid paper. When the paper is folded, they should match exactly.

CHECK What You Know

Graph each figure after a reflection across the line. Then write the ordered pairs for the new vertices. See Example 1 (p. 583)

1.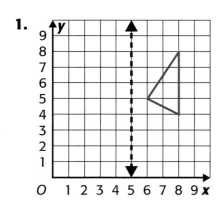

2.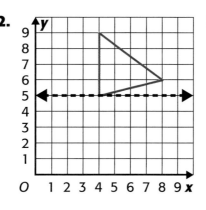

3.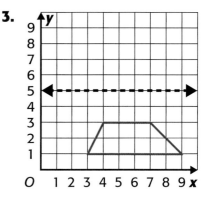

4. Which letters in GEOMETRY can be reflected over a vertical line and remain the same?

5. **Talk About It** Compare and contrast translations and reflections.

Graph each figure after a reflection across the line. Then write the ordered pairs for the new vertices. See Example 1 (p. 583)

6.

7.
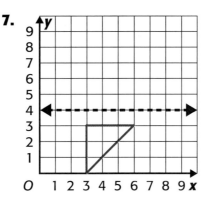

8.
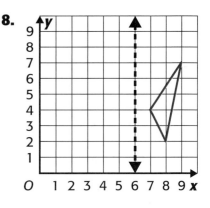

9.
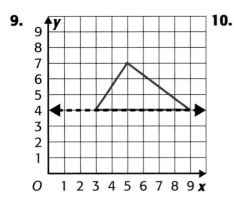

10.
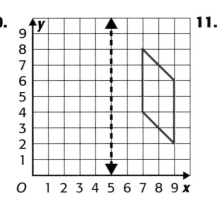

11.
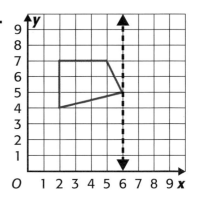

12. Name four capital letters that look the same after being reflected across a horizontal line.

13. A cartoonist draws a figure whose head is at (3, 8) and whose feet are at (2, 1) and (5, 1). If the figure is reflected over a vertical line, what are possible coordinates for the new points? Explain.

14. Sketch a pattern that can be made by reflecting the figure at the right both horizontally and vertically.

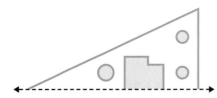

15. The figure below shows paper that was folded once along the dotted line. The colored parts are holes cut out of the folded paper. Make a sketch of what you will see when the paper is unfolded.

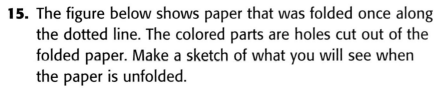

Music Some melodies have patterns of notes that are reflections. In the figure below, notice that the notes on each side of the dashed line are mirror images of each other.

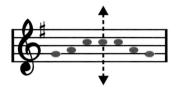

Copy and complete each set of notes so that the right and left sides are reflections of each other.

16.

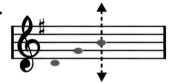

17.

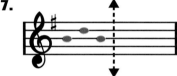

H.O.T. Problems

18. **OPEN ENDED** Copy the figure at the right on graph paper. Draw two different lines of reflection and use them to draw the reflected images of the triangle.

19. **CHALLENGE** Draw a figure on a coordinate grid and its reflection over the *y*-axis. Explain how the *x*- and *y*-coordinates of the image relate to the *x*- and *y*-coordinates of the original figure.

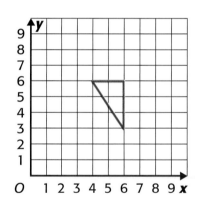

20. **FIND THE ERROR** Alexis and Devon are reflecting a triangle across a vertical line. Who is correct? Explain your reasoning.

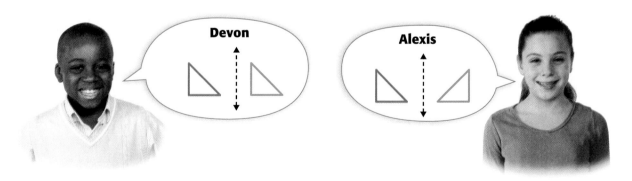

21. **WRITING IN ►MATH** Describe the steps for sketching the reflection of a quadrilateral over a line on a coordinate grid.

Rotations and Graphs

MAIN IDEA

I will sketch rotations on a coordinate grid.

NYS Core Curriculum

5.G.13 Plot points to form **basic geometric shapes** (identify and classify)
Also addresses 5.CM.11.

New Vocabulary

rotation

NY Math Online

macmillanmh.com

• Extra Examples
• Personal Tutor
• Self-Check Quiz

GET READY to Learn

The movement of the gymnast around the bar is an example of a *rotation*.

A rotation is another type of transformation.

Rotation	Key Concept

Rotating a figure about a point is called a **rotation**. A rotation is also called a turn. It does not change the size or shape of a figure.

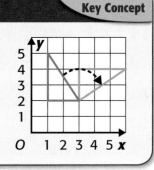

Hands-On Mini Activity

A triangle has vertices *A*(5, 4), *B*(1, 4), and *C*(1, 6). Draw a coordinate grid on graph paper. Copy the triangle.

a. With a different colored pencil, graph points *A*, *B*, and *C* after they are rotated 90° clockwise about point *A*.

b. Connect the points.

c. What are the vertices of the image?

To check the new vertices, use tracing paper. Trace the original triangle. Then turn it to see if it is congruent to the new triangle.

Sketch a Rotation

1 A triangle has vertices *G*(1, 1), *H*(5, 4), and *J*(5, 1). Graph the triangle. Then graph its rotation 180° clockwise about point *H*. Write the ordered pairs for the new vertices.

Step 1 Graph the original triangle.

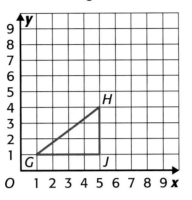

Step 2 Graph the rotated image.

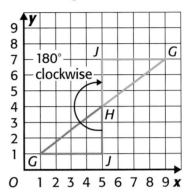

The ordered pairs for the new vertices are *G*(9, 7), *H*(5, 4), and *J*(5, 7).

CHECK What You Know

Graph the triangle after each rotation about point *P*. Then write the ordered pairs for the new vertices.
See Example 1 (p. 587)

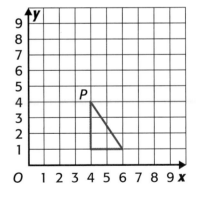

1. 90° clockwise

2. 180° counterclockwise

Graph each triangle with the given vertices and the rotation described. Write the ordered pairs for the new vertices.
See Example 1 (p. 587)

3. *L*(5, 5), *M*(5, 2), *N*(1, 5); 90° counterclockwise about point *L*

4. *A*(6, 5), *B*(6, 9), *C*(9, 8); 180° clockwise about point *A*

5. Name two lowercase letters that are transformations of the letter b. Describe the transformation.

6. **Talk About It** Explain the differences between a rotation and reflection.

Graph the triangle after each rotation. Then write the ordered pairs for the new vertices. See Example 1 (p. 587)

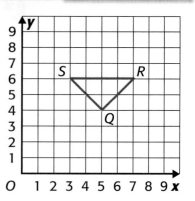

7. 90° clockwise about point *Q*

8. 180° clockwise about point *Q*

9. 90° counterclockwise about point *S*

10. 90° clockwise about point *S*

Graph each triangle with the given vertices and the rotation described. Write the ordered pairs for the new vertices. See Example 1 (p. 587)

11. *J*(7, 2), *K*(5, 2), *L*(5, 5); 90° clockwise about point *L*

12. *T*(5, 5), *U*(4, 8), *V*(9, 8); 180° counterclockwise about point *T*

13. *L*(1, 4), *M*(5, 1), *N*(5, 3); 90° counterclockwise about point *L*

14. *W*(2, 7), *X*(2, 1), *Y*(0, 8); 90° clockwise about point *X*

15. The sign was incorrectly rotated 90° counterclockwise. Sketch how the sign was supposed to look.

16. Geometry Describe the transformation of the letter F shown below.

17. A triangle with vertices at (4, 6), (8, 6), and (7, 8) is transformed so that the new vertices are at (3, 3), (7, 3), and (6, 5). Then that figure is transformed so that the final figure has vertices at (3, 3), (3, 7), and (1, 6). Describe the transformations.

18. A rectangular trampoline at (2, 4), (2, 9), (5, 9) and (5, 4) is being moved to a new location. The corner at (2, 4) becomes the corner at (2, 4). The corner at (2, 9) becomes the corner at (7, 4). Describe the type of move made for the trampoline. Name the new location of the other two corners. Include a drawing.

Science Some objects in nature have *rotational symmetry*. This means that if they are rotated less than 360°, they look the same as in their original position. An example is the snowflake shown below.

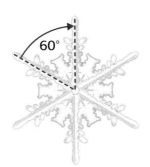

60°

Determine whether each object has rotational symmetry. Write *yes* or *no*.

19. starfish

20. clover

21. dragonfly

H.O.T. Problems

22. OPEN ENDED Draw a figure on a coordinate plane. Then draw the figure after it is rotated 180° clockwise. Describe the coordinates of the point around which the figure was rotated.

23. NUMBER SENSE A triangle graphed on the coordinate plane has a vertex at (0, 9). What type of rotation would move the vertex to (9, 0)? Explain your reasoning.

24. **WRITING IN ►MATH** Rotate the original figure that you drew in Exercise 22 180° counterclockwise. Describe the difference between rotating a figure 180° clockwise and 180° counterclockwise.

25. Which of these does NOT show a reflection? (Lesson 13-7)

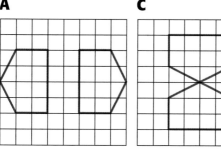

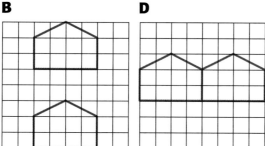

A   C

B   D

26. Which represents a rotation of the shaded figure? (Lesson 13-8)

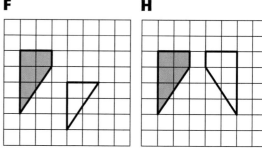

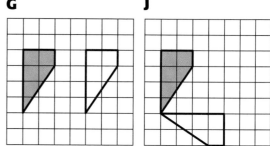

F   H

G   J

Spiral Review

Graph each figure after a reflection across the line. Then write the ordered pairs for the vertices of the image. (Lesson 13-7)

27.

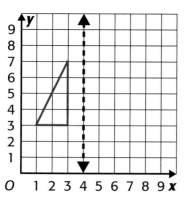

28.

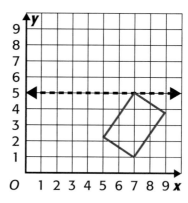

29. Graph triangle *ABC* with vertices *A*(3, 4), *B*(4, 8), and *C*(1, 4). Then graph the triangle after it is translated 4 units right and 2 units down. Write the ordered pairs for the new vertices. (Lesson 13-6)

30. Suppose today's forecast says it will be 10°C. Could you go on a picnic? Explain your reasoning. (Lesson 12-6)

Complete. (Lesson 11-1)

31. 36 in. = ▪ ft   **32.** 15 ft = ▪ yd   **33.** 4 ft = ▪ in.

Identify Transformations

GET READY to Learn

Many decorative patterns are made using translations, reflections, or rotations. The pattern at the right could be made by reflecting or rotating the portion of the design in the black triangle.

EXAMPLE   Identify a Transformation

1 Determine whether the transformation shown below is a *translation*, *reflection*, or *rotation*.

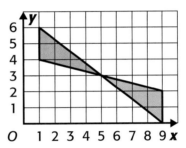

The triangle has been turned about the point at (4, 3) to a new position.

So, this is a rotation.

Real-World EXAMPLE   Identify a Transformation

2 ART What transformation could be used to create the design?

The top and bottom half are mirror images of each other. So, a reflection across a horizontal line is one way to create the design.

Determine whether each transformation is a *translation, reflection,* or *rotation.* See Examples 1, 2 (p. 591)

1.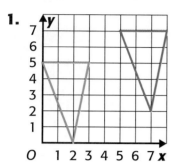

2.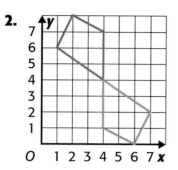

3.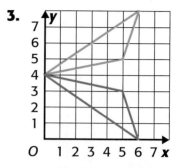

4. Which transformations appear in the pattern of bricks shown at the right?

5. *Talk About It* Describe how you could use a symmetrical shape on grid paper to show a translation, reflection, and rotation.

Practice and Problem Solving

NYSCC • NYSMT
Extra Practice, p. R37

Determine whether each transformation is a *translation, reflection,* or *rotation.* See Examples 1, 2 (p. 591)

6.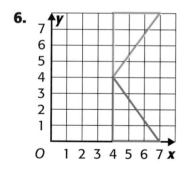

7.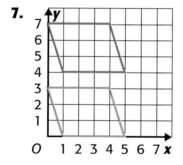

8.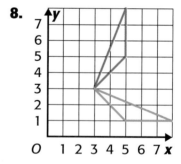

9.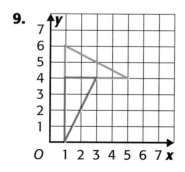

10.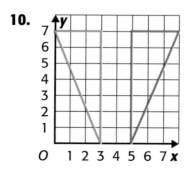

11.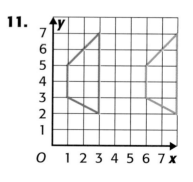

12. Was a translation, reflection, or rotation used to create the pattern below?

13. Two different transformations were used to change figure *A* to figure *B*. Describe them.

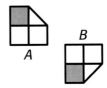

14. Analyze the pattern below. Which transformations could be used to create the design?

15. Describe how you could use a transformation to complete the figure below.

New York Data File

At the Adirondack International Speedway, race car drivers travel around the $\frac{1}{2}$ mile track at speeds of over 100 miles per hour.

For Exercises 16–18, describe the transformations found in the patterns.

16. End of race

17. Faster car is approaching

18. Track is slippery

H.O.T. Problems

19. OPEN ENDED Create a pattern using translations, reflections, and rotations. Describe the basic shape that you used and the transformations that you used.

20. WRITING IN ►MATH Write about a real-world situation that involves transformations. Describe the transformation that is used.

Problem Solving in Art

POMPEII PATTERNS

Pompeii was a popular vacation spot for wealthy members of the ancient Roman Empire. The city had houses that were designed in classic Roman style. This style was characterized by using a variety of geometrical shapes and patterns. Many of the houses included murals painted on the walls, decorative fountains, and patterned mosaic floors. In the year 79, nearby Mount Vesuvius erupted violently, spewing lava and ash throughout Pompeii. For 1,600 years, the city and its residents were lost under Mount Vesuvius' ashes. Today, scientists continue to uncover buildings and artworks at the site.

Did You Know?

The city of Pompeii was accidentally rediscovered by an Italian architect named Fontana in 1599.

5.CN.8 Investigate the presence of mathematics in careers and **areas of interest**
5.A.8 **Create** algebraic or **geometric patterns using** concrete objects or **visual drawings** (e.g., rotate and shade geometric shapes)   *Also addresses 5.CN.9.*

Real-World Math

Use the image above of the design on a Pompeii building to solve each problem.

1. Identify all of the geometric figures in the design.

2. Where do you see acute angles in the design?

3. Where do you see obtuse angles in the design?

4. Are there any right angles in the design? If so, where?

5. Where in the design do you see parallel lines?

6. Where in the design do you see perpendicular lines?

7. What can you tell about the triangles in the design?

8. Identify any transformations that could have been used to create the design.

FOLDABLES Study Organizer GET READY to Study

Be sure the following Big Ideas are written in your Foldable.

Point
Line
Plane
Line Segment
Ray
Parallel
Perpendicular
Intersecting
Congruent

Key Concepts

Triangles

• Triangles can be classified by the lengths of their sides. (p. 566)

Triangle	Description
Isosceles	at least 2 sides congruent
Equilateral	all sides congruent
Scalene	no sides congruent

• Triangles can be classified by the measures of their angles. (p. 567)

Triangle	Description
Acute	3 acute angles
Right	1 right angle, 2 acute angles
Obtuse	1 obtuse angle, 2 acute angles

Quadrilaterals (p. 571)

• A parallelogram has both pairs of opposite sides parallel and congruent.
• Rectangles, rhombi, and squares are parallelograms.
• A trapezoid has exactly one pair of opposite sides parallel.

Transformations

• A **translation** is a slide. (p. 578)
• A **reflection** is a flip. (p. 582)
• A **rotation** is a turn. (p. 586)

Key Vocabulary

parallel lines (p. 558)
perpendicular lines (p. 558)
reflection (p. 582)
rotation (p. 586)
translation (p. 578)

Vocabulary Check

State whether each sentence is true or false. If false, replace the underlined word or number to make a true sentence.

1. In a <u>rotation</u>, a figure is moved without being turned or flipped.

2. <u>Intersecting lines</u> are lines that cross each other at right angles.

3. Parallel lines <u>always</u> intersect.

4. A <u>rectangle</u> has opposite sides congruent and parallel.

5. A <u>ray</u> is a line that has one endpoint and goes on forever in one direction.

6. Flipping a figure over a line to create a mirror image of the figure is called a <u>reflection</u>.

7. A translation <u>changes</u> the size of the figure.

Lesson-by-Lesson Review

13-1 **Geometry Vocabulary** (pp. 557–560)

4.G.2

Example 1
Identify the figure. Then name it using symbols.

The figure is a line segment. In symbols, this is written as $\overline{LM}$ or $\overline{ML}$.

Example 2
Describe the pair of lines as *intersecting*, *perpendicular*, or *parallel*.

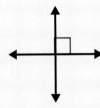

The lines intersect to form right angles. They are intersecting perpendicular lines.

Identify each figure. Then name it using symbols.

8. 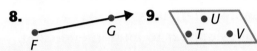   9.

Describe each pair of lines as *intersecting*, *perpendicular*, or *parallel*.

10. 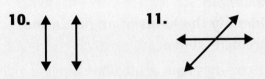   11.

12. Draw a ray that can be used to show the direction north on a map.

13-2 **Problem-Solving Strategy:** Use Logical Reasoning (pp. 562–563)

5.PS.9

Example 3
Angie, Carlo, and Camille each play a different sport: basketball, soccer, or football. Angie does not like soccer. Carlo's favorite sport is not played with a round ball. Who plays each sport?

Make a table to organize the information.

	Basketball	Soccer	Football
Angie	yes	X	X
Carlo	X	X	yes
Camille	X	yes	X

Angie likes basketball, Carlo likes football, and Camille likes soccer.

Solve. Use the *use logical reasoning* strategy.

13. Two walls intersect. Is the intersection an example of a point, line, ray, or line segment?

14. Steve is taller than Lorena. Riley is shorter than Steve. Lorena is not the shortest. List the people from shortest to tallest.

15. Five dogs are getting groomed. Duke is groomed after Daisy and before Spike. Sadie is groomed after Duke and before Spike and Rusty. Spike is groomed immediately after Sadie. Which dog is groomed last?

13-3 Triangles (pp. 566–569)

5.G.6

Example 4
Measure each side of the triangle. Then find the number of congruent sides. State whether any of the sides appear to be perpendicular.

Two sides of the triangle are congruent. Two sides are perpendicular.

Example 5
Identify the kinds of angles in the triangle above.

Two angles are acute. One angle is right.

Measure the sides of each triangle. Then find the number of congruent sides. State whether any of the sides appear to be perpendicular. Write *yes* or *no*.

16. 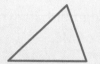 17.

18. Find the number of congruent sides in the triangular sign.

13-4 Quadrilaterals (pp. 560–574)

5.G.4

Example 6
Describe the congruent sides in the quadrilateral. Then state whether any sides appear to be parallel or perpendicular.

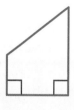

No sides are congruent. Two sides appear to be parallel. Two pairs of adjacent sides appear to be perpendicular.

Example 7
Refer to the figure in Example 6. Find the number of acute angles.

The figure has 1 acute angle.

Describe the sides that appear congruent in each quadrilateral. Then state whether any sides appear to be parallel or perpendicular.

19. 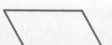 20.

Find the number of acute angles in each quadrilateral.

21.   22.

23. Miss Cruz is cutting out a quadrilateral. It has four congruent sides and no right angles. What figure is it?

13-5 Problem-Solving Investigation: Choose a Strategy (pp. 576–577)

5.PS.3

Example 8
Algebra Find the eighth number in the pattern below.

18, 19, 15, 16, 12, 13,...

Find the pattern in the list of numbers.

18, 19, 15, 16, 12, 13,...
+1 −4 +1 −4 +1

The pattern is to add 1, and then subtract 4.

So, the seventh number in the pattern is 13 − 4 or 9. The eighth number is 9 + 1 or 10.

Solve.

24. Holly is 6 years younger than her sister. Their mother is 44 years old, and her age is twice the sum of her two children's ages. How old is Holly?

25. How many 2-inch squares fit inside a rectangle 6 inches by 8 inches?

26. Caden uses one pencil the first week of drawing class, and twice as many pencils each week as he did the week before. How many pencils does he use the fifth week?

13-6 Translations and Graphs (pp. 578–581)

Example 9
A triangle has vertices A(2, 2), B(1, 4), and C(5, 2). Graph the triangle. Then graph its translation image 1 unit right and 5 units up. Write the ordered pairs for the vertices of the image.

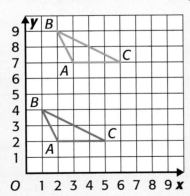

The new vertices are A(3, 7), B(2, 9), and C(6, 7).

Graph each figure and the translation image described. Write the ordered pairs for the vertices of the image.

27. quadrilateral with vertices F(2, 9), G(7, 9), H(8, 7), J(5, 7); translated 6 units down

28. triangle with vertices T(7, 3), U(9, 8), V(9, 4); translated 3 units left, 1 unit up

29. A triangular stool has legs at (5, 3), (9, 3), and (7, 6). It is moved 5 units to the right. What are the new coordinates?

13-7 Reflections and Graphs (pp. 582–585)

5.G.13

Example 10
Graph the figure after a reflection across the line. Then write the ordered pairs for the vertices of the image.

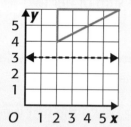 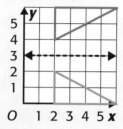

The ordered pairs for the new vertices are (2, 0), (2, 2), and (6, 0).

Graph each figure after a reflection across the line. Then write the ordered pairs for the vertices of the image.

30. 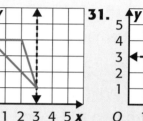   31.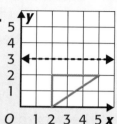

13-8 Rotations and Graphs (pp. 586–590)

5.G.13

Example 11
Graph the rotation of the triangle clockwise about point *W*. Write the ordered pairs for the new vertices.

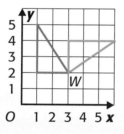

The ordered pairs for the new vertices are (3, 2), (3, 4), and (6, 4).

Graph each figure and the rotation described. Write the ordered pairs for the new vertices.

32. triangle with vertices *C*(2, 6), *D*(5, 4), *E*(3, 2); rotated 90° counterclockwise about *C*

33. triangle with vertices *M*(2, 8), *N*(5, 6), *P*(4, 4); rotated 180° clockwise about *N*

13-9 Identify Transformations (pp. 591–593)

5.G.13

Example 12
Determine whether the transformation is a *translation*, *reflection*, or *rotation*.

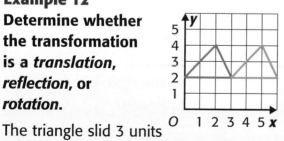

The triangle slid 3 units right. This is a translation.

Determine whether each transformation is a *translation, reflection,* or *rotation*.

34. 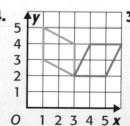   35.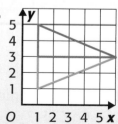

CHAPTER

Chapter Test

Describe each pair of lines as *intersecting*, *perpendicular*, or *parallel*.

1.   2.

3. Hiroshi has been at a baseball game for 1 hour 50 minutes. The time is 5:20 P.M. At what time did he arrive?

Measure each side of the triangle. Then find the number of congruent sides. State whether any of the sides appear to be perpendicular. Write *yes* or *no*.

4.   5.

Find the number of acute angles in each quadrilateral.

6.   7.

8. MULTIPLE CHOICE Wendy will show her friend an example of an acute angle. Which figure could she NOT use?

   A quadrilateral   **C** square

   B rhombus   **D** trapezoid

9. Which single transformation is represented by the figure and its image?

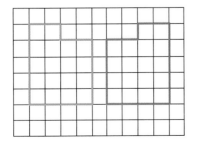

Graph the figure and the translation image described. Write the ordered pairs for the vertices of the image.

10. triangle with vertices $N(2, 2)$, $P(6, 3)$, $Q(4, 1)$; translated 5 units up

Graph each figure after a reflection across the line. Then write the ordered pairs for the vertices of the image.

11. 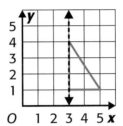   12.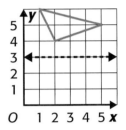

13. Graph a triangle with vertices $A(1, 4)$, $B(5, 4)$, and $C(5, 2)$. Sketch the triangle rotated 180° about point B. Write the ordered pairs for the new vertices.

14. MULTIPLE CHOICE Which pair of figures shows a translation?

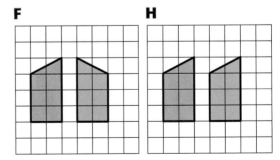

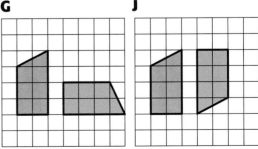

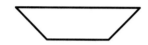

Read each question. Then fill in the correct answer on the answer sheet provided by the teacher or on a sheet of paper.

1. Which statement about the trapezoid shown below is true?

A The figure has 4 congruent sides.

B The figure contains 4 right angles.

C The figure has two parallel bases.

D The figure has a perimeter of 10 units.

---

2. Which of the following shapes could never have perpendicular sides?

F circle   **H** square

G rectangle   **J** triangle

---

3. Which diagram shows only a translation of the figure?

A 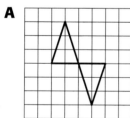   **C**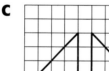

B 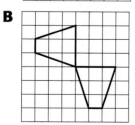   **D**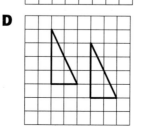

---

4. Which single transformation is shown below?

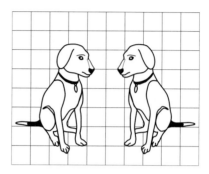

F rotation   **H** reflection

G translation   **J** not here

---

5. Which of these shapes could never have parallel opposite sides?

A rectangle   **C** trapezoid

B rhombus   **D** triangle

---

6. What part of the model is shaded?

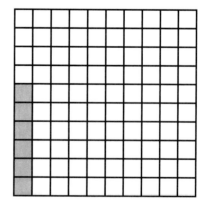

F 0.006

G 0.06

H 0.6

J 6

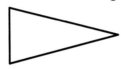
7. Mr. Cortez determined that the cost of renting a popcorn machine for 9 hours was $82. Which shows that his solution is NOT reasonable?

Number of Hours	Cost ($)
1	32
3	47
5	62
7	77

A The terms are decreasing.

B The terms are multiples of 11.

C The terms are increasing by 15.

D The terms are multiples of 15.

8. An isosceles triangle is shown. Which statement about the triangle is true?

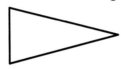

F None of the sides are congruent.

G All the angles are right angles.

H The triangle has only 2 sides that are congruent.

J Two of the sides are perpendicular.

9. What fraction is equivalent to 0.32?

A $\frac{32}{1000}$

B $\frac{32}{100}$

C $\frac{32}{10}$

D $3\frac{2}{10}$

PART 2   Short Response

Record your answers on the answer sheet provided by your teacher or on a sheet of paper.

10. Julie practiced the piano one afternoon, as shown. Find the number of minutes she practiced the piano.

Start    **Finish**

11. What type of angle will the hands of a clock show at 1:15?

PART 3   Extended Response

Record your answers on the answer sheet provided by your teacher or on a sheet of paper. Show your work.

12. Use a Venn diagram to compare characteristics of perpendicular lines and intersecting lines.

13. Describe two ways to represent $1.76 using dollars and coins. You may NOT use more than 6 coins.

NEED EXTRA HELP?													
If You Missed Question...	1	2	3	4	5	6	7	8	9	10	11	12	13
Go to Lesson...	13–4	13–1	13–9	13–9	13–3	8–2	6–6	13–3	1–4	11–7	13–3	13–1	1–8
NYS Core Curriculum	5.G.4	4.G.2	5.G.13	5.G.13	5.G.6	5.N.20	5.A.4	5.G.6	5.N.3	5.M.7	5.G.6	4.G.2	5.PS.12

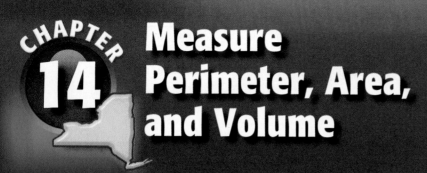

CHAPTER 14 Measure Perimeter, Area, and Volume

 **What are perimeter and area?**

Perimeter is the distance around a closed figure. **Area** is the number of square units needed to cover a surface.

Example A Kentucky farm has 6 acres of woods with horseback riding trails. The perimeter is the distance around the woods. The area is the total surface of the woods, 6 acres.

What will I learn in this chapter?

- Find perimeters of polygons.
- Find and estimate the areas of figures by counting squares and using formulas.
- Identify characteristics of three-dimensional figures.
- Select and use appropriate units and formulas to measure length, perimeter, area, and volume.
- Solve problems by using the *make a model* strategy.

 **Key Vocabulary**

area

perimeter

polygon

prism

three-dimensional figure

 **Student Study Tools**
at macmillanmh.com

FOLDABLES®
Study Organizer

Make this Foldable to help you organize information about perimeter, area, and volume. Begin with a sheet of 11″ × 17″ paper and six index cards.

1 **Fold** the paper lengthwise about 3″ from the bottom.

2 **Fold** in thirds. Open and staple the edges on either side to form three pockets.

3 **Label** each pocket as shown. Place two index cards in each pocket.

Perimeter Area Volume

You have two ways to check prerequisite skills for this chapter.

Option 2

NY Math Online Take the Chapter Readiness Quiz at macmillanmh.com.

Option 1

Complete the Quick Check below.

QUICK Check

Add. (Lessons 2-4, 2-6, and 10-7)

1. $15 + 20 + 25 + 7$

2. $9\frac{1}{2} + 11 + 14\frac{1}{2}$

3. $8\frac{1}{4} + 12 + 12$

4. $5 + 13 + 19$

5. $16.3 + 16.3 + 16.3$

6. $4 + 9.1 + 3.2 + 8$

7. The amount of money that Tyrese spent shopping is shown in the table. Find the total amount that he spent.

Item	Amount ($)
CD	14.99
T-shirt	26.30
Snack	5.20

Multiply. (Lessons 3-4 and 3-6)

8. 10×26

9. 12×14

10. 75×2

11. 25×48

12. 25×6

13. 5×32

14. 132×13

15. 45×45

16. Mrs. Ohlin sold 3 handmade bookshelves for $160 each. How much money did she earn in all?

Multiply. (Lessons 3-4 and 3-6)

17. $12 \times 3 \times 5$

18. $8 \times 6 \times 4$

19. $14 \times 10 \times 3$

20. $15 \times 9 \times 6$

21. $13 \times 9 \times 11$

22. $12 \times 7 \times 14$

Measurement Activity for 14-1

Perimeters of Rectangles

The **perimeter** of a figure is the distance around the figure. Perimeter is a measure of length. The perimeter of the rectangle at the right is 6 + 4 + 6 + 4 or 20 centimeters.

6 cm

4 cm

MAIN IDEA

I will use models to find the perimeters of rectangles.

NYS Core Curriculum

5.R.7 Use mathematics to show and understand physical phenomena (e.g., determine the perimeter of a bulletin board)

5.A.6 Evaluate the perimeter formula for given input values *Also addresses 5.G.14.*

New Vocabulary

perimeter

ACTIVITY Copy and complete the table.

Rectangle	Length (ℓ)	Width (w)	2ℓ	2w	Perimeter (P)
	2	1	4	2	2 + 1 + 2 + 1 = 6

CHECK What You Know

1. **WRITING IN ►MATH** Refer to the table above. How are ℓ and w related to the perimeter of the rectangles? Then use P, ℓ, and w to write an equation for the perimeter of a rectangle.

2. Use the formula you wrote in Exercise 1 to find the perimeter of the rectangle. Select and use appropriate units.

8 in.

5 in.

3. In Exercise 2, only two sides of the rectangle are labeled. Explain why this is enough information to find the perimeter.

4. Find 2ℓ + 2w for the rectangle in Exercise 2. Then write an equation to describe the relationship between P, ℓ, and w.

Perimeters of Polygons

MAIN IDEA

I will find perimeters of polygons.

NYS Core Curriculum

5.G.1 Calculate the perimeter of regular and irregular polygons
Also addresses 5.R.7, 5.A.6.

New Vocabulary

polygon

NY Math Online

macmillanmh.com
• Extra Examples
• Personal Tutor
• Self-Check Quiz

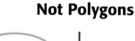

A city park is building a fence around a dog run. They need to know the *perimeter*, or distance around the run, to determine how much fencing they will need.

A **polygon** is a closed figure made up of line segments that do not cross each other.

The perimeter of a polygon is measured in units of length, such as inches, feet, meters, or yards.

   **Find the Perimeter by Adding Side Lengths**

1 Find the perimeter of the figure below.

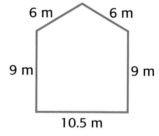

Estimate $10 + 10 + 10 + 10 + 10 = 50$ m

$P = 6 + 6 + 9 + 10.5 + 9$ Add the length of each side.
$ = 40.5$

The perimeter is 40.5 meters. This is close to the estimate, so the answer is reasonable.

Hands-On Mini Activity

Copy and complete the table.

Square	 1	2	3	4
Side Length (s)	1			
Perimeter (P)	4			

Describe the relationship between the perimeter of a square and side length. Then write an equation using *P* and *s*.

Perimeter of a Square

Key Concept

Words	The perimeter *P* of a square is 4 times the side length *s*.	**Model**
Symbols	$P = s + s + s + s$ or $4s$	*s*

Real-World EXAMPLE   **Perimeter of a Square**

2   **ART** Hai and his uncle tiled the kitchen floor using square tiles like the one shown at the right. What is the perimeter of the tile?

$P = 4s$ Perimeter of a square

$P = 4(2)$ Replace *s* with 2.

$P = 8$ Multiply.

2 ft

The perimeter of the tile is 8 feet.

Perimeter of a Rectangle

Key Concept

Words	The perimeter *P* of a rectangle is two times the length ℓ plus two times the width *w*.	**Model**
Symbols	$P = \ell + \ell + w + w$ or $2\ell + 2w$	

ℓ
w w
ℓ

| Real-World EXAMPLE | Perimeter of a Rectangle |

③ CRAFTS Christa is sewing a lace border around the edges of her scrapbook. How many inches of lace will Christa need?

7 in.

9 in.

Find the perimeter of the scrapbook.

$P = 2\ell + 2w$ Perimeter of a rectangle

$P = 2(7) + 2(9)$ $\ell = 7$ and $w = 9$

$P = 14 + 18$ Multiply.

$P = 32$ Add.

So, Christa will need 32 inches of lace.

CHECK What You Know

Find the perimeter of each figure. See Example 1 (p. 608)

1.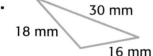
30 mm
18 mm
16 mm

2.
11 in.
$9\frac{1}{2}$ in. $9\frac{1}{2}$ in.
7 in.

Find the perimeter of each square or rectangle.
See Examples 2, 3 (pp. 609–610)

3.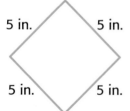
5 in.   5 in.
5 in.   5 in.

4.
$7\frac{1}{2}$ ft
12 ft

5.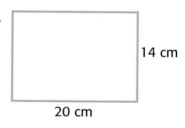
14 cm
20 cm

6. A rectangular playground is 32 feet long and 14 feet wide. How many feet of edging are needed to enclose the playground?

7. **Talk About It** Describe two ways to find the perimeter of a rectangle.

Find the perimeter of each figure. See Example 1 (p. 608)

8.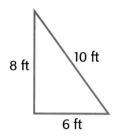

9.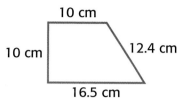

10.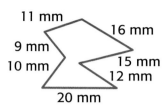

Find the perimeter of each square or rectangle. See Examples 2, 3 (pp. 609–610)

11.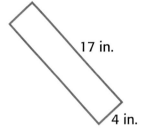

12.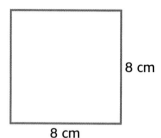

13.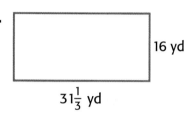

14.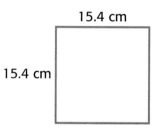

15.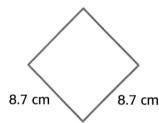

16.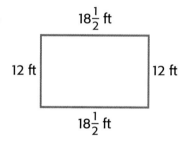

17. An octagon-shaped table has two sides measuring 4 feet and the other sides each measuring 1 foot each. What is the perimeter of the table?

18. A billiards table is twice as long as it is wide. If the perimeter of a billiards table is 24 feet, what is the length and width of the table?

19. Use a centimeter ruler to measure the side lengths rectangle shown at the right. Select and use appropriate units to find the perimetter of the rectangle.

H.O.T. Problems

20. **OPEN ENDED** Use a ruler to draw two different rectangles that have the same perimeter.

21. **WRITING IN ►MATH** Write a real-world problem that can be solved by finding the perimeter. Then solve the problem.

GET READY to Learn

A checkerboard is made up of sixty-four 1-inch squares. You can describe the board by saying that it has an *area* of 64 square inches.

MAIN IDEA

I will find and estimate the areas of figures by counting squares.

NYS Core Curriculum

Preparation for 6.G.2 Determine the area of triangles and quadrilaterals (squares, rectangles, rhombi, and trapezoids) and develop formulas *Also addresses 6.M.7.*

New Vocabulary

area

NY Math Online

macmillanmh.com
• Extra Examples
• Personal Tutor
• Self-Check Quiz

Area is the number of square units that cover the surface of a closed figure.

1 square unit   2 square units   4 square units

If the figure is not a square or a rectangle, count the number of whole squares and the number of half squares.

EXAMPLE   **Estimate Areas**

1 **Find the area of the figure at the right.**

Step 1 Count the number of whole squares in the figure.

9 whole squares = 9 square units

Step 2 Count the number of half squares in the figure.

5 half squares = $2\frac{1}{2}$ square units

Step 3 Add the number of whole and half squares.

9 square units + $2\frac{1}{2}$ square units = $11\frac{1}{2}$ square units

So, the area of the figure is $11\frac{1}{2}$ square units.

When you cannot count square units or half square units exactly, you can estimate the area.

Real-World EXAMPLES Estimate Areas

2 **TREE HOUSES** The diagram shows the floor plan for a tree house. One square on the grid represents 1 square foot. About how many square feet is the area of the floor?

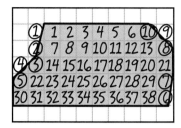

Step 1 Count the number of whole squares in the diagram.

38 whole squares = 38 square feet

Step 2 Count the partial squares circled in the diagram.

10 partial squares is about 5 square feet

Step 3 Add the number of whole and partial squares.

38 + 5 = 43 square feet

The tree house floor has an area of about 43 square feet.

3 **LANDSCAPING** A landscape architect designed the pond at the right. Each square represents 1 square meter. Estimate the area of the pond.

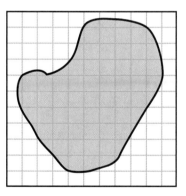

Step 1 Count the number of whole squares. There are 44 whole squares which is 44 square meters.

Step 2 Count the partial squares.

26 partial squares is about 13 square meters.

Step 3 Add the whole squares and partial squares.

44 + 13 = 57 square meters

The area of the pond is about 57 square meters.

**Estimate the area of each figure. Each square represents
1 square centimeter.** See Examples 1-3 (pp. 612–613)

1.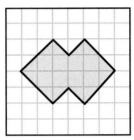

2.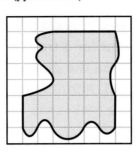

3.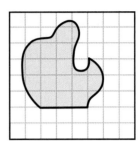

4. A cake decorator is drawing a heart on a cake. Each square
represents 1 square inch. Estimate the area of the heart.

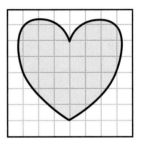

5. (Talk About It) Describe one way to estimate the area of an
irregular figure that is drawn on grid paper.

Practice and Problem Solving

NYSCC • NYSMT
Extra Practice, p. R37

**Estimate the area of each figure. Each square represents
1 square centimeter.** See Examples 1-3 (pp. 612–613)

6.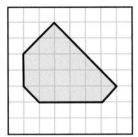

7.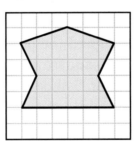

8.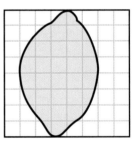

9.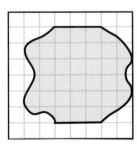

10.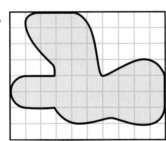

11.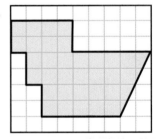

12. Isaiah made a sign for his yard sale shown at the right.
If each square represents 1 square inch, estimate the
area of the sign.

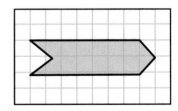

13. The flower patch at the right is on Cindy's backpack. One square represents 1 square centimeter. Estimate the total area of the patch.

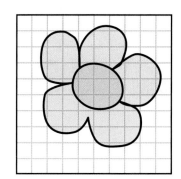

H.O.T. Problems

14. OPEN ENDED Draw a figure on grid paper with an approximate area of 38 square units.

15. **WRITING IN** ▸**MATH** Describe some real-life examples of when it would be useful to know how to estimate the area of figures.

NYSMT Practice ⟩ 5.G.1, 6.G.2

16. The student council is making a sign 8 feet long and 3 feet wide. They want to glue a colorful border around the four edges of the sign. How many feet of border will be needed? (Lesson 14-1)

A 24 ft

B 22 ft

C 19 ft

D 14 ft

17. Which is the best estimate for the area of the figure? (Lesson 14-2)

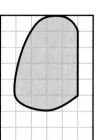

F 12 square units

G 15 square units

H 18 square units

J 24 square units

Spiral Review

Find the perimeter of each figure. (Lesson 14-1)

18.

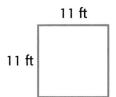
11 ft
11 ft

19.

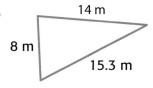
14 m
8 m
15.3 m

20.

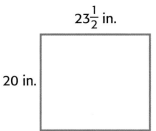
$23\frac{1}{2}$ in.
20 in.

21. Triangle *ABC* has vertices at *A*(1, 1), *B*(4, 1), and *C*(3, 5). After a transformation, the vertices are at *A*(4, 1), *B*(7, 1), and *C*(6, 5). Determine whether the transformation is a translation, reflection, or rotation. (Lesson 13-9)

22. The temperature was 54°F at 3:00. Three hours later, the temperature was 48°F. Use an integer to represent the change. (Lesson 12-6)

Areas of Rectangles and Squares

MAIN IDEA

I will find the areas of rectangles.

NYS Core Curriculum

Preparation for 6.G.2 Determine the area of triangles and quadrilaterals (squares, rectangles, rhombi, and trapezoids) and develop formulas

NY Math Online

macmillanmh.com

• Extra Examples
• Personal Tutor
• Self-Check Quiz

GET READY to Learn

The largest flying American Flag is located in Gaston, North Carolina. The flag is 114 feet long and 65 feet wide. What is the area of the flag?

Hands-On Mini Activity

Copy and complete the table below. Use centimeter cubes to create and measure the rectangles shown.

Rectangle				
Length (ℓ)	3			
Width (w)	1			
Area (A)	3			

a. Study the pattern in the table. How are the length and width of the rectangles related to the areas?

b. Use A, ℓ, and w to write a formula for the area of a rectangle.

Area of a Rectangle   Key Concept

Words	The area A of a rectangle equals length ℓ times the width w.	Model
Symbols	$A = \ell w$	

Remember

Different shapes have different formulas for area.

Real-World EXAMPLE Area of a Rectangle

① **FLAGS** Refer to the information at the beginning of the lesson. Find the area of the flag that is described.

The rectangle at the right represents the flag. The flag is 114 feet long and 65 feet wide.

65 ft

114 ft

$A = \ell w$	Formula for area of a rectangle
$A = 114 \times 65$	Replace ℓ with 114 and w with 65.
$A = 7,410$	Multiply.

The area of the flag is 7,410 square feet.

Recall that a square is a rectangle with four congruent sides. Each side length is represented by s. So, you can replace ℓ and w in the formula $A = \ell w$ with s.

Area of a Square   Key Concept

Words   The area A of a square equals   **Model**
             the square of the side length s.

Symbols $A = s \times s$ or $A = s^2$ s

Remember

The expression s^2 is read s *squared* because its model forms a square with side s.

Real-World EXAMPLE Area of a Square

② **SPORTS** A baseball diamond is actually a square. Find the area of the baseball diamond at the right.

90 ft

$A = s^2$	Formula for area of a square
$A = 90 \times 90$	Replace s with 90.
$A = 8,100$	Simplify.

The area of the baseball diamond is 8,100 square feet.

Find the area of each rectangle or square. See Examples 1, 2 (p. 617)

1.
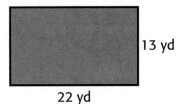
13 yd
22 yd

2.
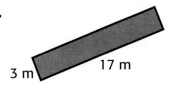
3 m
17 m

3.
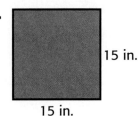
15 in.
15 in.

4. $\ell = 9$ km, $w = 1$ km

5. $\ell = 8$ cm, $w = 6$ cm

6. The Parthenon of ancient Greece had the rectangular floor plan shown at the right. How much area does the building cover?

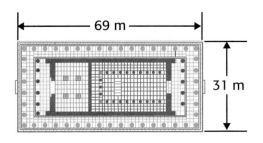
69 m
31 m

7. **Talk About It** Write the formulas for the area of a rectangle and a square. Explain what each variable represents.

Practice and Problem Solving

NYSCC • NYSMT
Extra Practice, p. R38

Find the area of each rectangle or square. See Examples 1, 2 (p. 617)

8.
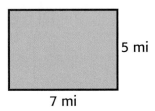
5 mi
7 mi

9.
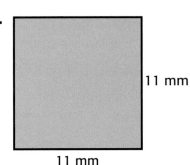
11 mm
11 mm

10.
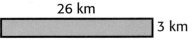
26 km
3 km

11.
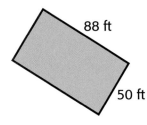
88 ft
50 ft

12.
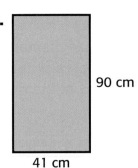
90 cm
41 cm

13.
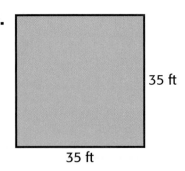
35 ft
35 ft

14. $\ell = 18$ m
$w = 5$ m

15. $\ell = 24$ m
$w = 37$ m

16. $\ell = 12$ cm
$w = 10$ cm

17. Use a centimeter ruler to draw two different rectangles and one square that each have an area of 16 square centimeters.

18. Use a centimeter ruler to measure the side lengths of the figures shown. Select and use appropriate formulas and units to find the area.

19. A square has an area of 196 square inches. What is the side length?

20. The four boxes whose bases are described in the table are being used as props for the school's spring play. They can not take up more than 90 square feet of area on the stage. Can all the boxes be used? Explain.

Box	Length (ft)	Width (ft)
1	4	3
2	5	4
3	6	2
4	2	8

21. A soccer field has to be 100 to 130 yards long and 50 to 100 yards wide. Find the least and greatest areas for the soccer field.

22. The door of a new building measures 7 feet by 3 feet. It is to be covered with 12-inch square metal tiles that cost $15 each. How much will it cost to cover the door? Explain.

 New York Data File

All of the license plates in the United States may have a different design, but they all come in one standard size.

License Plate Size	
Customary Units	Metric Units
12 in. × 6 in.	300 mm × 150 mm

Find the area of the license plate using each type of unit.

23. square inches

24. square millimeters

25. square centimeters (Hint: 10 = 1cm)

H.O.T. Problems

26. OPEN ENDED Give the dimensions of a rectangle whose area is between 100 and 200 square centimeters. Find the area.

27. CHALLENGE Suppose you double the length and the width of a rectangle. Would the area also double? Explain.

28. WRITING IN ►MATH Write about a real-life situation that can be solved by finding the area of a rectangle. Then solve.

You can create a parallelogram from a rectangle. The area of the parallelogram will be the same as the area of the rectangle.

MAIN IDEA

I will use models to find the area of parallelograms.

NYS Core Curriculum

Preparation for 6.G.2 Determine the area of triangles and quadrilaterals (squares, rectangles, rhombi, and trapezoids) and develop formulas

You Will Need
graph paper

① **Step 1** Cut out a rectangle using grid paper like the one shown below. The area is 8 square units.

Step 2 Cut a triangle from one side of the rectangle and move it to the other side to form a parallelogram.

The area is still 8 square units.

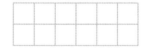

② **Step 1** Cut out a rectangle using graph paper like the one shown below. The area is 12 square units.

Step 2 Cut a triangle from one side of the rectangle and move it to the other side to form a parallelogram.

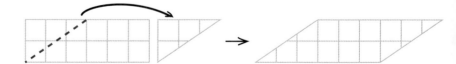

The area is still 12 square units.

ACTIVITY

③ Find the area of the parallelogram to the right by using a model.

Step 1 Draw the parallelogram on grid paper.

Step 2 Fold and cut along the dotted line.

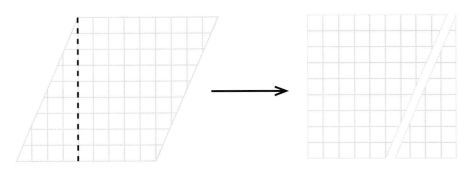

Step 3 Move the triangle to the right to make a square.

Step 4 Count up the number of units in the square or use the formula $A = \ell w$.

$A = 81$ square units

Think About It

1. Explain how to use a model to find the area of a parallelogram.

✓ CHECK What You Know

Use a model to find the area of each parallelogram.

2.

3.

4.

5.

6. **WRITING IN ►MATH** The formula for finding the area of a rectangle is $A = \ell w$. Can the same formula be used to find the area of a parallelogram?

What's the Area?

Measuring Areas

Get Ready!

Players: 2 to 4

You will need: 18 cards with sketches of different sized rectangles, centimeter ruler, paper, pencils

Get Set!

Shuffle and turn the cards facedown in a pile. Give paper and pencil to each player.

Go!

- Turn the first card face up.

- Each player estimates the area of the figure in square centimeters and records that number.

- Players work together to measure the figure and calculate the area. Select and use appropriate units and formulas.

- Each player compares the actual area to their estimate. The player with the closest estimate earns 1 point.

- Continue playing until all the cards are used. The player with the most points wins.

Find the perimeter of each square or rectangle. (Lesson 14-1)

1.

5 ft

2.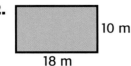

10 m

18 m

3. **MULTIPLE CHOICE** Chelsea wants to plant flowers around her triangle-shaped garden. The sides of the garden measure 2 yards, 3 yards 2 feet, and 8 feet. What is the perimeter of the garden in feet? (Lesson 14-1)

A 15 ft

B 25 ft

C 41 ft

D 47 ft

4. A horse stall is a square with a side length of 12 feet. What is the perimeter of the stall? (Lesson 14-1)

5. A doghouse is a rectangle that measures $2\frac{1}{3}$ feet by 3 feet. What is the perimeter of the doghouse? (Lesson 14-1)

Estimate the area of each figure. Each square represents 1 square foot.

(Lesson 14-2)

6.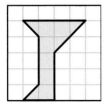

7.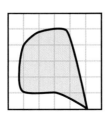

8. Estimate the area of the stop sign below. (Lesson 14-2)

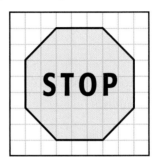

Find the area of each rectangle or square. (Lesson 14-3)

9.

7 in.

3 in.

10.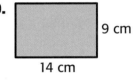

9 cm

14 cm

11.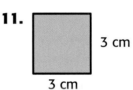

3 cm

3 cm

12.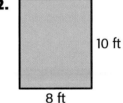

10 ft

8 ft

13. **MULTIPLE CHOICE** A square has a length of 20 inches. What is the area? (Lesson 14-3)

F 40 square inches

G 80 square inches

H 200 square inches

J 400 square inches

14. **WRITING IN ▶MATH** Describe how to estimate the area of the figure in Exercise 7. (Lessons 14-1 and 14-3)

14-4 Three-Dimensional Figures

GET READY to Learn

The building at the right is made up of shapes called *rectangular prisms*.

A two-dimensional figure is a plane figure that has length and width. A **three-dimensional figure** has length, width, and height. A three-dimensional figure with faces that are polygons is called a **polyhedron**. A **prism** is a polyhedron with two parallel congruent faces, called **bases**.

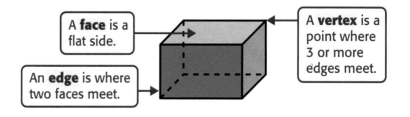

A **face** is a flat side.

A **vertex** is a point where 3 or more edges meet.

An **edge** is where two faces meet.

Three-dimensional Figures   Key Concepts

Figure	Example	Characteristics
rectangular prism		a prism with six rectangular faces including two rectangular bases
triangular prism		a prism that has triangular bases
cylinder		a solid with two parallel congruent circular bases; a curved surface connects the bases
cone		a solid that has a circular base and one curved surface from the base to a vertex

EXAMPLE   Characteristics of Solids

Remember

Bases, faces, edges, and vertices are all parts of three-dimensional figures.

1 Describe parts of the figure that are parallel and congruent. Then identify the figure.

faces	This figure has 5 faces. The triangular bases are parallel and congruent. The rectangular faces appear to be congruent.
edges	There are 9 edges. The edges that form the vertical sides of the rectangles are parallel and congruent.
vertices	This figure has 6 vertices.

So, the figure is a triangular prism.

Real-World EXAMPLE   Characteristics of Solids

2 **SPORTS** Describe parts of the tennis ball container that are perpendicular and congruent. Then identify the shape of the container.

faces	The circular bases are congruent. They are perpendicular to the curved surface of the container.
edges	The container has no edges. So the container is a cylinder.

 CHECK What You Know

1. Describe parts of the figure that are parallel and congruent. Then identify the figure. See Examples 1, 2 (p. 625)

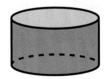

2. Describe parts of the hamster cage that are perpendicular and congruent. Then identify the shape of the cage.

3. **Talk About It** Describe the differences between a cylinder and a rectangular prism.

Describe parts of each figure that are parallel and congruent. Then identify the figure. See Examples 1, 2 (p. 625)

4.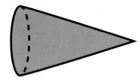

5.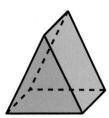

6.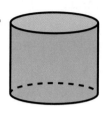

7.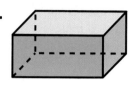

Describe parts of each figure that are perpendicular and congruent. Then identify the figure. See Examples 1, 2 (p. 625)

8.

9.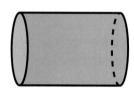

10.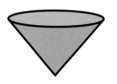

11.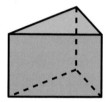

12. What kind of figure is the tomato soup can at the right?

13. Describe the number of vertices and edges in a closed book. Identify the shape of the book.

14. Vera's closet is in the shape of a rectangular prism. Describe the pairs of parallel planes that make up her closet.

H.O.T. Problems

15. **WHICH ONE DOESN'T BELONG?** Which figure does not belong with the other three? Explain your reasoning.

 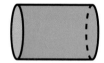

16. **CHALLENGE** Suppose the figure is folded on the dashed lines. What three-dimensional figure is formed?

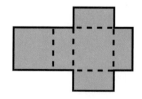

17. **WRITING IN ►MATH** Describe the similarities and differences of a rectangular prism and a triangular prism.

18. A rectangular fish tank is shown below.

10 in.

8 in.

16 in.

What is the area of the bottom of the fish tank? (Lesson 14-3)

A 24 square inches

B 56 square inches

C 80 square inches

D 128 square inches

19. Look at the figure below.

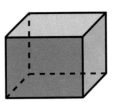

Which statement is true? (Lesson 14-4)

F The figure has a triangular base.

G The figure has exactly 3 pairs of parallel faces.

H The figure has exactly 2 pairs of parallel faces.

J The figure has no perpendicular sides.

Spiral Review

Find the area of each rectangle or square. (Lesson 14-3)

20.
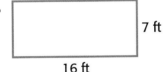
7 ft

16 ft

21.
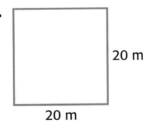
20 m

20 m

22.

2 cm

8 cm

23. Estimate the area of the figure at the right. Each square represents 1 square centimeter. (Lesson 14-2)

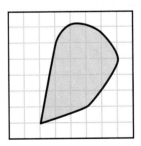

24. What is the perimeter of a rectangular building measuring 42 feet by 30 feet? (Lesson 14-1)

Graph each figure and the translation described. Write the ordered pairs for the new vertices. (Lessons 13-6 and 13-8)

25. triangle XYZ with vertices X(1, 5), Y(5, 8), Z(7, 6); translated 4 units down

26. triangle ABC with vertices A(3, 0), B(3, 3), C(5, 0); translated up 1 unit and to the right 3 units.

Complete. (Lesson 12-4)

27. 40 L = ▦ mL

28. 2 L = ▦ mL

29. 16,000 mL = ▦ L

Problem-Solving Strategy

MAIN IDEA I will solve problems by making a model.

 **5.PS.13 Model problems with pictures/diagrams or physical objects**

Nick is helping his younger sister put away her alphabet blocks. She has already put away one layer of blocks. To fill up one layer it takes nine blocks. If the box is filled with six layers of blocks, how many blocks would be in the box?

Understand	**What facts do you know?** • The number of blocks in one layer of a box. • The number of layers in the box. **What do you need to find?** • The number of blocks in the box when there are six layers.
Plan	Solve the problem by making a model.
Solve	Use your plan to solve the problem. Make a model of one layer of the box by arranging 9 cubes in a 3 × 3 array. Continue stacking the cubes until there are six layers. There are a total of 54 cubes. So, the box would have 54 blocks.
Check	Look back. Use logical reasoning and multiplication. There are 6 layers and each layer has 9 cubes. So, the total number of cubes is 6 × 9 or 54. The answer is correct. ✔

Refer to the problem on the previous page.

1. How many blocks would the box contain if it had only five layers of blocks?

2. If you stacked two boxes of the original size on top of each other, what would be the total number of blocks in the boxes?

3. What are the advantages of the *make a model* strategy?

4. List some objects that you could use to make a model.

PRACTICE the Strategy

NYSCC • NYSMT
Extra Practice, p. R38

Solve. Use the *make a model* strategy.

5. **Measurement** On an assembly line that is 150 feet long, there is a work station every 15 feet. The first station is at the beginning of the line. How many work stations are there?

6. A store is stacking cans of food into a pyramid-shaped display. The bottom layer has 9 cans. There are 5 layers. If there are two less cans in each layer, how many cans are in the display?

7. **Measurement** The distance around the center ring at the circus is 80 feet. A clown stands every 10 feet along the circle. How many clowns are there?

8. **Measurement** Martino wants to arrange 18 square tiles into a rectangular shape with the least perimeter possible. How many tiles will be in each row?

9. In the figure below, there are 22 marbles in Box A. To go from Box A to Box B, four marbles can pass through the triangular machine at a time. Five marbles can pass through the square machine at a time. Describe how to move all the marbles from Box A to Box B in the fewest moves possible.

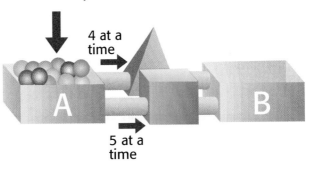

10. Drake lined up 15 pennies on his desk. He replaced every third penny with a nickel. Then he replaced every fourth coin with a dime. Finally, he replaced every fifth coin with a quarter. What is the value of the remaining 15 coins on his desk? Explain.

11. **WRITING IN ►MATH** Describe when you would use the *make a model* strategy.

You can use centimeter cubes to build rectangular prisms like the ones shown at the right.

MAIN IDEA

I will use models to find the volumes of prisms.

NYS Core Curriculum

Preparation for 6.G.4 Determine the volume of rectangular prisms by counting cubes and develop the formula

ACTIVITY

Step 1 Use centimeter cubes to build four different rectangular prisms.

Step 2 For each prism, record the dimensions and the number of cubes used in a table like the one below.

Prism	Length (ℓ)	Width (w)	Height (h)	Area of Base (B)	Number of Cubes
A					
B					
C					
D					

Since volume can be measured using cubes, volume is measured in cubic units.

✓ CHECK What You Know

1. Describe the relationship between the dimensions of the prism and number of cubes.

2. Use ℓ, w, and h to write a formula for the volume V of a rectangular prism.

3. Use the formula you wrote in Exercise 2 to find the volume of the prism at the right in appropriate units. Verify your solution by counting the number of cubes.

Volumes of Prisms

MAIN IDEA

I will find the volumes of rectangular prisms.

NYS Core Curriculum

Preparation for 6.G.4 Determine the volume of rectangular prisms by counting cubes and develop the formula

Preparation for 6.M.1 Measure capacity and calculate volume of a rectangular prism

New Vocabulary

volume

NY Math Online

macmillanmh.com
• Extra Examples
• Personal Tutor
• Self-Check Quiz

GET READY to Learn

Armando makes sand paintings by filling clear plastic cases with colored sand. The amount of sand he uses depends on the amount of space in the cases.

Volume is the amount of space that a three-dimensional figure contains. Volume is measured in cubic units. A cubic unit has length, width, and height.

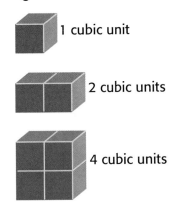

1 cubic unit

2 cubic units

4 cubic units

Some common units of volume are *cubic inch*, *cubic foot*, *cubic yard*, *cubic centimeter*, and *cubic meter*.

You can find the volume of a rectangular prism by using models or a formula.

Volume of a Rectangular Prism	Key Concept
Words	The volume *V* of a rectangular prism is length ℓ times width *w* times height *h*.
Symbols	$V = \ell wh$
Model	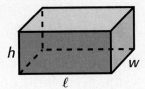

1 **GAMES** **What is the volume of a video game system that is 6 inches long, 4 inches wide, and 4 inches tall?**

Remember

A cube with 1 unit on an edge is a standard unit for measuring volume. When cubes are placed in a prism to determine volume, there are no gaps or overlaps between the cubes.

One Way: **Use a Model**

Count the number of 1-inch cubes that will fill the bottom of the rectangular prism. The prism is 6 cubes long and 4 cubes wide. There are 24 cubes on the bottom.

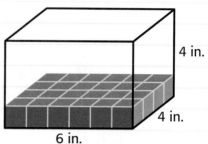

There are 4 layers of cubes. So, there are 4 × 24 or 96 cubes.

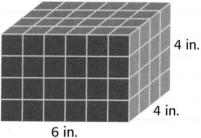

Another Way: **Select and Use a Formula**

$V = \ell wh$ Formula for the volume of a rectangular prism
$V = 6 \times 4 \times 4$ $\ell = 6$, $w = 4$, $h = 4$
$V = 96$ Multiply.

The volume of the video game system is 96 cubic inches.

EXAMPLE   Volume of a Prism

2 **Find the volume of the prism.**

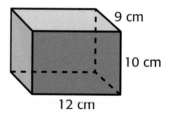

$V = \ell wh$ Formula for the volume

Estimate $10 \times 10 \times 10 = 1,000$

$V = \mathbf{12} \times \mathbf{9} \times \mathbf{10}$ $\ell = 12$, $w = 9$, $h = 10$

$V = 1,080$ Multiply.

The volume of the prism is 1,080 cubic centimeters. This is close to the estimate, 1,000. So, the answer is reasonable.

Find the volume of each prism. See Examples 1, 2 (p. 632)

1.
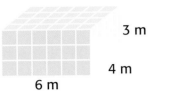
3 m
4 m
6 m

2.
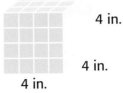
4 in.
4 in.
4 in.

3.
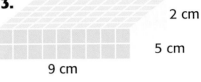
2 cm
5 cm
9 cm

4. $\ell = 21$ cm, $w = 8$ cm, $h = 4$ cm

5. $\ell = 19$ ft, $w = 9$ ft, $h = 16$ ft

6. Find the cubic feet of air in a room that is 13 feet long, 10 feet high, and 11 feet wide.

7. **Talk About It** Describe which units would be appropriate to measure the volume of a jewelry box. What other units might be reasonable to use? Would it be reasonable to use the same units to measure the volume of a garage? Explain.

Practice and Problem Solving

NYSCC • NYSMT

Extra Practice, p. R39

Find the volume of each prism. See Examples 1, 2 (p. 632)

8.
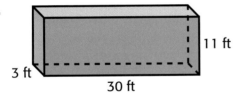
11 ft
3 ft
30 ft

9.
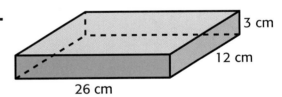
3 cm
12 cm
26 cm

10.
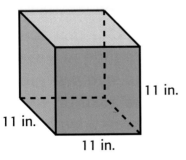
11 in.
11 in.
11 in.

11. 16 m
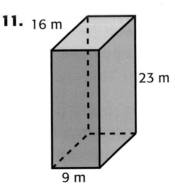
23 m
9 m

12.
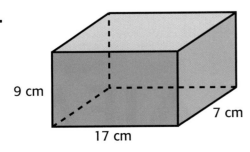
9 cm
7 cm
17 cm

13.
3 in.
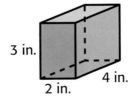
2 in.
4 in.

Find the volume of each prism. See Examples 1, 2 (p. 632)

14. $\ell = 5$ yd, $w = 16$ yd, $h = 6$ yd

15. $\ell = 2$ m, $w = 8$ m, $h = 10$ m

16. $\ell = 13$ in., $w = 3$ in., $h = 2$ in.

17. $\ell = 13$ cm, $w = 8$ cm, $h = 10$ cm

18. Find the volume of a bank vault that is 14 feet by 20 feet by 19 feet.

19. Which size container has the greater volume? Explain.

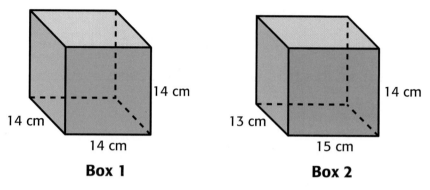

Box 1   **Box 2**

20. Sherita needs 1,400 cubic meters of storage space for her furniture. The space available at a storage company has a length of 11 meters, width of 10 meters, and height of 12 meters. Is the space large enough for Sherita's furniture? Explain.

H.O.T. Problems ·······································

21. OPEN ENDED Estimate the volume of a shoe box. Then measure the box. Check your estimate by finding the actual volume.

22. NUMBER SENSE Describe the dimensions of two different prisms that have a volume of 2,400 cubic centimeters.

23. CHALLENGE A store sells lunch boxes that measure 11 inches by 7 inches by 4 inches. How many lunch boxes will fit in a box that measures 22 inches by 15 inches by 8 inches? Explain.

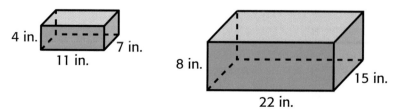

24. WRITING IN ►MATH Write about a real-life situation that can be solved by finding the volume of a prism. Then solve.

25. Popcorn tins are stacked in a display so that there are 12 tins in the bottom row. There are 10 tins in the next row, and 8 tins in the row above that. There are five rows of tins. If the pattern continues, how many popcorn tins are there in all? **(Lesson 14-5)**

A 22

B 30

C 40

D 42

26. SHORT RESPONSE Find the volume in cubic inches of a rectangular prism with length 8 inches, width 5 inches, and height 11 inches. **(Lesson 14-6)**

27. Which of these rectangular prisms has a volume of 20 cubic units? **(Lesson 14-6)**

F

G

H

J

Spiral Review

28. Estimate the volume of one of your textbooks in cubic centimeters. Explain how you could make a model to test your estimate. **(Lesson 14-5)**

29. What kind of three-dimensional shape is shown below? **(Lesson 14-4)**

30. Estimate the area of the figure shown below. **(Lesson 14-2)**

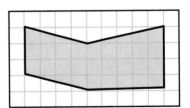

Identify whether each group of objects represents a prime number or a composite number. (Lesson 9-2)

31.

32.

Problem Solving in Science

BIRDSEYE VIEW

You probably eat packaged frozen food every day. Frozen food might seem like a simple concept, but there's more to it than just putting a container of food in the freezer.

Clarence Birdseye is sometimes called "the father of frozen food" because he was the first to develop a practical way to preserve food by flash freezing.

Birdseye experimented with freezing fruits and vegetables, as well as fish and meat. His method of freezing food preserved the food's taste, texture, and appearance. He also was the first to package food in waxed cardboard packages that could be sold directly to consumers.

Did You Know?

148 patents were issued that related to Clarence Birdseye's flash-freezing method, his type of packaging, and the packaging materials he used.

DIMENSIONS OF FROZEN FOOD PACKAGES IN INCHES

Item	Length	Width	Height
Pizza	12	12	2
Vegetables	5	6	2
Frozen Dinner	11	8	2
Fish Sticks	9	5	3
Hamburger Patties	9	10	4

 # Real-World Math

Use the information above to solve each problem.

1. What is the volume of a frozen pizza package?

2. How much more space does a package of fish sticks occupy than a package of vegetables?

3. Is 175 cubic inches a reasonable estimate for the volume of a frozen dinner package? Explain.

4. A freezer has 2,600 cubic inches of available space. After seven packages of hamburger patties are placed inside, how much available freezer space is left?

5. A larger package of frozen vegetables has the same length and width but twice the height. What is the volume of this package?

6. Use a centimeter ruler to measure the length, width, and height of an actual frozen food package to the nearest whole unit. Then find the volume of the package.

7. **WRITING IN ▶MATH** Explain the differences between area and volume and the units used to represent them.

Surface Area of Prisms

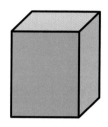

To find the *surface area* of a rectangular prism, you add the areas of all the faces of the prism.

All six faces can be seen by using a *net*. A **net** is a two dimensional pattern of a three dimensional figure.

MAIN IDEA

I will use models to find the surface area of rectangular prisms.

NYS Core Curriculum

Preparation for 6.G.2 Determine the area of triangles and quadrilaterals (squares, rectangles, rhombi, and trapezoids) and develop formulas *Also addresses 6.M.7.*

You Will Need
graph paper
scissors

New Vocabulary

net

ACTIVITY

1 **Create a net to find the surface area of the prism.**

Step 1 Draw and cut out the net below.

Step 2 Fold along the dotted lines. Tape the edges together to form a prism.

Step 3 Find the area of each of the six faces of the prism.

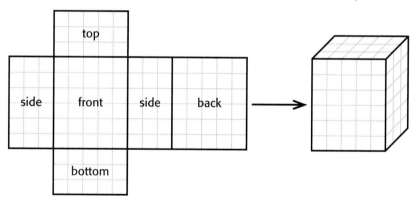

Face	front and back	top and bottom	two sides
Model			
Area (cm²)	30	15	18

Step 4 Find the sum of the areas.

$A = 30 + 30 + 18 + 18 + 15 + 15$

$A = 126$ cm² Surface area has square units because it measures area.

2 **Find the surface area of the rectangular prism.**

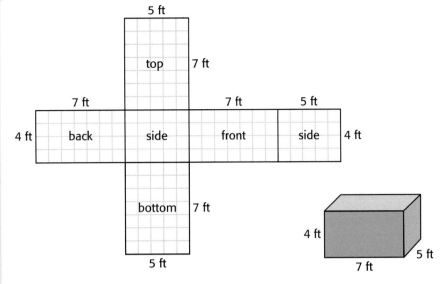

Find the area of each face. Then add.

Face	front and back	top and bottom	two sides
Model			
Area (cm²)	28	35	20

$A = 28 + 28 + 35 + 35 + 20 + 20$ or 166 square feet

Think About It

1. Explain how to find the surface area of a prism by using a net.

✓ CHECK What You Know

Make a net to find the surface area of each rectangular prism.

2.

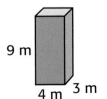

9 m

4 m   3 m

3.

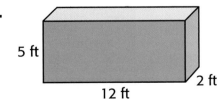

5 ft

12 ft   2 ft

4. **WRITING IN ▶MATH** Will the top side of a rectangular prism always have the same area as the bottom side? Explain.

14-7 Surface Areas of Prisms

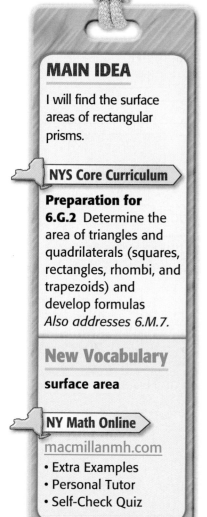

MAIN IDEA

I will find the surface areas of rectangular prisms.

NYS Core Curriculum

Preparation for 6.G.2 Determine the area of triangles and quadrilaterals (squares, rectangles, rhombi, and trapezoids) and develop formulas *Also addresses 6.M.7.*

New Vocabulary

surface area

NY Math Online

macmillanmh.com
• Extra Examples
• Personal Tutor
• Self-Check Quiz

GET READY to Learn

Wrapping paper is used to cover the surface area of a box.

The sum of the areas of all the faces of a prism is called the **surface area** of the prism.

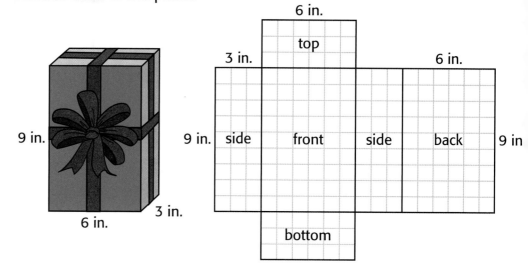

To find the surface area, you could add the areas of all six faces.

In the diagram above each face has a congruent opposite face. The front is congruent to the back, the top is congruent to the bottom, and the two sides are congruent.

So, the following formula can also be used to find surface area.

Surface Area of a Rectangular Prism	Key Concept
Words	The surface area S of a rectangular prism with length ℓ, width w, and height h is the sum of the areas of the faces.
Symbols	$S = 2\ell w + 2\ell h + 2wh$
Model	

① **GIFTS Find the surface area for the amount of wrapping paper needed to cover the gift on page 640.**

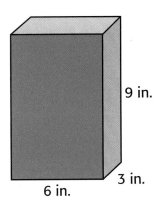

9 in.

3 in.

6 in.

Find the area of each face.

top and bottom:
$2(\ell w) = 2(6 \times 3)$ or 36

front and back:
$2(\ell h) = 2(6 \times 9)$ or 108

two sides:
$2(wh) = 2(3 \times 9)$ or 54

Add to find the surface area.

The surface area is 36 + 108 + 54 or 198 square inches.

Remember

The top face has the same area as the bottom face. The front face has the same area as the back face. Both side faces have the same area.

② **CAMERAS Digital cameras are made small enough to fit in a pocket. This camera is shaped like a rectangular prism. Find the surface area of the camera.**

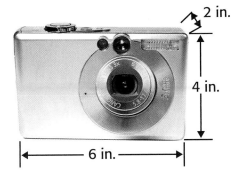

2 in.

4 in.

6 in.

Find the area of each face.

top and bottom: $2(\ell w) = 2(6 \times 2)$ or 24

front and back: $2(\ell h) = 2(6 \times 4)$ or 48

two sides: $2(wh) = 2(2 \times 4)$ or 16

Add to find the surface area.

The surface area is 24 + 48 + 16 or 88 square inches.

Find the surface area of each rectangular prism. See Example 1 (p. 641)

1.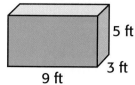
5 ft
3 ft
9 ft

2.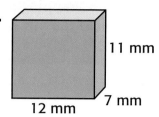
11 mm
12 mm
7 mm

3.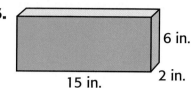
6 in.
15 in.
2 in.

4. A box of animal crackers is shaped like a rectangular prism. What is the surface area of the box of crackers?

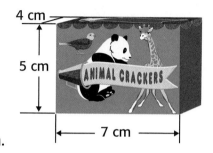
4 cm
5 cm
7 cm

5. 💬 Talk About It
The formula for the surface area of a rectangular prism is $S = 2\ell w + 2\ell h + 2wh$. Explain why there are three 2s in the formula.

Find the surface area of each rectangular prism. See Example 1 (p. 641)

6.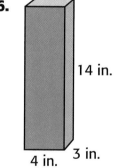
14 in.
4 in.
3 in.

7.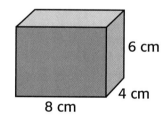
6 cm
8 cm
4 cm

8.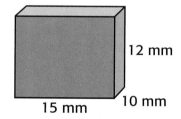
12 mm
15 mm
10 mm

9.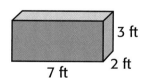
3 ft
7 ft
2 ft

10.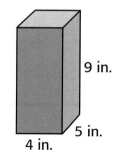
9 in.
4 in.
5 in.

11.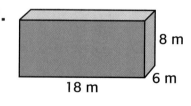
8 m
18 m
6 m

12. Alyssa owns a toolbox that is 16 inches by 22 inches by 5 inches. What is the surface area of the toolbox?

13. Michelle put her sister's birthday present in a box with a length of 13 mm, a width of 4 mm, and a height of 8 mm. How many square millimeters of wrapping paper will Michelle need to completely cover the box?

14. A package of three golf balls comes in the box shown. What is the surface area of the box?

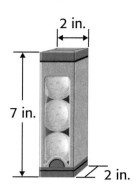

2 in.

7 in.

2 in.

H.O.T. Problems

15. OPEN ENDED What is the possible length, width, and height of a rectangular prism with the surface area of 110 square centimeters?

CHALLENGE **For Exercises 16 and 17, use the rectangular prism shown.**

16. How many rectangles and how many squares would the net of the prism make?

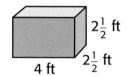

$2\frac{1}{2}$ ft

$2\frac{1}{2}$ ft

4 ft

17. Find the surface area of the rectangular prism.

18. WRITING IN ►MATH Write a real-world problem about a time when you would need to find the surface area of a rectangular prism.

NYSMT Practice   6.G.2

19. A shoebox has a length of 10 inches, a width of 5 inches, and a height of 6 inches. What is the surface area of the shoebox? (Lesson 14-7)

   A 220 in²   **C** 325 in²

   B 280 in²   **D** 340 in²

20. SHORT RESPONSE If the surface area of the top of a rectangular prism is 16 square centimeters, what is the surface area of the bottom? (Lesson 14-7)

Spiral Review

21. Find the volume of a cube that has a length, width, and height of 7 inches. (Lesson 14-6)

22. Identify the kinds of angles in the triangle shown at the right. (Lesson 13-3)

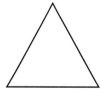

Select Appropriate Measurement Formulas

MAIN IDEA

I will select and use appropriate units and formulas to measure length, perimeter, area, and volume.

NYS Core Curriculum

5.M.6 Determine the tool and technique to measure with an appropriate level of precision: lengths and angles

NY Math Online

macmillanmh.com

• Extra Examples
• Personal Tutor
• Self-Check Quiz

GET READY to Learn

The 2007 Women's World Cup was played in China. The field at Chengdu Stadium is 109 meters long by 75 meters wide.

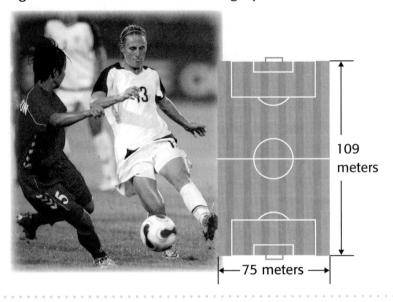

You have learned to find the perimeter, area, and volume of figures. It is important to be able to choose the appropriate measurement for a given situation.

Measurement Formulas			Key Concept
Measure	**Used to Find**	**Model**	**Formula**
Perimeter	distance around a figure		$P = 2\ell + 2w$
Area	space covered by a figure		$A = \ell w$
Volume	space enclosed by a figure		$V = \ell wh$

Remember

Perimeter is given in units, area is given in square units, and volume is given in cubic units.

Real-World EXAMPLES · Determine the Appropriate Measurement

1 SOCCER A grounds crew will be cutting the grass on the field at Chengdu stadium. Determine whether they will be cutting the perimeter, area, or volume of the grass. Then solve.

The field is a rectangle that is 109 meters long and 75 meters wide.

They need to find the area to determine the size of the surface that needs to be cut.

$A = \ell w$	Formula for area of a rectangle
$A = 109 \times 75$	$\ell = 109$ and $w = 75$
$A = 8{,}175$	Multiply.

The area of the field is 8,175 square meters.

2 SWIMMING Mr. Clive needs to install a rubber strip around the edge of the swimming pool shown below. Determine whether he should find the perimeter, area, or volume of the swimming pool. Then solve.

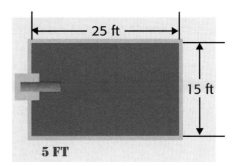

Mr. Clive needs to know the distance around the pool. So, he needs to find the perimeter.

$P = 2\ell + 2w$	Formula for perimeter of a rectangle
$P = 2(25) + 2(15)$	$\ell = 25$ and $w = 15$
$P = 80$	Simplify.

The distance around the pool is 80 feet.

3 **DESIGN** An architect needs to calculate how
much cement to use for a decorative column.
The figure represents the column. Determine
whether she should find the perimeter,
area, or volume of the column. Then solve.

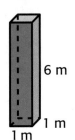

6 m

1 m

1 m

The architect needs to know how much space the
column encloses. So, she needs to find the volume.

$V = \ell wh$ 　　　　Formula for volume of a rectangular prism

$V = 1 \times 1 \times 6$ 　$\ell = 1$, $w = 1$, and $h = 6$

$V = 6$ 　　　　Simplify.

So, 6 cubic meters of cement are needed.

CHECK What You Know

**Determine whether you need to find the perimeter, area, or volume.
Then solve.** See Examples 1–3 (pp. 644–645)

1. Carmella is making a rectangular flower garden in her backyard. The
space she wants to use is 4 meters in length and 2 meters wide. How
much space will she have in her garden?

2. Mrs. Hernandez is sewing fringe around curtains that are used in a
school play. There are four rectangular panels, each 3 feet wide and
$5\frac{1}{2}$ feet long. How much fringe does she need to buy?

3. How much water is needed to fill a pool that is 50 meters long,
25 meters wide, and 3 meters deep?

4. Which units would be most appropriate to measure the volume of a
cake pan: cubic inches, cubic feet, or cubic yards? Explain.

5. A basketball court that is 50 feet wide and
84 feet long needs to be refinished. The cost
for refinishing is $6.00 per square foot. What
will be the total cost?

6. **Talk About It** Explain how you determine whether
to use the formula for perimeter,
area, or volume for a given situation.

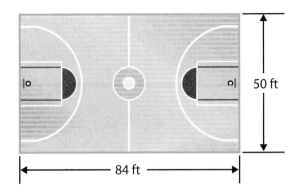

50 ft

84 ft

Determine whether you need to find the perimeter, area, or volume.
Then solve. See Examples 1–3 (pp. 644–645)

7. A path is 3 feet wide and 14 feet long. How much gravel will Mr. James need if he wants to add 2 inches of gravel over the entire path?

8. A room is 8 meters by 16 meters. How much carpet is needed?

Refer to the pool shown at the right for Exercises 9 and 10.

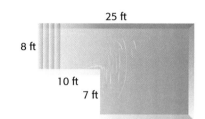

9. Decorative tiles 6 inches long are to be placed around the edges of the pool. How many tiles will be needed?

10. What size tarp would be needed to cover the pool?

Real-World PROBLEM SOLVING

Measurement In a fish tank, 30 square centimeters of water surface are needed for each centimeter of fish length. So, two fish that are 6 centimeters long need 360 square centimeters of water.

11. An angelfish is 12 centimeters long. How many angelfish could be placed in Tank B?

12. A fancy guppy is 5 centimeters long. Which tank could hold 2 angelfish and 4 fancy guppies?

Tank	Size (cm)
A	$\ell = 24, w = 12, h = 12$
B	$\ell = 45, w = 25, h = 25$
C	$\ell = 60, w = 30, h = 38$

H.O.T. Problems

13. **FIND THE ERROR** Martin and Ryan are finding the volume of a prism with length 3 meters, height 8 meters, and width 17 meters. Who is correct? Explain your reasoning.

Martin
$V = 2(3) + 2(8)$
$= 22$ cubic meters

Ryan
$V = 3 \times 8 \times 17$
$= 408$ cubic meters

14. **WRITING IN ▸MATH** Describe the steps you would take to find the area of your bedroom floor.

Problem-Solving Investigation

MAIN IDEA I will choose the best strategy to solve a problem.

 5.PS.3 Interpret information correctly, identify the problem, and generate possible strategies and solutions

P.S.I. TEAM +

JACINDA: I am helping my mom cover the swing set area with mulch. The base of the swing set is rectangular in shape and measures 4 meters by 2 meters. The area we want to cover extends 1 meter in each direction from the edge of the swing set.

YOUR MISSION: Find the area of the space covered with mulch.

Understand	You know the dimensions of the swing set. You need to find the area of the space covered with mulch.
Plan	Solve the problem by drawing a diagram.
Solve	Draw a diagram of the area to be covered with mulch. Find the length. 4 m + 1 m + 1 m, or 6 m Find the width. 2 m + 1 m + 1 m, or 4 m $A = \ell w$ Formula for area of a rectangle. $A = 6 \times 4$ Replace ℓ with 6 and w with 4. $A = 24$ Multiply. The area of the space to be covered is 24 square meters.
Check	Look back. Reread the problem to see if the diagram matches the information given. ✓

(Diagram: rectangle labeled "base of swing set" 2 m by 4 m, surrounded by 1 m on each side — top 1 m, bottom 1 m, left 1 m, right 1 m.)

Use any strategy shown below to solve each problem.

PROBLEM-SOLVING STRATEGIES
- Guess and check.
- Look for a pattern.
- Make a table.
- Draw a diagram.

1. **Geometry** Mariana stacked 8 cubes on top of each other to make a tower 8 cubes high. How many of the cubes' faces can Mariana see?

2. **Measurement** A hexagon that has each side equal to 1 inch has a perimeter of 6 inches.

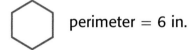 perimeter = 6 in.

Two hexagons placed side by side have a perimeter of 10 inches. Three hexagons have a perimeter of 14 inches.

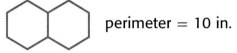 perimeter = 10 in.

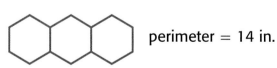 perimeter = 14 in.

What would be the perimeter of five hexagons placed side by side?

3. Five friends are standing in a circle and playing a game where they toss a ball of yarn to one another. If each person tosses the yarn to each other only once, how many lines of yarn will be between them?

4. Pedro has $42 in his pocket. He has only $5 and $1 bills. He has a total of 14 bills. What combination of bills does he have?

5. **Algebra** The table below shows the number of minutes Danielle spent practicing the trumpet over the last 7 days. If she continues this pattern of practicing, in how many days will she have practiced 555 minutes?

Day	Time (min)
1	20
2	20
3	35
4	20
5	20
6	35
7	20

For Exercises 6 and 7, use the following information.

Marita wants to make a rectangle with a perimeter of 20 inches.

6. How many rectangles can Marita make if she only uses whole numbers for the side lengths? List the dimensions.

7. Which rectangle has the greatest area?

8. **WRITING IN ►MATH** One wall of a building is 80 feet long and 16 feet high. A one-gallon can of paint covers up to 450 square feet. If each can of paint costs $22.50, find the total cost of paint for the wall. Explain the steps you used to solve the problem.

FOLDABLES® Study Organizer GET READY to Study

Be sure the following Big Ideas are written in your Foldable.

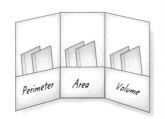

Perimeter   Area   Volume

Key Concepts

Perimeters of Polygons

• The perimeter P of a square is 4 times the side length s. (p. 609)

$$P = s + s + s + s \quad \text{or} \quad 4s$$

• The perimeter P of a rectangle is two times the length ℓ plus two times the width w. (p. 609)

$$P = \ell + \ell + w + w \quad \text{or} \quad 2\ell + 2w$$

Areas of Rectangles

• The area A of a rectangle is the length ℓ times the width w. (p. 616)

$$A = \ell w$$

• The area A of a square is the square of the side length s. (p. 617)

$$A = s^2 \quad \text{or} \quad s \times s$$

Surface Areas of Rectangular Prisms

• The surface area S of a rectangular prism is the sum of the areas of the faces. (p. 640)

$$S = 2\ell w + 2\ell h + 2wh$$

Volumes of Prisms

• The volume V of a rectangular prism is length ℓ times width w times height h. (p. 631)

$$V = \ell w h$$

Key Vocabulary

area (p. 612)

cone (p. 624)

cylinder (p. 624)

perimeter (p. 607)

polygon (p. 608)

prism (p. 624)

rectangular prism (p. 624)

surface area (p. 640)

triangular prism (p. 624)

volume (p. 631)

Vocabulary Check

State whether each sentence is *true* or *false*. If false, replace the underlined word or number to make a true sentence.

1. The <u>perimeter</u> of a rectangle is the length times the width.

2. A rectangular prism with all sides 4 centimeters long has a volume of <u>64</u> cubic centimeters.

3. The area of a square with a side length of 8 inches is <u>32</u> square inches.

4. A three-dimensional figure with faces that are polygons is called a <u>polyhedron</u>.

5. A <u>cylinder</u> has two parallel congruent circular bases.

Lesson-by-Lesson Review

14-1   Perimeters of Polygons (pp. 608–611)

5.G.1

Example 1
Find the perimeter of the rectangle.

9 in.

16 in.

$P = 2\ell + 2w$ Perimeter of rectangle

$P = 2(16) + 2(9)$ $\ell = 16, w = 9$

$P = 50$ in.   Simplfiy.

The perimeter is 50 inches.

Find the perimeter of each figure.

6.
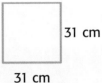
15 yd   18 yd
10 yd

7.
31 cm
31 cm

8. A garden in the shape of a square is 15 feet on each side. What is the perimeter?

14-2   Areas (pp. 612–615)

6.G.2

Example 2
Estimate the area of the figure. Each square represents 1 square inch.

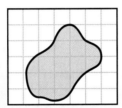

7 whole squares = 7 square inches

11 partial squares is about $5\frac{1}{2}$ square inches

The area is about $7 + 5\frac{1}{2} = 12\frac{1}{2}$ square centimeters.

Estimate the area of each figure. Each square represents 1 square centimeter.

9.
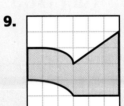

10.
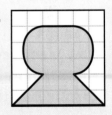

14-3   Areas of Rectangles and Squares (pp. 616–619)

6.G.2

Example 3
Find the area of the rectangle.

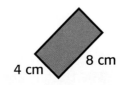
4 cm   8 cm

$A = \ell w$

$A = 8 \times 4$ $\ell = 8, w = 4$

$A = 32$ square centimeters

Find the area of each rectangle or square.

11.
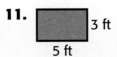 3 ft
5 ft

12.
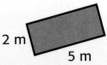
2 m
5 m

13. A new building measures 42 feet by 30 feet. How much land does it cover?

Study Guide and Review

 Three-Dimensional Figures (pp. 624–627)

6.M.1

Example 4
Describe parts of the figure that are parallel, perpendicular and congruent. Then identify the figure.

Opposite faces are parallel and congruent. Adjacent faces form right angles, so they are perpendicular.

The figure is a rectangular prism.

Describe parts of each figure that are parallel, perpendicular, and congruent. Then identify the figure.

14.    **15.**

16. Describe parts of the vase that are parallel and congruent. Then identify the shape of the vase.

 Problem-Solving Strategy: Make a Model (pp. 628–629)

5.PS.13

Example 5
How many centimeter cubes will fit in the container at the right?

You can use cubes to model the situation.

First, arrange 2 rows of 5 cubes.

Next, add three more layers of cubes.

The total number of cubes used is 40. So, 40 centimeter cubes will fit in the container.

Solve by making a model.

17. A box is filled with 48 cubes that measure 1 inch on each side. The cubes completely fill the box. What are possible dimensions of the box?

18. Haley is making a bracelet by placing beads and charms on a 6-inch chain. She places a charm at 1 inch from each end, and at every $\frac{1}{2}$ inch in between. How many charms does she use?

19. Destiny has 24 feet of fencing material to make a pet enclosure. Describe three different rectangular areas that can be enclosed by the fencing.

14-6 Volumes of Prisms (pp. 631–635)

6.M.1

Example 6
Find the volume of the prism.

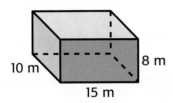

10 m — 8 m — 15 m

$V = \ell wh$ Volume of a prism

$V = 15 \times 10 \times 8$ $\ell = 15, w = 10, h = 8$

$V = 1{,}200$ Multiply.

The volume of the prism is 1,200 cubic meters.

Find the volume of each prism.

20.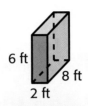
6 ft   8 ft   2 ft

21.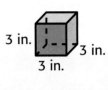
3 in.   3 in.   3 in.

22.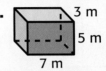
3 m   5 m   7 m

23.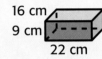
16 cm   9 cm   22 cm

24. Victoro keeps his pet rabbit in a cage that is shaped like a rectangular prism. The cage measures 2 feet by 3 feet by 2 feet. What is the volume of the cage?

14-7 Surface Area of Prisms (pp. 640-643)

6.G.2

Example 7
Find the surface area of the rectangular prism.

8 cm   4 cm   5 cm

$S = 2\ell w + 2\ell h + 2wh$

top and bottom: $2(\ell w) = 2(8 \times 5)$ or 80

front and back: $2(\ell h) = 2(8 \times 4)$ or 64

two sides: $2(wh) = 2(5 \times 4)$ or 40

The surface area is 80 + 64 + 40 or 184 square centimeters.

Find the surface area of each rectangular prism.

25.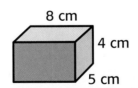
2 in.   8 in.   3 in.

26.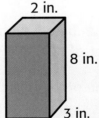
3 ft   4 ft   10 ft

27. A DVD player measures 17 inches by 15 inches by 3 inches. What is the minimum surface area of a box to hold the DVD player?

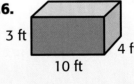

14-8 Select Appropriate Measurement Formulas (pp. 644–647)

5.M.6

Example 8

The park shown below is to be covered with new sod. How much sod is needed? Determine whether you need to find the perimeter, area, or volume. Then solve.

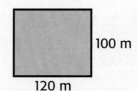

100 m

120 m

The sod is to cover the entire surface of the park, so the area needs to be found.

$A = \ell w$ Area of a rectangle

$A = 120 \times 100$ $\ell = 120, w = 100$

$A = 12{,}000$ Multiply.

The area that needs to be covered with sod is 12,000 square meters.

Determine whether you need to find the perimeter, area, or volume. Then solve.

28. Ray is sweeping a rectangular floor that is 12 feet long and 9 feet wide. How much does he have to sweep?

29. A gym mat measures 8 feet by 4 feet. The edges of the mat need to be repaired. What is the total length of the edges?

30. Planters that are 16 inches long, 7 inches wide, and 5 inches high are to be placed around a restaurant patio. How much soil is needed to fill 8 planters?

14-9 Problem-Solving Investigation: Choose a Strategy (pp. 648–649)

5.PS.3

Example 9

What two whole numbers have a sum of 12 and a product of 32?

One way to solve the problem is to use the guess and check strategy.

Guess: 3 and 9

Check: $3 + 9 = 12, 3 \times 9 = 27 \neq 32$

Guess: 4 and 8

Check: $4 + 8 = 12, 4 \times 8 = 32$ ✔

The whole numbers are 4 and 8.

Use any strategy to solve.

31. Barrett has 18 sports cards. He collects football and baseball cards. He has twice as many baseball cards. How many of each kind does he have?

32. Leon has $5 to buy a bottle of water that costs $1.49, a granola bar for $1.09, and a newspaper for $2.25. Does he have enough money? Explain.

Find the perimeter of each rectangle or square.

1.

15 cm
15 cm

2.
14 ft
22 ft

3. MULTIPLE CHOICE A rectangular picture frame is 10 inches by 12 inches. Jodie wants to add a lace border around the frame. Which length would fit around the frame with the least amount left?

A 1 foot   **C** 4 feet

B 2 feet   **D** 5 feet

Find the area of each rectangle or square.

4.

5 ft
8 ft

5.

6 m
6 m

6. Estimate the area of the figure. Each square represents 1 square centimeter.
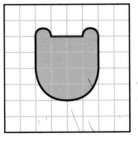

7. If you place one cube on a table, you can see 5 faces of the cube. If you place a second cube on top of the first, you can see 9 faces. How many faces can you see in a stack of 6 cubes?

8. A backyard is in the shape of a right triangle. The sides measure 30 feet, 40 feet, and 50 feet. How much fencing is needed to enclose the entire backyard?

9. MULTIPLE CHOICE Which figure below has 3 more edges than faces?

F

H

G

J

Find the volume of each prism.

10.
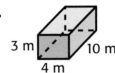
3 m
10 m
4 m

11.
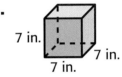
7 in.
7 in.
7 in.

A pool is 50 meters long, 20 meters wide, and 3 meters deep. For each problem, determine whether you need to find the perimeter, area, or volume. Then solve.

12. The bottom of the pool needs to be painted. How much paint is needed?

13. How many lifeguards are needed if they are posted every 35 meters?

14. Find the surface area of the rectangular prism.

7 cm
4 cm
2 cm

15. **WRITING IN ►MATH** Describe the difference between finding the area of a rectangle and finding the volume of a rectangular prism.

PART I **Multiple Choice**

Read each question. Then fill in the correct answer on the answer sheet provided by the teacher or on a sheet of paper.

1. A square has a perimeter of 36 meters. What is the area of the square?

   A 81 m²   **C** 9 m²

   B 72 m²   **D** 6 m²

2. Which of the following would you use to find the volume of the figure shown?

   F $V = \ell \times w$

   G $V = 2\ell + 2w$

   H $V = \ell \times w \times h$

   J $V = 2\ell \times 2w \times 2h$

3. How many faces, edges, and vertices does the figure have?

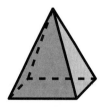

   A 5 faces, 8 edges, 5 vertices

   B 5 faces, 6 edges, 8 vertices

   C 5 faces, 8 edges, 6 vertices

   D 6 faces, 10 edges, 6 vertices

4. Bansi needs 48 ounces of buttermilk for a recipe. How many cups of buttermilk does she need?

   F 4 c   **H** 6 c

   G 5 c   **J** 7 c

5. Which transformation is represented in the diagram?

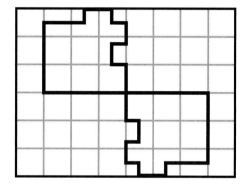

   A Reflection   **C** Rotation

   B Translation   **D** Not here

6. Look at the pattern of numbers shown below.

     7, ___, 17, 22, 27, 32

Which expression could be used to find the missing number in the pattern?

   F $(27 - 18) + 3$

   G $(7 + 12) - 5$

   H $(17 - 12) + 5$

   J $(28 - 23) + 3$

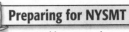
7. Which statement about the figures shown below is true?

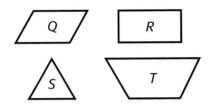

A Figures *Q* and *R* are congruent.

B Figures *S* and *T* are squares.

C Figures *S* and *R* have the same number of sides.

D Figures *Q* and *T* each have at least two acute angles.

8. The drawing below represents a parking lot at a pet store.

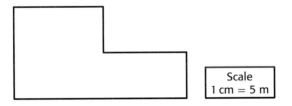

Scale
1 cm = 5 m

Use the ruler on the Mathematics Chart to measure the dimensions of the parking lot to the nearest tenth of centimeter. Which is the closest to the perimeter of the parking lot in meters?

F 125 m   **H** 75 m

G 100 m   **J** 18 m

PART 2   Short Response

Record your answers on the answer sheet provided by your teacher or on a sheet of paper.

9. A rectangular driveway measures 16 feet by 12 feet. What is the area of the driveway in square feet?

---

10. Find the number of millimeters that are equivalent to 50 centimeters.

PART 3   Extended Response

Record your answers on the answer sheet provided by your teacher or on a sheet of paper.

11. Derrick is painting a toy chest that is 14 inches tall, 9 inches wide, and 11 inches long. Draw a diagram of Derrick's toy chest. Then, find the surface area and volume of the chest.

---

12. It takes 3 feet of wood to make 1 birdhouse. If you have 23 feet of wood, can you make 8 birdhouses? Explain.

NEED EXTRA HELP?												
If You Missed Question...	1	2	3	4	5	6	7	8	9	10	11	12
Go to Lesson...	14–3	14–6	14–4	12–4	13–9	6–6	13–1	14–1	14–3	12–1	14–6	4–6
NYS Core Curriculum	6.G.2	6.M.1	6.M.1	5.M.5	5.G.13	5.A.4	5.G.11	5.G.1	6.G.2	5.M.4	6.M.1	5.N.17

CHAPTER 15 Use Probability to Make Predictions

BIG Idea **What is probability?**

Probability is the chance that a given event will happen.

Example In his pocket, Jeremy has the three state quarters shown below. If he takes a quarter from his pocket without looking, what is the probability that it is the New Jersey quarter?

The probability is **1 out of 3**, or $\frac{1}{3}$, that it will be the New Jersey quarter.

What will I learn in this chapter?

- Determine the likelihood of an event.
- Use fractions to describe the results of an experiment.
- Use experimental results to make a prediction.
- List outcomes of a probability experiment.
- Solve problems by *making an organized list*.

Key Vocabulary

probability

outcome

probability experiment

tree diagram

NY Math Online **Student Study Tools**
at macmillanmh.com

FOLDABLES® Study Organizer

Make this Foldable to help you organize information about probability. Begin with a sheet of 11" × 17" paper.

❶ **Fold** the short sides toward the middle.

❷ **Fold** the top to the bottom.

❸ **Open.** Cut as shown to make four tabs.

❹ **Label** each tab as shown.

Probability | Probability as a Fraction

Make a Prediction | Count Outcomes

ARE YOU READY for Chapter 15?

You have two ways to check prerequisite skills for this chapter.

Option 2

NY Math Online > Take the Chapter Readiness Quiz at macmillanmh.com.

Option 1

Complete the Quick Check below.

QUICK Check

Choose from *certain*, *impossible*, *likely*, or *unlikely* to describe each probability. (Prior Grade)

1. If you choose a letter from the word EAR, it will be a vowel.

2. If you spin the spinner at the right, the number will be 8.

3. If you spin the spinner at the right, the number will be 5.

4. If you choose a letter from the word MATHEMATICS, it will be Q.

5. If you toss a coin, it will come up either heads or tails.

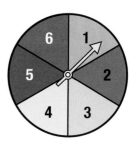

Write each fraction in simplest form. (Lesson 9-4)

6. $\frac{10}{12}$ 7. $\frac{4}{8}$ 8. $\frac{5}{15}$ 9. $\frac{14}{21}$

10. $\frac{6}{10}$ 11. $\frac{9}{24}$ 12. $\frac{12}{16}$ 13. $\frac{28}{36}$

14. Paloma goes to school 20 out of the 30 days in April. Write the number of days out of the month that she goes to school as a fraction in simplest form. (Lesson 9-4)

15. Daryl is meeting his friends on either Saturday or Sunday. They are either going to lunch or going to see a movie. Describe two different situations that could happen. (Prior Grade)

16. Manning is choosing a sandwich and a beverage from the table at the right. Describe three different choices. (Prior Grade)

Sandwich	Beverage
Cheese	Iced tea
Tuna	Lemonade
Turkey	

Probability

GET READY to Learn

One cube is drawn from each bag without looking. Write *certain*, *impossible*, or *equally likely* to make each a true sentence.

Bag 1	Bag 2	Bag 3
It is ___?___ that a black cube will be drawn.	It is ___?___ that a yellow cube will be drawn.	It is ___?___ that a yellow cube will be drawn.

Probability is the chance that an event will happen.

Probability		
Description	**Meaning**	**Example**
Certain	The event will definitely happen.	Drawing a yellow cube from Bag 2.
Impossible	There is no chance the event will happen.	Drawing a yellow cube from Bag 3.
Equally likely	There is an equal chance the event will happen.	Drawing a black cube from Bag 1.

An **outcome** is a possible result in a **probability experiment**. So, when drawing a cube from Bag 1 above, the possible outcomes are a black cube and a green cube.

EXAMPLE   List Outcomes

① **Cole spins the spinner at the right. List the possible outcomes.**

The spinner could land on the red space, the blue space, or the orange space.

outcomes: red, blue, orange

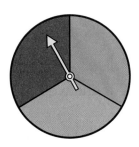

If the probability that an event will occur is *more* than equally likely, use the phrase *likely*. If the probability is *less* than equally likely, use the phrase *unlikely* to describe it.

Remember

At random or randomly means choosing a marble without looking. Each marble is equally likely to be chosen.

EXAMPLE Describe Probability

2 One marble is chosen at random. Describe the probability of choosing a green marble. Write *certain, impossible, likely, unlikely,* or *equally likely.*

event: choosing a green marble

outcomes: red, blue, green, yellow

There is only 1 green marble, compared to 5 yellow marbles. So, the probability of choosing a green marble is *unlikely.*

CHECK What You Know

List the possible outcomes in each probability experiment. See Example 1 (p. 661)

1. spinning the spinner

2. tossing a quarter

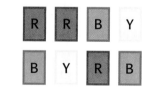

3. choosing a card at random

R	R	B	Y
B	Y	R	B

One disc is randomly drawn from the bag. Describe the probability of drawing each disc. Write *certain, impossible, likely, unlikely,* or *equally likely.* See Example 2 (p. 662)

4. blue

5. red

6. green

7. blue, red, or yellow

8. How many possible outcomes are there for choosing a letter in the word CERTAIN?

9. *Talk About It* Describe outcomes that are likely and unlikely to occur when a number cube labeled 1 to 6 is tossed. Explain.

List the possible outcomes in each probability experiment. See Example 1 (p. 661)

10. choosing one coin at random

11. randomly choosing one can of soup

12. choosing one cube without looking

13. spinning the spinner

14. randomly choosing one letter from the word EVENT

One card is drawn without looking. Describe the probability of drawing each card. Write *certain*, *impossible*, *likely*, *unlikely*, or *equally likely*. See Example 2 (p. 662)

B   A   N   A   N   A

15. B

16. A

Suppose you spin the spinner at the right. Describe the probability of landing on each color. Write *certain*, *impossible*, *likely*, *unlikely*, or *equally likely*. See Example 2 (p. 662)

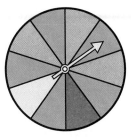

17. orange rather than red

18. green

19. orange rather than blue

20. *not* purple

H.O.T. Problems

21. **CHALLENGE** Describe a group of 10 cubes that have the following characteristics.

• There are 4 different colors.

• When a cube is drawn, one color is more likely to be drawn than any other.

• Exactly two of the remaining colors are equally likely to be drawn.

22. **WRITING IN ►MATH** Write a real-world problem that can be solved by describing its probability. Then solve the problem.

WILD ABOUT WILDFLOWER HABITATS

Many people like to grow flowers in their yards. The National Wildlife Federation encourages people to grow wildflowers and also to include plants that provide protective cover and food for another type of wildlife—animals!

A wildlife habitat for animals needs to have four essential ingredients: food, water, protective cover, and places for animals to raise their young. If you can provide these elements, you can enjoy a wildlife habitat in your own backyard!

Real-World Math

Use the table below to solve each problem.

1. Suppose you pick one seed at random from the packet of wildflower habitat mix. Is the probability of picking a grain *greater than* or *less than* picking a grass?

2. If you pick one seed at random from the packet of wildflower habitat mix, is the probability of picking a clover *likely* or *unlikely*?

3. If there are 700 seeds in the wildflower habitat mix, how many would be annual flowers?

4. Suppose you pick one seed at random from the packet of wildflower habitat mix. What is the probability that you would pick a flower seed? Write your answer as a fraction.

5. Describe your answer for Exercise 4 as *certain, impossible,* or *equally likely.*

6. **WRITING IN ►MATH** Explain how the fraction of seeds in the wildlife habitat mix will result in a well-balanced wildlife habitat.

WILDFLOWER HABITAT MIX

Grasses	$\frac{7}{20}$
Clovers	$\frac{1}{20}$
Grains	$\frac{1}{10}$
Annual flowers	$\frac{1}{4}$
Perennial flowers	$\frac{1}{4}$

Did You Know?
A lawn costs about $700 per acre each year. A wildflower meadow costs about $30 per acre each year.

Explore

Probability Activity for 15-2
Make a Prediction

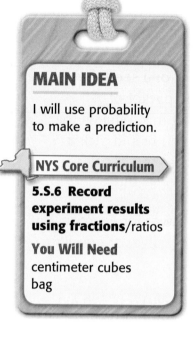

MAIN IDEA

I will use probability to make a prediction.

NYS Core Curriculum

5.S.6 Record experiment results using fractions/ratios

You Will Need
centimeter cubes
bag

ACTIVITY

Step 1 Place 5 blue cubes, 3 yellow cubes, and 2 red cubes in a bag.

What fraction of the cubes is blue? yellow? red? Write each fraction in a table like the one below.

Outcome	Fraction	Prediction	Tally	Number
Blue	$\frac{1}{2}$			
Yellow	$\frac{3}{10}$			
Red	$\frac{1}{5}$			

Step 2 Suppose you draw a cube and then return it to the bag. If you do this 40 times, predict the number of times a blue, a yellow, and a red cube will be drawn. Record your predictions in the table.

Step 3 Without looking, draw a cube from the bag. Record the color in the Tally column of your table.

Step 4 Replace the cube and repeat Step 3 for a total of 40 times. Add the tally marks and record the numbers in the table.

Hands-On
Activity

Think About It

1. Explain how you predicted the number of blue, yellow, and red cubes that would be drawn.

2. Compare your predictions in Step 2 with the actual number of cubes that were drawn. Describe any differences.

3. In your experiment, what fraction of the cubes drawn is blue? yellow? red? How do these compare to the actual fractions? Explain any differences.

4. Suppose this experiment was performed an additional 20 times for a total of 60 times. Based on the experimental results, predict the number of times you would draw a red cube.

CHECK What You Know

5. Perform this experiment an additional 20 times for a total of 60 times. Copy and complete the table below with your predictions and results.

Outcome	Fraction	Prediction	Tally	Number
Blue	$\frac{1}{2}$			
Yellow	$\frac{3}{10}$			
Red	$\frac{1}{5}$			

A bag has 6 marbles. One marble is drawn and replaced 30 times. The results are shown in the table.

Color	Number of Times Drawn
Red	25
White	5

6. Predict the number of red marbles in the bag. Explain.

7. Based on the experiment, describe the likelihood that there is a blue marble in the bag. Explain.

8. Predict the number of white marbles in the bag. Explain.

9. **WRITING IN ▶MATH** The same experiment was performed with a bag containing 18 marbles and the same results were achieved. Predict the number of red marbles in the bag. Explain.

MAIN IDEA

I will use fractions to describe probability.

NYS Core Curriculum

5.S.6 Record experiment results using fractions/ratios

5.S.7 Create a sample space and determine the probability of a single event, given a simple experiment (e.g., rolling a number cube)

New Vocabulary

favorable outcome

NY Math Online

macmillanmh.com

• Extra Examples
• Personal Tutor
• Self-Check Quiz

GET READY to Learn

When the spinner shown is spun, what is the probability that it will land on G?

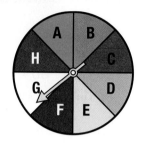

The probability that the spinner above will land on G can be described using a fraction.

$$P(G) = \frac{1}{8} \quad \begin{array}{l} \leftarrow \text{number of ways to land on G} \\ \leftarrow \text{number of possible outcomes} \end{array}$$

Since you are finding the probability of landing on G, the outcome of landing on G is called a **favorable outcome**.

Probability		Key Concept
Words	The probability of an event is a fraction that compares the number of favorable outcomes to the number of possible outcomes.	
Symbols	$P(\text{event}) = \dfrac{\text{number of favorable outcomes}}{\text{number of possible outcomes}}$	

The probability of an event can be described by a number from 0 to 1.

• An event that is *impossible* has a probability of 0.

• An event that is *certain* to happen has a probability of 1.

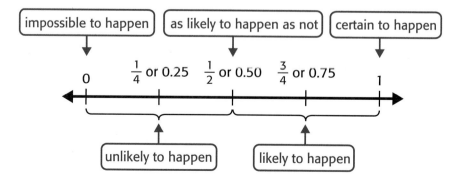

1 One marble is randomly chosen from the bag. Find the probability that a blue marble is chosen.

Use a fraction to describe the probability that a blue marble is chosen.

Remember

P(blue) means the probability of choosing blue.

$$P(\text{event}) = \frac{\text{number of favorable outcomes}}{\text{number of possible outcomes}}$$

$$P(\text{blue}) = \frac{4}{12} \quad \begin{matrix} \leftarrow \text{number of blue marbles} \\ \leftarrow \text{total number of marbles} \end{matrix}$$

$$P(\text{blue}) = \frac{1}{3} \quad \text{Simplify.}$$

So, the probability of choosing a blue marble is $\frac{1}{3}$.

Real-World EXAMPLE

2 **BALLOONS** Latanya has a bag of different colored balloons, as shown in the table. If she takes one balloon without looking, what is the probability that she gets a pink or white balloon?

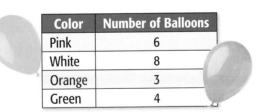

Color	Number of Balloons
Pink	6
White	8
Orange	3
Green	4

There are 6 + 8 + 3 + 4 or 21 balloons in all. There are 6 + 8 or 14 balloons that are either pink or white.

$$P(\text{event}) = \frac{\text{number of favorable outcomes}}{\text{number of possible outcomes}}$$

$$P(\text{pink or white}) = \frac{6 + 8}{6 + 8 + 3 + 4} \quad \begin{matrix} \leftarrow \text{pink or white balloons} \\ \leftarrow \text{total number of balloons} \end{matrix}$$

$$= \frac{14}{21} \quad \text{Add.}$$

$$= \frac{2}{3} \quad \text{Simplify.}$$

So, the probability that Latanya gets a pink or white balloon is $\frac{2}{3}$.

The spinner is spun once. Find the probability of each event. Write as a fraction in simplest form. See Examples 1, 2 (p. 669)

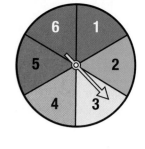

1. $P(4)$

2. $P(\text{odd number})$

3. $P(\text{number less than 6})$

4. $P(1 \text{ or } 6)$

5. $P(9)$

6. $P(\text{positive number})$

7. There are 9 kittens in a large basket. Three are gray, two are white, and four are striped. Miss Perez reaches in and randomly picks up one of the kittens. What is the probability that she picks up a striped kitten?

8. **Talk About It** Use an example to describe the difference between a favorable outcome and an outcome that is not favorable.

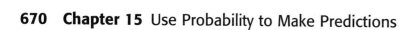

Practice and Problem Solving

NYSCC • NYSMT
Extra Practice, p. R40

A number cube labeled 1 through 6 is rolled. Find the probability of each event. Write as a fraction in simplest form. See Examples 1, 2 (p. 669)

9. $P(6)$

10. $P(\text{even number})$

11. $P(\text{a number less than 5})$

12. $P(\text{a negative number})$

13. $P(\text{a number less than 13})$

14. $P(\text{a prime number})$

One block is drawn from the blocks shown. Find the probability of each event. Write as a fraction in simplest form.

See Examples 1, 2 (p. 669)

15. $P(\text{red})$

16. $P(\text{blue})$

17. $P(not \text{ yellow})$

18. $P(\text{yellow, red, or blue})$

19. $P(\text{white})$

20. $P(\text{red or yellow})$

21. A letter is chosen at random from the word FRACTION. What is the probability that the letter chosen is a consonant?

22. An amusement park has a ride with 20 cars numbered 1 through 20. Leroy chooses a car at random. What is the probability that he chooses an even-numbered car?

23. Dawn has 16 pennies, 19 nickels, and 15 dimes in a piggy bank. If she turns the bank over and a coin falls out, what is the probability that it will be a dime?

24. A band has a drummer, 2 guitar players, a keyboard player, and a lead singer. One of their names is randomly chosen. What is the probability that it is the name of the drummer or lead singer?

25. Darius has a magnetic construction set that has plastic pieces in different geometric shapes, as shown in the table. If he chooses one piece from the box without looking, what is the probability that he chooses a square or pentagon?

Shape	Number of Pieces
Triangle	26
Square	16
Rhombus	16
Pentagon	12

Real-World PROBLEM SOLVING

Science When one pea plant fertilizes another pea plant, a seed forms that can grow into an offspring plant. Each pea plant has two genes, one from each parent. Whether the plant grows to be tall or short depends on which pair of genes the plant has.

- If the plant has the genes TT, then it will be tall.
- If the plant has the genes Tt, then it will be tall.
- If the plant has the genes tt, then it will be short.

The table shows the possible outcomes for the offspring of two plants that each have Tt genes. Each of the four outcomes is equally likely.

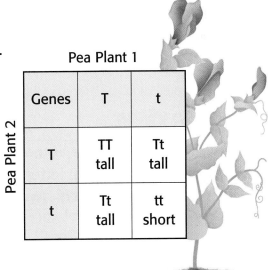

Pea Plant 1

Genes	T	t
T	TT tall	Tt tall
t	Tt tall	tt short

(Pea Plant 2)

Find each probability.

26. The offspring will have the genes TT.

27. The offspring will be tall.

28. The offspring will have the genes Tt.

H.O.T. Problems

29. OPEN ENDED Create a spinner so that the probability of landing on red is less than the probability of landing on any other single color. Use red and at least two other colors. State the probability of each color using a fraction.

30. CHALLENGE Suppose a 6-sided number cube is rolled. Describe two different events that have a probability of $\frac{1}{3}$.

31. WRITING IN ►MATH Write a real-world problem that can be solved by finding the probability. Then solve the problem.

32. One cube is drawn at random from the bag. Which is a true statement? (Lesson 15–1)

A Drawing a red cube is impossible.

B Drawing an orange cube is certain.

C Drawing a red cube is unlikely.

D Drawing an orange cube is equally likely.

33. Ronada has a bag of coins, as shown in the table.

Coin	Number of Coins
Penny	10
Nickel	8
Dime	6
Quarter	3

If she takes one coin without looking, what is the probability that she will pick a dime or quarter? (Lesson 15-2)

F $\frac{1}{4}$

G $\frac{1}{3}$

H $\frac{1}{2}$

J $\frac{3}{4}$

Spiral Review

Suppose you spin the spinner at the right. Describe the probability of landing on each letter. Write *certain, impossible, likely, unlikely,* or *equally likely.* (Lesson 15–1)

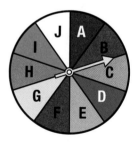

34. F

35. M

36. a consonant

37. *not* Z

Determine whether you need to find the perimeter, area, or volume. Then solve. (Lesson 14-8)

38. Measurement A wall 12 feet long and 8 feet high is being painted with chalkboard paint. How much space is to be painted?

39. Measurement Elijah is making a rectangular wooden picture frame that is $5\frac{1}{2}$ inches wide and 7 inches long. What length of wood does he need?

Find the area of each rectangle. (Lesson 14–3)

40. $\ell = 16$ cm, $w = 13$ cm

41. $\ell = 12$ m, $w = 8$ m

42. $\ell = 18$ yd, $w = 16$ yd

43. $\ell = 15$ ft, $w = 19$ ft

Juana and Chad are playing a game that uses a spinner. The spinner is divided into 4 equal sections. Each section is a different color. If they spin the spinner 40 times, predict how many times the outcome would be green.

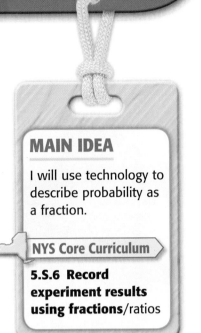

MAIN IDEA

I will use technology to describe probability as a fraction.

NYS Core Curriculum

5.S.6 Record experiment results using fractions/ratios

You can use the Math Tool Chest™ to conduct an experiment.

- Choose Spinner.
- Increase the number of trials to 40.
- Set speed to spin slow and click go.
- Click on the Link button in the bottom right-hand corner.
- Select table.

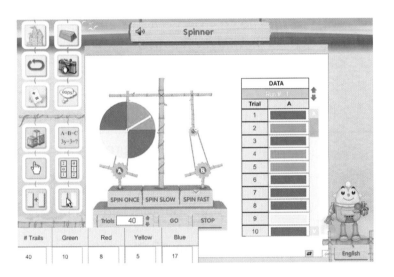

In this experiment, green was the outcome 10 times.

CHECK What You Know

1. How many times out of 40 spins would you have expected the outcome to be green? Explain.

2. If you were to spin the spinner 100 times, how many outcomes would you predict to be green? 1,000 times?

3. If you were to spin the spinner 100 times, what would you predict to be the probability for green, yellow, or blue?

4. **WRITING IN ►MATH** Write your own real-world probability problem. Use the spinner from Math Tool Chest.™

Problem-Solving Strategy

MAIN IDEA I will solve problems by making an organized list.

 **NYSCC** **5.PS.15 Make organized lists** or charts **to solve numerical problems**
5.S.5 List the possible outcomes for a single-event experiment

Edgar saw the following items at a store: a batting glove for $8.95, inline skates for $39.75, weights for $5.50 each, and a can of tennis balls for $2.75. Which items can Edgar buy and spend about $15?

Understand	**What facts do you know?**
	• The cost of the items and that Edgar has $15 to spend.
	What do you need to find?
	• You need to find which items Edgar can buy and spend about $15.
Plan	One way to solve the problem is by making an organized list.
Solve	Since the inline skates cost more than $15, eliminate the inline skates as an option. Round the other costs to the nearest dollar.
	Batting glove: $8.95 ≈ $9 Weights: $5.50 ≈ $6 Can of tennis balls: $2.75 ≈ $3
	Start with the batting glove: • 1 glove + 1 weight ≈ $9 + $6, or $15 • 1 glove + 2 cans of tennis balls ≈ $9 + $6, or $15
	List other combinations that contain the weights: • 2 weights + 1 can of tennis balls ≈ $12 + $3, or $15 • 1 weight + 3 cans of tennis balls ≈ $6 + $9, or $15
	List any remaining combination that contain the tennis balls: • 5 cans of tennis balls ≈ $15
Check	Check the list to be sure that all of the possible combinations of sporting good items that total no more than $15 are included. ✓

674 Chapter 15 Use Probability to Make Predictions

Refer to the problem on the previous page.

1. Which items can Edgar buy and spend between $20 and $25?

2. What is the least amount of money Edgar would need if he wanted to buy the inline skates and one other item?

3. What strategy is similar to *making an organized list*?

4. Describe how making an organized list is helpful in solving a problem.

PRACTICE the Strategy

NYSCC • NYSMT
Extra Practice, p. R41

Solve by *making an organized list.*

5. How many different products are possible using the digits 1, 3, 5, and 7?

6. Lawrence has $0.20 in his pocket. How many different possibilities of coins could he have? List the possibilities.

7. Laura hit the dartboard shown below with 3 darts. How many total scores are possible?

8. Awenita is selecting 2 charms for her charm bracelet. She has 4 charms to choose from. How many different arrangements of 2 charms can she choose? Describe the possibilities.

9. A red marble, a blue marble, a green marble, and a yellow marble are placed in a brown paper bag. Suppose if you take one marble out of the bag at a time. How many different orders can all four marbles be removed from the bag? List all possibilities.

10. Sean has the three cards shown below. How many different ways can he arrange the three letters? List them.

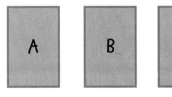

11. The following four numbers are used for employee identification at a small company: 1, 2, 3, and 4. How many different employee identification numbers can be made if 1 is always the first number?

12. **WRITING IN ►MATH** Mrs. Glover has four pictures to display in a row on her desk. Explain how to use the *make an organized list* strategy to find the different ways she can display the pictures.

List the possible outcomes in each probability experiment. (Lesson 15-1)

1. choosing one card without looking

D   E   F   G

2. spinning the spinner

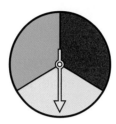

One marble is randomly drawn from the bag. Describe the probability of drawing each marble. Write *certain*, *impossible*, *likely*, *unlikely*, or *equally likely*.
(Lesson 15-1)

3. blue

4. purple

5. red, blue, green, or yellow

6. yellow or green

7. MULTIPLE CHOICE Desiree has 4 red pens, 6 blue pens, and 2 purple pens in her desk drawer. If she takes 1 pen from her drawer without looking, what is the probability that it will be a blue pen? (Lesson 15-2)

A $\frac{2}{5}$ **C** $\frac{6}{11}$

B $\frac{1}{2}$ **D** $\frac{3}{4}$

One cube is drawn from the bag. Find the probability of each event. Write as a fraction in simplest form. (Lesson 15-2)

8. P(green)   **9.** P(blue)

10. P(green or black) **11.** P(*not* black)

12. MULTIPLE CHOICE The table shows the results of 20 spins on a spinner. Based on these results, what is the probability that the spinner will land on green? (Lesson 15-2)

Color	Number of Spins
Red	7
Orange	2
Green	8
Blue	3

F $\frac{4}{5}$ **H** $\frac{1}{4}$

G $\frac{2}{5}$ **J** $\frac{1}{9}$

13. A quarter and a nickel are tossed. How many different outcomes are possible? Make a list. (Lesson 15-3)

14. Pete's Pizza offers thin or thick crust and pepperoni, sausage, mushroom, onion, and green peppers as toppings. How many different 1-topping pizzas are possible? Make a list. (Lesson 15-3)

15. **WRITING IN MATH** Explain why one event may be more likely to occur than another event in an experiment.

Counting Outcomes

GET READY to Learn

The stone shown is made from topaz. Topaz stones come in different colors, such as blue, pink, or clear. They can have different cuts such as a regular cut or a star cut.

MAIN IDEA

I will list outcomes of a probability experiment.

NYS Core Curriculum

5.PS.15 Make organized lists or charts to solve numerical problems

5.S.5 List the possible outcomes for a single-event experiment

New Vocabulary

tree diagram

NY Math Online

macmillanmh.com
• Extra Examples
• Personal Tutor
• Self-Check Quiz

You can use a tree diagram to show all possible color-cut combinations of topaz. A **tree diagram** is a diagram that shows all possible outcomes of an event.

Real-World EXAMPLE Use Tree Diagrams to List Outcomes

1 **GEMSTONES Refer to the information above. Make a tree diagram to show all possible color-cut combinations of the topaz described.**

The colors are blue, pink, and clear. List the colors. The cuts are a regular cut and a star cut. For each color, list the cuts.

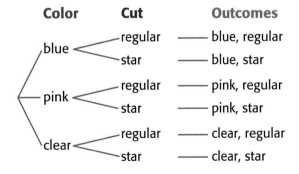

There are six possible combinations. These are listed as outcomes on the tree diagram.

EXAMPLE Find Probability

2 **Suppose you toss a penny, a nickel, and a dime. What is the probability of getting 3 heads?**

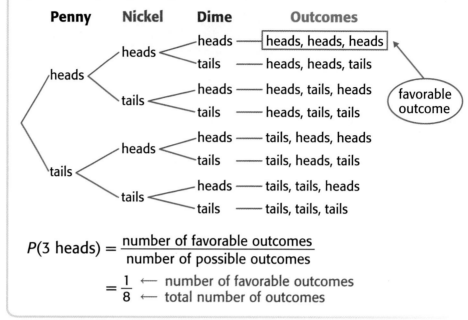

Remember

Outcomes are written at branch ends.

$$P(3 \text{ heads}) = \frac{\text{number of favorable outcomes}}{\text{number of possible outcomes}}$$

$$= \frac{1}{8} \begin{array}{l} \leftarrow \text{ number of favorable outcomes} \\ \leftarrow \text{ total number of outcomes} \end{array}$$

CHECK What You Know

A coin is tossed twice. See Examples 1, 2 (pp. 677–678)

1. Make a tree diagram to show all possible outcomes.

2. What is the probability of tossing two tails?

3. What is the probability of tossing one tail and one head?

The spinner is spun and two coins are tossed. See Examples 1, 2 (pp. 677–678)

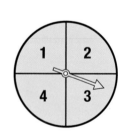

4. Make a tree diagram to show all possible outcomes. Tell how many outcomes are possible.

5. What is the probability of landing on 2 and tossing two tails?

6. How many outcomes involve landing on 3 and tossing a head and a tail (in any order)? What is the probability of landing on 3 and tossing both a head and a tail?

7. Trent randomly chooses a belt and a pair of pants from his closet. What is the probability of choosing a black belt and black pants?

Belt	Pants
brown	tan
black	black
	blue

8. **Talk About It** Describe the steps you take to make a tree diagram when there are two probability experiments involved.

A 4-sided die, called a tetrahedron, numbered 1 through 4 is tossed and a coin is tossed. See Examples 1, 2 (pp. 677–678)

9. Make a tree diagram to show all possible outcomes. Tell how many outcomes are possible.

10. What is the probability of tossing an odd number and a tail?

The two spinners at the right are spun.

See Examples 1, 2 (pp. 677–678)

11. Make a tree diagram to show all possible outcomes. How many outcomes are possible?

12. What is the probability of spinning an A and a 1?

13. What is the probability of spinning *not* C?

Use the table at the right. A customer randomly chooses a type of bread, one meat, and one vegetable for a sandwich. See Examples 1, 2 (pp. 677–678)

Bread	Meat	Vegetable
white	turkey	lettuce
wheat	ham	tomato
	beef	

14. Make a tree diagram to show all possible outcomes. How many outcomes are possible?

15. How many sandwiches include wheat bread and turkey?

16. What is the probability that the sandwich has ham and tomato?

17. A store has 6 different shades of blue paint. The paint can be either oil or latex. The shine can be gloss, semi-gloss, or flat. How many combinations include blue latex paint?

New York Data File

There are over 7,500 lakes and ponds, 50,000 miles of rivers and streams, and hundreds of miles of coastline in New York. The table shows some different fishing possibilities that fisherman can choose from when visiting a New York lake.

18. Make a tree diagram to show all of the different fishing possibilities.

19. Tell how many different ways there are to fish.

New York Fishing		
Lake	**Location**	**Type of Fish**
Lake Champlain	boat	bass
Lake George	shoreline	salmon
Seneca Lake		trout

H.O.T. Problems

20. OPEN ENDED Suppose two number cubes are rolled. Describe one possible event. What is the probability of the event occurring?

21. FIND THE ERROR Jack and Makayla are finding the probability of tossing heads twice when a dime is tossed twice. Who is correct? Explain your reasoning.

Jack
$\frac{1}{2}$, since each toss has a probability of $\frac{1}{2}$.

Makayla
$\frac{1}{4}$, since there is one outcome out of four that has two heads.

22. **WRITING IN** ►**MATH** Describe how the number of possible outcomes changes if a spinner is spun twice rather than once.

NYSMT Practice 5.PS.15, 5.S.5

23. The eye color of an Abyssinian cat can be green, blue, gold, or hazel. Their fur color can be brown or black. How many different eye and fur color combinations are possible?
(Lessons 15-3 and 15-4)

  A 4

  B 6

  C 8

  D 10

24. The spinners are spun once. What is the probability of spinning a 5 and a B? (Lesson 15–4)

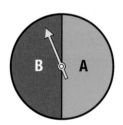

  F $\frac{1}{12}$ **H** $\frac{1}{5}$

  G $\frac{1}{6}$ **J** $\frac{2}{7}$

Spiral Review

25. How many different 3-letter arrangements can be made from the letters in Ben's first name? Make a list. (Lesson 15-3)

A spinner with eight equal sections numbered 1–8 is spun once. Find the probability of each event. Write as a fraction in simplest form. (Lesson 15-2)

26. $P(6)$ **27.** $P(10)$ **28.** $P(7 \text{ or } 8)$

Bean Game

Counting Outcomes

Get Ready!

Players: 2, 3, or 4

You will need: 6 dry beans
bowl
marker

Get Set!

Color one side of each bean with the marker.

Go!

The first player places the beans in the bowl, gently tosses the beans into the air, and catches them in the bowl. Points are scored as follows.

- If all of the beans land with the unmarked sides up, score 6 points.

- If all of the beans land with the marked sides up, score 4 points.

- If exactly one bean lands with the marked or unmarked side up, score 2 points.

- If three beans are marked and three beans are unmarked, score 1 point.

If a toss scores points, the player takes another turn. If a toss does not score any points, it is the next player's turn.

The winner is the player with the most points after a given number of rounds.

Problem-Solving Investigation

MAIN IDEA I will choose the best strategy to solve a problem.

P.S.I. TEAM +

DREW: I am making a flag to represent our class at the school assembly. The flag must have three solid-colored horizontal stripes (one red, one blue, and one yellow) with a gray star in the center of the middle stripe.

YOUR MISSION: Find how many different flags Drew can make.

Understand	You know that the flag will have a red, blue, and yellow stripe and that a star will be in the center of the middle stripe. You need to find how many different flags Drew can make with three stripes and one star.
Plan	You can use the *make a picture* strategy.
Solve	Continue drawing flags until no more flags can be made. After drawing the flags, you find that 6 different flags can be made with 3 horizontal stripes with a star in the center of the middle stripe.
Check	Look back. Make a list of all the possible flags. RBY, RYB, YBR, YRB, BYR, BRY Since there are 6 items in the list and 6 different flags, the answer is correct. ✓

Use any strategy shown below to solve each problem.

PROBLEM-SOLVING STRATEGIES
• Make an organized list.
• Draw a picture.
• Solve a simpler problem.

1. Vince is ordering lunch from Taco Express. The choices are shown in the table below.

Tacos	Filling	Salsa
soft	beef	mild
hard	chicken	medium
	pork	hot
	vegetables	

How many different possibilities are there if Vince orders a taco with one filling and one type of salsa?

2. **Geometry** A window design is made from a rectangle divided by two diagonals. How many sections are there? What are their shapes?

3. Isabel is playing a game with the set of cards shown below. She takes one card from this set without looking. What is the probability that the card will have either a triangle or circle on it?

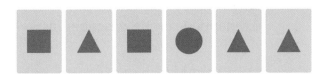

4. Monya has three different shirts and two pairs of pants. She wants to make different outfits, each with one pair of pants and one shirt. How many different outfits can she make?

5. **Geometry** A student divides a triangle into sections by drawing a line from each vertex to the center of the opposite side. How many sections are there, and what are their shapes?

6. **Measurement** Three students can make 9 posters in 45 minutes. How many posters can 6 students make at the same rate in 90 minutes?

7. Logan is buying a digital music player. The choices are shown below.

Color	Capabilities
black	music
blue	music and photos
pink	music, photos, and movies
silver	
white	

How many different possibilities of color and capabilities are there?

8. **WRITING IN ►MATH** Jeff said that since $3 + 3 = 6$, there are 6 different possibilities of cereal and juice for breakfast. Tell what mistake he made. Explain how to correct it.

Cereal	Juice
oatmeal	orange
corn flakes	apple
wheat squares	pineapple

Study Guide and Review

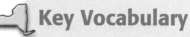

FOLDABLES Study Organizer GET READY to Study

Be sure the following Big Ideas are written in your Foldable.

Probability | Probability as a Fraction

Make a Prediction | Count Outcomes

Key Concepts

Probability

- **Probability** is the chance that an event will happen. (p. 661)

Probability	Meaning
Certain	The event will definitely happen.
Impossible	There is no chance the event will happen.
Equally likely	There is an equal chance the event will happen.

- An **outcome** is a possible result in a **probability experiment.** (p. 661)

Describe Probability using Fractions

- The probability of an event can be described using a fraction. (p. 668)

$$P(\text{event}) = \frac{\text{number of favorable outcomes}}{\text{number of possible outcomes}}$$

- An event that is impossible has a probability of 0.

- An event that is certain to happen has a probability of 1.

Key Vocabulary

certain (p. 661)

impossible (p. 661)

outcome (p. 661)

probability (p. 661)

probability experiment (p. 661)

tree diagram (p. 677)

Vocabulary Check

Complete. Use a word from this Key Vocabulary list.

1. An event that will definitely happen is ___?___ to happen.

2. When a coin is tossed, the two ___?___ are heads and tails.

3. ___?___ is the chance that an event will occur.

4. An outcome is a possible result in a(n) ___?___.

5. A(n) ___?___ shows all possible outcomes of an experiment.

6. An event that can never happen can be described as ___?___ to occur.

Lesson-by-Lesson Review

15-1 Probability (pp. 661–663)

5.S.5

Example 1
Describe the probability of the spinner landing on 1.

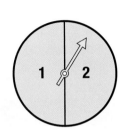

The chance of landing on 1 is equally likely.

One letter is randomly chosen from the word OUTCOME. Describe the probability of choosing each letter. Write *certain*, *impossible*, *likely*, *unlikely*, or *equally likely*.

7. T   **8.** E   **9.** A

15-2 Probability as a Fraction (pp. 668–672)

5.S.6

Example 2
One marble is randomly chosen from the bag. Find the probability that a green marble is chosen.

$P(\text{event}) = \dfrac{\text{number of favorable outcomes}}{\text{number of possible outcomes}}$

$P(\text{green}) = \dfrac{2}{7}$

So, the probability that a green marble is chosen is $\dfrac{2}{7}$.

The spinner is spun once. Find the probability of each event. Write as a fraction in simplest form.

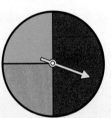

10. $P(\text{blue})$ **11.** $P(\text{red})$

12. $P(\text{green, red, or blue})$

15-3 Problem-Solving Strategy: Make an Organized List (pp. 674–675)

5.PS.15

Example 3
How many different sums are possible using the digits 1, 2, and 3?

12 + 3 = 15	13 + 2 = 15
21 + 3 = 24	23 + 1 = 24
31 + 2 = 33	32 + 1 = 33

There are 3 possible sums.

Solve by *making an organized list*.

13. There are 2 movies that Bailey wants to see. Each movie is showing at 5 different times. How many choices does she have?

Counting Outcomes (pp. 677–680)

5.PS.15

Example 4
A coin is tossed and the spinner is spun. What is the probability that the outcome is tails and red?

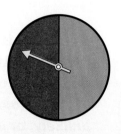

Coin	Spinner	Outcomes
heads	red	heads, red
	blue	heads, blue
tails	red	tails, red
	blue	tails, blue

There are four possible outcomes. One outcome is tails and red. So, the probability of that outcome is $\frac{1}{4}$.

A number cube labeled 1 to 6 is rolled and a coin is tossed.

14. Make a tree diagram to show all possible outcomes. Tell how many outcomes are possible.

15. What is the probability of rolling the number 2 and tossing heads?

16. What is the probability of rolling an even number and tossing tails?

17. A store has roses, tulips, and carnations. They each come in red and yellow. How many outcomes are possible?

 Problem-Solving Investigation: **Choose a Strategy**
(pp. 682–683)

5.PS.3

Example 5
Miranda has a black purse and a tan purse. She has a black hat and a red hat. How many different purse-hat possibilities are there?

Make a list of the different possibilities.

black purse and black hat
black purse and red hat
tan purse and black hat
tan purse and red hat

So, there are 4 different purse-hat possibilities.

18. For lunch, Mazo can choose a soup or salad, a hamburger or grilled cheese, and a fruit cup or yogurt. How many different lunch possibilities are there?

19. A student divides a hexagon into sections by drawing three diagonals from one vertex. How many sections are there? What are their shapes?

1. Marissa spins the spinner. List the possible outcomes.

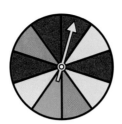

One block is randomly drawn from the bag. Describe the probability of drawing each marble. Write *certain, impossible, likely, unlikely,* or *equally likely*.

2. red

3. green

4. yellow

5. not green

6. **MULTIPLE CHOICE** Each letter in the word HOMEWORK is written on a separate note card. If one card is picked without looking, what is the probability that it will have a vowel on it?

A $\frac{1}{4}$

B $\frac{3}{8}$

C $\frac{1}{2}$

D $\frac{3}{4}$

7. **Geometry** Mrs. Hong has two sets of math shapes. One set has a square and a triangle. The other set has a circle, a rectangle, and a pentagon. If she chooses one shape from each set, how many possibilities are there?

8. **MULTIPLE CHOICE** Jana tossed a coin and a number cube marked 1 to 6. What is the probability that the results were tails and 3?

F $\frac{1}{4}$

H $\frac{1}{8}$

G $\frac{1}{6}$

J $\frac{1}{12}$

Marlon grabs a pair of shoes and a pair of socks without looking. He has black, brown, and red shoes. He has four pairs of socks: white, blue, yellow, and red.

9. Make a tree diagram to show the possible outcomes. Tell how many outcomes are possible.

10. What is the probability that the shoes and socks are both red?

11. What is the probability that the socks are *not* white?

The spinner is spun once. Find the probability of each event. Write as a fraction in simplest form.

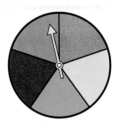

12. *P*(red)

13. *P*(blue or yellow)

14. *P*(black)

15. *P*(*not* purple)

16. **WRITING IN ►MATH** Gabe is downloading 3 songs from a group of 5 songs. Explain how to find the different possibilities for downloading the 3 songs.

PART 1   Multiple Choice

Read each question. Then fill in the correct answer on the answer sheet provided by your teacher or on a sheet of paper.

1. The table shows the tips that Stella earned each week. Based on these results, what is the probability that Stella will earn more than $100 in tips next week?

Week	Tips Earned ($)
1	94
2	132
3	115
4	104

   A $\frac{1}{4}$ **C** $\frac{1}{2}$

   B $\frac{1}{3}$ **D** $\frac{3}{4}$

2. If each digit 1, 3, and 5 is used only once, which group shows all the possibilities of 3-digit numbers?

   F 135, 315, 531

   G 315, 135, 513, 531

   H 135, 315, 531, 153, 513

   J 315, 351, 135, 153, 513, 531

3. The table shows the choices for frozen yogurt sundaes. From how many different combinations of 1 type of yogurt and 1 type of topping can a customer choose?

Yogurt	Topping
Strawberry	Nuts
Vanilla	Granola
Lemon	Strawberry
	Pineapple

   A 12   **C** 7
   B 9   **D** 6

4. Eleven cards spell the word MATHEMATICS when put together. If one card is chosen without looking, what is the probability that it will have the letter M on it?

   F $\frac{1}{11}$ **H** $\frac{4}{11}$

   G $\frac{2}{11}$ **J** $\frac{9}{11}$

5. A fifth grade class voted for the class mascot. Based on these results, which is the most reasonable prediction of the number of votes a bear would receive if 50 students voted?

Mascot	Number of Students
Bear	7
Falcon	4
Panther	11
Ram	3

   A 22   **C** 8

   B 14   **D** 6

6. Look for the pattern in the sequence of numbers below.

   5, 10, 7, 14, 11, 22, 19, …

   Which rule describes this pattern best?

   F Add 5, subtract 3.

   G Multiply by 2, subtract 3.

   H Add 5, multiply by 2.

   J Multiply by 2, add 3.

Preparing for NYSMT
For test-taking strategies and
practice, see pages R42–R55.

7. Teams are formed for a game so they each have 1 boy and 1 girl. There are 5 girls and 5 boys. How many different combinations are possible?

A 5

C 25

B 10

D 50

8. The table shows the grades Jake earned on 13 tests. Based on these results, what is the probability that Jake will earn a B on his next spelling test?

Spelling Tests	
Grade	Number
A	10
B	2
C	1

F $\frac{1}{13}$

H $\frac{3}{13}$

G $\frac{2}{13}$

J $\frac{10}{13}$

9. Five horses were in a race. They wore different colored blankets. Use the clues below to name a possible order of the horses from first to last.

Blanket	Finish
Red	First
Orange	Between blue and yellow
Green	Fifth

A green, yellow, orange, blue, red

B red, green, yellow, blue, orange

C blue, red, orange, yellow, green

D red, blue, orange, yellow, green

PART 2 Short Response

Record your answers on the answer sheet provided by your teacher or on a sheet of paper.

10. The temperature outside at 6:45 A.M. was 56°F. By noon, the temperature was 62°F. Write an integer to represent this situation.

11. Name one object that would be measured using milligrams, one that would be measured using grams, and one that would be measured with kilograms.

PART 3 Extended Response

Record your answers on the answer sheet provided by your teacher or on a sheet of paper.

12. Write a real-world problem that can be solved using the equation $24 = 3p$.

13. Which shape would have a larger perimeter, an equilateral triangle with sides that are each 14 inches, or a square with sides that are each 1 foot? Explain.

NEED EXTRA HELP?													
If You Missed Question...	1	2	3	4	5	6	7	8	9	10	11	12	13
Go to Lesson...	15-2	15-4	15-4	15-2	15-2	9-6	15-4	15-2	15-3	12-5	12-3	6-2	13-3
NYS Core Curriculum	5.S.6	5.PS.15	5.PS.15	5.S.6	5.S.6	5.PS.14	5.PS.15	5.S.6	5.PS.15	6.N.14	5.M.5	5.A.5	5.G.6

Looking Ahead

to Next Year

Let's Look Ahead!

Multiplying Decimals

MAIN IDEA

What You'll Learn
I will multiply a decimal by a whole number and by another decimal.

Materials:
grid paper
colored pencils
scissors

NYS Core Curriculum

5.N.23 Use a variety of strategies to add, subtract, **multiply,** and divide **decimals to thousandths**

NY Math Online

macmillanmh.com

• Extra Examples
• Personal Tutor
• Self-Check Quiz

 Hands-On Mini Lab

Recall that a 10-by-10 grid represents the number one.

ACTIVITY

1 **Model 0.7 × 0.3 using decimal models.**

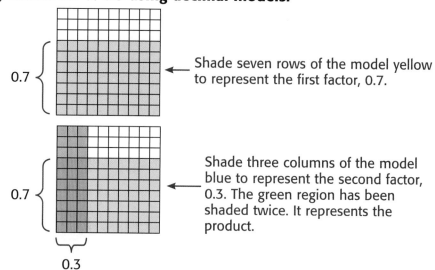

Shade seven rows of the model yellow to represent the first factor, 0.7.

Shade three columns of the model blue to represent the second factor, 0.3. The green region has been shaded twice. It represents the product.

There are 21 hundredths in the region where the colors overlap. So, 0.7 × 0.3 = 0.21.

Draw decimal models to show each product.

a. 3 × 0.2   **b.** 2 × 0.5   **c.** 0.4 × 0.8   **d.** 0.6 × 0.4

2 **Model 0.4 × 2 using decimal models.**

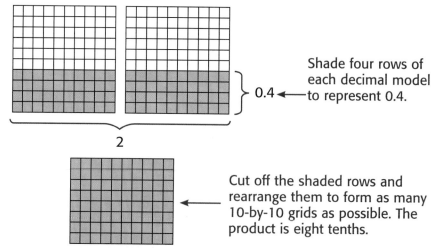

Shade four rows of each decimal model to represent 0.4.

Cut off the shaded rows and rearrange them to form as many 10-by-10 grids as possible. The product is eight tenths.

So, 0.4 × 2 = 0.8.

 **EXAMPLES** **Multiply Decimals by a Whole Number**

① **Find 7 × 0.96.**

One Way: **Use estimation.**

Round 0.96 to 1. $7 \times 0.96 \longrightarrow 7 \times 1$ or 7

$$
\begin{array}{r}
4 \\
0.96 \\
\times\ \ 7 \\
\hline
6.72
\end{array}
$$

Since the estimate is 7, place the decimal point after the 6.

Another Way: **Count decimal places.**

$$
\begin{array}{r}
4 \\
0.96 \\
\times\ \ 7 \\
\hline
6.72
\end{array}
$$

There are two places to the right of the decimal point.

Count two decimals places from right to left.

② **Measurement Find the area of a board that is 4 feet by 3.62 feet.**

Estimate $4 \times 3.62 \longrightarrow 4 \times 4$ or 16

$$
\begin{array}{r}
2 \\
3.62 \\
\times\ \ \ 4 \\
\hline
14.48
\end{array}
$$

There are two places to the right of the decimal point.

Count two decimals places from right to left.

The area of the bulletin board is 14.48 feet.

EXAMPLE **Multiply Decimals**

③ **Find 5.2 × 3.4.** **Estimate** $5.2 \times 3.4 \longrightarrow 5 \times 3$ or 15

$$
\begin{array}{r}
5.2 \\
\times\ 3.4 \\
\hline
208 \\
+156\ \ \ \\
\hline
17.68
\end{array}
$$

one decimal place

one decimal place

two decimal places

The product is 17.68.

Check for Reasonableness Compare 17.68 to the estimate.

$$17.68 \approx 15 ✓$$

Multiply. (See Examples 1–3, p. LA3)

1. 6 × 0.5   **2.** 4 × 2.6   **3.** 7 × 0.89

4. 3 × 2.49   **5.** 52 × 2.1   **6.** 3.4 × 2.7

7. 5.4 × 0.9   **8.** 8.2 × 5.8   **9.** 5.7 × 0.6

10. A recipe for a cake calls for 3.5 cups of sugar. How many cups of sugar are needed for 4 cakes?

11. **Talk About It** Is the product of 2.8 and 1.5 greater than 6 or less than 6? How do you know?

Practice and Problem Solving

Multiply. (See Examples 1–3, p. LA3)

12. 2 × 1.3   **13.** 3 × 0.5   **14.** 1.8 × 9

15. 2.4 × 8   **16.** 4 × 0.02   **17.** 0.66 × 5

18. 0.7 × 0.4   **19.** 1.5 × 2.7   **20.** 0.4 × 3.7

21. 0.8 × 7.3   **22.** 2.4 × 3.8   **23.** 6.2 × 0.3

Algebra Evaluate each expression if $x = 3$, $y = 0.2$, and $z = 4.5$.

24. xy **25.** $7.3y$ **27.** xyz

28. $(7 \times 2) \times y$ **29.** xz **30.** $(9 - x) \times y$

31. Miguel is trying to eat less than 750 Calories at dinner. A 4-serving, thin crust cheese pizza has 272.8 Calories per serving. A dinner salad has 150 Calories. Will Miguel be able to eat the salad and two pieces of pizza for under 750 Calories? Explain.

Science A panda spends about 0.5 of the day eating. They can eat up to 33 pounds of bamboo in a single day.

32. How long will the panda spend eating in 7 days?

33. How many pounds of bamboo will a panda eat in 30 days?

Measurement Find the area of each rectangle.

34.

3 in.

5.4 in.

35.

6.2 ft

9.4 ft

H.O.T. Problems

36. OPEN ENDED Write a multiplication problem in which the product has two decimal places.

37. FIND THE ERROR Armando and Kellis are finding the product of 0.52 and 21. Who is correct? Explain.

Armando

0.52
× 21
_____
1,092

Kellis

21
× 0.52
_____
10.92

38. NUMBER SENSE Place the decimal point in the answer to make it correct. Explain your reasoning.
4.98 × 8.32 = 414336

39. WRITING IN ▶MATH Write a real-world problem that can be solved using multiplication. One factor should be a decimal.

Multiplying Fractions

Looking Ahead 2

MAIN IDEA

I will multiply fractions.

NYS Core Curriculum

**Preparation for
6.N.17** Multiply and
divide fractions with
unlike denominators
Also addresses 5.PS.20.

NY Math Online

macmillanmh.com

• Extra Examples
• Personal Tutor
• Self-Check Quiz

GET READY to Learn

Michael planted a vegetable
garden. Two-thirds of the
vegetables that he planted
were green. Two-fifths of the
green vegetables were
peppers. The expression
$\frac{2}{3} \times \frac{2}{5}$ represents the fraction of all the vegetables that
Michael planted that were green peppers.

EXAMPLE   Multiply Fractions

① Find $\frac{2}{3} \times \frac{2}{5}$ using a model. Write in simplest form.

To find $\frac{2}{3} \times \frac{2}{5}$, find $\frac{2}{5}$ of $\frac{2}{3}$.

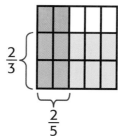

Shade $\frac{2}{3}$ of the square yellow.

Shade $\frac{2}{5}$ of the square blue.
The green region has been
shaded twice. It represents
the product.

Four out of 15 parts are shaded green. So, $\frac{2}{3} \times \frac{2}{5} = \frac{4}{15}$.

Multiplying Fractions	Key Concept
Words	To multiply fractions, multiply the numerators and multiply the denominators.

Numbers

$\frac{3}{5} \times \frac{1}{2} = \frac{3 \times 1}{5 \times 2}$

Algebra

$\frac{a}{b} \times \frac{c}{d} = \frac{a \times c}{b \times d}$, where b and d are not 0.

LA6   Looking Ahead to Next Year

You can simplify the fractions before or after you multiply them.

EXAMPLE   **Multiply Fractions**

2 Find $\frac{3}{4} \times \frac{5}{9}$.

One Way: Simplify after multiplying.

$$\frac{3}{4} \times \frac{5}{9} = \frac{3 \times 5}{4 \times 9}$$

$$= \frac{\overset{\div 3}{\cancel{15}}}{\underset{\div 3}{\cancel{36}}} = \frac{5}{12} \quad \text{Simplify.}$$

Another Way: Simplify before multiplying.

The numerator and denominator have a common factor, 3.

$$\frac{3}{4} \times \frac{5}{9} = \frac{\overset{1}{\cancel{3}} \times 5}{4 \times \underset{3}{\cancel{9}}}$$

Divide both the numerator and the denominator by 3.

$$= \frac{5}{12} \quad \text{Simplify.}$$

Real-World EXAMPLE

3 **FOOD** The student council voted for the kind of food served at their school's year-end celebration. There are 10 council members, and $\frac{4}{8}$ of them voted for pizza. How many students voted for pizza?

$$\frac{4}{8} \times 10 = \frac{4 \times 10}{8 \times 1} \qquad \text{Rewrite 10 as } \frac{10}{1}.$$

$$= \frac{\overset{\div 8}{\cancel{40}}}{\underset{\div 8}{\cancel{8}}} = \frac{5}{1} \qquad \text{Simplify.}$$

$$\frac{5}{1} = 5$$

So, 5 of the students voted for pizza.

Multiply. Write in simplest form. (See Examples 1–3, pp. LA6–LA7)

1. $\frac{1}{7} \times \frac{1}{2}$ **2.** $\frac{4}{5} \times \frac{3}{4}$ **3.** $\frac{5}{6} \times \frac{3}{4}$

4. $\frac{3}{10} \times \frac{5}{6}$ **5.** $\frac{3}{4} \times \frac{2}{7}$ **6.** $\frac{3}{5} \times \frac{5}{6}$

7. $\frac{3}{4} \times \frac{5}{12}$ **8.** $\frac{2}{9} \times \frac{1}{3}$ **9.** $\frac{6}{7} \times \frac{3}{4}$

10. Melody is putting together a puzzle that has 50 pieces. She has $\frac{7}{10}$ of the puzzle complete. How many pieces does Melody have in place?

11. Adults should sleep $\frac{1}{3}$ of the day. How many hours of the day should adults sleep?

12. **Talk About It** Will the product of $\frac{2}{9} \times \frac{1}{3}$ be the same as the product of $\frac{2}{9} \times \frac{2}{6}$? Explain.

Practice and Problem Solving

Multiply. Write in simplest form. (See Examples 1–3, pp. LA6–LA7)

13. $\frac{2}{3} \times \frac{1}{4}$ **14.** $\frac{5}{6} \times \frac{2}{3}$ **15.** $\frac{3}{4} \times \frac{2}{5}$

16. $\frac{1}{3} \times \frac{2}{5}$ **17.** $\frac{3}{5} \times \frac{5}{7}$ **18.** $\frac{4}{9} \times \frac{3}{8}$

19. $\frac{3}{4} \times \frac{5}{8}$ **20.** $\frac{1}{8} \times \frac{3}{4}$ **21.** $\frac{1}{2} \times \frac{4}{9}$

22. Carrie ate $\frac{1}{5}$ of the oranges that her mother brought home from the grocery store. If there were 10 oranges, how many oranges did Carrie eat?

Algebra Evaluate each expression if $a = \frac{3}{4}$, $b = \frac{2}{3}$, and $c = \frac{1}{6}$.

23. ab

24. cb

25. ac

26. $\frac{3}{5}a$

27. $\frac{5}{6}a$

28. abc

29. Lydia is 63 inches tall. Her baby brother is $\frac{1}{3}$ of her height.

How many inches tall is Lydia's baby brother?

30. Collin and his family are going on vacation for 6 days. They plan on spending $\frac{2}{3}$ of the days at the beach.

How many days will Collin and his family spend at the beach?

H.O.T. Problems

31. OPEN ENDED How can you determine if the product of $\frac{1}{2} \times \frac{4}{9}$ will be larger or smaller than $\frac{1}{2}$?

REASONING State whether each statement is true or false. If the statement is false, provide a counterexample.

32. The product of a whole number and a fraction is always a whole number.

33. The product of two fractions that are each between 0 and 1 is also between 0 and 1.

34. NUMBER SENSE If you toss a coin 20 times is it possible to land on heads $10\frac{1}{2}$ times?

35. **WRITING IN ►MATH** When multiplying $\frac{5}{6} \times \frac{3}{4}$, can you simplify before you multiply?

Ratios

GET READY to Learn

CLOTHES The table shows how many shirts of each color are on a shelf.

Shirts	
Color	**Number**
Black	6
Yellow	10
Blue	5
Red	4
Green	7

1. Write a sentence that compares the number of green shirts to the number of red shirts. Use the word *less* in your sentence.

2. Write a sentence that compares the number of blue shirts to the number of yellow shirts. Use the word *half* in your sentence.

3. Write a sentence comparing the number of black shirts to the total number of shirts. Use a fraction in your sentence.

MAIN IDEA

What You'll Learn
Express ratios and rates in fraction form.

NYS Core Curriculum

5.N.6 Understand the concept of ratio

5.N.7 Express ratios in different forms

New Vocabulary

ratio

equivalent ratios

NY Math Online

macmillanmh.com

• Extra Examples
• Personal Tutor
• Self-Check Quiz

There are many ways to compare numbers. A **ratio** is a comparison of two numbers by division. A ratio of 7 green shirts to 10 yellow shirts can be written in three ways.

Ratio	Using *to*	Using:	Using a *Fraction*
green shirts to yellow shirts	7 to 10	7:10	$\frac{7}{10}$

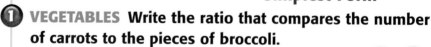

Real-World EXAMPLE Write a Ratio in Simplest Form

1 **VEGETABLES** Write the ratio that compares the number of carrots to the pieces of broccoli.

$$\text{carrots} \longrightarrow \frac{4}{6} = \frac{2}{3} \longleftarrow \text{broccoli}$$

The ratio of carrots to broccoli is $\frac{2}{3}$, 2 to 3, or 2:3. $\frac{4}{6}$ and $\frac{2}{3}$ are said to be **equivalent ratios** since $\frac{4}{6} = \frac{2}{3}$.

EXAMPLE   Use Ratios to Compare Parts to a Whole

2 **FLOWERS** Write the ratio that compares the number of red flowers to the total number of flowers.

red flowers ⟶ $\dfrac{4}{12} = \dfrac{1}{3}$
total flowers ⟶

The ratio of red flowers to the total number of flowers is $\dfrac{1}{3}$, 1 to 3, or 1:3. For every one red flower, there are three total flowers.

EXAMPLE   Use Ratio Tables

3 **FOOD** To make 5 peach pies, you need 2 pounds of peaches. How many pounds of peaches do you need to make 20 pies?

Set up a ratio table.

Number of Pies	5		20
Pounds of Peaches	2		

Label the rows with the two quantities being compared. Then fill in what is given.

Multiply to find the desired quantity.

Number of Pies	5	× 4	20
Pounds of Peaches	2	× 4	8

Multiply each quantity by 4.

So, use 8 pounds of peaches to make 20 pies.

CHECK What You Know

Write each ratio as a fraction in simplest form. (See Examples 1–3 pp. LA10–LA11)

1. 6 dogs to 8 cats

2. 15 pens to 45 pencils

3. 10 mosquitoes out of 30 insects

4. 4 pretzels out of 24 snacks

5. 14 dimes to 24 nickels

6. 15 rubies to 25 emeralds

7. Example 1 gave a part to part ratio, and Example 2 gave a part to whole ratio. Explain the difference between a ratio comparing part to part and a ratio comparing part to whole.

Practice and Problem Solving

Write each ratio as a fraction in simplest form. (See Examples 1–3 pp. LA10–LA11)

8. 15 elm trees to 10 pine trees

9. 8 circles to 22 squares

10. 6 iguanas out of 21 lizards

11. 4 cell phones out of 18 phones

12. 10 girls out of 24 students

13. 32 apples out of 72 pieces of fruit

Write an equivalent ratio to each ratio given.

14. 2:3

15. 4 to 7

16. $\frac{5}{9}$

17. 5:6

18. 3 to 11

19. $\frac{3}{8}$

20. Draw a picture showing 4 pencils and a number of pens in which the ratio of pencils to pens is 2:3.

21. In a certain store, the ratio of high definition televisions sold to regular televisions is 1 to 4. Explain the meaning of this ratio.

22. Find the ratio of the number of vowels in the word *Mississippi* to the number of consonants. Write as a fraction in simplest form.

Real-World PROBLEM SOLVING

Social Studies There are 23 states in the United States that border an ocean. Only 5 of those states border the Pacific Ocean.

23. Write a ratio for the number of states bordering the Pacific Ocean to the number of states bordering any ocean.

24. Write a ratio for the number of states that border an ocean to the number of states in the United States.

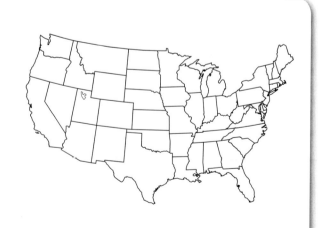

25. It is school policy that for field trips there is 1 adult to go along with every 8 students. How many adults will go on a field trip with 48 students?

Number of Adults	1	× ?	
Number of Students	8	× ?	48

26. At a school cafeteria, 3 out of every 5 students order a hamburger. If 60 students are eating in the cafeteria, how many students order a hamburger?

Number of Hamburgers	3	× ?	
Number of Students	5	× ?	60

For Exercises 27 and 28, use the graphic at the right. Write each ratio in simplest form.

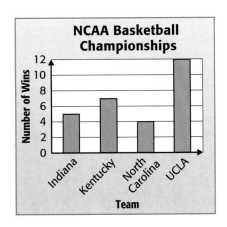

27. What ratio compares the number of wins for Indiana to the number of wins for Kentucky?

28. What ratio compares the number of wins for North Carolina to the number of wins for UCLA?

H.O.T. Problems

29. NUMBER SENSE Write the ratio 6 robins out of 15 birds in three different ways.

30. CRITICAL THINKING If 12 out of 40 students received above a 95% on the test, what ratio of students received a 95% or below?

31. FIND THE ERROR There are 6 red, 5 blue, 8 green, and 4 yellow marbles in a bag. Ivan and Martha are each writing a part to whole ratio for the number of blue marbles. Who is correct? Explain.

Ivan
$$\frac{blue}{red} = \frac{5}{6}$$

Martha
$$\frac{blue}{total\ marbles} = \frac{5}{24}$$

32. **WRITING IN ►MATH** The ratio of quarters to pennies in a piggy bank is 1 to 3. Explain how to write an equivalent ratio showing the number of pennies in the bank if there are 7 quarters.

Rates

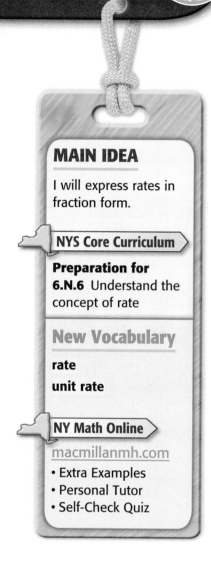

MAIN IDEA

I will express rates in fraction form.

NYS Core Curriculum

Preparation for 6.N.6 Understand the concept of rate

New Vocabulary

rate

unit rate

NY Math Online

macmillanmh.com

• Extra Examples
• Personal Tutor
• Self-Check Quiz

 GET READY to Learn

One of the most famous marathons in the world is the Boston Marathon. The push rim wheel chair race at the marathon is about 26 miles. Some athletes must have a qualifying time of 2 hours in order to race.

$$26 \text{ miles in 2 hours} = \frac{26 \text{ mi}}{2 \text{ h}} = \frac{13 \text{ mi}}{1 \text{ h}}$$

The average rate, of the athlete must be 13 miles per hour.

A ratio that compares two quantities with different kinds of units is called a **rate**. The example above compares miles and hours.

When a rate is simplified so that it has a denominator of 1 unit, it is called a **unit rate**. The table shows common unit rates.

Ratio	Unit Rate	Name
$\frac{\text{number of miles}}{1 \text{ hour}}$	miles per hour	speed
$\frac{\text{number of miles}}{1 \text{ gallon}}$	miles per gallon	gas mileage
$\frac{\text{number of dollars}}{1 \text{ hour}}$	dollars per hour	hourly wage

EXAMPLE   Find Unit Rates

① **Write 300 feet in 30 seconds as a unit rate in feet per second.**

$= \dfrac{300 \text{ ft}}{30 \text{ s}}$ Write the rate as a fraction.

$= \dfrac{300 \text{ ft} \div 30}{30 \text{ s} \div 30}$ Divide the numerator and the denominator by 30.

$= \dfrac{10 \text{ ft}}{1 \text{ s}}$ Simplify.

So, the unit rate is 10 feet per second.

2 A family of four attend a baseball game and want to eat hot dogs. Find the unit rate if it costs $12 for 4 hot dogs.

$12 for 4 hot dogs $= \dfrac{\$12}{4 \text{ hot dogs}}$ Write the rate as a fraction.

$= \dfrac{\$12 \div 4}{4 \div 4}$ Divide the numerator and the denominator by 4.

$= \dfrac{\$3}{1 \text{ hot dog}}$ Simplify.

So, the unit rate is $3 per hot dog.

In Example 2, you found a special kind of unit rate, called the *unit price*. This is the price per unit and is useful when you want to compare the cost of an item that comes in different sizes.

EXAMPLE   Choose the Best Buy Using Estimation

3 The costs of different sized bags of sand used to fill a sandbox are shown. Which bag costs the least per pound?

Size	Price
3 lb	$12.05
4 lb	$19.99
8 lb	$40.25

Find the unit price, or the cost per pound, of each bag. Divide the price by the number of pounds.

Estimated cost

3-pound bag $12 ÷ 3 pounds = $4 per pound
4-pound bag $20 ÷ 4 pounds = $5 per pound
8-pound bag $40 ÷ 8 pounds = $5 per pound

The 3-pound bag costs the least per pound.

CHECK What You Know

Find each unit rate. (See Examples 1–3, pp. LA14–LA15)

1. $36 for 12 gallons

2. 1,500 words in 25 minutes

3. 55 pounds for $11

4. 28 cans of juice for $7

5. A person jumps rope 36 times in 18 seconds. What is the unit rate?

6. Which has the better unit price: a 6-pack of soda for $3 or a 12-pack for $4?

7. **WRITING IN ►MATH** Ethan can buy 4 DVDs for $72.12 at DVD World or 9 DVDs for $153.25 at Movie Town. Estimate to find which has the better unit price. Explain.

Practice and Problem Solving

Find each unit rate. (See Examples 1–3, pp. LA14–LA15)

8. $45 for 5 pounds

9. $96 for 8 ounces

10. 150 people for 5 classes

11. 420 miles in 6 hours

12. 210 visitors in 35 days

13. 510 Calories in 3 servings

14. 40 meters in 4 seconds

15. 84 miles in 14 gallons

16. 70 yards in 7 minutes

17. $45 in 5 hours

Use estimation to choose the better value.

18. $47.99 for a 16-ounce bag or $23.60 for a 12-ounce bag

19. vitamins sold in bottles of 24 for $3.69, 50 for $5.49, 100 for $10.29, or 180 for $11.99

Use the table at the right for Exercises 20 and 21.

20. Estimate the cost of each container to the nearest dollar amount. Which container has the best value?

21. Which two containers have about the same unit price?

Container	Serving Size (oz)	Price
A	18	$5.80
B	16	$4.34
C	12	$3.72
D	10	$2.30

22. A fountain pumps 60,000 gallons of water every 15 minutes. What is the unit rate?

23. Find the unit rate if 40 tickets are sold in 8 minutes.

24. Rebecca blinks her eyes 60 times in 5 minutes. At this rate, how many times does she blink in one minute?

25. Luke can type 300 words in 5 minutes. At this rate, how many words can he type in one minute?

Use the table at the right for Exercises 26–27.

26. Lannie is looking for a job that pays at least 64 dollars a day. However, she must work at least 3 days a week. Use the table to determine which job fits Lannie's needs the best. Explain.

Job	Total Paid	Days Per Week
Server	$160	4
Valet	$168	3
Cashier	$144	2
Librarian	$256	4

27. Which job pays the most money per day?

SHARKS The Shortfin Mako uses its incredible speed to track down fish like the tuna or the sword fish. The Mako is the fastest shark in the ocean. It can travel as far as 60 miles in only 3 hours.

28. How many miles can the Mako shark travel in one hour?

29. How long would it take the Mako shark to travel 80 miles if were traveling at top speed?

H.O.T. Problems

30. NUMBER SENSE In which situation will the rate $\frac{x \text{ ft}}{y \text{ min}}$ increase? Explain your reasoning.
a. x increases, y is unchanged
b. x is unchanged, y increases

31. CHALLENGE A rate is always a ratio, but a ratio is not always a rate. Write a sentence or two to explain this statement, and give an example of when a ratio is not a rate.

32. WHICH ONE DOESN'T BELONG? Identify the measurement that is different from the other three. Explain your reasoning.

8 ft per s	25 mi
6 cans per pack	$16 per lb

33. CHALLENGE The stationery store sold 6 boxes of colored notebook paper in 15 minutes. At this rate, how many boxes will they sell per hour?

34. WRITING IN ►MATH Write a sentence describing how unit price can help you spend less money at the grocery store.

Order of Operations

GET READY to Learn

CHORES The table shows the number of minutes Erica spends doing each activity after school.

Activity	Time Spent (min)
walking the dog	25
watering plants	10

1. How many total minutes are spent if Erica walks the dog for five days after school?

2. How many total minutes are spent if Erica walks the dog and waters plants for four days after school?

3. What two operations did you use in Exercise 2? Explain how to find the answer to Exercise 2 using these operations.

A numerical expression like 25 × 4 + 10 × 4 is a combination of numbers and operations. The **order of operations** tells you which operation to perform to evaluate the expression.

Order of Operations   Key Concept

1. Do the operations in the parentheses first.
2. Multiply and divide in order from left to right.
3. Add and subtract in order from left to right.

EXAMPLES   Use Order of Operations

1 Find 25 × 4 + 10 × 4.

25 × 4 + 10 × 4   Write the expression.

100 + 40   Since there are no parentheses, multiply 25 by 4 and 10 by 4.

140   Add 100 and 40.

2 Find 7 × (9 − 3).

7 × (9 − 3)   Write the expression.

7 × 6   Find 9 − 3 first because it is in parentheses.

42   Multiply 7 and 6.

MAIN IDEA

I will use the order of operations to find the value of expressions.

NYS Core Curriculum

5.N.18 Evaluate an arithmetic expression using order of operations including multiplication, division, addition, subtraction and parentheses

New Vocabulary

order of
  operations

NY Math Online

macmillanmh.com

• Extra Examples
• Personal Tutor
• Self-Check Quiz

Write and Find the Value of Expressions

3 CHORES Refer to the lesson opener. Write an expression to find the total number of minutes Erica spends walking the dog and watering plants for three days after school. Then find the value of the expression.

First, write the expression.

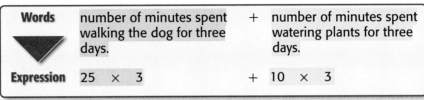

Words	number of minutes spent walking the dog for three days.	+	number of minutes spent watering plants for three days.
Expression	25 × 3	+	10 × 3

$25 \times 3 + 10 \times 3 = 75 + 30$

$= 105$ First, multiply 25 by 3 and 10 by 3.

Add.

So, Erica spends a total of 105 minutes walking the dog and watering the plants for three days after school.

CHECK What You Know

Find the value of each expression. (See Examples 1, 2, p. LA18)

1. $8 + 3 \times 2$

2. $5 + 4 \times 6$

3. $10 \div 2 + 1$

4. $13 + 16 \div 4$

5. $4 \times 3 + 3 \times 9$

6. $6 \times 5 + 2 \times 2$

7. $8 + (7 \times 3)$

8. $20 - (3 \times 5)$

9. $(4 + 2) \times 8$

10. $9 \times (3 + 4)$

11. $18 \div (3 + 3)$

12. $1 + (15 \div 3)$

13. Makayla and Samson are entered in a two-person relay race. Makayla will run 2 miles and Samson will bicycle 4 miles. Makayla can run one mile in 9 minutes and Samson can bicycle one mile in 4 minutes. Write an expression to find the total time to finish the race. Then find the value of the expression (See Example 3, p. LA19)

14. A store sells DVDs for $18 each and CDs for $12 each. Write an expression to find the total cost of four DVDs and four CDs. Then find the value of the expression. See Example 3 (p. LA19)

15. Talk About It What operation would you perform first in evaluating the expression $8 - (3 \times 4) + 5$? Explain.

Find the value of each expression. (See Examples 1, 2, p. LA18)

16. 7 + 5 × 4

17. 3 + 3 × 3

18. 14 + 2 × 6

19. 8 + 5 × 7

20. 25 ÷ 5 + 3

21. 12 ÷ 4 − 1

22. 28 ÷ 4 + 3

23. 18 ÷ 9 + 11

24. 5 × 7 + 3 × 4

25. 8 × 4 + 3 × 7

26. 9 × 3 + 3 × 2

27. 6 × 3 + 2 × 8

28. 3 + (6 × 3)

29. 17 − (2 × 3)

30. (7 + 3) × 4

31. 9 × (12 ÷ 4)

32. 25 (3 + 2)

33. 4 + (16 ÷ 8)

34. On Monday, Mrs. Hinderer drove at an average speed of 50 miles per hour. On Tuesday, she drove at an average speed of 55 miles per hour. Write an expression to find the total number of miles she drove if she drove for 4 hours on Monday and 2 hours on Tuesday. Then find the value of the expression. (See Example 3, p. LA19)

35. One apple contains 70 Calories and one pear contains 100 Calories. Write an expression to find the total number of Calories that are in 3 apples and 2 pears. Then find the value of the expression. (See Example 3, p. LA19)

70 calories   **100 calories**

36. Philip earns $12 an hour for mowing lawns and $9 an hour for raking leaves. Write an expression to find the total amount Philip would earn mowing and raking for 5 hours each. Then find the value of the expression. (See Example 3, p. LA19)

37. The table gives the price of each type of admission to the Museum of Natural History. Seven eleven-year olds and three adults will buy tickets for admission. Write an expression to find the total admission cost. Then find the value of the expression.

Museum of Natural History Admission Prices	
Type of Admission	**Price ($)**
Under 2 years	Free
2–12 years	3
over 12 years	6

Science A housecat spends about 16 hours a day asleep. It also spends about 4 hours grooming.

38. In 3 days, how long will a cat spend sleeping? grooming?

39. How much total time does a housecat spend sleeping and grooming in 7 days?

40. Write an expression to find the total time a housecat spends sleeping and grooming in 30 days.

H.O.T. Problems

41. OPEN ENDED Write a numerical expression involving parentheses for which you would use the order of operations to find its value. Then find the value of the expression.

42. FIND THE ERROR Marty and Shenequa are finding the value of the expression $7 + (21 \div 7) - 4$. Who is correct? Explain.

Marty	Shenequa
$7 + (21 \div 7) - 4$	$7 + (21 \div 7) - 4$
$= 7 + 3 - 4$	$= 28 \div 7 - 4$
$= 10 - 4$	$= 4 - 4$
$= 6$	$= 0$

CHALLENGE For Exercises 43–46, use the order of operations to find the value of each expression.

43. $5 + (6 \times 2) - 3 + (4 \times 4)$

44. $30 - (3 \times 6) + (12 \div 4) - 2$

45. $24 \div (7 + 1) \times 2 + 11$

46. $9 + (49 \div 7) - 1 + (5 \times 3)$

47. WRITING IN ►MATH Write a real-world problem that can be solved by first writing a numerical expression and then by using the order of operations. Then solve.

Algebraic Expressions

Looking 6 Ahead

MAIN IDEA

I will use the order of operations to evaluate algebraic expressions.

NYS Core Curriculum

5.A.3 Substitute assigned values into variable expressions and evaluate using order of operations

NY Math Online

macmillanmh.com

• Extra Examples
• Personal Tutor
• Self-Check Quiz

GET READY to Learn

Tom is counting his money. His piggybank is full of quarters and dimes. He has four additional quarters.

1. Let x represent the number of quarters that are in Tom's piggybank. Write an expression to represent the total number of quarters that Tom has.

2. Let y represent the number of dimes in Tom's piggybank. Write an expression to represent the total number of coins that Tom has.

3. If there are 37 quarters in Tom's piggybank and 15 dimes, how many total coins does he have?

In Chapter 5, you learned to evaluate simple algebraic expressions such as $x + 4$, $5x$, and $x - 9$. You can also use the order of operations to evaluate algebraic expressions when more than one operation is involved.

EXAMPLES   Evaluate Algebraic Expressions

1 **Evaluate the expression $x + 2y$ if $x = 5$ and $y = 7$.**

$x + y = 5 + 2(7)$	Replace x with 5 and y with 7.
$= 5 + 14$	Multiply 2 and 7.
$= 19$	Add 5 and 14.

2 **Evaluate the expression $3a - b$ if $a = 9$ and $b = 4$.**

$3a - b = 3(9) - 4$	Replace a with 9 and b with 4.
$= 27 - 4$	Multiply 3 and 9.
$= 23$	Subtract 4 from 27.

3 **Evaluate the expression $6w + 7(z - 2)$ if $w = 8$ and $z = 11$.**

$6w + 7(z - 2) = 6(8) + 7(11 - 2)$	$w = 8$ and $z = 11$
$= 6(8) + 7(9)$	Subtract 2 from 11.
$= 48 + 63$	Multiply 6 by 8 and 7 by 9.
$= 111$	Add 48 and 63.

④ AMUSEMENT PARKS An amusement park has an admission cost of $25. Paulo has a gift certificate for two free admissions. The expression $25(n - 2)$ represents the total admission cost in dollars for n friends to go to the park. Find the total cost of admission if $n = 6$.

$$25(n - 2) = 25(6 - 2) \qquad \text{Replace } n \text{ with 6.}$$

$$= 25(4) \qquad \text{Find } 6 - 2.$$

$$= 100 \qquad \text{Multiply 25 by 4.}$$

So, the total cost of admission for six friends is $100.

CHECK What You Know

Evaluate each expression if $m = 7$ and $n = 3$. (See Examples 1-3, p. LA22)

1. $m + 3n$ **2.** $4m + n$ **3.** $5m + 2n$

4. $2m + 7n$ **5.** $m - n$ **6.** $6m - 2n$

7. $m - 2n$ **8.** $3m - n$ **9.** $4m + 3(n - 1)$

10. $3m + 2(n + 4)$ **11.** $m + 5(n + 2)$ **12.** $2m + 3(n - 3)$

13. The cost of a large pizza at Papa Pepperoni's is $9. Meghan has a coupon for a total of $3 off any order. The expression $9p - 3$ represents the total cost in dollars for p large pizzas with Meghan's coupon. Find the total cost if $p = 4$.
(See Example 4, p. LA23)

14. Tyler has k baseball cards. His friend Antwon has five more baseball cards. Tyler's brother Keith has twice as many baseball cards as Antwon. The expression $2(k + 5)$ represents the number of baseball cards that Keith has. Find how many baseball cards Keith has if $k = 17$. (See Example 4, p. LA23)

15. When evaluating the expression $5h + 4(h + 3)$ for $h = 7$, which operation would you perform first? Explain.

Evaluate each expression if $c = 8$ and $d = 2$. (See Examples 1-3, p. LA22)

16. $c + 5d$ **17.** $2c + d$ **18.** $3c + 4d$

19. $6c + 7d$ **20.** $c - d$ **21.** $5c - 3d$

22. $c - 2d$ **23.** $4c - d$ **24.** $3(c + 2d)$

25. $3(3c + d)$ **26.** $2(c - d)$ **27.** $4(3c - d)$

28. $2(2c + 3d)$ **29.** $2(3c + 4d)$ **30.** $2c + 5(d - 1)$

31. $4c + 2(d + 7)$ **32.** $c + 3(d + 2)$ **33.** $4c + 6(d + 1)$

34. Measurement The perimeter of a rectangle is given by the expression $2\ell + 2w$. Find the perimeter of a rectangle if $\ell = 13$ centimeters and $w = 9$ centimeters. (See Example 4, p. LA23)

w

ℓ

35. Mrs. Hamilton's class is selling magazine subscriptions. The subscription costs are shown in the table. The expression $30a + 18b$ gives the total amount earned from selling a 12-month subscriptions and b 6-month subscriptions. Find the total amount earned if $a = 4$ and $b = 3$. (See Example 4, p. LA23)

Costs of Magazine Subscriptions	
Type of Subscription	Cost per Month ($)
12 months	30
6 months	18

36. Movie tickets at Studio 19 cost $8 each. Celeste and five of her friends will buy tickets. The cost of a large popcorn is $3 each. The expression $6 \times 8 + 3m$ gives the total cost for the six friends to see a movie if m of the friends also buy a large popcorn. Find the total cost if $m = 4$. (See Example 4, p. LA23)

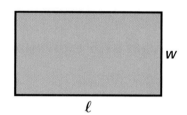

37. At a pet store, goldfish cost $2 each and hamsters cost $9 each. The expression $2g + 9h$ gives the total cost of g goldfish and h hamsters. Find the total cost if $g = 8$ and $h = 2$. (See Example 4, p. LA23)

Real-World PROBLEM SOLVING

Science An airplane is flying at an average speed of 500 miles per hour. A car below is traveling at an average speed of 60 miles per hour. The expression 500h gives the total distance in miles that the airplane will travel in h hours. The expression 60h gives the total distance in miles that the car will travel h hours.

38. How many total miles will the airplane travel in 4 hours? The car?

39. The expression 500h – 60h gives the difference in the number of miles that the airplane and car have traveled after h hours. How many miles farther will the airplane travel in 6 hours than the car?

40. Measurement The expression $\frac{1}{2}bh$ gives the area of a triangle, where b is the length of the base of the triangle and h is the height of the triangle. Find the area of a triangle if b = 12 inches and h = 10 inches.

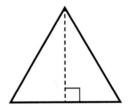

H.O.T. Problems

41. OPEN ENDED Write an algebraic expression for which x = 5 and y = 8. Then evaluate your expression.

CHALLENGE For Exercises 42–45, use the order of operations to evaluate each expression if a = 6, b = 3, and c = 9.

42. $4a + 2(b + 7) - 3c$

43. $a \times b + 36 \div 2c$

44. $3c \div b + 5a \div b$

45. $6a + 3b \div c + a$

46. **WRITING IN ▶MATH** You and a friend are each evaluating the expression $2(n - 1) + n$ if n = 3. Your friend says the answer is $2 \times 3 - 1 + 3$, or 8. Write one or two sentences explaining their error. Then find the correct answer.

Problem-Solving Projects

Problem-Solving Projects

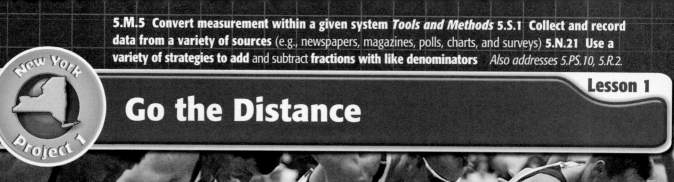

Go the Distance

Lesson 1

New York Project 1

Go the Distance

The first Olympic Games with a recorded winner was in Greece in 776 BCE. In the beginning, there was only one event, a sprint. The winner received a wreath of olive branches to place on his head because olive trees were thought to be sacred.

Getting Started

Day 1 The Long Jump Challenge

- Many Olympic long jumpers are able to jump over 20 feet. Estimate how far you think you can jump. Suppose the lengths of all of the jumps of everyone in your class were added together. About how long do you think this would be?
- Go outside or in your gymnasium and set up a long jump site. Everyone should jump once. Record the exact measures.
- Add the distances to find the total length of jumps for the class. Then compare the actual amount to the estimate. Who had the closest estimate?

Day 2 On Your Mark, Get Set, GO!

- One Olympic event is the 100-meter dash. Today you will run the 50-yard dash. Go outside and mark off an area that is 50 yards long.
- Find a partner. Time each other running the 50-yard dash. Record your times.
- Find the median and mode of the times for everyone in your class.

Day 3 Sponge Relay

- Another Olympic event is the 4-by-400 meter relay. Today you will run a relay. Work in teams that have the same number of members. Each team has an equal-size empty container. Each team races to fill their container to the appropriate line by dunking the sponge into a large bucket, running to the empty container, and wringing the water into it. Record the times for each team to fill their container. Compare the times. Order the times from least to greatest.

Day 4 Frisbee Frenzy

The Olympic event, the discus, focuses on distance. Today you will throw a frisbee but will focus on accuracy.

- Set up a Frisbee toss outside. Make a bull's-eye target like the one shown. The outer section is $\frac{1}{4}$, or 0.25, of a point. The middle section is $\frac{1}{2}$, or 0.5, of a point. The center circle or bull's-eye is worth 1 point. Each person gets three tosses.

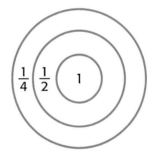

- After your three tosses, add up your total points. Find the median and mode of total points for everyone in your class.

Day 5 Now You Are the Olympic Judge!

- Now it is time to take what you have learned and teach other classes. You may need to make a few adjustments for the younger grades.
- Divide your class into four groups of equal size. Each group is in charge of one of the activities.

Wrap-Up

- How did you use math in this project?
- Describe how you used measurement in the above events.
- Explain why exact measurements and not estimates are need for Olympic events.

5.G.1 Calculate the perimeter of regular and irregular polygons
5.CM.6 Understand mathematical solutions shared by other students
Also addresses 5.RP.7, 5.CM.5.

Lesson 2

Arranging Space

Do you know an interior designer? Some people go to college to learn how to arrange rooms in an appealing and practical fashion. Practice your design skills by rearranging your classroom and by creating a design of your own dream home.

Getting Started

Day 1 Measure and Map It

- Measure to find the perimeter and area of your classroom to the nearest yard. Then convert your measurements to feet.
- Measure the furniture and study its placement in the classroom. Could it be set up in a different way?
- Use graph paper to create a drawing of a rearrangement of the classroom furniture. Be sure to label everything.

Day 2 Persuading the Client

- Create a persuasive speech to explain to the class why your design should be used to rearrange the classroom. Tell why you decided to place objects where you did. Think about how your design might make it easier for the teacher to teach and your classmates to learn.
- Deliver your speech and share your design with the class.

Day 3 The Winning Model

- Walk around the room and look at all of the designs. Consider the speeches that were presented yesterday. Vote for the one that you think will work the best for your classroom.
- Discuss the probability of certain designs being selected.
- Record the votes of everyone in the class. Then rearrange the classroom to match the winning design.

Day 4 Dream Design

You will create a model of a dream house.
- Work with a group to glue smaller boxes inside of a larger box to create walls in your group's dream home.
- Find the perimeter and area of each room in your group's dream home.
- Cut out pictures of furniture, swimming pools, and other features you want in your group's dream home from magazines and catalogs and place them in the correct rooms in the box.

Day 5 Show it Off

- Use the Internet to find information and floor plans from real homes in your area.
- With your group, create a brochure highlighting all the amazing features your dream home has to offer. Make sure to include the home's dimensions.
- Have a "Tour of Homes" and invite other classes to visit.

Wrap-Up

- How did you use math to design your dream home?
- Explain why you needed exact measurements when designing your dream classrooms.
- Which type of graph would you use to display the number of votes for the best design? Explain why. Then make the graph.

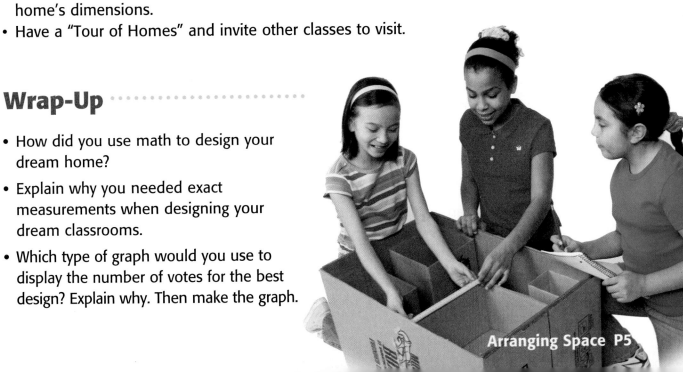

5.G.12 Identify and plot points in the first quadrant
5.CM.7 Raise questions that elicit, extend, or challenge others' thinking
Also addresses 5.CM.8, 5.PS.16.

Lesson 3

Mail Mania

14611

One way people communicate with each other is through mail. Sending mail across the country today is easy. You just apply the proper postage and drop it off at the post office or in a mailbox.

Getting Started

Day 1 The Old Pony Express

- In 1860, there were no mail trucks or planes. But there was the Pony Express. The Pony Express was a team of horses and riders that carried mail from St. Joseph, Missouri, to Sacramento, California. Look at a United States map. Use the scale to find this approximate distance in miles. How long might it have taken them?
- If there was a Pony Express station every 20 miles along the route, how many stations were there in all?
- Write a journal entry as if you were a Pony Express rider back in 1860.

Day 2 Coordinate Your School

- Each day, many mail carriers walk their mail routes. Why do you think it is important to have specific routes?
- Draw a mail route for your school. Using grid paper, draw a coordinate grid labeled 0 to 20. Mark and label the coordinates of the classrooms you want on your mail route.

Day 3 Weighing In

- The price of sending packages through the United States Postal Service depends on the type of package, its weight, and how far it will be sent. Pick a city in the United States to send a 3-pound package. Use the Internet or another source to find the cost.
- Your teacher has set out different packages that need to be mailed. Based on what you have learned above, weigh each package, and calculate the cost of sending it to the city you selected.

Day 4 Overseas Friends

- If you were to send a package from your local post office to a friend overseas, it might travel in many ways. It might be sent in a truck, a plane, or via a mail carrier. Pick one city overseas in which you would like to send a 3-pound package. Track how many miles your package would have to travel from your school to that city. Then find the cost of sending the package.
- Suppose someone is sending you a 3-pound package from the same city you chose. Research the currency that is used in that country to find out how much it will cost to send the package.

Day 5 A Trip to the Post Office

- Using the Internet, find the cost of a stamp for the following years: 1950, 1960, 1970, 1980, 1990, and 2000. Make a table to display the data.
- What is the difference between the cost of a stamp from 1950 to 1960? 1960 to 1970? 1970 to 1980? 1980 to 1990? 1990 to 2000?
- Which years had the greatest increase in price? Which years had the least increase in price?

Wrap-Up

- Almost every year, the price of sending mail increases. Why do you think this happens?
- Why do you think it costs more to send mail overseas?
- Which type of graph would you use to best display the cost of a stamp from 1950 to 2000? Explain your reasoning.

New York
Project 4

It's How Big?

This pie holds the Guinness World Record for the largest pumpkin pie. It was baked in October of 2005 in New Bremen, Ohio. How much do you think it weighs? How many people do you think it would serve?

Getting Started

Day 1 Find out the Favorite

- As a class, create a survey about favorite types of pie.
- Have the entire class take the survey and determine the results.
- Survey other students in the school to find their favorite type of pie.

Day 2 Chart the Results

- Record the data received from your surveys in a frequency table.
- Work in small groups to create bar graphs, pictographs, and line plots on poster board.

Day 3 Make the World's Largest Pie

- Look at the picture of the world record pie. Draw a large pie resembling the world's largest pumpkin pie on construction paper.
- Work in groups to convert a recipe for a normal sized pumpkin pie into this large sized pie. Determine the amount of ingredients needed for the largest pie. Then find the cost of making the largest pie using a calculator.
- Record all the information and display your pie for the school.

Day 4 Tell Everyone!

- Pretend that your class broke the record for the world's largest pie and write a newspaper article about it. Make sure to include all the information that was recorded about the pie yesterday.

Day 5 Magnificent Mud

- In small groups, use the Internet or cookbooks to find a recipe for "mud pie."
- Make the pie using the recipe.
- As a class, set up a taste test for teachers. Survey the teachers about the taste test.
- Record and display the taste test results in a bar graph.
- Discuss the results of the taste test.

Wrap-Up

- Explain why it was important to display the data about favorite types of pies.
- Explain which type of graph best displays this data.
- You used a calculator to find the cost of making the largest pie. Explain the benefits of using a calculator to find total costs.
- Explain how you use math to make your mud pie.

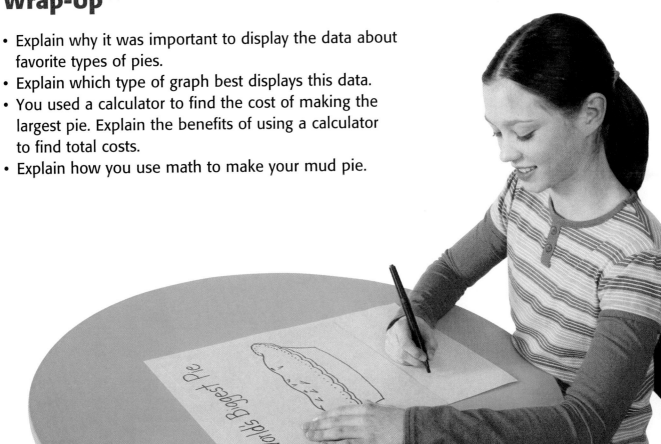

Student Handbook

Built-In Workbook

Reference

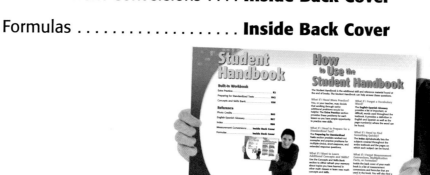

How to Use the Student Handbook

The Student Handbook is the additional skill and reference material found at the end of books. The Student Handbook can help answer these questions.

What If I Need More Practice?

You, or your teacher, may decide that working through some additional problems would be helpful. The **Extra Practice** section provides these problems for each lesson so you have ample opportunity to practice new skills.

What If I Need to Prepare for a Standardized Test?

The **Preparing for Standardized Tests** section provides worked-out examples and practice problems for multiple-choice, short-response, and extended response questions.

What if I Want to Learn Additional Concepts and Skills?

Use the Concepts and Skills Bank section to either refresh your memory about topics you have learned in other math classes or learn new math concepts and skills.

What If I Forgot a Vocabulary Word?

The **English-Spanish Glossary** provides a list of important, or difficult, words used throughout the textbook. It provides a definition in English and Spanish as well as the page number(s) where the word can be found.

What If I Need to Find Something Quickly?

The **Index** alphabetically lists the subjects covered throughout the entire textbook and the pages on which each subject can be found.

What If I Forget Measurement Conversions, Multiplication Facts, or Formulas?

Inside the back cover of your math book is a list of measurement conversions and formulas that are used in the book. You will also find a multiplication table inside the back cover.

Extra Practice

Lesson 1-1

Pages 17–19

Name the place value of the underlined digit. Then write the number it represents.

1. 5̲1,424
2. 3̲24,856
3. 8̲0,885,004
4. 65̲,080,050,000
5. 4̲13,800,560,399
6. 79,7̲07,010

Write each number in standard form.

7. 7 million, 760 thousand, 400
8. six billion, four hundred five million, three hundred

Write in expanded form. Then read and write in word form.

9. 850,120
10. 30,335,012
11. 61,850,002,050

Lesson 1-2

Pages 20–23

Replace each ● with <, >, or = to make a true sentence.

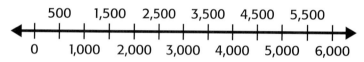

1. 600 ● 1,100
2. 775 ● 875
3. 1433 ● 1973
4. 5,551 ● 5,545
5. 775 ● 775
6. 205 ● 3,205

Replace each ● with <, >, or = to make a true sentence.

7. 890 ● 4,080
8. 10,600 ● 340
9. 7,500 ● 7,000
10. 105,706 ● 90,805
11. 12 ● 1,200
12. 7,900 ● 9,700

Lesson 1-3

Pages 24–25

Use the four-step plan to solve each problem.

1. A sprinter set three Olympic records. Her times were 2:02 minutes, 53.7 seconds, and 26.5 seconds. She competed in the 400-meter dash, the 800-meter run, and the 200-meter dash. What were her times for each event? Explain how you know.

2. Fernando gets out of school at 4:00 P.M. He goes to bed at 9:00 P.M. How much time does he have left if he spends 2 hours at football practice, 1 hour and 30 minutes on his homework, and 50 minutes eating?

3. Your mother agrees to triple whatever you put into a savings account at the bank. If you have deposited $25 each year for the last 3 years, how much money has been deposited?

Lesson 1-4

Pages 28–30

Use a model to write each fraction as a decimal.

1. $\frac{1}{2}$

2. $\frac{8}{10}$

3. $\frac{94}{100}$

4. $\frac{34}{100}$

5. $\frac{187}{1,000}$

6. $\frac{333}{1,000}$

7. $\frac{7}{100}$

8. $\frac{17}{1,000}$

9. $\frac{500}{1,000}$

10. $\frac{775}{1,000}$

11. $\frac{663}{1,000}$

12. $\frac{250}{1,000}$

13. The average snowfall in Amarillo, Texas is 15.4 inches. Write this decimal as a fraction.

14. In a survey, $\frac{56}{100}$ of the students preferred hamburgers to hot dogs. Write this fraction as a decimal.

Lesson 1-5

Pages 32–35

Name the place value of each underlined digit. Then write the number it represents.

1. 42.2<u>3</u>

2. 7.<u>3</u>5

3. 1.09<u>6</u>

4. 36.<u>9</u>37

Write each number in standard form.

5. 16 and 7 tenths

6. thirty-three and two hundredths

7. $11 + 2 + 0.4 + 0.06 + 0.005$

8. $9 + 0.09 + 0.001$

Write each number in expanded form. Then read and write in word form.

9. 6.78

10. 0.775

11. 50.05

12. 84.993

Lesson 1-6

Pages 36–39

Replace each ● with <, >, or = to make a true sentence.

1. 2.2 ● 2.8

2. 0.55 ● 0.66

3. 0.27 ● 0.277

4. 9.456 ● 9.45

5. 11.74 ● 10.25

6. 4.55 ● 4.54

7. 0.09 ● 0.090

8. 75.75 ● 75.70

9. 5.8 ● 8.5

10. 25.5 ● 25.00

11. 0.01 ● 0.010

12. 82.02 ● 82.20

13. Roy can run the 100 meter dash in 11.04 seconds. Malik can run the same distance in 11.40 seconds. Who is faster, Roy or Malik?

Lesson 1-7

Order each set of numbers from least to greatest.

1. 55, 42, 43, 29
2. 109, 167, 87, 99
3. 2,984, 2,893, 4,367, 2,335, 4,387
4. 3.8, 5.9, 2.7, 1.9, 5.6
5. 59,033, 52,456, 59,999, 51,092
6. 63.09, 61.99, 68.47, 63.10
7. 44.4, 4.44, 0.444, 444, 0.044
8. 7.27, 7.79, 0.772, 77.5, 76.903
9. 7.5, 5.7, 7.55, 5.77
10. 9, 8.9, 8.96, 9.01, 9.001

11. Clara's cat weighs 9.72 pounds. Lucia's cat weighs 9.8 pounds. Write a sentence comparing the cats' weights.

Lesson 1-8

Solve. Use the *guess and check* strategy.

1. Hunter saw 16 wheels on a total of 5 cars and motorcycles at the store. How many cars and motorcycles are there at the store?

2. The sum of two numbers is 17. Their product is 72. What are the two numbers?

3. Shirley bought two hot dogs from a street vendor and received $2.50 back in change. The vendor gave her the change in quarters and nickels. If she received 14 coins, how many of each coin did she get?

4. A total of 23 students and teachers from Western Middle School went to the zoo. Student admission price was $3 for each student. Each teacher had to pay $4 for admission. The total cost was $71. How many students went to the zoo?

Lesson 2-1

Round each number to the underlined place.

1. 1̲6
2. 82̲3
3. 2,5̲99
4. 4̲,999
5. 1̲7,347
6. 409,16̲8
7. 5,5̲55
8. 33̲3,225

Round each decimal to the place indicated.

9. 7.8; ones
10. 2.34; tenths
11. 0.928; hundredths
12. 56.10; ones
13. 4.298; tenths
14. 22.399; hundredths
15. 5.345; ones
16. 0.687; tenths

17. The thickness of a United States penny is 1.27 millimeter. Round this number to the nearest tenth.

Lesson 2-2

Pages 64–67

Estimate each sum or difference. Use rounding or compatible numbers. Show your work.

1. 44
   − 21

2. 1,833
   + 3,109

3. 472
   − 268

4. 6.9
   + 3.5

5. 299.5
   + 700.3

6. 8,723
   − 3,114

7. Shanti has 472 baseball cards. Her brother has 835 baseball cards. About how many baseball cards do they have altogether? Show your work.

Lesson 2-3

Pages 68–69

Solve. Use the *work backward* strategy.

1. The local girl scout troop is selling cookies for a fundraiser. They sold all 30 of the boxes that cost $3 and the rest of the boxes they sold were $2 each. If they made $170, how many boxes of cookies did they sell?

2. Calvin's mother gave him $3.35 in change that was left over after she bought groceries. The grocery receipt was for $32.23. How much money did Calvin's mother have before she went grocery shopping?

3. Lola went to Chicago with friends. She wanted to be home no later than 9:00 P.M. on Sunday. It will take Lola 7 hours to ride the train home or 6 hours if she takes the bus. What time will she need to leave Chicago if she rides the bus home?

Lesson 2-4

Pages 70–72

Add or subtract.

1. 45
   + 18

2. 620
   − 430

3. 4,320
   + 6,109

4. 560
   − 350

5. 17,700
   + 13,356

6. 4,350
   + 360

7. 934
   − 275

8. 20,020
   − 12,987

9. Corey bought a pair of shoes for $49, a shirt for $28, and jeans for $55. How much did he spend on his new clothes?

For each problem, determine whether you need an estimate or an exact answer. Then solve.

1. A giant submarine sandwich can feed 13 students. Mr. Smith's science class is having a party for perfect attendance, and they want to order enough food to feed 37 students. How many subs will they need to order?

2. Four friends are sharing 3 pizzas. Each pizza costs $12.96. How much will each person need to pay?

3. A school spends $132 on art supplies for each student. There are 186 students in the school, and the school's art budget is $27,000. Does the school have enough money in the budget to cover the students' supplies?

Lesson 2-6

Add or subtract.

1. $\begin{array}{r} 2.4 \\ + 4.7 \\ \hline \end{array}$

2. $\begin{array}{r} 7.6 \\ + 2.56 \\ \hline \end{array}$

3. $\begin{array}{r} 0.78 \\ - 0.04 \\ \hline \end{array}$

4. $\begin{array}{r} 8 \\ - 3.5 \\ \hline \end{array}$

5. $5.14 + 3.66$

6. $0.6 - 0.11$

7. Brody, Elvio, Jamil and Tito were on the relay team for track and field. The table lists their times. What was the team's total time?

Name	Time (in seconds)
Brody	58.6
Elvio	57.93
Jamil	59.2
Tito	56.8

Lesson 2-7

Identify the addition property used to rewrite each problem.

1. $10 + 5 = 5 + 10$

2. $(22 + 50) + 25 = 22 + (50 + 25)$

3. $9 + 23 + 75 = 9 + 75 + 23$

4. $45 + 0 + 5 = 45 + 5$

Use properties of addition to find each sum mentally. Show your steps and identify the properties that you used.

5. $5 + 30 + 11$

6. $22 + 54 + 6$

7. $3.5 + 7.6 + 19.5$

8. $10.6 + 74 + 2$

9. $49 + 27$

10. $50.4 + 13.6 + 4.5$

Find the value that makes each sentence true.

11. $21 + (45 + 7) = 7 + (21 + \blacksquare)$

12. $13.3 + 2.6 + 6 = \blacksquare + 21$

13. $52 + 0 = \blacksquare$

14. $17 + 32 + 3 = 17 + \blacksquare + 32$

Lesson 2-8

Pages 88–91

Add or subtract mentally. Use compensation.

1. 43 + 21   **2.** 57 + 35   **3.** 79 − 31

4. 88 − 29   **5.** 25 − 15   **6.** 205 + 675

7. 4.3 − 3.2   **8.** 95 − 77   **9.** 29.4 + 22.6

10. 74.2 − 41.2   **11.** 59.4 + 38.6   **12.** 60.5 − 20.3

13. 398 + 492   **13.** 62.6 − 41.9   **14.** 492 − 398

15. In a fish tank, one angelfish measures 5.7 inches and another one measures 4.9 inches. What is the total length of both angelfish?

Lesson 3-1

Pages 103–105

Find each product mentally.

1. 4 × 30   **2.** 70 × 3   **3.** 22 × 10

4. 50 × 40   **5.** 300 × 5   **6.** 620 × 10

7. 30 × 400   **8.** 800 × 700   **9.** 1,000 × 40

10. 4,000 × 5   **11.** 300 × 70   **12.** 25 × 500

13. 25 × 20   **14.** 600 × 600   **15.** 3,000 × 20

16. Celeste is making bracelets for her friends. Each bracelet uses 50 beads. If she wants to make 20 bracelets, how many beads does she need?

Lesson 3-2

Pages 108–111

Rewrite each expression using the Distributive Property. Then evaluate.

1. 5 × (8 + 2)   **2.** 3 × (20 + 7)   **3.** 8 × (40 + 2)

4. 4 × (7 + 7)   **5.** 6 × (5 + 9)   **6.** 2 × (90 + 40)

Find each product mentally using the Distributive Property. Show the steps that you used.

7. 3 × 12   **8.** 5 × 48   **9.** 7 × 23   **10.** 2 × 76

11. 33 × 6   **12.** 94 × 5   **13.** 2 × 43   **14.** 55 × 6

15. Arnaldo is packing 8 red model cars and 5 blue model cars into each box. If he needs to pack 25 boxes, how many model cars will he need? Use the Distributive Property. Show your steps.

16. Maurice is a sports cards dealer. On Tuesday, he sold 13 cards that cost $15 each. He also sold 10 cards that cost $8 each. How much money did Maurice make on Tuesday?

Lesson 3-3

Pages 112–115

Estimate by rounding. Show your work.

1. 38
    × 5

2. 52
    × 7

3.   49
    × 79

4. 102
    × 38

5. 320
    × 73

6. 320
    × 17

7.   79
    × 59

8.   520
    × 437

9.   289
    × 132

Estimate by using compatible numbers. Show your work.

10. 85 × 221

11. 118 × 94

12. 327 × 75

13. Thi's class is ordering books for the reading club. Each book costs $7.55. If there are 12 people in the reading club, about how much will the books cost? Show how you estimated.

Lesson 3-4

Pages 116–118

Multiply.

1. 32
    × 8

2. 47
    × 6

3. 257
    × 5

4. 442
    × 2

5. 321 × 4

6. 63 × 5

7. 7 × 321

8. 94 × 2

9. Willy wants to buy diet soda for 6 people. The sodas cost $1.39 each and he has $10. Will he have enough money? How much will be left over?

Lesson 3-5

Pages 120–121

Solve. Use the *draw a picture* strategy.

1. Denitra is making bracelets from a piece of string that is 50 inches long. After she cuts eight equal size pieces, she has 2 inches left. How long was each piece?

2. Mr. Morris is hanging a light from a ceiling. The height from the ceiling to the floor is 12 feet. If the fixture is 2 feet 4 inches from the ceiling, how far is the fixture to the floor?

4. A bike trail has markers at every other mile beginning with mile one. There is also one at the end of the trail. The trail is 16.3 miles long. How many markers are there?

Lesson 3-6

Pages 122–124

Multiply.

1. 45
    $\times$ 41

2. 62
    $\times$ 68

3. 17
    $\times$ 59

4. 172
    $\times$ 48

5. 17×13

6. 56×72

7. 473×59

8. 182×35

9. Kate swims 18 laps every day in the school's pool. The length of the pool is 50 meters. How many meters will she swim in 28 days?

Lesson 3-7

Pages 126–129

Identify the multiplication property used to rewrite each problem.

1. $13 \times 4 = 4 \times 13$

2. $46 = 1 \times 46$

3. $7 \times 15 \times 42 = 7 \times 42 \times 15$

4. $5 \times (8 \times 10) = (5 \times 8) \times 10$

Use properties of multiplication to find each product mentally. Show your steps and identify the properties that you used.

5. $10 \times 4 \times 7$

6. $15 \times (4 \times 5)$

7. $100 \times 32 \times 3$

8. $4 \times (5 \times 18)$

9. $2 \times 24 \times 5$

10. $25 \times (4 \times 17)$

11. Colby delivers papers every weekday. It takes him 80 minutes each day. If he works 5 days a week for 4 weeks, how many total minutes will it take him to deliver the papers?

Lesson 3-8

Pages 132–135

Estimate by rounding.

1. $\$2.30 \times 8$

2. $\$5.87 \times 4$

3. $\$38.09 \times 6$

4. $\$19.95 \times 3$

5. $3{,}272 \times 9$

6. 485×724

7. Lauren bought 3.2 pounds of lunch meat. It costs $4 per pound. About how much did Lauren pay for the lunch meat?

8. Rodrigo is buying DVDs. He buys two DVDs that cost $19.98 each and three that cost $22.50 each. Estimate the total cost of the DVDs.

Lesson 3-9

Pages 136–137

Solve each problem. If there is extra information, identify it. If there is not enough information, tell what information is needed.

1. Hayden purchases a new bicycle for $149. The color of the bicycle is blue with red stripes. He needs to make 12 monthly payments of $9 to pay off the balance on the bike. How much was the down payment?

2. Shawnel and Cynthiana are participating in a magazine sale. Each magazine subscription costs $2 per week. How many more magazine subscriptions did Cynthiana sell than Shawnel?

Person	Subscriptions
Shawnel	38
Cynthiana	77

3. An arts and crafts store sells three sizes of candles. The prices for the candles are $1.50 for the small size, $2.50 for the medium size, and $5.00 for the large size. The store averages $335 in candle sales each week. How many large candles do they sell on average per week?

Lesson 4-1

Pages 149–151

Divide mentally.

1. $400 \div 4$
2. $600 \div 3$
3. $270 \div 10$
4. $160 \div 8$

5. $5,400 \div 6$
6. $800 \div 8$
7. $2,700 \div 9$
8. $16,000 \div 8,000$

9. $28,000 \div 2$
10. $45,000 \div 5$
11. $90,000 \div 300$
12. $42,000 \div 6$

13. Griffen made $350 doing yard work. If he makes $10 per hour, how many hours did he work?

Lesson 4-2

Pages 152–155

Estimate by using compatible numbers. Show your work.

1. $277 \div 3$
2. $778 \div 21$
3. $990 \div 333$

4. $721 \div 34$
5. $110 \div 9$
6. $320 \div 37$

7. $499 \div 23$
8. $655 \div 222$
9. $5,322 \div 63$

10. $8,672 \div 218$
11. $4,776 \div 239$
12. $21,356 \div 3,200$

13. Mr. Jerome can drive 320 miles on one tank of gas. If his gas tank holds 11 gallons of gasoline, about how many miles can he drive on one gallon? Show how you estimated.

Lesson 4-3

Pages 158–161

Divide.

1. $76 \div 4$ 2. $235 \div 5$ 3. $244 \div 8$

4. $333 \div 2$ 5. $222 \div 3$ 6. $632 \div 4$

7. $933 \div 3$ 8. $420 \div 4$ 9. $302 \div 4$

10. $622 \div 3$ 11. $721 \div 7$ 12. $432 \div 6$

13. Trey used a total of 13,335 Calories for the week. On average, how many Calories a day did he use?

14. If Trey eats 3 meals a day, how many Calories per meal can he have?

Lesson 4-4

Pages 162–164

Divide.

1. $73 \div 11$ 2. $81 \div 30$ 3. $43 \div 13$

4. $82 \div 44$ 5. $443 \div 66$ 6. $211 \div 17$

7. $525 \div 75$ 8. $321 \div 11$ 9. $150 \div 30$

10. $756 \div 50$ 11. $923 \div 71$ 12. $388 \div 24$

13. Paz's class is making birdhouses for a project. They have 524 inches of wood. If each birdhouse takes 24 inches to complete, how many birdhouses can they build? What does your remainder represent?

Lesson 4-5

Pages 166–167

Solve. Use the *act it out* strategy.

1. The top three finishers in the local swimming competition were Melanie, Yasmin, and Francisca. In how many different ways can first, second, and third place be awarded?

2. Elio's mother asked him to roll the family's extra change. The table shows the coins he rolled, how many rolls he made, and the value of money in the rolls. How many total coins did Elio roll?

Coin	Number of rolls	Value of coins (in dollars)
Quarter	2	20.00
Dime	2	10.00
Nickel	3	6.00

Solve. Tell how you interpreted the remainder.

1. Deborah decided to purchase T-shirts at an amusement park to give as souvenirs. How many T-shirts can she buy with $35?

2. It takes 5 bags of beads to make 3 necklaces. How many necklaces can be made with 36 bags of beads?

3. Mrs. Heaton cuts her pie into 7 pieces. She needs to have 83 pieces for a charity event. How many pies must she bake to have enough pieces? How many pieces will be left over?

Estimate.

1. $5\overline{)\$8.25}$

2. $7\overline{)\$19.88}$

3. $2\overline{)\$33.50}$

4. Papina, Malik, and Silvia made a total of $63.21 at a yard sale. They divide the money evenly. About how much does each person get?

Use any strategy to solve each problem.

1. An artist painted twice as many pieces on Tuesday as he did on Monday. He painted 36 pieces total on the two days. How many did he paint on Monday?

2. Ruth has 43 cents in coins in her pocket. If you know that one of the coins is a quarter and she has six coins in her pocket, what are the other coins?

3. Luz is saving up to buy a pair of inline skates that cost $34.98. If she saves $5.00 each week, how many weeks will it take until she can buy the skates?

4. Amiel is heading out for his daily jog. He needs to be home by 6:15 P.M. to do his homework. It takes him 15 minutes to warm up, 45 minutes to jog, and 10 minutes to cool down. What time should he leave for his jog?

5. Akiko is buying books to hold her stamp collection. Each book can hold 120 stamps. If she has 76 envelopes that contain 4 stamps each, how many books will she need?

Lesson 5-1

Pages 193–195

Evaluate each expression if $x = 4$ and $y = 7$.

1. $x + 6$ **2.** $3 + y$ **3.** $2 + x$ **4.** $y + 27$

5. $17 + y$ **6.** $x + 21$ **7.** $x + 29$ **8.** $x + y$

Write an expression for the real-world situation. Then evaluate it.

9. Sareeta is t years old. Her sister is 6 years older. If $t = 10$, how old is Sareeta's sister?

Lesson 5-2

Pages 196–197

Solve. Use the *solve a simpler problem* strategy.

1. For a play, five students can paint 5 props in 5 hours. At this rate, how many props can 7 students paint in 10 hours?

2. What is the sum of the whole numbers from 10 through 19? 20 through 29? 30 through 39? Can you predict the sum of the numbers 50 through 59?

3. Monty is cutting wood for shelves. He has 40 feet of lumber. Each shelf needs to be 5 feet long. If each cut takes 90 seconds, how long will it take Monty to make the cuts?

4. A newspaper delivery person can fit 35 newspapers into their carry bag on Monday through Saturday. On Sunday they can fit 21 papers. They deliver the newspaper to 88 customers every day. How many times do they have to load their carry bag on Wednesdays?

Lesson 5-3

Pages 198–201

Evaluate each expression if $x = 5$ and $y = 3$.

1. $3x$ **2.** $6y$ **3.** $7x$ **4.** $13y$

Evaluate each expression if $a = 9$ and $b = 5$.

5. $4b$ **6.** $11a$ **7.** $20b$ **8.** $8a$

9. $17b$ **10.** $31a$ **11.** $45b$ **12.** $9b$

13. Mei can walk 3 miles in one hour. Saturday she walked for t hours. Write an expression to show the distance she walked.

14. Mrs. Turner is providing fruit slices for the football team. She can get 8 slices from one orange. Write an expression to show how many slices she can get from f oranges. How many slices can Mrs. Turner get from 15 oranges?

Lesson 5-4

Write an expression for each phrase.

1. half of *c*

2. 12 times *w*

3. 19 more than *k*

4. 20 less than *x*

5. twice *p*

6. the sum of *m* and 5

Evaluate each expression if $r = 3$, $s = 5$, and $t = 9$.

7. $r \times 31$

8. $13t$

9. $4r$

10. $t \div 3 \times s$

11. There were *t* questions on a test. Eva missed 4 questions. If there were 35 questions on the test, write and evaluate an expression for the number of questions answered correctly.

Lesson 5-5

Use any strategy to solve each problem.

1. Jonas' parents give him $15 each week for school lunches. If Jonas buys one of each item every day, how much money does he have left on Friday?

Item	Price (in dollars)
pizza	1.50
drink	0.65
fruit	0.75

2. Marlo is twice as old as his sister Naomi. Four years ago he was three times as old. What are their ages now?

3. A large commercial jet seats 416 passengers. On a recent flight, there was one empty seat for every three passengers. How many passengers were on the flight?

Lesson 5-6

Copy and complete each function table for each real-world situation.

1. Cora has 11 more trains than Luis.

Input (x)	x + 11	Output
12		
14		
17		

2. Each package weighs 10 pounds.

Input (x)	10x	Output
7		
11		
15		

Lesson 5-7

Pages 218–222

Evaluate each expression.

 1. $(14 \times 7) - 3$ **2.** $14 \times (7 - 3)$ **3.** $7 + (2 \times 9)$

 4. $(7 + 2) \times 9$ **5.** $(23 + 17) \times 5$ **6.** $23 + (17 \times 5)$

 7. Mrs. Walker is making banners for the middle school sports teams. She needs 8 yards of gold fabric and 6 yards of maroon fabric. The gold fabric costs $6 per yard and the maroon fabric costs $10 per yard. How much will she spend for the fabric?

Lesson 6-1

Pages 237–239

Solve each equation. Check your solution.

 1. $x + 8 = 14$ **2.** $7 - y = 2$ **3.** $e + 15 = 29$ **4.** $q + 4 = 17$

 5. $17 - w = 5$ **6.** $9 + h = 21$ **7.** $t - 19 = 6$ **8.** $29 - y = 1$

Write an equation and then solve. Check your solution.

 9. Lei is thinking of a number. Elsa incorrectly guessed the number to be 25. Lei said the difference between the two numbers is 36. What was her number?

10. The school's lacrosse team has won 5 straight games. Their record is now 13 wins and 4 losses. What was their record before the winning streak?

11. Tyran owns 24 movies. He bought 11 with his own money. The other movies were gifts from others. How many did he receive as gifts?

Lesson 6-2

Pages 242–245

Solve each equation. Check your solution.

 1. $6c = 24$ **2.** $21 = 3c$ **3.** $9g = 45$ **4.** $66 = 2p$

 5. $17y = 102$ **6.** $93 = 31h$ **7.** $49 = 7k$ **8.** $21s = 42$

Write an equation and then solve. Check your solution.

 9. Every player on a basketball team practiced for 30 hours during the two week summer camp. The team practiced for a total of 330 hours. How many players are on the basketball team?

10. A shoe store sold 84 pairs of shoes last weekend. Each clerk sold the same number of shoes. There are 7 clerks at the store. How many pairs of shoes did each sell?

Lesson 6-3

Pages 248–249

Solve. Use the *make a table* strategy.

1. Francisco is 17 years old. His grandfather is 77. How old will Francisco's grandfather be when he is exactly 4 times as old as Francisco?

2. The first week of track practice Cesar ran the 400 meter dash in 1 minute 8 seconds. The third week he ran the 400 meter dash in 1 minute 5 seconds. He continued this pattern until the end of the season. How fast could Cesar run the 400 meter dash in week 9?

3. Marsha's little brother tells her he will clean her room every day for the next two weeks if she pays him by doubling the amount of money paid from the day before. He offers to start for $0.10. How much will he make on the seventh day?

4. If Marsha agrees to his plan, did she make a good deal? Explain.

Lesson 6-4

Pages 250–252

Name the ordered pair for each point.

1. B   2. F   3. E

4. A   5. K   6. G

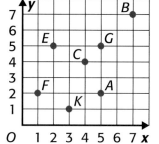

7. Suppose point C was moved one unit to the right and 2 units down. After the move what point will be the same as point C?

8. Garcia located a point that was 6 points to the right of the origin and 3 points above the origin. What was the ordered pair?

Lesson 6-5

Pages 254–257

Graph and label each point on a coordinate grid.

1. W (3, 4)   2. R (1, 8)   3. H (7, 3)   4. T (5, 5)

5. B (5, 2)   6. J (3, 6)   7. P (6, 8)   8. C (2, 4)

9. Mr. Rollins wants to plant trees. Each tree costs $25, and he must pay a delivery charge of $10. Given the function rule $25t + 10$, make a function table to find the total amount Mr. Rollins would pay if he purchased 3 trees, 4 trees, 5 trees, and 6 trees.

10. The Williams family is taking a trip. They travel for 20 miles before they begin timing the length of the trip. Given the function rule $55h + 20$, make a function table to find the distance traveled if they drove for 3 hours, 4 hours, 5 hours, and 6 hours.

Lesson 6-6

Pages 258–260

Solve using a function table or equation.

1. A vendor sells gyros. How much would it cost for a group of 6 people to each eat one gyro?

2. On average Elizabeth reads 82 pages of her book each night. If her book is 548 pages, how long will it take her to read the entire book?

3. A pet store sells goldfish for $0.30 each. Alesha bought 12 goldfish. How much did she spend at the pet store?

4. A pumpkin pie recipe calls for 2 cups of sugar. How much sugar is needed to make 4 pumpkin pies?

Lesson 6-7

Pages 266–267

Use any strategy to solve each problem.

1. Olinda, Danica, and Kimi each like different flavors of ice cream. The flavors they like are vanilla, chocolate, and strawberry. Danica does not like vanilla. Kimi does not like chocolate or vanilla. What type of ice cream does each girl like?

2. A store is selling a television at a clearance price. The clearance price of the television is listed with its original price. If the store sold 7 televisions, what was the total difference between selling them at clearance price and selling them at regular price?

3. Yasu is painting eggs for the local egg hunt. He can paint 3 eggs in 20 minutes. How many eggs can he paint in 1 hour and 40 minutes?

Lesson 7-1

Pages 279–281

Find the median and mode of each set of data.

1. points scored by a basketball team: 55, 67, 55, 98, 87

2. weight of rocks in pounds: 5, 12, 45, 17, 12

3. cups of flour: 8, 2.5, 4.25, 2.5, 1.75

Lesson 7-2

Use any strategy to solve each problem.

1. Henry bought two greeting cards. One card was $0.50 more than the other. The total cost was $7.00. How much did Henry spend for each card?

2. Waban, Josie, and Jacylyn all like different types of books. Josie does not like mysteries or biographies. Jacylyn does not like mysteries or fairytales. Which type of book does each like to read?

3. Wanda wants to drive 300 miles to visit her brother. If she can drive 25 miles on one gallon of gasoline, how many gallons of gasoline will she need to make the trip?

Lesson 7-3

Draw a line plot for each set of data. Then find the median, mode, range, and any outliers of the data shown in the line plot.

1.

Student Height in inches for Mrs. Foster's 5th grade class			
52	48	52	51
52	65	58	48
60	45	50	52
56	48	53	58
62	49	51	49

2.

Daily Low Temperatures for January				
23	17	30	20	17
14	22	31	32	22
32	20	8	31	32
33	27	15	32	30
32	28	20	40	27
33	29	18	14	15

3.

Distances of Paper Airplanes (ft)					
1	5	5	8	3	2
1	4	3	3	6	9
0	2	2	6	3	1
4	7	5	2	4	8

4.

Number of Birds Counted			
30	20	18	22
20	18	21	23
20	20	21	19
18	19	20	23

Lesson 7-4

The following are speed limits for different roads located in a city's limits:

55, 35, 25, 25, 35, 45, 40, 40, 25, 20, 25, 50, 35, 40, 25, 25

1. Make a frequency table of the data.

2. Find the median, mode, and range of the data. Identify any outliers.

The table shows the cost of athletic shoes.

Athletic Shoe Prices (in dollars)				
75	60	60	110	60
100	90	90	85	45
90	75	65	65	55
60	85	110	60	80

1. Choose an appropriate scale and interval size for a frequency table that will represent the sales. Describe the intervals.

2. Create a frequency table using the scale and interval size you described.

3. Write a sentence or two to describe how the prices are distributed among the intervals.

Lesson 7-6

Pages 299–303

The table shows the number of each type of pie sold at a restaurant during lunch.

Pie Sales	
Flavor	Number
cherry pie	3
pumpkin pie	8
pecan pie	7
raspberry pie	6
apple pie	10

1. Make a bar graph of the data. Describe the scale and interval size that you used.

2. Which pie was purchased the most?

3. Which pie represents the median number sold? Explain.

For Exercises 4 and 5, use the bar graph below.

4. Based on the graph below, which state has about twice the area as Kansas? Which state is about $\frac{1}{3}$ the size of Texas?

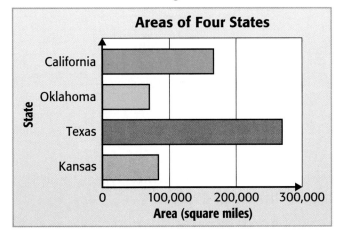

5. About how many more people live in California than Oklahoma?

Extra Practice

The table shows the amount of growth of two sunflower plants Juanita grew for her science fair project.

Sunflower growth control plant												
Week	0	1	2	3	4	5	6	7	8	9	10	11	12
Height (inches)	0	7	14	27	40	52	68	82	90	99	100	101	101
Sunflower growth experimental plant												
Height (inches)	0	3	10	15	18	21	24	28	28	28	32	32	32

1. Make a double line graph of the data.

2. What is the scale of each axis?

3. Would your scale be different if you only had the top data to graph? Explain.

4. Write a sentence or two for each line describing the changes over time.

5. Give a possible explanation for the differences between the two lines.

Which type of graph would you use to display the data in each table? Write *line plot, bar graph, double bar graph, line graph, double line graph*, or *pictograph*. Explain why. Then make the graph.

1.

Students' Favorite Drinks In School Cafeteria	
White Milk	157
Chocolate Milk	93
Water	45
Orange Juice	140
Apple Juice	65

2.

Neighborhood Pets	Cats	Dogs
House 1	2	0
House 2	0	3
House 3	1	2
House 4	2	2
House 5	3	0
House 6	0	1
House 7	0	0
House 8	3	1

3. You want to show your friends how easy it is to save money and what happens to that money over time. Which type of graph would be best to display the data? Explain.

4. Orlando took a survey of his classmates' favorite cafeteria food. What type of graph should he use if he wants to present the data to the principal? Explain.

Lesson 7-9

Pages 320–321

Solve by using a graph.

1. The table shows the number of books read by students during the summer. What was the most common number of books to read? How can you determine the smallest amount of books read just by looking at the graph? What kind of graph did you make?

Number of Books Read					
5	4	1	6	7	4
3	2	3	1	4	2
2	1	3	4	5	9
2	4	5	3	3	4

2. Ty wrote down the amount of time that he read on school nights. What day was the peak of his reading? What kind of graph did you make? How can you determine the peak of his reading just by looking at the graph?

Day of the Week	Sunday	Monday	Tuesday	Wednesday	Thursday
Time (hours)	2	1.5	3.5	2.5	1

Lesson 8-1

Pages 333–335

Represent each situation using a fraction. Then solve.

1. Seven gallons of water are needed to wash 9 cars. How much water was needed to wash each car?

2. Three tons of sand is put into 4 volleyball courts. How many tons of sand did each court receive?

3. One pizza is divided between 6 people. How much pizza did each person receive?

4. Twenty six bags of soil are used to fill in 6 holes. How many bags of soil does each hole use?

Lesson 8-2

Pages 338–342

Write each improper fraction as a mixed number.

1. $\frac{6}{5}$ 2. $\frac{7}{2}$ 3. $\frac{19}{8}$ 4. $\frac{42}{5}$

5. $\frac{27}{7}$ 6. $\frac{15}{4}$ 7. $\frac{8}{7}$ 8. $\frac{21}{8}$

9. $\frac{10}{3}$ 10. $\frac{44}{6}$ 11. $\frac{11}{3}$ 12. $\frac{38}{5}$

Solve by *using logical reasoning*.

1. In a class of 30 students, 18 say their favorite subject is math, 5 say their favorite subject is social studies, and 3 say they love both math and social studies. How many students have favorite subjects other than math or social studies?

2. In a school of 500 students, 185 students are in the band, 300 are on sports teams, and 160 participate in both activities. How many students are involved in either band or sports?

3. There were six dogs, four cats, and two snakes in a vet's office. Two people owned a cat and dog, and one person owned a dog and snake. If no one else owned multiple animals, how many people were in the office?

Write each mixed number as an improper fraction.

1. $6\frac{1}{2}$ 2. $4\frac{2}{3}$ 3. $9\frac{5}{7}$ 4. $7\frac{4}{9}$

5. $2\frac{5}{8}$ 6. $5\frac{2}{13}$ 7. $2\frac{3}{5}$ 8. $4\frac{7}{8}$

9. $3\frac{7}{12}$ 10. $1\frac{5}{6}$ 11. $13\frac{5}{12}$ 12. $5\frac{1}{4}$

13. Ines can make $4\frac{1}{3}$ necklaces out of one bag of beads. Write this number as an improper fraction.

Replace each ● with < or > to make a true statement.

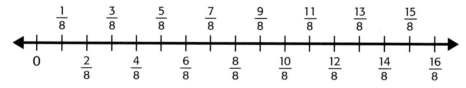

1. $\frac{5}{8}$ ● $\frac{3}{8}$ 2. $2\frac{4}{8}$ ● $2\frac{2}{8}$ 3. $10\frac{7}{8}$ ● $10\frac{5}{8}$

Replace each ● with < or > to make a true statement.

4. $\frac{6}{9}$ ● $\frac{4}{9}$ 5. $\frac{9}{5}$ ● $3\frac{5}{9}$ 6. $10\frac{3}{4}$ ● $2\frac{1}{3}$

5. $\frac{2}{3}$ ● $\frac{1}{2}$ 6. $2\frac{5}{8}$ ● $1\frac{1}{4}$ 7. $\frac{21}{3}$ ● $7\frac{1}{8}$

8. Ricky said he could make $\frac{4}{5}$ of the baskets he shot at practice. Omar said he could make $\frac{6}{7}$ of the baskets he shot. Who claimed to make more baskets at practice?

Lesson 8-6

Pages 356–359

State whether each fraction is closest to 0, $\frac{1}{2}$, or 1.

1. $\frac{7}{9}$

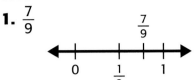

2. $\frac{1}{5}$

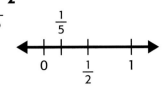

Round each fraction to 0, $\frac{1}{2}$, or 1.

3. $\frac{4}{13}$ **4.** $\frac{5}{7}$ **5.** $\frac{12}{15}$ **6.** $\frac{8}{12}$

7. $\frac{7}{11}$ **8.** $\frac{6}{10}$ **9.** $\frac{15}{17}$ **10.** $\frac{1}{16}$

11. Lewis has finished running $\frac{5}{8}$ of a mile. Has he run half a mile or almost all of a mile?

Lesson 8-7

Pages 360–361

Use any strategy to solve each problem.

1. Billiards players use the dots on the edge of the table to guide their shots. If there are 6 dots on each side of the table and 3 dots on each end, how many total dots are there around the perimeter of the billiards table?

2. What two positive integers have a sum of 17 and a product of 72?

3. A salesperson at a department store makes the following commissions. In one day, the sales person sold 8 shirts, 3 pairs of pants, and 4 pairs of shoes. How much did the salesperson make in commissions on that day?

Article of Clothing	Commission
Shirt	$2
Pants	$4
Shoes	$7

Lesson 9-1

Pages 373–375

Find the common factors of each set of numbers.

1. 7, 28   **2.** 12, 40   **3.** 6, 30   **4.** 27, 45

Find the GCF of each set of numbers.

5. 6, 18   **6.** 20, 24   **7.** 44, 12   **8.** 35, 14

9. There are 36 dogs and 48 cats in a pet show. The show planner wants to put an equal number of dogs and cats in each row. What is the greatest number of cats that can be in each row?

Lesson 9-2

Tell whether each number is *prime* or *composite*.

1. 12   **2.** 23   **3.** 28   **4.** 30

5. 55   **6.** 43   **7.** 17   **8.** 62

9. Kaya wants to arrange her 12 field hockey trophies on a shelf. How many different ways can she arrange her trophies so an equal number of trophies are in each row? List the ways.

10. What is the only even prime number?

Lesson 9-3

Pages 382–384

Find two fractions that are equivalent to each fraction.

1. $\frac{6}{7}$ **2.** $\frac{3}{9}$ **3.** $\frac{8}{9}$ **4.** $\frac{3}{10}$

5. $\frac{6}{18}$ **6.** $\frac{8}{14}$ **7.** $\frac{4}{20}$ **8.** $\frac{7}{8}$

9. Khalid wants to buy $\frac{24}{32}$ of a yard of chain. How many fourths of a yard is this?

10. A craft project takes $\frac{16}{24}$ of a yard of fabric. Ito wants to buy enough for one project. The store only sells fabric in thirds. How many thirds should Ito buy?

Lesson 9-4

Pages 386–389

Write each fraction in simplest form. If the fraction is already in simplest form, write *simplified*.

1. $\frac{4}{6}$ **2.** $\frac{4}{10}$ **3.** $\frac{9}{21}$ **4.** $\frac{8}{12}$

5. $\frac{12}{32}$ **6.** $\frac{17}{35}$ **7.** $\frac{20}{45}$ **8.** $\frac{6}{42}$

9. $\frac{22}{44}$ **10.** $\frac{9}{12}$ **11.** $\frac{5}{15}$ **12.** $\frac{10}{25}$

13. Victoria has 16 white socks, 10 pink socks, 4 green socks and 6 blue socks in her drawer. Express in simplest form the fraction of socks in her drawer that are white; pink; blue.

14. Marta and Nicki were sharing a pizza. Marta wanted $\frac{1}{4}$ of the pizza and Nicki wanted $\frac{3}{8}$ of the pizza. Should they get the pizza cut into 4 or 8 pieces? How many pieces would each girl get?

R24   Extra Practice

Lesson 9-5

Pages 391–393

Write each decimal as a fraction in simplest form.

1. 0.5   **2.** 0.7   **3.** 0.13   **4.** 0.75

5. 0.321   **6.** 0.340   **7.** 0.08   **8.** 0.50

9. In 1911, Ty Cobbs' batting average was 0.420. Write this rate as a fraction in simplest form.

Lesson 9-6

Pages 394–395

Solve. Use the *look for a pattern* strategy.

1. Look at the pattern below.

> 17, 58, 99, 140

Describe the rule for determining the last 3 numbers shown in this pattern.

2. Mrs. Hintz's fifth grade class is raising money for the American Red Cross. They raise $66 the first week. The next two weeks are shown on the table. If this pattern continues, how much should the class expect to raise in the fourth week?

Week	1	2	3
Amount raised ($)	66	87	108

3. Jalen's test scores are continually improving. Here is a record of four of his first five tests. Based on the pattern, what was his third test score?

Test 1	Test 2	Test 3	Test 4	Test 5
63	69		81	87

Lesson 9-7

Pages 396–399

List multiples to find the first two common multiples of each pair of numbers.

1. 3 and 6   **2.** 4 and 16   **3.** 5 and 20   **4.** 7 and 14

Find the LCM of each set of numbers.

5. 4 and 5   **6.** 7 and 9   **7.** 4, 6, and 8   **8.** 7 and 15

9. The ages of Mrs. Thorne's children are 6, 8, and 12. What is the least common multiple of their ages?

Lesson 9-8

Pages 400–401

Use any strategy to solve each problem.

1. Brad, Landon, and Amanda each play different sports. Amanda does not play baseball or tennis. Landon does not play basketball or baseball. What sport does each person play?

2. A DNA strip follows this pattern: TCTTCGTCTTCGT _ _ _ What three letters finish the pattern?

3. A total of 42 students were on the quiz bowl team. There were twice as many boys as girls. How many girls were on the team?

Lesson 9-9

Pages 402–405

Compare each pair of fractions using models or the LCD.

1. $\frac{1}{2}$ and $\frac{5}{6}$ 2. $\frac{3}{8}$ and $\frac{1}{12}$ 3. $\frac{1}{2}$ and $\frac{3}{10}$ 4. $\frac{1}{3}$ and $\frac{4}{7}$

Replace each ● with <, >, or = to make a true statement.

5. $\frac{3}{4}$ ● $\frac{2}{3}$ 6. $\frac{5}{8}$ ● $\frac{10}{16}$ 7. $\frac{3}{8}$ ● $\frac{1}{3}$ 8. $\frac{5}{9}$ ● $\frac{7}{12}$

9. Mr. Torres assigned thirty math problems for homework. Aisha worked for $\frac{1}{3}$ of an hour, Taro worked for $\frac{2}{5}$ of an hour, and Lucas worked for $\frac{1}{2}$ of an hour. Who worked the longest on the math homework?

10. Marcela made punch for the class party. She used $\frac{2}{3}$ quart of orange juice and $\frac{3}{4}$ quart of grape juice. Did she use more orange juice or more grape juice? Explain.

Lesson 10-1

Pages 423–425

Add. Write each sum in the simplest form.

1. $\frac{3}{6} + \frac{5}{6}$ 2. $\frac{7}{15} + \frac{11}{15}$ 3. $\frac{2}{8} + \frac{4}{8}$ 4. $\frac{2}{4} + \frac{4}{4}$

5. $\frac{7}{5} + \frac{2}{5}$ 6. $\frac{7}{13} + \frac{3}{13}$ 7. $\frac{2}{9} + \frac{7}{9}$ 8. $\frac{11}{20} + \frac{17}{20}$

9. Mr. Chang and his daughter Ping were building shelves for her room. One day they worked $\frac{2}{3}$ of an hour, and the second day they worked twice as long. How much total time did they work on the shelves?

10. Delmar was mixing paint to use on a school project. He mixed $\frac{3}{4}$ gallon of white paint, $\frac{3}{4}$ gallon of red paint, and $\frac{2}{4}$ gallon of yellow paint. How much total paint did Delmar have?

Lesson 10-2

Pages 428–431

Subtract. Write each difference in simplest form. Check your answer by using fraction tiles or drawing a picture.

1. $\frac{3}{6} - \frac{2}{6}$

2. $\frac{12}{15} - \frac{11}{15}$

3. $\frac{7}{8} - \frac{4}{8}$

4. $\frac{3}{4} - \frac{1}{4}$

5. $\frac{7}{5} - \frac{2}{5}$

6. $\frac{7}{13} - \frac{3}{13}$

7. $\frac{9}{9} - \frac{7}{9}$

8. $\frac{19}{20} - \frac{11}{20}$

9. $\frac{15}{16} - \frac{3}{16}$

10. Ken runs $\frac{3}{8}$ of a mile. Isabel runs $\frac{5}{8}$ of a mile in the same time. How much farther does Isabel run?

Lesson 10-3

Pages 434–436

Add. Write in simplest form.

1. $\frac{5}{14} + \frac{1}{7}$

2. $\frac{1}{3} + \frac{1}{2}$

3. $\frac{2}{9} + \frac{1}{3}$

4. $\frac{1}{2} + \frac{3}{4}$

5. $\frac{1}{4} + \frac{3}{12}$

6. $\frac{9}{12} + \frac{13}{24}$

7. $\frac{8}{15} + \frac{2}{3}$

8. $\frac{5}{14} + \frac{11}{28}$

9. $\frac{7}{16} + \frac{3}{4}$

10. Ahmed ate $\frac{2}{5}$ of the cookies and Sarah ate $\frac{1}{3}$ of the cookies. What fraction of the cookies were eaten altogether?

Lesson 10-4

Pages 439–441

Subtract. Write in simplest form.

1. $\frac{13}{20} - \frac{3}{10}$

2. $\frac{5}{9} - \frac{1}{3}$

3. $\frac{5}{8} - \frac{2}{5}$

4. $\frac{3}{4} - \frac{1}{2}$

5. $\frac{7}{8} - \frac{3}{16}$

6. $\frac{2}{3} - \frac{1}{6}$

7. $\frac{9}{16} - \frac{1}{2}$

8. $\frac{5}{8} - \frac{11}{20}$

9. $\frac{9}{12} - \frac{2}{3}$

10. Terrell finished $\frac{4}{9}$ of his report on Wednesday and $\frac{1}{3}$ of his report on Thursday. What fraction of the report does Terrell have left to finish?

Solve. Determine which answer is reasonable.

1. Teak wants to buy a new skateboard with special wheels. The skateboard costs $38.45, the wheels cost $8.95, and the tools needed to install them are $10.49. Which is a more reasonable estimate for the money Teak needs to save: $55, $60, or $65?

2. A shoe store had a total of 3,868 pairs of shoes in stock. A week later, 997 pairs of shoes were sold. Which is a more reasonable estimate for the number of pairs of shoes remaining in the store: 3,000 or 2,500?

3. After school, Trina spends $\frac{2}{4}$ of an hour cleaning her room, $\frac{3}{4}$ of an hour practicing the flute, and $\frac{3}{4}$ of an hour doing her homework. Which is a more reasonable estimate for the amount of time she has spent working: 1 hour, 2 hours or 3 hours?

Estimate.

1. $3\frac{4}{9} + 7\frac{2}{9}$
2. $10\frac{3}{11} - 4\frac{2}{11}$
3. $5\frac{7}{12} + 7\frac{2}{3}$
4. $10\frac{2}{11} - 3\frac{3}{22}$
5. $7\frac{5}{6} - 4\frac{1}{6}$
6. $7\frac{7}{15} + 4\frac{6}{15}$
7. $6\frac{5}{8} - 5\frac{1}{4}$
8. $19\frac{1}{15} + 11\frac{1}{15}$
9. $4\frac{5}{7} - 1\frac{6}{7}$

10. Clarissa's first long jump attempt was $4\frac{5}{6}$ feet. Her second attempt was $5\frac{1}{2}$ feet. About how much longer was Clarissa's second attempt?

Add. Write each sum in simplest form. Check your answer by using fraction tiles or drawing a picture.

1. $2\frac{4}{7} + 6\frac{2}{7}$
2. $8\frac{1}{3} + 2\frac{2}{9}$
3. $3\frac{7}{10} + 5\frac{4}{5}$
4. $6\frac{1}{5} + 12\frac{9}{20}$
5. $1\frac{1}{8} + 2\frac{5}{8}$
6. $7\frac{7}{17} + 6\frac{6}{17}$
7. $4\frac{1}{2} + 3\frac{2}{10}$
8. $17\frac{1}{13} + 13\frac{1}{13}$
9. $2\frac{4}{6} + 1\frac{2}{3}$

10. Mr. Woods needs $1\frac{3}{4}$ pounds of ground beef to make hamburgers and $2\frac{1}{2}$ pounds to make meatloaf. How much ground beef does Mr. Woods need altogether?

Lesson 10-8

Pages 452–454

Subtract. Write each difference in simplest form. Check your answer by using fraction tiles or drawing a picture.

1. $7\frac{9}{10} - 4\frac{7}{10}$

2. $10\frac{4}{7} - 2\frac{3}{7}$

3. $9\frac{2}{3} - 7\frac{7}{12}$

4. $16\frac{1}{3} - 12\frac{4}{27}$

5. $7\frac{5}{9} - 2\frac{4}{9}$

6. $7\frac{7}{19} - 6\frac{6}{19}$

7. The average rainfall in Abilene for the month of August is $2\frac{4}{5}$ inches. The average rainfall in Zapata is $1\frac{7}{10}$ inches. What is the difference in the average amount of rainfall between the two cities?

Lesson 10-9

Pages 456–457

Use any strategy to solve each problem.

1. A one topping pizza with eight slices costs $6. If the cost per slice remains the same, how much would a one topping pizza with fourteen slices cost?

2. What is the next figure in the pattern? $\longrightarrow \longleftarrow \uparrow \downarrow \longrightarrow$

3. At the Henderson's garage sale, they are selling T-shirts for $0.80 each and bicycles for $15.50 each. If someone bought 3 T-shirts and 1 bicycle, how much did they spend at the garage sale?

Lesson 10-10

Pages 458–461

Subtract. Write each difference in simplest form. Check your answer by using fraction tiles or drawing a picture.

1. $9\frac{2}{6} - 5\frac{5}{6}$

2. $8\frac{4}{9} - 6\frac{7}{9}$

3. $5\frac{1}{5} - 1\frac{2}{5}$

4. $7\frac{1}{3} - 3\frac{2}{3}$

5. $13 - 10\frac{5}{8}$

6. $15\frac{1}{4} - 12\frac{3}{4}$

7. $10\frac{3}{7} - 5\frac{5}{7}$

8. $15 - 11\frac{7}{10}$

9. Hala's dog Max weighs $45\frac{3}{8}$ pounds. Berto's dog Teddy weighs $23\frac{5}{8}$ pounds. How much more does Max weigh than Teddy?

Lesson 11-1

Pages 477–480

Complete.

1. 4 ft = ▨ in.

2. 14 yd = ▨ in.

3. 39 ft = ▨ yd

4. 132 in. = ▨ ft.

5. 24 yd 3 ft = ▨ ft

6. 8 ft 24 in. = ▨ ft

7. The beluga whale grows to be about 15 feet in length. What is the length of the whale in yards? In inches?

Solve. Use the *draw a diagram* strategy.

1. Jai is taking her dog for a walk. She leaves the house, turns left and walks three blocks. Then she turns right, walks three blocks, turns left, walks 2 more blocks, then turns left again and walks 5 blocks. How far from home is she?

2. Mr. Costa is making cookies for a party. He has two cookie sheets. One is 14 inches wide by 16 inches long and the other is 12 inches by 18 inches. If each cookie is 2 inches in diameter and he places them 1 inch apart, which cookie sheet holds more cookies?

Lesson 11-3

Complete.

1. 80 oz = ▨ lb

2. 3 T = ▨ lb

3. 12 lb = ▨ oz

4. 3,000 lb = ▨ T ▨ lb

5. 23 lb 48 oz = ▨ lb

6. 144 oz = ▨ lb

7. Mrs. Wilson needs 240 ounces of potatoes for her school potluck dinner. How many pounds of potatoes does she need?

Lesson 11-4

Complete.

1. 6 c = ▨ fl oz

2. 6 gal = ▨ fl oz

3. 34 c = ▨ pt

4. 8 qt = ▨ gal

5. 5 qt 3 c = ▨ c

6. 16 pt = ▨ qt

7. 9 c = ▨ pt ▨ c

8. 7 gal = ▨ qt

9. 22 fl oz = ▨ c ▨ fl oz

10. Alvar's mother brought home 24 bottles of water. Each bottle contained 20 ounces. How many quarts of water did she bring home?

11. Mr. Chen's car holds $12\frac{1}{2}$ gallons of gasoline. How many quarts is this? How many fluid ounces?

Lesson 11-5

Complete.

1. 660 s = ▨ min

2. 3 wk = ▨ d

3. 1,825 d = ▨ y

4. 1,990 s = ▨ min ▨ s

5. 240 min = ▨ h

6. 3,211 d = ▨ wk ▨ d

7. The average lifespan of a Border Collie is 13 years. The average lifespan of a Jack Russell Terrier is 163 months. On average, which breed of dog lives longer? How much longer?

Lesson 11-6

Pages 496–497

Use any strategy to solve each problem.

1. Mount Kilimanjaro, the highest mountain in Tanzania, is 5,895 meters tall. Mount Meru, which is near Kilimanjaro, is 4,566 meters tall. What is the difference in height between the two?

2. Tory's cow is 3 times heavier than Tom's. If Tory's cow weighs 840 pounds, how much does Tom's cow weigh?

3. Marla and Angelina are hiking. They can hike 6 miles in 2 hours, 9 miles in 3 hours, and 12 miles in 4 hours. How many miles can they hike in 5 hours?

4. Mr. Stevens grades a test with 20 questions. Each correct answer is worth 2 points. Each wrong answer takes one point away from the total. Lana's score is 25. Continue the table to find how many of her answers are correct.

Number Correct	20	19	18
Number Wrong	0	1	2
Total Score	40	37	34

Lesson 11-7

Pages 500–503

Find the elapsed time.

1. 7:00 A.M. to 12:15 P.M.

2. 1:30 P.M. to 8:15 A.M.

3. 4:46 P.M. to 5:39 P.M.

4. 8:04 P.M. to 6:37 A.M.

5. Bryce started babysitting at 6:45 P.M. and finished at 9:54 P.M. How long did he babysit?

Lesson 12-1

Pages 517–521

Complete.

1. 6 cm = ▇ mm

2. 4,000 mm = ▇ m

3. 700 cm = ▇ m

4. 5 m = ▇ cm

5. 14,000 mm = ▇ m

6. 18 cm = ▇ mm

Select an appropriate unit to measure the length of each of the following. Write millimeter, centimeter, meter, or kilometer.

7. lightpole

8. notebook

9. postage stamp

10. Mira has a cordless phone that allows her to talk up to 20 meters from the base of the phone. Can she continue to talk on the phone while going to her mail box which is 2,200 centimeters away from the base of the phone? Explain.

Solve. Determine *reasonable* answers.

1. A label on a mountain bike states that the weight of the bike is 100 pounds. Is this label accurate? Explain.

2. Mrs. Cashman estimates that she uses a cup and a half of sugar in her pumpkin pie recipe. Does this seem like a reasonable amount to use? Explain.

3. Parker is at the lumber yard looking at plywood to build a toy chest. The toy chest needs 36 square feet of lumber to build it. The plywood comes in sheets of 4 feet × 8 feet. Parker reasons that 4 sheets of plywood will be just enough. Is this a reasonable assumption? Explain.

4. Shaniqua was measuring her locker to see if her books would fit. She claimed her notebooks were 21 centimeters wide and 30 centimeters long. Is she correct? Explain.

Lesson 12-3

Complete.

1. 4 g = ▒ mg
2. 9 kg = ▒ g
3. 12 g = ▒ mg
4. 6,000 g = ▒ kg
5. 2,000 mg = ▒ kg
6. 1 kg = ▒ g

7. Which is a more reasonable estimate for the mass of a stapler: 130 milligrams, 130 grams, or 130 kilograms?

8. A sugar company donated 50 kg of sugar to a local high school. If the sugar was divided into equal bags of 250 g, how many bags are there?

Lesson 12-4

Complete.

1. 40 L = ▒ mL
2. 8,000 mL = ▒ L
3. 7 L = ▒ mL
4. 4,000 mL = ▒ L
5. 5 L = ▒ mL
6. 8 L = ▒ mL

7. Which metric unit would you use to measure the capacity of a bath tub?

8. A coffee mug holds 600 milliliters. Find the capacity in liters.

9. Jenn bought 6 bottles of juice that were marked 750 mL. How many liters of juice did she buy?

Lesson 12-5
Pages 533–535

Write an integer to represent each situation. Then graph the integer on a number line.

1. spent $12 on a CD

2. 8 degrees warmer

3. The puppy gained 2 pounds

4. lost $10

Write an integer to represent each situation. Then write its opposite.

5. earned $56 mowing grass

6. scored a three point basket in basketball

7. 40 plants were dead

8. 2 inches of rain in a gauge

Lesson 12-6
Pages 538–541

Choose the more reasonable temperature for each situation.

1. skiing: 56°F or 7°C

2. frozen fish: 40°F or 0°C

3. July 4th in Florida: 18°C or 92°F

4. playing tennis: 5°C or 75°F

The table shows the highest recorded temperatures for several U.S. states.

State	Temperature (°F)	State	Temperature (°F)
Alabama	112	Florida	109
Connecticut	100	Idaho	118
Arizona	128	California	134
Arkansas	120	Texas	120
Colorado	118	Maine	105

Source: Fact Monster

5. How much greater is California's highest temperature than Maine's highest temperature?

6. How much greater is Arizona's highest temperature than Florida's highest temperature?

Lesson 12-7

Pages 544–545

Extra Practice

Use any strategy to solve each problem.

1. Tyler runs for 8 minutes then walks for 4 minutes. How many sets of this pattern will he complete if he exercises for 65 minutes?

2. Tickets for a movie cost $3 for children and $5 for adults. The movie took in $126 in one showing. At that showing there were 12 children. How many adults were there?

3. The Empire State Building is 1,250 ft tall. How many inches is half of the building?

4. Gary claimed that he is older than Diane. Diane is twice as old as Marty. Marty is 3 years short of being half as old as Gary. Is Gary's claim true?

Lesson 13-1

Pages 557–560

Identify each figure. Then name it using symbols.

1.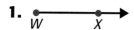

2. •B

3.

4. Are these two lines parallel? Explain your answer.

Lesson 13-2

Pages 562–563

Solve. Use *logical reasoning*.

1. If Tiara continues making the figures shown below, how many triangular blocks will be in the fifth figure?

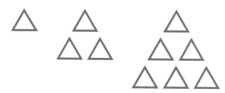

2. Sebastian made 44 more necklaces than Tina made. Together they made 196 necklaces. How many necklaces did Tina make?

3. Quinn, Andy, and Chase are friends with three different hobbies: motocross, art, and skating. Andy has no artistic skill. Chase can not draw or skate. Quinn is a tremendous painter. Who is the friend that rides motocross?

4. There are three fish bowls with five fish in each bowl. Two of the bowls have two orange fish, two bowls have two yellow fish, two bowls have two gold fish and all three have one silver fish. What are the colors of fish in each bowl?

Lesson 13-3

Pages 566–569

Measure the sides of each triangle. Then find the number of congruent sides. State whether any of the sides appear to be perpendicular. Write yes or no.

1.

2.

3.

4.

Lesson 13-4

Pages 570–574

Determine whether each statement is *true* or *false*. Explain.

1. Some rhombi are rectangles.

2. Some trapezoids are parallelograms.

3. All parallelograms are rectangles.

4. All squares are rhombi.

Lesson 13-5

Pages 576–577

Use any strategy to solve each problem.

1. Seven trains pass through a town every day. The times for the first four trains are 9:10 A.M., 9:45 A.M., 10:20 A.M., and 10:55 A.M. At what time will the last train of the day pass through the town?

2. There are 12 pieces of red candy in a jar for every 8 pieces of blue candy. If there are 60 pieces of red candy in the jar, how many total pieces of candy are in the jar?

3. Ramous' batting average is 0.050 points higher than Albert's. Albert's average is 0.180 points lower than Rashid's. List the players in order of their batting average from least to greatest.

4. The Fibonacci Sequence is a special mathematical sequence that occurs frequently in nature. The first six numbers of the sequence are 1, 1, 2, 3, 5, and 8. What is the seventh term? The tenth?

Lesson 13-6

Pages 578–581

Graph each figure and the translation described. Then write the ordered pairs for the vertices of the translation image.

1. triangle *XYZ* with vertices *X*(3, 2), *Y*(5, 4), *Z*(2, 6); translated 2 units right

2. quadrilateral *LMNO* with vertices *L*(1, 8), *M*(1, 6), *N*(5, 6), *O*(5, 8); translated 3 units up

3. triangle *KLM* with vertices *K*(2, 5), *L*(4, 7), and *M*(5, 5); translated 3 units right, 4 units down

4. triangle *ABC* with vertices *A*(3, 6), *B*(3, 9), *C*(7, 6); translated 2 units left and 3 units down

Lesson 13-7

Pages 582–585

Graph each figure after a reflection across the line. Then write the ordered pairs for the vertices of the relection image.

1.
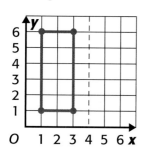

2.
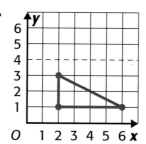

Lesson 13-8

Pages 586–590

Graph the triangle after each rotation. Then write the ordered pairs for the vertices of the rotation image.

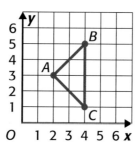

1. 90' clockwise about point *C*

2. 90' counterclockwise about point *B*

3. 90' counterclockwise about point *A*

Lesson 13-9

Pages 591–593

Determine whether each transformation is a *translation*, *reflection*, or *rotation*.

1.

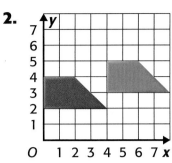

2.

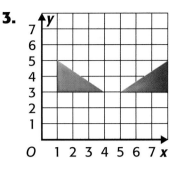

3.

Lesson 14-1

Pages 608–611

Find the perimeter of each figure.

1.

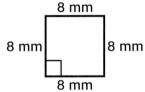

8 mm
8 mm 8 mm
8 mm

2.

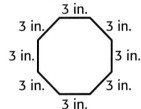

3 in.
3 in. 3 in.
3 in. 3 in.
3 in. 3 in.
3 in.

3.

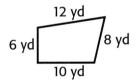

12 yd
6 yd 8 yd
10 yd

4.

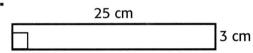

25 cm
3 cm

Lesson 14-2

Pages 612–615

Estimate the area of each figure. Each square represents 1 square centimeter.

1.

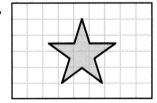

2.

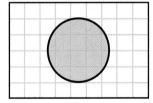

3.

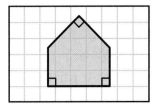

4.

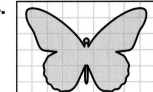

Lesson 14-3

Pages 616–619

Find the area of each rectangle.

1.

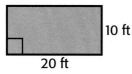

10 ft

20 ft

2.

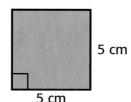

5 cm

5 cm

3. $\ell = 6$ cm
$w = 12$ cm

4. $\ell = 15$ yd
$w = 10$ yd

5. $\ell = 7$ ft
$w = 21$ ft

6. Mrs. Ortega is painting three walls in a room. The walls are 8 feet high and 13 feet long. One gallon of paint will cover 350 ft². If she buys one gallon of paint, will she have enough? Explain.

Lesson 14-4

Pages 624–627

Describe parts of each figure that are parallel and congruent. Then identify the figure.

1.

2.

3.

Lesson 14-5

Pages 628–629

Solve. Use the *make a model* strategy

1. Ms. Jacobson is passing out notebooks to her class of 27 students. She has four different colors of notebooks; red, green, blue, and yellow. If she passes out a red notebook to every fourth student, how many red notebooks does she pass out?

2. The students in Mr. Lincoln's gym class were asked to run around three cones placed in a line. The students must run down and back to complete one run. How many times will the students go between the cones in their attempt to complete six runs?

3. Pentominoes are tiles made by placing five squares in different designs. One way to place the squares is in a straight line. Another is to form an L. How many different designs are there?

Lesson 14-6

Find the volume of each prism.

1.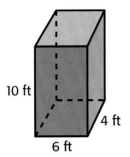

10 ft

6 ft   4 ft

2.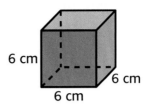

6 cm

6 cm

6 cm

3. Prism A has dimensions of 9 yards × 6 yards × 3 yards and Prism B has dimensions of 3 yards × 2 yards × 1 yard. How much larger is the volume of Prism A than Prism B in cubic feet?

Lesson 14-7

Find the surface area of each rectangular prism.

1.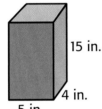

15 in.

5 in.   4 in.

2.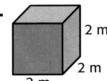

2 m

2 m

2 m

3.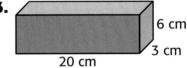

6 cm

20 cm   3 cm

4. Natalie finds the measurements of a rectangular prism. The length is 13 feet, the width is 7 feet, and the height is 9 feet. Find the surface area.

Lesson 14-8

Determine whether you need to find the perimeter, area, or volume. Then solve.

1. The basketball team warms up by running around the gym, which is 120 feet by 86 feet. If Chet runs 6 laps, how far has he run?

2. Freda is laying mulch in her garden. The garden is 8 feet by 12 feet and the mulch should be 3 inches deep. How much mulch does she need?

3. Maya wants new carpet for her bedroom. The room is 5 yards wide and 4 yards long. The carpet she wants costs $23.00 per square yard. How much will it cost to carpet her room?

Use any strategy to solve each problem.

1. Tamika has 33 stuffed animals. She gave $\frac{1}{3}$ to her sister and $\frac{1}{2}$ of the rest to charity. She says she has more than 10 stuffed animals left. Is she correct? How many stuffed animals are left?

2. Mr. Ruiz is making cookies. If each batch of cookies requires 14 ounces of milk, how many quarts of milk will he need to make 8 batches?

3. The middle school soccer team had the following record for the past five years. What fraction of the games did they win?

Year	2002	2003	2004	2005	2006
Won	12	10	4	7	13
Lost	3	5	11	8	2

List the possible outcomes in each probability experiment.

1. spinning the spinner

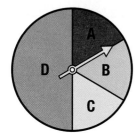

2. choosing one number out of a bowl

3. Sarah randomly chose one letter from the word BEEKEEPER. Which letter did she most likely pick? How likely is it that she chose a vowel?

The spinner is spun once. Find the probability of each event. Write as a fraction in simplest form.

1. $P(1)$

2. $P(2)$

3. $P(\text{prime number})$

4. $P(\text{odd number})$

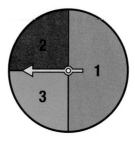

Lesson 15-3

Pages 674–675

Solve by making an organized list.

1. Two years ago, Mr. Braxton counted seven hickory trees in his yard. Last year he counted 14 trees in his yard. This spring he counted 28 hickory trees. In how many years will there be 224 hickory trees?

2. Thomas has four books colored blue, red, green, and yellow. How many different ways can he combine them on a shelf?

Lesson 15-4

Pages 677–680

Two bags each contain three different colored marbles: green, blue, and yellow. Make a tree diagram to show all possible outcomes if you choose a marble from each bag.

1. What is the probability of pulling a green marble from the first bag, then a blue marble from the second bag?

2. What is the probability of pulling a yellow marble from each bag?

3. What is the probability that you will pull the same colored marble from each bag?

Lesson 15-5

Pages 682–683

Use any strategy to solve each problem.

1. Sydney has been randomly tossing a coin. She has landed on heads 16 times and tails 8 times. Based on these results, if she tosses a coin what is the probability that she will land on tails?

2. A train engineer said that he traveled 1,458 miles in his train during a single 8 hour work day. Is his claim reasonable? Explain.

3. Mona is cutting different size pieces of fabric for a quilt. The first piece is 1 inch long, the second piece is 2 inches long, the third piece is 4 inches long, and so on. If she has 55 inches of fabric, how many pieces can she cut, and how long is each piece?

Preparing for Standardized Tests

Throughout the school year, you may be required to take several tests, and you may have many questions about them. Here are some answers to help you get ready.

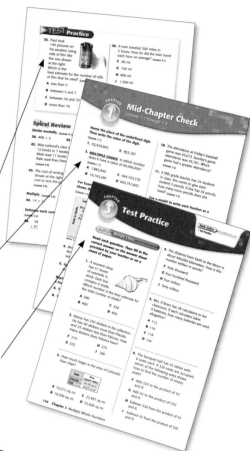

How Should I Study?

The good news is that you've been studying all along— a little bit every day. Here are some of the ways your textbook has been preparing you.

- **Every Day** The lessons had multiple-choice practice questions.

- **Every Week** The Mid-Chapter Check and Chapter Test also had several multiple-choice practice questions.

- **Every Month** The Test Practice pages at the end of each chapter had even more questions, including short-response and extended-response questions.

Are There Other Ways to Review?

Absolutely! The following pages contain even more practice for standardized tests.

Tips for SUCCESS

Before the Test

- Go to bed early the night before the test. You will think more clearly after a good night's rest.
- Become familiar with common measurement units and when they should be used.
- Think positively.

During the Test

- Read each problem carefully. Underline key words and think about different ways to solve the problem.
- Watch for key words like *not.* Also look for order words like *least, greatest, first,* and *last.*
- Answer questions you are sure about first. If you do not know the answer to a question, skip it and go back to that question later.
- Check your answer to make sure that it is reasonable.
- Make sure that the number of the question on the answer sheet matches the number of the question on which you are working in your test booklet.

Whatever you do...

- Don't try to do it all in your head. If no figure is provided, draw one.
- Don't rush. Try to work at a steady pace.
- Don't give up. Some problems may seem hard to you, but you may be able to figure out what to do if you read each question carefully or try another strategy.

RELAX!
Just do your best.

Multiple-Choice Questions

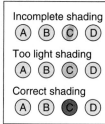

Incomplete shading
Ⓐ Ⓑ Ⓒ Ⓓ

Too light shading
Ⓐ Ⓑ Ⓒ Ⓓ

Correct shading
Ⓐ Ⓑ ● Ⓓ

Multiple-choice questions are the most common type of questions on standardized tests. You are asked to choose the best answer from four possible answers.

To record a multiple-choice answer, you may be asked to shade in a bubble that is a circle or an oval. Always make sure that your shading is dark enough and completely covers the bubble.

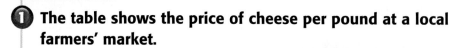

Example

1. **The table shows the price of cheese per pound at a local farmers' market.**

Amount (lb)	Price
1	$5
2	$10
3	$15

If the price increases at the same rate, how much would you pay for 5 pounds of cheese?

A $35   **B** $25   **C** $20   **D** $15

> STRATEGY
>
> **Patterns** Can you find a pattern to solve the problem?

Read the Problem Carefully You know the price of cheese per pound in dollars. Find how much you will pay if you buy 5 pounds of cheese.

Solve the Problem Look for a pattern. One pound of cheese costs $5. Two pounds cost $10. Three pounds cost $15. So, for each pound of cheese, the price increases by $5.

Extend the pattern to find the price of five pounds of cheese.

4 pounds   ⟶ $15 + $5 or $20

5 pounds   ⟶ $20 + $5 or $25

So, 5 pounds of cheese will cost $25.

The correct choice is B.

Example

STRATEGY

Key Words When reading a question, look for words such as *not* or *both*.

2 The shaded part of the figure below represents the fraction $\frac{2}{3}$.

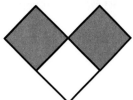

Which fraction is NOT equivalent to $\frac{2}{3}$?

F $\frac{6}{9}$ G $\frac{4}{6}$ H $\frac{2}{6}$ J $\frac{10}{15}$

Read the Problem Carefully You are asked to use the diagram to find which fraction is NOT equivalent to $\frac{2}{3}$.

Solve the Problem Find the fraction that is not equivalent to $\frac{3}{9}$.

$\frac{2}{3} \times \frac{3}{3} = \frac{6}{9}$ ◄── equivalent $\frac{2}{3} \times \frac{1}{2} = \frac{2}{6}$ ◄── NOT equivalent

$\frac{2}{3} \times \frac{2}{2} = \frac{4}{6}$ ◄── equivalent $\frac{2}{3} \times \frac{5}{5} = \frac{10}{15}$ ◄── equivalent

The correct choice is H.

Example

3 A book has five chapters. Each chapter has 5 more pages than the previous chapter. Chapter 5 has 38 pages. How many pages were in Chapter 2?

A 18   B 23   C 25   D 33

Read the Problem Carefully You are asked to find the number of pages in Chapter 2. You know how many pages were in Chapter 5.

Solve the Problem You need to find the number of pages in Chapter 2. To find the number of pages, count backward by five.

STRATEGY

Work Backward Can you work backward from the total to find the unit cost?

Chapter 5   38 pages
Chapter 4   33 pages   ─5
Chapter 3   28 pages   ─5
Chapter 2   23 pages   ─5

The correct choice is B.

Multiple-Choice Practice

DIRECTIONS
Read each question. Choose the best answer.

1. A car wash company charges $8 per car. If 94 cars were washed in one day, how much money would the company collect?

   A $752

   B $740

   C $702

   D $688

2. Which fractional part of the model is shaded?

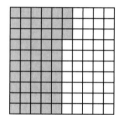

   F $\frac{53}{1,000}$

   H $\frac{53}{10}$

   G $\frac{53}{100}$

   J 53

3. Which group shows all the numbers that are common factors of 24 and 32?

   A 1, 2, 4, 8

   B 1, 2, 3, 4, 8

   C 1, 2, 4, 6, 8

   D 1, 2, 4, 8, 12

4. Brittany is having a party on a date in May that is NOT a prime number. Which of the following could be the date of her party?

   F May 11   **H** May 21

   G May 17   **J** May 31

5. The table shows how much money Mrs. Stoehr spends on bus fare.

Bus Fare	
Number of Weeks	Total Amount Spent ($)
4	48
5	60
6	72
7	84

What is the relationship between the number of weeks and the total amount spent?

   A The total amount spent is 12 times the number of weeks.

   B The number of weeks is 44 less than the total amount spent.

   C The total amount spent is 55 more than the number of weeks.

   D The number of weeks is 12 times the total amount spent.

6. Which figure does NOT contain any right angles?

   F

   G

   H

   J

7. Suppose the temperature outside at 5:15 P.M. was 54°F. By midnight, the temperature was 37 °F. How many degrees did the temperature drop by midnight?

A 13°F

B 17°F

C 23°F

D 27°F

8. Which pair of moons shows only a translation?

F

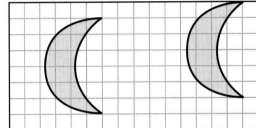

G

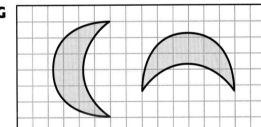

H

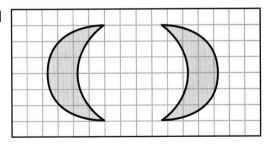

J

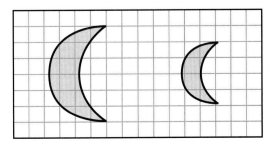

9. What fractional part of a kilogram is a gram?

A $\frac{1}{4}$

B $\frac{1}{10}$

C $\frac{1}{100}$

D $\frac{1}{1,000}$

10. Nico has 10 letter cards that spell the word *ELEMENTARY* when put together. If he picks one card without looking, what is the probability that it will have the letter *E* on it?

F $\frac{3}{10}$ **H** $\frac{3}{5}$

G $\frac{2}{5}$ **J** $\frac{7}{10}$

11. Paulo spun each spinner once.

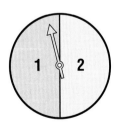 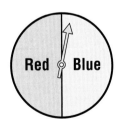

Which shows all the unique combinations of letters and numbers that are possible?

A Red, Blue, 1, 2

B Red 1, Blue 2, Red 1

C Red 1, Blue 1, Red 2, Blue 2

D Blue Red, Red Blue, 21, 12

Multiple-Choice Questions   **R47**

Short-Response Questions

Short-response questions ask you to find the answer to the problem as well as any method, explanation, and/or justification you used to arrive at the solution. You are asked to solve the problem, showing your work.

The following is a sample rubric, or scoring guide, for scoring short-response questions.

Credit	Scores	Criteria
Full	2	Full Credit: The answer is correct and a full explanation is provided that shows each step in arriving at the final answer.
Partial	1	Partial Credit: There are two different ways to receive partial credit. • The answer is correct, but the explanation provided is incomplete or incorrect. • The answer is incorrect, but the explanation and method of solving the problem is correct.
None	0	No credit: Either an answer is not provided or the answer does not make sense.

Example

1. **A restaurant received a shipment of 36 cartons of eggs. Each carton had 12 eggs. How many eggs did the restaurant receive in all?**

Full Credit Solution

First, I will decide which operation to use. Since each carton has the same number of eggs, I can use repeated addition or multiplication. I will use multiplication to find 36 × 12.

$$
\begin{array}{r}
1 \\
36 \text{ cartons} \\
\times\ 12 \text{ eggs} \\
\hline
72 \\
+360 \\
\hline
432 \text{ total eggs}
\end{array}
$$

The steps, calculations, and reasoning are clearly stated.

The correct answer is given.

The restaurant received 432 eggs in all.

Partial Credit Solution

In this sample solution, the answer is correct. However, there is no explanation for any of the calculations.

36 cartons, 12 eggs

There are 432 eggs in all.

There is no explanation of how the problem was solved.

Partial Credit Solution

In this sample solution, the answer is incorrect. However, the calculations and reasoning are correct.

Each carton has the same number of eggs, so I can use repeated addition or multiplication. I will use multiplication to find 36 × 12.

```
    36   cartons
  ×  12  eggs
    62
+  360
   422   total eggs
```

The student forgot to carry the ten.

There are 422 eggs in all.

The answer is incorrect.

No Credit Solution

In this sample solution, the answer is incorrect, and there is no explanation for any calculations.

36 + 12 = 48

There are 48 eggs.

The student does not understand the problem and adds 36 and 12.

Short-Response Practice

DIRECTIONS
Solve each problem.

1. The table shows the cost of Miss Rodriguez's lunch items.

Lunch	
Item	**Cost**
Sandwich	$3.85
Salad	$0.90
Pudding	$0.63
Iced Tea	$1.10

She has a $5 bill in her pocket. How much more money does Miss Rodriguez need?

2. Buses are being used to transport students on a field trip. Each bus can hold 62 students. How many buses are needed to transport 180 students?

3. Mr. Solis is buying supplies to install a ceiling fan. The fan costs $64, the support brace costs $8, and a roll of electrical tape costs $2. All prices include sales tax. If Mr. Solis pays with a $100 bill, how much change in dollars should he receive?

4. Look for a pattern in the sequences of numbers shown below.

   3, 6, 9, 12, 15, 18, …

   5, 10, 15, 20, 25, …

   8, 16, 24, 32, 40, 48, …

   Another sequence begins with the number 4 and follows the same pattern. Which is the third number in this sequence?

5. The table shows the numerators and denominators of fractions that are equivalent to $\frac{2}{3}$. What is the denominator if the numerator is 54?

Numerator	Denominator
2	3
6	9
18	27
54	?

6. Mrs. Smith told her class she was thinking of a number. She told them that when 12 is subtracted from the number and the result is doubled, the final number is 26. What was the original number that Mrs. Smith was thinking of?

7. Sarika wants to go to a movie that starts at 9:10 P.M. The movie is 1 hour 45 minutes long. At what time will the movie end?

8. A rectangular prism made of 1-inch cubes is shown below.

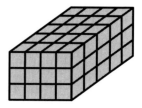

   What is the volume of the prism?

9. Natalie needs 24 ounces of milk for a recipe. How many cups of milk does she need?

10. What single transformation is shown below?

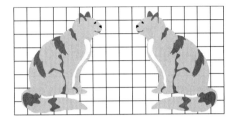

11. What is the perimeter of the rectangular field shown below?

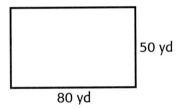

50 yd

80 yd

12. Shada's quiz scores are shown in the table.

Quiz	Score
1	84
2	90
3	88
4	92
5	89

On which quiz did Shada receive the median score?

13. The ages of the students in Mr. Jeffrey's reading group are 11, 12, 10, 9, 11, 13, 12, and 11. What is the mode of the ages?

14. Jenny counted the number of coins in her wallet. She had 4 pennies, 3 nickels, 6 dimes, and 2 quarters. What fraction represents the probability of picking a nickel?

15. The table shows the results of 20 spins that Kendra made with a spinner.

Spinner Results	
Color	Number of Spins
Blue	3
Red	8
Green	5
White	4

Based on these results, what is the probability that Kendra's spinner will land on red on her next spin?

16. Jermaine spent 32, 38, 36, 28, 40, 33, and 36 minutes working on homework. What is the range of the data?

17. The graph below represents the number of birds at a bird feeder one afternoon.

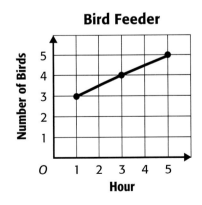

If the pattern continues, how many birds will be at the feeder at the seventh hour?

Short-Response Practice   **R51**

Extended-Response Questions

Most extended-response questions have multiple parts. You must answer all parts to receive full credit.

In extended-response questions, you must show all of your work in solving the problem. A rubric is used to determine if you receive full, partial, or no credit. The following is a sample rubric for scoring extended-response questions.

Credit	Scores	Criteria
Full	4	Full Credit: The answer is correct and a full explanation is given that shows each step in finding the answer.
Partial	3, 2, 1	Partial Credit: Most of the solution is correct but it may have some mistakes in the explanation or solution. The more correct the solution, the greater the score.
None	0	No credit: Either an answer is not provided or the answer does not make sense.

Make sure that when the problem says to *show your work*, you show every part of your solution. This includes figures, graphs, and any explanations for your calcutlations.

Example

1. **The bar graph shows the top speeds of four roller coasters. Explain how to use the bar graph to find the range of the roller coaster speeds shown.**

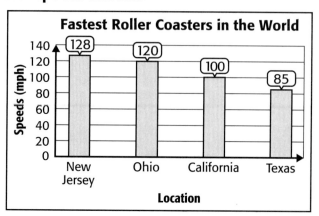

Fastest Roller Coasters in the World

Full Credit Solution

In this sample answer, the student explains how to read the bar graph, what calculations need to be done and finds the correct solution.

The steps, calculations, and reasoning are clearly stated.

First, I will use the bar graph to find the fastest speed and slowest speed. Then I will find the difference of the two speeds.

The bar graph shows the speeds (mph) in each of the four states: New Jersey: 128, Ohio: 120, California: 100, and Texas: 85.

$$
\begin{array}{ll}
128 \text{ mph} & \text{fastest roller coaster} \\
-\ 85 \text{ mph} & \text{slowest roller coaster} \\
\hline
43 \text{ mph} &
\end{array}
$$

The range of the given speeds is 43 mph.

The correct answer is given.

Partial Credit Solution

In this sample answer, the student explains what calculations need to be done. However, there is an error in the calculations.

The steps, calculations, and reasoning are clearly stated.

First, I will use the bar graphs to find the fastest speed and slowest speed. Then I will find the difference of the two speeds.

The bar graph shows the speeds (mph) in each of the four states: New Jersey: 128, Ohio: 120, California: 100, Texas: 85

128 mph - 85 mph = 143 mph

There is an error.
$128 - 85 \neq 143$

The range of the given speeds is 143 mph.

No Credit Solution

A solution for this problem that will receive no credit may include incorrect answers and an inaccurate explanation.

I will find the range by listing all of the speeds.
New Jersey: 128, Ohio: 120, California: 110, Texas: 85
$228 + 120 + 110 + 85 = 433$ mph

The range is 143 mph.

Extended-Response Practice

DIRECTIONS:
Solve each problem. Show all your work.

1. Each month Carmina saves $24.80 from her paychecks. How can she estimate the amount of money she will save in 4 months?

2. The table below shows the amount of rain in a city during a 3-month period.

Amount of Rainfall	
Month	Amount of Rain (centimeters)
1	15.1
2	18.5
3	20.2

Estimate the total rainfall in these three months. Explain how to find the difference between your estimate and the actual total rainfall.

3. Write the instructions of how to make $4\frac{1}{5}$ into an improper fraction.

4. Shawnda needed 12 yards of fabric. How many feet of fabric did she need? What operation did you use to solve the problem?

5. Jane is sorting the numbers 2 through 20 into two groups.

Group 1: 2, 3, 5, 7, 11, 13, 17

Group 2: 4, 6, 8, 9, 12, 14, 15, 16, 18

How is she sorting them? In which groups should she place 19 and 20?

6. The dimensions of a rectangle are shown. Find the area. Show your work.

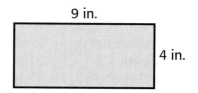

9 in.

4 in.

7. The figure below is made of 1-unit cubes. Describe how to find the volume of the figure.

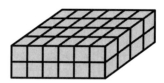

8. Mykia's dance class started at 10:45 A.M. and ended at 12:00 P.M. How many hours and minutes was her dance class? Explain your reasoning.

9. The coordinate grid below represents a playground.

Playground

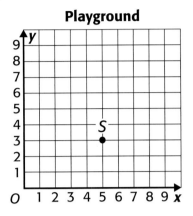

A slide is at point S on the playground. A set of swings that is not shown on the grid is 4 units up from the slide. Explain how to find the coordinates of the swings.

10. The figure below is a rectangular prism.

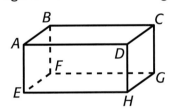

Face *ABFE* is congruent to face CDHG. Name another two faces that are congruent. Explain why they are congruent.

11. The table shows the prices at a used media store including tax. Ty has $24 to spend at the store. List two combinations of items that he can buy. Show your work.

Item	Price
CD	$4
DVD	$5
Video Game	$6

12. The table shows the results of a survey.

Class Pets	
Pet	**Number of Students**
Cat	7
Dog	8
Fish	6
Bird	2

A student made the following graph to display the data.

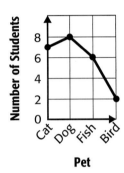

Explain why this type of a graph is not appropriate for the data shown in the table.

13. The graph shows how much time Jasmine spent on her project. How many total minutes were spent on this project? How many hours and minutes is this? Explain your reasoning.

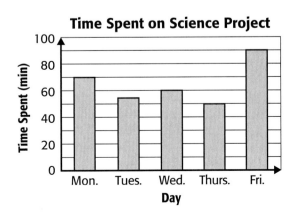

Concepts and Skills Bank

 Number Sense 5.N.11 Understand that percent means part of 100, and write percents as fractions and decimals

1 Percents as Fractions

The model to the right shows 25 squares shaded out of 100. This can be written as the fraction $\frac{25}{100}$ or $\frac{1}{4}$. It can also be written as the decimal 0.25.

A **percent** is a ratio that compares a number to 100. $25\% = 25$ out of 100 or $\frac{25}{100}$.

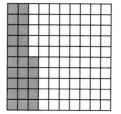

EXAMPLE Write a percent as a fraction

1 Write 75% as a fraction in simplest form.

75% means "75 out of 100."

$75\% = \dfrac{75}{100}$ Write as a fraction with a denominator of 100. Simplify.

$= \dfrac{\overset{3}{\cancel{75}}}{\underset{4}{\cancel{100}}} = \dfrac{3}{4}$

EXAMPLE Write a percent as a decimal

2 Write 32% as a decimal in simplest form.

32% means "32 out of 100."

$32\% = 0.32$ Write as a decimal.

Exercises

Write each percent as a fraction in simplest form.

1. 29%   **2.** 30%   **3.** 60%   **4.** 84%

5. 92%   **6.** 8%   **7.** 15%   **8.** 22%

Write each percent as a decimal.

9. 4%   **10.** 17%   **11.** 12%   **12.** 50%

13. Malak bought a box of colored paper clips. If 15% are green, what fraction of the paper clips are green?

14. Of the students in a class, 65% have more than 1 pet. Write this amount as a decimal.

 ## Squared Numbers

The product of a number and itself is the **square** of that number.

A square with an area of 16 square units is shown. The number 16 is a square number because the product of 4 and itself is 16.

4 units

4 units

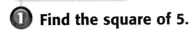 **EXAMPLES**

① Find the square of 5.

$5 \times 5 = 25$ Multiply 5 by itself.

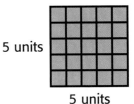

5 units

5 units

② Use models to determine if 9 is a square number.

3 units

9 units can be arranged to make a square because $3 \times 3 = 9$.

3 units

Yes, 9 is a square number.

Exercises

Find the square of each number.

1. 6   **2.** 10   **3.** 15   **4.** 12

5. 17   **6.** 22   **7.** 37   **8.** 50

Use models to determine if each number is a square number. Write yes or no.

9. 4   **10.** 12   **11.** 17   **12.** 36

13. 49   **14.** 50   **15.** 64   **16.** 81

17. How much greater is the area of a square that is 10 meters by 10 meters than the area of a square that is 9 meters by 9 meters?

18. A square garden has an area of 121 square feet. How much fencing is needed to place a fence around the entire garden?

Geometry

5.G.2 Identify pairs of similar triangles 5.G.3 Identify the ratio of corresponding sides of similar triangles 5.G.9 Identify pairs of congruent triangles 5.G.10 Identify corresponding parts of congruent triangles

Concepts and Skills

  Congruent and Similar Triangles

Congruent and Similar Triangles	Key Concepts

Words If two triangles are congruent, they have the same angle measures and side lengths.

Model

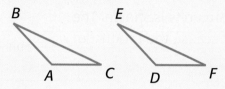

Symbols The symbol $\cong$ means congruent. $\triangle ABC \cong \triangle DEF$

Congruent sides: $\overline{AB} \cong \overline{DE}$; $\overline{AC} \cong \overline{DF}$; $\overline{BC} \cong \overline{EF}$

Congruent angles: $\angle A \cong \angle D$; $\angle B \cong \angle E$; $\angle C \cong \angle F$

Words If two triangles are similar, they have the same angle measures, but different side lengths.

Model

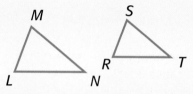

Symbols The symbol ~ means similar. $\triangle LMN \sim \triangle RST$

Congruent angles: $\angle L \cong \angle R$; $\angle M \cong \angle S$; $\angle N \cong \angle T$

note: Congruent figures are also similar.

EXAMPLE   **Congruent Triangles**

① IF $\triangle JKM \cong \triangle STU$ name the congruent sides and angles.

$\cong$ **sides:** $\overline{JM} \cong \overline{SU}$; $\overline{KM} \cong \overline{TU}$; $\overline{JK} \cong \overline{ST}$

$\cong$ **angles:** $\angle J \cong \angle S$; $\angle K \cong \angle T$; $\angle M \cong \angle U$

EXAMPLE   **Similar Triangles**

② IF $\triangle MNP \sim \triangle ABC$ name the congruent angles.

$\cong$ **sides:** $\dfrac{MP}{AC} \approx \dfrac{MN}{AB} ; \dfrac{NP}{BC}$

$\cong$ **angles:** $\angle P \cong \angle C$; $\angle M \cong \angle A$; $\angle N \cong \angle B$

 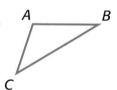

Exercises

Tell whether the triangles appear to be *congruent*, *similar*, or *neither*.

1.

2.

3.

4.

Identify the corresponding angle in the similar triangles shown.

5. ∠A

6. ∠F

7. ∠B

8. ∠D

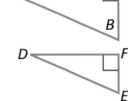

Identify the corresponding side in the congruent triangles shown.

9. $\overline{GH}$

10. $\overline{IH}$

11. $\overline{LJ}$

12. $\overline{GH}$

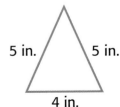

Solve.

13. Two triangles are similar. The height of one triangle is 4 times greater than the other triangle. If the smaller triangle is 33 centimeters tall, how tall is the larger triangle?

14. Mia is cutting out 12 triangles for a project. She decides to speed up the process by cutting multiple sheets of paper at once. Is Mia cutting congruent triangles or similar triangles? Explain.

15. Marcus is building a triangular frame for his garden. Before he cuts the wood for the frame, he draws the triangle shown. If one inch represents 2 feet, find the dimensions of the sides of the frame.

5 in.   5 in.

4 in.

16. In Exercise 15, is Marcus' drawing similar or congruent to the frame he built? Explain.

Concepts and Skills

Geometry 5.G.7 Know that the sum of the interior angles of a triangle is 180 degrees 5.G.8 Find a missing angle when given two angles of a triangle

④ Interior Angle Measures of Triangles

Sum of Angle Measures in a Triangle **Key Concept**

Words
The sum of the measures of the angles in a triangle is 180°.

Model 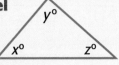   **Symbols** $x° + y° + z° = 180°$

EXAMPLE   **Find Angle Measures**

① **Find the value of x in the triangle.**

Since the sum of the angle measures
in a triangle is 180°, $x + 37 + 84 = 180$.

$$x + 37 + 84 = 180$$ Write the equation.
$$x + 121 = 180$$ Add 37 and 84.
$$-121 = -121$$ Subtract 121 from each side.
$$x = 59$$

So, the value of x is 59.

Exercises

Find the value of the missing angle x.

1. 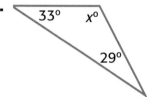   **2.** 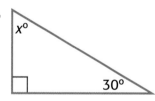   **3.**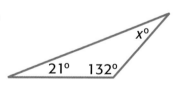

4. 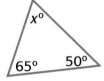   **5.** 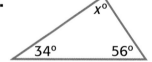   **6.**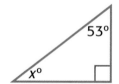

7. Lamar drew a triangle with three equal sides. What is the measure of each angle? How did you find the answer?

8. Adrian was asked to draw a triangle in which each angle is 10° greater than the next angle. If the largest angle is 70°, what is the measure of the other two angles? How can you check your solution?

5 Interior Angle Measures of Quadrilaterals

Sum of Angle Measures in a Quadrilateral Key Concept

Words
The sum of the measures of the angles in a quadrilateral is 360°

Model
360°

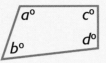

Symbols $a° + b° + c° + d° =$

EXAMPLE Find Angle Measures

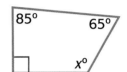

1 **Find the value of x in the quadrilateral.**

The sum of the angle measures in a
quadrilateral is 360°.

$$x + 65 + 85 + 90 \ = \ 360$$
$$x + 240 \ = \ 360 \qquad \text{Add 65, 85, and 90.}$$
$$\underline{ - 240 \ = \ - 240} \qquad \text{Subtract 240 from each side.}$$
$$x \ = \ 120$$

So, the value of x is 120.

Exercises

Algebra Find the value of x in each quadrilateral.

1.

2.
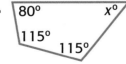

3.
79°
103°
$x°$

4.
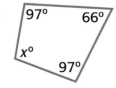

5.

6.
105° $x°$
85°
75°

7. Jacob was asked to draw a quadrilateral in which each angle is 10° greater
than the next angle. If the smallest angle is 75°, what is the measure of the
other three angles? How can you check your solution?

Concepts and Skills

Geometry **Reinforcement of 4.G.1 Identify and name polygons, recognizing that their names are related to the number of sides and angles (triangle, quadrilateral, pentagon, hexagon, and octagon)**

⑥ Two–Dimensional Figures

A two-dimensional figure is a closed figure with length and width. Two-dimensional figures are also known as plane figures.

A **polygon** is a simple closed figure formed by three or more sides. The number of sides determines the name of the polygon.

A circle is not a polygon because it is a curve.

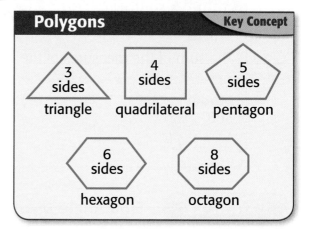

| Polygons | | Key Concept |

triangle — 3 sides, quadrilateral — 4 sides, pentagon — 5 sides, hexagon — 6 sides, octagon — 8 sides

Polygons	Not Polygons

EXAMPLES

Tell whether each shape is a polygon. If it is a polygon, identify the polygon.

1.

No. It has curves.

2.

Yes. It is a closed figure with 6 sides. It is a hexagon.

Exercises

Tell whether each shape is a polygon. If it is a polygon, identify the polygon.

1.

2.

3.

Identify the type polygon for each sign.

4.

5.

6.

Data Analysis > **5.S.3 Calculate the mean for a given set of data and use to describe a set of data**

 Mean

The **mean** is a type of average. To find the mean of a set of data, you can add the data, then divide by the total number of data.

EXAMPLE **Find the Mean**

1 **Find the mean of the following test scores:**
75, 77, 89, 95, 66, 81, 54, 99

$$75 + 77 + 89 + 95 + 66 + 81 + 54 + 99 = 636 \quad \text{Add the data.}$$

$$= \frac{636}{8} \quad \begin{array}{l} \text{Divide by the number} \\ \text{of test scores.} \end{array}$$

$$= 79.5$$

So, the mean is 79.5.

Exercises

Find the mean.

1. Number of DVDs: 21, 23, 25, 27, 19

2. Test scores: 99, 87, 81, 95, 94, 84, 67

3. Number of pets: 2, 3, 7, 4, 5, 8, 6

4. Points scored: 11, 17, 34, 57, 14, 49, 35

5. Coins collected: 105, 112, 155, 142, 164, 187, 123

6. Yards gained: 751.1, 857.1, 801.4, 610.1

7. Miles traveled: 21.5, 25.9, 34.1, 24.7, 22.6

8. Students from Mrs. Whittier's class went on a field trip to collect different kinds of leaves for their science project. Use the chart to determine the mean number of leaves collected.

Student	Number of leaves
Manny	17
Tanya	4
Jai	7
Randy	11
Kelly	21

9. Trisha went to the mall and walked by several jewelry displays. There were 30 pairs of earrings in the first display. There were 40 necklaces in the next display. The third display had 25 rings. The final display had 50 bracelets. Find the mean number of jewelry in the displays.

Data Analysis ▷ **5.S.1 Collect and record data from a variety of sources** (e.g., newspapers, magazines, polls, charts, and surveys)

8 Stem-and-Leaf Plots

A **stem-and-leaf plot** is a way to organize and distribute data.

- The leaf is the last digit of the number.
- The other digits to the left of the leaf form the stem.

Stem	Leaf
2	1 4
3	5 8

For the numbers 21, 24, 35, and 38, 2 and 3 are the stems. The numbers 1, 4, 5 and 8 are the leaves.

EXAMPLE

1 SPORTS Make a stem-and-leaf plot of the basketball scores below.

68, 52, 85, 64, 59, 51, 62, 66

51, 52, 59, 62, 64, 66, 68, 85   Write the data from least to greatest.

51, 52, 59
62, 64, 66, 68   Group the numbers with the same first digit.
85

Stem	Leaf
5	1 2 9
6	2 4 6 8
8	5

Seperate each stem from each leaf.

Exercises

Make a stem-and-leaf plot for each set of numbers.

1. 83, 86, 99, 43, 75, 91   **2.** 33, 31, 62, 20, 32, 25

Write the set of numbers from least to greatest used to form each stem-and-leaf plot.

3.

Stem	Leaf
0	4 5 8
1	3 4 7
2	6

4.

Stem	Leaf
4	1
5	1 2 6 8

5. Sarah wants to use a stem-and-leaf plot to organize her test scores. List the digits that will make up the stem portions of the plot for the scores 80, 92, 88, 85, 76, 94, 98.

Photo Credits

Unless otherwise credited, all currency courtesy of the US Mint.
v Thomas Barwick/Getty Images; **vi** Doug Martin;
vii (br)courtesy Dinah Zike, (others)Doug Martin; **viii-ix** Alan
Schein Photography/CORBIS; **xx-xxi** Kerrick James Photog/
Getty Images; **xxii-xxiii** Miles Ertman/Masterfile;
xxiv-xxv George H. H. Huey/CORBIS; **xxvi-xxvii** Taxi/Getty
Images; **xxviii-xxix** Robert Landau/CORBIS; **xxx-xxxi** Richard
Cummins/CORBIS; **xxxii-xxxiii** Eduardo Garcia/Photographer's
Choice/Getty Images; **xxxiv-xxxv** Darrell Gulin/The Image
Bank/Getty Images; **xxxvii** Purestock/PunchStock;
NY0 Jupiterimages/Comstock Images/Alamy Images; **xxxviii** Tim
Fuller; **xxxix** Eclipse Studios; **1** D. Hurst/Alamy Images;
2 Visions of America, LLC/Alamy Images; **3** imagebroker/Alamy
Images; **4** Alan Schein/Alamy Images; **5** Neal and Molly Jansen/
Alamy Images; **6** MEYERS, STEFAN/Animals Animals; **7** Ron
Niebrugge/Alamy Images; **8** Sandra Baker/Alamy Images;
9 Radlund & Associates/Getty Images; **10** Andre Jenny/Alamy
Images; **11** Eric Kamp/Index Stock Imagery NY; **12** Matteo Del
Grosso/Alamy Images; **13** Pegaz/Alamy Images; **14–15** Richard
Broadwell/Alamy Images; **17–19** CORBIS; **22** Darrell Gulin/
Getty Images; **24** Ed-imaging; **28** A & L Sinibaldi/Stone/Getty
Images; **30** Ed-Imaging; **32** Al Bello/Getty Images; **34** Dennis
Flaherty/Getty Images; **36** Ed-Imaging; **38** Archivo Iconografico,
S.A./CORBIS; **40–41** Melba Photo Agency/PunchStock;
44 Stephen Simpson/Getty Images; **45** (t)Joseph T. Collins/
Photo Researchers, (b)Ed-Imaging; **46** David Andrews/
Tennessee Aquarium; **47** Ed-Imaging; **48** George Holton/Photo
Researchers; **58–59** Getty Images; **61** A. Fifis/AP Images; **66** Ed-
Imaging; **68** Flip De Nooyer/Foto Natura/Minden Pictures; **70**
Deborah Feingold/CORBIS; **74** Ed-Imaging; **76–77** (bkgd)Janusz
Wrobel/Alamy Images; (inset)Alan Jakubek/CORBIS; **78** Ed-
Imaging; **80** Barry Gregg/CORBIS; **81** Bernard Annebicque/
CORBIS; **82** John Lamb/Stone/Getty Images; **83** Ed-Imaging;
84 Richard Hutchings/Digital Light Source; **90** (tr)Christian
Darkin/Photo Researchers, (others)Ed-Imaging; **91** Jeff Vanuga/
CORBIS; **100–101** Antony Nagelmann/Getty Images; **103**
Courtesy Schlitterbahn Waterpark Resort; **105** Arco Images/
Alamy Images; **108** Bob Krist/CORBIS; **109** Jim Zipp/Photo
Researchers; **110** Ed-Imaging; **112** Norbert Rosing/National
Geographic Image Collection; **115** Ed-imaging; **116** Elyse
Lewin/Getty Images; **117** Rich Reid/National Geographic/Getty
Images; **120** Doug Menuez/Getty Images; **122** Creatas/
PunchStock; **123** Bloomimage/CORBIS; **125–126** Ed-Imaging;
127 C Squared Studios/Getty Images; **130–131** (bkgd)Anthony
Johnson/Getty Images; (inset)D. Hurst/Alamy Images;
132 Catapult/Getty Images; **136** Ed-Imaging; **146–147** Tom
Brakefield/Digital Vision/Getty Images; **149** Altrendo Nature/
Altrendo/Getty Images; **150** Gary Neil Corbett/SuperStock;
151 Ed-Imaging; **152** Yellow Dog Productions/The Image Bank/
Getty Images; **158** Cedar Fair Entertainment Company; **164** (tr)
Image Source White/Alamy Images, (others)Ed-Imaging;

166 168 169 Ed-Imaging; **170** Greg Pease/Stone/Getty Images;
172 Douglas Johns Studio/StockFood; **174** Thinkstock/CORBIS;
175 CORBIS; **176** Nick Koudis/Getty Images;
178–179 (bkgd)Everett C. Johnson/eStock Photo;
(inset)CORBIS; **180** Ed-Imaging; **190–191** Richard Cummins/
CORBIS; **195** The McGraw-Hill Companies; **196** Petrified
Collection/The Image Bank/Getty Images; **202** Doug Pensinger/
Time Life Pictures/Getty Images; **206** Ed-Imaging; **210** Millard
H. Sharp/Photo Researchers; **212** Ed-Imaging; **216–217** Jeff
Rotman/Getty Images; **221** Don Farrall/Getty Images;
232–233 Theo Allofs/zefa/CORBIS; **239** (l)Image Source/
SuperStock, (r)George Doyle/Getty Images; **245** (l)CORBIS, (r)C
Squared Studios/Getty Images; **246** imagebroker/Alamy
Images; **247** Ryan McVay/Getty Images; **248** Ed-Imaging;
256 Patricio Robles Gil/Sierra Madre/Minden Pictures;
258–259 (bkgd)SIME s.a.s/eStock Photo; (inset)CORBIS;
260 Tom Stewart/CORBIS; **261** Brand X Pictures/PunchStock;
262 through 266 Ed-Imaging; **276–277** Taxi/Getty Images;
282 Ed-Imaging; **285** Purestock/Getty Images; **286** Eric Meola/
The Image Bank/Getty Images; **287** Ryan McVay/Getty Images;
288 Eric Meola/The Image Bank/Getty Images; **292** Jean-Paul
Ferrero/Minden Pictures; **296** Mark Raycroft/Minden Pictures;
297 Howard C. Smith/CORBIS; **298** Friso Gentsch/epa/CORBIS;
299 Margarette Mead/The Image Bank/Getty Images; **301** Tim
Davis/Riser/Getty Images; **303** Ed-Imaging; **304–305** Tim Cuff/
Alamy Images; **311** Ed-Imaging; **312** Jose Fuste Raga/CORBIS;
317 Ed-Imaging; **320** ThinkStock LLC/Index Stock Imagery;
330–331 Janis Christie/Photodisc Green/Getty Images;
341 (tr)Gerry Ellis/Science Faction/Getty Images, (others)Ed-
Imaging; **343** Ed-Imaging; **344** Ariel Skelley/CORBIS;
345 Photodisc/PunchStock; **346** Juniors Bildarchiv/Alamy
Images; **347** David Steele/Gallo Images/Getty Images; **348**
Kevin Schafer/CORBIS; **350** Eising/Getty Images; **353** Ed-
Imaging; **354–355** Getty Images; **356** age fotostock/SuperStock;
360 Ed-Imaging; **370–371** Arnaldo Pomodoro, Disk in the Form
of a Desert Rose, Frederik Meijer Gardens & Sculpture Park cast
1999–2000. Gift of Fred and Lena Meijer. Photo by William J.
Hebert; **373** Laura Doss/Brand X/CORBIS; **375** Dr. Nick
Kurzenko/Photo Researchers; **384** Ed-Imaging; **386** Gail
Shumway/Taxi/Getty Images; **388** Ambient Images Inc./Alamy
Images; **393** Dorling Kindersley/Getty Images; **394** David
Madison/Getty Images; **398** Wilfried Krecichwost/Getty Images;
399 (l)Paul Burns/Getty Images, (r)Ed-Imaging; **400** Ed-
Imaging; **407** Ryan McVay/Getty Images; **408–409** (bkgd)Franck
Jeannin/Alamy Images, (l)Getty Images, (r)Oleg Moiseyenk/
Alamy Images; **418–419** Martin Harvey Cart/Gallo Images/
CORBIS; **425** John A. Rizzo/Getty Images; **430** Geostock/Getty
Images; **434** Laurence Mouton/Photoalto/PictureQuest/
Jupiterimages; **436** (l)Stockdisc/Getty Images, (r)image100 Ltd;
439 Samuel R. Maglione/Photo Researchers, Inc.; **442** Bob
Daemmrich/PhotoEdit; **444** Cosmo Condina/Stone/Getty

Photo Credits

Images; **448** Lew Robertson/FoodPix/Jupiterimages; **449** Norgert Wu/Minden Pictures; **450** Ed-Imaging; **451** Purestock/Getty Images; **452** ImageShop/CORBIS; **453** (l)age fotostock/SuperStock, (r)Dan Johnson; **455–456** Ed-Imaging; **458** Darrell Gulin/CORBIS; **460** Pete Turner/The Image Bank/Getty Images; **461** (l)Ed-Imaging, (r)Ben Blackenburg/CORBIS; **462–463** (bkgd t)Getty Images; (b)Philip James Corwin/CORBIS; **472–473** Robert Glusic/Getty Images; **475** C Squared Studios/Getty Images; **476** (tl)C Squared Studios/Getty Images, (tr)G.K. Vikki Hart/Getty Images, (bl)Photodisc/Getty Images, (br)C Squared Studios/Getty Images; **477** Randy Faris/CORBIS; **481** Ed-Imaging; **482** (bl)Darlyne A Murawski/National Geographic/Getty Images; (others)Getty Images; **484** Anup Shah/Getty Images; **488** Jose Luis Pelaez/Iconica/Getty Images; **490** Ed-Imaging; **492** Marc Debnam/Digital Vision/Getty Images; **494** David Grossman/Alamy Images; **496** Ed-Imaging; **498–499** EuroStyle Graphics/Alamy Images; **502** Ed-Imaging; **512–513** Tim De Waele/Isosport/CORBIS; **515** Dorling Kindersley/Dorling Kindersley/Getty Images; **516** (l)Jupiterimages, (r)Jonathan Kitchen/Getty Images; **517** Laurence Parent Photography/Laurence Parent Photography, Inc.; **520** Chris Cheadle/Photographer's Choice/Getty Images; **521** NASA/Photo Researchers; **522** C Borland/PhotoLink/Getty Images; **524** Piotr Naskrecki/Minden Pictures; **525** CORBIS; **526** (l)Stockbyte/Getty Images, (tr)IT Stock/PunchStock, (br)Ed-Imaging; **527** Foodcollection/Foodcollection/Getty Images; **528** Veronique Rolland/Stone/Getty Images; **529** Ed-Imaging; **535** Daniel J Cox/The Image Bank/Getty Images; **537** Joe McDonald/Visuals Unlimited/Getty Images; **540** Philip Scalia/Alamy Images; **542–543** (bkgd)PhotoLink/Getty Images; (l)Museum of Flight/CORBIS; (r)CORBIS; **544** Ed-Imaging; **548** The McGraw-Hill Companies; **554–555** Eduardo Garcia/Photographer's Choice/Getty Images; **557** Courtesy New Tech Kites; **559** Photodisc/Getty Images; **561** Ed-Imaging; **562** MTR Photography; **566** Andrew Ward/Life File/Getty Images; **567** Kazuyoshi Nomachi/CORBIS; **568** (l)Colin Mead Enterprises/Getty Images, (tr)Matthias Kulka/zefa/CORBIS, (br)Ryman Cabannes/photocuisine/CORBIS; **569** (t)Michael Houghton/StudiOhio, (b)Purestock/Getty Images; **570** Purestock/Getty Images; **573** (tr)Gail Mooney/CORBIS, (others)Ed-Imaging; **576** Blend Images/SuperStock; **585** Ed-Imaging; **586** image100 Ltd/CORBIS; **589** (r)Creatas/PunchStock; (others)Getty images; **592** MTR Photography; **593** (r)Lew Robertson/CORBIS; (l)Getty Images; **594–595** (bkgd)Robert Harding Picture Library/Alamy Images; (inset)Martin Moos/Lonely Planet Images; **598** David Frazier/CORBIS; **604–605** Darrell Gulin/The Image Bank/Getty Images; **608** Photoalto/Photolibrary; **609** Jules Frazier/Getty Images; **610** Andrea Rugg/Beateworks/CORBIS; **612** Siede Preis/Getty Images; **616** Courtesy of United Veterans of America; **619** Ron Chapple Stock/CORBIS; **622** Ed-Imaging;

624 pixie/Emporis; **625** (t)Image Source Pink/Getty Images, (b)Paul Bricknell/Dorling Kindersley/Getty Images; **626 through 631** The McGraw-Hill Companies; **636–637** Elisabeth Coelfen/Alamy Images; **641** Judith Collins/Alamy Images; **644** Getty Images; **647** (l)Ed-Imaging, (tr)Purestock/Getty Images, (br)Ed-Imaging; **648** Ned Frisk/CORBIS; **658–659** Digital Vision/Getty Images; **664–665** Ace Stock Limited/Alamy Images; **666** Ed-Imaging; **669** Getty Images; **674** (l)Ryan McVay/Getty Images, (c)Getty Images, (r)CORBIS; **677** Nona Darryl Whittington/Darmar Enterprises; **679** Little Blue Wolf Productions/CORBIS; **680–681** Ed-Imaging; **682** George Doyle/Stockdisc Classic/Getty Images; **683** Masterfile; **LA00** Mark Steinmetz; **LA02** Amos Morgan/Getty Images; **LA03** PunchStock; **LA04** Ingram Publishing/Alamy Images; **LA05** Purestock/PunchStock; **LA06** imagebroker/Alamy Images; **LA08** Stockdisc/PunchStock; **LA09** Creatas/PunchStock; **LA10** (t)Stockdisc/PunchStock, (b)D. Hurst/Alamy Images; **LA11** Getty Images; **LA14** Oleg Raisky/Alamy Images; **LA17** Richard Herrmann/Visuals Unlimited/Getty Images; **LA18** G.K. & Vikki Hart/Getty Images; **LA21** CORBIS; **LA25** CORBIS/PunchStock; **P00** (r)PunchStock, (bl)Bob Daemmrich/PhotoEdit, (tl)Getty Images; **P01** Tim Fuller; **P02** Reuters/CORBIS; **P03** Jason Reed/Reuters/CORBIS; **P04** Mika/zefa/CORBIS; **P05** Ed-Imaging; **P06** Nati Harnik/AP Images; **P07** Ed-Imaging; **P08** Jeff Pape/New Bremen Giant Pumpkin Growers; **P09** STOCK4B/STOCK4B-RF/Getty Images; **R43** Tim Fuller.

McGraw-Hill would like to acknowledge the artists and agencies who contributed to illustrating this program: **Cover** Mick McGinty represented by Mendola Artists; Argosy Publishing; Richard Carbajal, Mark Collins, Dick Gage represented by Deborah Wolfe Ltd.; Kristine Walsh represented by Bill Smith Studios; Terri Chico Represented by Cornell & McCarthy; Tim Pack represented by Quebecor World.

Glossary/Glosario

Math Online ⟩ A mathematics multilingual glossary is available at www.macmillanmh.com. The glossary includes the following languages.

Arabic	Cantonese	Korean	Tagalog
Bengali	English	Russian	Urdu
Brazilian	Haitian Creole	Spanish	Vietnamese
Portuguese	Hmong		

Cómo usar el glosario en español:
1. Busca el término en inglés que desees encontrar.
2. El término en español, junto con la definición, se encuentran en la columna de la derecha.

English

Español

acute angle (p. 564) An *angle* with a measure between 0° and 90°.

ángulo agudo *Ángulo* que mide entre 0° y 90°.

acute triangle (p. 567) A *triangle* with all three *angles* less than 90°.

triángulo acutángulo *Triángulo* cuyos tres *ángulos* miden menos de 90°.

addition (p. 70) An operation on two or more *addends* that results in a *sum*.

$$9 + 3 = 12$$

sumar (suma) Operación en dos o más *sumandos* que resulta en una *suma*.

$$9 + 3 = 12$$

algebra (p. 193) A branch of mathematics that uses symbols, usually letters, to explore relationships between quantities.

álgebra Rama de las matemáticas que usa símbolos, generalmente letras para explorar relaciones entre cantidades.

algebraic expression (p. 193) A group of numbers, symbols, and variables that represent an operation or series of operations.

$$3x + 5 \text{ or } y + 5$$

expresión algebraica Grupo de números, símbolos y variables que representan una operación o una serie de operaciones.

$$3x + 5 \text{ o } y + 5$$

angle (p. 564) Two rays with a common endpoint.

endpoint

ángulo Dos rectas con un extremo común.

extremo

area (p. 612)   The number of *square units* needed to cover the surface of a closed figure.

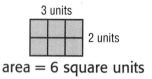

area = 6 square units

área   Número de *unidades cuadradas* necesarias para cubrir la superficie de una figura cerrada.

área = 6 unidades cuadrados

Associative Property of Addition (p. 84) Property that states that the way in which numbers are grouped does not change the sum.

propiedad asociativa de la suma Propiedad que establece que la manera en que se agrupan los números no altera la suma.

Associative Property of Multiplication (p. 126)   Property that states that the way in which factors are grouped does not change the product.

propiedad asociativa de la multiplicación Propiedad que establece que la manera en que se agrupan los factores no altera el producto.

axis (p. 250)   A horizontal or vertical number line on a graph. Plural is *axes*.

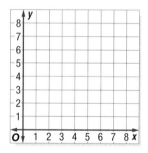

eje   Recta numérica horizontal o vertical en una gráfica.

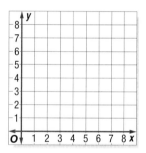

B

bar graph (p. 299)   A graph that compares *data* by using bars to display the number of items in each group.

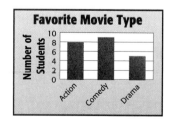

gráfica de barras   Gráfica que compara *datos* usando barras para mostrar el número de artículos en cada grupo.

base (p. 624)   One of two parallel congruent faces in a prism.

base   Una de dos caras congruentes paralelas en un prisma.

C

capacity (p. 488)   The amount a container can hold.

capacidad   Cantidad que puede contener un envase.

Celcius (°C) (p. 537)   The unit used to measure temperature in the metric system.

Celsios (°C)   Unidad que se usa para medir la temperatura en el sistema métrico.

centimeter (cm) (p. 517)   A *metric unit* for measuring *length*.

> 100 centimeters = 1 meter

centímetro (cm)   *Unidad métrica* de *longitud*.

> 100 centímetros = 1 metro

certain (p. 659)   The probability that an event will definitely happen.

cierto   La probabilidad de que ocurra un evento.

clustering (p. 113)   An estimation method in which a group of numbers close in value are rounded to the same number.

agrupar   Método de estimación en el cual se redondea a un mismo número un grupo de números cercanos a un valor.

coefficient (p. 402)   The numerical factor of a term that contains a variable.

coeficiente   Un factor numérico de un término que contiene una variable.

common denominator (p. 404)   A number that is a multiple of the denominators of two or more fractions.

denominador común   Número que es múltiplo de los denominadores de dos o más fracciones.

common factor (p. 373)   A number that is a *factor* of two or more numbers.

> 3 is a common factor of 6 and 12.

factor común   Un número *entero factor* de dos o más números.

> 3 es factor común de 6 y de 12.

common multiple (p. 396)   A *whole number* that is a *multiple* of two or more numbers.

> 24 is a common multiple of 6 and 4.

múltiplo común   *Número entero múltiplo* de dos o más números.

> 24 es un múltiplo común de 6 y 4.

Commutative Property of Addition (p. 84)   Property that states that the order in which numbers are added does not change the sum.

propiedad conmutativa de la suma   Propiedad que establece que el orden en que se suman los números no altera la suma.

Commutative Property of Multiplication (p. 126)   Property that states that the order in which factors are multiplied does not change the product.

propiedad conmutativa de la multiplicación   Propiedad que establece que el orden en que se multiplican los factores no altera el producto.

Glossary/Glosario

compatible numbers (p. 64) Numbers in a problem that are easy to work with mentally.

720 and 90 are compatible numbers for division because 72 ÷ 9 = 8.

números compatibles Números en un problema con los cuales es fácil trabajar mentalmente.

720 y 90 son números compatibles en la división porque 72 ÷ 9 = 8.

compensation (p. 88) Adding a number to one addend and subtracting the same number from another addend to add mentally.

compensación Sumar un número a un sumando y restar el mismo número de otro sumando con el fin de sumar mentalmente.

composite number (p. 376) A whole number that has more than two factors.

12 has the factors 1, 2, 3, 4, 6, and 12.

número compuesto Número entero que tiene más de dos factores.

12 tiene a los factores 1, 2, 3, 4, 6 y 12.

cone (p. 624) A solid that has a circular base and one surved surface from the base to a vertex.

cono Sólido con una base circular y una superficie curva desde la base hasta el vértice.

congruent line segments (p. 559) Line segments that have the same length.

segmentos congruentes de recta Segmentos de recta que tienen la misma medida.

convert (p. 477) To change one unit to another.

convertir Cambiar una unidad en otra.

coordinate (p. 250) One of two numbers in an *ordered pair*.

The 1 is the number on the *x*-axis, the 5 is on the *y*-axis. A coordinate can be positive or negative.

coordenada Uno de los dos números de un *par ordenado*.

El 1 es el número en el eje *x* y el 5 está en el eje *y*. Una coordenada puede ser positiva o negativa.

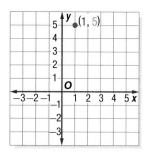

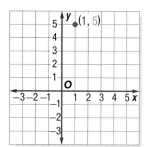

coordinate grid (p. 250) A grid that is formed when two number lines intersect at a right angle.

plano de coordenadas cuadriculado que se forma cuando dos rectas numéricas se intersecan a ángulos rectos.

cube (p. 624) A rectangular *prism* with six faces that are congruent squares.

cubo *Prisma* rectangular con seis caras que son cuadrados congruentes.

Glossary/Glosario

cubic unit (p. 631)   A unit for measuring *volume*, such as a cubic inch or a cubic centimeter.

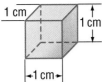

cup (p. 488)   A *customary unit* of *capacity* equal to 8 fluid ounces.

customary units (p. 477)   The units of measurement most often used in the United States. These include foot, pound, quart, and degrees Fahrenheit.

cylinder (p. 624)   A solid with two parallel congruent circular bases and a curved surface that connects the bases.

unidad cúbica   Unidad de *volumen*, como una pulgada cúbica o un centímetro cúbico.

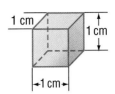

taza   *Unidad inglesa* de *capacidad* igual a 8 onzas líquidas.

unidades inglesas   Las unidades de medida de uso más frecuente en Estados Unidos. Incluyen el pie, la libra, el cuarto de galón y los grados Fahrenheit.

cilindro   Sólido con dos bases paralelas y congruentes y una superficie curva que las conecta.

data (p. 279)   Pieces of information that are often numerical.

decimal (p. 26)   A number that has a digit in the tenths place, hundredths place, and beyond.

decimal point (p. 26)   A period separating the ones and the *tenths* in a decimal number.

0.8 or $3.77

defining the variable (p. 238)   Choosing a variable to represent an unknown value.

degree (°) (pp. 537, 564)   **a.** A unit of measure used to describe temperature. **b.** A unit for measuring *angles*.

denominator (p. 333)   The bottom number in a *fraction*. It represents the number of parts in the whole.

In $\frac{5}{6}$, 6 is the denominator.

digit (p. 17)   A symbol used to write numbers. The ten digits are 0, 1, 2, 3, 4, 5, 6, 7, 8, and 9.

datos   Piezas de información que con frecuencia son numéricas.

decimal   Número que tiene un dígito en el lugar de las décimas, centésimas y más allá.

punto decimal   Punto que separa las unidades y las *décimas* en un número decimal.

0.8 ó $3.77

definir la variable   Elegir una variable para representar un valor desconocido.

grado (°)   **a.** Unidad de medida que se usa para describir la temperatura. **b.** Unidad para medir ángulos.

denominador   El número inferior en una *fracción*. Representa el número de partes en el todo.

En $\frac{5}{6}$, 6 es el denominador.

dígito   Símbolo que se usa para escribir números. Los diez dígitos son 0, 1, 2, 3, 4, 5, 6, 7, 8 y 9.

Glossary/Glosario

Distributive Property (p. 108)   To multiply a *sum* by a number, you can multiply each *addend* by the same number and add the *products*.

$$8 \times (9 + 5) = (8 \times 9) + (8 \times 5)$$

propiedad distributiva   Para multiplicar una *suma* por un número, puedes multiplicar cada *sumando* por el mismo número y sumar los *productos*.

$$8 \times (9 + 5) = (8 \times 9) + (8 \times 5)$$

divide (division) (p. 149)   An operation on two numbers in which the first number is split into the same number of equal groups as the second number.

12 ÷ 3 means 12 is divided into 3 equal size groups

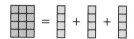

dividir (división)   Operación en dos números en que el primer número se separa en tantos grupos iguales como indica el segundo número.

12 ÷ 3 significa que 12 se divide en 3 grupos de igual tamaño.

dividend (p. 149)   A number that is being divided.

3)‾429‾   429 is the dividend

dividendo   Número que se divide.

3)‾429‾   429 es el dividendo

divisible (p. 149)   Describes a number that can be divided into equal parts and has no remainder.

39 is divisible by 3 with no remainder.

divisible   Describe un número que puede dividirse en partes iguales, sin residuo.

39 es divisible entre 3 sin residuo.

divisor (p. 149)   The number by which the dividend is being divided.

3)‾19‾   3 is the divisor

divisor   Número entre el que se divide el dividendo.

3)‾19‾   3 es el divisor

double bar graph (p. 306)   A graph used to display two sets of data dealing with the same subject.

gráfica de barras dobles   Gráfica que se usa para mostrar dos conjuntos de datos que tienen que ver con el mismo tema.

double line graph (p. 307)   A graph used to display two different sets of data using a common scale.

gráfica lineal doble   Gráfica que se usa para mostrar dos conjuntos diferentes de datos usando una escala común.

E

edge (p. 624)   The *line segment* where two *faces* of a *3-dimensional figure* meet.

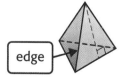

edge

arista   Segmento de recta donde concurren dos caras de una *figura tridimensional*.

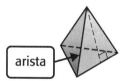

arista

elapsed time (p. 501)   The difference in time between the start and the end of an event.

tiempo transcurrido   La diferencia en tiempo entre el comienzo y el final de un evento.

Glossary/Glosario

equally likely (p. 659) Having the same chance of occurring.

> In a coin toss you are equally likely to flip a head or a tail.

equiprobable Que tienen la misma posibilidad de ocurrir.

> Al lanzar una moneda, tienes la misma posibilidad de sacar cara o cruz.

equals sign (p. 235) A symbol of equality, =.

signo de igualdad Símbolo de igual, =.

equation (p. 235) A number sentence that contains an equal sign, showing that two expressions are equal.

ecuación Expresión numérica que contiene un signo de igualdad que muestra que dos expresiones son iguales.

equilateral triangle (p. 566) A *triangle* with three *congruent* sides.

triángulo equilátero *Triángulo* con tres lados *congruentes*.

equivalent decimals (p. 37) Decimals that have the same value.

> 0.3 and 0.30

decimales equivalentes Decimales que tienen el mismo valor.

> 0.3 y 0.30

equivalent fractions (p. 382) *Fractions* that have the same value.

$$\frac{3}{4} = \frac{6}{8} = \frac{9}{12}$$

fracciones equivalentes *Fracciones* que representan el mismo número.

$$\frac{3}{4} = \frac{6}{8} = \frac{9}{12}$$

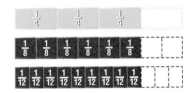

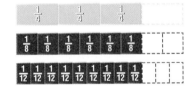

estimate (p. 64) A number close to an exact value. An estimate indicates *about* how much.

47 + 22 (round to 50 + 20)
The estimate is 70.

estimación Un número cercano a un valor exacto. Una estimación indica *aproximadamente* cuánto.

47 + 22 se redeondea a 50 + 20
La estimación es 70.

evaluate (p. 193) To find the *value* of an *expression* by replacing variables with numbers.

evaluar Calcular el *valor* de una expresión reemplazando las variables con números.

even number (p. 377) A whole number that is divisible by 2.

número par Número entero divisible entre 2.

expanded form (p. 17) A way of writing a number as the sum of the values of its digits.

forma desarrollada Una manera de escribir un número como la suma de los valores de sus dígitos.

expression (p. 193) A combination of numbers, variables, and at least one operation.

expresión Combinación de números, variables y por lo menos una operación.

Glossary/Glosario

F

face (p. 624)   The flat part of a 3-dimensional figure.

A square is a face of a cube.

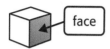

cara   La parte llana de una figura tridimensional.

Un cuadrado es una cara de un cubo.

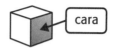

factor (p. 103)   A number that is multiplied by another number.

factor   Número que se multiplica por otro número.

Fahrenheit (°F) (p. 537)   The unit used to measure temperature in the customary system.

Fahrenheit   Unidad que se usa para medir la temperatura en el sistema inglés.

favorable outcome (p. 666)   Desired results in a *probability experiment*.

resultados favorables   Resultados deseados en un *experimento probabilístico*.

fluid ounce (p. 488)   A *customary unit* of *capacity*.

onzas líquidas   *Unidad inglesa* de *capacidad*.

foot (ft) (p. 477)   A *customary unit* for measuring *length*. Plural is *feet*.

1 foot = 12 inches

pie (pie)   *Unidad inglesa* de *longitud*.

1 pie = 12 pulgadas

fraction (p. 333)   A number that represents part of a whole or part of a set.

$$\frac{1}{2}, \frac{1}{3}, \frac{1}{4}, \frac{3}{4}$$

fracción   Número que representa parte de un todo o parte de un conjunto.

$$\frac{1}{2}, \frac{1}{3}, \frac{1}{4}, \frac{3}{4}$$

frequency (p. 289)   The number of times a result occurs or something happens in a set amount of time or collection of data.

frecuencia   Número de veces que ocurre un resultado o sucede algo en un período de tiempo dado o en una colección de datos.

frequency table (p. 289)   A table for organizing a set of *data* that shows the number of times each result has occurred.

tabla de frecuencias   Tabla para organizar un conjunto de *datos* que muestra el número de veces que ha ocurrido cada resultado.

function (p. 210)   A relationship between two variables in which one input quantity is paried with exactly one output quantity.

función   Relación entre dos variables en que una cantidad de entrada se relaciona exactamente con una cantidad de salida.

function rule (p. 210)   An expression that describes the relationship between each input and output.

regla de funciones   Expresión que describe la relación entre cada valor de entrada y cada valor de salida.

Glossary/Glosario

function table (p. 210)   A table of ordered pairs that is based on a rule.

Rule: $8h = r$	
Input (*h*)	Output (*r*)
1	8
2	16
3	24
4	32

tabla de funciones   Tabla de pares ordenados que se basa en una regla.

Regla: $8h = r$	
Entrada (*h*)	Salida (*r*)
1	8
2	16
3	24
4	32

G

gallon (gal) (p. 488)   A *customary unit* for measuring *capacity* for liquids.

1 gallon = 4 quarts

galón (gal)   Unidad de *medida inglesa* de *capacidad* de líquidos.

1 galón = 4 cuartos

gram (g) (p. 524)   A *metric unit* for measuring *mass*.

gramo (g)   Una *unidad métrica* para medir *masa*.

graph (p. 254)   Place a point named by an ordered pair on a coordinate grid.

graficar   Colocar un punto indicado por un par ordenado en un plano de coordenadas.

greater than > (p. 20)   An inequality relationship showing that the number on the left of the symbol is greater than the number on the right.

5 > 3
5 is greater than 3

mayor que >   Relación de desigualdad que muestra que el número a la izquierda del símbolo es mayor que el número a la derecha.

5 > 3
5 es mayor que 3

Greatest Common Factor (GCF) (p. 374) The greatest of the common factors of two or more numbers.

The greatest common factor of
12, 18, and 30 is 6.

máximo común divisor (MCD)   El mayor de los factores comunes de dos o más números.

El máximo común divisor de
12, 18 y 30 es 6.

H

horizontal axis (p. 250)   The axis in a coordinate plane that runs left and right (↔). Also known as the *x*-axis.

eje horizontal   Eje en un plano de coordenadas que va de izquierda a derecha (↔). También conocido como eje *x*.

Glossary/Glosario

hundredth (p. 17)   A place value position. One of one hundred equal parts.

In the number 0.57, 7 is in the hundredths place.

centésima   Valor de posición. Una de cien partes iguales.

En el número 0.57, 7 está en el lugar de las centésimas.

I

Identity Property of Addition (p. 84) Property that states that the sum of any number and 0 equals the number.

propiedad de identidad de la suma Propiedad que establece que la suma de cualquier número y 0 es igual al número.

Identity Property of Multiplication (p. 126)   Property that states that the product of any number and 1 equals the factor.

propiedad de identidad de la multiplicación   Propiedad que establece que el producto de cualquier número por 0 es igual al factor.

image (p. 578)   The resulting image after a geometric figure has been transformed.

imagen   La imagen que resulta después de transformar una figura geométrica.

impossible (p. 659)   There is no chance an event will happen. An *outcome* or *event* is impossible if it has a *probability* of 0.

It is impossible to choose a yellow tile.

imposible   Un *resultado* o un *evento* es imposible si tiene una *probabilidad* igual a 0.

Es imposible que elijas un azulejo amarillo.

improper fraction (p. 337)   A fraction with a numerator that is greater than or equal to the denominator.

$$\frac{17}{3} \text{ or } \frac{5}{5}$$

fracción impropia   Fracción con un numerador mayor que o igual al denominador.

$$\frac{17}{3} \text{ o } \frac{5}{5}$$

inch (in.) (p. 477)   A *customary unit* for measuring *length*. The plural is *inches*.

pulgada (pulg)   *Unidad inglesa* de *longitud*.

inequality (p. 20)   Two quantities that are not equal.

desigualdad   Dos cantidades que no son iguales.

integer (p. 533)   Whole numbers and their opposites, including zero.

$$\ldots-3, -2, -1, 0, 1, 2, 3\ldots$$

entero   Los números enteros y sus opuestos, incluyendo el cero.

$$\ldots-3, -2, -1, 0, 1, 2, 3\ldots$$

intersecting lines (p. 558)   *Lines* that meet or cross at a common *point*.

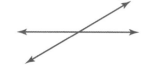

rectas secantes   *Rectas* que se intersecan o se cruzan en un *punto* común.

Glossary/Glosario

interval (p. 294)   The distance between successive values on a scale.

intervalo   Distancia entre dos valores sucesivos en una escala.

isosceles triangle (p. 566)   A *triangle* with at least 2 *sides* of the same *length*.

triángulo isósceles   *Triángulo* que tiene por lo menos 2 *lados* del mismo largo.

K

kilogram (kg) (p. 524)   A *metric unit* for measuring *mass*.

kilogramo (kg)   *Unidad métrica* de *masa*.

kilometer (km) (p. 517)   A *metric unit* for measuring *length*.

kilómetro (km)   *Unidad métrica* de *longitud*.

L

Least Common Denominator (LCD) (p. 404)   The *least common multiple* of the *denominators* of two or more *fractions*.

$$\frac{1}{12}, \frac{1}{6}, \frac{1}{8};\ \text{LCD is 24.}$$

mínimo común denominador (mcd)   El *mínimo común múltiplo* de los *denominadores* de dos o más *fracciones*.

$$\frac{1}{12}, \frac{1}{6}, \frac{1}{8};\ \text{el mcd es 24.}$$

Least Common Multiple (LCM) (p. 397) The smallest *whole number* greater than 0 that is a common *multiple* of each of two or more numbers.

The LCM of 2 and 3 is 6.

mínimo común múltiplo (mcm)   El menor *número entero*, mayor que 0, *múltiplo* común de dos o más números.

El mcm de 2 y 3 es 6.

length (p. 475)   Measurement of the distance between two points.

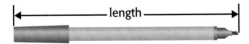

longitud   Medida de la distancia entre dos puntos.

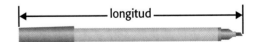

less than $<$ (p. 20)   The number on the left side of the symbol is smaller than the number on the right side.

$$4 < 7$$
4 is smaller than 7

menor que $<$ El número a la izquierda del símbolo es más pequeño que el número a su derecha.

$$4 < 7$$
4 es menor que 7

like fractions (p. 421)   Fractions that have the same denominator.

$$\frac{1}{5} \text{ and } \frac{2}{5}$$

fracciones semejantes   Fracciones que tienen el mismo denominador.

$$\frac{1}{5} \text{ y } \frac{2}{5}$$

Glossary/Glosario

likely (p. 660)   An event that will probably happen.

It is likely you will choose a red cube.

line (p. 557)   A set of *points* that form a straight path that goes on forever in opposite directions.

line graph (p. 306)   A graph that uses points connected by *line segments* to show changes in data over time.

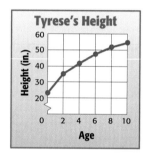

line of reflection (p. 582)   The line an image is reflected over.

line plot (p. 284)   A graph that uses columns of Xs above a *number line* to show the number of times values in a set of data occur.

line segment (p. 557)   A part of a *line* that connects two points.

liter (L) (p. 527)   A *metric unit* for measuring *volume* or *capacity*.

1 liter = 1,000 milliliters

posible   Un evento que probablemente sucederá.

Es posible que elijas un cubo rojo.

recta   Conjunto de *puntos* que forman una trayectoria recta sin fin en direcciones opuestas.

gráfica lineal   Gráfica que usa puntos unidos por *segmentos de recta* para mostrar cambios en los datos con el tiempo.

línea de reflexión   Línea sobre la cual se refleja una imagen.

esquema lineal   Gráfica que usa columnas de X sobre una *recta numérica* para mostrar el número de veces que en un conjunto de datos.

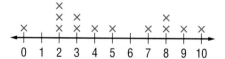

segmento de recta   Parte de una *recta* que conecta dos puntos.

litro (L)   *Unidad métrica* de *volumen* o *capacidad*.

1 litro = 1,000 mililitros

M

mass (p. 524)   Measure of the amount of matter in an object.

masa   Medida de la cantidad de material en un objeto. Dos ejemplos de unidades de esta medida son la libra y el kilogramo.

Glossary/Glosario

median (p. 279)   The middle number in a set of data that has been written in order from least to greatest. If the set contains an even number of numbers, the median is the number exactly halfway between the two middle numbers.

$$3, 4, 6, 8, 9, 9$$

The median is $7 = \dfrac{(6 + 8)}{2}$.

meter (p. 517)   A *metric unit* used to measure length.

metric system (SI) (p. 517)   The decimal system of measurement. Includes units such as meter, gram, liter, and degrees Celsius.

mile (mi) (p. 477)   A *customary unit* of measure for length.

$$1 \text{ mile} = 5{,}280 \text{ feet}$$

milligram (mg) (p. 524)   A *metric unit* used to measure *mass*.

$$1{,}000 \text{ milligrams} = 1 \text{ gram}$$

milliliter (mL) (p. 527)   A *metric unit* used for measuring *capacity*.

$$1{,}000 \text{ milliliters} = 1 \text{ liter}$$

millimeter (mm) (p. 517)   A *metric unit* used for measuring *length*.

$$1{,}000 \text{ millimeters} = 1 \text{ meter}$$

mixed number (p. 336)   A number that has a *whole number* and a *fraction*.

$$6\tfrac{3}{4}$$

mode (p. 280)   The number(s) that occurs most often in a set of data.

$$7, 4, 7, 10, 7, \text{ and } 2$$
The mode is 7.

multiple (multiples) (p. 396)   A multiple of a number is the *product* of that number and any whole number.

15 is a multiple of 5 because $3 \times 5 = 15$.

mediana   Número central de un conjunto de datos escritos en orden de menor a mayor. Si el conjunto contiene una cantidad par de números, la mediana es el número que está exactamente a mitad de camino entre los dos números centrales.

$$3, 4, 6, 8, 9, 9$$

La mediana es $7 = \dfrac{(6 + 8)}{2}$.

metro   *Unidad métrica* que se usa para medir la longitud.

sistema métrico (sm)   Sistema de medición que se basa en potencias de 10 el cual incluye unidades como el metro, el gramo, el litro y los grados Celsius.

milla (mi)   *Unidad inglesa* de longitud.

$$1 \text{ milla} = 5{,}280 \text{ pies}$$

miligramo (mg)   *Unidad métrica* de *masa*.

$$1{,}000 \text{ miligramos} = 1 \text{ gramo}$$

mililitro (mL)   *Unidad métrica* de *capacidad*.

$$1{,}000 \text{ mililitros} = 1 \text{ litro}$$

milímetro (mm)   *Unidad métrica* de *longitud*.

$$1{,}000 \text{ milímetros} = 1 \text{ metro}$$

número mixto   Número que tiene un *número entero* y una *fracción*.

$$6\tfrac{3}{4}$$

moda   Número o números que ocurren con mayor frecuencia en un conjunto de datos.

$$7, 4, 7, 10, 7, \text{ y } 2$$
La moda es 7.

múltiplo (múltiplos)   Un múltiplo de un número es el *producto* de ese número por cualquier otro número entero.

15 es múltiplo de 5 porque $3 \times 5 = 15$.

Glossary/Glosario

multiplication (p. 103)   An operation on two numbers to find their *product*. It can be thought of as repeated *addition*.

4 × 3 is another way to write the *sum* of four 3s, which is 3 + 3 + 3 + 3 or 12.

multiplicación   Operación que se realiza en dos números para calcular su *producto*. También se puede interpretar como una *suma* repetida.

4 × 3 es otra forma de escribir la *suma* de cuatro veces 3, la cual es 3 + 3 + 3 + 3 o 12.

N

negative integer (p. 533)   Integers less than zero. Written with a − sign.

entero negativo   Enteros menores que cero. Se escriben con un signo −.

negative number (p. 533)   Numbers less than zero.

número negativo   Números menores que cero.

number line (p. 20)   A line that represents numbers as points.

recta numérica   Recta que representa números como puntos.

numerator (p. 333)   The top number in a *fraction*; the part of the fraction that tells the number of parts you have.

numerador   Número que se escribe arriba de la barra de *fracción*; la parte de la fracción que indica el número de partes que tienes.

numerical expression (p. 193)   A combination of numbers and operations.

expresión numérica   Combinación de números y operaciones.

O

obtuse angle (p. 564)   An *angle* that measures between 90° and 180°.

ángulo obtuso   *Ángulo* que mide entre 90° y 180°.

obtuse triangle (p. 567)   A *triangle* with one *obtuse angle*.

triángulo obtusángulo   *Triángulo* con un *ángulo obtuso*.

odd number (p. 377)   A number that is not divisible by 2; such a number has 1, 3, 5, 7, or 9 in the ones place.

número impar   Número que no es divisible entre 2, tal número tiene 1, 3, 5, 7 ó 9 en el lugar de las unidades.

operation (p. 190)   A mathematical process such as addition (+), subtraction (−), multiplication (×), division (÷), and raising to a power.

operación   Proceso matemático como la suma (+), la resta (−), la multiplicación (×), la división (÷) y la potenciación.

Glossary/Glosario

opposite integers (p. 534)   Two different integers that are the same distance from 0 on a number line.

5 and −5

enteros opuestos   Dos enteros diferentes que equidistan de 0 en una recta numérica.

5 y −5

ordered pair (p. 250)   A pair of numbers that is used to name a point on the coordinate grid.

par ordenado   Par de números que se usan para nombrar un punto en un cuadriculado de coordenadas.

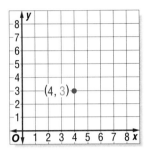

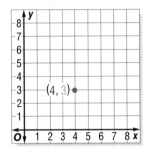

origin (p. 250)   The point (0, 0) on a *coordinate grid* where the vertical axis meets the horizontal axis.

origen   El punto (0, 0) en un *cuadriculado de coordenadas* donde el *eje* vertical interseca el eje horizontal.

ounce (oz) (p. 484)   A *customary unit* for measuring *weight* or *capacity*.

onza (oz)   *Unidad inglesa* de *peso* o *capacidad*.

outcome (p. 639)   A possible result of a probability experiment.

resultado   Resultado posible de un experimento probabilístico.

outlier (p. 285)   A number in a set of data that is much larger or much smaller than most of the other numbers in the set.

valor atípico   Número en un conjunto de datos que es mucho mayor o mucho menor que la mayoría de los otros números del conjunto.

P

parallel lines (p. 558)   Lines that are the same distance apart. Parallel lines do not intersect.

rectas paralelas   Rectas separadas por la misma distancia. Las rectas paralelas no se intersecan.

parallelogram (p. 571)   A quadrilateral with four sides in which each pair of opposite sides are parallel and congruent.

paralelogramo   Cuadrilátero de cuatro lados en que cada par de lados opuestos son paralelos y congruentes.

Glossary/Glosario

perimeter (p. 608)   The *distance* around a polygon.

perímetro   *Distancia* alrededor de un polígono.

period (p. 17)   Each group of three digits on a place-value chart.

período   Cada grupo de tres dígitos en una tabla de valor de posición.

perpendicular lines (p. 558)   *Lines* that cross each other at *right angles*.

rectas perpendiculares   *Rectas* que se cruzan a *ángulos rectos*.

pint (pt) (p. 488)   A customary *unit* for measuring *capacity*.

1 pint = 2 cups

pinta (pt)   *Unidad inglesa* de *capacidad*.

1 pinta = 2 tazas

place value (p. 26)   The value given to a digit by its position in a number.

valor de posición   Valor dado a un dígito según su posición en el número.

place-value chart (p. 17)   A chart that shows the value of the digits in a number.

tabla de valor de posición   Tabla que muestra el valor de los dígitos en un número.

plane (p. 557)   A flat surface that goes on forever in all directions.

plano   Superficie plana que se extiende infinitamente en todas direcciones.

point (p. 557)   An exact location in space that is represented by a dot.

punto   Ubicación exacta en el espacio que se representa con un marca puntual.

polygon (p. 608)   A closed figure made up of line segments that do not cross each other.

polígono   Figura cerrada compuesta por segmentos de recta que no se intersecan.

polyhedron (p. 624)   A three-dimensional figure with faces that are polygons.

poliedro   Figura tridimensional con caras en forma de polígonos.

population (p. 526)   The entire group of items or individuals from which the samples under consideration are taken.

población   Todo el grupo de cosas o individuos del cual se toman las muestras a considerar.

positive integer (p. 533)   Integers greater than zero. They can be written with or without a + sign.

entero positivo   Enteros mayores que cero. Se pueden escribir con o sin el signo +.

positive number (p. 533)   Numbers that are greater than zero.

número positivo   Números mayores que cero.

possible outcomes (p. 512)   Any of the results that could occur in an experiment.

resultados posibles   Cualquiera de los resultados que puede ocurrir en un experimento.

pound (lb) (p. 484)   A *customary unit* for measuring *weight* or *mass*.

1 pound = 16 ounces

libra (lb)   *Unidad inglesa* de *peso* o *masa*.

1 libra = 16 onzas

power (p. 22)   A number obtained by raising a *base* to an *exponent*.

$5^2 = 25$ 25 is a power of 5.

prime factorization (p. 379)   A way of expressing a *composite number* as a product of its *prime factors*.

prime number (p. 376)   A *whole number* with exactly two *factors*, 1 and itself.

7, 13, and 19

prism (p. 624)   A polyhedron with two *parallel, congruent faces,* called *bases.*

probability (p. 659)   The chance that an event will happen. It can be described as a number from 0 to 1.

probability experiment (p. 659)   An experiment to determine the chance that an event will happen.

product (p. 103)   The answer to a multiplication problem.

proper fraction (p. 333)   A fraction in which the numerator is less than the denominator.

$\frac{1}{2}$

potencia   Número que se obtiene elevando una *base* a un *exponente*.

$5^2 = 25$ 25 es una potencia de 5.

factorización prima   Una manera de escribir un *número compuesto* como un producto de sus *factores primos.*

número primo   *Número entero* que tiene exactamente dos *factores*, 1 y sí mismo.

7, 13, y 19

prisma   Poliedro con dos *caras paralelas* y *congruentes* llamadas *bases.*

probabilidad   La posibilidad de que ocurra un evento. Se puede describir como un número de 0 a 1.

experimento probabilístico   Experimento para determinar la posibilidad de que ocurra un evento.

producto   Repuesta a un problema de multiplicación.

fracción propia   Fracción en que el numerador es menor que el denominador.

$\frac{1}{2}$

quadrilateral (p. 570)   A polygon that has 4 sides and 4 angles.

square, rectangle, and parallelogram

cuadrilátero   Polígono con 4 lados y 4 ángulos.

cuadrado, rectángulo y paralelogramo

quart (qt) (p. 488)   A *customary unit* for measuring *capacity.*

1 quart = 4 cups

quotient (p. 149)   The result of a *division* problem.

cuarto (ct)   *Unidad inglesa* de *capacidad.*

1 cuarto = 4 tazas

cociente   El resultado de un problema de *división.*

range (p. 285)   The *difference* between the greatest and the least values in a set of data.

rango   La *diferencia* entre el mayor y el menor de los valores en un conjunto de datos.

Glossary/Glosario

ray (p. 557)   A line that has one endpoint and goes on forever in only one direction.

rayo   Recta con un extremo y la cual se extiende infinitamente en una sola dirección.

rectangle (p. 571)   A *quadrilateral* with four *right angles*; opposite *sides* are equal and *parallel*.

rectángulo   *Cuadrilátero* con cuatro *ángulo rectos*; los *lados* opuestos son iguales y *paralelos*.

rectangular prism (p. 159)   A polyhedron with six rectangular faces.

prisma rectangular   Poliedro con seis caras rectangulares.

reflection (p. 582)   An figure that is flipped over a line to create a mirror image of the figure.

reflexión   Figura que se vuelca sobre una línea para crear una imagen especular de la figura.

remainder (p. 159)   The number that is left after one whole number is divided by another.

residuo   Número que queda después de dividir un número entero entre otro número entero.

rhombus (p. 571)   A *parallelogram* with four *congruent sides*.

rombo   *Paralelogramo* con cuatro *lados congruentes*.

right angle (p. 564)   An *angle* with a measure of 90°.

ángulo recto   *Ángulo* que mide 90°.

right triangle (p. 567)   A *triangle* with one *right angle*.

triángulo rectángulo   *Triángulo* con un *ángulo recto*.

rotation (p. 586)   Rotating a figure about a point.

rotación   Rotar una figura alrededor de un punto.

round (p. 61)   To find the approximate value of a number.

6.38 rounded to the nearest tenth is 6.4.

redondear   Calcular el valor aproximado de un número.

6.38 redondeado a la décima más cercana es 6.4.

S

scale (p. 294)   A set of numbers that includes the least and greatest values separated by equal intervals.

escala   Conjunto de números que incluye los valores menor y mayor separados por intervalos iguales.

scalene triangle (p. 566)   A *triangle* with no *congruent sides*.

simplest form (p. 386)   A fraction in which the GCF of the numerator and the denominator is 1.

solution (p. 235)   The value of a variable that makes an equation true. The solution of $12 = x + 7$ is 5.

solve (p. 239)   To replace a variable with a value that results in a true sentence.

square (p. 571)   A rectangle with four *congruent sides*.

square unit (p. 612)   A unit for measuring *area*, such as *square inch* or *square centimeter*.

standard form (p. 17)   The usual or common way to write a number using digits.

subtraction (subtract) (p. 64)   An operation on two numbers that tells how many are left (*difference*), when some or all are taken away. Subtraction is also used to compare two numbers.

$$14 - 8 = 6$$

sum (p. 64)   The answer to an addition problem.

surface area (p. 638)   The sum of the areas of all the faces of a prism.

triángulo escaleno   *Triángulo* sin *lados congruentes*.

forma reducida   Fracción en que el MCD del numerador y del denominador es 1.

solución   Valor de una variable que hace verdadera la ecuación. La solución de $12 = x + 7$ es 5.

resolver   Despejar una variable y reemplazar este valor en la variable para hacer verdadera la ecuación.

cuadrado   Rectángulo con cuatro *lados congruentes*.

unidad cuadrada   Unidad de *área*, como una *pulgada cuadrada* o un *centímetro cuadrado*.

forma estándar   La manera usual o común de escribir un número usando dígitos.

restar (resta)   Operación que se realiza en dos números y que indica cuántos quedan (*diferencia*), cuando se eliminan algunos o todos. La resta también se usa para comparar dos números.

$$14 - 8 = 6$$

suma   Respuesta a un problema de suma.

área total   La suma de todas las área de todas las caras de un prisma.

tally mark(s) (p. 289)   A mark made to keep track and display data recorded from a survey.

ten thousandth (p. 18)   A place value in a decimal number.

In the decimal 0.7891, the 1 is in the ten thousandths place.

marcas(s) de conteo   Marca que se hace para llevar la cuenta y representar datos reunidos en una encuesta.

diezmilésima   Valor de posición en un número decimal.

En el decimal 0.7891, el 1 está en el lugar de las diezmilésimas.

Glossary/Glosario

tenth (p. 18)   A place value in a decimal number or one of ten equal parts or $\frac{1}{10}$.

thousandth(s) (p. 18)   One of a thousand equal parts or $\frac{1}{1,000}$. Also refers to a place value in a decimal number. In the decimal 0.789, the 9 is in the thousandth place.

three-dimensional figure (p. 624)   A solid figure that has *length*, *width*, and *height*.

ton (T) (p. 484)   A customary unit to measure weight.   1 ton = 2,000 pounds

transformation (p. 578)   A movement of a figure that does not change the size or shape of the figure.

translation (p. 578)   Sliding a figure in a straight line horizontally, vertically, or diagonally.

trapezoid (p. 571)   A *quadrilateral* with exactly one pair of *parallel* sides.

tree diagram (p. 675)   A diagram that shows all the *possible outcomes* of an event.

triangle (p. 566)   A *polygon* with three sides and three angles.

triangular prism (p. 624)   A prism that has triangular bases.

décima   Valor de posición en un número decimal o una de diez partes iguales ó $\frac{1}{10}$.

milésima(s)   Una de mil partes iguales ó $\frac{1}{1,000}$. También se refiere a un valor de posición en un número decimal. En el decimal 0.789, el 9 está en el lugar de las milésimas.

figura tridimensional   Figura sólida que tiene *largo, ancho* y *alto*.

tonelada (T)   Unidad inglesa de peso   1 tonelada = 2,000 libras

transformación   Movimiento de una figura que no cambia el tamaño o la forma de la figura.

traslación   Deslizar una figura horizontal, vertical o diagonalmente en línea recta.

trapecio   *Cuadrilátero* con exactamente un par de lados *paralelos*.

diagrama de árbol   Diagrama que muestra todos los *resultados posibles* de un evento.

triángulo   *Polígono* con tres lados y tres ángulos.

prisma triangular   Prisma con bases triangulares.

U

unlike fractions (p. 432)   Fractions that have different denominators.

unlikely (p. 660)   An event that is improbable or will probably *not* happen.

It is unlikely you will choose a blue cube.

fracciones no semejantes   Fracciones que tienen denominadores diferentes.

improbable   Evento que es improbable o que es probable que *no* suceda.

Es improbable que elijas un cubo azul.

value (p. 17)   A number amount or the worth of an object.

variable (p. 193)   A letter or symbol used to represent an unknown quantity.

vertex (pp. 564, 608)   **a.** The *point* where two rays meet in an *angle*. **b.** The point on a three-dimensional figure where 3 or more edges meet.

vertical axis (p. 250)   A vertical number line on a graph ($\updownarrow$). Also known as the *y*-axis.

volume (p. 631)   The amount of space that a *3-dimensional figure* contains.

valor   Cantidad numérica o lo que vale un objeto.

variable   Letra o un símbolo que se usa para representar una cantidad desconocida.

vértice   **a.** *Punto* donde concurren dos rayos de un *ángulo*. **b.** *Punto* en *una figura tridimensional* donde se intersecan 3 ó más aristas.

eje vertical   Recta numérica vertical en una gráfica ($\updownarrow$). También conocido como eje *y*.

volumen   Cantidad de espacio que contiene una *figura tridimensional*.

weight (p. 484)   A measurement that tells how heavy an object is.

whole number (p. 20)   The numbers 0, 1, 2, 3, 4…

width (p. 616)   The measurement of distance from side to side telling how wide.

peso   Medida que indica la pesadez un cuerpo.

número entero   Los números 0, 1, 2, 3, 4…

ancho   Medida de la distancia de lado a lado y que indica amplitud.

***x*-axis** (p. 250)   The horizontal axis ($\leftrightarrow$) in a coordinate plane.

***x*-coordinate** (p. 250)   The first part of an ordered pair that indicates how far to the right of the *y*-axis the corresponding point is.

eje *x*   Eje horizontal ($\leftrightarrow$) en un plano de coordenadas.

coordenada *x*   Primera parte de un par ordenado que indica la distancia a que está el punto correspondiente a la derecha del eje *y*.

yard (p. 477)   A *customary unit* of *length* equal to 3 feet or 36 inches.

***y*-axis** (p. 250)   The vertical axis ($\updownarrow$) in a coordinate plane.

***y*-coordinate** (p. 250)   The second part of an ordered pair that indicates how far above the *x*-axis the corresponding point is.

yarda   *Unidad inglesa* de *longitud* igual a 3 pies ó 36 pulgadas.

eje *y*   El eje vertical ($\updownarrow$) en un plano de coordenadas.

coordenada *y*   Segunda parte de un par ordenado que indica la distancia a que está el punto correspondiente por encima del eje *x*.

Index

G

Gallons, 488–490, 506, 706

Game Time
Bean Game, 681
Decimal War, 47
Decimos, 177
Find the Least Sum, 83
Four in a Row!, 311
Fraction Subtraction, 455
Geometry Concentration, 561
Match Up, 385
Metric Pairs!, 531
Mystery Measurements, 481
Order Matters, 223
That's Not Proper, 343
What's the Area?, 622
What's the Difference?, 125
Where's My Line, 263

Geometric shapes, 8–9

Geometric symbols, 557–560

Geometry, 250–257, 554, 575, 578–593, 599–603
Acute angles, 564–569, 598
Acute triangles, 566–569, 598
Cones, 624–627, 651
Congruent, 566–569, 598
Congruent lines segments, 558–561, 597
Cylinders, 624–627, 651
Edges, 624–627, 651
Equilateral triangles, 566–569, 598
Faces, 624–627, 651
Geometry Concentration Game, 561
Identify Angles, 564–565
Intersecting lines, 558–561, 597
Isosceles triangles, 566–569, 598
Lines, 557–561, 597
Line segments, 557–561, 597
Obtuse angles, 564–569, 598

Parallel lines, 558–561, 597
Perpendicular lines, 558–561, 597
Planes, 557–561, 597
Points, 557–561, 597
Polygons, 608–611
Polyhedron, 624–627, 651
Prisms, 624–627, 651
Quadrilaterals, 570–574, 598
Rays, 557–561, 597
Rectangles, 571–574, 598
Rhombuses, 571–574, 598
Right angles, 564–569, 598
Right triangles, 566–569, 598
Scalene triangles, 566–569, 598
Solid figures, 624–627, 651
Squares, 571–574, 598
Symbols, 557–560
Symmetry, 8–9
Three-dimensional figures, 624–627, 651
Trapezoids, 571–574, 598
Triangles, 566–569, 598
Triangular prisms, 624–627, 651
Vertex (vertices), 564–565, 598, 624–627, 651

Grams, 524–526, 548

Graphs
Bar Graphs, 12–13, 76–77, 299–303, 313, 316, 318–319, 325
Choose appropriate, 312–319, 326
Coordinate grid, 250–252, 254–257, 261–262, 270, 578–593, 599, 600
Double bar graphs, 300, 316
Double line graphs, 307–310, 316, 536
Four in a Row! Game, 311
Horizontal axis, 76–77, 299–303
Intervals, 294–298, 325
Line graphs, 306–311, 313, 316, 317, 326, 536

Ordered pairs, 250–257, 261, 262, 270, 271
Origin, 250–252
Pictographs, 312–317
Picture graphs, 312–317
Points, 250–257, 263, 709
Reflections, 582–585, 591–593, 600
Rotations, 586–593, 600
Scales, 294–298, 325
Temperature, 536
Translations, 578
Vertical axis, 76, 77, 299–303
Where's My Line Game, 263
X-coordinate, 250–252, 254–257, 270
Y-coordinate, 250–252, 254–257, 270

Greater than (>), 20–23, 42–46, 51, 350–353, 365, 402–405, 414

Greatest common factor (GCF), 374, 375, 386–389, 411

H

Hands-On Activity, 421, 422, 570, 578, 582, 586, 609, 616

Hands-On Mini Activity, 132, 174, 396

Horizontal axis, 76, 77, 299–303

H.O.T. Problems
Challenge, 23, 38, 72, 87, 105, 110, 115, 128, 135, 172, 200, 221, 239, 252, 287, 297, 303, 317, 341, 348, 358, 381, 399, 431, 441, 446, 480, 486, 490, 503, 521, 541, 543, 560, 569, 619, 626, 634, 643, 663, 671
Find the Error, 30, 45, 66, 90, 110, 115, 151, 164, 212, 239, 260, 303, 317, 341, 353, 384, 399, 436, 450, 461, 490, 500, 526, 529, 541, 573, 585, 611, 646, 680

Index

Index

Index

Value, 17–19

Variables, 193–195, 198–201, 202–204, 205

Venn diagram, 344–345

Vertex (vertices), 564–565, 598, 624–627, 651

Vertical axis, 76–77, 299–303

Volume

    Formula, 630, 631–635, 643–646, 652, 654

    Rectangular prism, 631–635, 643–646, 652, 654, 714

Weeks, 492–495, 507, 706

Weight, 10–11, 484–487, 506

    Converting, 484–487, 506

    Ounces, 484–487, 506

    Pounds, 484–487, 506

    Tons, 484–487, 506

Whole numbers

    Ordering, 42–46, 54

    Rounding, 61–63, 64–67, 93

Word form, 18–19, 33–35, 53

Writing expressions, 193–195, 198–201, 202–204, 205, 577

Writing in Math, 3, 5, 7, 9, 11, 13, 19, 23, 25, 27, 30, 31, 35, 38, 45, 49, 63, 66, 69, 72, 73, 75, 79, 82, 87, 90, 97 105, 107, 110, 115, 118, 119, 121, 124, 128, 135, 137, 143, 151, 154, 157, 161, 164, 165, 167, 169, 172, 176, 181, 187, 195, 197, 200, 204, 205, 207, 209, 212, 215, 221, 229, 236, 239, 241, 245, 249, 252, 253, 257, 260, 262, 267, 273, 281, 283, 287, 292, 293, 297, 303, 309, 317, 319, 321, 327, 335, 337, 341, 345, 348, 349, 353, 358, 361, 367, 375, 377, 381, 384, 388, 390, 393, 395, 399, 401, 404, 415, 422, 425, 427, 431, 433, 436, 438, 441, 443, 446, 447, 450, 454, 457, 461, 469, 476, 480, 483, 486, 490, 491, 494, 497, 500, 509, 516, 521, 523, 526, 529, 532, 535, 541, 545, 551, 560, 563, 565, 569, 573, 575, 577, 580, 585, 589, 593, 607, 611, 615, 619, 621, 623, 626, 629, 630, 634, 639, 643, 646, 648, 655, 663, 671, 673, 675, 676, 680, 683

Writing numbers

    Expanded form, 18–19, 33–35, 53

    Standard form, 18–19, 33–35, 53

    Word form, 18–19, 33–35, 53

***X*-coordinate,** 250–252, 254–257, 270

Yards, 475–476, 477–480, 505

***Y*-coordinate,** 250–252, 254–257, 270

Years, 492–495, 507

Zeros and division, 149–151

Zeros and multiplication, 104–105, 139

Measurement Conversions

Measure	Metric	Customary
Length	1 kilometer (km) = 1,000 meters (m) 1 meter = 100 centimeters (cm) 1 centimeter = 10 millimeters (mm)	1 foot (ft) = 12 inches (in.) 1 yard (yd) = 3 feet or 36 inches 1 mile (mi) = 1,760 yards or 5,280 feet
Volume and Capacity	1 liter (L) = 1,000 milliliters (mL) 1 kiloliter (kL) = 1,000 liters	1 cup (c) = 8 fluid ounces (fl oz) 1 pint (pt) = 2 cups 1 quart (qt) = 2 pints 1 gallon (gal) = 4 quarts
Weight and Mass	1 kilogram (kg) = 1,000 grams (g) 1 gram = 1,000 milligrams (mg) 1 metric ton = 1,000 kilograms	1 pound (lb) = 16 ounces (oz) 1 ton (T) = 2,000 pounds

Time	1 minute (min) = 60 seconds (s) 1 hour (h) = 60 minutes 1 day (d) = 24 hours 1 week (wk) = 7 days 1 year (yr) = 12 months (mo) 1 year = 52 weeks 1 year = 365 days 1 leap year = 366 days

Formulas

Perimeter	square	$P = 4s$
	rectangle	$P = 2\ell + 2w$ or $P = 2(\ell + w)$
Area	square	$A = s^2$
	rectangle	$A = \ell w$
	parallelogram	$A = bh$
	triangle	$A = \frac{1}{2}bh$
Surface Area	rectangular prism	$S = 2\ell w + 2\ell h + 2wh$
Volume	prism	$V = \ell wh$ or Bh